HAMLYN
ITALIAN
DICTIONARY

ITALIAN-ENGLISH   ENGLISH-ITALIAN

Published by
The Hamlyn Publishing Group Limited
London · New York · Sydney · Toronto
Astronaut House, Feltham, Middlesex, England
© The Hamlyn Publishing Group Limited 1976

ISBN 0 600 36566 2

Compiled by
Laurence Urdang Associates Ltd,
Aylesbury

Printed in Great Britain by
Butler and Tanner Ltd, Frome, Somerset

Foreword

This dictionary aims to give concise and accurate definitions of 24,000 of the most important words in use in the English and Italian languages today.

A pronunciation system based on the International Phonetic Alphabet is used (see *Key to symbols used in pronunciation*). Pronunciation is given for all headwords in both sections of the dictionary, and also for selected subentries in the Italian-English section.

Modern technical, commercial, and informal usage is given particular attention, in preference to outmoded terms or other expressions not in common contemporary use. Definitions are numbered in order to distinguish senses, and abbreviations are used to indicate use in specific technical, scientific, or commercial fields (see *Abbreviations used in the Dictionary*). An additional feature is the inclusion of idiomatic expressions and phrases, so necessary for the understanding and use of the foreign language.

This dictionary, with its emphasis on modernity, together with its compact form and clear typeface, should prove indispensable in the home, at school, in the office, and abroad.

Abbreviations used in the Dictionary

adj	adjective	*indef art*	indefinite article	*poss*	possessive
adv	adverb	*inf*	informal	*pref*	prefix
anat	anatomy	*infin*	infinitive	*prep*	preposition
arch	architecture	*interj*	interjection	*pron*	pronoun
aux	auxiliary	*invar*	invariable	*rel*	religion
aviat	aviation	*lit*	literature	*s*	singular
bot	botany	*m*	masculine	*sci*	science
cap	capital	*math*	mathematics	*sl*	slang
comm	commerce	*med*	medical	*suff*	suffix
conj	conjunction	*mil*	military	*tab*	taboo
cul	culinary	*min*	minerals	*Tdmk*	trademark
def art	definite article	*mod*	modal	*tech*	technical
derog	derogatory	*mot*	motoring	*Th*	theatre
dom	domestic	*mus*	music	*US*	United States
educ	education	*n*	noun	*v*	verb
fam	familiar	*naut*	nautical	*vi*	intransitive verb
fml	formal	*neg*	negative	*v imp*	impersonal verb
game	cards, chess, etc.	*pers*	person	*vr*	reflexive verb
gram	grammar	*phot*	photography	*vt*	transitive verb
geog	geography	*pol*	politics	*zool*	zoology

Key to symbols used in pronunciation

English
Vowels

							Consonants	
i:	meet	u	put	ai	fly		θ	thin
i	bit	u:	shoot	au	how		ð	then
e	get	ʌ	cut	ɔi	boy		ŋ	sing
æ	hat	ə	ago	iə	here		j	yes
ɑ:	heart	ə:	sir	ɛə	air		ʃ	ship
ɔ	hot	ei	late	uə	poor		ʒ	measure
ɔ:	ought	ou	go				tʃ	chin
							dʒ	gin

ˈ indicates that the following syllable is stressed, as in ago (əˈgou).

ˌ placed under an *n* or *l* indicates that the *n* or *l* is pronounced as a syllable, as in *button* (ˈbʌtn̩) and *flannel* (ˈflænl̩).

Italian
Vowels

				Consonants			
i	vino	o	notte	j	ieri	ʎ	gli
e	sera	ɔ	brodo	ʃ	uscire	ʎʎ	aglio
ɛ	bello	u	rupe	tʃ	cercare	ɲɲ	bagno
a	gatto			dʒ	cagionare		

ˈ indicates that the following syllable is stressed, as in *bello* (ˈbɛllo).

Notes on the use of the Dictionary

Irregular plural forms of Italian nouns are shown immediately after the part of speech; the gender of the plural is given only if it differs from that of the singular:—

> e.g. **uomo** . . . *nm, pl* **uomini**
> **uovo** . . . *nm, pl* **uova** *f*

Nouns or adjectives that do not change in the plural are marked as invariable:—

> e.g. **re** . . . *nm invar* king.

Feminine forms of nouns are not shown when they can be derived in a regular way from the masculine form. Both masculine and feminine forms are shown when different translations are required, e.g. *figlio* son, *figlia* daughter.

When the same word may be both an adjective and a noun, the gender of the noun is given only when it is fixed. Thus, **segreto** . . . *adj,nm* (secret) indicates that the word is an adjective or a masculine noun; **adulto** . . . *adj,n* indicates that the word is an adjective or a masculine or feminine noun (*l'adulto, l'adulta*).

Adverbs derived from adjectives are not shown in either section of the dictionary unless a separate translation is required, or unless the formation is irregular. Italian adverbs are considered regular if they are formed by adding *-mente* to the feminine singular of the adjective, e.g. *lenta—lentamente*, or by dropping the final *e* of a feminine adjective ending in a vowel followed by *-le* or *-re* and adding *-mente*, e.g. *facile—facilmente*. English adverbs are considered regular if they are formed by adding *-ly* to the adjective.

Irregular verbs are marked with an asterisk in the headword list of both sections of the dictionary. The principal parts of all these verbs, except compounds, are shown in the verb tables. For the conjugation of compounds the reader should refer to the base form, e.g. for *aggiungere*, see *giungere*.

A swung dash (~) before a change of part of speech indicates that the part of speech refers to the headword, not the preceding subentry shown in heavy type.

Infinitive	Past Tense	Past Participle	Infinitive	Past Tense	Past Participle
abide	abode or abided	abode or abided	draw	drew	drawn
			dream	dreamed or dreamt	dreamed or dreamt
arise	arose	arisen			
awake	awoke or awaked	awoke or awaked	drink	drank	drunk
			drive	drove	driven
be	was	been	dwell	dwelt	dwelt
bear[1]	bore	borne or born	eat	ate	eaten
beat	beat	beaten	fall	fell	fallen
become	became	become	feed	fed	fed
begin	began	begun	feel	felt	felt
bend	bent	bent	fight	fought	fought
bet	bet	bet	find	found	found
beware[2]			flee	fled	fled
bid	bid	bidden or bid	fling	flung	flung
bind	bound	bound	fly	flew	flown
bite	bit	bitten or bit	forbid	forbade or forbad	forbidden or forbid
bleed	bled	bled			
blow	blew	blown	forget	forgot	forgotten or forgot
break	broke	broken			
breed	bred	bred	forgive	forgave	forgiven
bring	brought	brought	forsake	forsook	forsaken
build	built	built	freeze	froze	frozen
burn	burnt or burned	burnt or burned	get	got	got
			give	gave	given
burst	burst	burst	go	went	gone
buy	bought	bought	grind	ground	ground
can	could		grow	grew	grown
cast	cast	cast	hang[3]	hung or hanged	hung or hanged
catch	caught	caught			
choose	chose	chosen	have	had	had
cling	clung	clung	hear	heard	heard
come	came	come	hide	hid	hidden or hid
cost	cost	cost	hit	hit	hit
creep	crept	crept	hold	held	held
crow	crowed or crew	crowed	hurt	hurt	hurt
cut	cut	cut	keep	kept	kept
deal	dealt	dealt	kneel	knelt	knelt
dig	dug or digged	dug or digged	knit	knitted or knit	knitted or knit
do	did	done	know	knew	known

English irregular verbs

Infinitive	Past Tense	Past Participle	Infinitive	Past Tense	Past Participle
lay	laid	laid	shear	sheared	sheared *or* shorn
lead	led	led			
lean	leant *or* leaned	leant *or* leaned	shed	shed	shed
leap	leapt *or* leaped	leapt *or* leaped	shine	shone	shone
learn	learnt *or* learned	learnt *or* learned	shoe	shod	shod
leave	left	left	shoot	shot	shot
lend	lent	lent	show	showed	shown
let	let	let	shrink	shrank *or* shrunk	shrunk *or* shrunken
lie	lay	lain			
light	lit *or* lighted	lit *or* lighted	shut	shut	shut
lose	lost	lost	sing	sang	sung
make	made	made	sink	sank	sunk
may	might		sit	sat	sat
mean	meant	meant	sleep	slept	slept
meet	met	met	slide	slid	slid
mow	mowed	mown	sling	slung	slung
must			slink	slunk	slunk
ought			slit	slit	slit
panic	panicked	panicked	smell	smelt *or* smelled	smelt *or* smelled
pay	paid	paid			
picnic	picnicked	picnicked	sow	sowed	sown *or* sowed
put	put	put	speak	spoke	spoken
quit	quitted *or* quit	quitted *or* quit	speed	sped *or* speeded	sped *or* speeded
read	read	read			
rid	rid *or* ridded	rid *or* ridded	spell	spelt *or* spelled	spelt *or* spelled
ride	rode	ridden	spend	spent	spent
ring	rang	rung	spill	spilt *or* spilled	spilt *or* spilled
rise	rose	risen	spin	spun	spun
run	ran	run	spit	spat *or* spit	spat *or* spit
saw	sawed	sawn *or* sawed	split	split	split
say	said	said	spread	spread	spread
see	saw	seen	spring	sprang	sprung
seek	sought	sought	stand	stood	stood
sell	sold	sold	steal	stole	stolen
send	sent	sent	stick	stuck	stuck
set	set	set	sting	stung	stung
sew	sewed	sewn *or* sewed	stink	stank *or* stunk	stunk
shake	shook	shaken	stride	strode	stridden
shall	should		strike	struck	struck

Infinitive	Past Tense	Past Participle	Infinitive	Past Tense	Past Participle
string	strung	strung	**wake**	woke	woken
strive	strove	striven	**wear**	wore	worn
swear	swore	sworn	**weave**	wove	woven *or* wove
sweep	swept	swept	**weep**	wept	wept
swell	swelled	swollen *or* swelled	**will**	would	
			win	won	won
swim	swam	swum	**wind**	wound	wound
swing	swung	swung	**wring**	wrung	wrung
take	took	taken	**write**	wrote	written
teach	taught	taught			
tear	tore	torn			
tell	told	told			
think	thought	thought			
throw	threw	thrown			
thrust	thrust	thrust			
traffic	trafficked	trafficked			
tread	trod	trodden *or* trod			

[1] when *bear* means *give birth to*, the past participle is always *born*.

[2] used only in the infinitive or as an imperative.

[3] the preferred form of the past tense and past participle when referring to death by hanging is *hanged*.

Italian irregular verbs

Infinitive	Present Indicative	Past Definite	Future	Past Participle
accendere	accendo	accesi	accenderò	acceso
accludere	accludo	acclusi	accluderò	accluso
accorgersi	mi accorgo	mi accorsi	mi accorgerò	accorto
addurre[1]	adduco	addussi	addurrò	addotto
affiggere[2]	affiggo	affissi	affiggerò	affisso
affliggere	affliggo	afflissi	affliggerò	afflitto
alludere	alludo	allusi	alluderò	alluso
andare	vado	andai	andrò	andato
annettere	annetto	annessi	annetterò	annesso
apparire	apparisco *or* appaio	apparvi *or* apparsi	apparirò	apparso
appendere	appendo	appesi	appenderò	appeso
aprire	apro	aprii *or* apersi	aprirò	aperto
ardere	ardo	arsi	arderò	arso
assalire	assalgo *or* assalisco	assalsi *or* assalii	assalirò	assalito
assistere	assisto	assistei	assisterò	assistito
assolvere	assolvo	assolsi	assolverò	assolto
assumere	assumo	assunsi	assumerò	assunto
avere	ho	avessi	avrò	avuto
bere	bevo	bevvi *or* bevei	berrò	bevuto
cadere	cado	caddi	cadrò	caduto
chiedere	chiedo	chiesi	chiederò	chiesto
chiudere	chiudo	chiusi	chiuderò	chiuso
cingere	cingo	cinsi	cingerò	cinto
cogliere	colgo	colsi	coglierò	colto
coincidere	coincido	coincisi	coinciderò	coinciso
comparire	comparisco *or* compaio	comparvi *or* comparsi	comparirò	comparso
comprimere	comprimo	compressi	comprimerò	compresso
concedere	concedo	concessi *or* concedei	concederò	concesso *or* conceduto
concludere	concludo	conclusi	concluderò	concluso
connettere	connetto	connessi	connetterò	connesso
conoscere	conosco	conobbi	conoscerò	conosciuto
coprire	copro	coprii *or* copersi	coprirò	coperto
correre	corro	corsi	correrò	corso
costruire	costruisco	costrussi	costruirò	costrutto

Infinitive	Present Indicative	Past Definite	Future	Past Participle
crescere	cresco	crebbi	crescerò	cresciuto
cuocere	cuocio	cossi	cuocerò	cotto
dare	do	diedo *or* detti	darò	dato
decidere	decido	decisi	deciderò	deciso
deludere	deludo	delusi	deluderò	deluso
deprimere	deprimo	depressi	deprimerò	depresso
difendere	difendo	difesi	difenderò	difeso
dipendere	dipendo	dipesi	dipenderò	dipeso
dipingere	dipingo	dipinsi	dipingerò	dipinto
dire	dico	dissi	dirò	detto
dirigere	dirigo	diressi	dirigerò	diretto
discutere	discuto	discussi	discuterò	discusso
dissuadere	dissuado	dissuasi	dissuaderò	dissuaso
distinguere	distinguo	distinsi	distinguerò	distinto
dividere	divido	divisi	dividerò	diviso
dolere	dolgo	dolsi	dorrò	doluto
dovere	devo *or* debbo	dovei	dovrò	dovuto
eludere	eludo	elusi	eluderò	eluso
emergere	emergo	emersi	emergerò	emerso
erigere	erigo	eressi	erigerò	eretto
escludere	escludo	esclusi	escluderò	escluso
esigere	esigo	esigei	esigerò	esatto
esistere	esisto	esistei	esisterò	esistito
espellere	espello	espulsi	espellerò	espulso
esplodere	esplodo	esplosi	esploderò	esploso
esprimere	esprimo	espressi	esprimerò	espresso
essere	sono	fui	sarò	stato
estinguere	estinguo	estinsi	estinguerò	estinto
evadere	evado	evasi	evaderò	evaso
fare	faccio	feci	farò	fatto
fendere	fendo	fendei	fenderò	fesso *or* fenduto
figgere	figgo	fissi	figgerò	fisso
fingere	fingo	finsi	fingerò	finto
fondere	fondo	fusi	fonderò	fuso
frangere	frango	fransi	frangerò	franto
friggere	friggo	frissi	friggerò	fritto
giacere	giaccio	giacqui	giacerò	giaciuto
giungere	giungo	giunsi	giungerò	giunto
illudere	illudo	illusi	illuderò	illuso

Italian irregular verbs

Infinitive	Present Indicative	Past Definite	Future	Past Participle
immergere	immergo	immersi	immergerò	immerso
imprimere	imprimo	impressi	imprimerò	impresso
incidere	incido	incisi	inciderò	inciso
includere	includo	inclusi	includerò	incluso
infliggere	infliggo	inflissi	infliggerò	inflitto
invadere	invado	invasi	invaderò	invaso
istruire	istruisco	istrussi	istruirò	istrutto
leggere	leggo	lessi	leggerò	letto
mettere	metto	misi	metterò	messo
mordere	mordo	'morsi	morderò	morso
morire	muoio	morii	morrò *or* morirò	morto
mungere	mungo	munsi	mungerò	munto
muovere	muovo	mossi	muoverò	mosso
nascere	nasco	nacqui	nascerò	nato
nascondere	nascondo	nascosi	nasconderò	nascosto
negligere	negligo	neglessi	negligerò	negletto
nuocere	nuoccio	nocqui	nuocerò	nociuto
offendere	offendo	offesi	offenderò	offeso
offrire	offro	offersi	offrirò	offerto
opprimere	opprimo	oppressi	opprimerò	oppresso
parere	paio	parvi *or* parsi	parrò	parso
percuotere	percuoto	percossi	percuoterò	percosso
perdere	perdo	persi *or* perdei	perderò	perso *or* perduto
persuadere	persuado	persuasi	persuaderò	persuaso
piacere	piaccio	piacqui	piacerò	piaciuto
piangere	piango	piansi	piangerò	pianto
piovere	piove	piovve	pioverà	piovuto
porgere	porgo	porsi	porgerò	porto
porre	pongo	posi	porrò	posto
potere	posso	potei	potrò	potuto
premere	premo	premei *or* pressi	premerò	premuto
prendere	prendo	presi	prenderò	preso
presumere	presumo	presunsi	presumerò	presunto
propendere	propendo	propendei	propenderò	propenso
proteggere	proteggo	protessi	proteggerò	protetto
provvedere	provvedo	provvidi	provvederò	provveduto *or* provvisto

Infinitive	Present Indicative	Past Definite	Future	Past Participle
prudere	prudo	prudei	pruderò	
pungere	pungo	punsi	pungerò	punto
radere	rado	rasi	raderò	raso
redigere	redigo	redassi	redigerò	redatto
reggere	reggo	ressi	reggerò	retto
rendere	rendo	resi	renderò	reso
reprimere	reprimo	repressi	reprimerò	represso
ridere	rido	risi	riderò	riso
riflettere	rifletto	riflessi *or* riflettei	rifletterò	riflesso *or* riflettuto
rifulgere	rifulgo	rifulsi	rifulgerò	
rilucere	riluco	rilussi *or* rilucei	rilucerò	
rimanere	rimango	rimasi	rimarrò	rimasto
risolvere	risolvo	risolsi	risolverò	risolto
rispondere	rispondo	risposi	risponderò	risposto
rodere	rodo	rosi	roderò	roso
rompere	rompo	ruppi	romperò	rotto
salire	salgo	salii	salirò	salito
sapere	so	seppi	saprò	saputo
scegliere	scelgo	scelsi	sceglierò	scelto
scendere	scendo	scesi	scenderò	sceso
sciogliere	sciolgo	sciolsi	scioglierò	sciolto
scomparire	scomparisco *or* scompaio	scomparvi *or* scomparsi	scomparirò	scomparso
sconnettere	sconnetto	sconnessi	sconnetterò	sconnesso
scoprire	scopro	scoprii *or* scopersi	scoprirò	scoperto
scorgere	scorgo	scorsi	scorgerò	scorto
scrivere	scrivo	scrissi	scriverò	scritto
scuotere	scuoto	scossi	scuoterò	scosso
sedere	siedo *or* seggo	sedei	sederò	seduto
seppellire	seppellisco	seppellii	seppellirò	seppellito *or* sepolto
soffrire	soffro	soffersi *or* soffrii	soffrirò	sofferto
solere	soglio			solito
sommergere	sommergo	sommersi	sommergerò	sommerso
sopprimere	sopprimo	soppressi	sopprimerò	soppresso

Italian irregular verbs

Infinitive	Present Indicative	Past Definite	Future	Past Participle
sorgere	sorgo	sorsi	sorgerò	sorto
sospendere	sospendo	sospesi	sospenderò	sospeso
spandere	spando	spansi	spanderò	spanto
spargere	spargo	sparsi	spargerò	sparso
sparire	sparisco	sparvi	sparirò	sparso
	or spaio	*or* sparsi		
spegnere	spengo	spensi	spegnerò	spento
spendere	spendo	spesi	spenderò	speso
spingere	spingo	spinsi	spingerò	spinto
stare	sto	stetti	starò	stato
stringere	stringo	strinsi	stringerò	stretto
strudere	strudo	strudei	struderò	
struggere	struggo	strussi	struggerò	strutto
succedere	succedo	successi	succederò	successo
		or succedei		*or* succeduto
tacere	taccio	tacqui	tacerò	taciuto
tendere	tendo	tesi	tenderò	teso
tenere	tengo	tenni	terrò	tenuto
tingere	tingo	tinsi	tingerò	tinto
toglieré	tolgo	tolsi	toglierò	tolto
			or torrò	
torcere	torco	torsi	torcerò	torto
trarre	traggo	trassi	trarrò	tratto
uccidere	uccido	uccisi	ucciderò	ucciso
udire	odo	udii	udirò	udito
ungere	ungo	unsi	ungerò	unto
uscire	esco	uscii	uscirò	uscito
valere	valgo	valsi	varrò	valso
				or valuto
vedere	vedo	vidi	vedrò	veduto *or* visto
venire	vengo	venni	verrò	venuto
vincere	vinco	vinsi	vincerò	vinto
vivere	vivo	vissi	vivrò	vissuto
volere	voglio	volli	vorrò	voluto
volgere	volgo	volsi	volgerò	volto

[1] All other verbs ending in -urre are conjugated like *addurre*.
[2] Most -ere verbs have the alternative endings of -ei or -etti in the Past Definite.

A

a, ad (a, ad) *prep* **1** to. **2** at. **3** in. **4** with. **5** by. **a dieci chilometri** ten kilometres away.

abate (a'bate) *nm* abbot.

abbagliare (abbaʎˈʎare) *vt* dazzle. **abbagliante** *adj* dazzling.

abbaiare (abbaˈjare) *vi* bark. **can che abbaia non morde** his bark is worse than his bite.

abbaino (abbaˈino) *nm* skylight.

abbaio (abˈbajo) *nm* bark.

abbandonare (abbandoˈnare) *vt* abandon, leave, desert. **abbandonarsi a** *vr* **1** indulge in. **2** give free rein to. **abbandonato** *adj* abandoned, deserted. **abbandono** *nm* neglect.

abbassare (abbasˈsare) *vt* lower. **abbassarsi** *vr* **1** subside. **2** (of temperature) fall. **abbassamento** *nm* **1** lowering. **2** fall.

abbastanza (abbasˈtantsa) *adv* **1** enough. **2** rather, quite.

abbattere (abˈbattere) *vt* **1** knock down. **2** defeat, overthrow. **3** dishearten. **abbattimento** *nm* dejection.

abbazia (abbatˈtsia) *nf* abbey.

abbellire (abbelˈlire) *vt* adorn, embellish. **abbellimento** *nm* embellishment.

abbeveratoio (abbeveraˈtojo) *nm* drinking trough.

abbi (ˈabbi) *v* see **avere.**

abbia (ˈabbja) *v* see **avere.**

abbiamo (abˈbjamo) *v* see **avere.**

abbiente (abˈbjɛnte) *adj* well-to-do, wealthy.

abbigliare (abbiʎˈʎare) *vt* dress up, adorn. **abbigliamento** *nm* clothing.

abboccare (abbokˈkare) *vt* **1** bite. **2** grip. **abboccarsi** *vr* confer. **abboccamento** *nm* interview, talk.

abbonare (abboˈnare) *vt* **1** deduct. **2** subscribe. **abbonarsi** *vr* **1** subscribe. **2** take out a season ticket. **abbonamento** *nm* **1** subscription. **2** season ticket. **abbonato** *nm* subscriber.

abbondare (abbonˈdare) *vi* abound, be plentiful. **abbondante** *adj* abundant. **abbondanza** (abbonˈdantsa) *nf* abundance.

abbordare (abborˈdare) *vt* **1** approach. **2** broach.

abborracciare (abborratˈtʃare) *vt* bungle, do carelessly.

abbottonare (abbottoˈnare) *vt* button (up).

abbozzare (abbotˈtsare) *vt* sketch, outline. **abbozzo** (abˈbɔttso) *nm* sketch, rough draft.

abbracciare (abbratˈtʃare) *vt* **1** embrace, hug. **2** comprise. **abbraccio** *nm* embrace, hug.

abbreviare (abbreˈvjare) *vt* abbreviate, shorten. **abbreviazione** *nf* abbreviation.

abbronzare (abbronˈdzare) *vt* tan. **abbronzarsi** *vr* become sun-tanned. **abbronzato** *adj* sunburnt, tanned. **abbronzatura** *nf* suntan.

abbrustolire (abbrustoˈlire) *vt* **1** toast. **2** burn.

abbuono (abˈbwɔno) *nm* **1** discount. **2** handicap.

abdicare (abdiˈkare) *vi* **abdicare a** abdicate, renounce. **abdicazione** *nf* abdication.

aberrazione (aberratˈtsjone) *nf* aberration.

abete (aˈbete) *nm* fir tree.

abietto (aˈbjɛtto) *adj* abject, vile.

abiezione (abjetˈtsjone) *nf* abjection, degradation.

abile (ˈabile) *adj* **1** capable, skilful. **2** suitable. **abilità** *nf* ability, skill.

abilitare (abiliˈtare) *vt* **1** train, equip. **2** qualify. **abilitazione** *nf* qualification, diploma.

Abissinia (abisˈsinia) *nf* Abyssinia. **abissino** *adj,n* Abyssinian.

abisso (aˈbisso) *nm* abyss, chasm.

abitare (abiˈtare) *vt* inhabit, occupy. *vi* dwell, live. **abitante** *nm* inhabitant. **abitato** *adj* inhabited. *nm* built-up area. **abitazione** *nf* dwelling.

abito[1] (ˈabito) *nm* **1** clothes. **2** suit. **abito da sera** evening dress.

abito[2] (ˈabito) *nm* habit.

abituare (abitu'are) vt accustom. **abituarsi a** vr get used to. **abituale** adj habitual.

abitudine (abi'tudine) nf habit, custom.

abolire (abo'lire) vt 1 abolish. 2 annul. **abolizione** nf abolition.

abominevole (abomi'nevole) adj abominable.

aborigeno (abo'ridʒeno) adj native, aboriginal. nm Aborigine.

aborrire (abor'rire) vt abhor, loathe.

abortire (abor'tire) vi 1 abort, miscarry. 2 fail. **aborto** (a'bɔrto) nm abortion.

abrasione (abra'zjone) nf abrasion.

abrasivo (abra'zivo) adj,nm abrasive.

abside ('abside) nf apse.

abusare (abu'zare) vt abuse, misuse, take advantage of. **abusivo** adj unauthorized. **abuso** nm abuse, misuse.

accademia (akka'dɛmja) nf academy, institute. **accademico** adj academic.

accadere* (akka'dere) vi happen, occur, take place. **accaduto** nm event, occurrence.

accampare (akkam'pare) vt 1 camp. 2 allege. 3 set forth. **accamparsi** vr camp. **accampamento** nm encampment, camp.

accanirsi (akka'nirsi) vr 1 rage. 2 persist. **accanimento** nm 1 fury. 2 tenacity. **accanito** adj 1 fierce. 2 obstinate.

accanto (ak'kanto) adv,prep near. **accanto a** beside.

accantonare (akkanto'nare) vt set aside.

accappatoio (akkappa'tojo) nm beach or bath robe.

accarezzare (akkaret'tsare) vt caress, stroke.

accavallare (akkaval'lare) vt overlap. **accavallare le gambe** cross one's legs.

accecare (attʃe'kare) vt blind.

accelerare (attʃele'rare) vi accelerate. vt quicken. **accelerato** nm slow train. **acceleratore** nm accelerator.

accendere* (at'tʃɛndere) vt 1 light. 2 switch on. **accendersi** vr catch fire. **accendino** (attʃen'dino) nm also **accendisigaro** (attʃendi'sigaro) cigarette lighter.

accennare (attʃen'nare) vi 1 nod, beckon. 2 mention, refer. vt point out, indicate. **accenno** nm 1 sign, nod. 2 mention.

accensione (attʃen'sjone) nf ignition.

accento (at'tʃɛnto) nm 1 accent. 2 tone. 3 stress.

accentrare (attʃen'trare) vt centralize, concentrate.

accentuare (attʃentu'are) vt accentuate, stress.

accertare (attʃer'tare) vt assure, verify.

accesi (at'tʃesi) v see **accendere.**

acceso (at'tʃeso) v see **accendere.** adj 1 alight, bright. 2 flushed.

accesso (at'tʃɛsso) nm 1 access. 2 fit. **accessibile** (attʃes'sibile) adj accessible.

accessorio (attʃes'sɔrjo) adj,nm accessory.

accetta (at'tʃetta) nf hatchet.

accettare (attʃet'tare) vt accept, agree. **accettazione** nf acceptance.

acchiappare (akkjap'pare) vt catch, grab hold of, seize.

acciaio (at'tʃajo) nm steel. **acciaio inossidabile** stainless steel. **acciaieria** nf steelworks.

accidente (attʃi'dɛnte) nm 1 accident, misfortune. 2 med fit. **non capire un accidente** not to understand a thing. **accidentale** adj accidental. **accidenti!** interj damn!

accigliarsi (attʃiʎ'ʎarsi) vr frown, knit one's brow. **accigliato** adj 1 frowning. 2 preoccupied.

acciocché (attʃok'ke) conj so that, in order that.

acciuga (at'tʃuga) nf anchovy. **pigiati come acciughe** packed like sardines.

acclamare (akkla'mare) vt acclaim, cheer. **acclamazione** nf acclamation.

acclimatare (akklima'tare) vt acclimatize.

accludere* (ak'kludere) vt enclose.

accoccolarsi (akkokko'larsi) vr crouch, squat.

accogliere* (ak'kɔʎʎere) vt 1 greet, welcome, receive. 2 accept. **accogliente** (akkoʎ'ʎɛnte) adj hospitable, cosy.

accomodare (akkomo'dare) vt 1 repair. 2 adjust. 3 tidy. vi suit. **accomodarsi** vr take a seat. **accomodamento** nm compromise. **accomodante** adj easy-going.

accompagnare (akkompaɲ'ɲare) vt accompany, escort. **accompagnamento** nm 1 accompaniment. 2 procession.

acconciare (akkon'tʃare) vt 1 prepare. 2 adorn. **acconciatura** (akkontʃa'tura) nf hairstyle.

accondiscendere* (akkondiʃ'ʃendere) vi concede, condescend.

acconsentire (akkonsen'tire) vi consent, approve.

accorciare (akkor'tʃare) vt shorten. vi become shorter.

accordare (akkor'dare) vt 1 grant. 2 tune. 3 match. **accordarsi** vr agree.

accordo (ak'kɔrdo) nm agreement. **andare**

d'accordo get on well. **d'accordo** okay, very well. **essere d'accordo** agree.

accorgersi (ak'kɔrdʒersi) vr notice, realize.

accorrere (ak'korrere) vi run up, come running.

accorsi (ak'kɔrsi) v see **accorgersi**.

accorto (ak'kɔrto) v see **accorgersi**. adj shrewd. **accortezza** (akkor'tettsa) nf shrewdness.

accostare (akkos'tare) vt bring near. **accosto** adv near by.

accovacciarsi (akkovat'tʃarsi) vr crouch, huddle.

accreditare (akkredi'tare) vt credit.

accrescere (ak'kreʃʃere) vt increase.

accumulare (akkumu'lare) vt amass, store, accumulate.

accurato (akku'rato) adj thorough, careful. **accuratezza** (akkura'tettsa) nf care.

accusare (akku'zare) vt accuse, charge. **accusa** nf accusation, charge.

acerbo (a'tʃerbo) adj bitter, unripe, sour.

acero (a'tʃero) nm maple tree.

aceto (a'tʃeto) nm vinegar. **sott'aceto** in vinegar.

acido (a'tʃido) adj,nm acid. **acidità** nf acidity.

acne ('akne) nm acne.

acqua ('akkwa) nf water. **acqua potabile** drinking water.

acquaforte (akkwa'fɔrte) nf 1 nitric acid. 2 etching.

acquaio (ak'kwajo) nm kitchen sink.

acquaragia (akkwa'radʒa) nf turpentine.

acquario (ak'kwarjo) nm 1 aquarium. 2 cap Aquarius.

acquatico (ak'kwatiko) adj aquatic.

acquavite (akkwa'vite) nf eau-de-vie.

acquazzone (akkwat'tsone) nm heavy shower, downpour.

acquedotto (akkwe'dotto) nm aqueduct.

acquerello (akkwe'rɛllo) nm watercolour.

acquistare (akkwis'tare) vt 1 buy, acquire. 2 obtain. 3 gain. **acquisto** nm purchase.

acre ('akre) adj 1 bitter. 2 pungent. 3 acrid. **acredine** (a'krɛdine) nf bitterness.

acrilico (a'kriliko) adj acrylic.

acro ('akro) nm acre.

acrobata (a'krɔbata) nm acrobat. **acrobatico** (akro'batiko) adj acrobatic. **acrobazia** nf acrobatics.

acustica (a'kustika) nf acoustics. **acustico** (a'kustiko) adj acoustic.

acuto (a'kuto) adj 1 sharp, acute. 2 intense.

ad (ad) prep see **a**.

adaguarsi (ada'dʒarsi) vr settle oneself.

adagio (a'dadʒo) adv slowly, carefully.

adattabile (adat'tabile) adj adaptable.

adattare (adat'tare) vt adapt, convert. **adatto** adj suitable.

addensare (adden'sare) vt thicken. **addensarsi** vr thicken.

addetto (ad'detto) adj 1 assigned. 2 attached. nm attaché.

addietro (ad'djetro) adv 1 behind. 2 ago, before.

addio (ad'dio) interj goodbye! farewell!

addirittura (addirit'tura) adv even, quite.

additare (addi'tare) vt indicate, point out.

addizionare (additsjo'nare) vt add (up). **addizionatrice** nf adding machine. **addizione** nf addition.

addolcire (addol'tʃire) vt 1 sweeten. 2 soothe.

addome (ad'dɔme) nm abdomen.

addomesticare (addomesti'kare) vt tame, train.

addormentare (addormen'tare) vt put to sleep. **addormentarsi** vr fall asleep.

addossare (addos'sare) vt 1 lean. 2 saddle, burden. **addossarsi** vr undertake.

addosso (ad'dɔsso) prep,adv 1 on, upon. 2 close, against. **levarsi d'addosso** get rid of. **mettere le mani addosso** hit, manhandle. **mettersi addosso** put on.

addotto (ad'dotto) v see **addurre**.

adduco (ad'duko) v see **addurre**.

addurre (ad'durre) vt 1 allege. 2 quote.

addussi (ad'dussi) v see **addurre**.

adeguare (ade'gware) vt make equal. **adeguarsi** vr adapt. **adeguato** adj 1 fitting. 2 fair.

adempiere (a'dempjere) vt carry out, fulfil. **adempimento** nm fulfilment.

adenoidi (ade'nɔidi) nf pl adenoids.

aderire (ade'rire) vt 1 adhere, stick. 2 support. **aderente** (ade'rɛnte) nm adherent. adj close fitting.

adesione (ade'zjone) nf 1 adhesion. 2 assent. **adesivo** adj adhesive.

adesso (a'dɛsso) adv now. **per adesso** for the moment.

adiacente (adja'tʃɛnte) adj adjacent.

adibire (adi'bire) vt 1 use as. 2 convert, adapt.

adirarsi (adi'rarsi) vr get angry. **adirato** adj angry.

adito ('adito) nm access, entrance.

adocchiare (adok'kjare) vt eye up, ogle.

adolescente (adoleʃ'ʃɛnte) adj,n adolescent. **adolescenza** (adoleʃ'ʃɛntsa) nf adolescence, teens.

adombrare (adom'brare) vt 1 shade, conceal. 2 outline. **adombrarsi** vr take offence.

adoperare (adope'rare) vt use.

adorare (ado'rare) vt adore, worship. **adorabile** (ado'rabile) adj adorable, charming. **adorazione** (adorat'tsjone) nf adoration.

adornare (ador'nare) vt adorn.

adottare (adot'tare) vt adopt. **adozione** nf adoption.

adrenalina (adrena'lina) nf adrenaline.

adriatico (adri'atiko) adj Adriatic. (**Mare**) **Adriatico** nm Adriatic (Sea).

adulazione (adulat'tsjone) nf adulation.

adulterare (adulte'rare) vt 1 adulterate. 2 tamper with.

adulterio (adul'tɛrjo) nm adultery.

adulto (a'dulto) adj,n adult.

adunare (adu'nare) vt assemble, gather together. **adunanza** (adu'nantsa) nf meeting.

adunque (a'dunkwe) conj,adv then.

aerare (ae'rare) vt air, ventilate.

aereo (a'ɛreo) adj aerial. nm aeroplane.

aerodinamica (aerodi'namika) nf aerodynamics.

aerodromo (ae'rɔdromo) nm aerodrome, airfield.

aeronautica (aero'nautika) nf 1 aeronautics. 2 airforce.

aeroplano (aero'plano) nm aeroplane.

aeroporto (aero'porto) nm airport.

aerosol (aero'sɔl) nm invar aerosol.

afa ('afa) nf sultry heat.

affabile (af'fabile) adj affable, friendly.

affaccendarsi (affattʃen'darsi) vr busy oneself.

affacciarsi (affat'tʃarsi) vr appear.

affamato (affa'mato) adj 1 starving, hungry. 2 eager.

affannare (affan'nare) vt trouble, worry. **affanno** nm worry, anxiety.

affare (af'fare) nm 1 affair, thing. 2 pl business. **uomo d'affari** nm business man. **affarista** nm speculator.

affascinare (affaʃʃi'nare) vt fascinate, bewitch. **affascinante** adj fascinating.

affastellare (affastel'lare) vt bundle, pile up.

affaticare (affati'kare) vt 1 tire. 2 strain.

affatto (af'fatto) adv completely. **non...affatto** not at all.

affermare (affer'mare) vt assert, affirm. **affermazione** nf affirmation.

afferrare (affer'rare) vt grasp, hold on to.

affettare[1] (affet'tare) vt affect. **affettato** adj affected, studied. **affettazione** nf affectation.

affettare[2] (affet'tare) vt slice, cut. **affettato** nm sliced cold ham or salami.

affetto[1] (af'fɛtto) adj afflicted, suffering.

affetto[2] (af'fɛtto) nm affection, love. **affettuoso** (affettu'oso) adj affectionate, loving.

affezionarsi (affettsjo'narsi) vr **affezionarsi a** become fond of or attached to. **affezionato** adj affectionate. **affezione** nf 1 affection. 2 illness, ailment.

affidare (affi'dare) vt entrust.

affiggere* (af'fiddʒere) vt 1 affix. 2 display.

affilare (affi'lare) vt sharpen. **affilato** adj sharp.

affiliare (affi'ljare) vt affiliate, associate. **affiliarsi** vr become a member. **affiliazione** nf affiliation.

affinché (affin'ke) conj so that, in order that.

affinità (affini'ta) nf affinity, resemblance.

affissi (af'fissi) v see **affiggere**.

affissione (affis'sjone) nf billposting. **è vietata l'affissione** no bills.

affisso (af'fisso) v see **affiggere**. nm bill, poster.

affittare (affit'tare) vt 1 let. 2 rent. 3 hire. **affittasi** to let. **affitto** nm 1 rent. 2 lease. **dare in affitto** let.

affliggere* (af'fliddʒere) vt 1 afflict. 2 torment.

afflissi (af'flissi) v see **affliggere**.

afflitto (af'flitto) v see **affliggere**. adj afflicted.

afflizione (afflit'tsjone) nf affliction.

affluire (afflu'ire) vi 1 flow. 2 pour in. **affluenza** (afflu'ɛntsa) nf affluence, abundance.

affogare (affo'gare) vt,vi 1 drown. 2 suffocate.

affollare (affol'lare) vt crowd, throng. **affollarsi** vr gather round. **affollato** adj crowded.

affondare (affon'dare) vt,vi sink.

affresco (af'fresko) nm fresco.

affrettare (affret'tare) vt hurry, quicken. **affrettarsi** vr hurry.

affrontare (affron'tare) vt confront, face. **affronto** nm insult.

affumicare (affumi'kare) vt 1 smoke. 2 cul cure.

Afganistan (afganis'tan) nm Afghanistan. **afgano** adj,n Afghan.

afoso (a'foso) adj sultry, close.

Africa (ˈafrika) nf Africa. **Africa del Sud** South Africa. **africano** adj,n African.

agenda (aˈdʒɛnda) nf **1** diary. **2** notebook.

agente (aˈdʒɛnte) nm agent, representative. **agente di cambio** stockbroker.

agenzia (adʒenˈtsia) nf agency, office. **agenzia di viaggi** travel agency.

agevole (aˈdʒevole) adj **1** comfortable. **2** reasonable.

aggettivo (addʒetˈtivo) nm adjective.

agghiacciare (aggjatˈtʃare) vt freeze.

aggiornare (addʒorˈnare) vt **1** bring up to date. **2** adjourn. **aggiornamento** nm **1** revision, bringing up to date. **2** adjournment.

aggiudicare (addʒudiˈkare) vt award.

aggiungere (adˈdʒundʒere) vt add. **aggiunta** nf addition.

aggiustare (addʒusˈtare) vt **1** repair. **2** adjust. **3** settle.

aggrappare (aggrapˈpare) vt seize. **aggrapparsi** vr cling.

aggravare (aggraˈvare) vt aggravate. **aggravarsi** vr become worse, deteriorate.

aggregare (aggreˈgare) vt enrol. **aggregarsi** vr join.

aggressione (aggresˈsjone) nf assault, attack. **aggressivo** adj aggressive.

aggrottare (aggrotˈtare) vt **aggrottare le ciglia** frown.

aggruppare (aggrupˈpare) vt group together.

agguato (agˈgwato) nm ambush. **tendere un agguato** lay an ambush.

agile (ˈadʒile) adj **1** agile. **2** alert. **agilità** nf agility.

agio (ˈadʒo) nm ease, comfort.

agire (aˈdʒire) vi **1** act, behave. **2** work.

agitare (adʒiˈtare) vt **1** shake. **2** trouble. **agitarsi** vr **1** toss. **2** worry. **agitato** adj restless. **agitatore** nm agitator. **agitazione** nf agitation.

agli (ˈaʎʎi) contraction of **a gli.**

aglio (ˈaʎʎo) nm garlic.

agnello (anˈɲɛllo) nm lamb.

agnostico (anˈɲɔstiko) adj,nm agnostic.

ago (ˈago) nm needle.

agonia (agoˈnia) nf agony. **agonizzare** (agonidˈdzare) vi be on the point of death.

agopuntura (agopunˈtura) nf acupuncture.

agosto (aˈgosto) nm August.

agraria (aˈgrarja) nf agriculture. **agrario** adj agrarian.

agricoltore (agrikolˈtore) nm farmer. **agricolo** (aˈgrikolo) adj agricultural. **agricoltura** nf agriculture.

agrifoglio (agriˈfɔʎʎo) nm holly.

agro (ˈagro) adj **1** bitter. **2** harsh.

agrumi (aˈgrumi) nm pl citrus fruits.

aguzzare (agutˈtsare) vt **1** sharpen. **2** stimulate. **aguzzo** adj sharp, pointed.

ahimé (aiˈmɛ) interj alas!

ai (ˈai) contraction of **a i.**

aia (ˈaja) nf threshing floor. **menare il can per l'aia** beat about the bush.

Aia, L' (ˈaja) nf The Hague.

airone (aiˈrone) nm heron.

aiuola (aˈjwɔla) nf flowerbed.

aiutare (ajuˈtare) vt help, aid. **aiutante** nm **1** helper. **2** adjutant. **aiuto** nm help.

aizzare (aitˈtsare) vt provoke, incite.

al (al) contraction of **a il.**

ala (ˈala) nf, pl **ali** wing.

alabastro (alaˈbastro) nm alabaster.

alano (aˈlano) nm Great Dane.

alba (ˈalba) nf dawn, daybreak.

Albania (albaˈnia) nf Albania. **albanese** adj,n Albanian.

albatro (ˈalbatro) nm albatross.

albergare (alberˈgare) vt **1** house. **2** cherish. vi lodge.

albergo (alˈbɛrgo) nm hotel. **albergo diurno** toilet facilities. **albergo per la gioventù** youth hostel.

albero (ˈalbero) nm **1** tree. **2** mast. **3** shaft.

album (ˈalbum) nm album.

alcali (ˈalkali) nm invar alkali.

alchimia (alkiˈmia) nf alchemy. **alchimista** nm alchemist.

alcool (ˈalkool) nm invar alcohol. **alcoolico** (alkoˈɔliko) adj alcoholic.

alcoolismo (alkooˈlizmo) nm alcoholism. **alcoolizzato** (alkoolidˈdzato) adj,n alcoholic.

alcunché (alkuˈke) pron **1** anything. **2** something.

alcuno (alˈkuno) adj **1** any. **2** some. pron **1** somebody. **2** anybody.

alfabeto (alfaˈbɛto) nm alphabet. **alfabetico** (alfaˈbɛtiko) adj alphabetical.

alfiere (alˈfjɛre) nm game bishop.

alfine (alˈfine) adv at last.

alga (ˈalga) nf seaweed.

algebra (ˈaldʒebra) nf algebra.

Algeria (ald3e'ria) *nf* Algeria. **algerino** *adj,n* Algerian.

aliante (ali'ante) *nm* glider.

alibi ('alibi) *nm invar* alibi.

alice (a'litʃe) *nf* anchovy.

alienare (alje'nare) *vt* alienate. **alienato** *nm* lunatic. **alienazione** *nf* 1 alienation. 2 insanity.

alieno (a'ljɛno) *adj* **alieno da** averse to.

alimentare (alimen'tare) *vt* nourish, feed. **alimentari** *nm pl* foodstuffs. **negozio di alimentari** *nm* grocer's shop. **alimento** *nm* 1 food. 2 *pl* alimony.

aliscafo (alis'kafo) *nm* hydrofoil.

alito ('alito) *nm* breath.

all' (al) contraction of **a l'**.

alla ('alla) contraction of **a la.**

allacciare (allat'tʃare) *vt* lace up, fasten.

allagare (alla'gare) *vt* flood. **allagamento** *nm* flood.

allargare (allar'gare) *vt* widen, broaden.

allarmare (allar'mare) *vt* alarm. **allarmarsi** *vr* take fright. **allarmante** *adj* alarming. **allarme** *nm* alarm.

alle ('alle) contraction of **a le.**

alleanza (alle'antsa) *nf* alliance.

alleato (alle'ato) *adj* allied. **alleato** *nm* ally.

allegare (alle'gare) *vt* 1 allege. 2 enclose. **allegazione** *nf* allegation.

allegoria (allego'ria) *nf* allegory. **allegorico** (alle'gɔriko) *adj* allegorical.

allegro (al'legro) *adj* happy, gay. **allegria** *nf* gaiety, joy.

allenare (alle'nare) *vt* train. **allenamento** *nm* training. **allenatore** *nm* coach, trainer.

allentare (allen'tare) *vt* loosen, relax.

allergia (aller'dʒia) *nf* allergy. **allergico** *adj* allergic.

allestire (alles'tire) *vt* 1 prepare. 2 stage. **allestimento** *nm* preparation.

allettare (allet'tare) *vt* lure, entice.

allevare (alle'vare) *vt* 1 bring up. 2 breed.

alleviare (alle'vjare) *vt* alleviate.

allibratore (allibra'tore) *nm* bookmaker, turf accountant.

allievo (al'ljɛvo) *nm* pupil, student.

alligatore (alliga'tore) *nm* alligator.

allineare (alline'are) *vt* put in line, line up.

allitterazione (allitterat'tsjone) *nf* alliteration.

allo ('allo) contraction of **a lo.**

allodola (al'lɔdola) *nf* lark.

alloggiare (allod'dʒare) *vt,vi* lodge. **alloggio** (al'lɔddʒo) *nm* lodgings.

allontanare (allonta'nare) *vt* remove, take away, avert. **allontanarsi** *vr* go away. **allontanamento** *nm* removal.

allora (al'lora) *adv* 1 then. 2 at that time. 3 in that case. **d'allora in poi** from then on.

allorché (allor'ke) *conj* when.

alloro (al'lɔro) *nm* laurel.

allucinazione (allutʃinat'tsjone) *nf* hallucination.

alludere* (al'ludere) *vi* allude, hint.

alluminio (allu'minjo) *nm* aluminium.

allungare (allun'gare) *vt* 1 lengthen, let down (a hem). 2 dilute. 3 hand, pass. 4 quicken. **allungarsi** *vr* lengthen, stretch.

allusi (al'luzi) *v* see **alludere.**

allusione (allu'zjone) *nf* allusion.

alluso (al'luzo) *v* see **alludere.**

almeno (al'meno) *adv* at least.

Alpi ('alpi) *nf pl* Alps. **alpino** *adj* alpine.

alpinismo (alpi'nizmo) *nm* mountaineering, (mountain) climbing. **alpinista** *nm* mountaineer, (mountain) climber.

alquanto (al'kwanto) *adj* quite a lot (of). *adv* somewhat, rather.

alt (alt) *interj* halt! stop!

altalena (alta'lena) *nf* 1 swing. 2 seesaw.

altare (al'tare) *nm* altar.

alterare (alte'rare) *vt* alter, forge, falsify, adulterate. **alterarsi** *vr* 1 go bad, perish. 2 become angry. **alterazione** *nf* alteration, forgery.

alternare (alter'nare) *vt* alternate. **alternarsi** *vr* alternate. **alternativa** *nf* alternative. **alternativo** *adj* alternative. **alterno** (al'tɛrno) *adj* alternate.

altero (al'tero) *adj* haughty, arrogant.

altezza (al'tettsa) *nf* 1 height. 2 depth. 3 width. 4 *cap* Highness. **essere all'altezza** be capable.

altipiano (alti'pjano) *nm* plateau.

altitudine (alti'tudine) *nf* altitude.

alto ('alto) *adj* 1 high, tall. 2 loud. **ad alta voce** aloud. ~*adv* high. **in alto** upwards. **mani in alto** hands up. **altoparlante** *nm* loudspeaker.

altresì (altre'si) *adv* also, as well.

altrettanto (altret'tanto) *adj,pron* as much, as many. *interj* the same to you! *adv* equally.

altro ('altro) *adj* 1 other. 2 different. 3 previous. 4 next. **altro ieri** day before yesterday. ~*pron* another. **altro che!** yes indeed! **non**

volere altro want nothing more. **tutt'altro** on the contrary.

altronde (al'tronde) **d'altronde** adv 1 besides. 2 on the other hand.

altrove (al'trove) adv elsewhere.

altrui (al'trui) adj invar of others.

alunno (a'lunno) nm educ pupil.

alveare (alve'are) nm beehive.

alzare (al'tsare) vt 1 raise, lift up. 2 erect. **alzarsi** vr get up, rise. **alzarsi in piedi** stand up.

amaca (a'maka) nf hammock.

amare (a'mare) vt love. **amabile** (a'mabile) adj 1 lovable. 2 amiable. 3 (of wine) sweet. **amante** nm lover. **amato** adj loved. nm loved-one. **amatore** nm 1 lover. 2 connoisseur.

amarena (ama'rɛna) nf black cherry.

amaro (a'maro) adj bitter. nm aperitive. **amarezza** nf bitterness.

amatriciano (amatri't∫ano) **spaghetti all'amatriciana** nm pl spaghetti with a sauce made of pork, onion, tomato, and cheese.

ambasciata (amba∫'∫ata) nf embassy. **ambasciatore** (amba∫∫a'tore) nm ambassador.

ambedue (ambe'due) adj invar,pron invar both.

ambidestro (ambi'dɛstro) adj ambidextrous.

ambientarsi (ambjen'tarsi) vr get used to one's surroundings, find one's feet. **ambiente** (am'bjɛnte) nm surroundings, environment, habitat. adj surrounding. **temperatura ambiente** nf room temperature.

ambiguo (am'biguo) adj 1 ambiguous. 2 dubious. **ambiguità** nf ambiguity.

ambito (am'bito) nm range, scope.

ambivalente (ambiva'lɛnte) adj ambivalent.

ambizione (ambit'tsjone) nf ambition. **ambizioso** (ambit'tsjoso) adj ambitious.

ambo ('ambo) adj,pron invar both.

ambra ('ambra) nf amber.

ambulante (ambu'lante) adj wandering, itinerant.

ambulanza (ambu'lantsa) nf ambulance.

ambulatorio (ambula'tɔrjo) nm 1 surgery. 2 outpatients' department.

ameba (a'mɛba) nf amoeba.

ameno (a'mɛno) adj pleasant, enjoyable.

America (a'mɛrika) nf America. **America del Nord/Sud** North/South America. **americano** adj,n American.

ametista (ame'tista) nf amethyst.

amianto (a'mjanto) asbestos.

amichevole (ami'kevole) adj friendly.

amico (a'miko) nm, pl **amici** friend. **amicizia** (ami't∫ittsja) nf friendship.

amido ('amido) nm starch.

ammaccare (ammak'kare) vt bruise. **ammaccatura** nf bruise.

ammaestrare (ammaes'trare) vt train, teach. **ammaestrato** adj tame. **ammaestratore** nm trainer.

ammalarsi (amma'larsi) vr fall ill. **ammalato** adj sick. nm sick person, patient.

ammansire (amman'sire) vt 1 tame. 2 calm down.

ammassare (ammas'sare) vt amass, accumulate. **ammasso** nm heap, pile.

ammazzare (ammat'tsare) vt kill, murder. **ammazzarsi** vr 1 kill oneself. 2 wear oneself out. **ammazzatoio** nm slaughterhouse.

ammenda (am'mɛnda) nf 1 amends. 2 fine.

ammettere* (am'mettere) vt 1 admit. 2 allow, grant. 3 suppose.

ammiccare (ammik'kare) vi wink. **ammicco** nm wink.

amministrare (amminis'trare) vt 1 administer. 2 manage. **amministrativo** adj administrative. **amministratore** nm director, manager. **amministrazione** nf administration.

ammiraglio (ammi'raʎʎo) nm admiral. **ammiragliato** nm admiralty.

ammirare (ammi'rare) vt admire, praise. **ammiratore** nm admirer. **ammirazione** nf admiration.

ammissibile (ammis'sibile) adj permissible, acceptable.

ammissione (ammis'sjone) nf admission. **esame di ammissione** nm entrance exam.

ammobiliare (ammobi'ljare) vt furnish. **ammobiliato** adj furnished.

ammollare (ammol'lare) vt soak.

ammollire (ammol'lire) vt soften.

ammoniaca (ammo'niaka) nf ammonia.

ammonire (ammo'nire) vt warn, reprimand. **ammonimento** nm reprimand, reproof.

ammontare (ammon'tare) vi amount.

ammorbidire (ammorbi'dire) vt soften.

ammortire (ammor'tire) vt 1 deaden. 2 dull, tone down. **ammortizzatore** (ammortiddza'tore) nm shock absorber.

ammucchiare (ammuk'kjare) vt pile up, amass.

ammuffire (ammuf'fire) vi grow mouldy.

ammutinamento (ammutina'mento) nm mutiny.

amnistia (amnis'tia) *nf* amnesty.

amo ('amo) *nm* fishhook.

amorale (amo'rale) *adj* amoral.

amore (a'more) *nm* love. **amore proprio** self-esteem. **fare all'amore** or **l'amore** make love. **amoroso** (amo'roso) *adj* loving. *nm* lover.

ampère (ã'per) *nm* ampere.

ampio ('ampjo) *adj* ample, vast, spacious. **ampiezza** (am'pjettsa) *nf* breadth, abundance.

amplificare (amplifi'kare) *vt* amplify. **amplificatore** *nm* amplifier.

amputare (ampu'tare) *vt* amputate. **amputazione** *nf* amputation.

anacronismo (anakro'nizmo) *nm* anachronism.

anagramma (ana'gramma) *nm* anagram.

analcolico (anal'koliko) *adj* non-alcoholic.

anale (a'nale) *adj* anal.

analfabeta (analfa'bɛta) *adj* illiterate. *nm* illiterate person. **analfabetismo** *nm* illiteracy.

analizzare (analid'dzare) *vt* analyse. **analisi** (a'nalizi) *nf invar* analysis. **analitico** (ana-'litiko) *adj* analytical.

analogo (a'nalogo) *adj* analogous. **analogia** *nf* analogy.

ananas ('ananas) *nm* pineapple.

anarchia (anar'kia) *nf* anarchy. **anarchico** (a'narkiko) *nm* anarchist.

anatomia (anato'mia) *nf* anatomy. **anatomico** (ana'tomiko) *adj* anatomical.

anatra ('anatra) *nf* duck. **anatroccolo** (ana-'trokkolo) *nm* duckling.

anca ('anka) *nf* hip, thigh, haunch.

anche ('anke) *conj* 1 also, too. 2 moreover. 3 even. **quand'anche** even if.

ancora[1] ('ankora) *nf* anchor.

ancora[2] (an'kora) *adv* 1 still. 2 yet. 3 more. 4 again.

andare* (an'dare) *vi* 1 go. 2 work, function. 3 suit. 4 be popular. 5 please, be to one's taste. **a lungo andare** in the long run. **andare a finire** end up. **va'fan culo!** *tab* fuck off! **va'via!** *tab* piss off! **andarsene** *vr* go away, leave. **andante** *adj* current, ordinary. **andata** *nf* outward journey. **biglietto d'andata e ritorno** *nm* return ticket. **andatura** *nf* gait.

andirivieni (andir'vjɛni) *nm invar* coming and going.

andito ('andito) *nm* passageway.

andrò (an'drɔ) *v* see **andare.**

aneddoto (a'nɛddoto) *nm* anecdote.

anelare (ane'lare) *vi* pant, gasp.

anello (a'nɛllo) *nm* ring. **anello di fidanzamento/matrimonio** engagement/wedding ring.

anemia (ane'mia) *nf* anaemia. **anemico** (a'nɛmiko) *adj* anaemic.

anemone (a'nɛmone) *nm* anemone. **anestesista** (aneste'zista) *nm* anaesthetist.

anestetico (anes'tɛtiko) *adj,nm* anaesthetic. **anestetizzare** (anestetid'dzare) *vt* anaesthetize.

anfetamina (anfeta'mina) *nf* amphetamine.

anfibio (an'fibjo) *adj* amphibious. *nm* amphibian.

angariare (anga'rjare) *vt* harass.

angelica (an'dʒelika) *nf* angelica.

angelo ('andʒelo) *nm* angel. **angelico** *adj* angelic.

anglicano (angli'kano) *adj,n* Anglican.

angolo ('angolo) *nm* 1 corner. 2 angle. **angolare** *adj* angular.

angoscia (an'gɔʃʃa) *nf* anguish, desolation. **angoscioso** (angoʃ'ʃoso) *adj* painful, harrowing.

anguilla (an'gwilla) *nf* eel.

anguria (an'gurja) *nf* watermelon.

anice (a'nitʃe) *nm* aniseed.

anima ('anima) *nf* 1 spirit. 2 mind. 3 soul.

animale (ani'male) *nm* 1 animal. 2 brute. *adj* animal. **animalesco** *adj* bestial.

animare (ani'mare) *vt* 1 enliven. 2 encourage. **animato** *adj* animated, vivacious.

animo ('animo) *nm* 1 mind. 2 courage.

animosità (animosi'ta) *nf* animosity.

annacquare (annak'kware) *vt* dilute, water down.

annaffiare (annaf'fjare) *vt* water (plants, etc.). **annaffiatoio** *nm* watering-can.

annali (an'nali) *nm pl* annals.

annata (an'nata) *nf* 1 year. 2 crop.

annebbiare (anneb'bjare) *vt* cloud, obscure. **annebbiarsi** *vr* 1 become foggy. 2 grow dim.

annegare (anne'gare) *vt,vi* drown.

annettere* (an'nɛttere) *vt* annex. **annettere importanza** attach importance. **annesso** *nm* annexe.

annichilare (anniki'lare) *vt* annihilate, destroy.

annientare (annjen'tare) *vt* reduce to nothing, destroy.

anniversario (anniver'sarjo) *nm* anniversary.

anno ('anno) *nm* year. **anno scorso** last year. **capo d'anno** *nm* New Year's Day. **quanti anni hai?** how old are you?

annodare (anno'dare) vt **1** knot, tie. **2** conclude.

annoiare (anno'jare) vt **1** bore. **2** annoy. **annoiarsi** vr be bored.

annotare (anno'tare) vt annotate, note, jot down. **annotazione** nf entry, note.

annuario (annu'arjo) nm yearbook, directory.

annuire (annu'ire) vi nod in assent.

annullare (annul'lare) vt annul, cancel. **annullamento** nm annulment.

annunciare (annun'tʃare) vt **1** announce. **2** foretell. **annunciatore** nm announcer. **annuncio** nm announcement, notice.

Annunciazione (annuntʃæt'tsjone) nf Annunciation.

annusare (annu'sare) vt sniff, smell. **annusare tabacco** take snuff.

annuvolare (annuvo'lare) vt darken. **annuvolarsi** vr cloud over, darken.

ano ('ano) nm anus.

anodo ('anodo) nm anode.

anomalia (anoma'lia) nf anomaly.

anonimo (a'nɔnimo) adj anonymous. **società anonima** nf limited company.

anormale (anor'male) adj abnormal. **anormalità** nf abnormality.

ansare (an'sare) vi puff, pant.

ansia ('ansja) nf anxiety. **ansioso** (an'sjoso) adj anxious.

antagonismo (antago'nizmo) nm antagonism. **antagonista** nm antagonist.

antartico (an'tartiko) adj,nm Antarctic.

antenato (ante'nato) nm ancestor.

antenna (an'tenna) nf **1** antenna, feeler. **2** aerial.

anteprima (ante'prima) nf preview.

anteriore (ante'rjore) adj **1** front. **2** previous.

antiabbagliante (antiabbaʎ'ʎante) adj antiglare. **faro antiabbagliante** nm dipped headlight.

antiaereo (antia'ɛreo) adj anti-aircraft.

antibiotico (antibi'ɔtiko) adj,nm antibiotic.

anticamera (anti'kamera) nf antechamber, waiting room.

antichità (antiki'ta) nf antiquity.

anticiclone (antitʃi'klone) nm anticyclone.

anticipare (antitʃi'pare) vt **1** anticipate. **2** comm advance. vi be early.

anticipo (an'titʃipo) nm **1** anticipation. **2** deposit. **in anticipo** ahead of time.

antico (an'tiko) adj **1** ancient. **2** old-fashioned. **3** former.

anticonformista (antikonfor'miesta) nm nonconformist.

anticongelante (antikondʒe'lante) nm antifreeze.

anticorpo (an'tikɔrpo) nm antibody.

antidoto (an'tidoto) nm antidote.

antifecondativo (antifekonda'tivo) adj,nm contraceptive.

antifurto (anti'furto) adj anti-theft.

antilope (an'tilope) nm antelope.

antipasto (anti'pasto) nm hors d'oeuvre.

antipatia (antipa'tia) nf dislike, antipathy. **antipatico** (anti'patiko) adj disagreeable, unpleasant.

antiquario (anti'kwarjo) nm antique dealer.

antiquato (anti'kwato) adj antiquated.

antisemita (antise'mita) adj anti-Semitic. **antisemitismo** nm anti-Semitism.

antisettico (anti'sɛttiko) adj,nm antiseptic.

antisociale (antiso'tʃale) adj antisocial.

antitesi (an'titezi) nf invar antithesis.

antologia (antolo'dʒia) nf anthology.

antro ('antro) nm **1** cave. **2** den.

antropologia (antropolo'dʒia) nf anthropology. **antropologo** (antri'pɔlogo) nm anthropologist.

anulare (anu'lare) nm ring finger.

anzi ('antsi) adv **1** rather. **2** on the contrary.

anziano (an'tsjano) adj **1** old, aged. **2** senior. **anzianità** nf seniority.

anziché (antsi'ke) conj rather than.

anzitutto (antsi'tutto) adv first of all.

apatia (apa'tia) nf apathy. **apatico** adj apathetic.

ape ('ape) nf bee.

aperitivo (aperi'tivo) nm aperitive.

aperso (a'pɛrsi) v see **aprire**.

aperto (a'pɛrto) v see **aprire**. adj **1** open. **2** frank. **all'aperto** in the open air. **apertura** nf opening, gap.

apice ('apitʃe) nm summit, height.

apostolo (a'pɔstolo) nm apostle, disciple.

apostrofo (a'pɔstrofo) nm apostrophe.

appagare (appa'gare) vt **1** satisfy. **2** quench.

appaio (ap'pajo) v see **apparire**.

appalto (ap'palto) nm contract.

appannare (appan'nare) vt veil, blur.

apparato (appa'rato) nm **1** decoration, pomp. **2** apparatus. **3** equipment. **apparato scenico** props.

apparecchiare (apparek'kjare) vt set (the table). **apparecchio** nm **1** machine, device, set. **2** aeroplane.

apparenza (appa'rɛntsa) *nf* aspect, appearance. **salvare le apparenze** keep up appearances.

apparire* (appa'rire) *vi* appear, seem. **apparizione** *nf* apparition.

apparsi (ap'parsi) *v see* **apparire**.

apparso (ap'parso) *v see* **apparire**.

appartamento (apparta'mento) *nm* flat.

appartare (appar'tare) *vt* set aside, separate. **appartato** *adj* secluded.

appartenere* (apparte'nere) *vi* belong.

apparvi (ap'parvi) *v see* **apparire**.

appassionare (appassjo'nare) *vt* enthrall, captivate. **appassionarsi** *vr* grow very fond of.

appena (ap'pena) *adv* 1 hardly, scarcely. 2 as soon as. **appena un po'** just a little.

appendere* (ap'pɛndere) *vt* hang. **appendice** *nf* appendix.

appendicite (appendi't∫ite) *nf* appendicitis.

appesi (ap'pesi) *v see* **appendere**.

appeso (ap'peso) *v see* **appendere**.

appestare (appes'tare) *vt* infect.

appetito (appe'tito) *nm* appetite. **appetitoso** (appeti'toso) *adj* appetizing.

appianare (appja'nare) *vt* 1 flatten, level. 2 settle.

appiccare (appik'kare) *vt* 1 hang. 2 attach.

appiccicare (appitt∫i'kare) *vt* stick, glue. **appiccicoso** (appitt∫i'koso) *adj* sticky.

appiè (ap'pjɛ) *prep* at the foot.

appigionare (appidʒo'nare) *vt* let.

appisolarsi (appizo'larsi) *vr* doze.

applaudire (applau'dire) *vt* applaud, clap. **applauso** (ap'plauzo) *nm* applause.

applicare (appli'kare) *vt* 1 put on, affix. 2 apply. **applicazione** *nf* application.

appoggiare (appod'dʒare) *vt* lean, rest. **appoggio** (ap'pɔddʒo) *nm* support.

apporre* (ap'porre) *vt* add, affix.

apportare (appor'tare) *vt* bring.

apposito (ap'pɔzito) *adj* suitable, proper.

apposta (ap'pɔsta) *adv* on purpose, deliberately.

apprendere* (ap'prɛndere) *vt* learn. **apprendista** *nm* apprentice.

apprensione (appren'sjone) *nf* apprehension.

apprestare (appres'tare) *vt* prepare.

apprezzare (appret'tsare) *vt* appreciate.

approfittare (approfit'tare) *vi* gain, profit. **approfittarsi di** *vr* take advantage of.

approfondire (approfon'dire) *vt* go into thoroughly.

approssimativo (approssima'tivo) *adj* approximate, rough.

approvare (appro'vare) *vt* approve. **approvazione** *nf* approval.

appuntamento (appunta'mento) *nm* appointment.

appuntare (appun'tare) *vt* 1 sharpen. 2 point. 3 fix. **appuntare gli orecchi** prick up one's ears. **appuntalapis** (appunta'lapis) *nm invar* pencil-sharpener.

appunto[1] (ap'punto) *nm* 1 note. 2 mark.

appunto[2] (ap'punto) *adv* exactly, precisely.

appurare (appu'rare) *vt* verify.

aprile (a'prile) *nm* April.

aprire* (a'prire) *vt* 1 open. 2 inaugurate. 3 unlock. 4 switch on. **apribottiglie** *nm invar* bottle opener. **apriscatole** (apris'katole) *nm invar* tin-opener.

aquila ('akwila) *nf* eagle. **aquilone** (akwi'lone) *nm* kite.

Arabia (a'rabia) *nf* Arabia. **Arabia Saudita** (sau'dita) Saudi Arabia. **arabico** (a'rabiko) *adj* Arabic, Arabian. **arabo** *adj* Arab. *nm* 1 Arab. 2 Arabic.

arachide (a'rakide) *nf* peanut.

aragosta (ara'gosta) *nf* lobster.

araldo (a'raldo) *nm* herald. **araldico** *adj* heraldic.

arancia (a'rant∫a) *nf* 1 *bot* orange. 2 orange (colour). **aranciata** *nf* orangeade. **arancio** *nm* orange tree. **arancione** *adj* orange-coloured.

arare (a'rare) *vt* plough. **arabile** *adj* arable. **aratro** *nm* plough.

arazzo (a'rattso) *nm* tapestry.

arbitrare (arbi'trare) *vt* 1 judge. 2 umpire, referee. **arbitrario** *adj* arbitrary.

arbitrio (ar'bitrjo) *nm* will. **libero arbitrio** free will. **arbitro** *nm* 1 judge, arbitrator. 2 umpire, referee.

arbusto (ar'busto) *nm* shrub.

arca ('arka) *nf* ark.

arcaico (ar'kaiko) *adj* archaic.

arcata (ar'kata) *nf* 1 arch. 2 arcade.

archeologia (arkeolo'dʒia) *nf* archaeology. **archeologico** (arkeo'lɔdʒiko) *adj* archaeological. **archeologo** (arke'ɔlogo) *nm* archaeologist.

archetipo (ar'kɛtipo) *nm* archetype.

architetto (arki'tetto) *nm* architect. **architettura** *nf* architecture.

archivio (ar'kivjo) *nm* archive.

arciduca (art∫i'duka) *nm* archduke.

arciere (ar't∫ɛre) *nm* archer.

arcigno (ar'tʃiɲɲo) *adj* sullen.

arcipelago (artʃi'pɛlago) *nm* archipelago.

arcivescovo (artʃi'veskovo) *nm* archbishop.

arco ('arko) *nm* **1** bow. **2** arch. **3** *pl* string instruments.

arcobaleno (arkoba'leno) *nm* rainbow.

ardere* ('ardere) *vt,vi* burn. **ardente** *adj* burning.

ardesia (ar'dezja) *nf* slate.

ardire (ar'dire) *vi* dare. **ardito** *adj* daring, bold.

arduo ('arduo) *adj* **2** arduous. **2** steep.

area ('area) *nf* area, zone.

arena *nf* **1** (a'rena) sand. **2** (a'rɛna) arena. **2** arena.

arenare (are'nare) *vi* run aground.

argento (ar'dʒɛnto) *nm* silver. **argenteo** (ar'dʒɛnteo) *adj* silvery. **argenteria** *nf* silverware. **argentiere** (ardʒen'tjɛre) *nm* silversmith.

argilla (ar'dʒilla) *nf* clay.

argine ('ardʒine) *nm* dyke.

argomento (argo'mento) *nm* **1** topic, subject, theme. **2** summary.

arguto (ar'guto) *adj* shrewd, quick-witted.

aria ('arja) *nf* **1** air. **2** appearance. **3** melody.

arido ('arido) *adj* arid, dry.

arieggiare (arjed'dʒare) *vt* air.

ariete (a'rjɛte) *nm* **1** ram. **2** *cap* Aries.

aringa (a'ringa) *nf* herring.

aristocrazia (aristokrat'tsia) *nf* aristocracy. **aristocratico** (aristo'kratiko) *adj* aristocratic.

aritmetica (arit'mɛtika) *nf* arithmetic.

armadio (ar'madjo) *nm* **1** wardrobe. **2** cupboard.

armare (ar'mare) *vt* arm. **arma**, *nf, pl* **armi** arm, weapon.

armata (ar'mata) *nf* **1** army. **2** fleet.

armonia (armo'nia) *nf* harmony. **armonioso** (armo'njoso) *adj* harmonious. **armonizzare** *vt* harmonize, match.

armonica (ar'mɔnika) *nf* harmonica.

arnese (ar'nese) *nm* tool.

arnia ('arnja) *nf* beehive.

aroma (a'rɔma) *nm* smell, aroma.

arpa ('arpa) *nf* harp.

arrabbiarsi (arrab'bjarsi) *vr* lose one's temper, get angry. **arrabbiato** *adj* angry.

arrampicarsi (arrampi'karsi) *vr* climb.

arrangiare (arran'dʒare) *vt* adjust, arrange. **arrangiarsi** *vr* do the best one can.

arrecare (arre'kare) *vt* **1** cause. **2** bring.

arredare (arre'dare) *vt* furnish, equip. **arreda-**

mento *nm* furnishings. **arredi** (ar'rɛdi) *nm pl* furnishings, fittings.

arrendersi* (arren'dersi) *vr* surrender.

arrestare (arres'tare) *vt* **1** stop. **2** arrest. **arresto** (ar'rɛsto) *nm* arrest.

arretrare (arre'trare) *vi* recoil, withdraw. **arretrato** *adj* **1** underdeveloped. **2** in arrears, behind. *nm* arrears.

arricchire (arrik'kire) *vi* become rich. *vt* enrich, adorn. **arricchirsi** *vr* become rich.

arricciare (arrit'tʃare) *vt* **1** curl. **2** wrinkle.

arrischiare (arris'kjare) *vt* risk, endanger.

arrivare (arri'are) *vi* **1** arrive, reach. **2** manage. **3** happen. **arrivo** *nm* arrival. **ben arrivato!** welcome!

arrivederci (arrive'dertʃi) *interj also* **arrivederla** goodbye!

arrogante (arro'gante) *adj* haughty, arrogant. **arroganza** (arro'gantsa) *nf* arrogance.

arrossire (arros'sire) *vi* blush.

arrostire (arros'tire) *vt* roast. **arrosto** (ar'rɔsto) *nm*-roast meat. *adj invar* roast.

arrotolare (arroto'lare) *vt* roll up.

arrotondare (arroton'dare) *vt* make round.

arrovesciare (arrove'ʃʃare) *vt* **1** overturn. **2** turn inside out.

arruffare (aruf'fare) *vt* ruffle. **arruffarsi** *vr* bristle.

arrugginire (aruddʒi'nire) *vt,vi* rust. **arrugginito** *adj* rusty.

arruolare (arrwo'lare) *vt* enlist. **arruolarsi** *vr* join up, enlist.

arsenale (arse'nale) *nm* **1** shipyard. **2** arsenal.

arsenico (ar'sɛniko) *nm* arsenic.

arsi ('arsi) *v see* **ardere.**

arso ('arso) *v see* **ardere.**

arte ('arte) *nf* **1** art. **2** skill. **artefice** (ar'tefitʃe) *nm* craftsman.

arteria (ar'tɛrja) *nf* **1** artery. **2** main road or line.

artico ('artiko) *adj,nm* Arctic.

articolare (artiko'lare) *vt* pronounce clearly, articulate.

articolo (ar'tikolo) *nm* article. **articolo di fondo** newspaper leader.

artificiale (artifi'tʃale) *adj* artificial, false.

artificio (arti'fitʃo) *nm* **1** skill, cunning. **2** affectation.

artigiano (arti'dʒano) *nm* artisan, craftsman. **artigianato** *nm* **1** small industry. **2** handicraft.

artiglieria (artiʎʎe'ria) *nf* artillery.

artiglio (ar'tiʎʎo) *nm* claw, talon.

artista (ar'tista) *nm* **1** artist. **2** entertainer. **artistico** (ar'tistiko) *adj* artistic.

artrite (ar'trite) *nf* arthritis.

asbesto (az'bɛsto) *nm* asbestos.

ascella (aʃ'ʃɛlla) *nf* armpit.

ascensore (aʃʃen'sore) *nm* lift.

ascesa (aʃ'ʃesa) *nf* rise, ascent.

ascesso (aʃ'ʃɛsso) *nm* abscess.

asceta (aʃ'ʃɛta) *nm* ascetic.

ascia ('aʃʃa) *nf* axe, hatchet.

asciugare (aʃʃu'gare) *vt,vi* dry, wipe. **asciugacapelli** (aʃʃugaka'pelli) *nm invar* hair drier. **asciugamano** (aʃʃuga'mano) *nm* towel.

asciutto (aʃ'ʃutto) *adj* dry.

ascoltare (askol'tare) *vt* **1** listen to. **2** understand. *vi* listen. **ascoltatore** *nm* listener.

asfalto (as'falto) *nm* asphalt.

Asia ('azja) *nf* Asia. **asiatico** *adj,n* Asian.

asilo (a'zilo) *nm* **1** refuge, shelter. **2** nursery school. **asilo politico** political asylum.

asino ('asino) *nm* **1** donkey, ass. **2** fool.

asma ('azma) *nf* asthma.

asparago (as'parago) *nm, pl* **asparagi** asparagus.

aspettare (aspet'tare) *vt* **1** await, wait for. **2** expect. **aspettarsi** *vr* suspect, expect. **sala d'aspetto** *nf* waiting room.

aspetto (as'pɛtto) *nm* look, aspect.

aspirare (aspi'rare) *vt* inhale. *vi* aspire. **aspirapolvere** (aspira'polvere) *nm invar* vacuum cleaner.

aspirina (aspi'rina) *nf* aspirin.

aspro ('aspro) *adj* **1** bitter. **2** harsh, rough. **asprezza** (as'prettsa) *nf* harshness, severity.

assaggiare (assad'dʒare) *vt* taste, try.

assai (as'sai) *adv* **1** enough. **2** very, much.

assalire (assa'lire) *vt* attack. **assalitore** *nm* assailant. **assalto** *nm* attack, assault.

assassinare (assassi'nare) *vt* **1** murder, kill. **2** ruin. **assassinio** *nm* assassination, murder. **assassino** *nm* assassin, murderer. *adj* murderous.

asse[1] ('asse) *nm* axle, axis.

asse[2] ('asse) *nf* plank. **asse da stiro** ironing-board.

assediare (asse'djare) *vt* **1** beseige. **2** beset. **assedio** (as'sɛdjo) *nm* seige.

assegnare (asseɲ'ɲare) *vt* assign, attach, allot.

assegno (as'seɲɲo) *nm* **1** allowance. **2** cheque. **assegno per viaggiatore** traveller's cheque.

assemblea (assem'blɛa) *nf* meeting, assembly.

assembramento (assembra'mento) *nm* meeting, demonstration.

assenso (as'sɛnso) *nm* agreement, assent.

assente (as'sɛnte) *adj* absent. **assenza** *nf* absence.

assentire (assen'tire) *vi* assent, approve.

asserire (asse'rire) *vt* affirm, assert.

assestare (asses'tare) *vt* **1** put in order, arrange, settle. **2** deliver (blow).

assetato (asse'tato) *adj* thirsty, parched.

assettare (asset'tare) *vt* **1** tidy. **2** adjust. **assetto** (as'sɛtto) *nm* order.

assicurare (assiku'rare) *vt* **1** attach, secure. **2** assure. **3** insure. **assicurazione** *nf* **1** assurance. **2** insurance.

assiduo (as'siduo) *adj* **1** diligent. **2** constant.

assieme (as'sjɛme) *adv* together.

assieparsi (assje'parsi) *vr* crowd round.

assimilare (assimi'lare) *vt* assimilate.

assise (as'size) *nf pl* assizes.

assistere* (as'sistere) *vt* aid, assist. *vi* be present, attend. **assistente** (assis'tɛnte) *adj,nm* assistant. **assistenza** (assis'tɛntsa) *nf* aid, assistance. **assistenza sociale** welfare services.

asso ('asso) *nm* ace. **piantare in asso** leave in the lurch.

associare (asso't'ʃare) *vt* **1** associate. **2** admit. **3** unite. **associarsi** *vr* join. **associato** *nm* associate. **associazione** *nf* association.

assoggettare (assoddʒet'tare) *vt* subject, control.

assolsi (as'sɔlsi) *v see* **assolvere**.

assolto (as'sɔlto) *v see* **assolvere**.

assoluto (asso'luto) *adj* absolute, complete.

assolvere* (as'sɔlvere) *vt* acquit. **assoluzione** *nf* acquittal.

assomigliare (assomiʎ'ʎare) *vt* compare. *vi* resemble. **assomigliarsi** *vr* resemble one another, look alike.

assonnato (asson'nato) *adj* sleepy.

assopirsi (asso'pirsi) *vr* doze.

assorbire (assor'bire) *vt* absorb. **assorbente** (assor'bɛnte) *adj* absorbent. **assorbente igienico** *nm* sanitary towel. **carta assorbente** *nf* blotting paper.

assordare (assor'dare) *vt* deafen.

assortire (assor'tire) *vt* **1** arrange. **2** stock. **assortimento** *nm* assortment. **assortito** *adj* assorted.

assuefare (assue'fare) *vt* accustom. **assuefarsi** *vr* get used to.

assumere* (as'sumere) vt **1** undertake, assume. **2** employ. **3** raise.

assunsi (as'sunsi) v see **assumere.**

assunto (as'sunto) v see **assumere.**

Assunzione (assun'tsjone) nf Assumption.

assurdo (as'surdo) adj absurd.

asta ('asta) nf **1** lance. **2** mast, pole. **3** auction. **vendere all'asta** auction.

astante (as'tante) nm bystander. **astanteria** nf casualty ward.

astenersi* (aste'nersi) vr abstain. **astensione** nf abstention.

asterisco (aste'risko) nm asterisk.

astinenza (asti'nɛntsa) nf abstinence.

astio ('astjo) nm rancour, resentment. **astioso** (as'tjoso) adj spiteful.

astratto (as'tratto) adj,nm abstract.

astro ('astro) nm star.

astrologia (astrolo'dʒia) nf astrology. **astrologo** (as'trologo) nm, pl **astrologi** astrologer.

astronauta (astro'nauta) nm astronaut.

astronomia (astrono'mia) nf astronomy. **astronomico** (astro'nɔmiko) adj astronomical. **astronomo** (as'trɔnomo) nm astronomer.

astuccio (as'tuttʃo) nm box, case.

astuto (as'tuto) adj cunning, astute. **astuzia** (as'tuttsja) nf cunning, guile.

Atene (a'tene) nf Athens.

ateo ('ateo) nm atheist. **ateismo** nm atheism.

atlante (a'tlante) nm atlas.

atlantico (a'tlantiko) adj Atlantic. **(Oceano) Atlantico** nm Atlantic (Ocean).

atleta (a'tlɛta) nm athlete. **atletica** (a'tlɛtika) nf athletics. **atletico** (a'tlɛtiko) adj athletic.

atmosfera (atmos'fɛra) nf atmosphere. **atmosferico** (atmo'sfɛriko) adj atmospheric.

atomo ('atomo) nm atom. **atomico** (a'tɔmiko) adj atomic.

atrio ('atrjo) nm hall, entrance.

atroce (a'trotʃe) adj terrible, atrocious. **atrocità** nf atrocity.

attaccare (attak'kare) vt **1** attach, hang. **2** attack. **3** begin. vi stick. **attaccabrighe** nm invar quarrelsome person. **attaccapanni** nm invar hanger, peg. **attacco** nm attack.

attecchire (attek'kire) vi take root.

atteggiare (atted'dʒare) vt pose, arrange. **atteggiamento** nm **1** pose. **2** attitude.

attempato (attem'pato) adj elderly.

attendere* (at'tɛndere) vt await, wait for. vi apply oneself, attend to. **attendibile** (atten'dibile) adj reliable.

attentato (atten'tato) nm **1** assassination attempt. **2** outrage.

attento (at'tɛnto) adj careful, attentive, close. **attenzione** (atten'tsjone) nf attention.

attergare (atter'gare) vt endorse.

atterrare (atter'rare) vi land. **atterraggio** nm landing, touchdown.

attesa (at'tesa) nf wait, delay.

attestare (attes'tare) vt testify, declare. **attestato** nm certificate.

attiguo (at'tiguo) adj adjacent, next.

attimo ('attimo) nm moment.

attirare (atti'rare) vt attract.

attitudine[1] (atti'tudine) nf aptitude.

attitudine[2] (atti'tudine) nf attitude.

attivare (atti'vare) vt activate, start.

attivo (at'tivo) adj active. nm assets. **attività** nf activity.

attizzare (attit'tsare) vt **1** poke (fire). **2** incite.

atto[1] ('atto) nm act, action. **mettere in atto** put into effect.

atto[2] ('atto) adj suitable, apt.

attonito (at'tɔnito) adj surprised, amazed.

attorcigliare (attortʃiʎ'ʎare) vt twist, coil.

attore (at'tore) nm actor.

attorniare (attor'njare) vt surround, encircle.

attorno (at'torno) adv around. **attorno a** prep around.

attrarre (at'trarre) vt attract. **attraente** (attra'ɛnte) adj attractive. **attrazione** nf attraction.

attraversare (attraver'sare) vt cross. **attraverso** (attra'vɛrso) prep **1** across. **2** through.

attrezzo (at'trettso) nm tool, piece of equipment.

attribuire (attribu'ire) vt assign, attribute. **attributo** nm attribute.

attrice (at'tritʃe) nf actress.

attrito (at'trito) friction.

attuale (attu'ale) adj present, current. **attualmente** adv at this moment.

attualità (attuali'ta) nf **1** tropical subject. **2** pl news.

attuare (attu'are) vt **1** bring into being. **2** carry out.

attuario (attu'arjo) nm actuary.

audace (au'datʃe) adj bold, fearless. **audacia** nf boldness, daring.

audiovisuale (audjovizu'ale) adj audiovisual.

auditorio (audi'tɔrjo) nm hall, auditorium.

audizione (audit'tsjone) nf **1** hearing. **2** audition.

augurare (augu'rare) *vt* wish. **augurio** (au'gurjo) *nm* 1 wish. 2 *pl* best wishes.

aula ('aula) *nf* hall. **aula scolastica** classroom.

aumentare (aumen'tare) *vt,vi* increase, augment. **aumento** *nm* increase.

aureola (au'rɛola) *nf* halo.

aurora (au'rɔra) *nf* daybreak.

ausiliare (auzi'ljare) *adj,n* auxiliary. **ausiliario** (auzi'ljarjo) *adj* auxiliary.

austero (aus'tɛro) *adj* austere, severe.

Australia (aus'tralja) *nf* Australia. **australiano** *adj,n* Australian.

Austria ('austria) *nf* Austria. **austriaco** *adj,n* Austrian.

autentico (au'tɛntiko) *adj* real, genuine, authentic.

autista (au'tista) *nm* chauffeur.

autistico (au'tistiko) *adj* autistic.

auto ('auto) *nf invar* car.

autobiografia (autobiogra'fia) *nf* autobiography.

autoblinda (auto'blinda) *nf* armoured car.

autobus ('autobus) *nm* bus.

autocarro (auto'karro) *nm* lorry.

automa (au'tɔma) *nm* automaton.

automatico (auto'matiko) *adj* automatic.

automezzo (auto'mɛddzo) *nm* vehicle.

automobile (auto'mɔbile) *nf* car.

autonomo (au'tɔnomo) *adj* autonomous. **autonomia** (autono'mia) *nf* autonomy.

autopsia (autop'sia) *nf* post-mortem.

autore (au'tore) *nm* author, composer.

autorevole (auto'revole) *adj* authoritative.

autorimessa (autori'messa) *nf* garage.

autorità (autori'ta) *nf* authority.

autoritratto (autori'tratto) *nf* self-portrait.

autorizzare (autorid'dzare) *vt* authorize.

autostop (autos'tɔp) *nm invar* hitch-hiking. **fare l'autostop** hitch.

autostrada (autos'trada) *nf* motorway.

autotrasporto (autotras'pɔrto) *nm* road transport.

autoveicolo (autove'ikolo) *nm* vehicle.

autunno (au'tunno) *nm* autumn.

avambraccio (avam'brattʃo) *nm* forearm.

avanguardia (avan'gwardja) *nf* 1 vanguard. 2 forefront.

avanti (a'vanti) *adv* before, ahead. *prep* before. **avantieri** (avan'tjɛri) *adv* the day before yesterday.

avanzare (avan'tsare) *vt* 1 advance. 2 promote.

3 precede. 4 lend. 5 put aside. *vi* 1 proceed. 2 be left over. **avanzarsi** *vr* approach, near.

avanzo (a'vantso) *nm* 1 remainder. 2 *pl* leftovers.

avaro (a'varo) *adj* mean. **avarizia** (ava'rittsja) *nf* meanness.

avemmo (a'vemmo) *v see* **avere.**

avena (a'vena) *nf* oats.

avere* (a'vere) *vt* 1 have. 2 possess. 3 get. 4 wear. 5 be. *v aux* have. **avercela con uno** have something against someone. **avere da** have to. ~*nm* 1 property. 2 *pl* possessions.

aveste (a'veste) *v see* **avere.**

avesti (a'veste) *v see* **avere.**

avete (a'vete) *v see* **avere.**

avevo (a'vevo) *v see* **avere.**

aviazione (avjat'tsjone) *nf* 1 aviation. 2 Air Force. **aviatore** *nm* airman, pilot.

avido ('avido) *adj* 1 greedy. 2 eager. **avidità** *nf* greed.

avo ('avo) *nm* ancestor.

avocado (avo'kado) *nm invar* avocado.

avorio (a'vorjo) *nm* ivory.

avrei (a'vrɛi) *v see* **avere.**

avrò (a'vro) *v see* **avere.**

avuto (a'vuto) *v see* **avere.**

avvampare (avvam'pare) *vi* flare up, burn.

avvantaggiare (avvantad'dʒare) *vt* favour. **avvantaggiarsi** *vr* profit, make use.

avvedersi* (avve'dersi) *vr* become aware, realize.

avvelenare (avvele'nare) *vt* poison.

avvenire* (avve'nire) *vi* happen, occur. *nm* future. **avvenimento** *nm* event, happening.

avventato (avven'tato) *adj* rash, imprudent.

avventurare (avventu'rare) *vt* risk. **avventurarsi** *vr* venture. **avventura** *nf* adventure.

avverbio (av'vɛrbjo) *nm* adverb.

avversario (avver'sarjo) *nm* opponent, adversary.

avversione (avver'sjone) *nf* dislike, repugnance, aversion. **avverso** (av'vɛrso) *adj* adverse, hostile.

avvertire (avver'tire) *vt* 1 inform. 2 warn. **avvertenza** (avver'tɛntsa) *nf* 1 attention. 2 foreword. 3 *pl* instructions. **avvertimento** (avverti'mento) *nm* warning.

avvezzare (avvet'tsare) *vt* accustom. **avvezzarsi** *vr* become accustomed. **avvezzo** (av'vettso) *adj* accustomed.

avviare (avvi'are) *vt* 1 start, begin. 2 direct. **avviarsi** *vr* set out. **avviamento** *nm* start.

avvicinare (avvitʃi'nare) vt approach, bring near. **avvicinarsi** vr 1 approach. 2 resemble.

avvilire (avvi'lire) vt humiliate. **avvilirsi** vr 1 humble oneself. 2 lose heart. **avvilimento** nm 1 despondency. 2 degradation.

avviluppare (avvilup'pare) vt wrap up.

avvincere (av'vintʃere) vt 1 bind. 2 attract.

avvisare (avvi'zare) vt 1 announce, inform. 2 warn, advise. **avviso** nm 1 announcement. 2 opinion. 3 warning.

avvizzire (avvit'tsire) vi wither, fade.

avvocato (avvo'kato) nm lawyer.

avvolgere (av'vɔldʒere) vt 1 roll up. 2 cover.

avvoltoio (avvol'tojo) nm vulture.

azalea (addza'lɛa) nf azalea.

azienda (ad'dzjɛnda) nf business, firm.

azione (at'tsjone) nf 1 action. 2 comm share. **azionista** nm shareholder.

azoto (ad'dzɔto) nm nitrogen.

azzardare (addzar'dare) vt,vi risk, attempt. **azzardarsi** vr dare. **azzardo** nm 1 risk. 2 chance.

azzuffarsi (attsuf'farsi) vr fight, come to blows.

azzurro (ad'dzurro) adj blue.

B

babbo ('babbo) nm inf dad, daddy.

babbuino (babbu'ino) nm baboon.

babordo (ba'bordo) nm naut port.

bacca ('bakka) nf berry.

baccalà (bakka'la) nm invar dried cod.

baccano (bak'kano) nm din, uproar.

baccarà (bakka'ra) nm baccarat.

baccelliere (battʃel'ljɛre) nm educ bachelor.

baccello (bat'tʃɛllo) nm pod.

bacchetta (bak'ketta) nf 1 stick, baton. 2 wand.

baciare (ba'tʃare) vt kiss. **bacio** nm kiss.

bacino (ba'tʃino) nm 1 basin. 2 dock.

baco ('bako) nm 1 worm. 2 maggot.

badare (ba'dare) vi take care, pay attention. **badare ai fatti suoi** mind one's own business.

badessa (ba'dessa) nf abbess.

badia (ba'dia) nf abbey.

baffi ('baffi) nm pl 1 moustache. 2 whiskers. **leccarsi i baffi** lick one's lips.

bagaglio (ba'gaʎʎo) nm baggage, luggage. **fare i bagagli** pack.

bagattella (bagat'tɛlla) nf trinket, trifle.

bagliore (baʎ'ʎore) nm 1 dazzling light. 2 flash, ray.

bagnare (baɲ'ɲare) vt 1 wet. 2 bathe. **bagnarsi** vr 1 bathe. 2 get soaked. **bagnato** adj soaked.

bagnino (baɲ'ɲino) nm bathing attendant.

bagno ('baɲɲo) nm 1 bath. 2 bathroom. **fare il bagno** 1 take a bath. 2 go for a bathe. **mettere a bagno** soak.

baia ('baja) nf geog bay.

baio ('bajo) adj bay. nm bay horse.

baionetta (bajo'netta) nf bayonet.

balbettare (balbet'tare) vi stutter, stammer. vt mutter, mumble. **balbuzie** (bal'buttsje) nf invar stammer.

balcone (bal'kone) nm balcony.

baldacchino (baldak'kino) nm canopy.

baldanza (bal'dantsa) nf 1 audacity. 2 self-confidence. **baldanzoso** (baldan'tsoso) adj daring, bold.

baldoria (bal'dɔrja) nf merrymaking. **fare baldoria** make merry.

balena (ba'lena) nf whale.

balenare (bale'nare) vi 1 flash lightning. 2 flash. **baleno** nm flash of lightning. **in un baleno** in a moment.

balia[1] ('balja) nf nurse.

balia[2] (ba'lia) nf power, authority.

balistica (ba'listika) nf ballistics. **balistico** (ba'listiko) adj ballistic.

balla ('balla) nf bale.

ballare (bal'lare) vt dance. vi 1 dance. 2 sway. **via la gatta i topi ballano** when the cat's away the mice will play.

ballata (bal'lata) nf ballad.

ballerina (balle'rina) nf ballerina. **ballerino** nm dancer.

balletto (bal'letto) nm ballet.

ballo ('ballo) nm dance, ball.

balneare (balne'are) adj seaside.

balocco (ba'lɔkko) nm toy, plaything.

balordo (ba'lordo) adj foolish, stupid.

baltico ('baltiko) adj Baltic. (**Mare**) **Baltico** nm Baltic (Sea).

balzare (bal'tsare) vi 1 jump. 2 bounce. **balzo** nm 1 bounce. 2 crag.

bambagia (bam'badʒa) nf also **bambagio** nm cottonwool.

bambinaia (bambi'naja) nf children's nurse.

bambino (bam'bino) nm 1 baby. 2 child, little boy.

bambola ('bambola) nf doll.

bambù (bam'bu) nm invar bamboo plant.

banale (ba'nale) adj trivial, banal.

15

banana (ba'nana) *nf* banana. **banano** *nm* banana tree.

banca ('banka) *nf comm* bank. **biglietto di banca** *nm* banknote. **banchiere** (ban'kjɛre) *nm* banker.

bancarella (banka'rɛlla) *nf* stall, barrow.

bancarotta (banka'rotta) *nf* bankruptcy.

banchetto (ban'ketto) *nm* banquet.

banchina (ban'kina) *nf* 1 quay. 2 platform.

banco ('banko) *nm* 1 bench. 2 counter. 3 (in gambling) bank. 4 *geog* bank, reef. **banconota** (banko'nɔta) *nf* banknote.

banda[1] ('banda) *nf* side. **lasciare da banda** leave aside.

banda[2] ('banda) *nf* band, stripe.

banda[3] ('banda) *nf* band, group.

bandiera (ban'djera) *nf* flag.

bandire (ban'dire) *vt* 1 announce, proclaim. 2 banish, exile. **bando** *nm* 1 announcement. 2 ban. 3 banishment. **bandito** *nm* bandit, outlaw.

bangio ('bandʒo) *nm* banjo.

bar (bar) *nm invar* 1 bar, cafe. 2 cocktail cabinet. **barista** *nm* barman. *nf* barmaid.

bara ('bara) *nf* coffin.

baracca (ba'rakka) *nf* hut. **stentare a mandare avanti la baracca** have difficulty in making ends meet.

barattare (barat'tare) *vt* 1 exchange. 2 barter.

barattolo (ba'rattolo) *nm* 1 jar, pot. 2 tin, can.

barba ('barba) *nf* beard. **farsi la barba** shave. **barbuto** *adj* bearded.

barbabietola (barba'bjetola) *nf* beetroot.

barbaro ('barbaro) *adj,nm* barbarian.

barbiere (bar'bjere) *nm* barber.

barbiturato (barbitu'rato) *nm* barbiturate.

barca ('barka) *nf* boat. **barca a remi/vela** rowing/ sailing boat.

barcollare (barkol'lare) *vi* stagger, totter.

bardare (bar'dare) *vt* harness. **bardatura** *nf* harness.

barella (ba'rɛlla) *nf* stretcher.

barile (ba'rile) *nm* barrel, cask.

baritono (ba'ritono) *adj,nm* baritone.

barlume (bar'lume) *nm* glimmer, gleam.

barometro (ba'rɔmetro) *nm* barometer.

barone (ba'rone) *nm* baron. **baronessa** *nf* baroness.

barricare (barri'kare) *vt* barricade. **barricata** *nf* barricade.

barriera (bar'rjɛra) *nf* 1 barrier. 2 gate. 3 fence.

baruffa (ba'ruffa) *nf* scuffle, brawl.

barzelletta (bardzel'letta) *nf* joke.

basare (ba'zare) *vt* base, found.

bascula ('baskula) *nf* weighing machine.

base ('baze) *nf* 1 base. 2 basis, foundation. **in base a** on the basis of.

basetta (ba'zetta) *nf* sideburn, whisker.

basilica (ba'zilika) *nf* basilica.

basilico (ba'ziliko) *nm* basil.

basso ('basso) *adj* 1 low. 2 short in stature. 3 shallow. 4 vulgar, shameful. *nm* 1 bottom. 2 *mus* bass.

bassofondo (basso'fondo) *nm* shallow, sand-bank. **bassifondi** *nm pl* underworld, slums.

bastardo (bas'tardo) *adj,nm* 1 bastard. 2 *zool* mongrel.

bastare (bas'tare) *vi* 1 be enough or sufficient. 2 last. **basta!** *interj* enough!

bastonare (basto'nare) *vt* beat, cane.

bastone (bas'tone) *nm* 1 stick, cane. 2 *pl* game clubs. **bastone da passeggio** walking stick. **mettere un bastone tra le ruote** put a spoke in the wheel. **bastoncino** (baston't∫ino) *nm* little stick.

battaglia (bat'taʎʎa) *nf* battle.

battaglione (batta'ʎone) *nm* battalion.

battello (bat'tɛllo) *nm* boat, steamer.

battere ('battere) *vt* 1 beat, strike. 2 defeat, beat. *vi* beat, knock. **battere a macchina** type. **battere le mani** clap one's hands. **in un batter d'occhio** in a flash.

batteri (bat'tɛri) *nm pl* bacteria.

batteria (batte'ria) *nf* 1 *mil* battery. 2 set.

battesimo (bat'tezimo) *nm* baptism, christening. **battezzare** (batted'dzare) *vt* baptize, christen.

battibaleno (battiba'leno) **in un battibaleno** *adv* in an instant.

battistero (battis'tero) *nm* baptistry.

battitore (batti'tore) *nm* 1 *sport* server. 2 batsman.

battuta (bat'tuta) *nf* 1 blow. 2 witty remark. 3 *sport* service.

batuffolo (ba'tuffolo) *nm* wad.

baule (ba'ule) *nm* (luggage) trunk.

bava ('bava) *nf* 1 dribble. 2 foam.

bavaglino (bavaʎ'ʎino) *nm* bib.

bavaglio (ba'vaʎʎo) *nm* gag.

bavero ('bavero) *nm* coat collar.

bazzicare (battsi'kare) *vt* frequent.

beatitudine (beati'tudine) *nf* beatitude. **Sua Beatitudine** His Holiness.

beato (be'ato) *adj* **1** happy. **2** blessed. **beato te!** lucky you!

beccaccia (bek'kattʃa) *nf* woodcock. **beccaccino** (bekkat'tʃino) *nm* snipe.

beccare (bek'kare) *vt* **1** peck (food). **2** peck, nip. **3** get, catch. **beccarsi** *vr* obtain. **beccamorti** (bekka'morti) *nm invar* gravedigger. **becco** *nm* **1** beak. **2** point. **3** nib.

becchime (bek'kime) *nm* bird food.

becchino (bek'kino) *nm* gravedigger.

befana (be'fana) *nf* **1** old woman supposed to bring gifts to children on the feast of the Epiphany. **2** ugly old woman. **3** Epiphany.

beffare (bef'fare) *vt* mock, ridicule. **beffarsi di** *vr* make fun of. **beffa** ('bɛffa) *nf* **1** mockery. **2** practical joke.

begli ('beʎʎi) *adj* see **bello.**

bei ('bɛi) *adj* see **bello.**

bel (bɛl) *adj* see **bello.**

belare (be'lare) *vi* bleat.

Belgio ('bɛldʒo) *nm* Belgium. **belga** ('bɛlga) *adj,n* Belgian.

belletto (bel'letto) *nm* make-up.

bello ('bɛllo) *adj* **bello, bel** *ms.* **bella** *fs.* **belli, bei, begli** *m pl.* **belle** *f pl.* beautiful, handsome, lovely, fine. **bell'e fatto** well and truly done. **bellezza** (bel'lettsa) *nf* beauty. **bellino** *adj* pretty.

benché (ben'ke) *conj* although.

bendare (ben'dare) *vt* **1** bind, bandage. **2** blindfold. **benda** ('bɛnda) *nf* **1** bandage. **2** blindfold.

bene ('bɛne) *nm* **1** good. **2** *pl* goods, possessions. *adv* well. **voler bene** love, be fond of.

benedire* (bene'dire) *vt* bless. **benedetto** (bene'detto) *adj* holy, blessed.

beneducato (benedu'kato) *adj* well-mannered.

beneficenza (benefi'tʃɛntsa) *nf* charity.

beneficio (bene'fitʃo) *nm* **1** benefit. **2** profit.

benessere (be'nɛssere) *nm* well-being, welfare.

benestante (benes'tante) *adj* well-to-do.

benevolo (be'nɛvolo) *adj* well-disposed, kindly. **benevolenza** (benevo'lɛntsa) *nf* goodwill, benevolence.

beninteso (benin'teso) *adv* of course.

benvenuto (benve'nuto) *nm* welcome. **dare il benvenuto** welcome.

benzina (ben'dzina) *nf* petrol.

bere* ('bere) *vt* drink.

bernoccolo (ber'nɔkkolo) *nm* bump, lump.

berretto (ber'retto) *nm* cap, beret.

berrò (ber'rɔ) *v* see **bere.**

bersaglio (ber'saʎʎo) *nm* target.

bestemmia (bes'temmja) *nf* curse, oath. **bestemmiare** *vi* curse, swear.

bestia ('bestja) *nf* **1** beast, animal. **2** ignoramus. **bestiale** *adj* bestial, brutal.

bestiame (bes'tjame) *nm* livestock.

betoniera (beto'njera) *nf* cement-mixer.

bettola ('bettola) *nf* pub.

betulla (be'tulla) *nf* birch tree.

bevanda (be'vanda) *nf* drink, beverage.

bevo ('bevo) *v* see **bere.**

bevuto (be'vuto) *v* see **bere.**

bevvi ('bevvi) *v* see **bere.**

biada ('bjada) *nf* **1** fodder. **2** *pl* crops.

biancheria (bjanke'ria) *nf* household linen.

bianco ('bjanko) *adj,nm* white. **lasciare in bianco** leave blank. **pesce in bianco** *nm* boiled fish. **riso in bianco** *nm* boiled rice, usually with butter. **biancospino** (bjanko-'spino) *nm* hawthorn.

biascicare (bjaʃʃi'kare) *vt* **1** chew. **2** mumble.

biasimare (bjazi'mare) *vt* blame. **biasimo** ('bjazimo) *nm* blame.

Bibbia ('bibbja) *nf* Bible.

bibita ('bibita) *nf* drink, beverage.

biblico ('bibliko) *adj* biblical.

bibliografia (bibljogra'fia) *nf* bibliography.

biblioteca (bibljo'tɛka) *nf* library. **bibliotecario** *nm* librarian.

bicchiere (bik'kjɛre) *nm* glass.

bicicletta (bitʃi'kletta) *nf* bicycle.

bicipite (bi'tʃipite) *nm* biceps.

bidè (bi'dɛ) *nm* bidet.

bidone (bi'done) *nm* drum, bin.

bieco ('bjɛko) *adj* (of a glance or expression) threatening.

biennale (bien'nale) *adj* two yearly. *nf* two yearly event.

bietta ('bjetta) *nf* wedge.

biforcarsi (bifor'karsi) *vr* branch off, fork.

bigamia (biga'mia) *nf* bigamy. **bigamo** *nm* bigamist. *adj* bigamous.

bighellonare (bigello'nare) *vi* saunter, idle.

bigio ('bidʒo) *adj,nm* grey. **pane bigio** *nm* brown bread.

bigliardo (biʎ'ʎardo) *nm* **1** billiard table. **2** game of billiards. **bigliardino** *nm* pinball machine.

biglietto (biʎ'ʎetto) *nm* **1** note, card. **2** ticket. **3** banknote. **biglietto d'ingresso** platform tic-

bigliettaio nm ticket collector. **biglietteria** nf ticket office.

bigodino (bigo'dino) nm (hair) roller.

bigotto (bi'gɔtto) adj bigoted. nm bigot.

bilancia (bi'lantʃa) nf 1 scales. 2 cap Libra. **bilanciare** vt 1 balance. 2 weigh.

bilancio (bi'lantʃo) nm 1 budget. 2 balance sheet.

bilingue (bi'lingwe) adj bilingual.

bimbo ('bimbo) nm child.

binario (bi'narjo) nm 1 railway track or line. 2 platform.

binocolo (bi'nɔkolo) nm binoculars.

biografia (biogra'fia) nf biography. **biografico** (bio'grafiko) adj biographical.

biologia (biolo'dʒia) nf biology. **biologico** (bio-'lɔdʒiko) adj biological. **biologo** (bi'ɔlogo) nm biologist.

biondo ('bjondo) adj,nm blond.

birbante (bir'bante) nm rascal.

birbone (bir'bone) nm rogue.

birichino (biri'kino) adj naughty. nm mischievous child.

birillo (bi'rillo) nm skittle.

Biro ('biro) nf invar Tdmk Biro.

birra ('birra) nf beer.

bis (bis) adv, interj encore.

bisaccia (bi'zattʃa) nf knapsack.

bisbigliare (bizbiʎ'ʎare) vt,vi whisper. **bisbiglio** nm whisper.

biscia ('biʃʃa) nf snake.

biscotto (bi'skɔtto) nm biscuit.

bisestile (bizes'tile) **anno bisestile** nm leap year.

bisognare (bizoɲ'ɲare) v imp 1 be necessary, must. 2 need. **bisogno** nm need, want. **avere bisogno di** need.

bistecca (bis'tekka) nf steak.

bisticciare (bistit't'ʃare) vi quarrel, argue. **bisticcio** nm 1 quarrel. 2 pun.

bistrattare (bistrat'tare) vt ill-treat.

bivio ('bivjo) nm junction, fork.

bizzarro (bid'dzarro) adj odd, strange.

blandire (blan'dire) vt entice.

blando ('blando) adj 1 mild. 2 gentle.

blatta ('blatta) nf cockroach.

blindare (blin'dare) vt armour.

bloccare (blok'kare) vt block. **blocco** nm 1 block, lump. 2 blockade. 3 notepad.

blu (blu) adj,nm blue.

blusa ('bluza) nf blouse.

boa ('bɔa) nf buoy.

bobina (bo'bina) nf bobbin, spool.

bocca ('bokka) nf 1 mouth. 2 opening. **a bocca aperta** open-mouthed. **in bocca al lupo!** good luck! **boccata** nf mouthful. **boccone** nm mouthful, bite.

boccale (bok'kale) nm jug.

boccia ('bɔttʃa) nf 1 bud. 2 decanter. 3 sport bowl.

bocciare (bot'tʃare) vt fail. **essere bocciato** fail.

boccio ('bɔttʃo) nm bud.

bocconi (bok'koni) adv face downwards, flat on one's face.

boia ('bɔja) nm invar executioner.

boicottare (boikot'tare) vt boycott.

bolla ('bolla) nf 1 bubble. 2 blister.

bollare (bol'lare) vt stamp, seal.

bolletta (bol'letta) nf receipt, note. **bollettino** (bollet'tino) nm 1 bulletin. 2 receipt.

bollire (bol'lire) vt,vi boil. **bollito** nm boiled beef. **bollitore** nm kettle.

bollo ('bollo) nm seal, stamp.

bolognese (boloɲ'ɲese) adj Bolognese. **alla bolognese** with meat sauce.

bomba ('bomba) nf bomb.

bombardare (bombar'dare) vt bombard, bomb.

bombetta (bom'betta) nf bowler hat.

bombola ('bombola) nf cylinder.

bonario (bo'narjo) adj good-natured. **bonarietà** nf kindliness.

bontà (bon'ta) nf goodness, kindness.

borbottare (borbot'tare) vt mutter. vi rumble.

bordello (bor'dɛllo) nm 1 brothel. 2 uproar.

bordo ('bordo) nm 1 side (of a ship). 2 edge, border. **a bordo** on board. **giornale di bordo** nm ship's log.

borghese (bor'gese) adj bourgeois. **borghesia** nf middle class.

borgo ('borgo) nm 1 village. 2 suburb.

boria ('bɔrja) nf arrogance, pride. **borioso** (bo'rjoso) adj haughty.

borotalco (boro'talko) nm talcum powder.

borsa¹ ('bɔrsa) nf bag, purse. **borsa di studio** educ grant.

borsa² ('bɔrsa) nf stock exchange. **borsanera** (borsa'nera) nf black market.

bosco ('bɔsko) nm wood, forest.

botanica (bo'tanika) nf botany. **botanico** adj botanical. nm botanist.

botta ('bɔtta) nf blow, knock. **dare le botte a** spank.

botte ('botte) nf cask, barrel.

bottega (bot'tega) nf **1** shop. **2** workshop.
bottegaio (botte'gajo) nm shopkeeper.

bottiglia (bot'tiλλa) nf bottle.

bottone (bot'tone) nm **1** button. **2** knob, button. **3** bud.

boxe (bɔks) nf boxing.

bozza ('bɔttsa) nf draft, rough sketch. **bozzetto** (bot'tsetto) nm outline, sketch.

bozzolo ('bɔttsolo) nm cocoon.

braccetto (brat'tʃetto) **a braccetto** adv arm in arm.

braccialetto (brattʃa'letto) nm bracelet.

bracciante (brat'tʃante) nm workman, labourer.

braccio ('brattʃo) nm **1** pl **braccia** f anat arm. **2** pl **bracci** m arm, wing. **bracciuolo** (brat-'tʃɔlo) nm arm rest.

braciola (bra'tʃɔla) nf cul chop.

bramare (bra'mare) vt desire.

branchia ('brankja) nf zool gill.

branco ('branko) nm flock, herd.

brancolare (branko'lare) vi grope.

branda ('branda) nf camp bed.

brandello (bran'dɛllo) nm tatter, rag. **a brandelli** in shreds.

brano ('brano) nm **1** scrap, shred. **2** extract, passage.

branzino (bran'dzino) nm zool bass.

Brasile (bra'zile) nm Brazil. **brasiliano** adj,n Brazilian.

bravo ('bravo) adj **1** good, competent. **2** skilful. **3** honest. interj well done! **su** or **da bravo!** there's a good boy!

breccia ('brettʃa) nf breach.

Bretagna (bre'taɲɲa) nf Brittany. **bretone** adj,n Breton.

bretelle (bre'tɛlle) nf pl braces.

breve ('brɛve) adj short, brief. **brevità** nf brevity.

brevetto (bre'vetto) nm **1** patent. **2** licence.

brezza ('breddza) nf breeze.

bricco ('brikko) nm jug.

briccone (brik'kone) nm rascal, scamp.

briciola ('britʃola) nf crumb.

bridge (bridʒ) nm game bridge.

briga ('briga) nf quarrel, trouble.

brigadiere (briga'djɛre) nm **1** brigadier. **2** sergeant.

brigante (bri'gante) nm bandit, robber.

brigata (bri'gata) nf **1** company, group. **2** brigade.

briglia ('briλλa) nf bridle.

brillare (bril'lare) vi shine, glitter, sparkle. **brillante** adj brilliant. nm diamond.

brindare (brin'dare) vi toast, drink someone's health.

brindello (brin'dɛllo) nm rag, tatter.

brindisi ('brindizi) nm invar toast. **fare un brindisi** drink a toast.

brio ('brio) nm gaiety, vivacity.

brivido ('brivido) nm shiver. **fare venire i brividi a qualcuno** give someone the creeps.

brocca ('brɔkka) nf jug.

broccolo ('brɔkkolo) nm broccoli.

brodo ('brɔdo) nm soup, broth.

broglio ('brɔλλo) nm malpractice.

bronchite (bron'kite) nf bronchitis.

broncio ('brontʃo) nm pout, sulk.

brontolare (bronto'lare) vi grumble, mutter.

bronzo ('brondzo) nm bronze.

bruciapelo (brutʃa'pelo) **a bruciapelo** adv pointblank.

bruciare (bru'tʃare) vt burn, set fire to. vi burn, blaze. **bruciato** adj burnt.

bruco ('bruko) nm caterpillar.

brughiera (bru'gjɛra) nf moor.

brulicare (bruli'kare) vi swarm, teem.

bruno ('bruno) adj brown, dark-haired. nm brown. **bruna** nf brunette.

brusco ('brusko) adj **1** sharp. **2** rough. **3** brusque.

brusio (bru'zio) nm buzz, bustle.

bruto ('bruto) adj,nm brute. **brutale** adj brutal. **brutalità** nf brutality.

brutto ('brutto) adj **1** ugly. **2** bad, unpleasant. **fare brutta figura** disgrace oneself.

buca ('buka) nf hole, cavity, pit. **buca delle lettere** letter-box.

bucaneve (buk'aneve) nf snowdrop.

bucare (bu'kare) vt **1** pierce. **2** punch (ticket). vi get a puncture. **avere le mani bucate** be a spendthrift.

bucato (bu'kato) nm washing, laundry.

buccia ('buttʃa) nf peel, skin, rind.

buco ('buko) nm hole.

buddismo (bud'dizmo) nm Buddhism. **buddista** nm Buddhist.

budello (bu'dɛllo) nm,pl **budella** f intestine, bowel.

budino (bu'dino) nm pudding.

bue ('bue) nm,pl **buoi** ox.

bufalo ('bufalo) nm buffalo.

bufera (bu'fɛra) nf blizzard, hurricane.

buffè (buf'fɛ) nm invar **1** sideboard. **2** buffet.

19

buffo ('buffo) adj funny, amusing.
bugia[1] (bu'dʒia) nf candlestick.
bugia[2] (bu'dʒia) nf lie. **bugiardo** nm liar.
buio ('bujo) nm darkness, dark. adj dark, gloomy.
bulbo ('bulbo) nm 1 bulb. 2 eyeball.
Bulgaria (bulga'ria) nf Bulgaria. **bulgaro** adj,n Bulgarian.
buono ('bwɔno) adj 1 good. 2 kind. **buon mercaro** cheap. **buono a nulla** good for nothing. **di buon' ora** early. ~nm 1 good. 2 bill, bond. **con le buone** gently. **buongustaio** (bwongus'tajo) nm gourmet.
burattino (burat'tino) nm puppet.
burbanza (bur'bantsa) nf arrogance. **burbanzoso** (burban'tsoso) adj haughty.
burlare (bur'lare) vt play a trick on. vi joke. **burlarsi di** vr make fun of. **burla** nf joke.
burocrate (bu'rɔkrate) nm bureaucrat. **burocratico** (buro'kratiko) adj bureaucratic. **burocrazia** (burokrat'tsia) nf bureaucracy.
burrasca (bur'raska) nf tempest, storm.
burro ('burro) nm butter.
burrone (bur'rone) nm ravine, gorge.
bussare (bus'sare) vi knock.
bussola ('bussola) nf compass.
busta ('busta) nf 1 envelope. 2 case. **bustarella** (busta'rɛlla) nf bribe.
busto ('busto) nm 1 bust. 2 corset.
buttare (but'tare) vt throw. **buttare via** throw away. **buttarsi** vr throw oneself, jump.

C

cabina (ka'bina) nf 1 cabin. 2 cockpit. **cabina telefonica** telephone box.
cablogramma (kablo'gramma) nm cablegram.
cacao (ka'kao) nm cocoa.
caccia ('kattʃa) nf hunting. **dare la caccia a** hunt. **cacciatore** nm hunter.
cacciagione (kattʃa'dʒone) nf (hunting) game.
cacciare (kat'tʃare) vt 1 hunt, shoot. 2 chase. 3 thrust, put. **cacciare un urlo** let out a yell. **cacciavite** nm invar screwdriver.
cachi ('kaki) adj,nm khaki.
cacio ('katʃo) nm cheese.
cacto ('kakto) nm cactus.
cadavere (ka'davere) nm corpse.
caddi ('kaddi) v see **cadere.**
cadere* (ka'dere) vi fall. **caduta** nf 1 fall. 2 ruin.

cadetto (ka'detto) nm cadet.
cadrò (ka'drɔ) v see **cadere.**
caffè (kaf'fɛ) nm invar 1 coffee. 2 bar, cafe. **caffè corretto** coffee with liqueur. **caffè macchiato** coffee with a little milk. **caffèlatte** nm white coffee. **caffettiera** (kaffet'tjɛre) nf coffee pot.
caffeina (kaffe'ina) nf caffeine.
cagionare (kadʒo'nare) vt cause. **cagione** nf cause, reason.
cagna ('kaɲɲa) nf bitch. **quardare in cagnesco** scowl. **cagnolino** nm puppy.
calabrone (kala'brone) nm hornet.
calamaio (kala'majo) nm inkstand.
calamaro (kala'maro) nm squid.
calamita (kala'mita) nf magnet.
calare (ka'lare) vt lower, drop. vi 1 descend. 2 grow shorter. 3 (of the sun) set. 4 lose weight.
calcagno (kal'kaɲɲo) nm heel.
calcare (kal'kare) vt 1 tread, press down. 2 stress.
calce ('kaltʃe) nf lime.
calcestruzzo (kaltʃes'truttso) nm concrete.
calcio[1] ('kaltʃo) nm 1 kick. 2 football. **calciatore** nm footballer.
calcio[2] ('kaltʃo) nm calcium.
calcolare (kalko'lare) vt,vi calculate. **calcolatore** nm computer. **calcolatrice** nf calculator, calculating machine.
calcolo ('kalkolo) nm 1 calculation. 2 plan. 3 med stone.
caldaia (kal'daja) nf boiler.
caldo ('kaldo) adj hot, warm. **avere caldo** (of a person) be hot. **fare caldo** (of weather) be hot. ~nm heat.
caleidoscopio (kaleidos'kɔpjo) nm kaleidoscope.
calendario (kalen'darjo) nm calendar.
calice ('kalitʃe) nm chalice.
calligrafia (kalligra'fia) nf handwriting.
callo ('kallo) nm med corn.
calmare (kal'mare) vt soothe, calm (down). **calmante** nm sedative, tranquilliser. **calmo** adj calm.
calore (ka'lore) nm heat, warmth. **caloroso** adj warm, cordial.
caloria (kalo'ria) nf calorie.
calorifero (kalo'rifero) nm radiator.
caloscia (ka'lɔʃʃa) nf wellington, galosh.
calpestare (kalpes'tare) vt trample. **calpestio** nm tramping (of feet).
calunnia (ka'lunnja) nf slander.

calvo ('kalvo) *adj* bald. **calvizie** (kal'vittsje) *nf pl* baldness.

calza ('kaltsa) *nf* sock, stocking. **calzatura** (kaltsa'tura) *nf* footwear. **calzino** *nm* sock.

calzolaio (kaltso'lajo) *nm* cobbler, shoemaker. **calzoleria** (kaltsole'ria) *nf* shoemaker's shop.

calzoni (kal'tsoni) *nm pl* trousers. **calzoncini** *nm pl* shorts.

camaleonte (kamale'onte) *nm* chameleon.

cambiale (kam'bjale) *nf* bill of exchange.

cambiare (kam'bjare) *vt,vi* change, alter. **cambiamento** *nm* change, alteration. **cambio** *nm* 1 change. 2 *comm* exchange. 3 *mot* gears.

camera[1] ('kamera) *nf* 1 bedroom, room. 2 chamber. **Camera dei Comuni/Lords** House of Commons/Lords.

camera[2] ('kamera) *nf* camera.

camerata[1] (kame'rata) *nf* dormitory.

camerata[2] (kame'rata) *nm* comrade.

cameriera (kame'rjɛra) *nf* 1 waitress. 2 maid. **cameriere** (kame'rjɛre) *nm* waiter.

camicia (ka'mitʃa) *nf* shirt. **camicetta** (kami-'tʃetta) *nf* blouse.

camino (ka'mino) *nm* 1 fireplace. 2 chimney. **caminetto** *nm* 1 fireplace. 2 mantelpiece.

camion ('kamjon) *nm* lorry.

cammello (kam'mɛllo) *nm* camel.

camminare (kammi'nare) *vi* 1 walk. 2 go. **cammino** (kam'mino) *nm* way, path.

camoscio (ka'mɔʃʃo) *nm* chamois (leather).

campagna (kam'paɲɲa) *nf* 1 countryside. 2 campaign.

campana (kam'pana) *nf* bell. **sordo come una campana** deaf as a post. **campanello** (kam-pa'nɛllo) *nm* doorbell. **campanile** *nm* belltower.

campeggiare (kamped'dʒare) *vi* camp. **campeggio** *nm* 1 camping. 2 camp, camp site. **campeggiatore** *nm* camper.

campione (kam'pjone) *nm* 1 champion. 2 sample, specimen. **campionato** *nm* championship.

campo ('kampo) *nm* 1 field. 2 field, sphere. 3 *sport* ground. **campo di tennis** tennis court.

camposanto (kampo'santo) *nm,pl* **campisanti** cemetery.

camuffamento (kamuffa'mento) *nm* camouflage.

Canada (kana'da) *nm* Canada. **canadese** (kana'dese) *adj,n* Canadian.

canaglia (ka'naʎʎa) *nf* rabble, mob.

canale (ka'nale) *nm* 1 canal. 2 (television) channel.

canapa ('kanapa) *nf* hemp.

canapè (kana'pɛ) *nm invar* sofa.

Canarie (ka'narje) **Isole Canarie** *nf pl* Canary Islands.

canarino (kana'rino) *nm* canary.

cancellare (kantʃel'lare) *vt* 1 score out, cancel. 2 annul.

cancelliere (kantʃel'ljɛre) *nm* chancellor. **Cancelliere dello Scacchiere** Chancellor of the Exchequer.

cancello (kan'tʃɛllo) *nm* gate.

cancro ('kankro) *nm* 1 cancer. 2 *cap* Cancer.

candeggiare (kanded'dʒare) *vt* bleach.

candela (kan'dela) *nf* 1 candle. 2 spark plug. 3 watt.

candidato (kandi'dato) *nm* candidate.

candito (kan'dito) *adj* candied. *nm* candy, sweet.

cane ('kane) *nm* dog. **fatica da cani** *nf* great effort. **tempo da cani** *nm* bad weather.

canguro (kan'guro) *nm* kangaroo.

canile (ka'nile) *nm* kennel.

canna ('kanna) *nf* 1 reed, cane. 2 rod. 3 pipe, tube.

cannella (kan'nɛlla) *nf* cinnamon.

cannelloni (kannel'loni) *nm pl* tubes of pasta stuffed with a meat sauce and baked.

cannibale (kan'nibale) *nm* cannibal. **cannibalismo** *nm* cannibalism.

cannocchiale (kannok'kjale) *nm* 1 binoculars. 2 telescope.

cannone (kan'none) *nm* cannon.

cannuccia (kan'nuttʃa) *nf* (drinking) straw.

canoa (ka'nɔa) *nf* canoe.

canone ('kanone) *nm* canon, law.

canonico (ka'nɔniko) *nm rel* canon.

canonizzare (kanonid'dzare) *vt* canonize.

canottaggio (kanot'taddʒo) *nm* boating, rowing.

canottiera (kanot'tjɛra) *nf* vest, T-shirt.

canotto (ka'nɔtto) *nm* 1 canoe. 2 small boat.

cantare (kan'tare) *vt,vi* sing. *vi* (of a cock) crow. **cantante** *nm* singer.

cantiere (kan'tjɛre) *nm* 1 shipyard. 2 site, yard.

cantina (kan'tina) *nf* cellar.

canto[1] ('kanto) *nm* 1 song. 2 singing. 3 crow (of a cock).

canto[2] ('kanto) *nm* side, corner. **dall'altro canto** on the other hand.

cantone (kan'tone) *nm* 1 corner. 2 canton.

cantoniere (kanto'njɛre) *nm* signalman.

canuto (ka'nuto) *adj* white-haired.

canzonare (kantso'nare) *vt* make fun of. *vi* joke.

canzone (kan'tsone) *nf* song.

caos ('kaos) *nm invar* chaos.

capace (ka'patʃe) *adj* capable, able. **capacità** *nf* 1 capacity. 2 ability.

capanna (ka'panna) *nf* hut. **capannone** (kapan'none) *nm* hangar, shed.

caparbio (ka'parbjo) *adj* obstinate, stubborn.

capello (ka'pello) *nm* 1 hair. 2 *pl* hair (of head). **da fare rizzare i capelli** make one's hair stand on end. **spaccare un capello in quattro** split hairs.

capezzale (kapet'tsale) *nm* bolster.

capezzolo (ka'pettsolo) *nm* nipple, teat.

capire (ka'pire) *vt,vi* understand.

capitale (kapi'tale) *adj,nf* capital. *nm comm* capital. **capitalismo** *nm* capitalism. **capitalista** *nm* capitalist.

capitano (kapi'tano) *nm* captain.

capitare (kapi'tare) *vi* 1 happen. 2 turn up.

capitolo (ka'pitolo) *nm* chapter.

capo ('kapo) *nm* 1 head, mind. 2 top, end. 3 cape. 4 item. 5 chief, leader. **da capo** over again.

capodanno (kapo'danno) *nm* New Year's Day.

capofitto (kapo'fitto) **a capofitto** *adv* head-first.

capogiro (kapo'dʒiro) *nm, pl* **capogiri** fit of dizziness.

capolavoro (kapola'voro) *nm, pl* **capolavori** masterpiece.

capolinea (kapo'linea) *nm, pl* **capilinea** terminus.

caporale (kapo'rale) *nm* corporal.

capostazione (kapostat'tsjone) *nm, pl* **capistazione** station master.

capotreno (kapo'trɛno) *nm, pl* **capitreno** guard.

capovolgere (kapo'vɔldʒere) *vt* overturn.

cappa ('kappa) *nf* cloak, cape.

cappella (kap'pella) *nf* chapel.

cappello (kap'pɛllo) *nm* hat.

cappero (kap'pero) *nm bot* caper. **capperi!** *interj* gosh!

cappotta (kap'pɔtta) *nf mot* hood.

cappotto (kap'pɔtto) *nm* overcoat.

cappuccino (kapput'tʃino) *nm* coffee with milk.

cappuccio (kap'puttʃo) *nm* hood.

capriccio (ca'prittʃo) *nm* whim, caprice.

capriccioso (kaprit'tʃoso) *adj* capricious, wilful.

Capricorno (kapri'kɔrno) *nm* Capricorn.

caprifoglio (kapri'fɔʎʎo) *nm* honeysuckle.

capriola (kapri'ɔla) *nm* somersault.

capro (kapro) *nm* billy-goat. **capro espiatorio** scapegoat. **capretto** (ka'pretto) *nm* kid.

capsico ('kapsiko) *nm* capsicum.

capsula ('kapsula) *nf* capsule.

carabiniere (karabi'njɛre) *nm* military policeman.

caraffa (ka'raffa) *nf* carafe.

caraibo (kara'ibo) *adj* Caribbean. (**Mar dei) Caraibi** *nm* Caribbean (Sea).

caramella (kara'mɛlla) *nf* sweet.

carato (ka'rato) *nm* carat.

carattere (ka'rattere) *nm* 1 character, nature. 2 letter, character. **caratteristico** (karatte'ristiko) *adj* typical, characteristic.

carboidrato (karboi'drato) *nm* carbohydrate.

carbone (kar'bone) *nm* coal.

carbonio (kar'bɔnjo) *nm* carbon. **carbonico** (kar'bɔniko) *adj* carbonic.

carburante (karbu'rante) *nm mot* fuel.

carburatore (karbura'tore) *nm* carburettor.

carcassa (kar'kassa) *nf* skeleton, carcass.

carcere ('kartʃere) *nm, pl* **carceri** *f* prison.

carciofo (kar'tʃɔfo) *nm* artichoke.

cardiaco (kar'diako) *adj* cardiac. **attacco cardiaco** *nm* heart attack.

cardinale (kardi'nale) *nm rel* cardinal. *adj* cardinal, principal.

cardine ('kardine) *nm* hinge.

cardo ('kardo) *nm* thistle.

carena (ka'rɛna) *nf* keel.

carestia (kares'tia) *nf* scarcity, shortage.

carezzare (karet'tsare) *vt* caress, stroke. **carezza** *nf* caress.

cariarsi (ka'rjarsi) *vr* decay.

carica ('karika) *nf* appointment, office. **in carica** 1 in office. 2 in charge.

caricare (kari'kare) *vt* 1 load, fill. 2 overload. 3 wind up.

caricatura (karika'tura) *nf* caricature.

carico ('kariko) *nm* 1 load. 2 weight, responsibility. 3 *naut* cargo. *adj* laden, loaded.

carie ('karje) *nf invar* decay.

carità (kari'ta) *nf* charity, love. **per carità!** for heaven's sake! please!

carlinga (kar'linga) *nf* cockpit.

carnagione (karna'dʒone) *nf* complexion.

carne ('karne) *nf* 1 flesh. 2 meat. **carnale** *adj* carnal.

carneficina (karnefi't∫ina) *nf* slaughter, massacre.

carnevale (karne'vale) *nm* carnival.

caro ('karo) *adj* 1 dear, beloved. 2 expensive, dear. *adv* at a high price.

carosello (karo'zɛllo) *nm* merry-go-round.

carota (ka'rɔta) *nf* carrot.

carponi (kar'poni) *adv* on all fours.

carrello (kar'rɛllo) *nm* trolley.

carriera (kar'rjɛra) *nf* career, profession.

carro ('karro) *nm* 1 cart. 2 lorry, truck.

carrozza (kar'rɔttsa) *nf* coach, carriage. **carrozzeria** *nf* mot bodywork. **carrozzina** *nf* pram.

carrucola (kar'rukola) *nf* pulley.

carta ('karta) *nf* 1 paper. 2 document. 3 map, chart. 4 card. **carta da lettere** notepaper. **carta d'identità** identity card. **cartacarbone** *nf* carbon paper. **cartapecora** (karta'pɛkora) *nf* parchment. **cartapesta** (karta'pesta) *nf* papier-mâché. **cartella** (kar't∫lla) *nf* 1 folder, file. 2 satchel. **cartellino** *nm* 1 tag. 2 nameplate. **cartello** (kar'tɛllo) *nm* poster, notice. **cartolina** *nf* postcard. **cartone** *nm* cardboard.

cartilagine (karti'ladʒine) *nf* cartilage.

cartolaio (karto'lajo) *nm* stationer. **cartoleria** *nf* stationery shop.

cartuccia (kar'tutt∫a) *nf* cartridge.

casa ('kasa) *nf* 1 house, home. 2 company, firm. 3 family, house.

casalinga (kasa'linga) *nf* housewife. **casalingo** *adj* 1 domestic. 2 home-made. 3 plain.

cascare (kas'kare) *vi* fall, tumble. **cascata** *nf* waterfall.

casco ('kasko) *nm* helmet, crash helmet.

casella (ka'sella) *nf* pigeonhole. **casella postale** post office box.

caserma (ka'zɛrma) *nf* barracks.

casino (ka'sino) *nm* 1 casino. 2 *inf* brothel.

caso ('kazo) *nm* 1 chance. 2 event, occurrence. 3 case. 4 way, possibility. **caso mai** if by chance. **far caso di** take into account. **in ogni caso** in any case. **per caso** by chance.

cassa ('kassa) *nf* 1 box, case, chest. 2 cash desk. 3 bank, fund. 4 cash. **cassa da morto** coffin. **cassaforte** (kassa'fɔrte) *nf, pl* **casseforti** strongbox.

cassetta (kas'setta) *nf* box. **cassetta delle lettere** letter-box. **cassetto** (kas'setto) *nm* drawer. **cassettone** (kasset'tone) *nm* chest of drawers.

cassata (kas'sata) *nf* Neapolitan ice-cream.

casseruola (kasse'rwɔla) *nf* saucepan.

cassiere (kas'sjere) 1 cashier. 2 treasurer.

casta ('kasta) *nf* caste.

castagna (kas'tanna) *nf* chestnut. **castagno** *nm* chestnut tree. *adj* chestnut, brown.

castello (kas'tɛllo) *nm* castle.

castigare (kasti'gare) *vt* punish. **castigo** *nm* punishment.

casto ('kasto) *adj* chaste. **castità** *nf invar* chastity.

castoro (kas'tɔro) *nm* beaver.

castrare (kas'trare) *vt* castrate.

casuale (kazu'ale) *adj* chance.

catacomba (kata'komba) *nf* catacomb.

catalogo (ka'talogo) *nm* catalogue.

catapulta (kata'pulta) *nf* catapult.

catarro (ka'tarro) *nm* catarrh.

catastrofe (ka'tastrofe) *nf* disaster, catastrophe.

catechismo (kate'kizmo) *nm* catechism.

categoria (katego'ria) *nf* category, class. **categorico** (kate'gɔriko) *adj* categorical, explicit.

catena (ka'tena) *nf* chain. **catena di negozi** chain store.

catino (ka'tino) *nm* basin. **catinella** *nf* small basin. **piovere a catinelle** rain cats and dogs.

catodo ('katodo) *nm* cathode.

catrame (ka'trame) *nm* tar.

cattedrale (katte'drale) *nf* cathedral.

cattivo (kat'tivo) *adj* 1 bad, naughty. 2 evil.

cattolico (kat'tɔliko) *adj,n* Catholic. **cattolicesimo** (kattoli't∫ezimo) *nm* Catholicism.

catturare (kattu'rare) *vt* 1 capture. 2 arrest. **cattura** *nf* 1 capture. 2 arrest.

caucciù (kaut't∫u) *nm invar* rubber.

causa ('kauza) *nf* 1 cause, reason. 2 *law* case, action. **a causa di** owing to, because of.

causare (kau'zare) *vt* cause, produce.

caustico ('kaustiko) *adj* caustic.

cauto ('kauto) *adj* cautious, careful. **cautela** (kau'tɛla) *nf* 1 caution. 2 precaution.

cauzione (kaut'tsjone) *nf* 1 caution money, deposit. 2 bail.

cava ('kava) *nf* quarry, pit.

cavalcare (kaval'kare) *vt,vi* ride. **cavalcioni** *adv* astride.

cavaliere (kava'ljɛre) *nm* knight.

cavalleria (kavalle'ria) *nf* 1 cavalry. 2 chivalry. **cavalleresco** *adj* chivalrous.

cavallo (ka'vallo) *nm* 1 horse. 2 *game* knight. **a cavallo** on horseback. **cavallo a dondolo**

23

rocking horse. **cavallo di corsa** racehorse. **cavalletto** (kaval'letto) nm easel.

cavare (ka'vare) vt **1** extract, remove. **2** obtain. **cavarsela** vr get out of a difficult situation. **cavatappi** nm invar corkscrew.

caverna (ka'vɛrna) nf cavern, cave.

caviale (ka'vjale) nm caviar.

caviglia (ka'viʎʎa) nf ankle.

cavo[1] ('kavo) adj,nm hollow. **cavità** nf hollow, cavity.

cavo[2] ('kavo) nm cable, rope.

cavolo ('kavolo) nm cabbage. **cavolfiore** nm cauliflower.

ce (tʃe) pron 1st pers m,f pl us, to us. adv there.

cecità (tʃetʃi'ta) nf blindness.

Cecoslovacchia (tʃekoslo'vakkja) nf Czechoslovakia. **ceco** adj,n Czech. nm Czech (language). **cecoslovacco** adj,n Czechoslovakian.

cedere ('tʃɛdere) vi **1** collapse. **2** yield, give up. vt **1** hand over. **2** renounce.

cedola ('tʃedola) nf **1** coupon. **2** counterfoil.

cedro[1] ('tʃedro) nm **1** lime tree. **2** lime (fruit).

cedro[2] ('tʃedro) nm cedar.

celare (tʃe'lare) vt hide, conceal.

celebrare (tʃele'brare) vt celebrate.

celebre ('tʃɛlebre) adj famous, well-known. **celebrità** nf celebrity.

celeste (tʃe'lɛste) adj **1** heavenly, celestial. **2** azure.

celibe ('tʃɛlibe) nm bachelor.

cella ('tʃɛlla) nf cell.

cellula ('tʃɛllula) nf sci cell.

celluloide (tʃellu'lɔide) nf celluloid.

cemento (tʃe'mento) nm **1** cement. **2** concrete. **cemento armato** reinforced concrete.

cenacolo (tʃe'nakolo) nm painting of the Last Supper.

cenare ('tʃenare) vi dine, have dinner. **cena** nf dinner, supper.

cencio ('tʃentʃo) nm **1** rag. **2** duster, cloth.

cenere ('tʃenere) nf ash. **Ceneri** (tʃe'neri) nf pl Ash Wednesday.

cenno ('tʃenno) nm **1** nod. **2** sign. **3** hint. **fare cenno di** mention.

censimento (tʃensi'mento) nm census.

censurare (tʃensu'rare) vt censure, reprove. **censura** nf censorship. **censore** (tʃen'sore) nm censor.

centenario (tʃente'narjo) nm **1** centenary. **2** centenarian.

centigrado (tʃen'tigrado) adj centigrade.

centimetro (tʃen'timetro) nm centimetre.

cento ('tʃento) adj,nm one hundred. **per cento** per cent. **centesimo** (tʃen'tɛzimo) adj hundredth. **centinaio** (tʃenti'najo) nm, pl **centinaia** f about a hundred.

centrale (tʃen'trale) adj **1** central. **2** principal. **sede centrale** nf head office. ~nf centre of production, plant, station. **centrale elettrica** power station. **centralinista** nm operator. **centralino** nm telephone exchange. **centralizzare** (tʃentralid'dzare) vt centralize.

centro ('tʃɛntro) nm **1** centre, middle. **2** sport centre. **centro avanti** or **attacco** centreforward. **centro mediano** or **sostegno** halfback.

ceppo ('tʃeppo) nm **1** stump. **2** log. **3** block.

cera[1] ('tʃera) nf wax.

cera[2] ('tʃera) nf appearance.

ceramica (tʃe'ramika) nf ceramics.

cercare (tʃer'kare) vt **1** search. **2** look for, seek. vi try, attempt. **cercasi** (in newspaper advertisements) wanted. **cerca** nf search.

cerchio ('tʃerkjo) nm circle.

cereale (tʃere'ale) adj,nm cereal.

cerimonia (tʃeri'mɔnja) nf ceremony.

cerino (tʃe'rino) nm **1** wax match. **2** taper.

cerniera (tʃer'njɛra) nf hinge. **cerniera lampo** zip (fastener).

cerotto (tʃe'rɔtto) nm med plaster.

certificare (tʃertifi'kare) vt **1** certify. **2** confirm. **certificato** nm certificate.

certo ('tʃɛrto) adj **1** sure, certain. **2** certain, particular. adv certainly, of course.

cervello (tʃer'vɛllo) nm, pl **cervella** f or **cervelli** m brain.

cervo ('tʃervo) nm deer.

cesello (tʃe'zɛllo) nm chisel.

cesoie (tʃe'zɔje) nf pl shears.

cespo ('tʃespo) nm tuft.

cespuglio (tʃes'puʎʎo) nm bush.

cessare (tʃes'sare) vi stop, cease.

cesta ('tʃesta) nf basket, hamper. **cestino** nm wastepaper basket. **cestino da viaggio** lunch pack.

ceto ('tʃeto) nm class, rank.

cetriolo (tʃetri'ɔlo) nm cucumber.

che (ke) pron **1** who, whom. **2** which. **3** that. **un gran che** something important. **un non so che di** a hint of. ~adj **1** what? which? **2** what, what a. **3** how. conj **1** that **2** than. **3** as. **non...che** only. **ma che!** interj also **macchè!** rubbish!

cheto ('keto) *adj* quiet. **chetichella** (keti'kella) **alla chetichella** *adv* furtively, inconspicuously.

chi (ki) *pron* **1** who? whom? **2** those who, he who, whoever. **chi...chi** some...some. **di chi è?** whose is it?

chiacchierare (kjakkje'rare) *vi* chat, chatter, gossip. **chiacchiera** ('kjakkjera) *nf* chat, piece of gossip. **fare due chiacchiere** have a chat. **chiacchierata** *nf* chat.

chiamare (kja'mare) *vt* **1** call. **2** send for, summon. **chiamarsi** *vr* be called. **chiamata** *nf* call.

chiarire (klja'rire) *vt* clarify, clear up. **chiaro** *adj* clear, bright. **chiarore** *nm* glimmer. **chiaroscuro** *nm* Art light and shade. **chiaroveggente** (kjaroved'dʒɛnte) *adj* clear-sighted.

chiasso ('kjasso) *nm* hubbub, din. **chiassoso** (kjas'soso) *adj* noisy.

chiavare (kja'vare) *vt* have sexual intercourse with.

chiave ('kjave) *nf* key. **chiudere a chiave** lock. **tenere sotto chiave** keep under lock and key.

chiavistello (kjavi'stɛllo) *nm* bolt.

chiazzare (kjat'tsare) *vt* stain. **chiazza** *nf* stain.

chicchirichì (kikkiri'ki) *nm* cock-a-doodle-do.

chicco ('kikko) *nm* **1** grain. **2** (coffee) bean. **3** grape.

chiedere* ('kjɛdere) *vt* **1** ask. **2** ask for, request, beg.

chiesa ('kjɛza) *nf* church.

chiesi ('kjɛsi) *v see* **chiedere.**

chiesto ('kjɛsto) *v see* **chiedere.**

chiglia ('kiʎʎa) *nf* keel.

chilo ('kilo) *nm* kilo. **chilogrammo** (kilo'grammo) *nm* kilogram. **chilometro** (ki'lɔmetro) *nm* kilometre. **chilowatt** ('kilovat) *nm invar* kilowatt.

chimera (ki'mɛra) *nf* illusion.

chimica ('kimika) *nf* chemistry. **chimico** ('kimiko) *adj* chemical. *nm* chemist.

china ('kina) *nf* slope, descent.

chinare (ki'nare) *vt* lower, bend. **chinarsi** *vr* stoop, bend.

chincaglieria (kinkaʎʎe'ria) *nf* bric-a-brac, trinkets.

chiocciare (kjot'tʃare) *vi* cluck.

chiocciola ('kjɔttʃola) *nf* snail. **scala a chiocciola** *nf* spiral staircase.

chiodo ('kjɔdo) *nm* **1** nail. **2** debt.

chiosco ('kjɔsko) *nm* kiosk.

chiostro ('kjɔstro) *nm* cloister.

chirurgia (kirur'dʒia) *nf* surgery. **chirurgico** *adj* surgical. **chirurgo** *nm, pl* **chirurghi** or **chirurgi** surgeon.

chitarra (ki'tarra) *nf* guitar.

chiudere* ('kjudere) *vt* **1** close, shut. **2** end. **3** switch or turn off.

chiunque (ki'unkwe) *pron invar* whoever, anyone who.

chiusi ('kjusi) *v see* **chiudere.**

chiuso ('kjuso) *v see* **chiudere.** *adj* shut, closed.

chiusura (kju'sura) *nf* **1** closure. **2** fastening. **chiusura lampo** zip fastener.

ci (tʃi) *pron, 1st pers m,f pl* **1** us, to us. **2** ourselves. *adv* here, there.

cialda ('tʃalda) *nf* waffle.

ciambella (tʃam'bɛlla) *nf* **1** ring-shaped bun. **2** rubber ring.

ciambellano (tʃambel'lano) *nm* chamberlain.

cianuro (tʃa'nuro) *nm* cyanide.

ciao ('tʃao) *interj* **1** hello! **2** bye-bye! cheerio!

ciarlare (tʃar'lare) *vi* chatter, gabble.

ciarlatano (tʃarla'tano) *nm* charlatan.

ciascuno (tʃas'kuno) *also* **ciascheduno** *adj* each, every. *pron* each one, every one.

cibare (tʃi'bare) *vt* feed, nourish. **cibo** *nm* food.

cicala (tʃi'kala) *nf* cicada.

cicatrice (tʃika'tritʃe) *nf* scar.

cicca ('tʃikka) *nf* butt, cigarette end.

cicerone (tʃitʃe'rone) *nm* guide.

ciclamino (tʃikla'mino) *nm* cyclamen.

ciclo ('tʃiklo) *nm* **1** cycle. **2** bicycle, cycle. **ciclismo** *nm* cycling. **ciclista** *nm* cyclist.

ciclone (tʃi'klone) *nm* cyclone.

cicogna (tʃi'koɲɲa) *nf* stork.

cicoria (tʃi'kɔrja) *nf* chicory.

cieco ('tʃɛko) *adj* blind. **cieco** blind man.

cielo ('tʃɛlo) *nm* **1** sky. **2** heaven.

cifra ('tʃifra) *nf* **1** figure, number. **2** sum, amount.

ciglio ('tʃiʎʎo) *nm* **1** *pl* **ciglia** *f* eyelash. **2** *pl* **cigli** *m* edge, bring.

cigno ('tʃiɲɲo) *nm* swan.

cigolare (tʃigo'lare) *vi* squeak, creak.

ciliegia (tʃi'ljɛdʒa) *nf* cherry. **ciliegio** *nm* cherry tree.

cilindro (tʃi'lindro) *nm* cylinder.

cima ('tʃima) *nf* summit, top.

cimice ('tʃimitʃe) *nf* bug.

ciminiera (tʃimi'njɛra) *nf* **1** factory chimney. **2** *naut* funnel.

cimitero (tʃimi'tɛro) *nm* cemetery, graveyard.

Cina ('tʃina) nf China. **cinese** (tʃi'nese) adj,n Chinese. nm Chinese (language).

cinema ('tʃinema) nm invar cinema. **cineasta** nm person connected with the cinema.

cinetico (tʃi'nɛtiko) adj kinetic.

cingere ('tʃindʒere) vt surround, encircle.

cinghia ('tʃingja) nf strap, belt.

cinghiale (tʃin'gjale) nm 1 wild boar. 2 pigskin.

cinguettare (tʃingwet'tare) vi twitter, chirp.

cinico ('tʃiniko) adj cynical, sceptical.

cinquanta (tʃin'kwanta) adj,nm fifty. **cinquantesimo** adj fiftieth.

cinque ('tʃinkwe) adj,nm five. **cinquecento** (tʃinkwe'tʃɛnto) adj five hundred. nm 1 five hundred. 2 sixteenth century.

cintura (tʃin'tura) nm belt. **cintura di sicurezza** seat belt. **cinturino** nm strap.

ciò (tʃɔ) pron invar that, this. **ciò che** that which.

cioccolata (tʃokko'lata) nf also **cioccolato** nm chocolate. **cioccolatino** nm chocolate sweet.

cioè (tʃo'ɛ) adv that is to say, that is.

ciondolo ('tʃondolo) nm pendant.

ciottolo ('tʃɔttolo) nm 1 stone, pebble. 2 cobble.

cipiglio (tʃi'piʎʎo) nm scowl, frown.

cipolla (tʃi'polla) nf onion. **cipollina** nf spring onion.

cipresso (tʃi'prɛsso) nm cypress.

cipria ('tʃiprja) nf face powder.

Cipro ('tʃipro) nm Cyprus. **cipriota** adj,n Cypriot.

circa ('tʃirka) prep about, concerning. adv roughly, approximately, about.

circo ('tʃirko) nm circus.

circolare[1] (tʃirko'lare) vi 1 circulate, spread, flow. 2 move about, circulate. **circolante** adj mobile. nm currency. **circolazione** nf 1 circulation. 2 traffic.

circolare[2] (tʃirko'lare) adj circular. nf circular (letter).

circolo ('tʃirkolo) nm 1 circle. 2 group, club.

circoncidere (tʃirkon'tʃidere) vt circumcize.

circondare (tʃirkon'dare) vt surround.

circonferenza (tʃirkonfe'rɛntsa) nf circumference.

circonvallazione (tʃirkonvallat'tsjone) nf ringroad.

circoscrivere (tʃirkos'krivere) vt limit, restrict.

circostante (tʃirkos'tante) adj surrounding. nm bystander.

circostanza (tʃirkos'tantsa) nf circumstance.

circuito (tʃir'kuito) nm circuit.

cisterna (tʃis'tɛrna) nf tank, cistern. **nave cisterna** nf naut tanker.

citare (tʃi'tare) vt 1 quote, cite. 2 summon. **citazione** nf 1 quotation. 2 summons.

città (tʃit'ta) nf invar town, city. **cittadino** nm citizen.

ciuffo ('tʃuffo) nm tuft.

civetta (tʃi'vetta) nf 1 owl. 2 flirt.

civico ('tʃiviko) adj civic.

civile (tʃi'vile) adj civil, civilian. nm civilian.

civiltà (tʃivil'ta) nf civilization. **civilizzare** (tʃivilid'dzare) vt civilize. **civilizzazione** nf civilization.

clacson ('klakson) nm mot horn.

clamore (kla'more) nm 1 din, uproar. 2 outcry. **clamoroso** (klamo'roso) adj noisy, sensational.

clandestino (klandes'tino) adj clandestine.

clarinetto (klari'netto) nm clarinet.

classe ('klasse) nf 1 class. 2 classroom. **di classe** of high quality. **fuori classe** in a class of its own.

classico ('klassiko) adj classic, classical.

classificare (klassifi'kare) vt classify, class. **classificazione** nf classification.

clausola ('klauzola) nf clause.

claustrofobia (klaustrofo'bia) nf claustrophobia.

clavicembalo (klavi'tʃembalo) nm harpsichord.

clavicola (kla'vikola) nf collarbone.

clemenza (kle'mɛntsa) nf mercy, clemency.

cleptomane (klep'tomane) nm kleptomaniac. **cleptomania** nf kleptomania.

clero ('klɛro) nm clergy.

cliente (kli'ɛnte) nm client, customer. **clientela** (klien'tɛla) nf clientele.

clima ('klima) nm climate.

clinica ('klinika) nf 1 clinical medicine. 2 clinic, nursing home.

cloro ('klɔro) nm chlorine.

clorofilla (kloro'filla) nf chlorophyll.

cloroformio (kloro'fɔrmjo) nm chloroform.

cloruro (klo'ruro) nm chloride.

coabitare (koabi'tare) vi cohabit, live together.

coagulare (koagu'lare) vt coagulate. **coagularsi** vr coagulate. **coagulo** (ko'agulo) nm 1 clot. 2 curd.

coalizione (koalit'tsjone) nf coalition.

cobra ('kɔbra) nm invar cobra.

cocaina (koka'ina) nf cocaine.

cocchio ('kɔkkjo) nm coach, carriage.

coccinella (kottʃiˈnɛlla) nf ladybird.

cocco (ˈkɔkko) nm 1 coconut. 2 coconut palm.

coccodrillo (kokkoˈdrillo) nm crocodile. **lagrime di coccodrillo** nf pl crocodile tears.

cocente (koˈtʃɛnte) adj 1 hot, burning. 2 acute.

cociamo (koˈtʃamo) v see **cuocere.**

cocomero (koˈkomero) nm watermelon.

coda (ˈkoda) nf 1 tail. 2 queue. **guardare con la coda dell'occhio** look out of the corner of one's eye.

codardo (koˈdardo) adj cowardly.

codeina (kodeˈina) nf codeine.

codesto (koˈdesto) adj this, that. pron that one.

codice (ˈkɔditʃe) nm code.

coerente (koeˈrɛnte) adj coherent. **coerenza** (koeˈrɛntsa) nf 1 coherence. 2 consistency.

coesistere (koeˈzistere) vi coexist.

coetaneo (koeˈtaneo) adj,nm contemporary.

cofano (ˈkɔfano) nm 1 chest, casket. 2 mot bonnet.

cogliere* (ˈkɔʎʎere) vt 1 pick. 2 gather, collect. 3 catch. 4 hit, strike. **cogliere l'occasione** seize the opportunity.

cognato (koɲˈɲato) nm brother-in-law. **cognata** nf sister-in-law.

cognome (goɲˈɲome) nm surname.

coincidere (koinˈtʃidere) vi coincide. **coincidenza** (kointʃiˈdɛntsa) nf 1 coincidence. 2 (railway) connection.

coinvolgere (koinˈvɔldʒere) vt involve.

coito (ˈkoito) nm coitus, sexual intercourse.

colare (koˈlare) vt 1 strain. 2 pour. vi drip, trickle. **colare a picco** sink. **colapasta** nm invar pasta strainer. **colino** nm strainer.

colatoio (kolaˈtojo) nm colander.

colazione (kolatˈtsjone) nf lunch. **prima colazione** breakfast.

colei (koˈlɛi) pron fs she, that woman.

colera (koˈlɛra) nm cholera.

colgo (ˈkɔlgo) v see **cogliere.**

colla (ˈkɔlla) nf glue.

collaborare (kollaboˈrare) vi 1 collaborate. 2 contribute. **collaborazione** nf collaboration.

collana (kolˈlana) nf 1 necklace. 2 series. 3 collection.

collare (kolˈlare) nm collar.

collasso (kolˈlasso) nm collapse.

collaudare (kollauˈdare) vt test, try. **collaudo** nm 1 test. 2 approval.

colle (ˈkɔlle) nm hill.

collega (kolˈlɛga) nm colleague.

collegare (kolleˈgare) vt join, connect, link. **collegamento** nm link, connection.

collegio (kolˈlɛdʒo) nm 1 college. 2 boarding school.

collera (ˈkɔllera) nf anger. **montare in collera** get angry.

colletta (kolˈletta) nf collection.

collettivo (kolletˈtivo) adj collective, joint.

colletto (kolˈletto) nm collar.

collezionare (kollettsjoˈnare) vt collect. **collezione** nf collection. **fare collezione di** collect.

collina (kolˈlina) nf hill.

collo[1] (ˈkɔllo) nm neck.

collo[2] (ˈkɔllo) nm parcel, package.

collocare (kolloˈkare) vt place, put.

colloquio (kolˈlɔkwjo) nm 1 talk, discussion. 2 interview.

colmare (kolˈmare) vt fill. **colmo** adj full, overflowing. nm 1 top. 2 height.

colomba (koˈlomba) nf dove. **colombo** nm pigeon.

colonia (koˈlɔnja) nf 1 colony. 2 summer camp. **coloniale** adj colonial. **colonizzare** (kolonidˈdzare) vt colonize.

colonna (koˈlonna) nf column, pillar.

colonnello (kolonˈnɛllo) nm colonel.

colorire (koloˈrire) vt colour. **colore** nm 1 colour. 2 colouring. **di colore** coloured.

colossale (kolosˈsale) adj gigantic.

colpa (ˈkolpa) nf 1 offence. 2 blame. 3 fault.

colpevole (kolˈpevole) adj guilty. nm culprit.

colpire (kolˈpire) vt strike, hit. **rimanere colpito** be amazed.

colpo (ˈkolpo) nm 1 blow, stroke, knock. 2 shot. **colpo d'aria** draught. **colpo di sole** sunstroke. **colpo di Stato** coup d'état. **colpo di telefono** telephone call. **colpo d'occhio** glance.

colsi (ˈkɔlsi) v see **cogliere.**

coltello (kolˈtɛllo) nm knife. **coltello a serramanico** pen-knife.

coltivare (koltiˈvare) vt cultivate.

colto[1] (ˈkɔlto) v see **cogliere.**

colto[2] (ˈkɔlto) adj cultured, learned.

coltura (kolˈtura) nf 1 cultivation, breeding. 2 culture.

colui (koˈlui) pron ms he, that man. **coloro** pron m,f pl those, those people.

coma (ˈkɔma) nm coma.

comandare (komanˈdare) vt 1 command, order.

27

2 control. **comandante** *nm* commander. **comando** *nm* command, order.

combattere (kom'battere) *vi,vt* fight, combat. **combattente** (kombat'tɛnte) *nm* soldier. **combattimento** *nm* combat, fight.

combinare (kombi'nare) *vt* **1** combine. **2** arrange. *vi* **1** agree. **2** match. **cosa sta combinando?** what is he up to? **combinazione** *nf* **1** combination. **2** chance.

combustione (kombus'tjone) *nf* combustion.

come ('kome) *adv* **1** like, as. **2** as well as. **3** how. *prep* as soon as. **come se** as if. ~*interj* what! **come?** what did you say?

cometa (ko'meta) *nf* comet.

comico ('kɔmiko) *adj* **1** comic. **2** funny, comical. *nm* comedian, comic.

cominciare (komin'tʃare) *vt,vi* begin, start.

comitato (komi'tato) *nm* committee, board.

comitiva (komi'tiva) *nf* party, group.

comizio (ko'mittsjo) *nm* meeting.

commedia (kom'mɛdja) *nf* **1** comedy. **2** play. **commediante** *nm* **1** actor. **2** comedian. *nf* **1** actress. **2** comedienne.

commemorare (kommemo'rare) *vt* commemorate. **commemorativo** *adj* commemorative. **commemorazione** *nf* commemoration.

commentare (kommen'tare) *vt* **1** annotate. **2** comment upon. **commentatore** *nm* commentator. **commento** *nm* comment.

commercio (kom'mɛrtʃo) *nm* commerce, business, trade. **commerciale** *adj* commercial. **commerciante** *nm* **1** businessman. **2** merchant.

commesso (kom'messo) *nm* **1** shop assistant. **2** clerk. **commesso viaggiatore** travelling salesman.

commestibile (kommes'tibile) *adj* edible.

commettere (kom'mettere) *vt* commit.

commissariato (kommissa'rjato) *nm* commissariat. **commissariato di polizia** police station. **commissario** (kommis'sarjo) *nm* commissioner.

commissione (kommis'sjone) *nf* **1** errand. **2** order. **3** commission, committee.

commosso (kom'mɔsso) *adj* touched, moved.

commozione (kommot'tsjone) *nf* agitation. **commozione cerebrale** concussion.

commuovere (kom'mwɔvere) *vt* move, touch, affect.

commutare (kommu'tare) *vt* change.

commutatore (kommuta'tore) *nm* switch.

comodino (komo'dino) *nm* bedside table.

comodo ('kɔmodo) *adj* **1** comfortable. **2** handy. **3** convenient. **4** useful. **stia comodo!** please don't get up! ~*nm* **1** comfort. **2** convenience. **con comodo** at one's leisure. **comodità** *nf* **1** convenience. **2** comfort.

compagno (kompaɲ'ɲo) *nm* **1** companion, comrade. **2** partner. **compagnia** *nf* company.

comparativo (kompara'tivo) *adj* comparative.

comparire (kompa'rire) *vi* **1** appear. **2** seem.

compartimento (komparti'mento) *nm* compartment.

compassione (kompas'sjone) *nf* pity, compassion.

compasso (kom'passo) *nm* **1** compass. **2** pair of compasses.

compatire (kompa'tire) *vt* **1** pity. **2** sympathize with. **compatimento** *nm* pity.

compatriota (kompatri'ɔta) *nm* fellow countryman.

compatto (kom'patto) *adj* compact.

compendio (kom'pɛndjo) *nm* **1** compendium. **2** summary.

compensare (kompen'sare) *vt* compensate, make up for. **compenso** (kom'pɛnso) *nm* compensation.

competente (kompe'tɛnte) *adj* **1** apt, suitable. **2** competent.

competere (kom'pɛtere) *vi* compete. **competitore** (kompeti'tore) *nm* competitor. **competizione** *nf* competition.

compiacere (kompja'tʃere) *vt* **1** please. **2** humour. **compiacersi** *vr* **1** delight in. **2** deign. **compiacente** *adj* obliging. **compiacimento** *nm* pleasure.

compiangere (kom'pjandʒere) *vt* pity.

compiere ('kompjere) *vt* **1** complete, finish. **2** fulfil, accomplish. **compiere gli anni** have a birthday.

compilare (kompi'lare) *vt* compile.

compito (kom'pito) *nm* **1** task. **2** homework.

compleanno (komple'anno) *nm* birthday. **buon compleanno!** happy birthday!

complesso (kom'plɛsso) *adj* complex, complicated. *nm* **1** whole, mass. **2** complex. **3** group, band. **nel complesso** on the whole. **complessivo** *adj* total, comprehensive.

completare (komple'tare) *vt* complete. **completo** (kom'plɛto) *adj* **1** complete. **2** full. *nm* suit.

complicare (kompli'kare) *vt* complicate. **complicato** *adj* complicated. **complicazione** *nf* complication.

complice ('komplitʃe) nm accomplice.

complimentare (komplimen'tare) vt compliment. **complimento** nm 1 compliment. 2 pl congratulations. **fare complimenti** stand on ceremony. **senza complimenti** without ceremony.

complotto (kom'plɔtto) nm plot.

componente (kompo'nɛnte) adj component. nm,f 1 component. 2 member.

comporre* (kom'porre) vt compose.

comportare (kompor'tare) vt 1 tolerate, permit. 2 involve. **comportarsi** vr behave. **comportamento** nm behaviour.

compositore (kompozi'tore) nm composer.

composizione (kompozit'tsjone) nf composition.

composto (kom'posto) adj 1 compound. 2 calm, sedate, composed. nm compound.

comprare (kom'prare) vt buy.

comprendere* (kom'prɛndere) vt 1 include, comprise. 2 understand, comprehend. **comprensibile** (kompren'sibile) adj comprehensible, understandable. **comprensione** nf comprehension, understanding. **comprensivo** adj comprehensive.

compressa (kom'prɛssa) nf 1 compress. 2 tablet. **compressore** nm compressor.

comprimere* (kom'primere) vt compress.

compromettere (kompro'mettere) vt 1 compromise. 2 endanger. **compromesso** nm compromise.

compunto (kom'punto) adj 1 contrite. 2 solemn.

comune (ko'mune) adj common, ordinary, everyday. nm 1 town council. 2 municipal buildings. **comunale** adj 1 communal. 2 municipal. **comunità** nf community.

comunicare (komuni'kare) vt communicate, pass on. vi communicate, keep in contact. **comunicazione** nf communication.

comunione (komu'njone) nf communion.

comunismo (komu'nizmo) nm communism. **comunista** nm communist.

comunque (ko'munkwe) adv however, anyhow.

con (kon) prep 1 with. 2 by. 3 to.

conca ('konka) nf 1 container. 2 basin. 3 shell.

concavo ('konkavo) adj concave.

concedere* (kon'tʃɛdere) vt 1 grant, allow. 2 admit.

concentrare (kontʃen'trare) vt concentrate. **concentramento** nm concentration. **campo**

di concentramento nm concentration camp. **concentrazione** nf concentration.

concentrico (kon'tʃɛntriko) adj concentric.

concepire (kontʃe'pire) vt 1 conceive. 2 imagine, devise. 3 understand.

concernere (kon'tʃɛrnere) vt concern.

concerto (kon'tʃɛrto) nm concert.

concessi (kon'tʃessi) v see **concedere.**

concessione (kontʃes'sjone) nf concession.

concesso (kon'tʃesso) v see **concedere.**

concetto (kon'tʃɛtto) nm 1 concept, idea. 2 opinion.

concezione (kontʃet'tsjone) nf conception.

conchiglia (kon'kiʎʎa) nf shell.

conciliare (kontʃi'ljare) vt 1 reconcile. 2 induce. **conciliarsi** vr 1 be reconciled. 2 gain.

concilio (kon'tʃiljo) nm council.

concime (kon'tʃime) nm dung, manure.

conciso (kon'tʃizo) adj concise.

concittadino (kontʃitta'dino) nm fellow citizen.

concludere* (kon'kludere) vt conclude, finish. **concludersi** vr end, finish. **conclusione** nf conclusion. **conclusivo** (konklu'zivo) adj conclusive.

concorrere* (kon'korrere) vi 1 assemble. 2 contribute. 3 compete. 4 concur. **concorrente** (konkor'rɛnte) nm competitor. **concorrenza** (konkor'rɛntsa) nf rivalry, competition.

concorso (kon'korso) nm competition.

concreto (kon'krɛto) adj concrete, actual.

condannare (kondan'nare) vt 1 condemn. 2 sentence, convict. 3 blame. **condanna** nf law sentence. **condannato** nm convict.

condensazione (kondensat'tsjone) nf condensation.

condire (kon'dire) vt cul season. **condimento** nm seasoning, dressing.

condiscendere (kondiʃ'ʃɛndere) vi 1 yield. 2 condescend. **condiscendente** (kondiʃʃen-'dɛnte) adj 1 indulgent. 2 condescending.

condividere* (kondi'videre) vt share.

condizione (kondit'tsjone) nf condition. **condizionale** adj conditional. **condizionare** vt condition. **condizionato** adj 1 conditioned. 2 packed. **aria condizionata** nf air conditioning.

condoglianza (kondoʎ'ʎantsa) nf condolence, sympathy.

condolersi* (kondo'lersi) vr 1 grieve. 2 sympathize.

condotta (kon'dotta) nf 1 conduct, behaviour. 2

29

leadership. 3 medical practice controlled by local authority.

condotto (kon'dotto) v see **condurre**. nm tube, pipe.

conducente (kondu'tʃɛnte) nm driver.

conduco (kon'duko) v see **condurre**.

condurre* (kon'durre) vt 1 lead, accompany, take. 2 manage, run. 3 drive. **condursi** vr behave.

condussi (kon'dussi) v see **condurre**.

conduttore (kondut'tore) nm 1 driver. 2 sci conductor.

confarsi (kon'farsi) vr suit.

confederazione (konfederat'tsjone) nf federation.

conferire (konfe'rire) vt bestow, give. vi confer. **conferenza** (konfe'rɛntsa) nf 1 conference. 2 lecture. **conferenziere** (konferen'tsjɛre) nm 1 speaker. 2 lecturer.

confermare (konfer'mare) vt confirm. **conferma** nf confirmation.

confessare (konfes'sare) vt confess. **confessionale** nm confessional box. **confessione** nf confession.

confetto (kon'fɛtto) nm 1 sweet. 2 sugared almond.

confettura (konfet'tura) nf jam.

confezionare (konfettsjo'nare) vt make, manufacture. **confezione** nf 1 manufacture. 2 pl clothes. 3 packaging. **confezioni su misura** made-to-measure clothes.

confidare (konfi'dare) vt confide. vi trust. **confidenza** (konfi'dɛntsa) nf 1 confidence, trust. 2 familiarity. **confidenziale** adj confidential.

confinare (konfi'nare) vt confine, banish. **confinare con** be adjacent to, border on. **confine** nm 1 border. 2 boundary.

confiscare (konfis'kare) vt confiscate.

conflitto (kon'flitto) nm conflict, struggle.

confondere* (kon'fondere) vt 1 confuse, mix up, mistake. 2 perplex, blur. **confondersi** vr become confused.

conformare (konfor'mare) vt conform. **conformarsi a** vr conform to, comply with. **conforme** adj similar. **conformista** nm conformist.

confortare (konfor'tare) vt comfort, console. **conforto** (kon'fɔrto) nm comfort.

confrontare (konfron'tare) vt compare. **confronto** nm comparison. **in** or **a confronto di** compared with.

confusione (konfu'zjone) nf 1 disorder, confusion. 2 embarrassment. **confuso** adj 1 confused. 2 embarrassed.

congedare (kondʒe'dare) vt dismiss. **congedo** (kon'dʒɛdo) nm leave, leave of absence.

congelare (kondʒe'lare) vt freeze. **congelarsi** vr freeze.

congestionare (kondʒestjo'nare) vt overcrowd, congest. **congestione** nf congestion.

congiungere* (kon'dʒundʒere) vt join, link.

congiurare (kondʒu'rare) vi conspire, plot. **congiura** nf conspiracy, plot. **congiurato** nm conspirator.

congratularsi (kongratu'larsi) vr congratulate. **congratulazione** nf congratulation.

congregare (kongre'gare) vt assemble. **congregarsi** vr congregate.

congresso (kon'grɛsso) nm 1 congress. 2 conference.

coniare (ko'njare) vt coin.

conico ('kɔniko) adj conical.

conifero (ko'nifero) adj coniferous.

coniglio (ko'niʎʎo) nm rabbit. **conigliera** (koniʎ'ʎera) nf rabbit-hutch.

coniugare (konju'gare) vt conjugate. **coniugazione** nf conjugation.

coniuge ('kɔnjudʒe) nm,f spouse. **coniugale** adj conjugal.

connettere* (kon'nɛttere) vt connect.

cono ('kɔno) nm cone.

conobbi (ko'nobbi) v see **conoscere**.

conoscere* (ko'noʃʃere) vt know, be acquainted with. **conoscente** (konoʃ'ʃɛnte) nm acquaintance. **conoscenza** (konoʃ'ʃɛntsa) nf 1 knowledge. 2 acquaintance. 3 consciousness. **fare conoscenza di** get to know. **conoscitore** nm connoisseur, expert.

conquistare (konkwis'tare) vt conquer. **conquista** nf conquest.

consacrare (konsa'krare) vt 1 consecrate, ordain. 2 devote.

consapevole (konsa'pevole) adj aware, informed.

consecutivo (konseku'tivo) adj consecutive.

consegnare (konsen'ɲare) vt 1 hand over, deliver, entrust. 2 confine. **consegna** nf delivery. **pagamento alla consegna** cash on delivery.

conseguire (konse'gwire) vt,vi follow, result. **conseguente** (konse'gwɛnte) adj consequent. **conseguenza** (konse'gwɛntsa) nf consequence.

consenso (kon'sɛnso) *nm* 1 consent, approval. 2 consensus.

consentire (konsen'tire) *vi* consent, agree.

conservare (konser'vare) *vt* keep, preserve. **conserva** (kon'sɛrva) *nf* preserve. **frutta in conserva** *nf* preserved fruit. **conservazione** *nf* preservation.

considerare (konside'rare) *vt* 1 examine. 2 consider, regard. **considerabile** (konside-'rabile) *adj* considerable. **considerazione** *nf* consideration.

consigliare (consiʎ'ʎare) *vt* advise. **consigliarsi** *vr* take advice. **consigliere** (konsiʎ-'ʎere) *nm* councillor.

consiglio (kon'siʎʎo) *nm* 1 piece of advice, advice. 2 council.

consistere (kon'sistere) *vi* consist.

consolare (konso'lare) *vt* console. **consolazione** *nf* consolation.

console ('kɔnsole) *nm* consul. **consolato** *nm* consulate.

consolidare (konsoli'dare) *vt* consolidate.

consonante (konso'nante) *nf* consonant.

consorzio (kon'sɔrtsjo) *nm* consortium.

consueto (konsu'ɛto) *adj* usual. *nm* habit, custom. **consuetudine** (konsue'tudine) *nf* habit, custom.

consultare (konsul'tare) *vt* consult. **consultazione** *nf* consultation. **consulto** *nm* consultation.

consumare (konsu'mare) *vt* 1 consume, use up. 2 commit. **consumatore** *nm* consumer. **consumo** *nm* consumption.

contabile (kon'tabile) *nm* bookkeeper. **contabilità** *nf* bookkeeping.

contadino (konta'dino) *nm* peasant.

contado (kon'tado) *nm* countryside (around a town).

contagioso (konta'dʒoso) *adj* contagious, infectious.

contaminare (kontami'nare) *vt* contaminate, infect. **contaminazione** *nf* contamination.

contante (kon'tanti) *adj* (of money) ready. *nm* cash.

contare (kon'tare) *vt* 1 count. 2 consider. 3 intend. *vi* 1 count, have importance. 2 rely. **contatore** *nm* meter.

contatto (kon'tatto) *nm* contact.

conte ('konte) *nm* (title) count. **contea** *nf* county. **contessa** *nf* countess.

conteggio (kon'teddʒo) *nm* calculation. **conteggio alla rovescia** countdown.

contegno (kon'teɲɲo) *nm* appearance, bearing.

contemplare (kontem'plare) *vt* contemplate.

contemporaneo (kontempo'raneo) *adj,nm* contemporary.

contendere (kon'tɛndere) *vt* dispute, contest.

contenere (konte'nere) *vt* 1 contain, hold. 2 repress. **contenersi** *vr* restrain oneself. **contenuto** *nm* contents.

contentare (konten'tare) *vt* satisfy. **contentarsi** *vr* be satisfied. **contento** (kon'tɛnto) *adj* happy, glad, pleased.

contestare (kontes'tare) *vt* challenge.

contiguo (kon'tiguo) *adj* adjoining.

continente (konti'nɛnte) *nm* continent. **continentale** *adj* continental.

continuare (kontinu'are) *vt,vi* continue. **continuazione** *nf* continuation.

continuo (kon'tinuo) *adj* continual, continuous, unbroken. **di continuo** incessantly.

conto ('konto) *nm* 1 calculation. 2 bill, account. 3 esteem, regard. 4 notice. 5 report. **conto alla rovescia** countdown. **conto corrente** current account. **fare conto** imagine, suppose. **per conto mio** 1 on my behalf. 2 for my part.

contorcere (kon'tɔrtʃere) *vt* twist. **contorcersi** *vr* writhe.

contorno (kon'torno) *nm* 1 contour. 2 border. 3 vegetables served with meat course.

contrabbandare (kontrabban'dare) *vt* smuggle. **contrabbandiere** (kontrabban'djere) *nm* smuggler. **contrabbando** *nm* smuggling.

contrabbasso (kontrab'basso) *nm* double bass.

contraccolpo (kontrak'kolpo) *nm* repercussion.

contraddire (kontrad'dire) *vt* contradict. **contraddittorio** *adj* contradictory. **contraddizione** *nf* contradiction.

contraereo (kontra'ɛreo) *adj* anti-aircraft.

contraffare (kontraf'fare) *vt* 1 imitate. 2 forge, copy. **contraffatto** *adj* counterfeit.

contrapporre (kontrap'porre) *vt* oppose.

contrariare (kontra'rjare) *vt* 1 contradict. 2 annoy.

contrario (kon'trarjo) *adj* 1 opposite, contrary. 2 unfavourable, adverse. *nm* contrary, opposite. **al contrario** on the contrary.

contrarre (kon'trarre) *vt* contract.

contrastare (kontras'tare) *vt* 1 oppose, resist. 2 dispute. *vi* 1 struggle. 2 clash. **contrasto** *nm* 1 conflict, opposition, clash. 2 contrast.

contrattare (kontrat'tare) *vt,vi* negotiate.

contratto (kon'tratto) *nm* contract.

contravvenire* (kontravve'nire) *vi* infringe, violate. **contravvenzione** *nf* 1 infringement. 2 fine.

contribuire (kontribu'ire) *vi* 1 contribute. 2 help. **contributo** *nm* contribution.

contristare (kontris'tare) *vt* sadden, grieve.

contro ('kontro) *prep,adv* against. **controffensiva** *nf* counterattack.

controllare (kontrol'lare) *vt* inspect, examine. **controllo** (kon'trollo) *nm* control. **controllo delle nascite** birth control. **controllore** (kontrol'lore) *nm* ticket inspector.

controversia (kontro'vɛrsja) *nf* controversy. **controverso** (kontro'vɛrso) *adj* controversial.

conturbare (kontur'bare) *vt* disturb, upset.

contusione (kontu'zjone) *nf* bruise.

convalescenza (konvaleʃ'ʃɛntsa) *nf* convalescence.

convegno (kon'veɲɲo) *nm* meeting.

convenire* (konve'nire) *vi* 1 meet, converge. 2 agree. *v imp* 1 suit. 2 be in one's interest. **conveniente** (konve'njɛnte) *adj* 1 advantageous. 2 suitable. **convenienza** (konve'njɛntsa) *nf* 1 suitability. 2 propriety.

convento (kon'vɛnto) *nm* 1 convent. 2 monastery.

convenzione (konven'tsjone) *nf* convention.

convergere (kon'vɛrdʒere) *vi* converge.

conversare (konver'sare) *vi* talk, chat, converse. **conversazione** *nf* conversation.

conversione (konver'sjone) *nf* conversion.

convertire (konver'tire) *vt* convert. **convertito** *nm* convert.

convesso (kon'vɛsso) *adj* convex.

convincere* (kon'vintʃere) *vt* persuade, convince.

convitato (konvi'tato) *nm* guest.

convito (kon'vito) *nm* banquet.

convitto (kon'vitto) *nm* boarding school.

convocare (konvo'kare) *vt* summon, convene.

convoglio (kon'vɔʎʎo) *nm* convoy, escort.

convulsione (konvul'sjone) *nf* convulsion.

cooperare (koope'rare) *vi* cooperate. **cooperativa** *nf* cooperative. **cooperazione** *nf* cooperation.

coordinare (coordi'nare) *vt* coordinate.

coperchio (ko'pɛrkjo) *nm* lid, cover.

coperta (ko'pɛrta) *nf* 1 blanket. 2 cover. 3 *pl* bed clothes. **copertina** *nf* cover, jacket (of a book). **copertura** *nf* covering.

coperto (ko'pɛrto) *v* see **coprire**.

copia ('kɔpja) *nf* copy. **copiare** (ko'pjare) *vt* copy.

copioso (ko'pjoso) *adj* abundant, copious.

coppa ('kɔppa) *nf* 1 goblet. 2 *sport* cup. 3 tub of ice cream.

coppia ('kɔppja) *nf* pair, couple.

coprire* (ko'prire) *vt* 1 cover. 2 hide. **coprifuoco** (kopri'fwoko) *nm* curfew. **copriletto** (kopri'letto) *nm* bedspread.

coraggio (ko'raddʒo) *nm* courage, bravery. *interj* come on! **coraggioso** (korad'dʒoso) *adj* brave.

corallo (ko'rallo) *nm* coral.

corazzare (korat'tsare) *vt* armour-plate.

corbello (kor'bɛllo) *nm* basket.

corda ('kɔrda) *nf* 1 cord, rope. 2 *mus* string, bow. 3 *mus* chord. **cordone** (kor'done) *nm* 1 cord. 2 cordon.

cordiale (kor'djale) *adj* cordial.

coreografo (kore'ɔgrafo) *nm* choreographer. **coreografia** *nf* choreography.

coricare (cori'kare) *vt* lay down. **coricarsi** *vr* go to bed.

cornacchia (kor'nakkja) *nf* crow.

cornamusa (korna'muza) *nf* bagpipes.

cornice (kor'nitʃe) *nf* 1 frame. 2 cornice. **mettere in cornice** frame.

corno ('kɔrno) *nm* 1 *pl* **corna** *f* horn (of an animal). 2 *pl* **corni** *m* horn. **fare le corna a** be unfaithful to.

coro ('kɔro) *nm* 1 choir. 2 chorus. **coronare** (koro'nare) *vt* crown. **corona** *nf* crown. **corona funebre** wreath.

corpo ('kɔrpo) *nm* 1 body. 2 corpse. 3 corps.

corporazione (korporat'tsjone) *nf* company, corporation.

copulento (korpu'lento) *adj* stout.

corredo (kor'rɛdo) *nm* trousseau.

correggere* (kor'rɛddʒere) *vt* correct.

corrente (kor'rɛnte) *adj* 1 running. 2 current. *nf* current. **corrente d'aria** draught. **mettere al corrente** bring up-to-date. **tenere al corrente** keep informed.

correre* ('korrere) *vi* 1 run, flow. 2 pass. 3 circulate. *vt* run, race.

corretto (kor'rɛtto) *adj* correct.

correzione (korret'tsjone) *nf* correction. **correzione di bozze** proofreading.

corrida (kor'rida) *nf* bullfight.

corridoio (korri'dojo) *nm* corridor.

corridore (korri'dore) *nm* 1 runner. 2 rider.

corriera (kor'rjɛra) nf bus, coach. **corriere** (kor'rjɛra) nm 1 courier. 2 mail, post.

corrispondere* (korris'pondere) vi 1 correspond. 2 return. **corrispondente** (korrispon'dɛnte) nm correspondent. adj corresponding. **corrispondenza** (korrispon'dɛntsa) nf correspondence, mail.

corroborare (korrobo'rare) vt corroborate, reinforce.

corrompere* (kor'rompere) vt corrupt, contaminate. **corrotto** adj corrupt, contaminated.

corrucciarsi (korrut'tʃarsi) vr get angry.

corrugare (korru'gare) vt wrinkle. **corrugare la fronte** frown.

corruzione (korrut'tsjone) nf corruption.

corsa ('korsa) nf 1 run. 2 race. 3 journey. **di corsa** 1 running. 2 in a hurry. **fare una corsa** run.

corsi ('korsi) v see **correre.**

corsia (kor'sia) nf 1 passage. 2 med ward. 3 dormitory. 4 lane.

corso[1] ('korso) v see **correre.**

corso[2] ('korso) nm 1 course, progress. 2 main street. 3 educ course. **corso del cambio** exchange rate. **in corso** current, valid. **lavori in corso** nm pl roadworks.

corte ('korte) nf court. **fare la corte a** court.

corteccia (kor'tettʃa) nf bark.

corteggiare (korted'dʒare) vt court.

corteo (kor'tɛo) nm procession, cortege.

cortese (kor'teze) adj 1 kind. 2 courteous. **cortesia** nf courtesy. **fare una cortesia** do a favour. **per cortesia** please.

cortile (kor'tile) nm 1 courtyard. 2 farmyard.

cortina (kor'tina) nf curtain.

corto ('korto) adj short, brief. **per farla corta** cut a long story short.

corvo ('korvo) nm crow, raven.

cosa ('kɔsa) nf 1 thing, matter, affair. 2 act, deed. **che cosa?** what? **(ché) cosa hai?** what is the matter? **per prima cosa** first of all.

coscia ('kɔʃʃa) nf thigh, leg (of an animal).

cosciente (koʃ'ʃɛnte) adj conscious.

coscienza (koʃ'ʃɛntsa) nf conscience.

coscritto (kos'kritto) nm conscript.

coscrizione (koskrit'tsjone) nf conscription.

così (ko'si) adv 1 thus, in this way. 2 so, therefore. **così così** so-so. **e così via** and so on. **~adj** such, similar. **cosicché** (kosik'ke) conj so that. **cosiddetto** adj so-called.

cosmetico (koz'mɛtiko) adj,nm cosmetic.

cosmo ('kɔzmo) nm cosmos. **cosmico** ('kɔzmiko) adj cosmic. **cosmonauta** (kozmo'nauta) nm cosmonaut.

cosmopolita (kozmopo'lita) adj cosmopolitan.

coso ('kɔso) nm inf what's-its-name, what's-his-name.

cospicuo (kos'pikuo) adj notable, eminent.

cospirare (kospi'rare) vi conspire, plot. **cospiratore** nm conspirator. **conspirazione** nf conspiracy.

cossi ('kɔssi) v see **cuocere.**

costa ('kɔsta) nf 1 rib (of a ship). 2 slope, hillside. 3 coast.

costà (kos'ta) adv there.

costante (kos'tante) adj firm, constant.

costare (kos'tare) vi 1 cost. 2 require. **costo** ('kɔsto) nm cost, price. **a tutti i costi** at all costs. **costo della vita** cost of living. **costoso** (kos'toso) adj dear, expensive.

costeggiare (kosted'dʒare) vt skirt, run alongside.

costei (kos'tɛi) see **costui.**

costellazione (kostellat'tsjone) nf constellation.

costituire (kostitu'ire) vt 1 form, constitute, make up. 2 found. 3 elect. **costituzione** nf constitution.

costola ('kɔstola) nf rib.

costoro (kos'toro) see **costui.**

costringere* (kos'trindʒere) vt force, oblige.

costruire* (kostru'ire) vt build, construct.

costrussi (kos'trussi) v see **costruire.**

costui (kos'tui) pron ms that man. **costei** pron fs that woman. **costoro** pron m,f pl those people.

costumato (kostu'mato) adj well-bred.

costume (kos'tume) nm 1 custom, habit. 2 costume. **costume di bagno** swimsuit.

costura (kos'tura) nf seam.

cotesto (ko'testo) adj that. pron that one.

cotoletta (koto'letta) nf cutlet.

cotone (ko'tone) nm 1 cotton. 2 cotton thread.

cottimo ('kɔttimo) nm piecework.

cotto ('kɔtto) v see **cuocere.** adj 1 cooked. 2 sl in love.

cottura (kot'tura) nf cooking.

covare (ko'vare) vt,vi hatch. **covata** nf brood.

covile (ko'vile) nm also **covo** lair, den.

cozza ('kɔttsa) nf mussel.

cozzare (kot'tsare) vt,vi butt, collide.

crampo ('krampo) nm cramp.

cranio ('kranjo) nm skull.

cratere (kra'tɛre) nm crater.

33

cravatta (kra'vatta) nf tie.

creanza (kre'antsa) nf breeding, education.

creare (kre'are) vt 1 create. 2 establish. 3 appoint. **creativo** adj creative. **creatore** nm creator. **creatura** nf creature. **creazione** nf creation.

crebbi (v see **crescere**.

credenza[1] (kre'dɛntsa) nf belief, faith.

credenza[2] (kre'dɛntsa) nf sideboard.

credere ('kredere) vt,vi 1 believe. 2 think.

credito ('kredito) nm 1 credit. 2 esteem. 3 trust. **credulo** ('kredulo) adj credulous.

crema ('krɛma) nf cream. **cremoso** adj creamy.

cremare (kre'mare) vt cremate.

cremisi ('krɛmizi) adj,nm crimson.

crepare (kre'pare) vi 1 crack, split. 2 sl die. **crepa** ('krɛpa) nf crack.

crepitare (krepi'tare) vi crackle.

crepuscolo (kre'puskolo) nm dusk.

crescere* ('kreʃʃere) vi 1 grow. 2 increase. 3 rise. **crescita** ('kreʃʃita) nf growth.

crescione (kreʃ'ʃone) nm watercress.

cresima ('krɛzima) nf confirmation.

crespo ('krespo) adj 1 curly. 2 pleated.

cresta ('kresta) nf 1 crest. 2 comb (of a cock).

cretino (kre'tino) nm idiot, fool.

cricco ('krikko) nm tech jack.

criminale (krimi'nale) adj,nm criminal.

criniera (kri'njɛra) nf mane.

cripta ('kripta) nf crypt.

crisalide (kri'zalide) nf chrysalis.

crisantemo (krizan'tɛmo) nm chrysanthemum.

crisi ('krizi) nf invar crisis.

cristallizzare (kristallid'dzare) vt crystallize.

cristallo (kris'tallo) nm crystal.

cristiano (kris'tjano) adj,n Christian. **cristianesimo** nm Christianity.

critica ('kritika) nf 1 criticism. 2 lit review. **criticare** vt criticize. **critico** ('kritiko) adj critical. nm critic.

crivellare (krivel'lare) vt riddle (with holes). **crivello** (kri'vɛllo) nm sieve.

croccante (krok'kante) nm nutty sweet.

crocchia ('krɔkkja) nf bun, chignon.

crocchio ('krɔkkjo) nm group.

croce (kro'tʃe) nf cross. **crocevia** (krotʃe'via) nm crossroads.

crociata (kro'tʃata) nf crusade.

crocicchio (kro'tʃikkjo) nm crossroads.

crociera (kro'tʃɛra) nf cruise.

crocifiggere (krotʃi'fiddʒere) vt crucify.

crocifisso (krotʃi'fisso) nm crucifix. **crocifissione** nf crucifixion.

croco ('krɔko) nm crocus.

crollare (krol'lare) vt shake. vi collapse, crumble. **crollo** ('krɔllo) nm collapse, crash.

cromo ('krɔmo) nm chrome. **cromato** adj chromium-plated.

cromosoma (kromo'sɔma) nm chromosome.

cronaca ('krɔnaka) nf 1 chronicle. 2 news item, report.

cronico ('krɔniko) adj chronic.

cronista (kro'nista) nm reporter, columnist.

cronologico (krono'lɔdʒiko) adj chronological.

cronometro (kro'nɔmetro) nm chronometer.

crosta ('krɔsta) nf crust. **crostata** nf pie, tart.

crostacei (kros'tatʃei) nm pl shellfish.

crucciare (krut'tʃare) vt annoy. **crucciarsi** vr 1 get angry. 2 worry.

cruciale (kru'tʃale) adj crucial.

crudele (kru'dɛle) adj cruel, heartless. **crudeltà** nf cruelty.

crudo ('krudo) adj 1 raw. 2 harsh, severe.

crumiro (kru'miro) nm blackleg.

cruscotto (krus'kɔtto) nm dashboard.

cubo ('kubo) nm cube. adj cubic.

cuccetta (kut'tʃetta) nf couchette, berth.

cucchiaio (kuk'kjajo) nm 1 spoon. 2 spoonful. **cucchiaio da frutta/tavola** dessertspoon/ tablespoon. **cucchiaino** nm teaspoon.

cucciolo ('kuttʃolo) nm puppy.

cucinare (kutʃi'nare) vt cook. **cucina** nf 1 kitchen. 2 cooking.

cucire (ku'tʃire) vt sew. **cucitura** nf seam.

cuculo (ku'kulo) nm cuckoo.

cuffia ('kuffja) nf 1 bonnet. 2 bath cap. 3 headphones.

cugino (ku'dʒino) nm cousin.

cui ('kui) pron invar 1 whom, which. 2 whose, of whom.

culla ('kulla) nf cradle.

culto ('kulto) nm cult.

cultura (kul'tura) nf culture, learning. **culturale** adj cultural.

cumulo ('kumulo) nm pile, heap.

cuneo ('kuneo) nm wedge.

cunetta (ku'netta) nf gutter.

cuocere* ('kwɔtʃere) vt cook. **cuoco** nm cook, chef.

cuoio ('kwɔjo) nm leather. **cuoio capelluto** nm scalp.

cuore ('kwɔre) nm 1 heart. 2 courage. 3 game hearts. **amico del cuore** nm best friend.

cupido ('kupido) adj greedy. **cupidigia** nf greed.

cupo ('kupo) adj gloomy, sombre, dark.

cupola ('kupola) nf dome.

cura ('kura) nf 1 care, charge. 2 attention. 3 treatment. **a cura di** edited by. **aver cura di** look after. **curare** vt 1 look after, attend to. 2 edit. 3 treat, cure. **curabile** (ku'rabile) adj curable.

curioso (ku'rjoso) adj 1 curious, inquisitive. 2 strange, odd, curious. **curiosità** nf curiosity.

curvare (kur'vare) vt bend, curve. **curvarsi** vr bend. **curva** nf curve, bend. **curvo** adj bent, curved.

cuscino (kuʃ'ʃino) nm 1 pillow. 2 cushion.

custode (kus'tode) nm 1 guardian. 2 caretaker. 3 warder. **custodia** (kus'todja) nf 1 custody, care. 2 case. **custodire** vt 1 take care of. 2 guard.

cuticola (ku'tikola) nf cuticle.

D

da (da) prep 1 from. 2 by. 3 to, at. 4 since, for. 5 as, like. 6 with. 7 for the purpose of.

dà (da) v see **dare**.

dabbasso (dab'basso) adv 1 below. 2 downstairs.

dabbene (dab'bɛne) adj invar decent, respectable.

daccapo (dak'kapo) adv over again.

dacché (dak'ke) conj since.

dado ('dado) nm 1 dice. 2 stock cube. 3 tech nut.

daffare (daf'fare) nm invar work. **avere molto daffare** be very busy.

daga ('daga) nf dagger.

dagli ('daʎʎi) contraction of **da gli**.

dai[1] ('dai) contraction of **da i**.

dai[2] ('dai) v see **dare**.

daino ('daino) nm deer.

dal (dal) contraction of **da il**.

dalia ('dalja) nf dahlia.

dall' (dal) contraction of **da l'**.

dalla ('dalla) contraction of **da la**.

dalle ('dalle) contraction of **da le**.

dallo ('dallo) contraction of **da lo**.

daltonismo (dalto'nizmo) nm colour-blindness. **daltonico** (dal'tɔniko) adj colour-blind.

d'altronde (dal'tronde) adv on the other hand, besides.

dama ('dama) nf 1 lady. 2 draughts.

damasco (da'masko) nm damask.

dancing ('dansiŋ) nm dance hall.

Danimarca (dani'marka) nf Denmark. **danese** (da'nese) adj Danish. nm 1 Dane. 2 Danish (language).

dannare (dan'nare) vt damn. **dannazione** nf damnation.

danneggiare (danned'dʒare) vt damage, harm. **danno** nm 1 damage, harm. 2 loss.

danzare (dan'tsare) vi, vt dance. **danza** nf dance.

dappertutto (dapper'tutto) adv everywhere.

dappoco (dap'pɔko) adj invar worthless.

dappresso (dap'presso) adv close by.

dapprima (dap'prima) adv at first.

dardeggiare (darded'dʒare) vt shoot forth.

dardo ('dardo) nm dart.

dare[*] ('dare) vt 1 give. 2 yield, produce. 3 assign, attach. 4 show. **dare alla testa** go to one's head. **dare in prestito** lend. **dare nell'occhio** catch the eye. **dare su** overlook. **darsi** vr dedicate oneself. **darsi da fare** keep oneself busy. **può darsi** it is possible.

darsena ('darsena) nf dock, basin.

data ('data) nf date. **datare** vt, vi date.

dattero ('dattero) nm date.

dattilografa (datti'lɔgrafa) nf typist. **dattilografia** nf typing.

dattorno (dat'torno) prep, adv around, about. **levarsi dattorno** get rid of.

davanti (da'vanti) prep before, in front of. adv before, in front.

davanzale (davan'tsale) nm windowsill.

davvero (dav'vero) adv really, indeed.

dazio ('dattsjo) nm duty, toll. **daziare** vt tax, put duty on.

dea ('dɛa) nf goddess.

debito ('debito) nm debt. adj due, proper. **debitore** nm debtor.

debole ('debole) adj weak, feeble. nm weak point, weakness. **debolezza** (debo'lettsa) nf weakness.

debuttare (debut'tare) vi make one's debut.

decadere (deka'dere) vi decay, decline. **decadente** (deka'dɛnte) adj in decline, decadent. **decadenza** (deka'dɛntsa) nf decline.

decano (de'kano) nm rel dean.

decapitare (dekapi'tare) vt behead.

decennio (de'tʃennjo) nm decade.

decente (de'tʃɛnte) adj decent, respectable. **decenza** (de'tʃɛnsa) nf decency.

decentrare (detʃen'trare) vt decentralize.

decesso (de'tʃɛsso) nm death, decease.

decibel (detʃi'bɛl) nm decibel.

decidere* (de'tʃidere) vt, vi decide, settle. **decidersi** vr make up one's mind.

deciduo (de'tʃiduo) adj deciduous.

decifrare (detʃi'frare) vt decipher.

decimale (detʃi'male) adj, nm decimal.

decimo (de'tʃimo) adj tenth.

decisi (de'tʃizi) v see **decidere**.

decisione (detʃi'zjone) nf decision. **decisivo** adj decisive.

deciso (de'tʃizo) v see **decidere**.

declamare (dekla'mare) vt declaim.

declinare (dekli'nare) vt decline. vi decline, decay, sink. **declino** nm decline.

declivio (de'klivjo) nm slope.

decollare (dekol'lare) vi aviat take off. **decollo** (de'kɔllo) nm take-off.

decomporsi (dekom'porsi) vr decompose. **decomposizione** nf decomposition.

decorare (deko'rare) vt decorate. **decorativo** adj decorative. **decorazione** nf decoration.

decoro (de'kɔro) nm dignity, decorum.

decorrere* (de'korrere) vi run, have effect. **a decorrere da** starting from.

decrepito (de'krɛpito) adj decrepit.

decrescere* (de'kreʃʃere) vi decrease, diminish.

decreto (de'kreto) nm decree.

dedalo ('dɛdalo) nm labyrinth.

dedicare (dedi'kare) vt dedicate. **dedica** ('dɛdika) nf dedication.

dedito ('dɛdito) adj devoted.

dedurre* (de'durre) vt 1 deduce. 2 deduct, subtract.

deferente (defe'rɛnte) adj respectful, deferential. **deferenza** (defe'rɛntsa) nf deference.

deficiente (defi'tʃɛnte) adj, n idiot.

deficit ('dɛfitʃit) nm deficit.

definire (defi'nire) vt 1 define. 2 settle. **definitivo** adj definitive. **definizione** nf definition.

deflazione (deflat'tsjone) nf deflation.

deflettere (de'flɛttere) vi 1 deflect, swerve. 2 deviate.

deformare (defor'mare) vt deform. **deforme** adj deformed, disfigured. **deformità** nf deformity.

defunto (de'funto) adj dead, deceased. nm dead person.

degenerare (dedʒene'rare) vi degenerate, deteriorate. **degenerazione** nf degeneration, deterioration.

degente (de'dʒɛnte) adj bedridden.

degenza (de'dʒɛntsa) nf stay in hospital or bed.

degli ('deʎʎi) contraction of **di gli**.

degnare (deɲ'ɲare) vi deign. **degnarsi** vr condescend. **degno** adj worthy, deserving.

degradare (degra'dare) vt degrade. **degradazione** nf degradation.

degustare (degus'tare) vt try, taste.

dei[1] ('dei) contraction of **di i**.

dei[2] ('dɛi) nm pl gods.

deificare (deifi'kare) vt deify.

del (del) contraction of **di il**.

delegare (dele'gare) vt delegate. **delegato** nm delegate. **delegazione** nf delegation.

delfino (del'fino) nm dolphin.

deliberare (delibe'rare) vt decide. vi deliberate. **deliberazione** nf 1 deliberation. 2 decision.

delicato (deli'kato) adj 1 delicate. 2 gentle. 3 refined. **delicatezza** (delika'tettsa) nf delicacy.

delimitare (delimi'tare) vt define, delimit.

delineare (deline'are) vt outline, trace.

delinquente (delin'kwɛnte) adj, n delinquent, criminal. **delinquenza** (delin'kwɛntsa) nf delinquency. **delinquenza minorile** juvenile delinquency.

deliquio (de'likwjo) nm fainting fit.

delirare (deli'rare) vi be delirious. **delirante** adj delirious. **delirio** nm delirium, frenzy.

delitto (de'litto) nm crime.

delizia (de'littsja) nf delight. **delizioso** (delit-'tsjoso) adj delicious, delightful.

dell' (del) contraction of **di l'**.

della ('della) contraction of **di la**.

delle ('delle) contraction of **di le**.

dello ('dello) contraction of **di lo**.

delta ('dɛlta) nm delta.

deludere* (de'ludere) vt 1 disappoint. 2 deceive.

delusione (delu'zjone) nf 1 disappointment. 2 deception.

demanio (de'manjo) nm state property.

demente (de'mɛnte) adj insane, mad. **demenza** (de'mɛntsa) nf madness.

democrazia (demokrat'tsia) nf democracy. **democratico** (demo'kratiko) adj democratic.

democristiano (demokris'tjano) nm Christian Democrat.

demolire (demo'lire) vt demolish. **demolizione** nf demolition.

demone ('dɛmone) nm demon.

demonio (de'mɔnjo) nm **1** devil. **2** demon.

demoralizzare (demoralid'dzare) vt demoralize.

denaro (de'naro) nm money.

denigrare (deni'grare) vt denigrate, run down.

denominatore (denomina'tore) nm denominator.

denotare (deno'tare) vt denote, indicate.

denso ('dɛnso) adj dense, thick. **densità** nf density.

dente ('dɛnte) nm tooth. **dente del giudizio** wisdom tooth. **dentiera** (den'tjɛra) nf set of false teeth. **dentifricio** nm toothpaste.

dentista (den'tista) nm dentist.

dentro ('dentro) adv,prep inside, within, in.

denunciare (denun'tʃare) vt declare, denounce. **denuncia** nf declaration, denunciation.

deodorante (deodo'rante) nm deodorant.

deperire (depe'rire) vi fade or waste away. **deperimento** nm decline.

depilare (depi'lare) vt remove hair. **depilatorio** (depila'tɔrjo) adj,nm depilatory.

deplorare (deplo'rare) vt deplore. **deplorevole** (deplo'revole) adj deplorable.

deporre* (de'porre) vt **1** place, put down. **2** deposit. **3** remove. **4** depose. **5** testify.

deportare (depor'tare) vt deport. **deportazione** nf deportation.

deposito (de'pɔzito) nm **1** deposit. **2** store, warehouse. **3** left-luggage office. **4** sediment. **depositare** vt deposit.

depredare (depre'dare) vt plunder, loot.

depresso (de'prɛsso) adj depressed. **depressione** nf depression.

deprezzare (depret'tsare) vt depreciate.

deprimere* (de'primere) vt depress.

depurare (depu'rare) vt purify.

deputare (depu'tare) vt appoint. **deputato** nm deputy.

deragliare (deraʎ'ʎare) vi be derailed.

derelitto (dere'litto) adj abandoned, derelict.

deretano (dere'tano) nm sl bottom, backside.

deridere* (de'ridere) vt deride, mock. **derisione** nf scorn, derision.

derisorio (deri'zɔrjo) adj derisory.

deriva (de'riva) nf drift. **andare alla deriva** drift.

derivare (deri'vare) vt,vi derive. vt divert.

derogare (dero'gare) vi **1** revoke. **2** contravene.

derubare (deru'bare) vt rob.

descrivere* (des'krivere) vt describe. **descrit-**

tivo adj descriptive. **descrizione** nf description.

deserto (de'zɛrto) nm desert. adj deserted.

desiderare (deside'rare) vt **1** want, desire. **2** require. **desiderio** (desi'dɛrjo) nm wish, desire.

designare (dezin'ɲare) vt designate.

desinare (dezi'nare) vi dine. nm dinner.

desistere (de'sistere) vi cease, abandon.

desolare (dezo'lare) vt devastate. **desolato** adj **1** desolate. **2** upset. **desolazione** nf desolation.

destare (des'tare) vt **1** waken. **2** arouse.

desti ('deste) v see **dare.**

destinare (desti'nare) vt **1** destine. **2** appoint. **3** address (a letter). **destinazione** nf destination. **destino** nm destiny.

destituire (destitu'ire) vt dismiss.

destro ('dɛstro) adj **1** right. **2** agile. **destra** nf **1** right side. **2** right hand.

detenere (dete'nere) vt hold, detain. **detenuto** adj imprisoned. nm prisoner.

detergente (deter'dʒɛnte) adj,nm detergent.

deteriorare (deterjo'rare) vi deteriorate. **deterioramento** nm deterioration.

determinare (determi'nare) vt determine, fix.

deterrente (deter'rɛnte) nm deterrent.

detersivo (deter'sivo) nm detergent.

detestare (detes'tare) vt hate, abhor. **detestabile** (detes'tabile) adj detestable.

detonatore (detona'tore) nm detonator.

detrarre* (de'trarre) vt subtract.

detrito (de'trito) nm debris.

dettagliare (dettaʎ'ʎare) vt **1** give in detail. **2** sell retail. **dettaglio** nm **1** detail. **2** retail.

dettare (det'tare) vt dictate. **dettato** nm dictation.

detti ('dɛtti) v see **dare.**

detto ('detto) v see **dare.** adj **1** so-called. **2** aforesaid. nm **1** saying. **2** word. **detto fatto** no sooner said than done.

deturpare (detur'pare) vt deform, disfigure.

devastare (devas'tare) vt devastate. **devastazione** nf devastation.

deviare (devi'are) vi **1** swerve. **2** deviate. vt divert. **deviazione** nf deviation.

devo ('dɛvo) v see **dovere.**

devoto (de'voto) adj **1** devout. **2** devoted. **devozione** nf devotion.

di (di) prep **1** of. **2** from, out of. **3** with. **4** about. **5** by. **6** than. **7** at. **8** in.

diabete (dia'bɛte) nm diabetes. **diabetico** (dia-'bɛtiko) adj,nm diabetic.

diacono (di'akono) nm deacon.

diaframma (dia'framma) nm diaphragm.

diagnosi (di'aɲɲozi) nf diagnosis. **diagnosticare** vt diagnose.

diagonale (diago'nale) adj,nm diagonal.

diagramma (dia'gramma) nm diagram.

dialetto (dia'lɛtto) nm dialect. **dialettale** adj dialectal.

dialogo (di'alogo) nm dialogue.

diamante (dia'mante) nm diamond.

diametro (di'ametro) nm diameter.

diapositiva (diapozi'tiva) nf phot slide.

diario (di'arjo) nm diary.

diarrea (diar'rɛa) nf diarrhoea.

diavolo ('djavolo) nm devil.

dibattere (di'battere) vt debate, discuss. **dibattersi** vr struggle.

dibattito (di'battito) nm debate.

dicastero (dikas'tɛro) nm ministry.

dicembre (di'tʃembre) nm December.

dichiarare (dikja'rare) vt declare. **dichiarazione** nf declaration.

diciannove (ditʃan'nɔve) adj nineteen. nm or f nineteen. **diciannovesimo** (ditʃanno'vɛzimo) adj nineteenth.

diciassette (ditʃas'sɛtte) adj seventeen. nm or f seventeen. **diciassettesimo** (ditʃasset'tɛzimo) adj seventeenth.

diciotto (di'tʃɔtto) adj eighteen. nm or f eighteen. **diciottesimo** (ditʃot'tɛzimo) adj eighteenth.

dico ('diko) v see **dire.**

didattico (di'dattiko) adj didactic.

dieci ('djetʃi) adj ten. nm or f ten.

diedi ('djɛdi) v see **dare.**

dieta ('djɛta) nf diet.

dietro ('djɛtro) adv 1 behind. 2 back. prep 1 behind, after. 2 following, upon.

difatti (di'fatti) adv in fact.

difendire* (di'fɛndere) vt defend, protect.

difensiva (difen'siva) nf defensive. **difensivo** adj defensive.

difesa (di'fesa) nf defence.

difesi (di'fesi) v see **difendere.**

difeso (di'feso) v see **difendere.**

difetto (di'fɛtto) nm defect, fault. **difettoso** (difet'toso) adj defective.

diffamare (diffa'mare) vt slander.

differente (diffe'rɛnte) adj different.

differenza (diffe'rɛntsa) nf difference. **differenziare** vt differentiate.

differire (diffe'rire) vi differ, be different. vt put off, postpone.

difficile (dif'fitʃile) adj 1 difficult, hard. 2 hard to please. 3 improbable. **difficilmente** adv with difficulty.

difficoltà (diffikol'ta) nf difficulty.

diffidare (diffi'dare) vi distrust.

diffondere* (dif'fondere) vt 1 spread. 2 divulge.

diffusione (diffu'zjone) nf 1 circulation (of a newspaper). 2 diffusion.

diga ('diga) nf dyke.

digerire (didʒe'rire) vt digest. **digestione** (didʒes'tjone) nf digestion.

digitale (didʒi'tale) adj digital. nf foxglove. **impronta digitale** nf fingerprint.

digiunare (didʒu'nare) vi fast. **digiuno** nm fast.

dignità (diɲɲi'ta) nf dignity. **dignitoso** (diɲɲi-'toso) adj dignified.

digressione (digres'sjone) nf digression.

digrignare (digriɲ'ɲare) vt gnash (one's teeth).

dilapidare (dilapi'dare) vt squander, waste.

dilatare (dila'tare) vt expand, spread.

dileguare (dile'gware) vt 1 melt. 2 remove. **dileguarsi** vr fade away.

dilemma (di'lemma) nm dilemma.

dilettare (dilet'tare) vt,vi please. **dilettarsi a** vr take pleasure in. **dilettante** nm amateur. **diletto** (di'lɛtto) nm delight, pleasure.

diligente (dili'dʒɛnte) adj 1 diligent. 2 careful.

diligenza[1] (dili'dʒɛntsa) nf diligence.

diligenza[2] (dili'dʒɛntsa) nf stagecoach.

diluire (dilu'ire) vt dilute.

dilungare (dilun'gare) vt prolong. **dilungarsi** vr digress.

diluvio (di'luvjo) nm flood.

dimagrire (dima'grire) vi grow thin, lose weight.

dimenare (dime'nare) vt shake. **dimenare la coda** wag the tail. **dimenarsi** vr wriggle, writhe.

dimensione (dimen'sjone) nf dimension.

dimenticare (dimenti'kare) vt forget. **dimenticarsi** vr forget. **dimentico** (di'mentiko) adj forgetful.

dimettere (di'mettere) ʾvt dismiss, discharge. **dimettersi** vr resign.

dimezzare (dimed'dzare) vt halve.

diminuire (diminu'ire) vt reduce, diminish. vi decrease.

dimissione (dimis'sjone) *nf* resignation. **dare le dimissione** resign.

dimorare (dimo'rare) *vi* live, stay. **dimora** (di'mɔra) *nf* residence, home.

dimostrare (dimos'trare) *vt* show, prove. **dimostrazione** *nf* demonstration.

dinamica (di'namika) *nf* dynamics. **dinamico** (di'namiko) *adj* dynamic.

dinamite (dina'mite) *nf* dynamite.

dinamo ('dinamo) *nf invar* dynamo.

dinanzi (di'nantsi) *adv* in front. **dinazi a** *prep* in front of, before.

dinastia (dinas'tia) *nf* dynasty.

dinoccolato (dinokko'lato) *adj* lanky.

dinosauro (dino'sauro) *nm* dinosaur.

dintorno (din'torno) *prep,adv* **1** around. **2** about. *nm pl* outskirts.

Dio ('dio) *nm* God.

diocesi (di'ɔtʃezi) *nf* diocese.

dipartimento (diparti'mento) *nm* department.

dipendere* (di'pɛndere) *vi* **1** depend. **2** be subject. **dipendere da** depend on. **dipendente** (dipen'dɛnte) *adj* dependent. *nm* dependant. **dipendenza** (dipen'dɛntsa) *nf* dependence.

dipingere* (di'pindʒere) *vt* **1** paint. **2** portray.

diploma (diplo'ma) *nm* diploma. **diplomatico** (diplo'matiko) *adj* diplomatic. **diplomazia** (diploma'tsia) *nf* diplomacy.

diradare (dira'dare) *vt* reduce. *vi* become sparse. **diradarsi** *vr* become sparse, clear.

diramare (dira'mare) *vt* **1** circulate. **2** broadcast. **diramarsi** *vr* branch off.

dire* ('dire) *vt* **1** say. **2** tell. **per così dire** so to speak.

diressi (di'rɛssi) *v* see **dirigere**.

diretto (di'rɛtto) *v* see **dirigere**. *adj* direct, straight. *nm* fast train. **direttissimo** *nm* express train.

direttore (diret'tore) *nm* **1** director, manager. **2** editor. **3** headmaster. **4** *mus* conductor. **direttrice** *nf* **1** manageress. **2** headmistress.

direzione (diret'tsjone) *nf* **1** management. **2** direction.

dirigere* (di'ridʒere) *vt* **1** run, manage. **2** address, direct. **dirigente** (diri'dʒɛnte) *nm* director. *adj* ruling.

dirimpetto (dirim'pɛtto) *prep,adv* opposite.

diritto[1] (di'ritto) *adj* **1** direct, straight. **2** right-hand. *adv* straight on. *nm* right side (of material).

diritto[2] (di'ritto) *nm* **1** right, claim. **2** law. **diritti d'autore** *nm pl* royalties.

diroccare (dirok'kare) *vt* demolish.

dirottare (dirot'tare) *vt* **1** divert. **2** hijack.

dirotto (di'rotto) *adj* unrestrained. **pioggia dirotta** *nf* pouring rain.

dirupato (diru'pato) *adj* rugged, precipitous.

dirupo (di'rupo) *nm* ravine.

disabitato (dizabi'tato) *adj* uninhabited.

disaccordo (disak'kɔrdo) *nm* disagreement.

disadatto (diza'datto) *adj* unsuited.

disagevole (diza'dʒevole) *adj* **1** difficult. **2** uncomfortable.

disagio (di'zadʒo) *nm* discomfort. **a disagio** ill at ease.

disapprovare (dizappro'vare) *vt* disapprove. **disapprovazione** *nf* disapproval.

disappunto (dizap'punto) *nm* disappointment, displeasure.

disarmare (dizar'mare) *vt* disarm. **disarmo** *nm* disarmament.

disastro (di'zastro) *nm* disaster. **disastroso** (dizas'troso) *adj* disastrous.

disattento (dizat'tɛnto) *adj* inattentive. **disattenzione** (dizatten'tsjone) *nf* carelessness.

discendere* (diʃʃendere) *vi* **1** come down, descend. **2** descend, be descended. *vt* go or come down. **discendente** (diʃʃen'dɛnte) *nm* descendant. **discendenza** (diʃʃen'dɛntsa) *nf* origin, descent.

discepolo (diʃʃepolo) *nm* disciple.

discernere (diʃʃɛrnere) *vt* distinguish, discern. **discernimento** *nm* judgment, discernment.

discesa (diʃʃesa) *nf* descent.

disciplinare (diʃʃipli'nare) *vt* control, discipline. **disciplina** *nf* discipline.

disco ('disko) *nm* **1** disc. **2** record, gramophone. **3** discus. **disco orario** parking disc.

discolpare (diskol'pare) *vt* prove innocent, clear of blame.

discorrere* (dis'korrere) *vi* discuss, talk.

discorso (dis'korso) *nm* talk, speech. **cambiare il discorso** change the subject.

discoteca (disko'tɛka) *nf* discotheque.

discreto (dis'kreto) *adj* **1** reasonable, moderate, passable. **2** cautious, discreet. **discrezione** *nf* discretion.

discriminazione (diskriminat'tsjone) *nf* discrimination.

discussi (dis'kussi) *v* see **discutere**.

discussione (diskus'sjone) *nf* **1** discussion. **2** argument.

discusso (dis'kusso) v see **discutere**.

discutere* (dis'kutere) vt discuss, debate.

disdire (diz'dire) vt 1 retract, take back. 2 cancel.

disegnare (disen'nare) vt 1 draw. 2 design. **disegno** nm 1 drawing. 2 design.

diseredare (dizere'dare) vt disinherit.

disertare (dizer'tare) vi desert. **disertore** nm deserter.

disfare* (dis'fare) vt 1 undo. 2 unpack. 3 destroy. **disfarsi** vr melt. **disfarsi di** get rid of.

disgelare (duzdʒe'lare) vi thaw. **disgelo** (diz'dʒɛlo) nm thaw.

disgrazia (diz'grattsja) nf 1 misfortune. 2 mishap, accident. **disgraziato** adj unfortunate. nm wretch.

disgregare (dizgre'gare) vt break up, disintegrate.

disgustare (dizgus'tare) vt disgust. **disgusto** nm disgust. **disgustoso** (dizgus'toso) adj disgusting.

disidratare (dizidra'tare) vt dehydrate.

disimpegnare (dizimpen'nare) vt 1 discharge. 2 relieve. 3 redeem. **disimpegnarsi** vr manage.

disinfettare (dizinfet'tare) vt disinfect. **disinfettante** adj,nm disinfectant.

disintegrare (dizinte'grare) vt split. **disintegrarsi** vr disintegrate.

disinteressarsi (dizinteres'sarsi) vr ignore, not to be aware of.

disinvolto (dizin'volto) adj nonchalant, free and easy. **disinvoltura** nf ease.

disistima (dizis'tima) nf discredit.

dismisura (dizmi'sura) nf excess.

disoccupato (dizokku'pato) adj unemployed. nm unemployed person. **disoccupazione** nf unemployment.

disonesto (dizo'nɛsto) adj dishonest.

disonorare (dizono'rare) vt dishonour. **disonore** nm dishonour, shame.

disopra (di'sopra) adv 1 above. 2 upstairs.

disordinare (dizordi'nare) vt upset, disarrange. **disordinato** adj untidy. **disordine** (di'zordine) nm disorder, confusion.

disorientare (dizorjen'tare) vt disorientate, confuse.

dissossare (dizos'sare) vt bone, fillet.

disotto (di'sotto) adv 1 below, beneath. 2 downstairs. **al disotto di** prep below, beneath.

dispaccio (dis'pattʃo) nm dispatch.

disparato (dispa'rato) adj dissimilar, heterogeneous.

dispari ('dispari) adj invar uneven, odd. **disparità** nf invar disparity.

disparte (dis'parte) adv aside. **in disparte da** apart from, on one side.

dispensa (dis'prɛnsa) 1 larder. 2 number, volume. 3 pl duplicated university lectures. 4 exemption. 5 dispense. 2 exempt, exempt.

disperare (dispe'rare) vi despair. **disperato** adj 1 desperate, in despair. 2 hopeless. **disperazione** nf desperation.

disperdere* (dis'pɛrdere) vt 1 scatter. 2 waste.

dispetto (dis'pɛtto) nm 1 spite. 2 annoyance. **dispettoso** (dispet'toso) adj spiteful.

dispiacere* (dispja'tʃere) v imp 1 mind. 2 be sorry. nm 1 displeasure. 2 regret.

disponibile (dispo'nibile) adj available.

disporre* (dis'porre) vt 1 arrange. 2 prepare. **disporre di** 1 dispose of. 2 have at one's disposal.

dispositivo (dispozi'tivo) nm gadget, device.

disposizione (dispozit'sjone) nf 1 disposition, inclination. 2 order, command.

disprezzare (dispret'tsare) vt scorn, despise. **disprezzo** (dis'prɛttso) nm scorn, contempt.

disputare (dispu'tare) vi discuss, debate. vt contest. **disputa** ('disputa) nf 1 discussion. 2 quarrel.

dissecare (disse'kare) vt dissect.

disseccare (dissek'kare) vt dry up.

dissenteria (dissente'ria) nf dysentery.

dissentire (dissen'tire) vi dissent, disagree.

dissertazione (dissertat'tsjone) nf dissertation, thesis.

dissestare (disses'tare) vt ruin. **dissesto** (dis'sɛsto) nm financial disaster.

dissetare (disse'tare) vt quench the thirst of.

dissi ('dissi) v see **dire**.

dissidente (dissi'dɛnte) nm dissident.

dissidio (dis'sidjo) nm quarrel.

dissimile (dis'simile) adj unlike.

dissimulare (dissimu'lare) vt conceal, hide.

dissipare (dissi'pare) vt 1 disperse. 2 waste.

dissociare (disso'tʃare) vt separate, dissociate.

dissoluto (disso'luto) adj dissolute.

dissoluzione (dissolut'tsjone) nf dissolution.

dissolvere* (dis'solvere) vt dissolve, break up.

dissuadere* (dissua'dere) vt dissuade.

distaccare (distak'kare) vt separate, detach.

distaccarsi (dis'takkarsi) *vr* stand out. **distacco** *nm* **1** aloofness. **2** separation.

distante (dis'tante) *adj* distant, far away. **distanza** *nf* distance.

distendere (dis'tɛndere) *vt* spread, open out. **distendersi** *vr* stretch oneself.

disteso (dis'teso) *adj* **1** open, spread out. **2** spacious. **distesa** *nf* expanse.

distillare (distil'lare) *vt* distil. **distilleria** *nf* distillery.

distinguere (dis'tingwere) *vt* distinguish.

distinsi (dis'tinsi) *v* see **distinguere.**

distintivo (distin'tivo) *nm* badge.

distinto (dis'tinto) *v* see **distinguere.** *adj* **1** distinct, clear. **2** refined.

distinzione (distin'tsjone) *nf* distinction.

distogliere (dis'toʎʎere) *vt* dissuade.

distrarre (dis'trarre) *vt* divert, distract. **distrarsi** *vr* **1** relax. **2** let one's mind wander. **distratto** *adj* absent-minded, inattentive. **distrazione** *nf* distraction.

distretto (dis'tretto) *nm* district.

distribuire (distribu'ire) *vt* distribute. **distributore** *nm* distributor. **distributore automatico** slot-machine. **distributore di benzina** petrol pump. **distribuzione** *nf* distribution.

districare (distri'kare) *vt* unravel.

distruggere (dis'truddʒere) *vt* destroy. **distruttivo** *adj* destructive. **distruzione** *nf* destruction.

disturbare (distur'bare) *vt* disturb, interrupt. **disturbarsi** *vr* put oneself out. **disturbo** *nm* trouble.

disubbidire (dizubbi'dire) *vi,vt* disobey. **disubbidiente** (dizubbi'djɛnte) *adj* disobedient. **disubbidienza** (dizubbi'djɛntsa) *nf* disobedience.

disuguale (dizu'gwale) *adj* **1** unequal. **2** eneven.

disunire (dizu'nire) *vt* divide, disunite.

disuso (di'zuzo) *nm* disuse. **disusato** *adj* **1** disused. **2** out-of-date.

dito ('dito) *nm* **1** *pl* **dita** *f* finger. **2** *pl* **diti** finger, finger's breadth. **dito del piede** *nm* toe. **sulla punta della dita** at one's fingertips. **ditale** *nm* thimble.

ditta ('ditta) *nf* company, firm.

dittatore (ditta'tore) *nm* dictator. **dittatura** *nf* dictatorship.

dittico ('dittiko) *nm* diptych.

dittongo (dit'tongo) *nm* diphthong.

diurno (di'urno) *adj* diurnal, daily.

diva ('diva) *nf* film star.

divagare (diva'gare) *vi* wander, ramble.

divampare (divam'pare) *vi* burst into flames, burn.

divano (di'vano) *nm* **1** divan. **2** settee.

divenire (dive'nire) *vi* become.

diventare (diven'tare) *vi* become.

divergere (di'vɛrdʒere) *vi* diverge.

diverso (di'vɛrso) *adj* **1** different. **2** *pl* several. **diversione** (diver'sjone) *nf* diversion. **diversità** *nf* variety.

divertirsi (diver'tirsi) *vr* **1** amuse oneself. **2** enjoy oneself. **divertente** (diver'tɛnte) *adj* funny, amusing. **divertimento** *nm* **1** pastime. **2** amusement.

dividendo (divi'dɛndo) *nm* dividend.

dividere (di'videre) *vt* divide, share. **dividersi** *vr* separate, split.

divieto (di'vjɛto) *nm* restriction, ban. **divieto di sosta/transito** no parking/thoroughfare.

divincolare (divinko'lare) *vt* wriggle. **divincolarsi** *vr* writhe.

divino (di'vino) *adj* **1** divine. **2** wonderful.

divisa (di'viza) *nf* **1** uniform. **2** currency.

divisi (di'vizi) *v* see **dividere.**

divisione (divi'zjone) *nf* **1** division. **2** separation.

diviso (di'vizo) *v* see **dividere.**

divorare (divo'rare) *vt* devour.

divorzio (di'vɔrtsjo) *nm* divorce. **divorziare** *vt,vi* divorce.

divulgare (divul'gare) *vt* reveal, divulge. **divulgarsi** *vr* spread.

dizionario (dittsjo'narjo) *nm* dictionary.

dizione (dit'tsjone) *nf* **1** diction. **2** wording.

do (dɔ) *v* see **dare.**

dobbiamo (dob'bjamo) *v* see **dovere.**

doccia ('dottʃa) *nf* shower. **fare la doccia** take a shower.

docente (do'tʃɛnte) *nm* teacher.

docile ('dɔtʃile) *adj* docile. **docilità** *nf* docility.

documento (doku'mento) *nm* document, brief. **documentare** *vt* document. **documentario** *nm* documentary.

dodici ('doditʃi) *adj* twelve. *nm or f* twelve. **dodicesimo** (dodi'tʃezimo) *adj* twelfth.

dogana (do'gana) *nf* **1** customs. **2** duty. **doganiere** (doga'njɛre) *nm* customs officer.

doge ('dɔdʒe) *nm* doge, chief Venetian magistrate.

doglia ('dɔʎʎa) *nf* pain.

dogma ('dɔgma) *nm* dogma. **dogmatico** (dog'matiko) *adj* dogmatic.

dolce ('doltʃe) adj **1** sweet. **2** gentle. **3** mild. **4** (of water) fresh. nm sweet. **dolcezza** (dol'tʃettsa) nf sweetness. **dolciumi** nm pl sweet things, sweets.

dolere* (do'lere) v imp **1** hurt, ache. **2** be sorry. **dolersi** vr lament, regret. **dolore** nm **1** pain, ache. **2** sorrow. **doloroso** (dolo'roso) adj painful.

dollaro ('dɔllaro) nm dollar.

dolse ('dɔlse) v see **dolere**.

domandare (doman'dare) vt ask, request. **domandarsi** vr wonder. **domanda** nf **1** question. **2** request, application. **fare una domanda** ask a question.

domani (do'mani) adv,nm tomorrow. **domani a otto** tomorrow week. **domani l'altro** day after tomorrow.

domare (do'mare) vt tame. **domatore** nm trainer.

domattina (domat'tina) adv tomorrow morning.

domenica (do'menika) nf Sunday.

domestico (do'mɛstiko) adj **1** domestic, household. **2** tame. nm servant. **domestica** (do'mɛstika) nf maid, servant.

domiciliarsi (domitʃi'ljarsi) vr settle, take up residence.

domicilio (domi'tʃiljo) nm residence, dwelling.

dominare (domi'nare) vt **1** dominate, control. **2** overlook. vi dominate, rule. **dominarsi** vr restrain oneself. **dominante** adj dominant. **dominazione** nf domination, rule.

dominio (do'minjo) nm **1** control. **2** possession, property. **3** field, domain.

domino ('dɔmino) nm game dominoes.

donare (do'nare) vt give, present. **donatore** nm donor. **dono** nm gift.

dondolare (dondo'lare) vi swing, rock, sway. vt shake. **dondolo** ('dondolo) nm swing.

donna ('dɔnna) nm **1** woman, lady **2** cap Lady. **donna di servizio** nf charwoman.

donnola ('dɔnnola) nf weasel.

dopo ('dopo) prep after. adv **1** behind. **2** afterwards. **3** then. **dopo tutto** after all. **subito dopo** immediately afterwards. **dopo-domani** (dopodo'mani) adv,nm day after tomorrow. **dopopranzo** (dopo'prandzo) nm afternoon.

doppiare (dop'pjare) vt dub. **doppiaggio** nm dubbing.

doppio ('doppjo) adj,adv double. **doppiogio-chista** (doppjodʒo'kista) nm double-dealer.

doppiogioco (doppjo'dʒɔko) nm double-dealing.

dorare (do'rare) vt gild. **dorato** adj gilt.

dormire (dor'mire) vi sleep. **dormire come un ghiro** sleep like a log. **dormirci sopra** sleep on it.

dormitorio (dormi'tɔrjo) nm dormitory.

dorso ('dɔrso) nm **1** back. **2** spine (of a book). **dorsale** adj dorsal. **spina dorsale** nf spine.

dose ('dɔze) nf dose.

dosso ('dɔsso) nm back. **togliere di dosso** remove, get rid of.

dote ('dɔte) nf dowry.

dotto ('dɔtto) adj learned, scholarly.

dottore (dot'tore) nm med doctor. **dottorato** nm doctorate. **dottoressa** nf med female doctor.

dottrina (dot'trina) nf **1** doctrine. **2** catechism classes.

dove ('dove) adv **1** where. **2** wherever. **3** in which.

dovere* (do'vere) vt **1** have to, be obliged to, need. **2** owe. nm duty.

dovrò (do'vrɔ) v see **dovere**.

dovunque (do'vunkwe) adv wherever.

dozzina (dod'dzina) nf dozen.

dragare (dra'gare) vt dredge. **draga** nf dredger.

dragone (dra'gone) nm also **drago** nm dragon.

dramma¹ ('dramma) nm drama, theatre. **drammatico** (dram'matiko) adj dramatic.

dramma² ('dramma) nf drachma.

drammatizzare (drammatid'dzare) vt dramatize.

drammaturgo (dramma'turgo) nm dramatist, playwright.

drenare (dre'nare) vt drain. **drenaggio** nm drainage.

dritto ('dritto) adj **1** right. **2** upright. **3** straight. nm right side, upper side.

drizzare (drit'tsare) vt **1** erect. **2** straighten. **drizzare le orecchie** prick up one's ears.

drogare (dro'gare) vt **1** drug. **2** spice. **droga** ('drɔga) nf **1** drug. **2** drug-taking. **drogato** nm drug addict.

droghiere (dro'gjɛre) nm grocer. **drogheria** nf grocer's shop.

dromedario (drome'darjo) nm dromedary.

duale (du'ale) adj dual.

dubbio ('dubbjo) nm doubt, suspicion. adj doubtful, uncertain. **dubbioso** (dub'bjoso) adj doubtful.

dubitare (dubi'tare) vi **1** doubt, hesitate. **2** suspect.

duca ('duka) *nm* duke. **ducale** *adj* ducal. **ducato** *nm* **1** duchy. **2** ducat.

duce ('dutʃe) *nm* guide, leader.

duchessa (du'kessa) *nf* duchess.

due ('due) *adj,nm* two. **duecento** (due'tʃɛnto) *adj* two hundred. *nm* **1** two hundred. **2** thirteenth century. **due pezzi** *nm invar* **1** bikini. **2** suit.

duello (du'ɛllo) *nm* duel.

duetto (du'etto) *nm* duet.

duna ('duna) *nf* dune.

dunque ('dunkwe) *conj* **1** therefore, so. **2** then.

duole ('dwɔle) *v* see **dolere**.

duomo ('dwɔmo) *nm* cathedral.

duplicare (dupli'kare) *vt* duplicate. **duplicato** *nm* duplicate. **duplicatore** *nm* duplicator, duplicating machine. **durata** *nf* duration. **durabile** (du'rabile) *adj* durable. **durante** (du'rante) *prep* during.

durare (du'rare) *vi* **1** last. **2** resist. **durabile** *adj* durable. **durante** *prep* during. **durata** *nf* duration.

duro ('duro) *adj* **1** hard. **2** tough, stale. **3** severe. **4** difficult. **5** stupid, dull. **tener duro** hold firm. **durevole** *adj* lasting. **durezza** (du'rettsa) *nf* **1** hardness. **2** severity.

E

e, ed (e, ed) *conj* and, also. **e...e** both...and.

è (e) *v* see **essere**.

ebano ('ɛbano) *nm* ebony.

ebbe ('ebbe) *v* see **avere**.

ebbene (eb'bɛne) *conj* well then, well.

ebbero ('ɛbbero) *v* see **avere**.

ebbi ('ɛbbi) *v* see **avere**.

ebbro ('ɛbbro) *adj* **1** drunk. **2** elated. **ebbrezza** (eb'brettsa) *nf* intoxication.

ebdomadario (ebdoma'darjo) *adj* weekly. *nm* weekly publication.

ebete ('ɛbete) *adj* stupid.

ebollizione (ebollit'tsjone) *nf* boiling. **punto di ebollizione** *nm* boiling point.

ebraico (e'braiko) *adj* Jewish, Hebrew. *nm* Hebrew (language).

ebreo (e'brɛo) *adj* Jewish. *nm* Jew.

eccedere (et'tʃɛdere) *vt* surpass, exceed. **eccedenza** (ettʃe'dɛntsa) *nf* surplus.

eccellere* (et'tʃɛllere) *vi* excel, stand out. **eccellente** (ettʃel'lɛnte) *adj* excellent. **eccel-**

lenza (ettʃel'lɛntsa) *nf* **1** excellence. **2** *cap* Excellency.

eccentrico (et'tʃɛntriko) *adj* eccentric. **eccentricità** *nf* eccentricity.

eccesso (et'tʃɛsso) *nm* excess. **all'eccesso** in the extreme. **eccessivo** *adj* excessive.

eccetera (et'tʃɛtera) *nm invar* et cetera, and so on.

eccetto (et'tʃɛtto) *prep* except. **eccetto che 1** apart from. **2** unless.

eccettuare (ettʃettu'are) *vt* exclude, leave out.

eccezione (ettʃet'tsjone) *nf* exception. **eccezionale** *adj* exceptional.

eccitare (ettʃi'tare) *vt* excite, arouse, stimulate. **eccitabile** (ettʃi'tabile) *adj* excitable. **eccitato** *adj* excited.

ecclesiastico (ekkle'zjastiko) *adj* ecclesiastical. *nm* clergyman.

ecco ('ɛkko) *adv* here is or are, there is or are. **ecco fatto** that's it, done.

echeggiare (eked'dʒare) *vi* echo, resound.

eclissare (eklis'sare) *vt* eclipse. **eclissi** *nm,f* eclipse.

eco ('ɛko) *nm or f, pl* **echi** *m* echo.

ecologia (ekolo'dʒia) *nf* ecology.

economia (ekono'mia) *nf* **1** saving, economy. **2** economics. **economico** (eko'nɔmiko) *adj* **1** economic. **2** economical.

economizzare (ekonomid'dzare) *vi* economize.

economo (e'kɔnomo) *nm* bursar, treasurer.

edera ('edera) *nf* ivy.

edicola (e'dikola) *nf* newspaper kiosk.

edificare (edifi'kare) *vt* build, construct. **edificio** *nm* building.

edilizio (edi'littsjo) *adj* building. **speculazione edilizia** *nf* property speculation. **edile** *adj* building. **edilizia** (edi'littsja) *nf* building trade.

Edimburgo (edim'burgo) *nf* Edinburgh.

editore (edi'tore) *nm* publisher. *adj* publishing. **edito** ('ɛdito) *adj* published. **editoriale** *adj* editorial. *nm* newspaper editorial. **casa editrice** *nf* publishing house.

edizione (edit'tsjone) *nf* edition.

educare (edu'kare) *vt* **1** bring up. **2** educate, instruct. **educato** *adj* well-bred. **educazione** *nf* **1** education. **2** manners.

effeminato (effemi'nato) *adj* effeminate.

effetto (ef'fɛtto) *nm* **1** effect. **2** result. **in effetti** in fact.

effettuare (effettu'are) *vt* accomplish. **effettuarsi** *vr* take place.

efficace (effi'katʃe) adj sure, effectual.

efficiente (effi'tʃɛnte) adj efficient. **efficienza** (effi'tʃɛntsa) nf **1** efficiency. **2** working order.

effigie (ef'fidʒe) nf also **effigie** nf invar effigy.

effimero (ef'fimero) adj fleeting, ephemeral.

egeo (e'dʒɛo) adj Aegean. (**Mare**) **Egeo** nm Aegean (Sea).

Egitto (e'dʒitto) nm Egypt. **egiziano** adj,n Egyptian.

egli ('eʎʎi) pron 3rd pers ms he.

egoista (ego'ista) nm egoist, selfish person. **egoismo** (ego'izmo) nm egoism, selfishness.

egregio (e'grɛdʒo) adj distinguished.

elaborare (elabo'rare) vt elaborate. **elaborato** adj elaborate.

elastico (e'lastiko) pl **elastici** adj elastic. nm **1** elastic. **2** elastic band.

elefante (ele'fante) nm elephant. **fare d'una mosca un elefante** make a mountain out of a molehill.

elegante (ele'gante) adj elegant. **eleganza** nf elegance.

eleggere* (e'lɛddʒere) vt **1** elect. **2** choose.

elegia (ele'dʒia) nf elegy.

elemento (ele'mento) nm **1** element. **2** unit. **3** pl rudiments, principles. **elementare** adj elementary. **scuola elementare** nf primary school.

elemosina (ele'mɔzina) nf charity.

elenco (e'lɛnko) nm list. **elenco telefonico** telephone directory. **elencare** vt list.

elettore (elet'tore) nm constituent, voter. **elettorato** nm electorate.

elettrico (e'lɛttriko) adj electric. **elettricista** nm electrician. **elettricità** nf electricity. **elettrodomestico** (elettrodo'mɛstiko) nm electrical household appliance.

elettrificare (elettrifi'kare) vt electrify.

elettrizzare (elettrid'dzare) vt excite, electrify.

elettrodo (e'lɛttrodo) nm electrode.

elettrone (elet'trone) nm electron. **elettronico** (elet'troniko) adj electronic.

elevare (ele'vare) vt raise.

elezione (elet'tsjone) nf election.

elica ('ɛlika) nf propeller. **elicottero** (eli-'kɔttero) nm helicopter.

eliminare (elimi'nare) vt eliminate. **eliminazione** nf elimination.

ella ('ella) pron **1** 3rd pers fs she. **2** cap 2nd pers fs fml you.

elmo ('elmo) nm helmet.

eloquente (elo'kwɛnte) adj eloquent. **eloquenza** (elo'kwɛntsa) nf eloquence.

eludere* (e'ludere) vt evade, elude.

emaciato (ema'tʃato) adj emaciated.

emancipare (emantʃi'pare) vt free, emancipate. **emancipazione** nf emancipation.

embargo (em'bargo) nm embargo.

emblema (em'blɛma) nm emblem.

embrione (embri'one) nm embryo.

emendare (emen'dare) vt amend. **emendamento** nm amendment.

emergenza (emer'dʒɛntsa) nf emergency.

emergere* (e'mɛrdʒere) vi emerge.

emettere* (e'mettere) vt emit, issue.

emicrania (emi'kranja) nf migraine.

emigrare (emi'grare) vi emigrate. **emigrante** nm emigrant. **emigrato** nm **1** emigrant. **2** political exile. **emigrazione** nf emigration.

eminente (emi'nɛnte) adj eminent.

emisfero (emis'fɛro) nm hemisphere.

emissione (emis'sjone) nf **1** issue. **2** programme, broadcast.

emorragia (emorra'dʒia) nf haemorrhage.

emozionare (emottsjo'nare) vt move, affect. **emozionante** adj moving, thrilling. **emozione** nf emotion.

empio ('empjo) adj **1** impious. **2** evil. **3** pitiless.

empire (em'pire) vt fill.

empirico (em'piriko) adj empirical.

emporio (em'pɔrjo) nm market, emporium.

emù (e'mu) nm invar emu.

enciclopedia (entʃiklope'dia) nf encyclopedia.

endemico (en'dɛmiko) adj endemic.

energia (ener'dʒia) nf energy. **energico** (e'nɛrdʒiko) adj energetic.

enfasi ('ɛnfazi) nf invar emphasis. **enfatico** (en'fatiko) adj emphatic.

enfiare (en'fjare) vi swell. **enfiarsi** vr swell up.

enigma (e'nigma) nm **1** enigma. **2** puzzle. **enigmatico** (enig'matiko) adj enigmatic.

ennesimo (en'nɛzimo) adj umpteenth.

enorme (e'norme) adj huge, enormous.

ente ('ɛnte) nm corporation, society.

entità (enti'ta) nf invar entity.

entrambi (en'trambi) pron pl both.

entrare (en'trare) vi **1** enter, go or come in. **2** have relevance. **io non c'entro** it has nothing to do with me. **entrata** nf entrance.

entro ('entro) prep within.

entusiasmo (entu'zjazmo) nm enthusiasm. **entusiasta** nm enthusiast. adj enthusiastic. **entusiastico** (entu'zjastiko) adj enthusiastic.

enumerare (enume'rare) vt enumerate.

enzima (en'dzima) nm enzyme.

epico ('epiko) adj,nm epic.

epidemia (epide'mia) nf epidemic.

Epifania (epifa'nia) nf Epiphany.

epigramma (epi'gramma) nm epigram.

epilessia (epiles'sia) nf epilepsy.

epilogo (e'pilogo) nm epilogue.

episodio (epi'zɔdjo) nm episode.

epistola (e'pistola) nf epistle.

epitaffio (epi'taffjo) nm epitaph.

epiteto (e'piteto) nm epithet.

epoca ('epoka) nf epoch, period.

eppure (ep'pure) conj nevertheless, and yet.

epurare (epu'rare) vt purge.

equatore (ekwa'tore) nm equator.

equazione (ekwat'tsjone) nf equation.

equestre (e'kwɛstre) adj equestrian.

equilibrare (ekwili'brare) vt balance.

equilibrio (ekwi'librjo) nm balance. **equilibrista** nm tightrope walker.

equinozio (ekwi'nɔttsjo) nm equinox.

equipaggiare (ekwipad'dʒare) vt equip. **equipaggio** nm crew.

equitazione (ekwitat'tsjone) nf **1** riding. **2** horsemanship.

equivalere (ekwiva'lere) vi be equivalent. **equivalente** (ekwiva'lɛnte) adj,nm equivalent.

equivoco (e'kwivoko) adj ambiguous, doubtful.

era[1] ('ɛra) v see **essere**.

era[2] ('ɛra) nf era.

erba ('ɛrba) nf **1** grass. **2** herb.

erbaccia (er'battʃa) nf weed.

erbivendolo (erbi'vendolo) nm greengrocer.

ereditare (eredi'tare) vt inherit. **erede** (e'rɛde) nm,f heir. **eredità** nf inheritance. **ereditario** adj hereditary.

eremita (ere'mita) nm hermit.

eresia (ere'zia) nf heresy. **eretico** (e'rɛtiko) adj heretical.

eretto (e'rɛtto) adj erect, upright.

erezione (eret'tsjone) nf erection.

eri ('ɛri) v see **essere**.

erica ('ɛrika) nf heather.

erigere* (e'ridʒere) vt erect.

ermellino (ermel'lino) nm ermine.

ermetico (er'mɛtiko) adj hermetic.

ernia ('ɛrnja) nf hernia.

ero ('ɛro) v see **essere**.

eroe (e'rɔe) nm hero. **eroico** (e'rɔiko) adj heroic.

eroina[1] (ero'ina) nf heroine.

eroina[2] (ero'ina) nf heroin.

erosione (ero'zjone) nf erosion.

erotico (e'rɔtiko) adj erotic.

errare (er'rare) vi **1** wander, roam. **2** err.

erroneo (er'rɔneo) adj false, mistaken.

errore (er'rore) nm mistake, error.

erudito (eru'dito) adj erudite. **erudizione** nf erudition.

eruttare (erut'tare) vt erupt. **eruzione** (erut'tsjone) nf eruption.

esagerare (ezadʒe'rare) vt exaggerate, overdo, go too far. **esagerazione** nf exaggeration.

esagonale (ezago'nale) adj hexagonal.

esalare (eza'lare) vt exhale.

esaltare (ezal'tare) vt exalt.

esame (e'zame) nm **1** examination, inspection. **2** exam. **dare un esame** sit an exam.

esaminare (ezami'nare) vt examine, inspect.

esasperare (ezaspe'rare) vt irritate, exasperate. **esasperazione** nf exasperation.

esatto (e'zatto) adj exact, precise. **esattezza** (ezat'tettsa) nf precision.

esattore (ezat'tore) nm tax man, tax collector.

esaurire (ezau'rire) vt exhaust, wear out. **esaurimento** nm exhaustion. **esaurimento nervoso** nervous breakdown. **esaurito** adj **1** exhausted. **2** finished, sold out.

esca ('eska) nf bait.

esclamare (eskla'mare) vi exclaim. **esclamazione** nf exclamation.

escludere* (es'kludere) vt exclude. **esclusione** nf exclusion.

esclusivo (esklu'zivo) adj exclusive. **esclusiva** nf monopoly, sole rights.

esco ('ɛsko) v see **uscire**.

escursione (eskur'sjone) nf excursion.

esecutivo (ezeku'tivo) adj,nm executive.

esecutore (ezeku'tore) nm executor.

esecuzione (ezekut'tsjone) nf execution.

eseguire (eze'gwire) vt carry out, perform.

esempio (e'zɛmpjo) nm example, illustration. **per esempio** for example.

esemplare (ezem'plare) adj exemplary. nm **1** copy. **2** example.

esentare (ezen'tare) vt exempt. **esente** (e'zɛnte) adj exempt.

esequie (e'zɛkwje) nf pl funeral.

esercitare (ezertʃi'tare) vt **1** exercise. **2** practise. **esercito** (e'zɛrtʃito) nm army. **esercizio** (ezer'tʃittsjo) nm **1** exercise. **2** practice.

esibire (ezi'bire) vt show, exhibit. **esibizione** nf exhibition. **esibizionista** nm exhibitionist.

esigere* (e'zidʒere) vt demand, claim.

esilarare (ezila'rare) vt exhilarate.

esile ('ɛzile) adj slim, slender.

esiliare (ezi'ljare) vt exile. **esiliato** nm exile.

esilio (e'ziljo) nm exile.

esimere (e'zimere) vt exempt.

esistenzialismo (ezistentsja'lizmo) nm existentialism.

esistere* (e'zistere) vi exist. **esistenza** (ezis'tɛntsa) nf existence, life.

esitare (ezi'tare) vi hesitate. **esitazione** nf hesitation.

esito ('ɛzito) nm outcome, result.

esonerare (ezone'rare) vt release, dismiss. **esonero** (e'zɔnero) nm exemption.

esorbitante (ezorbi'tante) adj exorbitant.

esorcizzare (ezortʃid'dzare) vt exorcize. **esorcismo** (ezor'tʃizmo) nm exorcism. **esorcista** (ezor'tʃista) nm exorcist.

esortare (ezor'tare) vt encourage, urge.

esoso (e'zɔzo) adj 1 hateful. 2 mean.

esoterico (ezo'tɛriko) adj esoteric.

esotico (e'zɔtiko) adj exotic.

espandere (es'pandere) vt expand. **espansione** nf expansion. **espansivo** adj expansive.

espatriare (espa'trjare) vi emigrate.

espediente (espe'djɛnte) nm expedient.

espellere* (es'pɛllere) vt expel.

esperienza (espe'rjɛntsa) nf 1 experience. 2 experiment.

esperimento (esperi'mento) nm experiment.

esperto (es'pɛrto) adj skilled, expert. nm expert.

espiare (espi'are) vt expiate.

esplicito (es'plitʃito) adj explicit.

esplodere* (es'plɔdere) vi explode.

esplorare (esplo'rare) vt explore, investigate. **esploratore** nm explorer. **esplorazione** nf exploration.

esplosi (es'plɔzi) v see **esplodere.**

esplosione (esplo'zjone) nf explosion.

esplosivo (esplo'zivo) adj,nm explosive.

esploso (es'plɔzo) v see **esplodere.**

esporre* (es'porre) vt exhibit, expose.

esportare (espor'tare) vt export. **esportazione** nf export, exportation.

esposizione (espozit'tsjone) nf 1 exposition, explanation. 2 exhibition.

espressione (espres'sjone) nf expression.

espressivo (espres'sivo) adj expressive.

espresso (es'prɛsso) adj express. nm 1 express train. 2 express-letter.

esprimere* (es'primere) vt express.

espulsi (es'pulsi) v see **espellere.**

espulsione (espul'sjone) nf expulsion.

espulso (es'pulso) v see **espellere.**

esquimese (eskwi'mese) adj,n Eskimo.

essa ('essa) pron 3rd pers fs 1 she. 2 her, it.

esse ('esse) 3rd pers f pl them.

essenza (es'sɛntsa) nf essence. **essenziale** adj,nm essential.

essere* ('ɛssere) vi exist, be. v aux be. **che ore sono?** what time is it? **cosa c'è?** what is the matter? **essere di 1** belong to. **2** be from.

essi ('essi) 3rd pers m pl them.

esso ('esso) pron 3rd pers ms 1 he. 2 him, it.

est (ɛst) nm east. adj invar east, eastern. **del est 1** eastern. **2** easterly. **verso est** eastwards.

estasi ('ɛstazi) nf ecstasy. **estatico** (es'tatiko) adj ecstatic.

estate (es'tate) nf summer.

estendere* (es'tɛndere) vt extend, enlarge.

estensione (esten'sjone) nf extension.

esteriore (este'rjore) adj,nm outside, exterior.

esterno (es'tɛrno) adj external.

estero ('ɛstero) adj foreign. **all'estero** abroad.

estetico (es'tɛtiko) adj aesthetic. **estetica** nf aesthetics.

estetista (este'tista) nf beautician.

estinguere* (es'tingwere) vt 1 put out, extinguish. 2 quench. 3 pay off. **estintore** nm fire-extinguisher. **estinzione** nf extinction.

estivo (es'tivo) adj summer, summery.

estradare (estra'dare) vt extradite. **estradizione** nf extradition.

estraneo (es'traneo) adj alien, foreign. nm stranger.

estrarre* (es'trarre) vt 1 extract. 2 pick out. **estratto** nm 1 extract. 2 excerpt.

estremo (es'trɛmo) adj,nm extreme. **estremista** nm extremist.

estro ('ɛstro) nm 1 inspiration. 2 whim.

estrogeno (es'trɔdʒeno) nm oestrogen.

estroverso (estro'vɛrso) adj,n extrovert.

estuario (estu'arjo) nm estuary.

esuberante (ezube'rante) adj exuberant. **esuberanza** (ezube'rantsa) nf exuberance.

esule ('ɛzule) nm exile. adj exiled.

età (e'ta) nf age.

etere ('ɛtere) nm ether.

eterno (e'tɛrno) adj eternal, never-ending. **eternità** nf eternity.

etica ('ɛtika) nf ethics. **etico** ('ɛtiko) adj ethical.

etichetta (eti'ketta) *nf* 1 etiquette. 2 label, ticket.
etimologia (etimolo'dʒia) *nf* etymology.
etnico ('etniko) *adj* ethnic.
ettaro ('ettaro) *nm* hectare.
etto ('etto) *nm* also **ettogrammo** hundred grams, hectogram.
eucalipto (euka'lipto) *nm* eucalyptus tree.
eufemismo (eufe'mizmo) *nm* euphemism.
eunuco (eu'nuko) *nm* eunuch.
Europa (eu'rɔpa) *nf* Europe. **europeo** (euro-'pɛo) *adj,nm* European.
eutanasia (eutana'zia) *nf* euthanasia.
evacuare (evaku'are) *vt* evacuate. **evacuazione** *nf* evacuation.
evadere' (e'vadere) *vi* escape, flee.
evangelista (evandʒe'lista) *nm* Evangelist.
evaporare (evapo'rare) *vi* evaporate. **evaporazione** *nf* evaporation.
evasi (e'vazi) *v see* **evadere**.
evasione (eva'zjone) *nf* escape.
evasivo (eva'zivo) *adj* evasive.
evaso (e'vazo) *v see* **evadere**. *nm* 1 fugitive. 2 escaped convict.
evento (e'vɛnto) *nm* 1 outcome. 2 event. **eventuale** *adj* possible.
evidente (evi'dɛnte) *adj* evident, obvious. **evidenza** (evi'dɛntsa) *nf* clarity. **mettersi in evidenza** show oneself.
evitare (evi'tare) *vt* avoid.
evizione (evit'tsjone) *nf* eviction.
evocare (evo'kare) *vt* evoke.
evoluzione (evolut'tsjone) *nf* evolution.
evviva (ev'viva) *interj* 1 hurrah! 2 long live.

F

fa¹ (fa) *adv* ago.
fa² (fa) *v see* **fare**.
fabbrica ('fabbrika) *nf* 1 building. 2 factory. **fabbricare** *vt* 1 build. 2 make, manufacture. 3 invent.
fabbro ('fabbro) *nm* smith. **fabbro ferraio** *nm* blacksmith.
faccenda (fat't∫ɛnda) *nf* 1 task, chore. 2 matter, affair.
facchino (fak'kino) *nm* porter.
faccia ('fatt∫a) *nf* 1 face. 2 side (of a record). **facciata** *nf* facade.
facciano (fat't∫amo) *v see* **fare**.
faccio ('fatt∫o) *v see* **fare**.

facezia (fa't∫ettsja) *nf* joke.
facile ('fat∫ile) *adj* 1 easy, simple. 2 probable, likely. 3 easy-going. **facilità** *nf* 1 ease 2 aptitude.
facilitare (fat∫ili'tare) *vt* facilitate, make easier.
facoltà (fakol'ta) *nf* 1 faculty. 2 right, authority. 3 university faculty. **facoltativo** *adj* optional.
faggio ('faddʒo) *nm* beech tree.
fagiano (fa'dʒano) *nm* pheasant.
fagiolo (fa'dʒɔlo) *nm* bean. **fagiolino** *nm* French bean.
fagotto (fa'gɔtto) *nm* 1 bundle. 2 bassoon. **far fagotto** leave.
fai ('fai) *v see* **fare**.
falce ('falt∫e) *nf* scythe, sickle.
falciare (fal't∫are) *vt* 1 mow. 2 mow down. **falciatrice** *nf* mower.
falco ('falko) *nm* hawk. **falcone** *nm* falcon.
falda ('falda) *nf* 1 layer. 2 fold, pleat. 3 coat-tail. 4 brim. 5 slope. 6 foot (of a mountain). 7 flake.
falegname (faleɲ'ɲame) *nm* carpenter, joiner.
falena (fa'lɛna) *nf* moth.
falla ('falla) *nf* leak, leakage.
fallace (fal'lat∫e) *adj* false, deceptive.
fallire (fal'lire) *vi* fail. *vt* miss. **fallimento** *nm* 1 failure. 2 bankruptcy.
fallo¹ ('fallo) *nm* 1 error. 2 *sport* foul.
fallo² ('fallo) *nm* phallus.
falò (fa'lo) *nm* bonfire.
falsare (fal'sare) *vt* distort, falsify. **falsario** (fal'sarjo) *nm* counterfeiter, forger.
falsariga (falsa'riga) *nf* sheet of ruled paper.
falsificare (falsifi'kare) *vt* 1 forge, fake. 2 tamper with.
falso ('falso) *adj* 1 false, artificial. 2 wrong. 3 untrue. **falso allarme** *nm* false alarm.
fama ('fama) *nf* fame, renown.
fame ('fame) *nf* hunger. **avere fame** be hungry.
famelico (fa'mɛliko) *adj* ravenous, starving.
famiglia (fa'miʎʎa) *nf* family.
familiare (fami'ljare) *adj* 1 domestic, family. 2 intimate, familiar.
famoso (fa'moso) *adj* famous, well-known.
fanale (fa'nale) *nm* 1 lamp, lantern. 2 headlight.
fanatico (fa'natiko) *adj* fanatical. *nm* fanatic.
fanciullo (fan't∫ullo) *nm* child, boy. **fanciulla** *nf* child, girl. **fanciullezza** (fant∫ul'lettsa) *nf* childhood.
fandonia (fan'dɔnja) *nf* lie.
fanfara (fan'fara) *nf* brass band.

fango ('fango) nm mud. **fangoso** (fan'goso) adj muddy.

fanno ('fanno) v see **fare.**

fannullone (fannul'lone) nm lazybones.

fantascienza (fantaʃ'ʃɛntsa) nf science fiction.

fantasia (fanta'zia) nf imagination, fantasy.

fantasma (fan'tazma) nm ghost.

fante ('fante) nm 1 infantryman. 2 game knave, jack. **fanteria** nf infantry. **fantino** nm jockey.

fantoccio (fan'tɔttʃo) nm puppet.

farabutto (fara'butto) nm rogue, scoundrel.

faraone (fara'one) nm pharaoh.

farcire (far'tʃire) vt stuff.

fardello (far'dɛllo) nm bundle, load.

fare¹ ('fare) vt 1 make. 2 do. 3 say. 4 be. **fare acqua** leak. **fare benzina** fill up with petrol. **fare da** act as. **fare per** suit. **non fa niente** it doesn't matter.

farfalla (far'falla) nf butterfly.

farina (fa'rina) nf flour.

faringe (fa'rindʒe) nf pharynx.

farmacia (farma'tʃia) nf 1 pharmacy. 2 chemist's shop. **farmacista** nm chemist. **farmaco** ('farmako) nm medicine, drug.

faro ('faro) nm 1 lighthouse. 2 headlight, headlamp.

farragine (far'radʒine) nf jumble, medley.

farsa ('farsa) nf farce.

fascia ('faʃʃa) nf 1 band, strip. 2 bandage. **fasciare** (faʃ'ʃare) vt bind, bandage.

fascicolo (faʃ'ʃikolo) nm 1 dossier, file. 2 number, issue (of a journal).

fascino (faʃ'ʃino) nm fascination, charm.

fascio ('faʃʃo) nm bundle.

fascismo (faʃ'ʃizmo) nm fascism. **fascista** adj,nm fascist.

fase ('faze) nf phase.

fastidio (fas'tidjo) nm 1 annoyance, trouble. 2 disgust. **dare fastidio a** annoy. **fastidioso** (fasti'djoso) adj annoying.

fasto ('fasto) nm pomp. **fastoso** (fas'toso) adj ostentatious.

fata ('fata) nf fairy.

fatale (fa'tale) adj fatal.

faticare (fati'kare) vi 1 struggle, toil. **fatica** nf 1 toil, labour. 2 exhaustion, weariness. 3 trouble. **faticoso** (fati'koso) adj 1 tiring. 2 difficult.

fato ('fato) nm fate.

fatta ('fatta) nf kind, sort.

fattezze (fat'tettse) nf pl features.

fatto ('fatto) v see **fare.** nm 1 fact. 2 action,

deed. 3 event. 4 subject. **badare ai fatti propri** mind one's own business. **dire il fatto suo** speak one's mind. **in fatto di** with respect to. **venire al fatto** come to the point.

fattore (fat'tore) nm 1 creator. 2 factor.

fattoria (fatto'ria) nf farm, farmhouse.

fattorino (fatto'rino) nm 1 office boy. 2 telegraph boy.

fattucchiera (fattuk'kjera) nf witch. **fattucchiere** (fattuk'kjɛre) nm sorcerer, wizard.

fattura (fat'tura) nf 1 manufacture, workmanship. 2 bill, invoice.

fatturare (fattu'rare) vt 1 adulterate, tamper with. 2 charge, invoice.

fatuo ('fatuo) adj silly, fatuous.

fauna ('fauna) nf fauna.

fausto ('fausto) adj lucky, happy.

fautore (fau'tore) nm supporter, follower.

fava ('fava) nf bean.

favilla (fa'villa) nf spark.

favo ('favo) nm honeycomb.

favola ('favola) nf 1 fable, story. 2 laughingstock. **favoloso** (favo'loso) adj fabulous, fantastic, incredible.

favore (fa'vore) nm 1 goodwill. 2 favour. **a favore di** 1 in the interest of. 2 on behalf of. **entrata di favore** nf complimentary seat. **per favore** please.

favoreggiare (favored'dʒare) vt 1 favour. 2 aid and abet.

favorevole (favo'revole) adj favourable, suitable.

favorire (favo'rire) vt 1 favour. 2 back, assist. 3 oblige. **favorito** adj,nm favourite.

fazione (fat'tsjone) nf faction.

fazzoletto (fattso'letto) nm 1 handkerchief. 2 headscarf.

febbraio (feb'brajo) nm February.

febbre ('fɛbbre) nf fever. **avere la febbre** have a temperature.

feccia ('fɛttʃa) nf 1 dregs, sediment. 2 scum, riffraff.

feci ('fetʃi) v see **fare.**

fecondare (fekon'dare) vt fertilize. **fecondo** adj fertile.

fede ('fede) nf 1 belief, trust. 2 faith, religion. 3 word of honour. 4 honesty. 5 certificate, document. 6 wedding ring. **fedele** adj 1 faithful, loyal. 2 exact. **fedeltà** nf fidelity, loyalty.

federa ('fɛdera) nf pillowcase.

federale (fede'rale) adj federal.

federazione (federat'tsjone) nf federation.

fedina (fe'dina) nf 1 criminal record. 2 side-whisker.

fegato ('fegato) nm liver.

felce ('feltʃe) nf fern.

felice (fe'litʃe) adj 1 happy, contented. 2 lucky. **felicità** nf happiness.

felicitare (felitʃi'tare) vt make happy. **felicitarsi** vr congratulate. **felicitazioni** nf pl congratulations.

felino (fe'lino) adj,nm feline.

feltro ('feltro) nm felt.

femmina ('femmina) nf 1 female. 2 woman. **femminile** adj feminine.

fendere* ('fɛndere) vt split, crack, break. **fenditura** nf crack, fissure.

fenice (fe'nitʃe) nf phoenix.

fenicottero (feni'kɔttero) nm flamingo.

fenomeno (fe'nɔmeno) nm phenomenon. **fenomenale** adj phenomenal.

feria ('fɛrja) nf holiday. **feriale** adj working. **giorno feriale** nm weekday.

ferire (fe'rire) vt 1 wound, injure. 2 strike. **ferita** nf wound, injury.

fermare (fer'mare) vt 1 stop, halt. 2 fix, fasten. 3 arrest. **fermarsi** vr stop. **fermata** nf 1 stop. 2 pause. **fermacarte** nm invar paperweight. **fermacravatta** nm invar tiepin. **fermaglio** nm 1 fastener, clasp. 2 brooch.

fermentare (fermen'tare) vi ferment. **fermentazione** nf fermentation.

fermo ('fermo) adj 1 motionless, still. 2 firm, steady. **fermo in posta** poste restante. **tener per fermo** be convinced. **fermezza** (fer'mettsa) nf firmness.

feroce (fe'rotʃe) adj fierce, wild. **ferocia** (fe'rɔtʃa) nf ferocity.

ferragosto (ferra'gosto) nm feast of Assumption, 15th August.

ferraio (fer'rajo) nm blacksmith.

ferrare (fer'rare) vt shoe (a horse).

ferreo ('fɛrreo) adj 1 strong. 2 iron.

ferro ('fɛrro) nm iron. **ferro da calza** knitting needle. **ferro da cavallo** horse-shoe. **ferro da stiro** dom iron. **ferramento** nm pl **ferramenta** f 1 iron tool. 2 hardware. **negozio di ferramenta** nm ironmonger's shop.

ferrovia (ferro'via) nf railway. **ferroviario** adj rail, railway. **ferroviere** (ferro'vjere) nm railwayman.

fertile ('fertile) adj fertile. **fertilità** nf fertility.

fertilizzare (fertilid'dzare) vt fertilize. **fertilizzante** nm fertilizer.

fervore (fer'vore) nm fervour.

festa ('fɛsta) nf 1 feast, holiday. 2 birthday, name day. 3 party. **fare festa** take a holiday. **fare festa a** welcome. **festivo** adj festive. **giorni festivi** nm pl holidays.

festeggiare (fested'dʒare) vt celebrate.

festevole (fes'tevole) adj festive, merry.

fetido ('fetido) adj fetid.

feto ('fɛto) nm foetus.

fetore (fe'tore) nm stench.

fetta ('fetta) nf slice. **fettuccine** nf pl strips of pasta.

feudale (feu'dale) adj feudal.

fiaba ('fjaba) nf fairy tale.

fiaccare (fjak'kare) vt 1 weaken. 2 break. **fiacco** adj listless, weak.

fiaccola ('fjakkola) nf torch.

fiala ('fjala) nf phial.

fiamma ('fjamma) nf 1 flame. 2 pennant.

fiammeggiare (fjammed'dʒare) vi 1 blaze, flame. 2 flash.

fiancheggiare (fjanked'dʒare) vt flank.

fianco ('fjanko) nm side, flank. **a fianco di** at the side of. **di fianco** sideways.

fiasco ('fjasko) nm 1 flask. 2 failure, fiasco.

fiatare (fja'tare) vi breathe. **fiato** nm breath. **strumenti a fiato** nm pl wind instruments.

fibbia ('fibbja) nf buckle.

fibra ('fibra) nf fibre.

ficcare (fik'kare) vt thrust, drive in, fix. **ficcarsi** vr intrude. **ficcarsi in capo** get into one's head.

fico ('fiko) nm 1 fig. 2 fig tree.

fidanzarsi (fidan'tsarsi) vr get engaged. **fidanzamento** engagement. **fidanzata** nf fiancée. **fidanzato** nm fiancé.

fidarsi (fi'darsi) vr trust.

fiducia (fi'dutʃa) nf trust, faith. **voto di fiducia** nm vote of confidence.

fiele ('fjɛle) nm 1 bile. 2 bitterness.

fieno ('fjɛno) nm hay. **fienile** nm hay loft.

fiera¹ ('fjɛra) nf fair, exhibition.

fiera² ('fjɛra) nf wild beast.

fiero ('fjɛro) adj 1 fearsome, bold. 2 proud.

fifa ('fifa) nf inf fear, funk.

figgere* ('fiddʒere) vt fix, attach.

figlia ('fiʎʎa) nf daughter. **figliastra** nf stepdaughter.

figlio ('fiʎʎo) nm son. **figliastro** nm stepson.

figura (fi'gura) nf 1 form, shape. 2 figure. 3

appearance. **4** illustration. **fare la figura di** play the part of.

figurare (figu'rare) vt **1** figure. **2** represent, symbolize. vi **1** look well. **2** pretend. **figurarsi** vr think, imagine. **figurati!** interj **1** just imagine! **2** not at all!

fila ('fila) nf **1** row, line. **2** queue. **di fila** without interruption. **fare la fila** queue.

filantropo (fi'lantropo) nm philanthropist. **filantropico** (filan'trɔpiko) adj philanthropic.

filare[1] (fi'lare) vt **1** spin. **2** let out (rope). vi **1** trickle. **2** run. **3** be off. **filanda** nf spinning mill.

filare[2] (fi'lare) nm row, line.

filastrocca (filas'trɔkka) nf **1** yarn. **2** nonsense rhyme.

filatelia (filate'lia) nf philately, stamp-collecting. **filatelista** nm philatelist, stamp-collector.

filetto (fi'letto) nm fillet.

filiale (fi'ljale) nf branch office. adj filial.

filigrana (fili'grana) nf **1** filigree. **2** watermark.

film (film) nm invar film.

filmare (fil'mare) vt film.

filo ('filo) nm **1** thread. **2** yarn. **3** string. **4** wire. **5** edge. **filo di voce** weak voice. **filo d'erba** blade of grass. **per filo e per segno** minutely.

filobus ('filobus) nm trolleybus.

filologo (fi'lɔlogo) nm philologist.

filosofia (filozo'fia) nf philosophy. **filosofico** (filo'zɔfiko) adj philosophical. **filosofo** (fi'lɔzofo) nm philosopher.

filtrare (fil'trare) vt,vi filter. **filtro** nm filter.

filza ('filtsa) nf series.

finale (fi'nale) adj final, last. nm finale. nf finals. **finalista** nm finalist. **finalmente** adv finally, at last.

finanza (fi'nantsa) nf finance.

finanziare (finan'tsjare) vt finance. **finanziario** adj financial. **finanziere** (finan'tsjɛre) nm financier.

finchè (fin'ke) conj **1** until. **2** as long as.

fine[1] ('fine) nf end, conclusion. nm **1** purpose, aim. **2** outcome.

fine[2] ('fine) adj **1** fine, thin. **2** delicate, refined.

fine-settimana nm or f invar weekend.

finestra (fi'nɛstra) nf window. **finestrino** nm window (of train, etc.).

fingere* ('findʒere) vt **1** feign, fake, pretend. **2** imagine, suppose.

finire (fi'nire) vt finish, complete, end. vi end, be over. **andare a finire** end up.

Finlandia (fin'landja) nf Finland. **finlandese** adj Finnish. nm **1** Finn. **2** Finnish (language). **finnico** adj Finnish.

fino[1] ('fino) adj **1** fine, slender. **2** pure. **3** shrewd.

fino[2] ('fino) prep **1** until, as far as. **2** from.

finocchio (fi'nɔkkjo) nm fennel.

finora (fi'nora) adv until now.

finsi ('finsi) v see **fingere**.

finta ('finta) nf pretence. **far finta di** pretend to.

finto ('finto) v see **fingere**. adj fake, false, artificial. nm hypocrite.

finzione (fin'tsjone) nf deceit, sham.

fio ('fio) nm penalty.

fioccare (fjok'kare) vi **1** snow. **2** pour or flock in.

fiocco ('fjɔkko) nm **1** bow, knot. **2** flake, tuft.

fioco ('fjɔko) adj weak, feeble.

fionda ('fjonda) nf catapult.

fiordo ('fjɔrdo) nm fiord.

fiore ('fjore) nm **1** flower. **2** pl game clubs. **fiorario** nm florist. **fiorame** nm floral pattern. **a fiorami** floral patterned.

fiorire (fjo'rire) vi **1** flower. **2** flourish.

Firenze (fi'rɛntse) nf Florence. **fiorentino** adj,n Florentine.

firmare (fir'mare) vt sign. **firma** nf signature.

fisarmonica (fizar'mɔnika) nf accordion.

fischiare (fis'kjare) vi,vt **1** whistle. **2** hiss, boo. **fischietto** nm (child's) whistle. **fischio** nm whistle.

fisica ('fizika) nf physics.

fisico ('fiziko) adj physical. nm **1** physique. **2** physicist.

fisiologia (fizjolo'dʒia) nf physiology. **fisiologico** adj physiological.

fisionomia (fizjono'mia) nf countenance, aspect.

fisioterapia (fizjotera'pia) nf physiotherapy. **fisioterapista** nm physiotherapist.

fissare (fis'sare) vt **1** fix, direct. **2** arrange. **3** book. **fisso** adj fixed. **quardare fisso** stare.

fissione (fis'sjone) nf fission.

fittizio (fit'tittsjo) adj **1** fictitious. **2** artificial, false.

fitto[1] ('fitto) adj thick, dense. **a capo fitto** adv headlong.

fitto[2] ('fitto) nm rent.

fiume ('fjume) nm river.

fiutare (fju'tare) vt **1** sniff, smell, scent. **2** detect. **fiuto** nm smell, sense of smell.

flaccido ('flattʃido) *adj* flabby.

flacone (fla'kone) *nm* phial.

flagellare (fladʒel'lare) *vt* lash, whip. **flagello** *nm* **1** whip. **2** scourge.

flagrante (fla'grante) *adj* flagrant. **in flagrante** in the act.

flanella (fla'nɛlla) *nf* flannel.

flauto ('flauto) *nm* flute. **flautista** *nm* flautist.

flebile ('flɛbile) *adj* weak, plaintive.

flessibile (fles'sibile) *adj* flexible. **flessibilità** *nf* flexibility.

flessuoso (flessu'oso) *adj* pliable.

flipper ('flipper) *nm* pinball.

flirt (flirt) *nm* flirtation.

flora ('flɔra) *nf* flora.

florido ('flɔrido) *adj* **1** florid. **2** prosperous.

floscio ('flɔʃʃo) *adj* **1** limp. **2** languid. **cappello floscio** *nm* soft hat.

flotta ('flɔtta) *nf* fleet.

fluido ('fluido) *adj,nm* fluid.

fluire (flu'ire) *vi* flow.

fluorescente (fluoreʃ'ʃɛnte) *adj* fluorescent.

fluoro (flu'ɔro) *nm* fluoride.

flusso ('flusso) *nm* **1** flux. **2** discharge.

fluttuare (fluttu'are) *vi* fluctuate.

fobia (fo'bia) *nf* phobia.

foca ('fɔka) *nf zool* seal.

focaccia (fo'kattʃa) *nf* tart, bun.

foce ('fotʃe) *nf* **1** outlet. **2** river mouth.

focena (fo'tʃɛna) *nf* porpoise.

focolare (foko'lare) *nm* **1** hearth. **2** fireside.

fodera ('fɔdera) *nf* **1** lining. **2** cover. **foderare** (fode'rare) *vt* **1** line. **2** cover. **fodero** ('fɔdero) *nm* sheath.

foga ('fɔga) *nf* ardour.

foggia ('fɔddʒa) *nf* manner, style. **foggiare** *vt* form, mould.

foglia ('fɔʎʎa) *nf* leaf. **fogliame** *nm* foliage.

foglio ('fɔʎʎo) *nm* **1** sheet of paper, leaf. **2** pamphlet. **3** document. **4** note.

fogna ('fɔɲɲa) *nf* **1** drain. **2** sewer.

föhn (føn) *nm invar* hair drier.

folata (fo'lata) *nf* gust.

folclore (fol'klore) *nm* folklore. **folcloristico** (folklo'ristiko) *adj* folk. **canto folcloristico** *nm* folk song.

folgorare (folgo'rare) *vi* **1** (of lightning) flash. **2** shine brightly. **folgore** ('folgore) *nf* flash of lightning.

folla ('folla) *nf* crowd, throng.

folle ('fɔlle) *adj* mad, insane. **follia** *nf* madness.

follicolo (fol'likolo) *nm* follicle.

folto ('folto) *adj* thick, dense.

fomentare (fomen'tare) *vt* **1** foment. **2** incite.

fondamento (fonda'mento) *nm* **1** *pl* **fondamenti** *m* foundation, basis. **2** *pl* **fondamenta** *f arch* foundation. **fondamentale** *adj* fundamental.

fondare (fon'dare) *vt* **1** found. **2** base, found. **fondarsi** *vr* rely upon.

fondere* ('fondere) *vt* **1** melt. **2** fuse. **fondersi** *vr* dissolve.

fonderia (fonde'ria) *nf* foundry.

fondina (fon'dina) *nf* holster.

fondo[1] ('fondo) *nm* **1** bottom, base. **2** background. **3** estate. **4** *pl* capital, funds. **5** *pl* dregs. **a fondo** in depth. **andare a fondo** sink. **in fondo** basically. **in fondo a** at the bottom of.

fondo[2] ('fondo) *adj* deep.

fonetica (fo'nɛtika) *nf* phonetics. **fonetico** (fo'nɛtiko) *adj* phonetic.

fonografo (fo'nɔgrafo) *nm* gramophone.

fontana (fon'tana) *nf* fountain. **fontaniere** (fonta'njɛre) *nm* plumber.

fonte ('fonte) *nf* **1** fountain. **2** source. **3** font.

fontina (fon'tina) *nf* soft cheese.

foraggiare (forad'dʒare) *vt* supply.

forare (fo'rare) *vt* **1** pierce. **2** perforate. **3** bore. *vi* have a puncture.

forbici ('fɔrbitʃi) *nf pl* scissors.

forca ('forka) *nf* **1** pitchfork. **2** gallows.

forchetta (for'ketta) *nf* fork.

forcipe ('fɔrtʃipe) *nm* forceps.

foresta (fo'rɛsta) *nf* forest.

forestiere (fores'tjɛre) *adj* foreign. *nm* **1** foreigner. **2** stranger.

forfecchia (for'fekkja) *nf* earwig.

forfora ('forfora) *nf* dandruff.

formaggio (for'maddʒo) *nm* cheese.

formale (for'male) *adj* formal. **formalità** *nf* formality.

formare (for'mare) *vt* form, shape. **formare un numero** dial a number. **forma** *nf* **1** form, shape. **2** mould. **3** formality. **formato** *nm* format.

formica (for'mika) *nf* ant.

formicolare (formiko'lare) *vi* **1** swarm, abound. **2** have pins and needles. **formicolio** *nm* pins and needles.

formidabile (formi'dabile) *adj* formidable, tremendous.

formula ('fɔrmula) *nf* formula.

formulare (formu'lare) *vt* formulate, express.

fornace (for'natʃe) nf furnace.

fornaio (for'najo) nm baker.

fornire (for'nire) vt provide, furnish. **fornitore** nm supplier.

forno ('forno) nm 1 oven. 2 furnace. 3 bakery. **fornello** (for'nɛllo) nm 1 ring. 2 bowl (of a pipe). **fornello a gas** gas cooker.

foro[1] ('foro) nm hole.

foro[2] ('fɔro) nm forum.

forse ('forse) adv perhaps, maybe. **essere in forse** be in doubt.

forsennato (forsen'nato) adj mad, insane. nm madman.

forte ('fɔrte) adj 1 strong, powerful. 2 loud. 3 expert. 4 well-built. nm 1 strong point. 2 fort. adv 1 strongly. 2 loudly.

fortezza (for'tettsa) nf 1 fortitude. 2 fortress.

fortificare (fortifi'kare) vt fortify. **fortificazione** nf fortification.

fortuito (for'tuito) adj chance, accidental.

fortuna (for'tuna) nf 1 fortune, chance, luck. 2 riches. **per fortuna** luckily. **atterraggio di fortuna** nm emergency landing. **fortunato** adj lucky.

foruncolo (fo'runkolo) nm boil.

forza ('fɔrtsa) nf 1 strength. 2 power. 3 force. **a forza di** by dint of. **interj** come on! **forzare** (for'tsare) vt force.

foschia (fos'kia) nf mist, haze.

fosco ('fosko) adj dark, gloomy.

fosfato (fos'fato) nm phosphate.

fosforescente (fosforeʃ'ʃente) adj phosphorescent.

fossa ('fɔssa) nf 1 ditch, trench. 2 pit. 3 grave. **fossetta** nf dimple.

fossile ('fɔssile) nm fossil.

fosso ('fɔsso) nm ditch.

foste ('foste) v see **essere**.

fosti ('fosti) v see **essere**.

foto ('fɔto) nf photo. **fotocopia** (foto'kɔpja) nf photocopy. **fotomodella** (fotomo'dɛlla) nf phot model.

fotogenico (foto'dʒeniko) adj photogenic.

fotografare (fotogra'fare) vt photograph. **fotografia** nf photograph. **fotografico** (foto'grafiko) adj photographic. **fotografo** (fo'tɔgrafo) nm photographer.

fra (fra) prep 1 between, among. 2 in, within. **fra poco** soon.

frac (frak) nm invar evening dress.

fracassare (frakas'sare) vt smash, break. **fra-**

casso nm 1 crash, din. 2 commotion. 3 crowd.

fradicio ('freditʃo) adj 1 soaked, drenched. 2 rotten. **ubriaco fradicio** blind drunk.

fragile ('fradʒile) adj fragile. **fragilità** nf fragility.

fragola ('fragola) nf 1 strawberry. 2 strawberry plant.

fragore (fra'gore) nm crash, roar.

fragrante (fra'grante) adj fragrant. **fragranza** (fra'grantsa) nf fragrance, scent.

fraintendere* (frain'tɛndere) vi misunderstand.

frammassone (frammas'sone) nm freemason. **frammassoneria** nf freemasonry.

frammento (fram'mento) nm fragment.

frammettere* (fram'mettere) vt insert. **frammettersi** vr interfere.

frana ('frana) nf landslide.

Francia ('frantʃa) nf France. **francese** (fran'tʃeze) adj French. nm 1 Frenchman. 2 French (language).

franchezza (fran'kettsa) nf 1 frankness. 2 boldness.

franco[1] ('franko) adj 1 free. 2 frank, sincere.

franco[2] ('franko) nm franc. **francobollo** (franko'bollo) nm postage stamp.

frangere* ('frandʒere) vt 1 break. 2 crush.

frangia ('frandʒa) nf fringe.

frantumare (frantu'mare) vt smash, shatter. **frantume** nm fragment.

frapporre* (frap'porre) vt insert. **frapporsi** vr intervene.

frase ('fraze) nf 1 phrase. 2 sentence.

frassino ('frassino) nm ash tree.

frastuono (fras'twɔno) nm hubbub, din.

frate ('frate) nm friar, brother.

fratello (fra'tɛllo) nm brother.

fraterno (fra'tɛrno) adj fraternal.

frattaglie (frat'taʎʎe) nf pl giblets.

frattanto (frat'tanto) adv meanwhile.

frattempo (frat'tɛmpo) **nel frattempo** adv in the meantime.

fratturare (frattu'rare) vt fracture. **frattura** nf fracture.

frazione (frat'tsjone) nf fraction.

freccia ('frettʃa) nf arrow.

freddo ('freddo) adj 1 cold, cool. 2 indifferent. nm cold. **freddezza** (fre'dettsa) nf 1 coldness, coolness. 2 indifference.

fregare (fre'gare) vt 1 rub, polish. 2 inf cheat, swindle. (**io**) **me ne frego** I don't give a damn.

fregio ('frɛdʒo) nm 1 frieze. 2 decoration.

fremere ('frɛmere) vi 1 tremble, shake. 2 rage.

fremito ('frɛmito) nm 1 roar. 2 tremor.

frenare (fre'nare) vt restrain. vi brake.

freno ('frɛno) nm 1 horse's bit. 2 brake.

frequentare (frekwen'tare) vt 1 frequent. 2 attend. **frequente** adj frequent. **frequenza** (fre'kwɛntsa) nf frequency.

fresco ('fresko) adj 1 fresh. 2 cool. **freschezza** (fres'kettsa) nf freshness.

fretta ('frɛtta) nf hurry. **avere fretta** be in a hurry. **in fretta** hurriedly.

friggere* ('friddʒere) vt,vi fry.

frigido ('fridʒido) adj frigid.

frigo ('frigo) nm fridge.

frigorifero (frigo'rifero) nm refrigerator.

fringuello (frin'gwɛllo) nm chaffinch.

frissi ('frissi) v see **friggere**.

frittata (frit'tata) nf omelette.

fritto ('fritto) v see **friggere**. adj fried.

frivolo ('frivolo) adj frivolous.

frizione (frit'tsjone) nf friction.

frizzare (frid'dzare) vi 1 sting. 2 fizz, sparkle. **frizzante** adj sparkling.

frodare (fro'dare) vt defraud, cheat. **frode** ('frɔde) nf fraud.

fronda ('fronda) nf branch.

fronte ('fronte) nf 1 forehead. 2 front. **di fronte a** opposite.

fronteggiare (fronted'dʒare) vt confront.

frontiera (fron'tjɛra) nf border, frontier.

frottola ('frɔttola) nf 1 fib. 2 pl nonsense.

frugale (fru'gale) adj meagre, frugal.

frugare (fru'gare) vt search. vi rummage.

frullare (frul'lare) vi spin. vt whip, beat. **frullatore** nm whisk. **frullino** nm eggwhisk.

frumento (fru'mento) nm wheat.

frusciare (fruʃ'ʃare) vi rustle. **fruscio** nm rustle.

frustare (frus'tare) vt whip. **frusta** nf whip.

frustrazione (frustra'tsjone) nf frustration.

frutto ('frutto) nm, pl **frutti** 1 fruit (on the tree). 2 gain, reward. **frutta** nf fruit (on the table). **frutteto** nm orchard. **frutti di mare** nm pl seafood. **fruttivendolo** (frutti'vendolo) nm fruiterer.

fu (fu) v see **essere**. adj deceased, late.

fucilare (futʃi'lare) vt shoot. **fucile** nm rifle.

fucina (fu'tʃina) nf forge.

fucsia ('fuksja) nf fuchsia.

fuga ('fuga) nf 1 flight, escape. 2 leak. **fugace** adj fleeting.

fuggire (fud'dʒire) vi flee, run away. vt avoid. **fuggiasco** nm fugitive.

fui ('fui) v see **essere.**

fuliggine (fu'liddʒine) nf soot.

fulminare (fulmi'nare) vt 1 strike down. 2 electrocute. vi flash (lightning), lighten. **fulmine** ('fulmine) nm flash of lightning, thunderbolt.

fumare (fu'mare) vt,vi smoke. **fumaiolo** (fuma'jɔlo) nm 1 chimneypot. 2 funnel. **fumatore** nm smoker. **fumetto** nm strip cartoon. **fumo** nm 1 smoke. 2 vapour.

fummo ('fummo) v see **essere.**

funambolo (fu'nambolo) nm tightrope walker.

fune ('fune) nf rope. **funicolare** nf funicular railway. **funivia** nf cable car.

funebre ('funebre) adj funereal, gloomy. **pompe funebri** nf pl funeral service.

funerale (fune'rale) nm funeral. **funereo** (fu-'nɛreo) adj funereal, gloomy.

funesto (fu'nɛsto) adj grievous, distressing.

fungo ('fungo) nm 1 fungus. 2 mushroom.

funzionare (funtsjo'nare) vi work, function. **funzione** nf function.

funzionario (funtsjo'narjo) nm civil servant.

fuoco ('fwɔko) nm 1 fire. 2 focus. **dare fuoco a** set fire to. **fuoco d'artificio** firework.

fuorchè (fwor'ke) conj,prep except.

fuori ('fwɔri) prep beyond, out of. adv away, outside, out. **fuoribordo** nm outboard motor (boat). **fuorilegge** nm outlaw. **fuoruscito** nm exile.

furbo ('furbo) adj shrewd, cunning. **furberia** nf cunning.

furetto (fu'retto) nm ferret.

furfante (fur'fante) nm rogue, rascal.

furgone (fur'gone) nm van.

furia ('furja) nf anger, fury. **a furia di** by dint of.

furibondo (furi'bondo) adj furious, livid.

furioso (fu'rjoso) adj furious, angry.

furono ('furono) v see **essere.**

furore (fu'rore) nm 1 fury, vehemence. 2 craze.

furtivo (fur'tivo) adj furtive.

furto ('furto) nm theft.

fuscello (fuʃ'ʃɛllo) nm twig.

fusi ('fuzi) v see **fondere.**

fusibile (fu'zibile) nm fuse.

fusione (fu'zjone) nf fusion.

fuso[1] ('fuzo) v see **fondere.**

fuso[2] ('fuzo) nm 1 pl **fusi** m spindle. 2 pl **fusa** f. **fare le fusa** purr.

fusoliera (fuzo'ljɛra) nf fuselage.

fustagno (fus'taɲɲo) nm corduroy.

fusto ('fusto) nm 1 stem, stalk. 2 trunk (of tree or body). 3 cask, container.

futile ('futile) adj vain, futile. **futilità** nf futility.

futuro (fu'turo) adj,nm future.

G

gabbare (gab'bare) vt 1 trick, swindle. 2 mock.

gabbia ('gabbja) nf cage.

gabbiano (gab'bjano) nm seagull.

gabella (ga'bɛlla) nf tax, duty.

gabinetto (gabi'netto) nm 1 study, consulting room. 2 lavatory. 3 pol cabinet.

gaffe (gaf) nf blunder.

gagliardo (gaʎ'ʎardo) adj robust, vigorous.

gaio ('gajo) adj 1 gay, merry. 2 bright. **gaiezza** (ga'jettsa) nf gaiety.

gala ('gala) nf gala.

galantuomo (galan'twɔmo) nm gentleman.

galassia (ga'lassja) nf galaxy.

galea (ga'lea) nf galley.

galeone (gale'one) nm galleon.

galera (ga'lɛra) nf 1 naut galley. 2 prison.

galla ('galla) nf bot gall. **a galla** afloat. **stare a galla** float.

galleggiare (galled'dʒare) vi float.

galleria (galle'ria) nf 1 gallery. 2 tunnel.

Galles ('galles) nm Wales. **gallese** (gal'lese) adj Welsh. nm 1 Welshman. 2 Welsh (language).

gallo ('gallo) nm cock. **gallina** nf hen.

gallone[1] (gal'lone) nm 1 braid. 2 mil stripe.

gallone[2] (gal'lone) nm gallon.

galoppare (galop'pare) vi gallop. **galoppo** (ga'lɔppo) nm gallop.

galoscia (ga'lɔʃʃa) nf galosh, wellington.

galvanizzare (galvanid'dzare) vt galvanize.

gamba ('gamba) nf leg. **darsela a gambe** take to one's heels. **persona in gamba** nf competent person.

gambero ('gambero) nm crayfish. **gambero di mare** lobster. **gamberetto** nm shrimp.

gambo ('gambo) nm stalk, stem.

gamma ('gamma) nf range, gamut.

ganascia (ga'naʃʃa) nf jaw.

gancio ('gantʃo) nm hook.

ganghero ('gangero) nm hinge. **andare fuori dai gangheri** lose one's self-control.

gara ('gara) nf competition, race, match.

garage (ga'raʒ) nm garage.

garanzia (garan'tsia) nf guarantee. **garantire** vt guarantee.

garbare (gar'bare) vi please. **garbato** adj polite. **garbo** nm 1 taste, style. 2 courtesy.

garbuglio (garbuʎ'ʎo) nm muddle.

gareggiare (gared'dʒare) vi compete. **gareggiatore** nm competitor.

gargarismo (garga'rizmo) nm gargle. **gargarizzare** (gargarid'dzare) vt gargle.

garitta (ga'ritta) nf sentry-box.

garofano (ga'rɔfano) nm carnation. **chiodo di garofano** nm clove.

garrire (gar'rire) vi 1 twitter, chirp. 2 (of a flag, etc.) flutter.

garrulo ('garrulo) adj talkative.

garza ('gardza) nf gauze.

garzone (gar'dzone) nm errand boy, helper.

gas (gas) nm invar gas.

gasolina (gazo'lina) nf gasoline.

gasolio (ga'zɔljo) nm diesel fuel.

gassosa (gas'sosa) nf fizzy drink.

gastrico ('gastriko) adj gastric.

gastronomia (gastrono'mia) nf gastronomy.

gatto ('gatto) nm cat. **gattino** nm kitten. **gattoni** adv 1 on all fours. 2 stealthily. **gattopardo** nm leopard, tiger-cat.

gavitello (gavi'tello) nm buoy.

gazza ('gaddza) nf magpie.

gazzella (gad'dzɛlla) nf gazelle.

gazzetta (gad'dzetta) nf gazette.

gelare (dʒe'lare) vi,vt freeze. **gelateria** nf ice-cream shop. **gelatina** nf jelly. **gelato** nm ice-cream. **gelo** ('dʒɛlo) nm frost. **gelone** nm chilblain.

gelido ('dʒɛlido) adj icy, cold.

gelosia[1] (dʒelo'sia) nf jealousy, envy.

gelosia[2] (dʒelo'sia) nf shutter.

geloso (dʒe'loso) adj jealous, envious.

gelsomino (dʒelso'mino) nm jasmine.

gemello (dʒe'mɛllo) adj twin. nm 1 twin. 2 pl cuff links. 3 pl cap Gemini.

gemere (dʒe'mere) vi moan, groan. **gemito** ('dʒɛmito) nm groan, moan.

gemma ('dʒemma) nf 1 gem, precious stone. 2 bud.

gene ('dʒɛne) nm gene.

genealogia (dʒenealo'dʒia) nf genealogy. **genealogico** (dʒenea'lɔdʒiko) adj genealogical. **albero genealogico** nm family tree.

generale (dʒene'rale) adj general, common. nm

general. **star sulle generali** speak in general terms.

generalizzare (dʒeneralid'dzare) vt spread. vi generalize.

generare (dʒene'rare) vt produce, generate. **generatore** nm generator. **generazione** nf generation.

genere ('dʒɛnere) nm 1 type, sort, kind. 2 genre. 3 product. 4 gender. **genere umano** human race. **in genere** generally.

generico (dʒe'nɛriko) adj generic.

genero ('dʒɛnero) nm son-in-law.

generoso (dʒene'roso) adj generous. **generosità** nf generosity.

genetica (dʒe'nɛtika) nf genetics. **genetico** (dʒe'nɛtiko) adj genetic.

gengiva (dʒen'dʒiva) nf anat gum.

genio ('dʒɛnjo) nm 1 genius. 2 talent. **andare a genio** suit. **geniale** adj 1 clever. 2 pleasing.

genitali (dʒeni'tali) nm pl genitals.

genitore (dʒeni'tore) nm parent.

gennaio (dʒen'najo) nm January.

Genova ('dʒɛnova) nf Genoa.

gente ('dʒɛnte) nf people.

gentile (dʒen'tile) adj kind, courteous. **Gentile signore** Dear sir. **gentilezza** (dʒenti'lettsa) nf 1 kindness. 2 favour. **gentiluomo** (dʒenti-'lwɔmo) nm gentleman.

genuino (dʒenu'ino) adj genuine.

genziana (dʒen'tsjana) nf gentian.

geografia (dʒeogra'fia) nf geography. **geografico** adj geographic. **geografo** (dʒe'ɔgrafo) nm geographer.

geologia (dʒeolo'dʒia) nf geology. **geologico** adj geological. **geologo** (dʒe'ɔlogo) nm geologist.

geometra (dʒe'ɔmetra) nm surveyor.

geometria (dʒeome'tria) nf geometry. **geometrico** (dʒeo'mɛtriko) adj geometric.

geranio (dʒe'ranjo) nm geranium.

gerarchia (dʒerar'kia) nf hierarchy.

gerente (dʒe'rɛnte) nm director, manager. **gerenza** (dʒe'rɛntsa) nf management.

gergo ('dʒɛrgo) nm slang, jargon.

geriatria (dʒerja'tria) nf geriatrics.

Germania (dʒer'manja) nf Germany.

germe ('dʒɛrme) nm seed.

germogliare (dʒermoʎ'ʎare) vi sprout, bud.

germoglio nm shoot, bud.

gesso ('dʒɛsso) nm chalk.

gesticolare (dʒestiko'lare) vi gesticulate.

gestire (dʒes'tire) vt run, manage. **gestione** nf administration.

gesto ('dʒɛsto) nm gesture.

Gesù (dʒe'zu) nm Jesus.

gesuita (dʒezu'ita) nm Jesuit.

gettare (dʒet'tare) vt throw, hurl.

getto ('dʒetto) nm 1 jet. 2 shoot. **di getto** at a stroke. **primo getto** draft.

gettone (dʒet'tone) nm token, counter.

ghermire (ger'mire) vt clutch, seize.

ghetto ('getto) nm ghetto.

ghiacciaia (gjat'tʃaja) nf icebox. **ghiacciaio** nm glacier.

ghiacciare (gjat'tʃare) vt,vi freeze.

ghiaccio ('gjattʃo) nm ice. **ghiacciolo** (gjat-'tʃɔlo) nm 1 icicle. 2 ice lolly.

ghiaia ('gjaja) nf gravel.

ghianda ('gjanda) nf acorn.

ghigliottina (giʎʎot'tina) nf guillotine.

ghignare (giɲ'ɲare) vi grimace, sneer. **ghigno** nm sneer.

ghiotto ('gjotto) adj greedy. **ghiottone** nm glutton.

ghiribizzo (giri'biddzo) nm whim.

ghirlanda (gir'landa) nf garland, wreath.

ghiro ('giro) nm dormouse.

già (dʒa) adv 1 once, formerly. 2 already. 3 yes, indeed.

giacca ('dʒakka) nf jacket.

giacché (dʒak'ke) conj since.

giacchetta (dʒak'ketta) nf jacket.

giaccio ('dʒattʃo) v see **giacere.**

giacere* (dʒa'tʃere) vi lie.

giacinto (dʒa'tʃinto) nm hyacinth.

giacqui ('dʒakkwi) v see **giacere.**

giada ('dʒada) nf jade.

giaggiolo (dʒad'dʒɔlo) nm bot iris.

giaguaro (dʒa'gwaro) nm jaguar.

giallo ('dʒallo) adj 1 yellow. 2 detective. **romanzo giallo** nm thriller. ~nm 1 yellow. 2 yolk (of an egg).

giammai (dʒam'mai) adv never.

Giappone (dʒap'pone) nm Japan. **giapponese** (dʒappo'nese) adj,n Japanese. nm Japanese (language).

giardino (dʒar'dino) nm garden. **giardino d'infanzia** kindergarten. **giardino pubblico** park. **giardino zoologico** zoo. **giardinaggio** (dʒardi'naddʒo) nm gardening. **giardinetta** nf estate car. **giardiniere** (dʒardi'njɛre) nm gardener.

55

giarrettiera

giarrettiera (dʒarret'tjɛra) *nf* **1** garter. **2** suspender.

giavellotto (dʒavel'lɔtto) *nm* javelin.

gibboso (dʒib'boso) *adj* humped.

gigante (dʒi'gante) *nm* giant. *adj* huge. **gigantesco** *adj* gigantic.

giglio ('dʒiʎʎo) *nm* lily.

gilè (dʒi'lɛ) *nm* waistcoat.

gin (dʒin) *nm* gin.

ginecologo (dʒine'kɔlogo) *nm* gynaecologist. **ginecologia** *nf* gynaecology.

ginepro (dʒi'nepro) *nm* juniper.

ginestra (dʒi'nɛstra) *nf* bot broom.

Ginevra (dʒi'nevra) *nf* Geneva.

gingillarsi (dʒindʒil'larsi) *vr* loiter, dawdle. **gingillo** *nm* plaything.

ginnasio (dʒin'nazjo) *nm* **1** secondary school. **2** gymnasium. **ginnasta** *nm* gymnast. **ginnastica** (dʒin'nastika) *nf* gymnastics. **ginnastico** *adj* gymnastic.

ginocchio (dʒi'nɔkkjo) *nm* knee.

giocare (dʒo'kare) *vi,vt* play. *vi* gamble. **giocatore** *nm* player. **giocattolo** (dʒo'kattolo) *nm* toy. **gioco** ('dʒɔko) *nm* game. **giocoso** *adj* playful.

giogo ('dʒogo) *nm* yoke.

gioia[1] ('dʒɔja) *nf* joy. **gioioso** (dʒo'joso) *adj* joyful.

gioia[2] ('dʒɔja) *nf* precious stone. **gioielliere** (dʒojel'ljɛre) *nm* jeweller. **gioiello** (dʒo'jɛllo) *nm* jewel.

gioire (dʒo'ire) *vi* rejoice.

giornalaio (dʒorna'lajo) *nm* newsagent.

giornale (dʒor'nale) *nm* **1** newspaper. **2** journal. **giornalismo** *nm* journalism. **giornalista** *nm* journalist, reporter.

giorno ('dʒorno) *nm* day, daytime. **a giorni** sometimes. **al giorno d'oggi** nowadays. **di giorno** by day. **due volte al giorno** twice daily. **giornata** *nf* **1** day. **2** day's pay.

giostra ('dʒɔstra) *nf* merry-go-round.

giovane ('dʒovane) *adj* **1** young. **2** new. *nm* young man, youth. *nf* young girl. **giovanile** *adj* youthful. **giovanotto** (dʒova'nɔtto) *nm* youth.

giovare[*] (dʒo'vare) *vi* be of use. *vt* aid. **giovarsi di** *vr* make use of.

Giove ('dʒɔve) *nm* Jupiter (planet).

giovedì (dʒove'di) *nm* Thursday.

gioventù (dʒoven'tu) *nf* youth.

gioviale (dʒo'vjale) *adj* jovial.

giraffa (dʒi'raffa) *nf* giraffe.

girandolare (dʒirando'lare) *vi* wander.

girare (dʒi'rare) *vt* **1** turn, spin. **2** go round. **3** travel round. **4** shoot (film). *vi* **1** spin, revolve. **2** wander. **3** turn, veer. **mi gira la testa** my head is spinning. **giradischi** *nm invar* record-player. **giramondo** *nm* globetrotter. **girarrosto** (dʒirar'rosto) *nm cul* spit. **girasole** *nm* sunflower. **girata** *nf* **1** turn, twist. **2** stroll. **giro** *nm* **1** turn. **2** stroll. **3** circle, ring. **4** circulation. **5** circuit. **in giro** around. **prendere in giro** make fun of.

girino (dʒi'rino) *nm* tadpole.

gironzolare (dʒirondzo'lare) *vi* roam.

girovagare (dʒirova'gare) *vi* wander.

gita ('dʒita) *nf* excursion.

giù (dʒu) *adv* down. **in giù** downwards. **su per giù** thereabouts.

giubba ('dʒubba) *nf* jacket. **giubbotto** (dʒub'bɔtto) *nm* jerkin.

giubilare (dʒubi'lare) *vi* rejoice. *vt* pension off.

giudicare (dʒudi'kare) *vt* judge. **giudice** ('dʒuditʃe) *nm* judge. **giudice popolare** juror.

giudizio (dʒu'dittsjo) *nm* **1** judgment. **2** opinion. **3** common sense.

giugno ('dʒuɲɲo) *nm* June.

giulivo (dʒu'livo) *adj* joyful.

giullare (dʒul'lare) *nm* jester.

giunco (dʒu'unko) *nm* rush, reed.

giungere[*] ('dʒundʒere) *vi* arrive. *vt* join. **giungere a** reach.

giungla ('dʒungla) *nf* jungle.

giunsi ('dʒunsi) *v* see **giungere.**

giunta ('dʒunta) *nf* **1** addition. **2** town council. **3** junta.

giunto ('dʒunto) *v* see **giungere.**

giurare (dʒu'rare) *vi,vt* swear. **giuramento** *nm* oath.

giuria (dʒu'ria) *nf* jury. **giurato** *nm* juror.

giurisdizione (dʒurizdit'tsjone) *nf* jurisdiction.

giustificare (dʒustifi'kare) *vt* justify. **giustificazione** *nf* justification.

giustizia (dʒus'tittsja) *nf* justice.

giusto ('dʒusto) *adj* **1** just, right, fair. **2** correct, right. *adv* exactly.

glaciale (gla'tʃale) *adj* glacial, icy.

glandola ('glandola) *nf* gland.

gli[1] (ʎi) *def art, m pl* the.

gli[2] (ʎi) *pron* **1** *3rd pers ms* to him or it. **2** *3rd pers m,f pl* them.

glicerina (glitʃe'rina) *nf* glycerine.

glicine ('glitʃine) *nm* wisteria.

globo ('glɔbo) nm globe, sphere. **globale** adj global.

gloria ('glɔrja) nf glory. **glorioso** (glo'rjoso) adj glorious.

glorificare (glorifi'kare) vt glorify.

glucosio (glu'kɔzjo) nm glucose.

gnocco ('ɲɔkko) nm 1 small ball of pasta or flour. 2 lump.

gnomo ('ɲɔmo) nm gnome.

gobba ('gɔbba) nf hump. **gobbo** ('gɔbbo) nm hunchback. adj humped.

gocciolare (gottʃo'lare) vt,vi drip. **goccia** ('gɔttʃa) nf drop, drip. **gocciola** (gott'ʃola) nf drop.

godere (go'dere) vt enjoy. vi 1 rejoice. 2 benefit. **godimento** nm enjoyment.

goffo ('gɔffo) adj clumsy, awkward.

gol (gɔl) nm invar goal.

gola ('gola) nf throat.

golf (gɔlf) nm invar 1 golf. 2 sweater.

golfo ('golfo) nm gulf.

goloso (go'loso) adj greedy, avaricious. **golosità** nf greed.

golpe ('golpe) nf right-wing coup.

gomito ('gomito) nm elbow. **gomitata** nf nudge.

gomitolo (go'mitolo) nm ball of thread.

gomma ('gomma) nf 1 gum. 2 rubber. 3 tyre.

gondola ('gondola) nf gondola. **gondoliere** (gondo'ljere) nm gondolier.

gonfalone (gonfa'lone) nm banner.

gonfiare (gon'fjare) vt blow up, inflate. vi swell. **gonfiarsi** vr swell. **gonfio** ('gonfjo) adj swollen. **gonfiore** nm swelling.

gong (gɔng) nm invar gong.

gonna ('gonna) nf skirt.

gonzo ('gondzo) nm simpleton.

gorgheggiare (gorged'dʒare) vi,vt warble, trill. **gorgheggio** nm trill.

gorgo ('gorgo) nm whirlpool.

gorgogliare (gorgoʎ'ʎare) vi gurgle.

gorilla (go'rilla) nm invar gorilla.

gotta ('gɔtta) nf gout.

governante (gover'nante) nf governess.

governare (gover'nare) vt govern. **governatore** nm governor. **governo** (go'vɛrno) nm government.

gracchiare (grak'kjare) vi croak.

gracidare (gratʃi'dare) vi croak, cackle.

gracile ('gratʃile) adj frail, delicate.

gradasso (gra'dasso) nm boaster.

gradino (gra'dino) nm step, stair.

gradire (gra'dire) vt 1 accept. 2 wish, like. v

imp please. **gradevole** (gra'devole) adj pleasing.

grado ('grado) nm 1 degree. 2 grade, rank, position. **essere in grado di** be in a position to. **graduale** adj gradual.

graffiare (graf'fjare) vt scratch. **graffiatura** nf scratch. **graffio** ('graffjo) nm scratch.

grafico ('grafiko) adj graphic. nm graph.

grammatica (gram'matika) nf grammar.

grammo ('grammo) nm gramme.

grammofono (gram'mɔfono) nm gramophone.

granaglie (gra'naʎʎe) nf pl grain.

granaio (gra'najo) nm granary.

granata (gra'nata) nf 1 brush, broom. 2 mil shell.

Gran Bretagna nf Great Britain.

granchio (grankjo) nm 1 crab. 2 mistake.

grande ('grande) adj 1 big, tall. 2 great. nm,f adult. **grandezza** (gran'dettsa) nf 1 size. 2 greatness.

grandeggiare (granded'dʒare) vi stand out.

grandinare (grandi'nare) vi hail. **grandine** ('grandine) nf hail. **chicco di grandine** nm hailstone.

grandioso (gran'djoso) adj grandiose.

granduca (gran'duka) nm grand duke.

granito (gra'nito) nm granite.

grano ('grano) nm 1 wheat. 2 grain. **granello** (gra'nɛllo) nm grain, seed.

granturco (gran'turko) nm maize.

granulo ('granulo) nm granule.

grappolo ('grappolo) nm bunch.

grasso ('grasso) adj 1 fat. 2 greasy. **grassezza** (gras'settsa) nf fatness.

grata ('grata) nf grating. **gratella** (gra'tɛlla) nf grill.

graticola (gra'tikola) nf grill.

gratis ('gratis) adv free of charge, free.

gratitudine (grati'tudine) nf gratitude.

grato ('grato) adj 1 grateful. 2 pleasing.

grattare (grat'tare) vt 1 scratch. 2 grate. **grattacielo** (gratta'tʃɛlo) nm skyscraper. **grattugiare** (grattu'dʒare) vt grate. **grattugia** nf grater.

gratuito (gra'tuito) adj free.

gravare (gra'vare) vt oppress, burden.

grave ('grave) adj 1 heavy. 2 serious, grave, solemn. **gravità** nf gravity.

gravido ('gravido) adj 1 pregnant. 2 laden. **gravidanza** (gravi'dantsa) nf pregnancy.

grazia ('grattsja) nf 1 grace, charm. 2 favour,

goodwill. **3** mercy, pardon. **4** *pl* thanks. **grazioso** (grat'tsjoso) *adj* gracious, charming.

Grecia ('grɛtʃa) *nf* Greece. **greco** ('grɛko) *pl* **greci** *adj,n* Greek. nm Greek (language).

gregge ('greddʒe) *nm,pl* **greggi** *f* flock.

greggio ('greddʒo) *adj* raw, coarse.

grembiule (grem'bjule) *nm* apron.

grembo ('grɛmbo) *nm* lap.

gremire (gre'mire) *vt* cram. **gremirsi** *vr* fill up. **gremito** *adj* crammed.

gretto ('gretto) *adj* **1** mean, stingy. **2** petty.

gridare (gri'dare) *vt,vi* shout, cry. **grida** *nf* proclamation. **grido** *nm* **1** *pl* **grida** *f* shout, cry. **2** *pl* **gridi** *m* cry (of an animal). **di grido** famous.

grigio ('gridʒo) *adj,nm* grey.

griglia ('griʎʎa) *nf* grill.

grilletto (gril'letto) *nm* trigger.

grillo ('grillo) *nm* **1** *zool* cricket. **2** whim.

grinza ('grintsa) *nf* **1** crease. **2** wrinkle.

grippe ('grippe) *nf* influenza.

grissino (gris'sino) *nm* bread-stick.

grondare (gron'dare) *vi* **1** drip. **2** pour. **gronda** *nf* eaves. **grondaia** *nf* gutter.

groppa ('grɔppa) *nf* **1** back. **2** rump.

grossa ('grɔssa) *nf* gross.

grosso ('grɔsso) *adj* **1** big. **2** coarse, rough. **pezzo grosso** *nm* important person. **grossezza** (gros'settsa) *nf* **1** size. **2** thickness. **grossolano** *adj* rough, coarse.

grotta ('grɔtta) *nf* cave.

grottesco (grot'tesko) *adj* grotesque.

groviglio (go'viʎʎo) *nm* tangle.

gru (gru) *nf invar* **1** *zool* crane. **2** mechanical crane.

gruccia ('gruttʃa) *nf* **1** crutch. **2** coathanger.

grugnire (gruɲ'ɲire) *vi* grunt. **grugnito** *nm* grunt.

grugno ('gruɲɲo) *nm* snout.

grullo ('grullo) *adj* silly.

grumo ('grumo) *nm* clot (of blood, etc.).

gruppo ('gruppo) *nm* group.

gruviera (gru'vjera) *nm* Gruyère.

guadagnare (gwadaɲ'ɲare) *vt* **1** earn. **2** gain. **3** reach. **4** win. **guadagno** *nm* **1** gain. **2** earnings.

guado ('gwado) *nm* ford.

guaina (gwa'ina) *nf* sheath.

guaio ('gwajo) *nm* mishap, trouble.

guaire (gwa'ire) *vi* howl, whine. **guaito** *nm* whine.

guancia ('gwantʃa) *nf anat* cheek. **guanciale** *nm* pillow.

guanto ('gwanto) *nm* glove.

guardare (gwar'dare) *vt* **1** look at. **2** look after, watch, protect. **3** examine. *vi* **1** look. **2** take care, pay attention. **guardarsi** *vr* **1** look at oneself. **2** look at one another. **3** beware. **guardacaccia** *nm* gamekeeper. **guardacoste** (gwarda'kɔste) *nm* coastguard. **guardaroba** (gwarda'rɔba) *nm invar* **1** wardrobe. **2** cloakroom. **guardata** *nf* glance.

guardia ('gwardja) *nf* guard. **guardia del corpo** bodyguard. **guardiano** *nm* guardian, keeper.

guardingo (gwar'dingo) *adj* cautious.

guarire (gwa'rire) *vi* recover, get well. *vt* cure, heal.

guarnigione (gwarni'dʒone) *nf* garrison.

guarnire (gwar'nire) *vt* **1** equip, furnish. **2** trim, decorate. **guarnizione** *nf* **1** decoration. **2** *cul* garnish.

guastare (gwas'tare) *vt* spoil, destroy, ruin. **guastarsi** *vr* go bad. **guastafeste** (gwasta-'feste) *nm* spoilsport. **guasto** *adj* spoilt, damaged. *nm* **1** damage. **2** fault.

guazza ('gwattsa) *nf* dew.

guazzabuglio (gwattsa'buʎʎo) *nm* hotchpotch.

guazzare (gwat'tsare) *vi* splash. **guazzo** *nm* **1** puddle. **2** pool. **3** gouache.

guercio ('gwertʃo) *adj* cross-eyed.

guerra ('gwɛrra) *nf* war. **guerriero** (gwer'rjɛro) *nm* warrior.

guerreggiare (gwerred'dʒare) *vi* wage war.

guerresco (gwer'resko) *adj* warlike.

guerriglia (gwer'riʎʎa) *nf* guerrilla warfare. **guerrigliere** (gwerriʎ'ʎɛre) *nm* guerrilla.

gufo ('gufo) *nm* owl.

guglia ('guʎʎa) *nf* spire.

guidare (gwi'dare) *vt* **1** guide. **2** drive, pilot. **guida** *nf* **1** guidance. **2** guide. **3** guidebook, guide. **lezione di guida** *nf* driving lesson. **scuola guida** *nf* school of motoring.

guinzaglio (gwin'tsaʎʎo) *nm* leash.

guisa ('gwiza) *nf* manner, way. **a guisa di** like.

guizzare (gwit'tsare) *vi* **1** flash. **2** dart. **3** wriggle. **4** flicker.

guscio ('guʃʃo) *nm* shell.

gustare (gus'tare) *vt* **1** taste. **2** enjoy. **3** try, sample. **gusto** *nm* **1** taste. **2** pleasure. **3** good taste. **gustoso** (gus'toso) *adj* agreeable.

gutturale (guttu'rale) *adj* guttural.

H

ha (a) *v see* **avere.**

hai ('ai) *v see* **avere.**

hanno ('anno) *v see* **avere.**

hascisc (aʃ'ʃiʃ) *nm invar* hashish.

ho (ɔ) *v see* **avere.**

hockey ('hɔki) *nm* hockey.

I

i (i) *def art, m pl* the.

iarda ('jarda) *nf* yard (measurement).

iattanza (jat'tantsa) *nf* arrogance.

ibernazione (ibernat'tsjone) *nf* hibernation.

ibrido ('ibrido) *adj,nm* hybrid.

icona (i'kɔna) *nf* icon.

Iddio (id'dio) *nm* God.

idea (i'dɛa) *nf* 1 idea. 2 opinion. **cambiare idea** change one's mind. **ideale** *adj,nm* ideal. **idealista** *nm* idealist. **idealizzare** (idealid'dzare) *vt* idealize.

idem ('idɛm) *adv* the same.

identico (i'dɛntiko) *adj* identical.

identificare (identifi'kare) *vt* identify. **identificazione** *nf* identification.

identità (identi'ta) *nf* identity.

ideologia (ideolo'dʒia) *nf* ideology.

idillio (i'dilljo) *nm* idyll. **idillico** (i'dilliko) *adj also* **idilliaco** (idil'liako) idyllic.

idioma (i'djɔma) *nm* 1 language. 2 dialect. **idiomatico** (idjo'matiko) *adj* idiomatic.

idiota (i'djɔta) *nm* idiot. *adj* idiotic.

idiotismo (idjo'tizmo) *nm* idiom.

idolo ('idolo) *nm* idol.

idoneo (i'dɔneo) *adj* suitable, fit.

idraulico (i'drauliko) *adj* hydraulic. *nm* plumber.

idroelettrico (idroe'lɛttriko) *adj* hydro-electric.

idrogeno (i'drɔdʒeno) *nm* hydrogen.

idroplano (idro'plano) *nm* hydroplane.

idrosci (idroʃ'ʃi) *nm* water-skiing.

idrovolante (idrovo'lante) *nm* seaplane.

iena ('jɛna) *nf* hyena.

ieri ('jɛri) *adv* yesterday. **ieri l'altro** the day before yesterday.

igiene (i'dʒɛne) *nf* hygiene. **igienico** (i'dʒɛniko) *adj* hygienic. **carta igienica** *nf* toilet paper.

iglù (i'glu) *nm* igloo.

ignaro (iɲ'ɲaro) *adj* ignorant, unaware.

ignominia (iɲɲo'minja) *nf* 1 ignominy. 2 shameful deed.

ignorare (iɲɲo'rare) *vt* 1 not to know, be unaware of. 2 ignore. **ignorante** *adj* ignorant. *nm* ignoramus. **ignoranza** (iɲɲo'rantsa) *nf* ignorance.

ignoto (iɲ'ɲɔto) *adj* unknown.

ignudo (iɲ'ɲudo) *adj* naked.

il (il) *def art, ms* the.

ilare ('ilare) *adj* cheerful. **ilarità** *nf* hilarity.

illecito (il'letʃito) *adj* illicit.

illegale (ille'gale) *adj* illegal.

illeggibile (illed'dʒibile) *adj* illegible.

illegittimo (illed'dʒittimo) *adj* illegitimate.

illeso (il'lezo) *adj* unhurt.

illimitato (illimi'tato) *adj* unlimited.

illogico (il'lɔdʒiko) *adj* illogical.

illudere* (il'ludere) *vt* deceive, delude.

illuminare (illumi'nare) *vt* 1 illuminate, light up. 2 enlighten. **illuminare a giorno** floodlight. **illuminazione** *nf* lighting.

illusione (illu'zjone) *nf* illusion.

illusorio (illu'zɔrjo) *adj* deceptive.

illustrare (illus'trare) *vt* illustrate. **illustrazione** *nf* illustration.

illustre (il'lustre) *adj* famous, renowned.

imbaccucare (imbakuk'kare) *vt* muffle up. **imbaccucarsi** *vr* wrap oneself up.

imballaggio (imbal'laddʒo) *nm* packing. **carta d'imballaggio** *nf* brown paper, wrapping paper.

imballare (imbal'lare) *vt* pack.

imbalsamare (imbalsa'mare) *vt* embalm.

imbarazzare (imbarat'tsare) *vt* 1 impede. 2 embarrass. **imbarazzante** *adj* embarrassing. **imbarazzato** *adj* 1 embarrassed. 2 perplexed. **imbarazzo** *nm* 1 obstacle. 2 embarrassment.

imbarcare (imbar'kare) *vt* take on board. **imbarcarsi** *vr* embark. **imbarcadero** (imbarka'dɛro) *nm* landing stage.

imbastire (imbas'tire) *vt* 1 (sewing) tack. 2 rough out.

imbattersi (im'battersi) *vr* come across by chance, bump into.

imbattibile (imbat'tibile) *adj* unbeatable.

imbavagliare (imbavaʎ'ʎare) *vt* gag.

imbecille (imbe'tʃille) *adj,nm* imbecile.

imbellettare (imbellet'tare) *vt* 1 make up. 2 embellish. **imbellettarsi** *vr* put on make-up.

imbellire (imbel'lire) *vt* adorn. *vi* improve in looks.

59

imbiancare (imbjan'kare) *vt* **1** whiten. **2** whitewash. *vi* turn white.

imboccare (imbok'kare) *vt* **1** feed. **2** suggest. **3** enter. **imboccatura** *nf* opening, entrance.

imboscata (imbos'kata) *nf* ambush.

imbottigliare (imbotti'ʎare) *vt* bottle.

imbottire (imbot'tire) *vt* **1** stuff. **2** pad. **imbottito** *adj* stuffed. **panino imbottito** *nm* sandwich.

imbrattare (imbrat'tare) *vt* dirty.

imbrigliare (imbriʎ'ʎare) *vt* bridle.

imbrogliare (imbroʎ'ʎare) *vt* **1** confuse, muddle. **2** cheat. **imbrogliarsi** *vr* become involved. **imbroglio** *nm* **1** tangle, muddle. **2** trick, swindle.

imbronciarsi (imbron'tʃarsi) *vr* sulk.

imbrunire (imbru'nire) *vi* darken, grow dark. **sull'imbrunire** towards dusk.

imbruttire (imbrut'tire) *vt* make ugly. *vi* become ugly. **imbruttirsi** *vr* become ugly.

imbucare (imbu'kare) *vt* post.

imburrare (imbur'rare) *vt* butter.

imbuto (im'buto) *nm* funnel.

imitare (imi'tare) *vt* imitate. **imitazione** *nf* imitation.

immagazzinare (immagaddzi'nare) *vt* store.

immaginare (immadʒi'nare) *vt* **1** imagine. **2** suppose. **immaginazione** *nf* imagination. **immagine** (im'madʒine) *nf* **1** image. **2** figure.

immangiabile (imman'dʒabile) *adj* uneatable.

immatricolarsi (immatriko'larsi) *vr* **1** enrol. **2** *educ* matriculate.

immaturo (imma'turo) *adj* immature. **immaturità** *nf* immaturity.

immedesimarsi (immedezi'marsi) *vr* identify oneself.

immediato (imme'djato) *adj* immediate.

immemorabile (immemo'rabile) *adj* immemorial.

immenso (im'mɛnso) *adj* huge, immense.

immergere* (im'mɛrdʒere) *vt* **1** immerse. **2** plunge. **3** dip. **immersione** *nf* immersion.

immeritato (immeri'tato) *adj* undeserved.

immigrare (immi'grare) *vi* immigrate. **immigrante** *adj,n* immigrant. **immigrazione** *nf* immigration.

imminente (immi'nɛnte) *adj* imminent.

immischiare (immis'kjare) *vt* involve. **immischiarsi** *vr* interfere.

immobile (im'mɔbile) *adj* still, motionless. **beni immobili** *nm pl* real estate.

immobiliare (immobi'ljare) *adj* immovable. **società immobiliare** *nf* building society.

immobilizzare (immobilid'dzare) *vt* immobilize.

immoderato (immode'rato) *adj* excessive.

immondo (im'mondo) *adj* **1** filthy, foul. **2** unclean. **immondizia** (immon'dittsja) *nf* **1** filth. **2** *pl* rubbish, refuse.

immorale (immo'rale) *adj* immoral.

immortale (immor'tale) *adj* immortal. **immortalità** *nf* immortality.

immune (im'mune) *adj* **1** immune. **2** free. **immunità** *nf* immunity. **immunizzare** *vt* immunize.

immutabile (immu'tabile) *adj* unchangeable.

impaccare (impak'kare) *vt* pack. **impacco** *nm* compress.

impacchettare (impakket'tare) *vt* parcel.

impacciare (impat'tʃare) *vt* **1** hinder, impede. **2** trouble. **impacciarsi** *vr* meddle. **impaccio** *nm* hindrance.

impadronirsi (impadro'nirsi) *vr* **1** seize. **2** take possession. **3** master.

impagliare (impaʎ'ʎare) *vt* stuff.

impalcatura (impalka'tura) *nf* scaffolding, frame.

impallidire (impalli'dire) *vi* turn pale.

impanare (impa'nare) *vt* dip in breadcrumbs.

imparare (impa'rare) *vt* learn.

impareggiabile (impared'dʒabile) *adj* incomparable.

impari ('impari) *adj invar* **1** unequal. **2** uneven.

impartire (impar'tire) *vt* impart.

imparziale (impar'tsjale) *adj* impartial. **imparzialità** *nf* impartiality, fairness.

impassibile (impas'sibile) *adj* impassive.

impastare (impas'tare) *vt* **1** knead. **2** paste. **impasto** *nm* mixture.

impaurire (impau'rire) *vt* frighten. **impaurirsi** *vr* become frightened.

impazientirsi (impattsjen'tirsi) *vr* lose one's patience. **impaziente** *adj* impatient. **impazienza** (impat'tsjɛntsa) *nf* impatience.

impazzire (impat'tsire) *vi* go mad.

impeccabile (impek'kabile) *adj* impeccable.

impedire (impe'dire) *vt* **1** prevent. **2** hinder, obstruct. **impedimento** *nm* **1** obstacle. **2** hindrance.

impegnare (impeɲ'ɲare) *vt* **1** pawn. **2** pledge. **3** occupy. **4** oblige. **5** book, reserve. **impegnarsi** *vr* promise. **impegnativo** *adj* **1** binding. **2** exacting. **impegno** *nm* **1** obligation. **2** engagement. **3** attention.

impenetrabile (impene'trabile) *adj* impenetrabile.

impenitente (impeni'tɛnte) *adj* impenitent.

impennarsi (impen'narsi) *vr* **1** (of a horse) rear. **2** become annoyed.

imperativo (impera'tivo) *adj* imperative.

imperatore (impera'tore) *nm* emperor. **imperatrice** *nf* empress.

impercettibile (impertʃet'tibile) *adj* imperceptible.

imperdonabile (imperdo'nabile) *adj* unpardonable.

imperfetto (imper'fɛtto) *adj* **1** imperfect. **2** incomplete. **imperfezione** (imperfet'tsjone) *nf* imperfection.

imperioso (impe'rjoso) *adj* **1** imperious. **2** compelling.

impermalirsi (imperma'lirsi) *vr* take offence.

impermeabile (imperme'abile) *adj* **1** waterproof. **2** airtight. *nm* raincoat.

imperniare (imper'njare) *vt* **1** pivot. **2** base.

impero (im'pɛro) *nm* empire. **imperiale** *adj* imperial.

imperscrutabile (imperskru'tabile) *adj* inscrutable.

impersonale (imperso'nale) *adj* impersonal.

impersonare (imperso'nare) *vt* **1** personify. **2** play the role of.

imperterrito (imper'tɛrrito) *adj* intrepid, fearless.

impertinente (imperti'nɛnte) *adj* impertinent. **impertinenza** (imperti'nɛntsa) *nf* impertinence.

imperturbabile (impertur'babile) *adj* imperturbable.

imperturbato (impertur'bato) *adj* unperturbed.

impeto ('impeto) *nm* impetus.

impetuoso (impetu'oso) *adj* impetuous. **impetuosità** *nf* impetuosity.

impiantare (impjan'tare) *vt* **1** install. **2** establish.

impiantito (impjan'tito) *nm* floor. **impianto** *nm* **1** installation, fitting. **2** tech plant.

impiastrare (impjas'trare) *vt* smear. **impiastro** *nm* **1** poultice. **2** nuisance.

impiccare (impik'kare) *vt* hang.

impicciare (impit'tʃare) *vt* impede, hinder. **impicciarsi** *vr* interfere, meddle. **impiccio** *nm* **1** hindrance. **2** mess.

impiegare (impje'gare) *vt* **1** use, employ. **2** spend. **3** invest. **impiegato** *nm* **1** employee. **2** clerk. **impiego** (im'pjɛgo) *nm* job, employment.

impiombare (impjom'bare) *vt* fill (a tooth). **impiombatura** *nf* filling.

implacabile (impla'kabile) *adj* implacable.

implicare (impli'kare) *vt* implicate, involve. **implicazione** *nf* implication.

implicito (im'plitʃito) *adj* implicit.

implorare (implo'rare) *vt* beg, implore.

impolverare (impolve'rare) *vt* cover with dust. **impolverarsi** *vr* become dusty.

imponente (impo'nɛnte) *adj* imposing.

imponibile (impo'nibile) *adj* taxable.

impopolare (impopo'lare) *adj* unpopular.

imporre* (im'porre) *vt* **1** impose, give. **2** command. **imporsi** *vr* dominate.

importante (impor'tante) *adj* important. **importanza** (impor'tantsa) *nf* importance.

importare (impor'tare) *vt* **1** import. **2** imply. *v imp* matter, be important. **importatore** *nm* importer. **importazione** *nf* **1** importation. **2** import.

importunare (importu'nare) *vt* pester, annoy. **importuno** *adj* annoying. *nm* nuisance.

imposizione (impozit'tsjone) *nf* imposition.

impossessarsi (imposses'sarsi) *vr* **1** take possession. **2** master.

impossibile (impos'sibile) *adj* impossible.

imposta[1] (im'posta) *nf* shutter.

imposta[2] (im'posta) *nf* tax.

impostare[1] (impos'tare) *vt* **1** begin. **2** plan, set out.

impostare[2] (impos'tare) *vt* post.

impostore (impos'tore) *nm* impostor.

impotente (impo'tɛnte) *adj* **1** weak, powerless. **2** impotent. **impotenza** (impo'tɛntsa) *nf* impotence.

impoverire (impove'rire) *vt* impoverish. **impoverirsi** *vr* become poor.

impreciso (impre'tʃizo) *adj* inexact, vague.

impregnare (impreɲ'ɲare) *vt* impregnate.

imprenditore (imprendi'tore) *nm* **1** entrepreneur. **2** contractor.

impreparato (imprepa'rato) *adj* unprepared.

impresa (im'presa) *nf* **1** undertaking, venture. **2** firm, concern.

impressionare (impressjo'nare) *vt* **1** make an impression upon, affect. **2** frighten. **impressionante** *adj* **1** striking. **2** frightening. **impressione** *nf* impression. **impressionismo** (impressjo'nizmo) *nm* impressionism.

imprestare (impres'tare) *vt* lend.

imprevisto (impre'visto) *adj* unforeseen.

imprigionare (impridʒo'nare) *vt* imprison.

imprimere* (im'primere) *vt* **1** imprint, stamp. **2** print.

improbabile (impro'babile) *adj* improbable.

improduttivo (improdut'tivo) *adj* unproductive.

impronta (im'pronta) *nf* imprint, mark.

improprio (im'prɔprjo) *adj* improper.

improvvisare (improvvi'zare) *vt* improvise. **improvviso** *adj* sudden. **all'improvviso** unexpectedly.

imprudente (impru'dɛnte) *adj* unwise, rash.

impudente (impu'dɛnte) *adj* impudent. **impudenza** (impu'dɛntsa) *nf* impudence.

impudico (impu'diko) *adj* immodest.

impugnare (impuɲ'ɲare) *vt* **1** grip. **2** contest.

impulso (im'pulso) *nm* impulse. **impulsivo** *adj* impulsive.

impunito (impu'nito) *adj* unpunished. **impunità** *nf* impunity.

impuntarsi (impun'tarsi) *vr* be obstinate.

impuro (im'puro) *adj* impure.

imputare (impu'tare) *vt* ascribe.

imputridire (imputri'dire) *vi* rot.

in (in) *prep* **1** in, at. **2** to. **3** into. **4** by. **5** on. **in casa** at home. **in piedi** standing.

inabile (i'nabile) *adj* unable, unfit.

inabitabile (inabi'tabile) *adj* uninhabitable.

inaccessibile (inattʃes'sibile) *adj* inaccessible.

inaccettabile (inattʃet'tabile) *adj* unacceptable.

inadeguato (inade'gwato) *adj* inadequate.

inalare (ina'lare) *vt* inhale.

inalienabile (inalje'nabile) *adj* inalienable.

inalterabile (inalte'rabile) *adj* unalterable.

inamidare (inami'dare) *vt* starch.

inammissibile (inammis'sibile) *adj* unacceptable.

inapplicabile (inappli'kabile) *adj* inapplicable.

inarcare (inar'kare) *vt* **1** arch. **2** bend.

inaridire (inari'dire) *vi* dry up. **inaridirsi** *vr* become dried up.

inaspettato (inaspet'tato) *adj* unexpected.

inasprire (inas'prire) *vt* **1** embitter. **2** exacerbate.

inastare (inas'tare) *vt* hoist.

inattendibile (inatten'dibile) *adj* unreliable.

inatteso (inat'teso) *adj* unexpected.

inaudito (inau'dito) *adj* unheard of.

inaugurare (inaugu'rare) *vt* inaugurate. **inaugurale** *adj* inaugural. **inaugurazione** *nf* inauguration.

inavvertenza (inavver'tɛntsa) *nf* inadvertence.

incagliare (inkaʎ'ʎare) *vt* hamper, impede. **incagliarsi** *vr* run aground.

incalcolabile (inkalko'labile) *adj* incalculable.

incalzare (inkal'tsare) *vt* **1** follow closely. **2** press, be imminent. **incalzante** *adj* **1** urgent. **2** imminent.

incamminare (inkammi'nare) *vt* start. **incamminarsi** *vr* set off.

incantare (inkan'tare) *vt* enchant, charm. **incantesimo** (inkan'tezimo) *nm* spell. **incanto** *nm* enchantment.

incapace (inka'patʃe) *adj* incapable, unable.

incappare (inkap'pare) *vi* run into danger.

incarcerare (inkartʃe'rare) *vt* imprison.

incaricare (inkari'kare) *vt* entrust, charge. **incaricarsi** *vr* undertake. **incaricato** *nm* official.

incarico (in'kariko) *nm* task.

incartare (inkar'tare) *vt* wrap up.

incartocciare (inkartot'tʃare) *vt* put into a paper bag.

incassare (inkas'sare) *vt* **1** pack, encase. **2** collect. *vi* fit. **incasso** *nm* takings.

incastrare (inkas'trare) *vt* insert.

incatenare (inkate'nare) *vt* chain up.

incauto (in'kauto) *adj* imprudent.

incendiare (intʃen'djare) *vt* set fire to. **incendiarsi** *vr* catch fire. **incendio** (in'tʃendjo) *nm* fire.

incenso (in'tʃenso) *nm* incense.

incensurabile (intʃensu'rabile) *adj* irreproachable.

inceppare (intʃep'pare) *vt* obstruct. **incepparsi** *vr* jam.

incerto (in'tʃerto) *adj* uncertain, doubtful. **incertezza** (intʃer'tettsa) *nf* uncertainty.

incespicare (intʃespi'kare) *vi* stumble.

incessante (intʃes'sante) *adj* incessant.

incesto (in'tʃesto) *nm* incest.

inchiesta (in'kjesta) *nf* investigation, inquiry.

inchinare (inki'nare) *vt* bow. **inchinarsi** *vr* bow. **inchino** *nm* bow, curtsy.

inchiodare (inkjo'dare) *vt* nail, pin.

inchiostro (in'kjostro) *nm* ink.

inciampare (intʃam'pare) *vi* stumble, trip. **inciampo** *nm* obstacle.

incidente (intʃi'dɛnte) *nm* accident.

incidere* (in'tʃidere) *vt* **1** engrave, cut. **2** record.

incinta (in'tʃinta) *adj* pregnant.

incipriare (intʃi'prjare) *vt* powder.

incisione (intʃi'zjone) *nf* **1** incision. **2** engraving.

incivilire (intʃivi'lire) vt civilize. **incivile** adj 1 uncivilized. 2 rude.

inclinare (inkli'nare) vt bend. vi incline.

includere* (in'kludere) vt include. **incluso** (in'kluzo) adj 1 included. 2 enclosed. **inclusione** nf inclusion.

incoerente (inkoe'rɛnte) adj incoherent.

incognito (in'kɔɲɲito) adj incognito.

incollare (inkol'lare) vt glue, paste.

incolore (inko'lore) adj colourless.

incolpare (inkol'pare) vt accuse, charge.

incolto (in'kolto) adj 1 neglected. 2 uneducated.

incolume (in'kɔlume) adj safe, unhurt.

incombustibile (inkombus'tibile) adj fireproof.

incominciare (inkomin'tʃare) vt,vi begin, start.

incomodare (inkomo'dare) vt trouble. **incomodarsi** vr put oneself out. **incomodo** (in'kɔmodo) adj troublesome, inconvenient. nm trouble.

incomparabile (inkompa'rabile) adj incomparable.

incompatibile (inkompa'tibile) adj incompatibile.

incompetente (inkompe'tɛnte) adj incompetent. **incompetenza** (inkompe'tɛntsa) nf incompetence.

incompiuto (inkom'pjuto) adj incomplete, unfinished.

incompleto (inkom'plɛto) adj incomplete.

incomprensibile (inkompren'sibile) adj incomprehensible.

inconcepibile (inkontʃe'pibile) adj incredible.

inconcludente (inkonklu'dɛnte) adj inconclusive.

inconsapevole (inkonsa'pevole) adj ignorant, unaware.

inconsolabile (inkonso'labile) adj inconsolable.

inconsueto (inkonsu'ɛto) adj unusual.

incontrare (inkon'trare) vt meet.

incontro[1] (in'kontro) 1 meeting. 2 match. **andare incontro** (a) 1 meet. 2 face.

incontro[2] (in'kontro) prep,adv 1 towards. 2 against.

inconveniente (inkonve'njɛnte) nm snag, drawback.

incoraggiare (inkorad'dʒare) vt encourage. **incoraggiamento** nm encouragement.

incorniciare (inkorni'tʃare) vt frame.

incoronare (inkoro'nare) vt crown.

incorporare (inkorpo'rare) vt incorporate.

incorrere* (in'korrere) vi incur.

incorruttibile (inkorrut'tibile) adj incorruptible.

incosciente (inkoʃ'ʃɛnte) adj irresponsible.

incredibile (inkre'dibile) adj unbelievable, incredible.

incredulo (in'krɛdulo) adj incredulous. **incredulità** nf incredulity.

increspare (inkres'pare) vt 1 ruffle. 2 wrinkle. **incresparsi** vr ripple.

incrinare (inkri'nare) vt crack. **incrinarsi** vr crack.

incrociare (inkro'tʃare) vt cross. vi cruise. **incrociarsi** vr cross, interlace. **incrociato** adj crossed. **parole incrociate** nf pl crossword. **incrocio** nm crossing, crossroads.

incubatrice (inkuba'tritʃe) nf incubator.

incubo ('inkubo) nm nightmare.

incudine (in'kudine) nf anvil.

incuneare (inkune'are) vt wedge.

incupire (inku'pire) vt,vi darken. **incupirsi** vr become gloomy.

incurabile (inku'rabile) adj incurable.

incurante (inku'rante) adj careless.

incursione (inkur'sjone) nf raid, attack.

indagare (inda'gare) vt investigate. **indagine** (in'dadʒine) nf investigation, inquiry.

indebolire (indebo'lire) vt,vi weaken. **indebolirsi** vr weaken.

indecente (inde'tʃɛnte) adj indecent. **indecenza** (inde'tʃɛntsa) nf indecency.

indecisione (indetʃi'zjone) nf indecision.

indeciso (inde'tʃizo) adj undecided.

indefinito (indefi'nito) adj indefinite.

indegno (in'deɲɲo) adj unworthy.

indenne (in'dɛnne) adj unhurt. **indennità** nf 1 compensation, damages. 2 indemnity. **indennizzare** (indennid'dzare) vt compensate.

indescrivibile (indeskri'vibile) adj indescribable.

indesiderabile (indeside'rabile) adj undesirable.

indeterminato (indetermi'nato) adj vague, indefinite.

India ('indja) nf India. **indiano** adj,n Indian.

indicare (indi'kare) vt 1 point to, indicate. 2 show. 3 recommend. **indicatore** nm indicator, gauge. **indicatore stradale** road sign. **indicazione** nf indication.

indice ('inditʃe) nm 1 index finger, forefinger. 2 index. 3 needle, pointer. 4 sign.

indietreggiare (indjetred'dʒare) vi retreat, withdraw.

indietro (in'djɛtro) adv 1 back. 2 behind. 3

backwards. **all'indietro** backwards. **andare indietro** (of a watch) be slow.

indifeso (indi'feso) *adj* undefended.

indifferente (indiffe'rɛnte) *adj* indifferent. **indifferenza** (indiffe'rɛntsa) *nf* indifference.

indigesto (indi'dʒesto) *adj* indigestible. **indigestione** *nf* indigestion.

indignare (indiɲ'nare) *vt* make indignant. **indignarsi** *vr* become angry. **indignato** *adj* indignant. **indignazione** *nf* indignation.

indimenticabile (indimenti'kabile) *adj* unforgettable.

indipendente (indipen'dɛnte) *adj* independent, free. **indipendenza** (indipen'dɛntsa) *nf* independence.

indiretto (indi'rɛtto) *adj* indirect.

indirizzare (indirit'tsare) *vt* 1 direct. 2 address. **indirizzarsi** *vr* set out. **indirizzo** *nm* 1 direction. 2 address.

indiscreto (indis'kreto) *adj* indiscreet.

indispensabile (indispen'sabile) *adj* necessary, indispensable.

indistinto (indis'tinto) *adj* indistinct.

indivia (in'divja) *nf* endive.

individuale (individu'ale) *adj* individual. **individuo** (indi'viduo) *nm* individual.

indivisibile (indivi'zibile) *adj* inseparable, indivisible.

indizio (in'dittsjo) *nm* clue, sign.

indole ('indole) *nf* disposition, nature. **indolente** (indo'lɛnte) *adj* indolent.

indolenzire (indolen'tsire) *vi* go numb.

indomani (indo'mani) *adv* next day, day after.

indossare (indos'sare) *vt* put on, wear. **indossatrice** *nf* model.

indovinare (indovi'nare) *vt* guess. **indovinello** (indovi'nɛllo) *nm* riddle.

indù (in'du) *adj,n* Hindu.

indubbio (in'dubbjo) *adj* certain.

indubitato (indubi'tato) *adj* undoubted.

indugiare (indu'dʒare) *vi* delay, linger. **indugiarsi** *vr* loiter. **indugio** *nm* delay.

indulgente (indul'dʒɛnte) *adj* indulgent. **indulgenza** (indul'dʒɛntsa) *nf* indulgence.

indumento (indu'mento) *nm* 1 garment. 2 *pl* clothes.

indurire (indu'rire) *vt* harden.

indurre (in'durre) *vt* induce.

industria (in'dustrja) *nf* industry. **industriale** *adj* industrial. *nm* industrialist.

inebriare (inebri'are) *vt* intoxicate.

inedito (i'nɛdito) *adj* unpublished.

ineguale (ine'gwale) *adj* 1 unequal. 2 uneven. **ineguaglianza** (inegwaʎ'ʎantsa) *nf* inequality.

inerente (ine'rɛnte) *adj* inherent.

inerpicarsi (inerpi'karsi) *vr* climb.

inerte (i'nɛrte) *adj* inert. **inerzia** (i'nɛrtsja) *nf* inertia.

inesatto (ine'zatto) *adj* inexact.

inescusabile (inesku'zabile) *adj* inexcusable.

inesistente (inezis'tɛnte) *adj* non-existent.

inesorabile (inezo'rabile) *adj* inexorable.

inesperto (ines'pɛrto) *adj* inexperienced.

inesplicabile (inespli'kabile) *adj* inexplicable.

inetto (i'nɛtto) *adj* 1 inept. 2 unsuited.

inevitabile (inevi'tabile) *adj* inevitable.

inezia (i'nɛttsja) *nf* trifle, thing of no importance.

infagottare (infagot'tare) *vt* bundle up.

infallibile (infal'libile) *adj* infallible.

infame (in'fame) *adj* infamous.

infangare (infan'gare) *vt* spatter with mud.

infante (in'fante) *nm* infant. **infanzia** (in'fantsja) *nf* 1 infancy. 2 childhood. 3 children.

infarcire (infar'tʃire) *vt* stuff, cram.

infarinare (infari'nare) *vt* coat with flour.

infastidire (infasti'dire) *vt* annoy.

infatti (in'fatti) *adv* in fact.

infatuarsi (infatu'arsi) *vr* become infatuated.

infedele (infe'dele) *adj* unfaithful. **infedeltà** *nf* infidelity.

infelice (infe'litʃe) *adj* unhappy, unfortunate. **infelicità** *nf* unhappiness.

inferiore (infe'rjore) *adj* 1 lower. 2 inferior. **inferiorità** *nf* inferiority. **complesso d'inferiorità** *nm* inferiority complex.

infermeria (inferme'ria) *nf* sick bay. **infermiera** (infer'mjera) *nf* nurse. **infermiere** (infer'mjere) *nm* male nurse.

inferno (in'fɛrno) *nm* hell. **infernale** *adj* infernal.

infestare (infes'tare) *vt* infest.

infettare (infet'tare) *vt* infect. **infezione** *nf* infection.

infiacchire (infjak'kire) *vt* weaken.

infiammare (infjam'mare) *vt* inflame. **infiammarsi** *vr* 1 flare up. 2 *med* be inflamed. **infiammazione** *nf* inflammation.

infido (in'fido) *adj* unreliable.

infilare (infi'lare) *vt* 1 thread. 2 insert. **infilarsi** *vr* put on.

infiltrarsi (infil'trarsi) *vr* infiltrate.

infimo ('infimo) *adj* lowest.

infine (in'fine) *adv* at last.

infinito (infi'nito) *adj* infinite.

infischiarsi (infis'kjarsi) *vr* not to care.

inflazione (inflat'tsjone) *nf* inflation.

inflessibile (infles'sibile) *adj* inflexible.

infliggere* (in'fliddʒere) *vt* inflict.

influenzare (influen'tsare) *vt* influence. **influenza** (influ'ɛntsa) *nf* 1 influence. 2 influenza.

influire (influ'ire) *vi* have an influence.

infondato (infon'dato) *adj* unfounded.

informare (infor'mare) *vt* inform. **informarsi** *vr* make enquiries. **informazioni** *nf pl* information.

informe (in'forme) *adj* shapeless.

informicolirsi (informiko'lirsi) *vr* have pins and needles.

infornare (infor'nare) *vt* put in oven. **infornata** *nf* 1 batch (of bread). 2 group.

infortunio (infor'tunjo) *nm* accident.

infossato (infos'sato) *adj* hollow, sunken.

inframmettersi* (inframmet'tersi) *vr* interfere.

infrangere* (in'frandʒere) *vt* break. **infrangibile** (infran'dʒibile) *adj* unbreakable.

infrazione (infrat'tsjone) *nf* violation.

infreddarsi (infred'darsi) *vr* catch cold.

infuriare (infu'rjare) *vi* become angry. **infuriarsi** *vr* fly into a temper.

ingannare (ingan'nare) *vt* deceive, cheat. **inganno** *nm* deceit.

ingegnarsi (indʒeɲ'ɲarsi) *vr* strive. **ingegno** *nm* 1 intelligence. 2 talent. **ingegnoso** (indʒeɲ'ɲoso) *adj* ingenious.

ingegnere (indʒeɲ'ɲɛre) *nm* engineer. **ingegneria** *nf* engineering.

ingenuo (in'dʒɛnuo) *adj* naive, simple.

ingerirsi (indʒe'rirsi) *vr* meddle.

Inghilterra (ingil'tɛrra) *nf* England.

inghiottire (ingjot'tire) *vt* swallow.

inginocchiarsi (indʒinok'kjarsi) *vr* kneel (down).

ingiù (in'dʒu) *adv* 1 downwards. 2 down.

ingiuriare (indʒu'rjare) *vt* insult. **ingiuria** (in'dʒurja) *nf* insult. **ingiurioso** (indʒu'rjoso) *adj* insulting.

ingiusto (in'dʒusto) *adj* unjust, unfair. **ingiustizia** (indʒus'tittsja) *nf* injustice.

inglese (in'glese) *adj* English. *nm* 1 Englishman. 2 English (language).

ingoiare (ingo'jare) *vt* swallow, gulp.

ingombrare (ingom'brare) *vt* block, obstruct. **ingombro** *nm* obstacle.

ingommare (ingom'mare) *vt* gum.

ingordo (in'gordo) *adj* voracious.

ingorgarsi (ingor'garsi) *vr* be blocked or choked up. **ingorgo** *nm* blockage. **ingorgo stradale** traffic jam.

ingranare (ingra'nare) *vt* *mot* engage. **ingranare la marcia** put into gear.

ingrandire (ingran'dire) *vt* enlarge, increase, magnify. **ingrandimento** *nm* enlargement. **lente d'ingrandimento** *nf* magnifying glass.

ingrassare (ingras'sare) *vt* fatten. *vi* grow fat. **ingrassarsi** *vr* get fat.

ingrato (in'grato) *adj* 1 ungrateful. 2 disagreeable. **ingratitudine** (ingrati'tudine) *nf* ingratitude.

ingrediente (ingre'djɛnte) *nm* ingredient.

ingresso (in'grɛsso) *nm* entrance.

ingrossare (ingros'sare) *vt* enlarge. **all'ingrosso** *adv* 1 wholesale. 2 about.

inguine ('ingwine) *nm* groin.

inibire (ini'bire) *vt* inhibit. **inibizione** *nf* inhibition.

iniettare (injet'tare) *vt* inject. **iniezione** (injet'tsjone) *nf* injection.

inimicizia (inimi'tʃittsja) *nf* animosity.

inintelligibile (inintelli'dʒibile) *adj* unintelligible.

ininterrotto (ininter'rotto) *adj* unbroken.

iniziare (init'tsjare) *vt* 1 begin. 2 initiate. **iniziale** *adj,nf* initial. **iniziativa** *nf* initiative. **inizio** *nm* beginning.

innaffiare (innaf'fjare) *vt* water.

innalzare (innal'tsare) *vt* raise.

innamorare (innamo'rare) *vt* charm. **innamorarsi** *vr* fall in love. **innamorato** *nm* lover.

innanzi (in'nantsi) *adv* 1 before. 2 in front, ahead. **da oggi innanzi** from today onwards. ~*prep* before.

innato (in'nato) *adj* innate.

innegabile (inne'gabile) *adj* undeniable.

innestare (innes'tare) *vt* 1 graft. 2 vaccinate. 3 insert. **innestare la marcia** put into gear.

inno ('inno) *nm* 1 hymn. 2 anthem.

innocente (inno'tʃɛnte) *adj* innocent. **innocenza** (inno'tʃɛntsa) *nf* innocence.

innocuo (in'nɔkuo) *adj* harmless.

innovare (inno'vare) *vt* innovate.

innumerabile (innume'rabile) *adj* innumerable.

inoculare (inoku'lare) *vt* inoculate.

inoffensivo (inoffen'sivo) *adj* inoffensive.

inoltrare (inol'trare) *vt* forward. **inoltrarsi** *vr* advance.

inoltre (i'noltre) *adv* besides, moreover.

inondare (inon'dare) *vt* flood.

inoperoso (inope'roso) *adj* inactive.

inorridire (inorri'dire) vt horrify. vi feel horror.

inosservato (inosser'vato) adj unobserved.

inossidabile (inossi'dabile) **acciaio inossidabile** nm stainless steel.

inquadrare (inkwa'drare) vt frame. **inquadratura** nf shot (in a film).

inquietare (inkwje'tare) vt worry. **inquietarsi** vr become anxious. **inquieto** adj 1 anxious. 2 restless. **inquietudine** (inkwje'tudine) nf anxiety.

inquilino (inkwi'lino) nm tenant.

inquinare (inkwi'nare) vt pollute. **inquinamento** nm pollution.

insalata (insa'lata) nf salad. **insalatiera** (insala-'tjɛra) nf salad bowl.

insalubre (insa'lubre) adj unhealthy.

insanabile (insa'nabile) adj incurable.

insanguinare (insangwi'nare) vt stain with blood.

insaputa (insa'puta) **all'insaputa di** adv unknown to.

insaziabile (insat'tsjabile) adj insatiable.

insegna (in'seɲɲa) nf 1 flag, banner. 2 decoration. 3 sign (board).

insegnare (inseɲ'ɲare) vt 1 teach. 2 point out. **insegnamento** nm teaching. **insegnante** nm teacher.

inseguire (inse'gwire) vt pursue, chase.

insensato (insen'sato) adj stupid.

insensibile (insen'sibile) adj 1 imperceptible. 2 insensitive.

inseparabile (insepa'rabile) adj inseparable.

inserire (inse'rire) vt insert. **inserzione** nf 1 insertion. 2 advertisement, notice.

insetto (in'sɛtto) nm insect. **insetticida** nm insecticide.

insicuro (insi'kuro) adj unsure. **insicurezza** (insiku'rettsa) nf insecurity.

insidia (in'sidja) nf snare, trap.

insieme (in'sjɛme) adv,prep together.

insignificante (insiɲɲifi'kante) adj insignificant.

insinuare (insinu'are) vt insinuate.

insipido (in'sipido) adj insipid.

insistere* (in'sistere) vi insist, persist. **insistente** (insi'stɛnte) adj insistent.

insocievole (inso'tʃevole) adj unsociable.

insoddisfato (insoddis'fatto) adj dissatisfied.

insolente (inso'lɛnte) adj insolent. **insolenza** (inso'lɛntsa) nf insolence.

insolito (in'sɔlito) adj unusual.

insolubile (inso'lubile) adj insoluble.

insomma (in'somma) adv in short. interj well! for heaven's sake!

insonnia (in'sɔnnja) nf insomnia.

insopportabile (insoppor'tabile) adj unbearable.

instabile (in'stabile) adj unstable. **instabilità** nf instability.

installare (instal'lare) vt install.

insù (in'su) adv 1 up. 2 upwards.

insubordinato (insubordi'nato) adj insubordinate.

insudiciare (insudi'tʃare) vt dirty.

insufficiente (insuffi'tʃɛnte) adj inadequate.

insulina (insu'lina) nf insulin.

insultare (insul'tare) vt insult. **insulto** nm insult.

insurrezione (insurret'tsjone) nf rising, revolt.

intaccare (intak'kare) vt 1 cut into. 2 corrode.

intagliare (inta'ʎʎare) vt carve. **intaglio** nm carving.

intanto (in'tanto) adv meanwhile.

intascare (intas'kare) vt pocket.

intatto (in'tatto) adj intact.

integrale (inte'grale) adj complete. **pane integrale** nm wholemeal bread.

integrare (inte'grare) vt integrate. **integrazione** nf integration.

integro ('integro) adj 1 complete. 2 honest.

intelletto (intel'lɛtto) nm intellect. **intellettuale** adj,n intellectual.

intelligente (intelli'dʒɛnte) adj intelligent, clever. **intelligenza** (intelli'dʒɛntsa) nf intelligence.

intemperie (intem'pɛrje) nf pl bad weather.

intendente (inten'dɛnte) nm superintendent.

intendere* (in'tɛndere) vt 1 understand. 2 hear. 3 mean. 4 intend. **intendersi** vr 1 get on together, agree. 2 be an expert. **s'intende** of course.

intensificare (intensifi'kare) vt intensify.

intenso (in'tɛnso) adj intense. **intensità** nf intensity.

intento (in'tɛnto) adj intent, fixed. nm intent.

intenzione (inten'tsjone) nf intention. **avere l'intenzione di** intend. **intenzionale** adj intentional.

intercettare (intertʃet'tare) vt intercept.

interdire* (inter'dire) vt forbid, prohibit.

interessare (interes'sare) vt 1 interest. 2 concern. vi matter. **interessarsi** vr take an interest. **interessante** adj interesting. **interesse** (inte'rɛsse) nm interest.

interferire (interfe'rire) *vi* interfere. **interferenza** (interfe'rɛntsa) *nf* interference.

interiore (inte'rjore) *adj* interior, inner. *nm* interior, inside.

intermedio (inter'mɛdjo) *adj* intermediate. **intermediario** (interme'djarjo) *adj,nm* intermediary.

interminabile (intermi'nabile) *adj* endless.

internare (inter'nare) *vt* intern.

internazionale (internattsjo'nale) *adj* international.

interno (in'tɛrno) *adj* interior, internal. *nm* interior.

intero (in'tero) *adj* whole, complete, entire.

interpretare (interpre'tare) *vt* interpret. **interpretazione** *nf* 1 interpretation. 2 performance. **interprete** (in'tɛrprete) *nm,f* 1 interpreter. 2 performer.

interrogare (interro'gare) *vt* question, examine, interrogate. **interrogazione** *nf* 1 question. 2 interrogation.

interrompere* (inter'rompere) *vt* interrupt. **interruzione** *nf* interruption.

interruttore (interrut'tore) *nm* switch.

interurbano (inter'bano) *adj* inter-city. **chiamata interurbana** *nf* long-distance telephone call.

intervallo (inter'vallo) *nm* 1 space. 2 interval.

intervenire* (interve'nire) *vi* 1 happen. 2 take part, intervene. 3 *med* operate. **intervento** (inter'vɛnto) *nm* 1 intervention. 2 *med* operation.

intervistare (intervis'tare) *vt* interview. **intervista** *nf* interview.

intesa (in'tesa) *nf* 1 agreement. 2 understanding.

intestino (intes'tino) *nm* intestine.

intimidire (intimi'dire) *vt* intimidate.

intimo ('intimo) *adj* intimate.

intimorire (intimo'rire) *vt* frighten. *vi* be afraid. **intimorirsi** *vr* get frightened.

intingolo (in'tingolo) *nm* 1 sauce. 2 stew.

intirizzire (intirid'dzire) *vt* numb.

intitolare (intito'lare) *vt* 1 entitle. 2 dedicate. **intitolarsi** *vr* be called.

intollerabile (intolle'rabile) *adj* intolerable.

intollerante (intolle'rante) *adj* intolerant. **intolleranza** (intolle'rantsa) *nf* intolerance.

intonaco (in'tɔnako) *nm* plaster.

intontire (inton'tire) *vi* daze.

intoppare (intop'pare) *vi* stumble.

intorno (in'torno) *prep* around, round, about.

intorpidire (intorpi'dire) *vt* numb.

intralciare (intral'tʃare) *vt* hinder. **intralcio** *nm* obstacle.

intransitivo (intransi'tivo) *adj,nm* intransitive.

intraprendere* (intra'prɛndere) *vt* undertake. **intraprendente** (intrapren'dɛnte) *adj* go-ahead.

intrattenere* (intratte'nere) *vt* entertain. **intrattenersi** *vr* linger.

intravedere* (intrave'dere) *vt* catch a glimpse of.

intreccio (in'trettʃo) *nm* plot, story.

intrepido (in'trɛpido) *adj* bold, fearless.

intrigo (in'trigo) *nm* plot, intrigue.

introdurre* (intro'durre) *vt* 1 insert. 2 introduce. 3 show in. **introduzione** *nf* introduction.

intromettersi* (intro'mettersi) *vr* 1 intervene. 2 interfere. **intromissione** (intromis'sjone) *nf* 1 intervention. 2 interference.

intronare (intro'nare) *vt* deafen.

introspettivo (introspet'tivo) *adj* introspective.

introverso (intro'vɛrso) *adj* introverted. *nm* introvert.

intrusione (intru'zjone) *nf* intrusion. **intruso** *nm* intruder.

intuitivo (intui'tivo) *adj* intuitive. **intuizione** *nf* intuition.

inumano (inu'mano) *adj* inhuman, cruel.

inumidire (inumi'dire) *vt* damp, dampen.

inusitato (inuzi'tato) *adj* unusual.

inutile (i'nutile) *adj* useless.

invadere* (in'vadere) *vt* invade. **invasione** (inva'zjone) *nf* invasion. **invasore** *nm* invader.

invalido (in'valido) *adj* 1 invalid, not valid. 2 disabled. *nm* invalid.

invano (in'vano) *adv* in vain.

invariabile (inva'rjabile) *adj* invariable.

invecchiare (invek'kjare) *vt* age. *vi* age, grow old.

invece (in'vetʃe) *adv* 1 instead. 2 on the contrary. **invece di** instead of.

inventare (inven'tare) *vt* invent. **inventore** *nm* inventor. **invenzione** *nf* invention.

inverno (in'vɛrno) *nm* winter.

inverosimile (invero'simile) *adj* unlikely.

inverso (in'vɛrso) *adj* opposite, inverse.

invertebrato (inverte'brato) *adj,nm* invertebrate.

investigare (investi'gare) *vt* investigate. **investigatore** *nm* investigator. **investigazione** *nf* investigation.

investire (inves'tire) *vt* 1 invest. 2 assail. 3

knock down, run over. **investimento** *nm* 1 investment. 2 collision.

invetriare (inve'trjare) *vt* glaze.

inviare (invi'are) *vt* send. **inviato** *nm* 1 envoy. 2 correspondent. **invio** *nm* sending.

invidiare (invi'djare) *vt* envy. **invidia** *nf* envy. **invidioso** (invi'djoso) *adj* envious.

invigorire (invigo'rire) *vt* strengthen.

invisibile (invi'zibile) *adj* invisible.

invitare (invi'tare) *vt* invite. **invitato** *nm* guest. **invito** *nm* invitation.

involgere* (in'vɔldʒere) *vt* 1 wrap. 2 involve.

involontario (involon'tarjo) *adj* unintentional.

involto (in'vɔlto) *nm* package.

invulnerabile (invulne'rabile) *adj* invulnerable.

inzaccherare (intsakke'rare) *vt* splash with mud.

inzuppare (intsup'pare) *vt* soak.

io ('io) *pron 1st pers m,f s* l. **io stesso** *pron 1st pers s* myself.

iodio ('jɔdjo) *nm* iodine.

ione ('jone) *nm* ion.

ipnosi (ip'nɔsi) *nf invar* hypnosis.

ipnotizzare (ipnotid'dzare) *vt* hypnotize.

ipocondriaco (ipokon'driako) *adj,nm* hypochondriac.

ipocrisia (ipokri'zia) *nf* hypocrisy. **ipocrita** (i'pɔkrita) *adj* hypocritical. *nm* hypocrite.

ipoteca (ipo'tɛka) *nf* mortgage.

ipotesi (i'pɔtezi) *nf invar* hypothesis. **ipotetico** (ipo'tɛtiko) *adj* hypothetical.

ippica ('ippika) *nf* horseracing. **ippico** ('ippiko) *adj* of horses.

ippocampo (ippo'kampo) *nm* seahorse.

ippocastano (ippokas'tano) *nm* horse chestnut tree.

ippodromo (ip'pɔdromo) *nm* racecourse.

ippopotamo (ippo'pɔtamo) *nm* hippopotamus.

ira ('ira) *nf* anger.

iride ('iride) *nf* 1 rainbow. 2 *bot* iris. 3 *anat* iris.

Irlanda (ir'landa) *nf* Ireland. **irlandese** (irlan'dese) *adj* Irish. *nm* 1 Irishman. 2 Irish (language).

ironia (iro'nia) *nf* irony. **ironico** (i'rɔniko) *adj* ironic.

iraggiungibile (irraddʒun'dʒibile) *adj* unattainable.

irragionevole (irradʒo'nevole) *adj* unreasonable.

irrazionale (irratsjo'nale) *adj* irrational.

irregolare (irrego'lare) *adj* 1 irregular. 2 uneven.

irrequieto (irre'kwjɛto) *adj* troubled.

irresistibile (irresis'tibile) *adj* irresistible.

irresoluto (irreso'luto) *adj* irresolute.

irresponsabile (irrespon'sabile) *adj* irresponsible.

irrigare (irri'gare) *vt* irrigate. **irrigazione** *nf* irrigation.

irrigidire (irridʒi'dire) *vi* stiffen. **irrigidirsi** *vr* stiffen.

irritare (irri'tare) *vt* irritate. **irritabile** (irri'tabile) *adj* irritable. **irritazione** *nf* irritation.

irrompere* (ir'rompere) *vi* rush.

irto ('irto) *adj* 1 bristly. 2 bristling.

iscrivere* (is'krivere) *vt* enrol, register. **iscrizione** (iskrit'tsjone) *nf* 1 enrolment. 2 inscription.

Islanda (iz'landa) *nf* Iceland. **islandese** *adj* Icelandic. *nm* 1 Icelander. 2 Icelandic (language).

isola ('izola) *nf* island.

isolare (izo'lare) *vt* 1 isolate. 2 insulate. **isolamento** *nm* 1 isolation. 2 insulation.

ispettore (ispet'tore) *nm* inspector.

ispezionare (ispettsjo'nare) *vt* inspect. **ispezione** *nf* inspection.

ispirare (ispi'rare) *vt* inspire. **ispirazione** *nf* inspiration.

Israele (izra'ɛle) *nm* Israel. **israeliano** *adj,n* Israeli.

issare (is'sare) *vt* hoist.

istante (is'tante) *nm* instant. **istantaneo** (istan-'taneo) *adj* instantaneous.

isterico (is'tɛriko) *adj* hysterical. **isterismo** *nm* hysteria.

istinto (is'tinto) *nm* instinct. **istintivo** *adj* instinctive.

istituire (istitu'ire) *vt* institute, found. **istituzione** *nf* institution.

istituto (isti'tuto) *nm* institute. **istitutore** *nm* tutor. **istitutrice** *nf* governess.

istrice ('istritʃe) *nm,f* porcupine.

istruire* (istru'ire) *vt* instruct, teach. **instruttore** *nm* instructor. **istruzione** *nf* 1 instruction. 2 teaching, education.

Italia (i'talja) *nf* Italy. **italiano** *adj,n* Italian. *nm* Italian (language).

itinerario (itine'rarjo) *nm* route, itinerary.

itterizia (itte'rittsja) *nf* jaundice.

Iugoslavia (jugo'slavja) *nf* Yugoslavia. **iugoslavo** *adj,n* Yugoslav.

iuta ('juta) *nf* jute.

L

la[1] (la) *def art, fs* the.

la[2] (la) *pron* **1** *3rd pers fs* her, it. **2** *2nd pers m,f s fml* you.

là (la) *adv* there. **di là di** beyond. **più in là** further on.

labbro ('labbro) *nm* **1** *pl* **labbra** *f anat* lip. **2** *pl* **labbri** *m* lip, rim.

labirinto (labi'rinto) *nm* labyrinth.

laboratorio (labora'tɔrjo) *nm* **1** laboratory. **2** workshop.

laborioso (labo'rjoso) *adj* **1** laborious. **2** hard-working.

laburista (labu'rista) *nm* Labour Party member.

lacca ('lakka) *nf* lacquer.

laccio ('lattʃo) *nm* noose. **laccio delle scarpe** shoelace.

lacerare (latʃe'rare) *vt* tear.

lacrima ('lakrima) *nf* tear.

lacrimogeno (lakri'mɔdʒeno) **gas lacrimogeno** *nm* tear gas.

ladro ('ladro) *nm* thief, robber.

laggiù (lad'dʒu) *adv* down there.

lagnarsi (laɲ'narsi) *vr* complain, grumble.

lago ('lago) *nm* lake.

laguna (la'guna) *nf* lagoon.

laico ('laiko) *adj* lay, secular.

lama ('lama) *nf* blade. **lametta** *nf* razor blade.

lambiccarsi (lambik'karsi) *vr* **lambiccarsi il cervello** rack one's brains.

lambire (lam'bire) *vt* lick, lap.

lambrusco (lam'brusko) *nm* type of red wine.

lamentare (lamen'tare) *vt* lament. **lamentarsi** *vr* **1** complain, moan. **2** lament. **lamento** *nm* **1** lament. **2** complaint.

lampada ('lampada) *nf* lamp. **lampadina** *nf* light bulb.

lampeggiare (lamped'dʒare) *vi* **1** (of lightning) flash.

lampione (lam'pjone) *nm* streetlamp.

lampo ('lampo) *nm* **1** flash of lightning. **2** flash. **in un lampo** in a flash.

lampone (lam'pone) *nm* raspberry. **pianta di lampone** *nf* raspberry cane.

lana ('lana) *nf* wool.

lancetta (lan'tʃetta) *nf* **1** hand (of a watch). **2** pointer.

lancia[1] ('lantʃa) *nf* lance.

lancia[2] ('lantʃa) *nf* launch.

lanciare (lan'tʃare) *vt* **1** throw, hurl. **2** launch. **lancio** *nm* **1** throw. **2** launching.

languire (lan'gwire) *vi* **1** languish. **2** flag. **languido** ('langwido) *adj* **1** weak. **2** languid.

lanterna (lan'tɛrna) *nf* lantern.

lapide ('lapide) *nf* **1** tombstone. **2** plaque.

lapis ('lapis) *nm invar* pencil.

lardo ('lardo) *nm* lard.

largo ('largo) *adj* **1** wide, broad. **2** liberal. *nm* **1** breadth. **2** space. **3** open sea. **farsi largo** clear one's way. **larghezza** (lar'gettsa) *nf* **1** width, breadth. **2** generosity.

larice ('laritʃe) *nm* larch.

laringe (la'rindʒe) *nf* larynx. **laringite** *nf* laryngitis.

larva ('larva) *nf* larva.

lasagne (la'zaɲɲe) *nf pl* dish made of strips of pasta and covered with sauce.

lasciare (laʃ'ʃare) *vt* **1** leave. **2** let, allow. **3** abandon, give up. **4** keep. **5** leave. **lasciare cadere** drop. **lasciapassare** *nm invar* pass, permit.

lascivo (laʃ'ʃivo) *adj* lascivious.

lassativo (lassa'tivo) *adj,nm* laxative.

lassù (las'su) *adv* up there.

lastra ('lastra) *nf* **1** slab, sheet. **2** paving slab. **3** X-ray plate.

lastricare (lastri'kare) *vt* pave. **lastrico** ('lastriko) *nm* pavement.

latente (la'tɛnte) *adj* latent, hidden.

latino (la'tino) *adj,nm* Latin.

latitudine (lati'tudine) *nf* latitude.

lato[1] ('lato) *nm* side. **d'altro lato** on the other hand.

lato[2] ('lato) *adj* wide.

latrina (la'trina) *nf* public lavatory.

latta ('latta) *nf* **1** tin plate. **2** can, tin.

lattaio (lat'tajo) *nm* milkman.

latte ('latte) *nm* milk. **latteria** *nf* dairy. **lattiera** (lat'tjera) *nf* milk jug.

lattuga (lat'tuga) *nf* lettuce.

laurea ('laurea) *nf educ* degree. **laurearsi** (laure'arsi) *vr* graduate.

lauro ('lauro) *nm* laurel.

lava ('lava) *nf* lava.

lavagna (la'vaɲɲa) *nf* blackboard.

lavanda (la'vanda) *nf* lavender.

lavandaia (lavan'daja) *nf* washerwoman, laundress.

lavanderia (lavande'ria) *nf* laundry.

lavandino (lavan'dino) *nm* sink.

lavare (la'vare) *vt* **1** wash. **2** clean. **lavare a**

secco dry-clean. **lavapiatti** (lava'pjatti) *nm also* **lavastoviglie** *nf* dishwasher. **lavatrice** *nf* washing machine.

lavorare (lavo'rare) *vi,vt* work. **lavorante** *nm also* **lavoratore** *nm* worker. **lavoro** *nm* 1 work. 2 job.

le[1] (le) *def art, f pl* the.

le[2] (le) *pron* 1 *3rd pers f pl* them. 2 *3rd pers fs* to her or it. 3 *2nd pers m,f s fml* to you.

leale (le'ale) *adj* loyal. **lealtà** *nf* loyalty.

lebbra ('lebbra) *nf* leprosy. **lebbroso** (leb'broso) *nm* leper.

leccare (lek'kare) *vt* lick. **leccarsi le labbra** lick one's lips.

leccalecca (lekka'lekka) *nm* lollipop.

lecito (le'tʃito) *adj* permitted, allowed.

lega ('lega) *nf* 1 league. 2 alloy.

legale (le'gale) *adj* legal. *nm* lawyer. **legalizzare** (legalid'dzare) *vt* 1 legalize. 2 authenticate.

legare (le'gare) *vt* 1 tie (up), bind. 2 join. **legame** *nm* link, tie, bond. **legatura** *nf* binding.

legato (le'gato) *nm* legacy.

legge ('leddʒe) *nf* law, rule.

leggenda (led'dʒenda) *nf* legend.

leggere* ('leddʒere) *vt* read. **leggibile** (led'dʒibile) *adj* legible.

leggero (led'dʒero) *adj* 1 light. 2 slight. 3 agile. **leggerezza** (leddʒe'rettsa) *nf* 1 lightness. 2 agility.

leggiadro (led'dʒadro) *adj* 1 pretty. 2 lovely.

legione (le'dʒone) *nf* legion.

legislazione (ledʒizlat'tsjone) *nf* legislation. **legislativo** *adj* legislative.

legittimo (le'dʒittimo) *adj* legitimate.

legno ('leɲɲo) *nm* wood. **di legno** wooden. **legna** *nf* firewood. **legname** *nm* wood, timber.

lei ('lɛi) *pron* 1 *3rd pers fs* she, her, it. 2 *cap 2nd pers ms fml* you. **dare del lei** use the polite form of address. **lei stessa** *pron* 1 *3rd pers fs* herself, itself. 2 *cap 2nd pers fs fml* yourself. **Lei stesso** *pron* *2nd pers ms fml* yourself.

lembo ('lembo) *nm* 1 edge. 2 hem.

lente ('lɛnte) *nf* lens. **lente a contatto** contact lens.

lenticchia (len'tikkja) *nf* lentil.

lentiggine (len'tiddʒine) *nf* freckle.

lento ('lɛnto) *adj* 1 slow. 2 slack. **lentezza** (len'tettsa) *nf* slowness.

lenzuolo (len'tswɔlo) *nm* 1 *pl* **lenzuoli** *m* sheet. 2 *pl* **lenzuola** *f* pair of sheets.

leone (le'one) *n* 1 lion. 2 *cap* Leo.

leopardo (leo'pardo) *nm* leopard.

lepre ('lɛpre) *nf* hare.

lesbico ('lɛzbiko) *adj* lesbian.

lessare (les'sare) *vt* boil. **lesso** *adj* boiled. *nm* boiled beef.

lessi ('lessi) *v* see **leggere.**

lessico ('lɛssiko) *nm* lexicon, dictionary.

lesto ('lɛsto) *adj* 1 swift. 2 agile.

letame (le'tame) *nm* manure, dung.

letizia (le'tittsja) *nf* happiness.

lettera ('lɛttera) *nf* letter. **letterale** *adj* literal.

letterario (lette'rarjo) *adj* literary. **proprietà letteraria** *nf* copyright.

letteratura (lettera'tura) *nf* literature.

lettiga (let'tiga) *nf* stretcher.

letto[1] ('lɛtto) *v* see **leggere.**

letto[2] ('lɛtto) *nm* bed. **letto matrimoniale** double bed.

lettore (let'tore) *nm* reader.

lettura (let'tura) *nf* reading.

leucemia (leutʃe'mia) *nf* leukaemia.

leva[1] ('lɛva) *nf* lever.

leva[2] ('lɛva) *nf* conscription.

levante (le'vante) *nm* east.

levare (le'vare) *vt* 1 raise, lift up. 2 remove. **levarsi** *vr* 1 rise, get up. 2 take off. **levarsi di mezzo** get out of the way. **levata** *nf* 1 rising. 2 postal collection.

levatoio (leva'tojo) **ponte levatoio** *nm* drawbridge.

levigare (levi'gare) *vt* smooth.

levriere (le'vrjɛre) *nm* greyhound.

lezione (let'tsjone) *nf* lesson.

lezioso (let'tsjoso) *adj* affected.

lezzo ('leddzo) *nm* stench.

li (li) *pron 3rd pers m,f pl* them.

lì (li) *adv* there. **essere lì lì per** be on the point of.

Libano ('libano) *nm* Lebanon. **libanese** *adj,n* Lebanese.

libbra ('libbra) *nf* pound (weight).

libellula (li'bɛllula) *nf* dragonfly.

liberale (libe'rale) *adj* liberal.

liberare (libe'rare) *vt* free, liberate. **liberazione** *nf* liberation.

libero ('libero) *adj* 1 free. 2 vacant. 3 open. **libertà** *nf* freedom, liberty.

Libia (li'bia) *nf* Libya. **libico** *adj,n* Libyan.

Libra ('libra) *nf* Libra.

libro ('libro) nm book. **libro mastro** ledger. **libreria** nf 1 bookshop. 2 bookcase. **libretto** nm 1 notebook, booklet. 2 libretto. **libretto di assegni** chequebook.

licenza (li'tʃɛntsa) nf 1 licence. 2 permission. 3 leave. 4 notice. 5 diploma.

licenziare (litʃen'tsjare) vt dismiss.

liceo (li'tʃɛo) nm high school, grammar school.

lichene (li'kɛne) nm lichen.

lido ('lido) nm shore.

lieto ('ljɛto) adj happy, joyful.

lieve ('ljɛve) adj light.

lievito ('ljɛvito) nm yeast.

ligustro (li'gustro) nm privet.

lilla ('lilla) adj invar lilac (coloured). nm 1 lilac (colour). 2 bot lilac.

limare (li'mare) vt file. **lima** nf file.

limitare (limi'tare) vt limit, restrict.

limite ('limite) nm 1 limit. 2 boundary.

limone (li'mone) nm 1 bot lemon. 2 lemon (colour). 3 lemon tree. **limonata** nf lemonade. **limonato** adj lemon (coloured).

limpido ('limpido) adj clear, limpid.

lince ('lintʃe) nf lynx.

linciare (lin'tʃare) vt lynch.

lindo ('lindo) adj neat.

linea ('linea) nf line.

lineamenti (linea'menti) nm pl features.

lingua ('lingwa) nf also **linguaggio** nm 1 tongue. 2 language. **linguistica** (lin'gwistika) nf linguistics.

lino ('lino) nm 1 flax. 2 linen. **linoleum** (li'nɔleum) nm linoleum.

liocorno (lio'kɔrno) nm unicorn.

liquidare (likwi'dare) vt 1 settle, pay. 2 sell off. 3 eliminate. **liquidazione** nf 1 settlement, winding-up. 2 sale. 3 elimination.

liquido ('likwido) adj,nm liquid.

liquirizia (likwi'rittsja) nf liquorice.

liquore (li'kwore) nm liqueur.

lira[1] ('lira) nf lira. **lira sterlina** pound sterling.

lira[2] ('lira) nf lyre.

lirico (liriko) adj lyric. nm lyric poet.

lisca ('liska) nf fishbone.

lisciare (liʃ'ʃare) vt 1 smooth. 2 caress. **liscio** adj 1 smooth. 2 (of a drink) neat.

liso ('lizo) adj worn out.

lista ('lista) nf 1 list. 2 strip. **listino** nm list.

litania (lita'nia) nf litany.

lite ('lite) nf 1 lawsuit. 2 quarrel, argument.

litigare (liti'gare) vi quarrel. **litigio** nm quarrel.

litorale (lito'rale) nm coast.

litro ('litro) nm litre.

liuto (li'uto) nm lute.

livellare (livel'lare) vt level. **livello** (li'vɛllo) nm level. **passaggio a livello** nm level crossing.

livido ('livido) adj livid. nm bruise.

Livorno (li'vorno) nf Leghorn.

livrea (li'vrɛa) nf livery.

lo[1] (lo) def art, ms the.

lo[2] (lo) pron 3rd pers ms him, it.

lobo ('lɔbo) nm lobe.

locale[1] (lo'kale) adj local.

locale[2] (lo'kale) nm 1 room. 2 pl premises. 3 place.

localizzare (lokalid'dzare) vt localize.

locanda (lo'kanda) nf inn. **locandiere** (lokan'djɛre) nm innkeeper.

locomotiva (lokomo'tiva) nf locomotive.

lodare (lo'dare) vt praise. **lode** nf praise. **lodevole** (lo'devole) adj praiseworthy.

logaritmo (loga'ritmo) nm logarithm.

loggia ('lɔddʒa) nf 1 balcony. 2 loggia. 3 masonic lodge.

logica ('lɔdʒika) nf logic. **logico** ('lɔdʒiko) adj logical.

logorare (logo'rare) vt wear out. **logoro** ('logoro) adj worn, worn out.

Londra ('londra) nf London.

longitudine (londʒi'tudine) nf longitude.

lontano (lon'tano) adj 1 distant, far away. 2 far. adv far away, far. **di lontano** from a distance. **lontano un chilometro** a kilometre away. **lontananza** (lonta'nantsa) nf distance.

lontra ('lontra) nf otter.

loquace (lo'kwatʃe) adj talkative.

lordo ('lordo) adj filthy.

loro ('loro) pron 1 3rd pers m,f pl they, them, to them. 2 cap 2nd pers m,f fml you, to you. poss adj 1 3rd pers pl invar their. 2 2nd pers pl fml invar your. poss pron 1 3rd pers pl invar theirs. 2 2nd pers pl fml invar yours. **loro stesse** pron 1 3rd pers f pl themselves. 2 cap 2nd pers f pl yourselves. **loro stessi** pron 1 3rd pers m pl themselves. 2 cap 2nd pers m pl yourselves.

losco ('losko) adj 1 squint-eyed. 2 shady, suspicious.

loto ('lɔto) nm lotus.

lottare (lot'tare) vi 1 struggle. 2 wrestle. **lotta** nf struggle. **lottatore** nm wrestler.

lotteria (lotte'ria) nf lottery.

lozione (lot'tsjone) nf lotion.

lubrificare (lubrifiˈkare) vt lubricate. **lubrificante** nm lubricant.

lucchetto (lukˈketto) nm padlock.

luccicare (luttʃiˈkare) vi shine, gleam.

lucciola (luttˈʃola) nf firefly.

luce (ˈlutʃe) nf light. **fare luce su** throw light on. **lucente** (luˈtʃente) adj shining.

lucerna (luˈtʃerna) nf oil lamp.

lucernario (lutʃerˈnarjo) nm skylight.

lucertola (luˈtʃertola) nf lizard.

lucidare (lutʃiˈdare) vt shine, polish.

lucido (ˈlutʃido) adj 1 shining. 2 lucid. **lucidità** nf lucidity.

luglio (ˈluʎʎo) nm July.

lugubre (ˈlugubre) adj gloomy.

lui (ˈlui) pron 3rd pers ms 1 he. 2 him, it. **lui stesso** pron 3rd pers ms himself, itself.

lumaca (luˈmaka) nf 1 snail. 2 slug.

lume (ˈlume) nm light.

luminoso (lumiˈnoso) adj luminous.

luna (ˈluna) nf moon. **luna di miele** honeymoon. **lunare** adj lunar. **lunapark** (ˈlunapark) nm invar amusements park.

lunedì (luneˈdi) nm Monday.

lungo (ˈlungo) adj 1 long. 2 slow. 3 thin, diluted. prep along. **di gran lunga** by far. **per lungo e per largo** far and wide. **lunghezza** (lunˈgettsa) nf length. **lungi** adv far.

luogo (ˈlwɔgo) nm 1 place. 2 position, site. 3 passage (in a book). **avere luogo** take place.

lupo (ˈlupo) nm wolf. **cane lupo** nm Alsatian. **lupo di mare** old salt, old sailor.

luppolo (ˈluppolo) nm bot hop.

lurido (ˈlurido) adj filthy.

lusingare (luzinˈgare) vt flatter. **lusinga** nf flattery.

Lussemburgo (lussemˈburgo) nm Luxembourg.

lusso (ˈlusso) nm luxury. **di lusso** de luxe, luxury. **lussuoso** (lussuˈoso) adj luxurious.

lustrare (lusˈtrare) vt polish, shine. **lustrascarpe** nm invar shoeshine boy. **lustro** adj shiny.

lutto (ˈlutto) nm mourning.

M

ma (ma) conj 1 but. 2 yet.

macabro (ˈmakabro) adj macabre.

maccheroni (makkeˈroni) nm pl macaroni.

macchia[1] (ˈmakkja) nf stain, spot.

macchia[2] (ˈmakkja) nf bush, scrub.

macchiare (makˈkjare) vt stain, spot. **macchiato** adj spotted. **caffè macchiato** nm coffee with a drop of milk.

macchina (ˈmakkina) nf 1 engine, machine. 2 car. **macchina da cucire** sewing machine. **macchina da scrivere** typewriter. **macchina fotografica** camera. **macchinetta** nf 1 cigarette lighter. 2 coffee percolator. **macchinista** nm engine-driver.

macchinare (makkiˈnare) vt plot.

macedonia (matʃeˈdɔnja) nf fruit salad.

macellare (matʃelˈlare) vt butcher, slaughter. **macellaio** nm butcher. **macelleria** nf butcher's shop. **macello** (maˈtʃɛllo) nm abattoir, slaughterhouse.

macina (ˈmatʃina) nf millstone. **macinare** vt grind, mill. **macinino** nm 1 coffee grinder. 2 pepper-mill.

Madera (maˈdɛra) nm Madeira wine.

madido (ˈmadido) adj damp, moist.

Madonna (maˈdɔnna) nf 1 Our Lady. 2 Madonna.

madre (ˈmadre) nf mother. **madreperla** (madreˈperla) nf mother-of-pearl. **madrina** nf godmother.

madrigale (madriˈgale) nm madrigal.

maestà (maesˈta) nf 1 majesty, grandeur. 2 cap Majesty. **maestoso** (maesˈtoso) adj majestic.

maestro (maˈɛstro) nm 1 master. 2 schoolteacher. adj 1 main. 2 skilful. **maestra** nf schoolmistress.

mafia (ˈmafja) nf Mafia. **mafioso** (maˈfjoso) nm member of the Mafia.

magari (maˈgari) adv 1 even. 2 perhaps. conj if only. interj if only it were so!

magazzino (magadˈdzino) nm warehouse.

maggio (ˈmaddʒo) nm May. **primo maggio** nm May Day.

maggiorana (maddʒoˈrana) nf marjoram.

maggiore (madˈdʒore) adj 1 greater. 2 bigger. 3 older. 4 greatest. 5 biggest. 6 oldest. nm mil major. **maggiordomo** (maddʒorˈdɔmo) nm butler. **maggiorenne** (maddʒoˈrɛnne) adj law of age.

magia (maˈdʒia) nf magic. **magico** (ˈmadʒiko) adj magic, magical.

magistero (madʒisˈtɛro) nm 1 skill. 2 teaching profession.

magistrato (madʒisˈtrato) nm magistrate.

maglia (ˈmaʎʎa) nf 1 stitch, link. 2 pullover. 3 vest. **lavorare a maglia** knit.

magnete (maɲ'ɲɛte) *nm* magnet. **magnetico** (maɲ'ɲɛtiko) *adj* magnetic.

magnetofono (maɲɲe'tɔfono) *nm tech* tape-recorder.

magnifico (maɲ'ɲifiko) *adj* splendid, magnificent.

magnolia (maɲ'ɲɔlja) *nf* magnolia.

mago ('mago) *nm* magician, wizard. **maga** *nf* sorceress.

magro ('magro) *adj* 1 thin. 2 scanty, meagre. 3 lean. **mangiare di magro** abstain from eating meat. **magrezza** (ma'grettsa) *nf* thinness.

mai ('mai) *adv* 1 ever. 2 never. **come mai?** how is that? **mai più** never again.

maiale (ma'jale) *nm* 1 pig. 2 pork.

maionese (majo'nese) *nf* mayonnaise.

mais ('mais) *nm* maize.

maiuscolo (ma'juskolo) *adj* (of a letter) capital. **maiuscola** (ma'juskola) *nf* capital letter.

malaccorto (malak'korto) *adj* imprudent.

malafede (mala'fede) *nf* bad faith.

malanno (ma'lanno) *nm* misfortune.

malapena (mala'pena) **a malapena** *adv* hardly.

malaria (ma'larja) *nf* malaria.

malato (ma'lato) *adj* 1 sick, ill. 2 sore. *nm* sick person, patient. **malattia** *nf* illness.

malavoglia (mala'vɔʎʎa) *nf* ill will.

malcontento (malkon'tɛnto) *adj* discontented. *nm* discontent.

male ('male) *nm* 1 evil, wrong. 2 ache, pain. **andare a male** go bad. **di male in peggio** from bad to worse. **mal di denti** toothache. **mal di gola** sore throat. **mal di mare** seasickness. **mal di testa** headache. *adv* 1 badly. 2 ill. **non c'è male** not too bad.

maledire* (male'dire) *vt* curse. **maledetto** *adj* cursed. **maledizione** *nf* curse.

maleducato (maledu'kato) *adj* rude, ill-bred.

malefico (ma'lɛfiko) *adj* malign.

malerba (ma'lɛrba) *nf* weed.

malessere (ma'lɛssere) *nm* 1 uneasiness. 2 indisposition.

malevolo (ma'lɛvolo) *adj* malevolent. **malevolenza** (malevo'lɛntsa) *nf* malevolence.

malfamato (malfa'mato) *adj* notorious.

malfatto (mal'fatto) *adj* misshapen.

malfattore (malfat'tore) *nm* evildoer, criminal.

malfermo (mal'fermo) *adj* unstable.

malfido (mal'fido) *adj* unreliable.

malgrado (mal'grado) *prep* despite, in spite of. *conj* although.

malia (ma'lia) *nf* enchantment.

maligno (ma'liɲɲo) *adj* malignant.

malinconia (malinko'nia) *nf* melancholy. **malinconico** (malin'kɔniko) *adj* melancholy.

malinteso (malin'teso) *adj* misunderstood. *nm* misunderstanding.

malizia (ma'littsja) *nf* malice. **malizioso** (malit'tsjoso) *adj* malicious.

malmenare (malme'nare) *vt* ill-treat.

malnutrizione (malnutrit'tsjone) *nf* malnutrition.

malo ('malo) *adj* bad. **di mala voglia** *adv* unwillingly.

malsano (mal'sano) *adj* unhealthy.

malta ('malta) *nf* mortar.

malto ('malto) *nm* malt.

maltrattare (maltrat'tare) *vt* ill-treat.

malumore (malu'more) *nm* bad mood. **di malumore** in a bad mood.

malvagio (mal'vadʒo) *adj* evil.

malversare (malver'sare) *vt* embezzle. **malversazione** *nf* embezzlement.

malvolentieri (malvolen'tjeri) *adv* unwillingly.

mamma ('mamma) *nf* inf mummy, mum. **mamma mia!** my goodness!

mammella (mam'mɛlla) *nf* breast.

mammifero (mam'mifero) *nm* mammal.

mancare (man'kare) *vi* 1 lack, want. 2 miss, be missing. 3 fail. **non ci mancherebbe altro!** that's all we need! **mancante** *adj* 1 missing. 2 lacking. **mancanza** (man'kantsa) *nf* lack.

mancia ('mantʃa) *nf* tip, gratuity.

mancino (man'tʃino) *adj* 1 left. 2 left-handed. 3 disloyal.

mandare (man'dare) *vt* send. **mandare giù** swallow. **mandato** *nm* 1 mandate. 2 warrant.

mandarino[1] (manda'rino) *nm* mandarin.

mandarino[2] (manda'rino) *nm* mandarin, tangerine.

mandolino (mando'lino) *nm* mandolin.

mandorla ('mandorla) *nf* 1 almond. 2 kernel. **mandorlo** ('mandorlo) *nm* almond tree.

mandria ('mandrja) *nf* herd.

maneggiare (maned'dʒare) *vt* handle. **maneggio** *nm* 1 handling. 2 management.

manette (ma'nette) *nf pl* handcuffs.

mangano ('mangano) *nm* mangle.

mangianastri (mandʒa'nastri) *nm Tdmk* portable cassette recorder.

mangiare (man'dʒare) *vt* 1 eat. 2 corrode. 3 waste. 4 (in draughts, etc.) take. **mangiabile** (man'dʒabile) *adj* edible. **mangime** *nm* fodder.

mangiatoia (mandʒa'toja) nf manger.

mango ('mango) nm 1 mango. 2 mango tree.

mania (ma'nia) nf 1 mania. 2 obsession, craze. **maniaco** (ma'niako) adj 1 maniacal. 2 crazy. nm maniac.

manica ('manika) nf 1 sleeve. 2 cap English Channel. **essere un altro paio di maniche** be another kettle of fish.

manichino (mani'kino) nm tailor's dummy.

manico ('maniko) nm handle.

manicomio (mani'kɔmjo) nm lunatic asylum.

maniera (ma'njɛra) nf 1 way, manner, style. 2 pl manners. **in maniera che** so that. **manierato** adj affected.

manifattura (manifat'tura) nf 1 manufacture. 2 factory.

manifestare (manifes'tare) vt display, show. vi pol demonstrate. **manifestazione** nf pol demonstration. **manifesto** (mani'fɛsto) nm 1 poster. 2 manifesto.

maniglia (ma'niʎʎa) nf handle, knob.

manipolare (manipo'lare) vt handle, manipulate.

mannaggia (man'naddʒa) interj damn!

mano ('mano) nf,pl **mani** 1 hand. 2 power. 3 skill. 4 help. 5 coat (of paint). **alla mano** affable. **a mano** by hand. **battere le mani** clap. **di seconda mano** second-hand. **man mano** gradually. **sotto mano** at hand. **stringere la mano a** shake hands with. **manata** nf handful. **manicotto** (mani'kɔtto) nm muff. **manodopera** (mano-'dɔpera) nf labour. **manopola** (ma'nɔpola) nf knob. **manoscritto** (manos'kritto) nm manuscript. **manovella** (mano'vɛlla) nf handle.

manomettere (mano'mettere) vt ill-treat.

manovrare (mano'vrare) vt manoeuvre. **manovra** (ma'nɔvra) nf manoeuvre.

mansueto (mansu'ɛto) adj 1 tame. 2 meek.

mantello (man'tɛllo) nm cloak.

mantenere* (mante'nere) vt 1 keep, maintain. 2 support. **mantenimento** nm maintenance.

mantice (man'titʃe) nm bellows.

mantiglia (man'tiʎʎa) nf mantilla.

manuale (manu'ale) adj manual. nm manual, handbook.

manubrio (ma'nubrjo) nm 1 handle. 2 handle-bar.

manutenzione (manuten'tsjone) nf maintenance.

manzo ('mandzo) nm beef.

mappa ('mappa) nf map. **mappamondo** nm globe.

marca ('marka) nf mark. **marca di fabbrica** trademark.

marcare (mar'kare) vt 1 mark, note. 2 sport score.

marchese (mar'keze) nm marquis. **marchesa** nf marchioness.

marchio ('markjo) nm brand.

marcia[1] ('martʃa) nf 1 march. 2 mot gear. **marciapiede** (martʃa'pjede) nm 1 pavement. 2 platform.

marcia[2] ('martʃa) nf pus.

marciare (mar'tʃare) vi march.

marcire (mar'tʃire) vi go bad. **marcio** adj rotten, bad.

marco[1] ('marko) nm mark (coin).

marco[2] ('marko) nm mark, sign.

mare ('mare) nm sea, ocean. **mare grosso** heavy sea. **marea** (ma'rɛa) nf tide.

maremma (ma'remma) nf swamp.

maresciallo (mareʃ'ʃallo) nm marshal.

margarina (marga'rina) nf margarine.

margherita (marge'rita) nf daisy.

margine ('mardʒine) nm 1 edge, border. 2 margin.

marina (ma'rina) nf 1 sea. 2 coast. 3 navy. 4 Art seascape. **marinaio** nm sailor. **marino** nm marine.

marinare (mari'nare) vt marinade. **marinare la scuola** play truant.

marionetta (marjo'netta) nf puppet.

maritare (mari'tare) vt marry. **maritarsi** vr marry, get married. **maritale** adj marital.

marito (ma'rito) nm husband.

marittimo (ma'rittimo) adj maritime.

marmellata (marmel'lata) nf jam, marmalade.

marmo ('marmo) nm marble.

marra ('marra) nf hoe.

marrone (mar'rone) nm chestnut. adj brown.

marsupiale (marsu'pjale) nm marsupial.

martedì (marte'di) nm Tuesday. **martedì grasso** Shrove Tuesday.

martellare (martel'lare) vt,vi hammer. vi throb. **martello** (mar'tɛllo) nm hammer.

martire (mar'tire) nm,f martyr. **martirio** nm 1 martyrdom. 2 torment.

marxismo (mark'sizmo) nm Marxism. **marxista** adj,n Marxist.

marzapane (martsa'pane) nm marzipan.

marziale (mar'tsjale) adj martial.

marzo ('martso) nm March.

mascalzone (maskal'tsone) *nm* villain.

mascara (mas'kare) *nm* mascara.

mascella maʃ'ʃella) *nf* jaw.

mascherare (maske'rare) *vt* mask, conceal. **maschera** ('maskera) *nf* mask. **ballo in maschera** *nm* masked ball.

maschile (mas'kile) *adj* masculine, male, manly.

maschio ('maskjo) *adj* male, manly. *nm* **1** male. **2** boy.

masochismo (mazo'kizmo) *nm* masochism.

massa ('massa) *nf* pile, heap, mass.

massacrare (massa'krare) *vt* massacre. **massacro** *nm* massacre.

massaggiare (massad'dʒare) *vt* massage. **massaggio** *nm* massage.

massaia (mas'saja) *nf* housewife.

massiccio (mas'sittʃo) *adj* **1** solid. **2** huge. **oro massiccio** *nm* solid gold.

massima ('massima) *nf* maxim, rule.

massimo ('massimo) *adj* greatest. *nm* maximum. **al massimo** at the most.

massone (mas'sone) *nm* freemason. **massoneria** *nf* freemasonry.

masticare (masti'kare) *vt* chew.

mastro ('mastro) *nm* ledger.

matematica (mate'matika) *nf* mathematics. **matematico** (mate'matiko) *nm* mathematician. *adj* mathematical.

materasso (mate'rasso) *nm* mattress.

materia (ma'terja) *nf* **1** matter, material. **2** subject. **materiale** *adj,nm* material.

materno (ma'terno) *adj* maternal. **maternità** *nf* maternity, motherhood.

matita (ma'tita) *nf* pencil.

matriarcale (matriar'kale) *adj* matriarchal.

matrice (ma'tritʃe) *nf* **1** womb. **2** counterfoil.

matricolare (matriko'lare) *vt* enroll. **matricolarsi** *vr* matriculate. **matricola** (ma'trikola) *nf* **1** register. **2** first year student.

matrigna (ma'trippa) *nf* stepmother.

matrimonio (matri'monjo) *nm* marriage, matrimony. **matrimoniale** *adj* matrimonial.

matterello (matte'rεllo) *nm* rolling pin.

mattina (mat'tina) *nf also* **mattino** *nm* morning. **mattinata** *nf* **1** morning. **2** matinée.

matto ('matto) *adj* mad, crazy. *nm* madman.

mattone (mat'tone) *nm* brick. **mattonella** (matto'nεlla) *nf* tile.

maturare (matu'rare) *vi* **1** ripen. **2** mature. **maturità** *nf* maturity. **maturo** *adj* **1** ripe. **2** mature.

mausoleo (mauzo'lεo) *nm* mausoleum.

mazza ('mattsa) *nf* club.

mazzo ('mattso) *nm* bunch.

me (me) *pron 1st pers m,f s* **1** me. **2** myself.

meccanica (mek'kanika) *nf* mechanics. **meccanico** (mek'kaniko) *adj* mechanical. *nm* mechanic. **meccanismo** *nm* mechanism. **meccanizzare** (mekkanid'dzare) *vt* mechanize.

mèche (mεʃ) *nf* streak (in the hair).

medaglia (me'daʎʎa) *nf* medal.

medesimo (me'dezimo) *adj* same.

media ('mεdja) *nf* average. **in media** on average.

mediante (me'djante) *prep* by means of.

medicare (medi'kare) *vt med* treat, dress. **medicamento** *nm* treatment, remedy. **medicina** *nf* medicine. **medico** ('mεdiko) *nm* doctor. **medico condotto** panel doctor.

medio ('mεdjo) *adj* **1** middle. **2** average. *nm* middle finger. **scuola media** *nf* secondary school.

mediocre (me'djɔkre) *adj* **1** average. **2** mediocre. **mediocrità** *nf* mediocrity.

medioevo (medjo'εvo) *nm* Middle Ages. **medioevale** *adj* medieval.

meditare (medi'tare) *vt* **1** meditate upon. **2** ponder. *vi* meditate. **meditazione** *nf* meditation.

mediterraneo (mediter'raneo) *adj* Mediterranean. **(Mare) Mediterraneo** *nm* Mediterranean (Sea).

medusa (me'duza) *nf* jellyfish.

megafono (me'gafono) *nm* loudspeaker.

meglio ('mεʎʎo) *adv,adj invar* **1** better. **2** best. **tanto meglio** so much the better. ~*nm* best. **fare del proprio meglio** do one's best.

mela ('mela) *nf* apple. **melo** *nm* apple tree.

melagrana (mela'grana) *nf* pomegranate.

melanzana (melan'dzana) *nf* aubergine.

melassa (me'lassa) *nf* molasses.

melodia (melo'dia) *nf* melody.

melodramma (melo'dramma) *nm* melodrama. **melodrammatico** (melodram'matiko) *adj* melodramatic.

melone (me'lone) *nm* melon.

membrana (mem'brana) *nf* membrane.

membro ('mεmbro) *nm* **1** *pl* **membra** *f* limb. **2** *pl* **membri** *m* member.

memoria (me'mɔrja) *nf* **1** memory. **2** *pl* memoirs. **a memoria** by heart. **memorabile** (memo'rabile) *adj* memorable.

menare (me'nare) *vt* **1** lead, take. **2** deliver (a blow). **sapere a menadito** have at one's fingertips.

mendicare (mendi'kare) *vt,vi* beg. **mendicante** *nm* beggar.

meno ('meno) *adv* 1 less. 2 minus. 3 least. **a meno che** unless. **meno male** so much the better. **per lo meno** at least. **venire meno** 1 fail. 2 faint. ~*conj* except. *adj invar* 1 less, fewer. 2 least. *nm* least.

menopausa (meno'pauza) *nf* menopause.

mensa ('mɛnsa) *nf* canteen, refectory.

mensile (men'sile) *adj* monthly.

menta ('menta) *nf* mint.

mente ('mente) *nf* mind. **sapere a mente** know by heart. **mentale** *adj* mental. **mentalità** *nf* mentality.

mentire (men'tire) *vi* lie.

mento ('mento) *nm* chin.

mentre ('mentre) *conj* 1 while. 2 whereas.

menu (mə'ny) *nm also* **menù** menu.

menzionare (mentsjo'nare) *vt* mention. **menzione** *nf* mention.

menzogna (men'tsoɲɲa) *nf* lie.

meraviglia (mera'viʎʎa) *nf* amazement, wonder. **a meraviglia** wonderfully. **meraviglioso** (meraviʎ'ʎoso) *adj* wonderful. **meravigliarsi** *vr* be amazed.

mercante (mer'kante) *nm* merchant.

mercanzia (merkan'tsia) *nf* merchandise.

mercato (mer'kato) *nm* market. **a buon mercato** cheaply.

merce ('mɛrtʃe) *nf* goods.

mercenario (mertʃe'narjo) *adj,nm* mercenary.

merciaio (mer'tʃajo) *nm* haberdasher. **merceria** *nf* haberdashery (shop).

mercoledi (merkole'di) *nm* Wednesday.

mercurio (mer'kurjo) *nm* mercury.

merda ('mɛrda) *n tab* excrement *f.*

merenda (me'rɛnda) *nf* mid-afternoon snack.

meridiana (meri'djana) *nf* sundial.

meridionale (meridjo'nale) *adj* southern.

meringa (me'ringa) *nf* meringue.

meritare (meri'tare) *vt* deserve, merit, earn. **meritevole** (meri'tevole) *adj* deserving. **merito** ('merito) *nm* merit.

merletto (mer'letto) *nm* lace.

merlo[1] ('mɛrlo) *nm* blackbird.

merlo[2] ('mɛrlo) *nm arch* battlement.

merluzzo (mer'luttso) *nm* cod.

mero ('mɛro) *adj* mere.

meschino (mes'kino) *adj* 1 wretched. 2 scanty, poor, mean.

mescita ('meʃʃita) *nf* 1 bar. 2 public house.

mescolare (mesko'lare) *vt* 1 mix, blend. 2 shuffle (cards). **mescolanza** *nf* mixture.

mese ('mese) *nm* month.

messa[1] ('messa) *nf* Mass.

messa[2] ('messa) *nf* putting, placing. **messa in piega** (hair) set.

messaggio (mes'saddʒo) *nm* message, note. **messaggero** (messad'dʒɛro) *nm* messenger.

Messico ('mɛssiko) *nm* Mexico. **messicano** *adj,n* Mexican.

messo ('messo) *v see* **mettere.**

mestiere (mes'tjɛre) *nm* job, trade.

mesto ('mɛsto) *adj* sad.

mestolo ('mestolo) *nm also* **mestola** ('mestola) *nf* ladle.

mestruazione (mestruat'tsjone) *nf* menstruation. **avere le mestruazioni** have a period.

meta ('mɛta) *nf* aim, object.

metà (me'ta) *nf* half.

metabolismo (metabo'lizmo) *nm* metabolism.

metafisica (meta'fizika) *nf* metaphysics.

metafora (me'tafora) *nf* metaphor. **metaforico** *adj* metaphorical.

metallo (me'tallo) *nm* metal. **metallico** (me'talliko) *adj* metallic. **metallurgia** *nf* metallurgy.

metano (me'tano) *nm* methane.

meteora (me'tɛora) *nf* meteor.

meteorologia (meteorolo'dʒia) *nf* meteorology. **meteorologico** (meteoro'lɔdʒiko) *adj* meteorological.

meticcio (me'tittʃo) *adj,nm* half-breed.

meticoloso (metiko'loso) *adj* scrupulous, meticulous.

metodista (meto'dista) *nm* Methodist.

metodo ('mɛtodo) *nm* 1 method. 2 order. **metodico** (me'tɔdiko) *adj* methodical.

metro ('mɛtro) *nm* metre. **metrico** ('mɛtriko) *adj* metric.

metropoli (me'trɔpoli) *nf invar* metropolis. **metropolitana** *nf* underground, tube.

mettere* ('mettere) *vt* 1 put, place, set. 2 take (time). 3 suppose. 4 install. 5 put forth, sprout. **mettere in onda** transmit. **mettere su** set up. **mettersi** *vr* 1 place oneself. 2 put on. 3 begin.

mezzo ('mɛddzo) *adj* 1 half. 2 medium. *adv* half. *nm* 1 half. 2 middle. 3 means. **le due e mezzo** half past two. **mezzaluna** *nf* crescent. **mezzanotte** (meddza'nɔtte) *nf* midnight. **mezzogiorno** *nm* 1 midday, noon. 2 south. **mezz'ora** *adj,nf* half-hour.

mi (mi) *pron 1st pers m,f s* **1** me, to me. **2** myself.

mia ('mia) *poss adj, poss pron* see **mio.**

miagolare (mjago'lare) *vi* miaow.

mica ('mika) *adv* **mica male** not too bad. **non...mica** not at all.

miccia ('mittʃa) *nf* fuse.

micio ('mitʃo) *nm inf* cat.

microbo ('mikrobo) *nm also* **microbio** (mi'krobjo) microbe.

microfono (mi'krofono) *nm* microphone.

microscopio (mikros'kopjo) *nm* microscope.

midollo (mi'dollo) *nm anat* marrow.

mie ('mie) *poss adj, poss pron* see **mio.**

miei ('mjɛi) *poss adj,poss pron* see **mio.**

miele ('mjɛle) *nm* honey.

mietere ('mjɛtere) *vt* reap.

migliaio (miʎ'ʎajo) *nm,pl* **migliaia** *f* about a thousand.

miglio (miʎ'ʎo) *nm,pl* **miglia** *f* mile.

migliore (miʎ'ʎore) *adj* **1** better. **2** best. **miglioramento** *nm* improvement. **migliorare** *vt,vi* improve.

mignolo ('miɲɲolo) *nm* **1** little finger. **2** little toe.

migrare (mi'grare) *vi* migrate.

mila ('mila) *adj,n invar* thousands.

Milano (mi'lano) *nf* Milan.

milione (mi'ljone) *nm* million. **milionario** (miljo'narjo) *nm* millionaire. **milionesimo** *adj* millionth.

milite ('milite) *nm* soldier. **militare** *vi* **1** fight. **2** *mil* serve. *adj* military. **militante** *adj,nm* militant.

millantare (millan'tare) *vt* exaggerate. **millantatore** *nm* boaster.

mille ('mille) *adj,nm* thousand. **millennio** (mil-'lɛnnjo) *nm* millennium. **millepiedi** (mille-'pjɛdi) *nm invar* centipede. **millesimo** *adj* thousandth.

milligrammo (milli'grammo) *nm* milligram.

mimetizzare (mimetid'dzare) *vt* camouflage.

mimo ('mimo) *nm* **1** mimic. **2** mime.

minacciare (minat'tʃare) *vt* threaten. **minaccia** *nf* threat.

minare (mi'nare) *vt* **1** mine. **2** undermine. **mina** *nf* mine (explosive). **minatore** *nm* miner.

minareto (mina'reto) *nm* minaret.

minerale (mine'rale) *adj,nm* mineral.

minestra (mi'nɛstra) *nf* soup. **minestrone** *nm* thick vegetable and pasta soup.

miniatura (minja'tura) *nf* miniature.

miniera (mi'njɛra) *nf* mine, quarry.

minimo ('minimo) *adj* **1** least. **2** lowest. *nm* minimum.

ministero (minis'tero) *nm* **1** ministry. **2** office. **ministero degli affari esteri** Foreign Office. **ministero dell'interno** Home Office. **ministro** *nm* minister.

minore (mi'nore) *adj* **1** smaller, less. **2** younger. **3** minor. **4** smallest. **5** youngest. **minoranza** (mino'rantsa) *nf* minority. **minorenne** (mino-'rɛnne) *adj* under age. *nm law* minor.

minuetto (minu'etto) *nm* minuet.

minuscolo (mi'nuskolo) *adj* small, tiny. **minuscola** (mi'nuskola) *nf* small letter.

minuto¹ (mi'nuto) *adj* **1** minute. **2** precise. **al minuto** retail.

minuto² (mi'nuto) *nm* minute.

mio, mia, miei, mie ('mio, 'mia, 'mjɛi, 'mie) *poss adj 1st pers s* my. *poss pron 1st pers s* mine.

miope ('miope) *adj* short-sighted.

miracolo (mi'rakolo) *nm* miracle.

miraggio (mi'raddʒo) *nm* mirage.

mirare (mi'rare) *vt* gaze at, look at. *vi* aim. **mira** *nf* aim. **mirino** *nm* viewfinder.

miscela (miʃ'ʃɛla) *nf* mixture. **miscellaneo** (miʃʃel'laneo) *adj* miscellaneous.

mischia ('miskja) *nf* fray, fight.

mischiare (mis'kjare) *vt* mix.

miscuglio (mis'kuʎʎo) *nm* mixture.

miseria (mi'zɛrja) *nf* **1** poverty. **2** misery. **miserabile** (mize'rabile) *adj* wretched. **misero** ('mizero) *adj* **1** wretched. **2** poor.

misi ('mizi) *v* see **mettere.**

missile ('missile) *nm* missile.

missione (mis'sjone) *nf* mission. **missionario** *nm* missionary.

mistero (mis'tero) *nm* mystery. **misterioso** (miste'rjoso) *adj* mysterious.

mistico ('mistiko) *adj* mystical. **misticismo** *nm* mysticism.

misto ('misto) *adj* mixed. *nm* mixture.

mistura (mis'tura) *nf* mixture.

misurare (mizu'rare) *vt* measure. **misura** (mi'zura) *nf* **1** measure. **2** size, measurement. **a misura che** in proportion as. **su misura** made to measure.

mite ('mite) *adj* mild.

mito ('mito) *nm* myth. **mitologia** *nf* mythology.

mitra¹ ('mitra) *nf* mitre.

mitra² ('mitra) *nm* submachine gun.

mitragliatrice (mitraʎʎa'tritʃe) *nf* machine-gun.

mittente (mit'tɛnte) nm sender.

mobile ('mɔbile) adj movable, mobile. nm 1 piece of furniture. 2 pl furniture.

mobilio (mo'biljo) nm furniture.

mobilitare (mobili'tare) vt mobilize.

moda ('mɔda) nf fashion. **di moda** in fashion. **modista** nf milliner.

modellare (model'lare) vt model. **modella** (mo'dɛlla) nf Art model. **modello** (mo'dɛllo) nm 1 model. 2 pattern.

moderare (mode'rare) vt moderate. **moderato** adj moderate. **moderazione** nf moderation.

moderno (mo'dɛrno) adj modern, up-to-date. **modernizzare** (modernid'dzare) vt modernize.

modestia (mo'dɛstja) nf modesty. **modesto** (mo'dɛsto) adj modest.

modificare (modifi'kare) vt modify, alter.

modo ('mɔdo) nm 1 way, method. 2 mus key. 3 means. **a ogni modo** anyway. **in tutti i modi** in any case. **per modo di dire** so to speak.

modulare (modu'lare) vt modulate.

modulo ('mɔdulo) nm form.

mogano ('mɔgano) nm mahogany.

moglie ('mɔʎʎe) nf wife.

molecola (mo'lɛkola) nf molecule.

molesto (mo'lɛsto) adj annoying.

molla ('mɔlla) nf 1 spring. 2 pl tongs. **molletta** nf 1 clothes peg. 2 hairgrip.

molle ('mɔlle) adj soft.

mollusco (mol'lusko) nm mollusc, shellfish.

molo ('mɔlo) nm pier.

molteplice (mol'teplitʃe) adj 1 complex. 2 various.

moltiplicare (moltipli'kare) vt multiply.

moltitudine (molti'tudine) nf crowd.

molto ('molto) adj 1 much, a lot of. 2 pl many. 3 (of time) long. adv 1 much, a lot. 2 very.

momento (mo'mento) nm moment. **momentaneo** adj momentary.

monaco ('mɔnako) nm monk. **monaca** ('mɔnaka) nf nun.

Monaco ('mɔnako) nf Monaco. **Monaco di Baviera** Munich.

monarca (mo'narka) nm monarch. **monarchia** nf monarchy.

monastero (monas'tero) nm 1 monastery. 2 convent. **monastico** (mo'nastiko) adj monastic.

monco ('monko) adj 1 maimed. 2 incomplete.

mondezzaio (mondet'tsajo) nm rubbish tip.

mondo ('mondo) nm world. **mondiale** adj 1 world. 2 worldwide.

monello (mo'nɛllo) nm rascal.

moneta (mo'neta) nf 1 coin. 2 small change. **carta moneta** nf paper money.

monetario (mone'tarjo) adj monetary.

monocromo (mo'nɔkromo) adj monochrome.

monologo (mo'nɔlogo) nm monologue.

monopolio (mono'pɔljo) nm monopoly. **monopolizzare** (monopolid'dzare) vt monopolize.

monotono (mo'nɔtono) adj monotonous. **monotonia** nf monotony.

monsone (mon'sone) nm monsoon.

montaggio (mon'taddʒo) nm tech assembly.

montagna (mon'taɲɲa nf mountain. **montagnoso** adj mountainous. **montanaro** nm person living in the highlands.

montare (mon'tare) vi climb, mount. vt 1 mount. 2 assemble, put together. 3 whip (cream).

monte ('monte) nm 1 mountain. 2 pile, heap.

montone (mon'tone) nm 1 ram. 2 mutton.

monumento (monu'mento) nm monument. **monumentale** adj monumental.

mora ('mɔra) nf blackberry.

morale (mo'rale) nf morality. nm morale. **moralità** nf morality. **moraleggiare** (moraled'dʒare) vi moralize.

morbido ('mɔrbido) adj soft. **morbidezza** (morbi'dettsa) nf softness.

morbillo (mor'billo) nm measles.

mordere* ('mɔrdere) vt bite. **mordente** (mor'dɛnte) adj biting.

morfina (mor'fina) nf morphine.

morire* (mo'rire) vi die.

mormorare (mormo'rare) vi murmur, mutter.

moro ('mɔro) adj dark. nm Negro.

morsi ('mɔrsi) v see **mordere.**

morsicare (morsi'kare) vt 1 nibble. 2 sting. **morso** ('mɔrso) v see **mordere.** nm 1 bite. 2 sting. 3 horse's bit.

mortadella (morta'dɛlla) nf spicy pork sausage.

mortaio (mor'tajo) nm mortar.

mortale (mor'tale) adj 1 mortal. 2 deadly. nm mortal. **mortalità** nf mortality.

morte ('mɔrte) nf death.

morto ('mɔrto) v see **morire.** adj dead. nm dead man.

mosaico (mo'zaiko) nm mosaic.

mosca ('moska) nf fly.

moschea (mos'kɛa) nf mosque.

moschetto (mos'ketto) nm musket.

mossa ('mɔssa) nf **1** movement. **2** *game* move.

mossi ('mɔssi) v see **muovere.**

mosso ('mɔsso) v see **muovere.** adj agitated. **mare mosso** nm rough sea.

mostarda (mos'tarda) nf mustard.

mostrare (mos'trare) vt show, exhibit. **mostra** nf exhibition, show.

mostro ('mɔstro) nm monster. **mostruoso** (mostru'oso) adj monstrous.

motivo (mo'tivo) nm **1** cause, motive. **2** motif.

moto[1] ('mɔto) nm motion. **mettere in moto** start.

moto[2] ('mɔto) nf invar motorbike.

motocicletta (mototʃi'kletta) nf motorcycle. **motociclista** nm motorcyclist.

motocisterna (mototʃis'terna) nf mot tanker.

motore (mo'tore) nm motor, engine. **motorino** nm motorcycle.

motoscafo (motos'kafo) nm motorboat.

movesti (mo'vesti) v see **muovere.**

movimento (movi'mento) nm movement.

mozione (mot'tsjone) nf motion.

mozzare (mot'tsare) vt cut off.

mozzarella (mottsa'rɛlla) nf sweet Neapolitan cheese.

mozzicone (mottsi'kone) nm cigar or cigarette stub.

mucca ('mukka) nf cow.

mucchio ('mukkjo) nm heap, pile.

muco ('muko) nm mucus.

muffa ('muffa) nf mould, must.

mugghiare (mug'gjare) vi bellow, roar.

muggire (mud'dʒire) vi **1** moo. **2** bellow, roar. **muggito** nm roar.

mughetto (mu'getto) nm lily-of-the-valley.

mugnaio (muɲ'najo) nm miller.

mugolare (mugo'lare) vi **1** howl. **2** whine.

mulino (mu'lino) nm mill. **mulino a vento** windmill.

mulo ('mulo) nm mule.

multa ('multa) nf fine.

multicolore (multiko'lore) adj multicoloured.

mummia ('mummja) nf mummy.

mungere* ('mundʒere) vt milk.

municipio (muni'tʃipjo) nm **1** municipality. **2** town hall. **municipale** adj municipal.

munire (mu'nire) vt **1** fortify. **2** supply, provide. **munizioni** nf pl ammunition.

muoio ('mwɔjo) v see **morire.**

muori ('mwɔri) v see **morire.**

muovere* ('mwɔvere) vt,vi move. **muovere un passo** take a step. **muoversi** vr move, stir.

muraglia (mu'raʎʎa) nf **1** wall. **2** barrier.

muro ('muro) nm **1** pl **muri** m wall. **2** pl **mura** f city wall. **muratore** nm mason.

muschio ('muskjo) nm musk.

muscolo ('muskolo) nm muscle.

museo (mu'zɛo) nm museum, art gallery.

musica ('muzika) nf music. **musicale** adj musical.

muso ('muzo) nm snout.

mussolina (musso'lina) nf muslin.

mutande (mu'tande) nf pl pants, knickers. **mutandine** nf pl **1** bathing trunks. **2** pants.

mutare (mu'tare) vt change.

mutilare (muti'lare) vt mutilate.

muto ('muto) adj dumb, mute.

mutuo ('mutuo) adj mutual, reciprocal. nm loan.

N

nacchera ('nakkera) nf castanet.

nacqui ('nakkwi) v see **nascere.**

nafta ('nafta) nf diesel (oil).

nailon ('nailon) nm nylon.

nanna ('nanna) nf inf sleep.

nano ('nano) nm dwarf.

napalm ('napalm) nm napalm.

Napoli ('napoli) nf Naples. **napoletano** adj,n Neapolitan.

nappa ('nappa) nf tassel.

narcotico (nar'kɔtiko) adj,nm narcotic.

narice (na'ritʃe) nf nostril.

narrare (nar'rare) vt tell, relate. **narrativa** nf **1** narrative. **2** fiction. **narratore** nm narrative writer. **narrazione** nf narration, account.

nascere* ('naʃʃere) vi be born. **nascita** ('naʃʃita) nf birth.

nascondere* (nas'kondere) vt hide, conceal. **nascondersi** vr hide. **nascondiglio** nm **1** hiding place. **2** hide and seek.

nascosi (nas'kosi) v see **nascondere.**

nascosto (nas'kosto) v see **nascondere.** adj hidden. **di nascosto** secretly.

nasello (na'sɛllo) nm whiting.

naso ('naso) nm nose. **nasale** (na'sale) adj nasal.

nastro ('nastro) nm **1** ribbon. **2** tape. **nastro magnetico** recording tape.

nasturzio (nas'turtsjo) nm nasturtium.

natale (na'tale) adj native, natal. **natalità** nf birth rate.

Natale (na'tale) nm Christmas.

natatoia (nata'toia) nf fin.

natica ('natika) nf buttock.

nativo (na'tivo) adj,nm native.

nato ('nato) v see **nascere**. adj born. **nato morto** still-born.

natura (na'tura) nf 1 nature. 2 temperament. **naturale** adj natural. **naturalismo** nm naturalism.

naturalizzare (naturalid'dzare) vt naturalize.

naufragio (nau'fradʒo) nm shipwreck.

nausea ('nauzea) nf 1 nausea. 2 disgust. **nauseare** vt 1 nauseate. 2 disgust.

nautico ('nautiko) adj nautical.

navata (na'vata) nf nave.

nave ('nave) nf ship, boat, liner. **navale** adj naval.

navigare (navi'gare) vi sail. **navigazione** nf navigation.

nazionalizzare (nattsjonalid'dzare) vt nationalize. **nazionalizzazione** nf nationalization.

nazione (nat'tsjone) nf nation. **nazionale** adj national. **nazionalismo** nm nationalism. **nazionalista** nm nazionalist. **nazionalità** nf nationality.

nazismo (nat'tsizmo) nm Nazism. **nazista** nm Nazi.

ne (ne) pron 1 of him, her, it, or them. 2 about it or them. adv from there. partitive some, any.

nè (ne) conj neither, nor. **nè...nè** neither...nor.

neanche (ne'anke) adv,conj not even.

nebbia ('nebbja) nf 1 fog. 2 mist. **nebbioso** (neb'bjoso) adj 1 foggy. 2 misty.

necessario (netʃes'sarjo) adj essential, necessary. **necessità** nf necessity, need.

negare (ne'gare) vt 1 deny. 2 refuse. **negativa** nf negative. **negativo** adj negative.

negli ('neʎʎi) contraction of **in gli**.

negligere* (ne'glidʒere) vt neglect. **negligente** adj negligent. **negligenza** (negli'dʒɛntsa) nf negligence.

negoziare (negot'tsjare) vt negotiate. vi trade, deal. **negoziante** nm dealer. **negoziato** nm negotiation. **negoziatore** nm negotiator.

negozio (ne'gɔttsjo) nm 1 shop. 2 business.

negro ('negro) adj,n Negro.

nei ('nei) contraction of **in i**.

nel (nel) contraction of **in il**.

nell' (nel) contraction of **in l'**.

nella ('nella) contraction of **in la**.

nelle ('nelle) contraction of **in le**.

nello ('nello) contraction of **in lo**.

nemico (ne'miko) adj hostile. nm, pl **nemici** enemy.

nemmeno (nem'meno) adv,conj not even.

neo ('nɛo) nm beauty spot, mole.

neon ('nɛon) nm neon.

neonato (neo'nato) adj newborn. nm newborn child.

nepotismo (nepo'tizmo) nm nepotism.

neppure (nep'pure) adv,conj not even.

nero ('nero) adj black. nm 1 black. 2 cap Black.

nervo ('nɛrvo) nm nerve, sinew. **dare ai nervi** get on one's nerves. **nervoso** (ner'voso) adj 1 nervous. 2 excitable.

nessuno (nes'suno) adj 1 no, none. 2 any. pron invar no-one, nobody.

nettare ('nɛttare) nm nectar.

netto ('netto) adj 1 clean, pure. 2 net.

neutrale (neu'trale) adj neutral. **neutralità** nf neutrality. **neutralizzare** (neutralid'dzare) vt neutralize.

neutro ('nɛutro) adj 1 neuter. 2 neutral.

neve ('neve) nf snow.

nevicare (nevi'kare) vi snow. **nevicata** nf fall of snow.

nevischio (ne'viskjo) nm sleet.

nevrosi (ne'vrɔzi) nf invar neurosis.

nicchia ('nikkja) nf niche.

nichel ('nikel) nm invar nickel.

nicotina (niko'tina) nf nicotine.

nido ('nido) nm nest.

niente ('njɛnte) pron invar,nm invar nothing. adv not at all.

ninfa ('ninfa) nf nymph.

ninfea (nin'fɛa) nf waterlily.

ninna-nanna (ninna'nanna) nf lullaby.

ninnolo ('ninnolo) nm knick-knack, plaything.

nipote (ni'pote) nm 1 nephew. 2 grandson. 3 pl grandchildren. nf 1 niece. 2 grand-daughter.

nitido ('nitido) adj 1 clear. 2 bright.

nitrire (ni'trire) vi neigh.

no (nɔ) adv 1 no. 2 not.

nobile ('nɔbile) adj,nm noble. **nobiltà** nf nobility.

nocca ('nɔkka) nf knuckle.

nocciola (not'tʃɔla) nf hazelnut. **nocciuolo** (not'tʃwɔlo) nm hazelnut tree.

nocciolo ('nɔttʃolo) nm 1 kernel. 2 stone.

noce ('notʃe) nf walnut, nut. nm walnut tree.

nocivo (no'tʃivo) adj harmful.

nocqui ('nɔkkwi) v see **nuocere**.

nodo ('nɔdo) nm knot.

noi ('noi) pron 1st pers m,f pl 1 we. 2 us.

noialtri (pron 1st pers m,f pl **1** we. **2** us. **noi stessi** pron 1st pers pl ourselves.

noia ('nɔja) nf **1** boredom. **2** annoyance. **dare noia** annoy. **noioso** (no'joso) adj **1** boring. **2** irritating.

noleggiare (noled'dʒare) vt hire, rent. **noleggio** nm also **nolo** ('nɔlo) nm hire.

nomade ('nɔmade) adj nomadic. nm nomad.

nome ('nome) nm **1** name. **2** noun.

nominare (nomi'nare) vt name, elect. **nomina** ('nɔmina) nf nomination.

non (non) adv not. **non...che** only.

noncurante (nonku'rante) adj careless.

nondimeno (nondi'meno) conj nonetheless.

nonno ('nɔnno) nm inf grandfather, grandad, or grandpa. nm also **nolo** ('nɔlo) nm inf grandmother, grandma.

nono ('nɔno) adj ninth.

nonostante (nonos'tante) prep in spite of, despite.

non-ti-scordar-me nm invar forget-me-not.

nord (nɔrd) nm north. adj invar north, northern. **del nord 1** northern. **2** northerly. **verso nord** northwards. **nord-est** nm north-east. adj invar north-east, north-eastern. **del nord-est 1** north-eastern. **2** north-easterly. **nordico** adj northern. **nord-ovest** nm north-west. adj invar north-west, north-western. **del nord-ovest 1** north-western. **2** north-westerly.

norma ('nɔrma) nf **1** norm. **2** regulation.

normale adj normal, usual. **normalità** nf normality.

Norvegia (nor'vɛdʒa) nf Norway. **norvegese** adj,n Norwegian. nm Norwegian (language).

nostalgia (nostal'dʒia) nf nostalgia. **nostalgico** (nos'taldʒiko) adj nostalgic.

nostro ('nɔstro) poss adj 1st pers pl our. poss pron 1st pers pl ours.

notaio (no'tajo) nm notary.

notare (no'tare) vt **1** note (down), mark. **2** observe. **nota** ('nɔta) nf **1** note. **2** mark. **3** bill. **4** list. **notevole** (no'tevole) adj noteworthy.

notificare (notifi'kare) vt notify, inform.

notizia (no'tittsja) nf **1** piece of news. **2** pl news, information.

noto ('nɔto) adj well-known.

notorio (no'tɔrjo) adj notorious.

notte ('nɔtte) nf night. **notturno** adj nocturnal. **guardiano notturno** nm night-watchman.

novanta (no'vanta) adj,nm ninety. **novantesimo** adj ninetieth.

nove ('nɔve) adj,nm nine. **novecento** (nove-

'tʃɛnto) adj nine hundred. nm **1** nine hundred. **2** twentieth century.

novella (no'vɛlla) nf short story. **novelliere** (novel'ljere) nm short story writer.

novembre (no'vɛmbre) nm November.

novità (novi'ta) nf **1** novelty, innovation. **2** news.

novizio (no'vittsjo) nm novice.

nozze ('nɔttse) nf pl marriage, wedding.

nuca ('nuka) nf nape of the neck).

nucleo ('nukleo) nm nucleus. **nucleare** adj nuclear.

nudo ('nudo) adj **1** naked, nude. **2** bare, plain. nm nude. **nudismo** nm nudism. **nudista** nm nudist. **nudità** nf nudity.

nulla ('nulla) pron invar nothing. adv nothing.

nullo ('nullo) adj void, null.

numero ('numero) nm number. **numerico** (nu'mɛriko) adj numerical. **numeroso** (nume-'roso) adj numerous.

nuoccio ('nwottʃo) v see **nuocere.**

nuocere* ('nwɔtʃere) vi harm, hurt, damage.

nuora ('nwɔra) nf daughter-in-law.

nuotare (nwo'tare) vi swim. **nuotatore** nm swimmer. **nuoto** ('nwɔto) nm swimming.

nuovo ('nwɔvo) adj **1** new. **2** recent. **di nuovo** again.

nutrire (nu'trire) vt feed, nourish. **nutriente** (nutri'ɛnte) adj nutritious. **nutrimento** nm nourishment.

nuvola ('nuvola) nf cloud. **nuvoloso** (nuvo-'loso) adj cloudy.

O

o (o) conj or. **o...o** either...or.

oasi ('ɔazi) nf oasis.

obbedire* (obbe'dire) vt,vi see **ubbidire.**

obbligare (obbli'gare) vt oblige, compel. **obbligato** adj obliged, grateful. **obbligatorio** (obbliga'tɔrjo) adj compulsory. **obbligo** ('ɔbbligo) nm **1** obligation. **2** duty.

obeso (o'bɛzo) adj obese. **obesità** nf obesity.

obiettare (objet'tare) vt object. **obiettivo** (objet'tivo) adj,nm objective. **obiettore** nm objector. **obiezione** nf objection.

obitorio (obi'tɔrjo) nm mortuary.

oblio (o'blio) nm oblivion.

obliquo (o'blikwo) adj oblique, slanting.

obliterare (oblite'rare) vt obliterate.

oblò (o'blɔ) nm porthole.

oblungo (o'blungo) *adj* oblong.

oboe ('ɔboe) *nm invar* oboe.

oca ('ɔka) *nf* goose.

occasionare (okkazjo'nare) *vt* cause.

occasione (okka'zjone) *nf* opportunity, occasion. **oggetto d'occasione** *nm* bargain.

occhio ('ɔkkjo) *nm* eye. **a quattr'occhi** tete à tete. **dare nell'occhio** catch the eye. **occhiali** *nm pl* glasses, spectacles. **occhiali da sole** sunglasses. **occhiata** *nf* glimpse, glance. **occhiello** (ok'kjɛllo) *nm* buttonhole.

occidente (ottʃi'dɛnte) *nm* west. **occidentale** *adj* western

occorrere* (ok'korrere) *v imp* need. *vi* happen. **occorrente** (okkor'rɛnte) *adj* necessary. *nm* all that is necessary. **occorrenza** (okkor'rɛntsa) *nf* 1 need. 2 occasion. 3 occurrence.

occulto (ok'kulto) *adj* occult.

occupare (okku'pare) *vt* 1 occupy, take up. 2 use, employ. **occuparsi** *vr* busy oneself, concern oneself. **occupante** *nm* occupier. **occupato** *adj* 1 busy. 2 occupied, taken, engaged. **occupazione** *nf* 1 occupation. 2 job, employment.

oceano (o'tʃɛano) *nm* ocean.

ocra ('ɔkra) *nf* ochre.

oculista (oku'lista) *nm* oculist.

ode ('ɔde) *nf* ode.

odiare (o'djare) *vt* hate, detest. **odio** ('ɔdjo) *nm* hatred. **odioso** (o'djoso) *adj* hateful.

odo ('ɔdo) *v see* **udire.**

odorare (odo'rare) *vt,vi* smell. **odore** *nm* 1 smell. 2 *pl* herbs.

offendere* (of'fɛndere) *vt* offend, hurt. **offendersi** *vr* take offence. **offensiva** *nf* offensive. **offensivo** (offen'sivo) *adj* offensive.

offersi (of'fersi) *v see* **offrire.**

offerta (of'fɛrta) *nf* offer.

offerto (of'ferto) *v see* **offrire.**

offesa (of'fesa) *nf* offence.

officina (offi'tʃina) *nf* workshop.

offrire* (of'frire) *vt* offer.

offuscare (offus'kare) *vt* darken, obscure.

oggetto (od'dʒetto) *nm* object. **oggettivo** *adj* objective.

oggi ('ɔddʒi) *adv* today. **al giorno d'oggi** nowadays. **oggi a otto** a week today.

ogni ('oɲɲi) *adj* each, every. **in ogni modo** in any case. **ogni tanto** now and again.

Ognissanti (oɲɲis'santi) *nm* All Saints' Day.

ognuno (oɲ'ɲuno) *pron* each one, everyone, everybody.

ohimè (oi'mɛ) *interj* oh dear!

Olanda (o'landa) *nf* Holland. **olandese** (olan'dese) *adj* Dutch. *nm* 1 Dutchman. 2 Dutch (language).

olfatto (ol'fatto) *nm* sense of smell.

olimpiade (olim'piade) *nf* Olympic Games. **olimpico** (o'limpiko) *adj* Olympic.

olio ('ɔljo) *nm* oil.

oliva (o'liva) *nf* olive. **olivo** *nm* olive tree.

olmo ('olmo) *nm* elm tree.

oltraggiare (oltrad'dʒare) *vt* outrage, violate. **oltraggio** *nm* outrage, offence. **oltraggioso** (oltrad'dʒoso) *adj* outrageous.

oltre ('oltre) *prep* 1 beyond. 2 over. 3 besides. *adv* 1 ahead. 2 further.

oltrepassare (oltrepas'sare) *vt* exceed, overstep.

omaggio (o'maddʒo) *nm* homage.

ombelico (ombe'liko) *nm* navel.

ombra ('ombra) *nf* 1 shade, shadow. 2 ghost. **ombreggiare** *vt* shade.

ombrello (om'brɛllo) *nm* umbrella. **ombrellino** *nm* parasol. **ombrellone** *nm* beach umbrella.

omettere* (o'mettere) *vt* omit.

omicidio (omi'tʃidjo) *nm* murder. **omicida** (omi'tʃida) *nm* murderer.

omissione (omis'sjone) *nf* omission.

omogeneo (omo'dʒɛneo) *adj* homogeneous.

omosessuale (omosessu'ale) *adj,nm* homosexual.

oncia ('ontʃa) *nf* ounce.

onda ('onda) *nf* wave. **onde** ('onde) *adv* whence, from where. *pron* with or by which. *conj* so that.

ondeggiare (onded'dʒare) *vi* 1 undulate. 2 waver.

ondulare (ondu'lare) *vi,vt* wave, undulate. **ondulazione** *nf* 1 undulation. 2 (in hair) wave.

onesto (o'nɛsto) *adj* honest, decent. **onestà** *nf* honesty.

onice ('ɔnitʃe) *nf* onyx.

onnipotente (onnipo'tɛnte) *adj* omnipotent, almighty.

onomastico (ono'mastiko) *nm* name-day.

onore (o'nore) *nm* honour. **onorabile** *adj* honourable. **onorare** *vt* honour. **onorario** *adj* honorary. **onorevole** (ono'revole) *adj* honourable.

ontano (on'tano) *nm* alder.

opaco (o'pako) *adj* opaque.

opale (o'pale) *nm* opal.

opera ('ɔpera) nf 1 work. 2 mus opera.

operaio (ope'rajo) nm worker.

operare (ope'rare) vi work, act. vt med operate on. **operazione** nf operation. **operoso** (ope'roso) adj industrious.

opinione (opi'njone) nf opinion.

oppio ('ɔppjo) nm opium.

opponente (oppo'nɛnte) adj opposing. nm adversary.

opporre* (op'porre) vt oppose.

opportuno (oppor'tuno) adj timely.

opposizione (oppozit'tsjone) nf opposition.

opposto (op'posto) adj,nm opposite, contrary. **all'opposto** on the contrary.

oppressi (op'prɛssi) v see **opprimere.**

oppressione (oppres'sjone) nf oppression.

oppresso (op'prɛsso) v see **opprimere.** adj oppressed. **oppressivo** (oppres'sivo) adj oppressive.

opprimere* (op'primere) vt 1 oppress. 2 burden.

oppure (op'pure) conj or else.

opulento (opu'lɛnto) adj opulent.

opuscolo (o'puskolo) nm pamphlet.

ora[1] ('ora) nf 1 hour. 2 time. **che ore sono?** what time is it? **di buon'ora** early. **non vedere l'ora di** long to.

ora[2] ('ora) adv now, just now.

orale (o'rale) adj oral.

orario (o'rarjo) nm timetable.

orazione (orat'tsjone) nf oration.

orbene (or'bɛne) conj so, well.

orbita ('ɔrbita) nf orbit.

orchestra (or'kɛstra) nf orchestra.

orchidea (orki'dɛa) nf orchid.

ordinare (ordi'nare) vt 1 tidy, put in order. 2 order, command. 3 prescribe. 4 ordain. **ordinamento** nm regulation. **ordinazione** nf 1 ordination. 2 prescription.

ordinario (ordi'narjo) adj ordinary.

ordine ('ordine) nm 1 order. 2 command.

ordire (or'dire) vt plot, scheme.

orecchia (o'rekkja) nf dog-ear. **orecchio** nm ear. **orecchino** nm earring.

orefice (o'refitʃe) nm goldsmith.

orfano ('ɔrfano) adj,nm orphan. **orfanotrofio** (orfano'trɔfjo) nm orphanage.

organico (or'ganiko) adj organic.

organizzare (organid'dzare) vt organize. **organizzazione** nf organization.

organo ('ɔrgano) nm organ. **organista** nm organist.

orgasmo (or'gazmo) nm 1 orgasm. 2 agitation, anxiety.

orgia ('ɔrdʒa) nf orgy.

orgoglio (or'goʎʎo) nm pride, arrogance. **orgoglioso** (orgoʎ'ʎoso) adj proud, haughty.

orientare (orjen'tare) vt orientate.

oriente (o'rjɛnte) nm east. **orientale** adj eastern, oriental.

origano (o'rigano) nm oregano.

originare (oridʒi'nare) vi derive, originate.

origine (o'ridʒine) nf 1 origin, source. 2 cause. **originale** adj,nm original. **originalità** nf originality.

origliare (oriʎ'ʎare) vi eavesdrop.

orina (o'rina) nf urine.

orizzonte (orid'dzonte) nm horizon. **orizzontale** adj horizontal.

orlo ('orlo) nm 1 rim, edge. 2 hem.

orma ('orma) nf 1 footprint. 2 trace.

ormai (or'mai) adv 1 by now. 2 by then.

ormeggiare (ormed'dʒare) vt moor.

ormone (or'mone) nm hormone.

ornare (or'nare) vt decorate, adorn. **ornamento** nm decoration.

ornitologia (ornitolo'dʒia) nf ornithology.

oro ('ɔro) nm gold. **d'oro** golden.

orologio (oro'lɔdʒo) nm 1 clock. 2 watch. **orologio da polso** wristwatch.

oroscopo (o'rɔskopo) nm horoscope.

orpello (or'pɛllo) nm tinsel.

orribile (or'ribile) adj horrible, awful.

orrore (or'rore) nm horror.

orso ('orso) nm bear. **orso polare** polar bear.

ortica (or'tika) nf nettle.

orto ('ɔrto) nm garden, market garden. **orticultura** nf horticulture.

ortodosso (orto'dɔsso) adj orthodox.

ortografia (ortogra'fia) nf spelling.

orzo ('ɔrdzo) nm barley. **orzata** nf barley water.

osare (o'zare) vt,vi dare.

osceno (oʃ'ʃɛno) adj obscene. **oscenità** nf obscenity.

oscillare (oʃʃil'lare) vi 1 sway, swing. 2 vary. 3 hesitate.

oscurare (osku'rare) vt darken, obscure. **oscuramento** nm blackout. **oscurità** nf 1 darkness. 2 obscurity. **oscuro** adj 1 dark. 2 obscure.

ospedale (ospe'dale) nm hospital.

ospitare (ospi'tare) vt lodge, put up.

ospite ('ɔspite) nm 1 host. 2 guest. **ospitale**

adj hospitable, friendly. **ospitalità** *nf* hospitality.

ospizio (os'pittsjo) *nm* 1 (establishment) home. 2 hostel.

ossequio (os'sɛkwjo) *nm* respect, reverence.

osservare (osser'vare) *vt* 1 observe. 2 note, remark. **osservatore** *nm* observer. **osservatorio** (osserva'tɔrjo) *nm* observatory. **osservazione** *nf* observation.

ossessionare (ossessjo'nare) *vt* obsess. **ossessione** *nf* obsession. **ossesso** (os'sɛsso) *adj* obsessed.

ossia (os'sia) *conj* or rather.

ossigeno (os'sidʒeno) *nm* oxygen. **ossigenato** *adj* bleached.

osso ('ɔsso) *nm* 1 *pl* **ossi** *m* (of animals or figurative) bone. 2 *pl* **ossa** *f anat* bone. **ossatura** *nf* framework. **ossobuco** *nm* 1 marrow bone. 2 dish made with this.

ostacolare (ostako'lare) *vt* hinder, impede. **ostacolo** (os'takolo) *nm* obstacle.

ostaggio (os'taddʒo) *nm* hostage.

oste ('ɔste) *nm* innkeeper.

ostello (os'tɛllo) *nm* **ostello della gioventù** youth hostel.

osteria (oste'ria) *nf* inn.

ostetrica (os'tɛtrika) *nf* midwife.

ostile (os'tile) *adj* hostile. **ostilità** *nf* hostility.

ostinarsi (osti'narsi) *vr* persist. **ostinato** *adj* obstinate. **ostinazione** *nf* obstinacy.

ostrica ('ɔstrika) *nf* oyster.

ostruire (ostru'ire) *vt* block.

ottagono (ot'tagono) *nm* octagon. **ottagonale** *adj* octagonal.

ottano (ot'tano) *nm* octane.

ottanta (ot'tanta) *adj,nm* eighty. **ottantesimo** *adj* eightieth.

ottava (ot'tava) *nf* octave.

ottenere* (otte'nere) *vt* gain, get, obtain.

ottico ('ɔttiko) *nm* optician.

ottimo ('ɔttimo) *adj* excellent, very good. *nm* best. **ottimismo** *nm* optimism. **ottimista** *nm* optimist.

otto ('ɔtto) *adj,nm* eight. **ottocento** (otto'tʃento) *adj* eight hundred. *nm* 1 eight hundred. 2 nineteenth century. **ottavo** *adj* eighth.

ottobre (ot'tobre) *nm* October.

ottone (ot'tone) *nm* brass.

otturare (ottu'rare) *vt* fill (a tooth).

ottuso (ot'tuzo) *adj* blunt.

ovaia (o'vaja) *nf* ovary.

ovale (o'vale) *adj* oval.

ovatta (o'vatta) *nf* cottonwool.

ovazione (ovat'tsjone) *nf* ovation.

ovest ('ɔvest) *nm* west. *adj invar* west, western. **del ovest** 1 western. 2 westerly. **verso ovest** westwards.

ovile (o'vile) *nm* sheepfold.

ovulo ('ɔvulo) *nm* ovule.

ovvero (ov'vero) *conj* or else.

ovvio ('ɔvvjo) *adj* obvious.

oziare (ot'tsjare) *vi* idle. **ozio** ('ɔttsjo) *nm* 1 idleness. 2 leisure. **ozioso** (ot'tsjoso) *adj* idle.

P

pacchetto (pak'ketto) *nm* packet.

pacco ('pakko) *nm* parcel, package.

pace ('patʃe) *nf* peace. **pacifico** (pa'tʃifiko) *adj* peaceful. **(Oceano) Pacifique** *nm* Pacific (Ocean).

pacificare (patʃifi'kare) *vt* appease, pacify.

pacifismo (patʃi'fizmo) *nm* pacifism. **pacifista** *nm* pacifist.

padella (pa'dɛlla) *nf* frying pan.

padiglione (padiʎ'ʎone) *nm* 1 pavilion. 2 tent.

Padova ('padova) *nf* Padua.

padre ('padre) *nm* father. **padrino** *nm* godfather.

padrone (pa'drone) *nm* 1 owner, boss. 2 landlord.

paesaggio (pae'zaddʒo) *nm* landscape.

paese (pa'eze) *nm* 1 country. 2 village. **paesano** *nm* countryman.

paffuto (paf'futo) *adj* puffy.

pagaia (pa'gaja) *nf* paddle.

pagano (pa'gano) *adj,nm* pagan.

pagare (pa'gare) *vt* pay. **paga** *nf* pay, payment, salary. **pagamento** *nm* payment.

pagella (pa'dʒɛlla) *nf* report card.

paggio ('paddʒo) *nm* 1 page. 2 pageboy.

pagina ('padʒina) *nf* page (of a book).

paglia ('paʎʎa) *nf* straw. **paglietta** *nf* 1 steel wool. 2 boater (hat).

pagliaccio (paʎ'ʎattʃo) *nm* clown.

pagnotta (paɲ'ɲotta) *nf* round loaf.

pagoda (pa'gɔda) *nf* pagoda.

paio[1] ('pajo) *nm* pair.

paio[2] ('pajo) *v see* **parere.**

pala ('pala) *nf also* **paletta** shovel.

palato (pa'lato) *nm* palate.

palazzo (pa'lattso) *nm* **1** palace. **2** block, building.

palchetto (pal'ketto) *nm* **1** shelf. **2** *Th* box.

palco ('palco) *nm* **1** platform. **2** *Th* box. **palcoscenico** (palkoʃ'ʃɛniko) *nm* stage.

palese (pa'leze) *adj* clear, evident.

palestra (pa'lɛstra) *nf* gymnasium.

palio ('paljo) *nm* horserace at Siena.

palla ('palla) *nf* **1** ball. **2** bullet. **pallacanestro** (pallaka'nɛstro) *nf* basketball. **pallavolo** *nf* volleyball.

palleggiare (palled'dʒare) *vi sport* dribble.

pallido ('pallido) *adj* pale. **pallidezza** (palli'dettsa) *nf* paleness.

pallone (pal'lone) *nm* football. **palloncino** *nm* toy balloon.

pallottola (pal'lɔttola) *nf* **1** pellet. **2** bullet.

palma[1] ('palma) *nf also* **palmo** *nm anat* palm.

palma[2] ('palma) *nf bot* palm.

palo ('palo) *nm* pole, post.

palombaro (palom'baro) *nm* diver.

palpare (pal'pare) *vt* touch, feel.

palpebra ('palpebra) *nf* eyelid.

palpitare (palpi'tare) *vi* throb, palpitate. **palpito** ('palpito) *nm* beat.

paltò (pal'tɔ) *nm invar* overcoat.

palude (pa'lude) *nf* marsh.

panca ('panka) *nf* bench. **pancone** *nm* workbench.

pancetta (pan'tʃetta) *nf* bacon.

panchina (pan'kina) *nf* garden seat.

pancia ('pantʃa) *nf* belly. **panciotto** (pan'tʃɔtto) *nm* waistcoat.

pancreas ('pankreas) *nm invar* pancreas.

panda ('panda) *nm invar* panda.

pane ('pane) *nm* **1** bread. **2** loaf of bread. **pane grattato** *nm* breadcrumbs. **panforte** (pan'fɔrte) *nm* gingerbread. **panino** *nm* roll. **panino imbottito** sandwich.

panico ('paniko) *nm* panic.

paniere (pa'njere) *nm* basket.

panna[1] ('panna) *nf* cream. **panna montata** whipped cream.

panna[2] ('panna) *nf mot* breakdown.

panneggiare (panned'dʒare) *vt,vi* drape.

pannello (pan'nɛllo) *nm* panel.

panno ('panno) *nm* **1** cloth. **2** *pl* clothes. **pannolino** *nm* **1** nappy. **2** sanitary towel.

panorama (pano'rama) *nm* view, panorama.

pantaloni (panta'loni) *nm pl* trousers.

pantera (pan'tɛra) *nf* panther.

pantofola (pan'tɔfola) *nf* slipper.

pantomima (panto'mima) *nf* pantomime.

papà (pa'pa) *nm inf* daddy, dad.

Papa ('papa) *nm* pope. **papale** *adj* papal. **papato** *nm* papacy.

papavero (pa'pavero) *nm* poppy.

papero ('papero) *nm* gosling.

papiro (pa'piro) *nm* papyrus.

pappagallo (pappa'gallo) *nm* parrot.

paprica ('paprika) *nf* **1** red pepper. **2** paprika.

parabola (pa'rabola) *nf* parable.

parabrezza (para'breddza) *nm* windscreen.

paracadute (paraka'dute) *nm invar* parachute. **paracadutista** *nm* parachutist.

paradiso (para'dizo) *nm* paradise, heaven.

paradosso (para'dɔsso) *nm* paradox.

parafango (para'fango) *nm* mudguard.

paraffina (paraf'fina) *nf* paraffin.

parafuoco (para'fwɔko) *nm* fireguard.

paragonare (parago'nare) *vt* compare. **paragone** *nm* comparison.

paragrafo (pa'ragrafo) *nm* paragraph.

paralisi (pa'ralizi) *nf invar* paralysis. **paralizzare** (paralid'dzare) *vt* paralyse.

parallelo (paral'lɛlo) *adj,nm* parallel.

paralume (para'lume) *nm* lampshade.

paranoia (para'nɔja) *nf* paranoia.

parapetto (para'pɛtto) *nm* parapet.

parare (pa'rare) *vt* **1** adorn. **2** ward off. **3** avert.

parasole (para'sole) *nm* parasol.

parassita (paras'sita) *nm* parasite.

parata[1] (pa'rata) *nf* **1** *sport* parry. **2** defence.

parata[2] (pa'rata) *nf* parade.

paraurti (para'urti) *nm invar* bumper.

paravento (para'vɛnto) *nm* screen.

parcheggiare (parked'dʒare) *vt* park. **parcheggio** *nm* **1** parking. **2** car park.

parchimetro (par'kimetro) *nm* parking meter.

parco[1] ('parko) *nm* park.

parco[2] ('parko) *adj* sparing, economical.

parecchio (pa'rekkjo) *adj* **1** a lot of, a good deal of. **2** considerable, some. *pron* a good many. *adv* much.

pareggiare (pared'dʒare) *vt* level, balance. *vi sport* draw. **pareggio** *nm* **1** balance. **2** *sport* draw.

parente (pa'rɛnte) *nm,f* relation, relative. **parentela** (paren'tɛla) *nf* **1** relationship. **2** relatives.

parentesi (pa'rɛntezi) *nf invar* **1** parenthesis. **2** bracket.

parere[*] (pa'rere) *v imp* **1** seem, appear. **2** think. *nm* opinion.

parete (pa'rete) *nf* wall.

pari ('pari) *adj invar* 1 equal. 2 same. 3 (of a number) even. **parità** *nf* parity.

Parigi (pa'ridʒi) *nf* Paris.

parlamento (parla'mento) *nm* parliament.

parlare (par'lare) *vi* speak, talk. *vt* speak.

parmigiano (parmi'dʒano) *adj,nm* Parmesan.

parodia (paro'dia) *nf* parody.

parola (pa'rɔla) *nf* 1 word. 2 speech. 3 promise. **parolaccia** (paro'lattʃa) *nf* bad word, swearword.

parrò (par'rɔ) *v* see **parere.**

parrocchia (par'rɔkkja) *nf* parish.

parroco ('parroko) *nm* parish priest.

parrucca (par'rukka) *nf* wig.

parrucchiere (parruk'kjɛre) *nm* hairdresser.

parsi ('parsi) *v* see **parere.**

parso ('parso) *v* see **parere.**

parte ('parte) *nf* 1 part. 2 portion, share. 3 side, direction. 4 *law,comm* party. **a parte** separately. **da parte** aside. **da una parte...d'altra parte** on the one hand...on the other.

partecipare (partetʃi'pare) *vi* 1 take part, participate. 2 share. *vt* announce.

participio (parti'tʃipjo) *nm* participle.

particolare (partiko'lare) *adj* 1 particular. 2 strange. 3 special. 4 private. *nm* detail.

partigiano (parti'dʒano) *adj,n* partisan.

partire (par'tire) *vi* leave, go away, depart. **a partire da oggi** starting from today. **partenza** (par'tɛntsa) *nf* departure.

partita (par'tita) *nf* game, match.

partito (par'tito) *nm* 1 choice. 2 match (marriage). 3 *pol* party.

partitura (parti'tura) *nf mus* score.

partorire (parto'rire) *vt* give birth to. **parto** *nm* birth, delivery.

parvi ('parvi) *v* see **parere.**

parziale (par'tsjale) *adj* partial.

pascere* ('paʃʃere) *vi* graze.

pascolare (pasko'lare) *vt,vi* graze. **pascolo** ('paskolo) *nm* pasture, meadow.

Pasqua ('paskwa) *nf* Easter.

passabile (pas'sabile) *adj* passable.

passaggio (pas'saddʒo) *nm* 1 passage. 2 crossing. 3 lift (in a car). **essere di passaggio** be passing through.

passare (pas'sare) *vi* 1 pass (by). 2 cease, stop. 3 go away. 4 happen. *vt* 1 pass. 2 exceed. 3 spend (time). 4 strain. **passante** *nm* passerby. **passaporto** (passa'pɔrto) *nm* passport.

passatempo (passa'tɛmpo) *nm* hobby, pastime. **passato** *adj,nm* past.

passeggero (passed'dʒero) *nm* passenger.

passeggiare (passed'dʒare) *vi* go for a walk. **passeggiata** *nf* 1 walk. 2 drive, run, excursion.

passerella (passe'rɛlla) *nf* 1 gangplank. 2 catwalk.

passero ('passero) *nm* sparrow.

passione (pas'sjone) *nf* passion.

passivo (pas'sivo) *adj* passive. **passività** *nf* passivity.

passo ('passo) *nm* 1 step. 2 excerpt, passage. **fare due passi** go for a short walk.

pasta ('pasta) *nf* 1 dough, pastry. 2 pasta. 3 cake. **pasta dentifricia** toothpaste. **pastasciutta** (pastaʃ'ʃutta) *nf* pasta (with sauce).

pastello (pas'tɛllo) *nm* pastel.

pasticca (pas'tikka) *nf* tablet.

pasticceria (pastittʃe'ria) *nf* cake shop.

pasticciare (pastit'tʃare) *vt* bungle. **pasticcio** *nm* 1 pie. 2 mess.

pastiglia (pas'tiʎʎa) *nf* tablet.

pastinaca (pasti'naka) *nf* parsnip.

pasto ('pasto) *nm* meal. **vino da pasto** *nm* table wine.

pastore (pas'tore) *nm* shepherd.

pastorizzare (pastorid'dʒare) *vt* pasteurize.

pastrano (pas'trano) *nm* overcoat.

pastura (pas'tura) *nf* pasture.

patata (pa'tata) *nf* potato. **patata fritta** chip. **patatina** *nf* potato crisp.

patella (pa'tɛlla) *nf* limpet.

patente[1] (pa'tɛnte) *nf* licence, certificate.

patente[2] (pa'tɛnte) *adj* obvious, evident.

paterno (pa'tɛrno) *adj* paternal.

patetico (pa'tɛtiko) *adj* pathetic.

patibolo (pa'tibolo) *nm* scaffold.

patire (pa'tire) *vt,vi* suffer.

patria ('patrja) *nf* homeland, native land.

patrigno (pa'triɲɲo) *nm* stepfather.

patrimonio (patri'mɔnjo) *nm* 1 estate. 2 heritage.

patriota (patri'ɔta) *nm* patriot. **patriottico** (patri'ɔttiko) *adj* patriotic.

patrono (pa'trono) *nm* patron saint.

pattinare (patti'nare) *vi* skate. **pattinaggio** *nm* skating. **pattino** *nm* skate.

patto ('patto) *nm* agreement, pact.

pattuglia (pat'tuʎʎa) *nf* patrol.

pattume (pat'tume) *nm* rubbish, refuse. **pattumiera** (pattu'mjɛra) *nf* dustbin.

paura (pa'ura) *nf* fear, fright. **fare paura a** frighten. **pauroso** (pau'roso) *adj* 1 timid. 2 frightening.

pausa ('pauza) *nf* pause.

pavimento (pavi'mento) *nm* floor.

pavone (pa'vone) *nm* peacock.

pavoneggiarsi (pavoned'dʒarsi) *vr* show off.

paziente (pat'tsjɛnte) *adj* patient. *nm* med patient. **pazienza** (pat'tsjɛntsa) *nf* patience.

pazzo ('pattso) *adj* mad, insane. *nm* madman. **pazzia** *nf* madness.

peccare (pek'kare) *vi* sin. **peccato** *nm* sin. **che peccato!** what a shame! **peccatore** *nm* sinner.

pecora ('pɛkora) *nf* sheep. **pecorino** *nm* sheep's milk cheese.

peculiare (peku'ljare) *adj* peculiar.

pedale (pe'dale) *nm* pedal. **pedalare** *vi* pedal.

pedana (pe'dana) *nf* 1 rug. 2 *sport* springboard.

pedante (pe'dante) *adj* pedantic. *nm* pedant.

pedata (pe'data) *nf* 1 footstep. 2 kick.

pediatria (pedja'tria) *nf* paediatrics.

pedicure (pedi'kure) *nm,f* chiropodist.

pedina (pe'dina) *nf* game 1 draughtsman. 2 pawn.

pedone (pe'done) *nm* pedestrian. **pedonale** *adj* pedestrian.

peggio ('pɛddʒo) *adv, adj invar* 1 worse. 2 worst. *nm,f* worst.

peggiorare (peddʒo'rare) *vt* make worse. *vi* worsen, deteriorate.

peggiore (ped'dʒore) *adj* 1 worse. 2 worst.

pegno ('peɲɲo) *nm* 1 pledge, pawn. 2 token. 3 forfeit.

pelare (pe'lare) *vt* 1 peel, skin. 2 pluck (a bird). **pelame** *nm* hair, fur.

pelle ('pɛlle) *nf* 1 skin. 2 hide. 3 leather. **amici per la pelle** *nm pl* friends for life.

pellegrino (pelle'grino) *nm* pilgrim. **pellegrinaggio** *nm* pilgrimage.

pellicano (pelli'kano) *nm* pelican.

pelliccia (pel'littʃa) *nf* fur coat, fur.

pellicola (pel'likola) *nf* 1 film, layer. 2 *phot* film.

pelo ('pelo) *nm* 1 hair. 2 fur, coat. **peloso** (pe'loso) *adj* hairy.

peltro ('peltro) *nm* pewter.

peluria (pe'lurja) *nf* down, soft hair.

pelvi ('pɛlvi) *nf invar* pelvis.

pena ('pena) *nf* 1 penalty, punishment. 2 pain, distress. **vale la pena** it is worthwhile. **penale** *adj* penal. **penalizzare** (penalid'dzare) *vt* penalize. **penoso** (pe'noso) *adj* painful.

pendere ('pɛndere) *vi* 1 hang. 2 lean, slope. **pendente** (pen'dɛnte) *adj* leaning. *nm* pendant. **pendenza** (pen'dɛntsa) *nf also* **pendice** slope. **pendio** *nm* slope, slant.

pendolo ('pɛndolo) *nm* pendulum. **pendola** ('pɛndola) *nf* pendulum clock.

pene ('pene) *nm* penis.

penetrare (pene'trare) *vi* enter, penetrate. *vt* penetrate.

penicillina (penitʃil'lina) *nf* penicillin.

penisola (pe'nizola) *nf* peninsula.

penitente (peni'tɛnte) *adj,n* penitent. **penitenza** (peni'tɛntsa) *nf* penance.

penna ('penna) *nf* 1 feather. 2 pen.

pennello (pen'nɛllo) *nm* paintbrush.

penombra (pe'nombra) *nf* dim light.

pensare (pen'sare) *vi* think, consider. *vt* think over, ponder. **pensatore** *nm* thinker. **pensiero** (pen'sjɛro) *nm* thought. **stare in pensiero** be worried. **pensieroso** (pensje'roso) *adj* thoughtful.

pensile ('pɛnsile) *adj* hanging.

pensionare (pensjo'nare) *vt* pension (off). **pensionato** *nm* pensioner. **pensione** *nf* 1 pension. 2 board. 3 boarding house.

pentagono (pen'tagono) *nm* pentagon.

Pentecoste (pente'kɔste) *nf* Pentecost, Whitsun.

pentirsi (pen'tirsi) *vr* 1 repent. 2 regret, be sorry. **pentimento** *nm* 1 repentance. 2 regret.

pentola ('pentola) *nf* pot. **pentola a pressione** pressure cooker.

penzolare (pendzo'lare) *vi* dangle. **penzoloni** *adv* dangling.

pepe ('pepe) *nm* pepper. **peperone** *nm* pepper, capsicum.

pepita (pe'pita) *nf* nugget.

per (per) *prep* 1 for. 2 by. 3 through. 4 during. 5 towards. **per amico** as a friend.

pera ('pera) *nf* pear.

perbacco (per'bakko) *interj* by Jove!

perbene (per'bɛne) *adj invar* respectable.

percalle (per'kalle) *nm* gingham.

percentuale (pertʃentu'ale) *nf* percentage.

percepire (pertʃe'pire) *vt* 1 notice, perceive. 2 receive. **percezione** *nf* perception.

perché (per'ke) *conj* 1 why. 2 because. 3 so that.

perciò (per'tʃɔ) *conj* therefore.

percorrere (per'korrere) *vt* go through, cross.

percorso (per'korso) *nm* 1 distance. 2 journey.

percossa (per'kɔssa) *nf* blow.

percuotere* (per'kwɔtere) vt strike, hit.

percussione (perkus'sjone) nf percussion.

perdere* ('pɛrdere) vt 1 lose. 2 miss. vi leak. **perdersi** vr get lost. **perdita** ('pɛrdita) nf loss.

perdonare (perdo'nare) vt forgive, pardon. **perdono** nm pardon.

perfetto (per'fetto) adj perfect.

perfezionare (perfettsjo'nare) vt perfect. **perfezionarsi** vr specialize. **perfezione** nf perfection.

perfidia (per'fidja) nf treachery. **perfido** ('pɛrfido) adj treacherous.

perfino (per'fino) adv even.

perforare (perfo'rare) vt 1 pierce, perforate. 2 bore.

pergamena (perga'mɛna) nf parchment.

pericolo (pe'rikolo) nm danger. **pericoloso** (periko'loso) adj dangerous.

periferia (perife'ria) nf outskirts, suburbs.

perimetro (pe'rimetro) nm perimeter.

periodo (pe'riodo) nm period. **periodico** (peri'ɔdiko) adj periodic. nm periodical.

perire (pe'rire) vi perish.

periscopio (peris'kɔpjo) nm periscope.

perito (pe'rito) adj skilled, expert. nm expert.

perla ('pɛrla) nf pearl.

perlustrare (perlus'trare) vt search.

permaloso (perma'loso) adj touchy.

permanente (perma'nɛnte) adj permanent.

permeare (perme'are) vt permeate.

permesso (per'messo) adj permitted. nm 1 permission, permit. 2 leave. interj excuse me! **permesso?** may I come in?

permettere* (per'mettere) vt allow, permit.

pernice (per'nitʃe) nf partridge.

perno ('pɛrno) nm pivot.

pero ('pero) nm pear tree.

però (pe'rɔ) conj however, yet.

perossido (pe'rɔssido) nm peroxide.

perpendicolare (perpendiko'lare) adj,nf perpendicular.

perpetuo (per'pɛtuo) adj perpetual.

perplesso (per'plɛsso) adj perplexed.

perquisire (perkwi'zire) vt search. **perquisizione** nf search. **mandato di perquisizione** nm search warrant.

perseguitare (persegwi'tare) vt 1 pursue. 2 persecute. **persecutore** nm persecutor. **persecuzione** nf persecution.

perseverare (perseve'rare) vi persevere.

persi ('pɛrsi) v see **perdere**.

persiana (per'sjana) nf shutter.

persino (per'sino) adv even.

persistere* (per'sistere) vi continue, persist.

perso ('pɛrso) v see **perdere**.

persona (per'sona) nf person. **personale** adj personal. nm staff. **personalità** nf personality.

personaggio (perso'naddʒo) nm character.

personificare (personifi'kare) vt personify.

persuadere* (persua'dere) vt persuade, convince. **persuasione** nf persuasion. **persuasivo** adj persuasive.

pertanto (per'tanto) conj therefore.

pertosse (per'tosse) nf whooping cough.

pervenire* (perve'nire) vi reach.

pesare (pe'sare) vt,vi weigh. **pesante** (pe'sante) adj heavy. **peso** ('peso) nm 1 weight. 2 burden.

pesca[1] ('pɛska) nf peach. **pesco** nm peach tree.

pesca[2] ('peska) nf fishing. **pescare** vt 1 fish. 2 catch. **pescatore** nm fisherman.

pesce ('peʃʃe) nm 1 fish. 2 pl cap Pisces. **non sapere che pesci pigliare** not know which to choose. **pesce d'aprile** April fool. **pescecane** (peʃʃe'kane) nm shark. **pescheria** nf fishmonger's shop. **pescivendolo** (peʃʃi'vendolo) nm fishmonger.

pessimismo (pessi'mizmo) nm pessimism. **pessimista** nm pessimist. **pessimistico** adj pessimistic.

pessimo ('pɛssimo) adj 1 very bad. 2 worst.

pestare (pes'tare) vt 1 trample on. 2 crush. 3 stamp (feet). **pestello** (pes'tɛllo) nm pestle. **pesto** adj ground. nm kind of sauce. **carta pesta** nf papier-mâché.

peste ('pɛste) nf 1 plague. 2 nuisance.

petalo ('pɛtalo) nm petal.

petizione (petit'tsjone) nf petition.

petrolifero (petro'lifero) **pozzo petrolifero** nm oilwell.

petrolio (pe'trɔljo) nm 1 oil. 2 petroleum. **petroliera** (petro'ljɛre) nf oil tanker.

pettegolo (pet'tegolo) adj gossipy. nm also **pettegola** nf gossip. **pettegolezzo** (pettego-'leddzo) nm gossip.

pettinare (petti'nare) vt comb. **pettinarsi** vr comb one's hair. **pettinatura** nf hairstyle. **pettine** ('pɛttine) nm comb.

petto ('petto) nm 1 anat chest. 2 breast. **pettirosso** (petti'rosso) nm robin.

pezza ('pɛttsa) nf 1 patch. 2 cloth.

pezzo ('pεttso) nm **1** piece, bit. **2** portion. **pezzo di ricambio** spare part. **pezzo grosso** bigwig. **un gran pezzo** a long time.

piaccio ('pjattʃo) v see **piacere**.

piacere¹ (pja'tʃere) vi please, be pleasing. v imp like. **piacere a** please. ~nm **1** pleasure, enjoyment. **2** favour. **per piacere** please. **piacevole** adj pleasant.

piaga ('pjaga) nf wound, sore.

piagnucolare (pjaɲɲuko'lare) vi whimper.

pianerottolo (pjane'rɔttolo) nm arch landing.

pianeta (pja'neta) nm planet.

piangere¹ ('pjandʒere) vi cry, weep. vt lament.

pianista (pja'nista) nm pianist.

piano¹ ('pjano) adj flat, level. adv **1** quietly, gently. **2** slowly. **pian piano** very slowly.

piano² ('pjano) nm **1** plain. **2** plane. **3** floor, storey. **primo piano** foreground. **pianterreno** nm ground floor.

piano³ ('pjano) nm **1** plan. **2** project.

piano⁴ ('pjano) nm piano.

pianoforte (pjano'fɔrte) nm piano.

piansi ('pjansi) v see **piangere**.

piantare (pjan'tare) vt **1** plant. **2** fix, put. **3** abandon. **piantarsi** vr stand. **pianta** nf **1** bot plant. **2** anat sole. **3** plan. **piantagione** nf plantation.

pianto¹ ('pjanto) v see **piangere**.

pianto² ('pjanto) nm weeping.

pianura (pja'nura) nf plain.

piastra ('pjastra) nf slab. **piastrella** (pjas'trεlla) nf tile.

piattaforma (pjatta'forma) nf platform.

piatto ('pjatto) adj flat. nm **1** plate. **2** dish (of food). **3** cul course. **4** pl cymbals. **piattino** nm saucer.

piazza ('pjattsa) nf square, marketplace. **fare piazza pulita** make a clean sweep. **piazzale** nm square, open space.

picca ('pikka) nf **1** lance, pike. **2** pl game spades.

piccante (pik'kante) adj spicy, pungent.

picchiare (pik'kjare) vt hit, strike. vi knock. **picchiotto** (pik'kjɔtto) nm doorknocker.

picchio ('pikkjo) nm woodpecker.

piccino (pit'tʃino) adj small, tiny.

piccione (pit'tʃone) nm pigeon.

picco ('pikko) nm peak. **andare a picco** sink. **a picco** perpendicularly.

piccolo ('pikkolo) adj small, little. nm little child.

piccone (pik'kone) nm pickaxe.

pidocchio (pi'dɔkkjo) nm louse.

piede ('pjεde) nm foot. **a piedi** on foot. **stare in piedi** stand. **piedistallo** (pjedis'tallo) nm pedestal.

piegare (pje'gare) vt fold, bend. vi **1** turn. **2** lean. **piegarsi** vr bow. **piega** nf **1** fold. **2** pleat.

pieghevole (pje'gevole) adj flexible.

pieno ('pjεno) adj full, complete. **fare il pieno** mot fill up. **pieno zeppo** full up.

pietà (pje'ta) nf pity, mercy. **monte di pietà** nm pawnbroker's shop. **pietoso** (pje'toso) adj **1** pitiful. **2** compassionate.

pietanza (pje'tantsa) nf **1** dish. **2** cul course.

pietra ('pjεtra) nf stone.

piffero ('piffero) nm mus pipe.

pigiama (pi'dʒama) nm pyjamas.

pigione (pi'dʒone) nf rent.

pigliare (piʎ'ʎare) vt **1** take. **2** catch.

pigmeo (pig'mεo) adj,n Pigmy.

pigna ('piɲɲa) nf pine cone.

pigolare (pigo'lare) vi cheep, chirp.

pigro ('pigro) adj **1** lazy. **2** slow. **pigrizia** (pi'grittsja) nf laziness.

pila ('pila) nf **1** arch pile, support. **2** battery.

pilastro (pi'lastro) nm pillar.

pillola ('pillola) nf pill.

pilone (pi'lone) nm pylon.

pilotare (pilo'tare) vt **1** pilot. **2** mot drive. **pilota** nm pilot.

pimento (pi'mento) nm cayenne pepper.

pinacoteca (pinako'tεka) nf art gallery.

pingue ('pingwe) adj fat.

pinguino (pin'gwino) nm penguin.

pinna ('pinna) nf **1** fin. **2** flipper.

pinnacolo (pin'nakolo) nm pinnacle.

pino ('pino) nm pine tree. **pineta** nf pine forest.

pinta ('pinta) nf pint.

pinza ('pintsa) nf pliers, pincers. **pinzette** nf pl tweezers.

pio ('pio) adj devout, charitable.

pioggia ('pjɔddʒa) nf rain.

piombare¹ (pjom'bare) vi fall heavily. **piombare su** assail.

piombare² (pjom'bare) vt **1** seal. **2** fill (a tooth). **piombo** ('pjombo) nm lead.

pioniere (pjo'njεre) nm pioneer.

pioppo ('pjɔppo) nm poplar tree.

piovere¹ ('pjɔvere) vi **1** rain. **2** pour. **piovere a catinelle** rain cats and dogs.

piovigginare (pjoviddʒi'nare) vi drizzle.

piovra ('pjɔvra) nf octopus.

piovve ('pjɔvve) v see **piovere.**

pipa ('pipa) nf pipe.

pipistrello (pipis'trɛllo) nm zool bat.

piramide (pi'ramide) nf pyramid.

pirata (pi'rata) nm pirate.

piroscafo (pi'rɔskafo) nm steamship.

piscina (piʃ'ʃina) nf swimming pool.

pisello (pi'sɛllo) nm pea.

pisolino (pizo'lino) nm nap.

pista ('pista) nf **1** track. **2** runway.

pistola (pis'tɔla) nf pistol.

pistone (pis'tone) nm piston.

pitone (pi'tone) nm python.

pittore (pit'tore) nm painter.

pittoresco (pitto'resko) adj picturesque.

pittura (pit'tura) nf painting, picture.

più (pju) adv **1** more. **2** most. **di più** more. **non...più** no longer. **più tardi** later. **tanto più che** all the more since. ~prep plus. adj more. nm majority. **per lo più** generally.

piuma ('pjuma) nf **1** down. **2** feather. **peso piuma** nm sport featherweight.

piuttosto (pjut'tɔsto) adv rather, somewhat.

pizza ('pittsa) nf dough base covered with various tomato mixtures.

pizzicare (pittsi'kare) vt **1** nip, pinch. **2** sting, bite. vi itch. **pizzicotto** (pittsi'kɔtto) nm also **pizzico** ('pittsiko) nip. **pizzicagnolo** (pittsi-'kaɲɲolo) nm specialist grocer. **pizzicheria** (pittsike'ria) nf delicatessen.

pizzo ('pittso) nm **1** lace. **2** goatee beard.

placare (pla'kare) vt calm.

placca ('plakka) nf plaque.

placenta (pla'tʃɛnta) nf placenta.

placido ('platʃido) adj **1** tranquil, calm. **2** placid.

plagiare (pla'dʒare) vt plagiarize.

planare (pla'nare) vi glide.

plasmare (plaz'mare) vt mould. **plasma** nm plasma.

plastica ('plastika) nf plastic. **plastico** ('plastiko) adj plastic.

platano ('platano) nm plane tree.

platea (pla'tɛa) nf Th stalls, pit.

platino ('platino) nm platinum.

platonico (pla'tɔniko) adj platonic.

plausibile (plau'zibile) adj plausible.

plebaglia (ple'baʎʎa) nf rabble.

plebe ('plɛbe) nf common people.

plico ('pliko) nm **1** packet (of letters). **2** envelope.

plotone (plo'tone) nm platoon.

plumbeo ('plumbeo) adj leaden.

plurale (plu'rale) adj,nm plural.

pneumatico (pneu'matiko) adj pneumatic. nm tyre.

po' (pɔ) adj contraction of **poco.**

pochino (po'kino) adj,nm little.

poco ('pɔko) adj **1** little. **2** insufficient. **3** pl few. **da poco** worthless. ~pron **1** little. **2** pl few. **un altro poco po'** another little bit. ~adv little. **a poco a poco** little by little. **per poco non** almost. **vediamo un po'** let's have a look.

podere (po'dere) nm farm.

podestà (podes'ta) nm mayor.

poema (po'ɛma) nm poem. **poesia** (poe'zia) nf **1** poetry. **2** poem. **poeta** (po'ɛta) nm poet. **poetico** (po'ɛtiko) adj poetic.

poi ('pɔi) adv then, after. **d'allora in poi** from then on.

poiché (poi'ke) conj for, since.

polacco (po'lakko) adj Polish. nm **1** Pole. **2** Polish (language).

polarizzare (polarid'dzare) vt polarize.

polca ('pɔlka) nf polka.

polemica (po'lɛmika) nf controversy, polemic.

polenta (po'lɛnta) nf pudding made of maize flour.

poligamia (poliga'mia) nf polygamy.

poligono (po'ligono) nm polygon.

politecnico (poli'tɛkniko) nm polytechnic.

politica (po'litika) nf **1** politics. **2** policy. **politico** (po'litiko) adj political. nm politician.

polizia (polit'tsia) nf police. **poliziotto** (polit'tsiɔtto) nm policeman. **romanzo poliziesco** nm detective story.

polizza ('pɔlittsa) nf **1** voucher. **2** receipt. **3** bill. **polizza d'assicurazione** insurance policy.

pollaio (pol'lajo) nm poultry yard.

pollice ('pɔllitʃe) nm **1** thumb. **2** big toe. **3** inch.

polline ('pɔlline) nm pollen.

pollo ('pollo) nm chicken. **pollame** nm poultry.

polmone (pol'mone) nm lung. **polmonite** nf pneumonia.

polo[1] ('pɔlo) nm (astronomy) pole. **polare** adj polar.

polo[2] ('pɔlo) nm polo.

Polonia (po'lɔnja) nf Poland.

polpa ('pɔlpa) nf flesh, pulp. **polpetta** nf meatball.

polpaccio (pol'pattʃo) nm anat calf.

polso ('pɔlso) nm **1** pulse. **2** wrist. **polsino** nm shirt cuff.

poltrona (pol'trona) nf **1** armchair. stall.

poltrone (pol'trone) adj lazy.

polvere ('polvere) nf **1** dust. **2** powder. **polveroso** (polve'roso) adj dusty.

polverizzare (polverid'dzare) vt pulverize.

pomata (po'mata) nf ointment.

pomeriggio (pome'riddʒo) nm afternoon.

pomice ('pomitʃe) nf pumice.

pomo ('pomo) nm **1** apple. **2** apple tree. **pomo d'Adamo** Adam's apple.

pomodoro (pomo'dɔro) nm tomato.

pompa[1] ('pompa) nf pomp, splendour.

pompa[2] ('pompa) nf pump. **pompiere** (pom'pjɛre) nm fireman.

pompelmo (pom'pɛlmo) nm grapefruit.

ponce ('pontʃe) nm also **punch** (pʌntʃ) nm invar punch (drink).

ponderare (ponde'rare) vt ponder.

ponente (po'nɛnte) nm west.

ponesti (po'nesti) v see **porre.**

pongo ('pongo) v see **porre.**

poni ('poni) v see **porre.**

ponte ('ponte) nm **1** bridge. **2** naut deck.

pontefice (pon'tefitʃe) nm pontiff.

popolare (popo'lare) vt populate. adj popular. **popolarità** nf popularity.

popolo ('pɔpolo) nm people, nation. **popolazione** nf population.

popone (po'pone) nm melon.

poppa[1] ('poppa) nf stern.

poppa[2] ('poppa) nf breast.

poppare (pop'pare) vt suck.

porcellana (portʃel'lana) nf china, porcelain.

porco ('pɔrko) nm, pl **porci 1** pig. **2** pork. **porcellino** nm piglet. **porcile** nm pigsty. **porcospino** nm porcupine.

porgere* ('pordʒere) vt **1** hold out. **2** hand out. **porgere una mano** lend a hand.

pornografia (pornogra'fia) nf pornography. **pornografico** (porno'grafiko) adj pornographic.

poro ('pɔro) nm pore. **poroso** (po'roso) adj porous.

porpora ('porpora) nf purple. **porporino** adj purple.

porre* ('porre) vt **1** place, put, set. **2** suppose.

porro ('pɔrro) nm leek.

porta ('pɔrta) nf **1** door. **2** gate. **portiera** (por'tjɛra) nf door. **portiere** (por'tjɛre) nm **1** doorman, porter. **2** goalkeeper.

portabagagli (portaba'gaʎʎi) nm invar **1** luggage rack. **2** porter.

portacenere (porta'tʃenere) nm invar ashtray.

portachiavi (porta'kjavi) nm key ring.

portaerei (porta'ɛrei) nf invar aircraft-carrier.

portafoglio (porta'fɔʎʎo) nm invar **1** wallet. **2** portfolio.

portalettere (porta'lɛttere) nm invar postman.

portamonete (portamo'nete) nm invar purse.

portare (por'tare) vt **1** carry. **2** take. **3** bring. **4** wear. **5** lead. **6** feel. **portarsi** vr behave. **portamento** nm bearing. **portata** nf **1** range. **2** capacity. **portatile** adj portable.

portariviste (portari'viste) nm invar magazine rack.

portasapone (portasa'pone) nm invar soap dish.

portasigarette (portasiga'rette) nm invar cigarette case.

portaspilli (porta'spilli) nm invar pin cushion.

portauova (porta'wɔva) nm egg cup.

portavoce (porta'votʃe) nm invar **1** megaphone. **2** mouthpiece, spokesman.

portico ('pɔrtiko) nm porch.

portinaio (porti'najo) nm porter, doorman. **portineria** nf porter's lodge.

porto[1] ('pɔrto) nm **1** carriage, transport. **2** postage.

porto[2] ('pɔrto) nm naut port.

porto[3] ('pɔrto) nm port (drink).

Portogallo (porto'gallo) nm Portugal. **portoghese** (porto'gese) adj,nm Portuguese. nm Portuguese (language).

porzione (por'tsjone) nf **1** share, portion. **2** helping (of food).

posa ('pɔsa) nf **1** pause. **2** pose. **3** phot exposure.

posare (po'sare) vt put, place, set or lay down. vi pose. **posarsi** vr alight. **posata** nf piece of cutlery.

posatoio (posa'tojo) nm perch.

poscritto (pos'kritto) nm postscript.

posi ('posi) v see **porre.**

positivo (pozi'tivo) adj positive.

posizione (pozit'tsjone) nf **1** position. **2** site. **3** situation.

posporre* (pos'porre) vt postpone.

possedere* (posse'dere) vt possess, own, have. **possedimento** nm **1** estate. **2** possession. **possesso** (pos'sɛsso) nm possession. **possessore** nm possessor, owner.

possiamo (pos'sjamo) v see **potere.**

possibile (pos'sibile) adj possible. **possibilità** nf **1** possibility. **2** opportunity.

posso ('pɔsso) v see **potere**.

posta ('pɔsta) nf 1 post, mail. 2 post office. **postale** adj postal. **cassetta postale** nf postbox. **postino** nm postman.

posteggiare (posted'dʒare) vi park. **posteggio** nm parking place.

posteriore (poste'rjore) adj 1 back, hind. 2 later.

posterità (posteri'ta) nf posterity.

posticcio (pos'tittʃo) adj false, fake.

posto[1] ('posto) v see **porre**.

posto[2] ('posto) nm 1 place, spot, site. 2 place, seat. 3 job, position. 4 space, room. 5 post. **a posto** in order. **posto di primo soccorso** first-aid post.

postumo ('postumo) adj posthumous.

potabile (po'tabile) adj drinkable.

potare (po'tare) vt prune.

potassio (po'tassjo) nm potassium.

potente (po'tɛnte) adj powerful. **potenza** (po'tɛntsa) nf power.

potenziale (poten'tsjale) adj,nm potential.

potere[*1] (po'tere) vi 1 be able. 2 be allowed. **può darsi** it is possible.

potere[2] (po'tere) nm power.

potrò (po'trɔ) v see **potere**.

povero ('pɔvero) adj poor, needy. nm 1 poor man. 2 beggar. **poveretto** nm poor wretch. **povertà** nf poverty.

pozza ('pottsa) nf puddle, pool. **pozzanghera** (pot'tsangera) nf puddle. **pozzo** ('pottso) nm well.

pranzare (pran'dzare) vi 1 lunch. 2 dine. **pranzo** nm 1 lunch. 2 dinner.

pratica ('pratika) nf 1 experience. 2 practice. 3 knowledge, familiarity. **praticare** vt 1 practice. 2 exercise. **pratico** ('pratiko) adj 1 practical. 2 experienced.

prato ('prato) nm meadow.

preavvertire (preavver'tire) vt forewarn.

preavvisare (preavvi'zare) vt forewarn. **preavviso** nm notice, warning.

precario (pre'karjo) adj precarious.

precauzione (prekaut'tsjone) nf precaution.

precedere (pre'tʃedere) vt 1 precede, go before. **precedente** (pretʃe'dɛnte) adj preceding. nm precedent. **precedenza** (pretʃe'dɛntsa) nf 1 precedence. 2 nm right-of-way, priority.

precipitare (pretʃipi'tare) vt 1 hurl. 2 speed up. vi crash down, fall. **precipizio** (pretʃi'pittsjo) nm precipice.

precisare (pretʃi'zare) vt specify, relate precise-

ly. **precisione** nf precision. **preciso** adj exact, precise. **alle due precise** at exactly two o'clock.

precoce (pre'kɔtʃe) adj precocious.

preconcetto (prekon'tʃetto) adj preconceived. nm preconception.

precursore (prekur'sore) nm forerunner.

predare (pre'dare) vt pillage. **preda** nf 1 prey. 2 booty.

predecessore (predetʃes'sore) nm predecessor.

predestinare (predesti'nare) vt predestine. **predestinazione** nf predestination.

predica ('predika) nf sermon. **predicare** vt,vi preach.

prediletto (predi'letto) adj,nm favourite.

predire* (pre'dire) vt predict. **predizione** nf prediction.

predominare (predomi'nare) vi predominate, prevail. **predominio** nm predominance.

prefabbricato (prefabbri'kato) adj prefabricated.

prefazione (prefat'tsjone) nf preface.

preferire (prefe'rire) vt prefer. **preferenza** (prefe'rɛntsa) nf preference. **preferibile** (prefe'ribile) adj preferable.

prefetto (pre'fɛtto) nm prefect. **prefettura** nf prefecture.

prefiggere* (pre'fiddʒere) vt arrange in advance. **prefiggersi** vr intend.

prefisso (pre'fisso) nm prefix.

pregare (pre'gare) vt 1 pray. 2 beg, ask. **prego** interj 1 yes please! 2 pardon? 3 don't mention it!

pregevole (pre'dʒevole) adj valuable.

preghiera (pre'gjɛra) nf prayer.

pregiare (pre'dʒare) vt esteem. **pregio** ('prɛdʒo) nm 1 esteem. 2 merit.

pregiudicare (predʒudi'kare) vt prejudice. **pregiudizio** (predʒu'dittsjo) nm prejudice.

pregustare (pregus'tare) vt look forward to.

preistorico (preis'tɔriko) adj prehistoric.

prelato (pre'lato) nm prelate.

prelevare (prele'vare) vt 1 withdraw. 2 take.

preliminare (prelimi'nare) adj,nm preliminary.

preludio (pre'ludjo) nm prelude.

prematuro (prema'turo) adj premature.

premeditato (premedi'tato) adj premeditated.

premere* (prɛmere) vt,vi squeeze, press. vi 1 insist. 2 be urgent.

premiare (pre'mjare) vt reward. **premio** ('prɛmjo) nm 1 prize. 2 reward. 3 award.

preminente (premi'nɛnte) *adj* pre-eminent. **preminenza** (premi'nɛntsa) *nf* pre-eminence.

premura (pre'mura) *nf* 1 care, attention. 2 hurry, urgency. **premuroso** (premu'roso) *adj* thoughtful.

prenatale (prena'tale) *adj* antenatal.

prendere* (pre'prɛndere) *vt* 1 take. 2 seize, catch. 3 surprise. 4 receive, get, earn. 5 take up, occupy. 6 catch (illness). 7 treat, consider. 8 hit, catch. *vi* set, take root. **prendere a begin to. prendere a destra** turn right. **prendere con le buone** treat nicely. **prendere fuoco** catch fire. **prendersela con** *vr* get angry with.

prenotare (preno'tare) *vt* book, reserve.

preoccupare (preokku'pare) *vt* worry, be anxious. **preoccuparsi** *vr* get worried. **preoccupato** *adj* worried. **preoccupazione** *nf* worry.

preparare (prepa'rare) *vt* prepare. **prepararsi** *vr* get oneself ready. **preparazione** *nf* also **preparativo** *nm* preparation.

preposizione (prepozit'tsjone) *nf* preposition.

prepotente (prepo'tɛnte) *adj* overbearing, tyrannical. **prepotenza** (prepo'tɛntsa) *nf* arrogance.

prerogativa (preroga'tiva) *nf* privilege, prerogative.

presa ('presa) *nf* 1 capture, seizure. 2 dose. 3 pinch. 4 electric plug.

presbite ('prɛzbite) *adj* long-sighted.

prescrivere* (pres'krivere) *vt* prescribe.

presentare (prezen'tare) *vt* 1 present. 2 introduce. 3 offer. 4 show. **presentarsi** *vr* appear. **presentatore** *nm* compere. **presentazione** *nf* introduction.

presente (pre'zɛnte) *adj,nm* present.

presentire (presen'tire) *vt* foresee. **presentimento** (presenti'mento) *nm* premonition.

presenza (pre'zɛntsa) *nf* presence.

preservativo (preserva'tivo) *nm* contraceptive.

presi ('presi) *v* see **prendere.**

preside ('prɛside) *nm* 1 principal. 2 dean.

presidente (presi'dɛnte) *nm* president.

presidio (pre'sidjo) *nm* garrison.

presiedere (pre'sjɛdere) *vt,vi* preside over.

preso ('preso) *v* see **prendere.**

pressare (pres'sare) *vt* press. **pressa** ('prɛssa) *nf* press.

pressione (pres'sjone) *nf* pressure.

presso ('prɛsso) *adv* near, nearby. **da presso** closely. **presso a** about to. ~*prep* 1 nearby.

2 in, at. 3 care of. 4 in the opinion of. 5 among. **presso a** in comparison with. **pressi** *nm pl* vicinity. **pressappoco** (pressap'pɔko) *adv* roughly, more or less.

prestabilire (prestabi'lire) *vt* arrange in advance.

prestare (pres'tare) *vt* 1 lend. 2 give.

prestigio (pres'tidʒo) *nm* 1 trick. 2 prestige. **gioco di prestigio** *nm* conjuring trick.

prestito ('prɛstito) *nm* loan. **dare in prestito** lend.

presto ('prɛsto) *adv* 1 quickly. 2 early. 3 soon. **al più presto** as quickly as possible. **fare presto** hurry.

presumere* (pre'zumere) *vi* presume. **presuntuoso** *adj* presumptuous. **presunzione** *nf* presumption.

presupporre* (presup'porre) *vt* presuppose.

prete ('prɛte) *nm* priest.

pretendere* (pre'tɛndere) *vt* 1 claim. 2 assert. 3 demand. 4 want, ask (a price). *vi* claim.

pretenzioso (preten'tsjoso) *adj* pretentious.

pretesa (pre'tesa) *nf* 1 claim. 2 pretension.

pretesto (pre'tɛsto) *nm* pretext, excuse.

prevalere* (preva'lere) *vi* prevail. **prevalersi** *vr* take advantage.

prevedere* (preve'dere) *vt* 1 foresee. 2 forecast.

prevenire* (preve'nire) *vt* anticipate.

preventivare (preventi'vare) *vt* allocate. **preventivo** *nm* budget.

previdenza (previ'dɛntsa) *nf* foresight.

previsione (previ'zjone) *nf* expectation. **previsioni del tempo** *nf pl* weather forecast.

prezioso (pret'tsjoso) *adj* precious.

prezzemolo (pret'tsemolo) *nm* parsley.

prezzo ('prɛttso) *nm* 1 cost. 2 price.

prigione (pri'dʒone) *nf* prison. **prigioniero** *nm* prisoner.

prima ('prima) *adv* 1 first. 2 before. 3 beforehand. 4 formerly. *prep* before. *nf* 1 first night. 2 *mot* first gear. 3 first class. **prima o poi** sooner or later.

primavera (prima'vera) *nf* spring.

primitivo (primi'tivo) *adj* primitive.

primo ('primo) *adj* 1 first. 2 principal. *nm* first. **primogenito** (primo'dʒɛnito) *adj,nm* firstborn.

primula ('primula) *nf* primrose.

principale (printʃi'pale) *adj* main, chief, principal. *nm* manager, boss.

principe ('printʃipe) *nm* prince. **principessa** *nf* princess.

principio (prin'tʃipio) *nm* **1** start, beginning. **2** principle.

priore (pri'ore) *nm rel* prior.

priorità (priori'ta) *nf* priority.

prisma ('prizma) *nm* prism.

privare (pri'vare) *vt* deprive.

privato (pri'vato) *adj* private.

privilegio (privi'lɛdʒo) *nm* privilege.

privo ('privo) *adj* lacking, wanting.

probabile (pro'babile) *adj* probable, likely. **probabilità** *nf* probability.

problema (pro'blɛma) *nm* problem.

procacciare (prokat'tʃare) *vt* seek, obtain.

procedere (pro'tʃɛdere) *vi* **1** proceed, go on. **2** start. **3** act. **procedimento** *nm* **1** process. **2** *law* proceedings.

processione (protʃes'sjone) *nf* procession.

processo (pro'tʃɛsso) *nm* **1** process. **2** *law* trial, lawsuit.

proclamare (prokla'mare) *nf* proclaim, declare. **proclamazione** *nf* proclamation.

procreare (prokre'are) *vt* procreate.

procurare (proku'rare) *vt* **1** obtain. **2** cause.

proda ('prɔda) *nf* **1** bank, shore. **2** edge.

prodigare (prodi'gare) *vt* lavish. **prodigo** ('prɔdigo) *adj* lavish.

prodigio (pro'didʒo) *nm* miracle.

produrre* (pro'durre) *vt* **1** produce. **2** cause. **prodursi** *vr* happen. **prodotto** *nm* product. **produttivo** *adj* productive. **produttore** *nm* producer. **produzione** *nf* **1** production. **2** manufacture.

proemio (pro'ɛmjo) *nm* introduction.

profanare (profa'nare) *vt* profane. **profano** *adj* profane.

proferire* (profe'rire) *vt* pronounce.

professare (profes'sare) *vt* **1** profess. **2** practise. **professione** *nf* profession. **professionista** *nm* professional. **professore** *nm* **1** teacher. **2** professor.

profeta (pro'fɛta) *nm* prophet. **profetico** (pro'fɛtiko) *adj* prophetic. **profezia** (profet'tsia) *nf* prophecy.

profilo (pro'filo) *nm* profile, outline. **di profilo** in profile.

profittare (profit'tare) *vi* profit, gain. **profitto** *nm* profit, gain.

profondo (pro'fondo) *adj* **1** deep. **2** profound. **poco profondo** shallow. **profondità** *nf* depth.

profugo ('prɔfugo) *nm* refugee.

profumare (profu'mare) *vt* perfume. **profumo** *nm* perfume.

profusione (profu'zjone) *nf* profusion.

progettare (prodʒet'tare) *vt* plan. **progetto** (pro'dʒetto) *nm* plan, project.

prognosi ('prɔɲɲozi) *nf* prognosis.

programmare (program'mare) *vt* program. **programma** *nm* **1** programme. **2** program.

progredire (progre'dire) *vi* progress, advance. **progresso** (pro'grɛsso) *nm* progress.

proibire (proi'bire) *vt* forbid, prohibit.

proiettare (projet'tare) *vt* throw, project. *vi* project. **proiettile** (pro'jɛttile) *nm* **1** missile. **2** shot, shell, bullet. **proiettore** *nm* **1** searchlight. **2** projector.

proletario (prole'tarjo) *adj,nm* proletarian. **proletariato** *nm* proletariat.

prolifico (pro'lifiko) *adj* prolific.

prologo ('prɔlogo) *nm* prologue.

prolungare (prolun'gare) *vt* lengthen, extend, prolong. **prolungamento** *nm* extension.

promettere* (pro'mettere) *vt* promise. **promessa** *nf* promise.

prominente (promi'nɛnte) *adj* prominent.

promiscuo (pro'miskuo) *adj* **1** mixed. **2** promiscuous.

promontorio (promon'tɔrjo) *nm* headland, promontory.

promozione (promot'tsjone) *nf* promotion.

promuovere* (pro'mwɔvere) *vt* **1** promote. **2** encourage, provoke.

pronome (pro'nome) *nm* pronoun.

pronto ('pronto) *adj* **1** ready. **2** quick, prompt. **pronto soccorso** *nm* first aid. ~*interj* (on the telephone) hello!

prontuario (prontu'arjo) *nm* handbook.

pronunciare (pronun'tʃare) *vt* pronounce. **pronuncia** *nf* pronunciation.

propaganda (propa'ganda) *nf* propaganda.

propendere* (pro'pɛndere) *vi* incline. **propensione** *nf* inclination. **propenso** (pro'pɛnso) *adj* inclined.

propizio (pro'pittsjo) *adj* favourable.

proponimento (proponi'mento) *nm* resolution.

proporre* (pro'porre) *vt* propose, suggest. **proporsi** *vr* intend.

proporzione (propor'tsjone) *nf* proportion. **proporzionale** *adj* proportional.

proposito (pro'pɔzito) *nm* **1** aim, intention. **2** theme, subject. **a proposito 1** by the way. **2** to the point. **a proposito di** with regard to.

proposizione (propozit'tsjone) *nf* proposition.

proposta (pro'posta) nf proposal.
proprietà (proprje'ta) nf 1 property. 2 ownership. **proprietario** nm 1 owner, proprietor. 2
landlord.
proprio ('prɔprjo) adj 1 own. 2 suitable, convenient. 3 characteristic. 4 proper. nm one's
own. adv 1 exactly, just, precisely. 2 really.
propulsione (propul'sjone) nf propulsion.
prora ('prɔra) nf prow, bows.
prorogare (proro'gare) vt defer, postpone, put
off. **proroga** ('prɔroga) nf extension, adjournment.
prorompere* (pro'rompere) vi burst out.
prosa ('prɔza) nf prose.
prosciutto (proʃ'ʃutto) nm ham.
proscrivere* (pros'krivere) vt outlaw, proscribe.
proseguire (prose'gwire) vt continue, pursue. vi
proceed, continue.
prosperare (prospe'rare) vi flourish, thrive.
prosperità nf prosperity. **prospero** ('prɔ-
spero) adj 1 favourable. 2 prosperous.
prospettiva (prospet'tiva) nf 1 perspective. 2
view. 3 prospect.
prospetto (pros'petto) nm 1 view. 2 prospectus.
prossimo ('prɔssimo) adj 1 near. 2 next. nm 1
fellow human being. 2 neighbour. **prossimità**
nf nearness, proximity.
prostituire (prostitu'ire) vt prostitute. **prostituta** nf prostitute. **prostituzione** nf prostitution.
protagonista (protago'nista) nm 1 protagonist.
2 chief actor.
proteggere* (pro'tɛddʒere) vt protect, defend.
proteina (prote'ina) nf protein.
protendere* (pro'tɛndere) vt extend. **protendersi** vr lean forward.
protessi (pro'tɛssi) v see **proteggere.**
protestante (protes'tante) adj,n Protestant.
protestare (protes'tare) vi protest. **protesta**
(pro'tɛsta) nf protest.
protetto (pro'tɛtto) v see **proteggere.**
protettore (protet'tore) nm 1 protector. 2
patron.
protezione (protet'tsjone) nf 1 protection. 2
patronage.
protocollo (proto'kɔllo) nm 1 protocol. 2
register.
prototipo (pro'tɔtipo) nm prototype.
protrarre* (pro'trarre) vt 1 prolong. 2 put off.
provare (pro'vare) vt 1 prove. 2 test, try. 3 feel,
experience. **provarsi** vr try on. **prova** ('prɔ-
va) nf 1 trial, test. 2 examination. 3 proof,

evidence. 4 rehearsal. **prova generale** dress
rehearsal. **in prova** on trial.
provenire* (prove'nire) vi come from. **prove-
nienza** (prove'njentsa) nf origin, source.
proverbio (pro'vɛrbjo) nm proverb. **proverbiale** adj proverbial.
provincia (pro'vintʃa) nf province. **provinciale**
adj provincial.
provocare (provo'kare) vt provoke. **provocante** adj provocative. **provocazione** nf
provocation.
provvedere* (provve'dere) vt provide, furnish,
supply. vi attend to, take care of. **provvedimento** nm measure, precaution.
provvigione (provvi'dʒone) nf commission.
provvisorio (provvi'zorjo) adj provisional.
provvista (prov'vista) nf supply.
prua ('prua) nf prow.
prudente (pru'dɛnte) adj prudent, wise. **prudenza** nf prudence, caution.
prudere* ('prudere) vi itch. **prurito** nm itch.
prugna ('pruɲɲa) nf plum. **prugna secca**
prune. **prugno** nm plum tree.
pseudonimo (pseu'dɔnimo) nm pseudonym.
psicanalisi (psika'nalizi) nf invar psychoanalysis. **psicanalista** nm psychoanalyst.
psichiatra (psi'kjatra) nm psychiatrist. **psichiatria** nf psychiatry. **psichiatrico** (psi'kjatriko)
adj psychiatric.
psichico ('psikiko) adj psychic.
psicologo (psi'kɔlogo) nm psychologist. **psicologia** nf psychology. **psicologico** (psiko-
'lɔdʒiko) adj psychological.
psicopatico (psiko'patiko) adj psychopathic.
nm psychopath.
psicosi (psi'kɔzi) nf psychosis.
pubblicare (pubbli'kare) vt publish. **pubblicazione** nf publication. **pubblicità** nf publicity,
advertising.
pubblico ('pubbliko) adj 1 public. 2 state. nm 1
public. 2 audience.
pubertà (puber'ta) nf puberty.
pudico (pu'diko) adj modest, decent. **pudicizia**
(pudi'tʃittsja) nf modesty.
pudore (pu'dore) nm modesty, decency.
puerile (pue'rile) adj childish.
pugilato (pudʒi'lato) nm boxing. **pugile**
('pudʒile) nm boxer.
pugnalare (puɲɲa'lare) vt stab. **pugnale** nm
dagger.
pugno ('puɲɲo) nm 1 fist. 2 fistful. 3 punch.

fare a pugni fight. **prendersi a pugni** begin to fight. **tirare pugni** punch.

pulce ('pultʃe) nf flea.

pulcino (pul'tʃino) nm chick.

puledro (pu'ledro) nm foal.

puleggia (puled'dʒa) nf pulley.

pulire (pu'lire) vt 1 clean. 2 polish. **pulito** adj 1 clean. 2 tidy. **pulizia** (pulit'tsia) nf cleaning.

pullman ('pulman) nm invar 1 mot coach. 2 (railway) pullman coach.

pulpito ('pulpito) nm pulpit.

pulsare (pul'sare) vi throb.

pungere ('pundʒere) vt 1 prick. 2 sting.

punire (pu'nire) vt punish. **punizione** nf punishment.

punta ('punta) nf 1 point, tip, end. 2 top. 3 pinch, touch. 4 promontory. **camminare in punta di piedi** walk on tiptoe. **ore di punta** nf pl rush hours. **puntina** nf 1 pin. 2 gramophone needle. **puntina da disegno** drawing-pin.

puntare (pun'tare) vt 1 point, direct, aim. 2 set. 3 bet, vi push. **puntata** nf 1 thrust. 2 bet. 3 instalment, number.

punteggio (pun'teddʒo) nm score.

puntellare (puntel'lare) vt prop up. **puntello** (pun'tɛllo) nm prop.

puntiglioso (puntiʎ'ʎoso) adj 1 punctilious. 2 obstinate.

punto ('punto) nm 1 point, dot. 2 stitch. 3 mark. 4 section. **fare punto** score. **in punto** exactly. ~adv no, not at all.

puntuale (puntu'ale) adj punctual. **puntualità** nf punctuality.

puntura (pun'tura) nf 1 prick, sting, bite. 2 injection. 3 pain.

punzecchiare (puntsek'kjare) vt prick.

può (pwɔ) v see **potere.**

puoi ('pwɔi) v see **potere.**

pupattola (pu'pattola) nf doll.

pupazzo (pu'pattso) nm puppet.

pupilla (pu'pilla) nf anat pupil.

purché (pur'ke) conj provided that.

pure ('pure) conj 1 however, nonetheless, yet. 2 even, still. adv also, too.

purgare (pur'gare) vt purge, cleanse. **purga** nf purge.

purgatorio (purga'tɔrjo) nm purgatory.

purificare (purifi'kare) vt purify.

puritano (puri'tano) adj,n Puritan.

puro ('puro) adj pure. **purità** nf purity.

purpureo (pur'pureo) adj crimson.

purtroppo (pur'trɔppo) adv unfortunately.

pus (pus) nm invar pus.

putrefare (putre'fare) vi rot.

putrido ('putrido) adj rotten, putrid.

puzzare (put'tsare) vi stink. **puzzo** nm bad smell, stink. **puzzolente** (puttso'lɛnte) adj stinking.

Q

qua (kwa) adv here. **di qua** this way. **quaggiù** adv down here. **quassù** adv up here.

quacchero ('kwakkero) nm Quaker.

quaderno (kwa'dɛrno) nm 1 exercise book. 2 notebook.

quadrante (kwa'drante) nm 1 quadrant. 2 dial, face (of a clock).

quadrato (kwa'drato) adj square. nm 1 math square. 2 boxing ring.

quadretto (kwa'dretto) nm check (of material). **a quadretti** checked.

quadrifoglio (kwadri'fɔʎʎo) nm four-leaved clover.

quadro ('kwadro) adj square. nm 1 painting, picture. 2 math square. 3 pl game diamonds.

quadrupede (kwa'drupede) adj,nm quadruped.

quaglia ('kwaʎʎa) nf quail.

qualche ('kwalke) adj invar 1 some, a few. 2 any. **qualche volta** sometimes. **qualcheduno** pron someone. **qualcosa** (kwal'kɔsa) pron also **qualchecosa** something. **qualcuno** (kwal'kuno) pron 1 someone. 2 anyone. **qualora** (kwa'lora) conj if, in case. **qualsiasi** (kwal'siasi) adj 1 any. 2 whatever. 3 ordinary. **qualunque** adj invar any, whatever.

quale ('kwale) adj what, which. pron 1 who. 2 whom, which. 3 whose. adv like.

qualificare (kwalifi'kare) vt 1 qualify. 2 define. **qualificarsi** vr qualify. **qualifica** (kwa'lifika) nf qualification.

qualità (kwali'ta) nf 1 quality. 2 type, kind.

quando ('kwando) conj 1 when. 2 while.

quantità (kwanti'ta) nf quantity.

quanto ('kwanto) adj how much or many. **quanto tempo?** how long? ~pron 1 how much or many. 2 what. **tutto quanto** 1 the lot. 2 pl all. ~adv 1 how. 2 as much as. **quanto a** as regards. **quantunque** conj although.

quaranta (kwa'ranta) adj,nm forty. **quarantena**

(kwaran'tɛna) nf quarantine. **quarantesimo** adj fortieth.

quaresima (kwa'rezima) nf Lent.

quartiere (kwar'tjɛre) nm **1** district, zone, quarter. **2** mil quarters.

quarto ('kwarto) adj fourth. nm quarter. **quartetto** nm quartet.

quarzo ('kwartso) nm quartz.

quasi ('kwazi) adv almost, nearly. conj as if.

quatto ('kwatto) adj **1** crouched. **2** silent. **quatto quatto** quietly.

quattordici (kwat'torditʃi) adj fourteen. nm or f fourteen. **quattordicesimo** adj fourteenth.

quattrini (kwat'trini) nm pl money, cash.

quattro ('kwattro) adj four. **fare quattro passi** take a walk. ~nm or f four. **quattrocento** (kwattro'tʃɛnto) adj four hundred. nm **1** four hundred. **2** fifteenth century.

quegli ('kweʎʎi) adj see **quello**.

quei ('kwei) adj see **quello**.

quel (kewl) adj see **quello**.

quello, quel, quella ('kwello, kwel, 'kwella) pl **quelli, quegli, quelle** pron **1** that man, he. **2** that (one). **3** pl those, the ones. adj **1** that. **2** pl those.

quercia ('kwɛrtʃa) nf oak.

questionario (kwestjo'narjo) nm questionnaire.

questione (kwes'tjone) nf question, matter.

questo ('kwesto) pron **1** this man. **2** this (one). **3** pl these, the ones. adj **1** this. **2** pl these.

questore (kwes'tore) nm chief constable.

questura (kwes'tura) nf police station.

qui (kwi) adv here.

quietanza (kwje'tantsa) nf receipt.

quietare (kwje'tare) vt quieten. **quietarsi** vr calm down. **quiete** ('kwjɛte) nf calm.

quindi ('kwindi) adv therefore.

quindici ('kwinditʃi) adj fifteen. nm or f fifteen. **quindicesimo** adj fifteenth.

quinta ('kwinta) nf Th wing.

quinto ('kwinto) adj fifth. **quintetto** nm quintet.

quota ('kwɔta) nf **1** quota, share. **2** instalment. **3** altitude. **4** sport odds. **prendere quota** gain height.

quotidiano (kwoti'djano) adj daily. nm daily newspaper.

R

rabarbaro (ra'barbaro) nm rhubarb.

rabberciare (rabber'tʃare) vt patch up.

rabbia ('rabbja) nf **1** rabies. **2** rage.

rabbino (rab'bino) nm rabbi.

rabbonire (rabbo'nire) vt placate. **rabbonirsi** vr calm down.

rabbrividire (rabbrivi'dire) vi shiver, shudder.

rabbuffare (rabbuf'fare) vt ruffle.

rabbuiare (rabbu'jare) vi grow dark. **rabbuiarsi** vr get dark.

raccapezzare (rakkapet'tsare) vt **1** gather. **2** understand.

raccapricciare (rakkaprit'tʃare) vt horrify. **raccapricciarsi** vr be horrified.

raccattare (rakkat'tare) vt pick up.

racchetta (rak'ketta) nf tennis racket.

racchiudere* (rak'kjudere) vt contain.

raccogliere* (rak'kɔʎʎere) vt **1** gather, collect, pick. **2** pick up. **raccogliersi** vr **1** assemble. **2** concentrate.

raccolta (rak'kɔlta) nf **1** harvest, crop. **2** collection.

raccolto (rak'kɔlto) nm crop, harvest.

raccomandare (rakkoman'dare) vt **1** recommend. **2** register (a letter, etc.). **raccomandata** nf registered letter. **raccomandazione** nf recommendation.

raccomodare (rakkomo'dare) vt **1** repair, mend. **2** put in order.

racconciare (rakkon'tʃare) vt repair.

raccontare (rakkon'tare) vt tell, narrate, recount. **racconto** nm **1** account. **2** tale, story.

raccorciare (rakkor'tʃare) vt shorten.

raccordare (rakkor'dare) vt join, connect. **raccordo** nm **1** mech connection. **2** slip-road, link road.

raccostare (rakkos'tare) vt also **raccozzare** (rakkot'tsare) bring together.

radar ('radar) nm radar.

raddolcire (raddol'tʃire) vt sweeten.

raddoppiare (raddop'pjare) vt,vi double.

raddrizzare (raddrit'tsare) vt straighten.

radere* ('radere) vt shave.

radiare (ra'djare) vt cancel, cross out.

radiatore (radja'tore) nm radiator.

radiazione (radjat'tsjone) nf radiation.

radicale (radi'kale) adj,n radical.

radicchio (raˈdikkjo) nm chicory.

radice (raˈditʃe) nf root.

radio[1] (ˈradjo) nm radium. **radioattività** nf radioactivity. **radioattivo** adj radioactive.

radio[2] (ˈradjo) nf invar radio. **radioascoltatore** (radjoaskoltaˈtore) nm listener. **radiodiffusione** nf broadcasting.

radiografare (radjograˈfare) vt X-ray. **radiografia** nf X-ray.

rado (ˈrado) adj 1 sparse, thin. 2 infrequent. **di rado** rarely.

radunare (raduˈnare) vt gather, collect. **radunarsi** vr assemble.

rafano (ˈrafano) nm radish.

raffica (ˈraffika) nf 1 gust, squall. 2 mil hail, burst.

raffigurare (raffiguˈrare) vt represent.

raffinare (raffiˈnare) vt refine. **raffinamento** nm also **raffinatezza** (raffinaˈtettsa) nf refinement. **raffineria** nf refinery.

raffreddare (raffredˈdare) vt cool. vi get cold. **raffreddarsi** vr 1 get cold. 2 catch a cold. **raffreddore** nm cold, chill.

raffrenare (raffreˈnare) vt restrain.

rafia (ˈrafja) nf raffia.

raganella (ragaˈnɛlla) nf 1 frog. 2 rattle.

ragazzo (raˈgattso) nm 1 boy. 2 boyfriend. **ragazza** nf 1 girl. 2 girlfriend. **ragazza alla pari** au pair.

raggiare (radˈdʒare) vi shine, beam. **raggio** nm ray, beam.

raggirare (raddʒiˈrare) vt trick, cheat. **raggiro** nm trick.

raggiungere* (radˈdʒundʒere) vt 1 reach, arrive at. 2 catch up with. 3 achieve. 4 hit (a target).

raggiustare (raddʒusˈtare) vt 1 repair, mend. 2 put in order, tidy.

raggomitolare (raggomitoˈlare) vt wind into a ball. **raggomitolarsi** vr curl up.

raggrinzare (raggrinˈtsare) vt crease, wrinkle. vi become wrinkled.

raggruppare (raggrupˈpare) vt group, assemble. **raggrupparsi** vr assemble.

ragguagliare (raggwaˈʎʎare) vt 1 level. 2 brief, inform. **ragguaglio** nm 1 comparison. 2 information.

ragia (ˈradʒa) nf resin.

ragionare (radʒoˈnare) vi reason. **ragionamento** nm reasoning.

ragione (raˈdʒone) nf 1 reason. 2 right. **aver ragione** be right. **ragioneria** nf 1 accountancy. 2 bookkeeping. **ragionevole** (radʒo-

ˈnevole) adj reasonable. **ragioniere** (radʒoˈnjɛre) nm accountant.

ragliare (raˈʎʎare) vi bray.

ragno (ˈraɲɲo) nm spider. **ragnatela** nf spider's web.

ragù (raˈgu) nm sauce, ragout.

raion (ˈrajon) nm rayon.

rallegrare (relleˈgrare) vt cheer. **rallegrarsi** vr 1 cheer up. 2 rejoice. **rallegrarsi con** congratulate.

rallentare (rallenˈtare) vt slacken. **rallentarsi** vr slow down.

rame (ˈrame) nm copper.

rammaricare (rammariˈkare) vt vex. **rammaricarsi** vr 1 lament, complain. 2 regret. **rammarico** (ramˈmariko) nm regret.

rammendare (rammenˈdare) vt 1 mend. 2 darn.

rammentare (rammenˈtare) vt remember, recall. **rammentarsi** vr remember.

rammollire (rammolˈlire) vt 1 soften. 2 melt.

ramo (ˈramo) nm branch. **ramoscello** (ramoʃˈʃello) nm twig.

rampicare (rampiˈkare) vi climb.

rampollo (ramˈpollo) nm 1 bot shoot. 2 scion.

rampone (ramˈpone) nm harpoon.

rana (ˈrana) nf frog.

rancido (ˈrantʃido) adj rancid.

rancore (ranˈkore) nm rancour.

randagio (ranˈdadʒo) adj stray.

randello (ranˈdɛllo) nm club, stick.

rango (ˈrango) nm rank, status.

rannicchiarsi (rannikˈkjarsi) vr crouch.

rannuvolare (rannuvoˈlare) vt cloud. **rannuvolarsi** vr cloud over.

ranocchio (raˈnɔkkjo) nm frog.

ranuncolo (raˈnunkolo) nm buttercup.

rapa (ˈrapa) nf turnip.

rapace (raˈpatʃe) adj rapacious.

rapida (ˈrapida) nf rapid.

rapido (ˈrapido) adj rapid, quick. nm express train.

rapina (raˈpina) nf robbery.

rapire (raˈpire) vt 1 snatch. 2 abduct, kidnap. 3 delight. **rapitore** nm kidnapper.

rappezzare (rappetˈtsare) vt piece together. **rappezzo** (rapˈpɛttso) nm patch.

rapporto (rapˈpɔrto) nm 1 report. 2 relation, connection.

rappresaglia (rappreˈsaʎʎa) nf reprisal, retaliation.

rappresentare (rapprezenˈtare) vt 1 represent. 2 perform, act. **rappresentarsi** vr imagine.

rappresentante *nm* **1** representative. **2** salesman. **rappresentazione** *nf* performance.

raro ('raro) *adj* rare.

rasare (ra'sare) *vt* **1** shave. **2** level.

raschiare (ras'kjare) *vt* scrape. *vi* clear one's throat.

rasentare (razen'tare) *vt* go close to, skim. **rasente** *prep* close to.

rasi ('rasi) *v* see **radere**.

raso ('raso) *v* see **radere**. *nm* satin.

rasoio (ra'sojo) *nm* razor.

rassegnarsi (rasseŋ'narsi) *vr* resign oneself. **rassegna** *nf* **1** *mil* inspection. **2** review. **3** report.

rasserenarsi (rassere'narsi) *vr* clear up.

rassettare (rasset'tare) *vt* **1** tidy, arrange. **2** repair, mend.

rassicurare (rassiku'rare) *vt* reassure. **rassicurarsi** *vr* be reassured.

rassomigliare (rassomiʎ'ʎare) *vi* resemble, look like. **rassomigliarsi** *vr* look alike. **rassomiglianza** (rassomiʎ'ʎantsa) *nf* resemblance.

rastrello (ras'trɛllo) *nm* rake. **rastrelliera** (rastrel'ljɛra) *nf* **1** hay rack. **2** dish rack.

rata ('rata) *nf* instalment. **comprare a rate** buy on hire purchase.

ratificare (ratifi'kare) *vt* confirm, ratify.

ratto[1] ('ratto) *nm* kidnapping.

ratto[2] ('ratto) *nm* rat.

rattoppare (rattop'pare) *vt* patch, mend.

rattrappire (rattrap'pire) *vi* be stiff.

rattristare (rattris'tare) *vt* sadden. **rattristarsi** *vr* become sad.

rauco ('rauko) *adj* hoarse.

ravanello (rava'nɛllo) *nm* radish.

ravioli (ravi'ɔli) *nm pl* pieces of stuffed pasta.

ravviare (ravvi'are) *vt* put in order, tidy.

ravvisare (ravvi'zare) *vt* recognize.

ravvivare (ravvi'vare) *vt* revive.

ravvolgere* (rav'vɔldʒere) *vt* wrap.

razionale (rattsjo'nale) *adj* rational.

razionare (rattsjo'nare) *vt* ration. **razione** *nf* ration.

razza ('rattsa) *nf* race, breed.

razzia (rat'tsia) *nf* raid. **razzismo** (rat'tsizmo) *nm* racialism. **razzista** *nm* racialist.

razzo ('raddzo) *nm* rocket.

re (re) *nm invar* king.

reale[1] (re'ale) *adj* real. **realismo** *nm* realism. **realtà** *nf* reality.

reale[2] (re'ale) *adj* royal.

realizzare (realid'dzare) *vt* achieve, carry out. **realizzarsi** *vr* come about.

reato (re'ato) *nm* crime.

reattore (reat'tore) *nm* reactor.

reazione (reat'tsjone) *nf* reaction.

rebbio ('rebbjo) *nm* prong.

recapito (re'kapito) *nm* address.

recare (re'kare) *vt* **1** bring. **2** cause. **recarsi** *vr* go.

recensire (retʃen'sire) *vt* review. **recensione** *nf* review.

recente (re'tʃɛnte) *adj* recent, new.

recessione (retʃes'sjone) *nf* recession.

recingere* (re'tʃindʒere) *vt* surround, enclose. **recinto** *nm* enclosure.

recipiente (retʃi'pjɛnte) *nm* container.

reciproco (re'tʃiproko) *adj* mutual, reciprocal.

recitare (retʃi'tare) *vt* **1** recite. **2** perform. **recita** ('rɛtʃita) *nf* performance.

reclamare (rekla'mare) *vi* protest, complain. *vt* demand, claim. **reclamo** *nm* claim.

reclame (re'klam) *nf* **1** advertisement. **2** advertising.

reclusione (reklu'zjone) *nf* **1** seclusion. **2** imprisonment.

reclutare (reklu'tare) *vt* enlist, enrol, recruit. **recluta** *nf* recruit.

record ('rɛkord) *nm invar* record (in sport, etc.).

recriminare (rekrimi'nare) *vi* recriminate. **recriminazione** *nf* recrimination.

recto ('rɛkto) *nm* **1** recto, right-hand side of page. **2** reverse (of a coin).

redarguire (redargu'ire) *vt* reprove, reproach.

redattore (redat'tore) *nm* **1** writer. **2** editor. **redazione** *nf* **1** editing. **2** editorial staff.

reddito ('rɛddito) *nm* income, revenue.

redentore (reden'tore) *nm* redeemer. **redenzione** *nf* redemption.

redigere* (re'didʒere) *vt* compile, draft.

redine ('rɛdine) *nf* rein.

reduce ('rɛdutʃe) *nm* survivor. *adj* returned.

refe ('refe) *nm* thread.

referendum (refe'rɛndum) *nm invar* referendum.

referenza (refe'rɛntsa) *nf* reference.

refettorio (refet'tɔrjo) *nm* refectory.

regalare (rega'lare) *vt* give. **regalo** *nm* gift.

regale (re'gale) *adj* regal.

regata (re'gata) *nf* boat race.

reggere* ('rɛddʒere) *vt* **1** hold, support. **2** direct. **3** rule. *vi* resist. **reggersi** *vr* stand. **reggente** (red'dʒɛnte) *nm* regent.

reggia ('rɛddʒa) nf royal palace.

reggimento (reddʒi'mento) nm regiment.

reggipetto (reddʃi'pɛtto) nm invar also **reggiseno** nm bra, brassiere.

regia (re'dʒia) nf (film) direction.

regime (re'dʒime) nm 1 regime. 2 diet.

regina (re'dʒina) nf queen. **reginetta** nf beauty queen.

regio ('rɛdʒo) adj royal.

regione (re'dʒone) nf region. **regionale** adj regional.

regista (re'dʒista) nm 1 (of a film) director. 2 Th producer.

registrare (redʒis'trare) vt 1 note, register. 2 record. **registratore** nm tape-recorder. **registratore di cassa** cash register. **registrazione** nf 1 registration. 2 recording. **registro** nm register.

regnare (reɲ'ɲare) vi reign. **regno** nm 1 kingdom. 2 reign.

regola ('rɛgola) nf rule. **in regola** in order.

regolare (rego'lare) vt regulate, adjust. adj regular. **regolarità** nf regularity.

regolo ('rɛgolo) nm ruler. **regolo calcolatore** slide rule.

reincarnazione (reinkarnat'tsjone) nf reincarnation.

relativo (rela'tivo) adj 1 relative. 2 relevant. **relatività** nf relativity.

relazione (relat'tsjone) nf 1 relation, relationship. 2 report.

relegare (rele'gare) vt 1 confine. 2 relegate.

religione (reli'dʒone) nf religion. **religioso** (reli'dʒoso) adj religious.

reliquia (re'likwja) nf relic.

reliquiario (reli'kwarjo) nm shrine.

remare (re'mare) vi row. **rematore** nm oarsman. **remo** nm oar.

reminiscenza (remini'ʃʃɛntsa) nf 1 remembrance. 2 reminiscence.

remissivo (remis'sivo) adj submissive.

remoto (re'mɔto) adj remote.

rena ('rena) nf sand.

rendere* ('rɛndere) vt 1 give back, return. 2 give. 3 make. 4 yield. **rendersi** vr become. **rendersi conto** realize. **rendiconto** nm comm statement.

rendita ('rɛndita) nf income.

rene ('rɛne) nm anat kidney.

reni ('reni) nf pl anat back.

renna ('rɛnna) nf reindeer.

Reno ('rɛno) nm Rhine.

reparto (re'parto) nm 1 department, section. 2 mil detachment.

repellente (repel'lɛnte) adj repulsive.

repertorio (reper'tɔrjo) nm 1 index. 2 repertory.

replicare (repli'kare) vt 1 reply. 2 repeat. **replica** ('rɛplika) nf 1 reply. 2 Th repeat performance, run.

reprensibile (repren'sibile) adj blameworthy.

repressione (repres'sjone) nf repression. **repressivo** adj repressive.

reprimere* (re'primere) vt check, suppress.

repubblica (re'pubblika) nf republic. **repubblicano** adj,n republican.

reputare (repu'tare) vt consider, judge. **reputazione** nf reputation.

requie ('rɛkwje) nf rest.

requisire (rekwi'zire) vt requisition.

resa ('resa) nf 1 surrender. 2 return.

resi ('resi) v see **rendere**.

residente (resi'dɛnte) adj,nm resident. **residenza** (resi'dɛntsa) nf residence. **residenziale** adj residential.

residuo (re'siduo) nm remainder.

resina ('rezina) nf resin.

resistere (re'sistere) vi 1 resist, hold out. 2 endure. **resistente** adj resistant. **resistenza** (resis'tɛntsa) nf resistance.

reso ('reso) v see **rendere**.

resoconto (reso'konto) nm report.

respingere* (res'pindʒere) vt 1 repel, force back. 2 reject.

respirare (respi'rare) vi,vt breathe. **respirazione** nf respiration. **respiro** nm 1 breath. 2 rest.

responsabile (respon'sabile) adj responsible. **responsabilità** nf responsibility.

ressa ('rɛssa) nf crowd.

ressi ('rɛssi) v see **reggere**.

restare (res'tare) vi 1 stay, remain. 2 be left.

restaurare (restau'rare) vt restore. **restauro** nm restoration, repair.

restio (res'tio) adj reluctant.

restituire (restitu'ire) vt give back, restore.

resto ('rɛsto) nm 1 rest, remainder. 2 change (money). **del resto** besides.

restringere* (res'trindʒere) vt 1 tighten, squeeze. 2 restrict. 3 take in (clothes). **restringersi** vr 1 narrow. 2 shrink. 3 close up. **restrizione** nf restriction.

rete ('rete) nf 1 net. 2 network. 3 sport goal. **reticella** (reti'tʃɛlla) nf luggage rack.

reticente (reti'tʃɛnte) *adj* reticent. **reticenza** (reti'tʃɛntsa) *nf* reticence.

reticolato (retiko'lato) *nm* wire netting.

retina ('rɛtina) *nf* retina.

retorica (re'tɔrika) *nf* rhetoric. **retorico** (re'tɔriko) *adj* rhetorical.

retribuire (retribu'ire) *vt* **1** pay. **2** reward. **retribuzione** *nf* payment.

retro ('rɛtro) *nm* back, reverse side. **retrodatare** (retroda'tare) *vt* backdate. **retrogrado** (re'trɔgrado) *adj* backward, retrograde. **retroguardia** (retro'gwardja) *nf* rearguard. **retromarcia** (retro'martʃa) *nf* reverse gear. **retrospettivo** (retrospet'tivo) *adj* retrospective. **retrovisore** (retrovi'zore) *nm* driving mirror.

retrocedere* (retro'tʃɛdere) *vi* retreat.

retta ('rɛtta) *nf* **dare retta** listen, pay attention.

rettangolo (ret'tangolo) *nm* rectangle. **rettangolare** *adj* rectangular.

rettificare (rettifi'kare) *vt* correct, rectify.

rettile ('rɛttile) *nm* reptile.

retto[1] ('rɛtto) *adj* **1** straight. **2** honest. **3** correct, right. *nm* **1** right angle. **2** *anat* rectum.

retto[2] ('rɛtto) *v* see **reggere.**

rettore (ret'tore) *nm educ* rector.

reumatismo (reuma'tizmo) *nm* rheumatism. **reumatico** (reu'matiko) *adj* rheumatic.

reverendo (reve'rɛndo) *adj,nm* reverend.

revisione (revi'zjone) *nf* revision.

revocare (revo'kare) *vt* annul.

revolver (re'vɔlver) *nm invar* revolver.

riabbassare (riabbas'sare) *vt* lower again.

riabbracciare (riabbrat'tʃare) *vt* embrace again.

riabilitare (riabili'tare) *vt* **1** rehabilitate. **2** reinstate. **riabilitazione** *nf* rehabilitation.

riaccendere* (riat'tʃɛndere) *vt* relight.

riaccompagnare (riakkompaɲ'ɲare) *vt* take back.

riacquistare (riakkwis'tare) *vt* regain.

riaddormentarsi (riaddormen'tarsi) *vr* fall asleep again.

riaffermare (riaffer'mare) *vt* reaffirm.

rialto (ri'alto) *nm* hill, rise.

rialzare (rial'tsare) *vt* lift up, raise. **rialzarsi** *vr* rise. **rialzo** (ri'altso) *nm* rise.

riammettere* (riam'mettere) *vt* readmit.

rianimare (riani'mare) *vt* revive.

riapertura (riaper'tura) *nf* reopening.

riapparire* (riappa'rire) *vi* reappear.

riaprire* (ria'prire) *vt,vi* reopen.

riassumere* (rias'sumere) *vt* **1** resume. **2** re-employ. **3** summarize. **riassunto** *nm* summary.

riattaccare (riattak'kare) *vt* **1** reattach. **2** hang up (telephone).

riattivare (riatti'vare) *vt* put back into operation.

ribadire (riba'dire) *vt* rivet.

ribaldo (ri'baldo) *nm* rogue.

ribaltare (ribal'tare) *vt,vi* overturn. **ribaltarsi** *vr* capsize. **ribalta** *nf* **1** footlights. **2** flap.

ribassare (ribas'sare) *vt* lower. *vi* fall. **ribasso** *nm* fall, reduction.

ribattere (ri'battere) *vt* return (ball). *vi* retort.

ribellarsi (ribel'larsi) *vr* rebel, revolt. **ribelle** (ri'bɛlle) *nm* rebel. *adj* rebellious. **ribellione** *nf* rebellion.

ribes ('ribes) *nm invar* gooseberry. **ribes nero** blackcurrant. **ribes spinoso** gooseberry bush.

riboccare (ribok'kare) *vi* overflow.

ribrezzo (ri'breddzo) *nm* shudder.

ributtare (ribut'tare) *vt* repel.

ricacciare (rikat'tʃare) *vt* drive back.

ricadere* (rika'dere) *vi* fall again. **ricaduta** *nf* relapse.

ricamare (rika'mare) *vt* embroider. **ricamo** *nm* embroidery.

ricambiare (rikam'bjare) *vt* exchange. **ricambio** *nm* exchange.

ricapitolare (rikapito'lare) *vt* sum up.

ricaricare (rikari'kare) *vt* reload.

ricattare (rikat'tare) *vt* blackmail. **ricattatore** *nm* blackmailer. **ricatto** *nm* blackmail.

ricavare (rika'vare) *vt* obtain, gain.

ricchezza (rik'kettsa) *nf* wealth.

riccio[1] ('rittʃo) *nm* hedgehog. **riccio di mare** sea urchin.

riccio[2] ('rittʃo) *adj* curly. *nm* curl. **ricciuto** *adj* curly.

ricco ('rikko) *adj* rich.

ricercare (ritʃer'kare) *vt* **1** seek. **2** investigate. **ricerca** *nf* research.

ricetta (ri'tʃɛtta) *nf* **1** *med* prescription. **2** recipe.

ricevere (ri'tʃevere) *vt* receive. **ricevimento** *nm* reception. **ricevitore** *nm* receiver. **ricevuta** *nf* receipt.

richiamare (rikja'mare) *vt* **1** call back, recall. **2** attract, draw. **3** rebuke. **richiamo** *nm* **1** recall. **2** call.

richiedere* (ri'kjɛdere) *vt* **1** ask again. **2** demand, request. **3** need. **richiesta** (ri'kjɛsta) *nf* demand, request.

ricino ('ritʃino) *nm* castor-oil plant. **olio di ricino** castor oil.

ricominciare (rikomin't∫are) vt begin again.

ricompensa (rikom'pɛnsa) nf reward.

riconciliare (rikont∫i'ljare) vt reconcile. **riconciliarsi** vr be reconciled.

ricondurre* (rikon'durre) vt take back.

riconoscere* (riko'no∫∫ere) vt 1 recognize. 2 acknowledge. **riconoscente** (rikono∫'∫ɛnte) adj grateful. **riconoscenza** (rikono∫'∫ɛntsa) nf gratitude. **riconoscimento** nm recognition.

ricopiare (riko'pjare) vt copy out.

ricoprire* (riko'prire) vt cover.

ricordare (rikor'dare) vt 1 remember, recall. 2 remind of. 3 commemorate. **ricordarsi** vr remember. **ricordo** (ri'kɔrdo) nm 1 memory. 2 souvenir.

ricorrere* (ri'korrere) vi 1 turn to. 2 appeal. 3 recur.

ricostruire (rikostru'ire) vt reconstruct.

ricotta (ri'kɔtta) nf cottage cheese.

ricoverare (rikove'rare) vt 1 shelter. 2 admit to hospital. **ricovero** (ri'kɔvero) nm refuge.

ricrearsi (rikre'arsi) vr amuse oneself. **ricreazione** nf recreation.

ricredersi (rikre'dersi) vr change one's mind.

ricuperare (rikupe'rare) vt recover, salvage.

ricusare (riku'zare) vt refuse.

ridare* (ri'dare) vt give back.

ridere* ('ridere) vi laugh.

ridicolo (ri'dikolo) adj ridiculous.

ridire* (ri'dire) vt 1 repeat. 2 find fault.

ridurre* (ri'durre) vt 1 reduce. 2 adapt. **riduzione** nf 1 reduction. 2 mus arrangement.

riempire (riem'pire) vt 1 fill. 2 stuff. 3 fill in.

rientrare (rien'trare) vi 1 re-enter. 2 return.

rifare* (ri'fare) vt 1 do or make again. 2 repair.

riferire (rife'rire) vt 1 report. 2 ascribe. **riferirsi** vr refer. **riferimento** nm reference.

rifiutare (rifju'tare) vt 1 refuse. 2 reject. **rifiutarsi** vr refuse. **rifiuto** (ri'fjuto) nm 1 refusal. 2 pl refuse, rubbish. **merce di rifiuto** nf pl waste goods.

riflessione (rifles'sjone) nf reflexion.

riflessivo (rifles'sivo) adj thoughtful.

riflesso (ri'flɛsso) nm 1 reflection. 2 reflex.

riflettere* (ri'flɛttere) vt,vi reflect. **riflettersi** vr be reflected. **riflettore** nm searchlight, floodlight.

rifondere* (ri'fondere) vt refund.

riformare (rifor'mare) vt 1 reform. 2 mil discharge. **riforma** nf 1 reform. 2 Reformation. **riformatore** nm reformer.

rifornire (rifor'nire) vt supply, provide. **rifor-**

nimento nm supply. **stazione di rifornimento** nf filling station.

rifuggire (rifud'dʒire) vi 1 flee. 2 shun.

rifugiarsi (rifu'dʒarsi) vr take refuge. **rifugiato** nm refugee. **rifugio** nm refuge, shelter.

rifulgere* (ri'fuldʒere) vi shine.

rigaglie (ri'gaʎʎe) nf pl giblets.

rigare ('rigare) vt rule. **riga** nf 1 line, stripe. 2 row. 3 ruler. 4 parting (in hair). **a righe** striped. **rigato** adj lined, striped.

rigettare (ridʒet'tare) vt 1 throw back. 2 reject. **rigetto** (ri'dʒetto) nm rejection.

rigido ('ridʒido) adj 1 stiff, rigid. 2 strict, severe. **rigidezza** (ridʒi'dettsa) nf severity. **rigidità** nf rigidity.

rigirare (ridʒi'rare) vt turn. **rigirarsi** vr turn round. **rigiro** nm 1 turning. 2 trick.

rigo ('rigo) nm line.

rigoglioso (rigoʎ'ʎoso) adj exuberant.

rigore (ri'gore) nm rigour, harshness. **rigoroso** adj 1 severe. 2 rigorous.

rigovernare (rigover'nare) vt wash up (dishes).

riguardare (rigwar'dare) vt 1 look at again. 2 concern. 3 consider. vi overlook. **riguardarsi** vr take care of oneself. **riguardo** nm 1 regard, respect. 2 care. **riguardo a** as regards.

rilasciare (rila∫'∫are) vt 1 leave again. 2 release. 3 issue. **rilascio** nm 1 release. 2 issue.

rilassare (rilas'sare) vt relax. **rilassarsi** vr slacken.

rilegare (rile'gare) vt 1 bind (a book). 2 set (a jewel). **rilegatura** nf binding.

rileggere* (ri'lɛddʒere) vt re-read.

rilevare (rile'vare) vt 1 lift up. 2 notice. 3 point out. 4 survey. 5 understand. 6 relieve. 7 take over.

rilievo (ri'ljɛvo) nm relief.

rilucere* (ri'lut∫ere) vi glitter.

riluttante (rilut'tante) adj reluctant. **riluttanza** (rilut'tantsa) nf reluctance.

rima ('rima) nf rhyme.

rimandare (riman'dare) vt 1 send back. 2 put off, postpone. **rimando** nm 1 return. 2 postponement.

rimanere* (rima'nere) vi 1 stay, remain. 2 be left, remain. **rimanere ferito** be wounded.

rimango (ri'mango) v see rimanere.

rimarrò (rimar'rɔ) v see rimanere.

rimasi (ri'masi) v see rimanere.

rimasto (ri'masto) v see rimanere.

rimasugli (rima'suʎʎi) nm pl leftovers.

rimbalzare (rimbal'tsare) vi rebound. **rimbalzo** nm rebound.

rimbambire (rimbam'bire) vi become childish.

rimbeccare (rimbek'kare) vt retort.

rimboccare (rimbok'kare) vt turn or tuck up.

rimbombare (rimbom'bare) vi resound.

rimborsare (rimbor'sare) vt refund, repay.

rimediare (rime'djare) vi cure. **rimedio** (ri'mɛdjo) nm cure, remedy.

rimescolare (rimesko'lare) vt 1 mix. 2 shuffle (cards).

rimessa (ri'messa) nf 1 shed. 2 garage.

rimettere (ri'mettere) vt 1 replace, return. 2 put on again. 3 lose. 4 postpone. 5 send. 6 pardon. 7 entrust. **rimettersi** vr 1 return. 2 recover. 3 (of the weather) clear up. 4 rely.

rimodernare (rimoder'nare) vt update, modernize.

rimontare (rimon'tare) vt 1 reassemble. 2 go up again. 3 remount. vi 1 remount. 2 date.

rimorchiare (rimor'kjare) vt tow. **rimorchio** (ri'mɔrkjo) nm trailer.

rimorso (ri'mɔrso) nm remorse.

rimpasto (rim'pasto) nm reshuffle.

rimpatriare (rimpa'trjare) vi return home. vt repatriate. **rimpatrio** (rim'patrjo) nm repatriation.

rimpiangere* (rim'pjandʒere) vt regret.

rimpiattino (rimpjat'tino) nm hide-and-seek.

rimpiccolire (rimpikko'lire) vt make smaller. vi become smaller.

rimpinzarsi (rimpin'tsarsi) vr overeat.

rimproverare (rimprove'rare) vt rebuke. **rimprovero** (rim'prɔvero) nm rebuke, reproof.

rimuovere* (ri'mwɔvere) vt 1 remove. 2 dissuade.

Rinascimento (rinaʃʃi'mento) nm Renaissance.

rincagnato (rinkan'ɲato) adj snub (of a nose).

rincalzare (rinkal'tsare) vt 1 prop up. 2 tuck in. 3 chase.

rincarare (rinka'rare) vt increase the price of.

rincasare (rinka'sare) vi go home.

rinchiudere* (rin'kjudere) vt enclose, shut up.

rincontrare (rinkon'trare) vt meet.

rincorrere* (rin'korrere) vt chase, pursue. **rincorsa** nf short run.

rincrescere* (rin'kreʃʃere) vi cause regret. v imp be sorry.

rinculare (rinku'lare) vi recoil.

rinfiancare (rinfjan'kare) vt prop up.

rinforzare (rinfor'tsare) vt reinforce, strengthen.

rinforzo (rin'fɔrtso) nm 1 support. 2 mil reinforcement.

rinfrescare (rinfres'kare) vt 1 cool. 2 refresh. **rinfrescarsi** vr 1 cool down. 2 have a cool drink. **rinfrescante** adj refreshing. **rinfresco** nm refreshment.

rinfusa (rin'fuza) adv,adj **alla rinfusa** higgledy-piggledy.

ringhiare (rin'gjare) vi growl. **ringhio** nm growl.

ringhiera (rin'gjɛra) nf 1 railing. 2 pl banisters.

ringiovanire (rindʒova'nire) vt make younger. vi become younger.

ringraziare (ringrat'tsjare) vt thank. **ringraziamento** nm thanks.

rinnegare (rinne'gare) vt 1 deny. 2 disown.

rinnovare (rinno'vare) vt renew.

rinoceronte (rinotʃe'ronte) nm rhinoceros.

rinomato (rino'mato) adj famous.

rintoccare (rintok'kare) vi (of a clock) strike, (of a bell) toll.

rintoppare (rintop'pare) vt come across, bump into.

rintracciare (rintrat't ʃare) vt trace.

rintronare (rintro'nare) vt 1 shake. 2 stun. vi resound.

rintuzzare (rintut'tsare) vt blunt.

rinunciare (rinun'tʃare) vi give up, relinquish. vt renounce. **rinuncia** nf renunciation.

rinvenire* (rinve'nire) vt find. vi revive.

rinviare (rinvi'are) vt 1 send back. 2 put off, defer.

rinvigorire (rinvigo'rire) vt strengthen.

riordinare (riordi'nare) vt 1 tidy. 2 reorganize.

riorganizzare (riorganid'dzare) vt reorganize. **riorganizzazione** nf reorganization.

ripagare (ripa'gare) vt repay.

riparare (ripa'rare) vt 1 repair, mend. 2 protect. **riparazione** nf repair. **riparo** nm shelter. **senza riparo** irreparably.

ripartire (ripar'tire) vt divide, share. vi leave again.

ripassare (ripas'sare) vt 1 recross. 2 revise. 3 retouch. 4 look over. **ripassata** nf 1 revision. 2 look over, inspection. **ripasso** nm revision.

ripensare (ripen'sare) vi 1 reconsider. 2 change one's mind.

ripentirsi (ripen'tirsi) vr repent.

ripercussione (riperkus'sjone) nf repercussion.

ripetere (ri'pɛtere) vt repeat. **ripetizione** nf 1 repetition. 2 rehearsal.

ripiano (ri'pjano) nm shelf.

ripido ('ripido) *adj* steep.

ripiegare (ripje'gare) *vt* fold up.

ripiego (ri'pjɛgo) *nm* expedient.

ripieno (ri'pjɛno) *adj* stuffed. *nm* stuffing, filling.

riporre* (ri'porre) *vt* place.

riportare (ripor'tare) *vt* **1** take or bring back. **2** report. **3** win, obtain, receive. **riportarsi** *vr* refer.

riposare (ripo'sare) *vt* **1** put back. **2** rest. *vi* rest. **riposarsi** *vr* rest. **riposo** (ri'pɔso) *nm* rest. **a riposo** retired.

ripostiglio (ripos'tiʎʎo) *nm* **1** hiding place. **2** storeroom.

riprendere* (ri'prɛndere) *vt* **1** take back. **2** take again. **3** resume. **4** reprove. **5** film. *vi* revive. **riprendersi** *vr* **1** recover. **2** correct oneself.

ripresa (ri'presa) *nf* **1** resumption. **2** *sport* second half or round.

riprodurre* (ripro'durre) *vt* reproduce. **riproduzione** *nf* reproduction.

ripugnante (ripuɲ'ɲante) *adj* repugnant. **ripugnanza** (ripuɲ'ɲantsa) *nf* repugnance.

ripulsione (ripul'sjone) *nf* repulsion. **ripulsivo** *adj* repulsive.

risaia (ri'saja) *nf* paddy field.

risalire (risa'lire) *vt* **1** go up again. **2** go back to, date from.

risaltare (risal'tare) *vi* stand out. **risalto** *nm* relief, prominence. **fare risalto** stand out.

risanare (risa'nare) *vt* cure.

risarcire (risar't ʃire) *vt* compensate.

risata (ri'sata) *nf* laugh.

riscaldare (riskal'dare) *vt* **1** heat, heat up. **2** warm. **riscaldarsi** *vr* warm up. **riscaldamento** *nm* heating. **riscaldatore** *nm* heater.

riscatto (ris'katto) *nm* ransom.

rischiarare (riskja'rare) *vt* **1** light up. **2** enlighten. **3** clear. *vi* light up. **rischiararsi** *vr* clear up. clear up.

rischiare (ris'kjare) *vt* risk. *vi* run the risk. **rischio** *nm* risk. **rischioso** (ris'kjoso) *adj* risky.

risciacquare (riʃ ʃak'kware) *vt* rinse.

risciò (riʃ'ʃɔ) *nm* rickshaw.

riscontrare (riskon'trare) *vt* **1** compare. **2** verify. **riscontrarsi** *vr* correspond. **riscontro** *nm* **1** checking. **2** comparison.

riscossa (ris'kɔssa) *nf* insurrection.

riscuotere* (ris'kwɔtere) *vt* **1** cash, draw, collect (one's salary). **2** obtain. **3** shake. **riscuotersi** *vr* **1** start. **2** *med* come round.

risentire (risen'tire) *vt* feel, experience. *vi* show signs of. **risentirsi** *vr* take offence. **risentimento** *nm* resentment.

riserbo (ri'sɛrbo) *nm* reserve.

riservare (riser'vare) *vt* keep, reserve. **riserva** (ri'sɛrva) *nf* **1** stock, reserve. **2** reservation. **3** reserve, preserve. **4** *sport* reserve. **riservato** *adj* reserved.

risi ('risi) *v* see **ridere.**

risiedere (ri'sjɛdere) *vi* reside.

riso[1] ('riso) *v* see **ridere.**

riso[2] ('riso) *nm* rice.

riso[3] ('riso) *nm* **1** laugh. **2** laughter.

risolsi (ri'sɔlsi) *v* see **risolvere.**

risolto (ri'sɔlto) *v* see **risolvere.**

risoluto (riso'luto) *adj* determined. **risolutezza** (risolu'tettsa) *nf* determination.

risoluzione (risolut'tsjone) *nf* resolution.

risolvere* (ri'sɔlvere) *vt* **1** resolve, solve. **2** break down, dissolve. **3** decide. **4** annul. **risolversi** *vr* **1** dissolve. **2** make up one's mind.

risonare (riso'nare) *vi* resound, ring out. **risonanza** (riso'nantsa) *nf* **1** resonance. **2** echo.

risorgere* (ri'sɔrdʒere) *vi* rise again. **risorgimento** *nm* **1** revival. **2** *cap* Italian 19th-century independence movement.

risorsa (ri'sɔrsa) *nf* resource.

risparmiare (rispar'mjare) *vt* **1** save. **2** spare. **risparmio** (ris'parmjo) *nm* saving. **cassa di risparmio** *nf* savings bank.

rispettare (rispet'tare) *vt* respect. **rispettabile** (rispet'tabile) *adj* respectable. **rispettabilità** *nf* respectability. **rispetto** (ris'pɛtto) *nm* respect. **rispetto a** as regards. **rispettoso** (rispet'toso) *adj* respectful.

rispettivo (rispet'tivo) *adj* respective.

risplendere (ris'plɛndere) *vi* shine.

rispondere* (ris'pondere) *vt* **1** reply, answer. **2** be responsible for. **3** correspond. **4** respond. **rispondere di sì/no** answer yes/no.

risposi (ris'posi) *v* see **rispondere.**

risposta (ris'posta) *nf* **1** reply, answer. **2** response.

risposto (ris'posto) *v* see **rispondere.**

rissa ('rissa) *nf* brawl. **rissoso** (ris'soso) *adj* quarrelsome.

ristabilire (ristabi'lire) *vt* restore.

ristagnare (ristaɲ'ɲare) *vi* stagnate. **ristagno** *nm* stagnation.

ristampare (ristam'pare) *vt* reprint.

ristorante (risto'rante) *nm* restaurant.

ristorare (risto'rare) vt refresh, restore. **ristoro** (ris'tɔro) nm 1 relief. 2 refreshments.

ristretto (ris'tretto) adj 1 narrow. 2 restricted, limited.

risultare (risul'tare) vi result, ensue. **risultare chiaro** be clear. **risultato** nm result.

risuonare (risuo'nare) vi resound, ring out. **risuonanza** nf 1 resonance. 2 echo.

risurrezione (risurret'tsjone) nf resurrection.

risuscitare (risuʃʃi'tare) vt bring back to life, revive. vi rise again.

risvegliare (rizveʎ'ʎare) vt awaken, revive. **risveglio** nm revival.

ritaglio (ri'taʎʎo) nm 1 newspaper cutting. 2 scrap.

ritardare (ritar'dare) vt slow down, delay. vi 1 be late. 2 (of a watch) lose. **ritardo** nm delay. **in ritardo** late.

ritegno (ri'teɲɲo) nm restraint.

ritenere* (rite'nere) vt 1 keep back. 2 keep, hold. 3 consider. 4 remember. **ritenersi** vr consider oneself.

ritirare (riti'rare) vt 1 withdraw, draw back. 2 retract. 3 draw (money). **ritirarsi** vr 1 withdraw. 2 retire. **ritirata** nf 1 retreat. 2 lavatory. **ritiro** nm withdrawal.

ritmo ('ritmo) nm rhythm. **ritmico** ('ritmiko) adj rhythmic.

rito ('rito) nm rite. **rituale** adj ritual.

ritoccare (ritok'kare) vt touch up. **ritocco** (ri'tokko) nm retouch.

ritornare (ritor'nare) vi 1 return, come back. 2 recur. vt give back. **ritorno** nm return. **essere di ritorno** be back. **ritorno di fiamma** 1 backfire. 2 renewed passion.

ritrarre* (ri'trarre) vt 1 draw back. 2 reproduce. **ritrarsi** vr withdraw.

ritratto (ri'tratto) nm portrait.

ritroso (ri'troso) adj 1 reluctant. 2 shy.

ritrovare (ritro'vare) vt 1 find (again). 2 discover. 3 recover. **ritrovarsi** vr 1 meet. 2 find oneself. **ritrovo** (ri'trɔvo) nm 1 meeting. 2 meeting place. **ritrovo notturno** nightclub.

ritto ('ritto) adj 1 upright. 2 straight. **stare ritto** stand up. ~nm right side.

riunire (riu'nire) vt 1 gather, collect. 2 reunite. **riunirsi** vr 1 be reunited. 2 meet. **riunione** nf meeting.

riuscire* (riuʃ'ʃire) vi 1 go out. 2 work or turn out. 3 result. 4 succeed, manage. **riuscita** nf 1 result. 2 success.

riva ('riva) nf bank, shore.

rivale (ri'vale) adj,n rival. **rivaleggiare** vi rival. **rivalità** nf rivalry.

rivedere* (rive'dere) vt 1 see again. 2 revise, examine.

rivelare (rive'lare) vt reveal, disclose. **rivelazione** nf revelation.

riverberare (riverbe'rare) vt reverberate.

riverire (rive'rire) vt respect. **riverente** (rive-'rɛnte) adj reverent. **riverenza** (rive'rɛntsa) nf 1 reverence. 2 bow.

rivestire (rives'tire) vt 1 cover. 2 line.

riviera (ri'vjɛra) nf coast.

rivista (ri'vista) nf 1 mil parade. 2 magazine, review. 3 revue.

rivolgere* (ri'vɔldʒere) vt 1 turn (over). 2 direct. **rivolgersi** vr 1 turn round. 2 apply. 3 go towards. **rivolgimento** nm upheaval.

rivoltare (rivol'tare) vt turn. **rivoltarsi** vr revolt. **rivolta** nf revolt.

rivoltella (rivol'tɛlla) nf revolver.

rivoluzione (rivolut'tsjone) nf revolution. **rivoluzionario** adj revolutionary.

rizzare (rit'tsare) vt raise, erect. **rizzarsi** vr 1 stand up. 2 stand on end.

roba ('rɔba) nf stuff, things, possessions.

robusto (ro'busto) adj strong, sturdy.

rocca ('rɔkka) nf fortress. **roccaforte** nf stronghold.

roccia ('rɔttʃa) nf rock. **roccioso** (rot'tʃoso) adj rocky.

rodaggio (ro'daddʒo) nm mot running in. **in rodaggio** running in.

Rodano ('rɔdano) nm Rhône.

rodere* ('rodere) vt 1 gnaw. 2 nibble. **roditori** nm pl rodents.

Rodesia (ro'dɛzja) nf Rhodesia. **rodesiano** adj,n Rhodesian.

rododendro (rodo'dɛndro) nm rhododendron.

rogna ('rɔɲɲa) nf 1 itch. 2 scabies.

rognone (roɲ'ɲone) nm cul kidney.

rollare (rol'lare) vi naut roll.

Roma ('roma) nf Rome. **romano** adj,n Roman.

Romania (roma'nia) nf Rumania. **romeno** adj,n Rumanian.

romanico (ro'maniko) adj romanesque.

romantico (ro'mantiko) adj romantic. **romanticismo** nm romanticism.

romanzo[1] (ro'mandzo) adj romance (language).

romanzo[2] (ro'mandzo) nm 1 novel. 2 romance. **romanziere** (roman'dzjɛre) nm novelist.

romito (ro'mito) nm hermit.

rompere* ('rompere) vt break, smash. vi break.

105

rompere la testa annoy. **rompersi** *vr* break up. **rompersi la testa** rack one's brains.

rompicapo *nm* annoyance. **rompiscatole** (rompis'katole) *nm sl* pest, nuisance.

ronda ('ronda) *nf mil* rounds, patrol.

rondine ('rondine) *nf zool* swallow.

rondone (ron'done) *nm* swift.

ronzare (ron'dzare) *vi* buzz, hum, whirr. **ronzio** *nm* buzz, hum.

ronzino (rond'zino) *nm inf* nag.

rosa ('rɔza) *nf* rose. *adj invar,nm invar* pink.

rosario (ro'zarjo) *nm* rosary.

rosbif ('rozbif) *nm invar* roast beef.

rosicchiare (rosik'kjare) *vt* nibble.

rosmarino (rozma'rino) *nm* rosemary.

rosolare (rozo'lare) *vt* cul brown.

rosolia (rozo'lia) *nf* German measles.

rospo ('rɔspo) *nm* toad. **ingoiare un rospo** swallow an insult.

rosso ('rosso) *adj,nm* red. **rossetto** *nm* lipstick. **rossore** *nm* shame.

rosticceria (rostittʃe'ria) *nf* shop selling cooked food.

rostro ('rɔstro) *nm* rostrum.

rotaia (ro'taja) *nf* 1 rail. 2 rut.

rotare (ro'tare) *vt,vi* rotate. **rotazione** *nf* rotation.

roteare (rote'are) *vt* whirl. *vi* wheel.

rotella (ro'tɛlla) *nf* wheel. **pattino a rotelle** *nm* roller-skate.

rotolare (roto'lare) *vt* roll. *vi* roll down. **rotolo** ('rɔtolo) *nm* roll.

rotondo (ro'tondo) *adj* round.

rotta[1] (ro'tta) *nf* 1 break. 2 rout. **a rotta di collo** at breakneck speed.

rotta[2] ('rɔtta) *nf* course, route.

rotto ('rotto) *v see* **rompere**. *adj* broken. **rottame** *nm* 1 fragment. 2 *pl* wreckage, ruins. **rottami di ferro** *nm pl* scrap iron. **rottura** *nf* break, breaking off.

rovesciare (roveʃ'ʃare) *vt* 1 upset, spill. 2 overturn. 3 turn inside out. 4 overthrow. **rovesciarsi** *vr* 1 overturn, capsize. 2 fall down. **rovescio** (ro'veʃʃo) *nm* 1 wrong side, other side. **a rovescio** back to front. **capire a rovescio** misunderstand. **alla rovescia** 1 inside out. 2 upside down.

rovinare (rovi'nare) *vt* ruin. **rovina** *nf* fall, ruin.

rovistare (rovis'tare) *vt* ransack.

rovo ('rovo) *nm* bramble, blackberry bush.

rozzo ('roddzo) *adj* rough, coarse.

106

ruba ('ruba) *nf* **andare a ruba** sell like hot cakes.

rubacchiare (rubak'kjare) *vt* pilfer.

rubare (ru'bare) *vt* steal, rob. **rubacuori** (ruba-'kwɔri) *nm sl* lady-killer.

rubinetto (rubi'netto) *nm* tap.

rubino (ru'bino) *nm* ruby.

rubrica (ru'brika) *nf* 1 directory. 2 feature, column.

rude ('rude) *adj* rough.

rudere ('rudere) *nm* ruin.

ruga ('ruga) *nf* wrinkle. **rugoso** (ru'goso) *adj* wrinkled.

rugby ('rugbi) *nm* rugby. **rugbista** *nm* rugby-player.

ruggine ('ruddʒine) *nf* rust. **rugginoso** (ruddʒi-'noso) *adj* rusty.

ruggire (rud'dʒire) *vi* roar. **ruggito** *nm* roar.

rugiada (ru'dʒada) *nf* dew.

rullare (rul'lare) *vt* roll. *vi* 1 roll. 2 *aviat* taxi. **rullio** *nm* roll. **rullo** *nm* 1 roll. 2 *tech* roller. **rullo compressore** steamroller.

rum (rum) *nm* rum.

ruminare (rumi'nare) *vt* 1 chew. 2 ruminate.

rumore (ru'more) *nm* 1 noise, din. 2 rumour. **rumoroso** (rumo'roso) *adj* noisy.

rumoreggiare (rumored'dʒare) *vi* make a noise.

ruolo ('rwɔlo) *nm* 1 roll, list. 2 role.

ruota ('rwɔta) *nf* wheel. **ruota di ricambio** spare wheel.

rupe ('rupe) *nf* cliff.

rupia (ru'pia) *nf* rupee.

ruppi ('ruppi) *v see* **rompere**.

rurale (ru'rale) *adj* rural.

ruscello (ruʃ'ʃello) *nm* stream.

russare (rus'sare) *vi* snore.

Russia ('russja) *nf* Russia. **russo** *adj,n* Russian. *nm* Russian (language).

rustico ('rustiko) *adj* rustic.

ruttare (rut'tare) *vi* belch, burp. **rutto** *nm* belch.

ruvido ('ruvido) *adj* rough, coarse. **ruvidezza** (ruvi'dettsa) *nf* coarseness.

ruzzare (rud'dzare) *vi* gambol.

ruzzolare (ruttso'lare) *vi* roll down.

S

sa (sa) *v see* **sapere**.

sabato ('sabato) *nm* Saturday.

sabbia ('sabbja) nf sand. **sabbie mobili** n pl quicksands. **sabbioso** (sab'bjoso) adj sandy.

sabotare (sabo'tare) vt sabotage. **sabotaggio** nm sabotage. **sabotatore** nm saboteur.

sacca ('sakka) nf **1** bag, satchel. **2** pocket.

saccarina (sakka'rina) nf saccharin.

saccente (sat'tʃɛnte) nm know-all.

saccheggiare (sakked'dʒare) vt sack, plunder. **saccheggio** nm sack, pillage.

sacchetto (sak'ketto) nm paper bag.

sacco ('sakko) nm sack, bag. **sacco a pelo** sleeping-bag.

saccoccia (sak'kɔttʃa) nf pocket.

sacerdote (satʃer'dɔte) nm priest. **sacerdotale** adj priestly. **sacerdozio** (satʃer'dɔttsjo) nm priesthood.

sacramento (sakra'mento) nm sacrament.

sacrificare (sakrifi'kare) vt sacrifice. **sacrificio** nm sacrifice.

sacrilegio (sakri'lɛdʒo) nm sacrilege.

sacro ('sakro) adj holy, sacred.

sadico ('sadiko) adj sadistic. nm sadist. **sadismo** nm sadism.

saetta (sa'etta) nf arrow.

safari (sa'fari) nm safari.

saga ('saga) nf saga.

sagace (sa'gatʃe) adj clever, shrewd. **sagacità** nf sagacity.

saggezza (sad'dʒettsa) nf wisdom.

saggio[1] ('saddʒo) adj wise, prudent. nm sage.

saggio[2] ('saddʒo) nm **1** trial, test. **2** sample. **3** study, essay.

Sagittario (sadʒit'tarjo) nm Sagittarius.

sagoma ('sagoma) nf outline, profile.

sagra ('sagra) nf festival.

sagrestia (sagres'tia) nf sacristy. **sagrestano** nm sacristan.

sai ('sai) v see **sapere.**

sala ('sala) nf room, hall. **sala da pranzo** dining room. **sala operatoria** operating theatre.

salamandra (sala'mandra) nf salamander.

salame (sa'lame) nm pork sausage, salami.

salamoia (sala'moja) nf brine.

salario (sa'larjo) nm wages, salary.

saldare (sal'dare) vt **1** join, weld. **2** settle, pay (a bill). **saldezza** (sal'dettsa) nf firmness. **saldo** adj solid, firm.

sale ('sale) nm salt. **salare** vt salt. **salato** adj **1** salt, salty. **2** expensive. **saliera** (sal'jɛra) nf saltcellar.

salgo ('salgo) v see **salire.**

salice ('salitʃe) nm willow.

salire* (sa'lire) vt,vi climb, go up. vi rise, increase. **salire in macchina** get into a car. **salita** nf ascent, climb.

saliva (sa'liva) nf saliva.

salma ('salma) nf corpse.

salmo ('salmo) nm psalm.

salmone (sal'mone) nm salmon.

salone (sa'lone) nm **1** hall. **2** assembly room.

salotto (sa'lɔtto) nm sitting room.

salpare (sal'pare) vi set sail.

salsa ('salsa) nf **1** sauce. **2** gravy. **salsiera** (sal'sjɛra) nf sauceboat.

salsiccia (sal'sittʃa) nf pork sausage.

salso ('salso) adj salt, salty.

saltare (sal'tare) vi jump, leap. vt **1** jump over. **2** miss. **saltare in aria** explode.

saltatoio (salta'tojo) nm perch.

saltellare (saltel'lare) vi skip, hop. **saltello** (sal'tɛllo) nm jump.

salterellare (salterel'lare) vi hop, skip. **salterello** (salte'rɛllo) nm skip, jump.

saltimbanco (saltim'banko) nm acrobat.

saltimbocca (saltim'bokka) nm invar meat in anchovy sauce.

salto ('salto) nm jump, leap. **salto mortale** somersault.

salubre ('salubre) adj healthy.

salume (sa'lume) nm salted meat. **salumeria** nf delicatessen.

salutare (salu'tare) vt greet, say hello or goodbye to. **andare a salutare** go and see. **saluto** nm **1** greeting. **2** salute. **tanti saluti** best regards.

salute (sa'lute) nf health. **salutare** adj salutary.

salva ('salva) nf salvo.

salvaguardare (salvagwar'dare) vt safeguard. **salvaguardia** nf safeguard.

salvare (sal'vare) vt **1** save. **2** rescue. **salvarsi** vr escape. **salvagente** (salva'dʒɛnte) nm invar lifebelt. **salvazione** nf salvation. **salvezza** (sal'vettsa) nf safety. **salvo** adj safe. prep except.

salvataggio (salva'taddʒo) nm rescue.

salvia ('salvja) nf bot sage.

sambuco (sam'buko) nm elder tree.

san (san) adj contraction of **santo.**

sanare (sa'nare) vt **1** cure, heal. **2** put right. **sanabile** (sa'nabile) adj curable.

sanatorio (sana'tɔrjo) nm sanatorium.

sancire (san'tʃire) vt sanction.

sandalo ('sandalo) nm sandal.

sangue ('sangwe) nm blood. **fare sangue** bleed.

sanguinare (sangwi'nare) vi bleed. **sanguigno** adj 1 blood. 2 blood-red. **sanguinoso** (sangwi'noso) adj bloody.

sanitario (sani'tarjo) adj sanitary.

sanno ('sanno) v see **sapere**.

sano ('sano) adj healthy, sound. **di sana pianta** entirely. **sano e salvo** safe and sound. **sanità** nf sanity.

santificare (santifi'kare) vt sanctify.

santo ('santo) adj holy, sacred. nm saint. **santità** nf holiness.

santuario (santu'arjo) nm sanctuary.

sanzionare (santsjo'nare) vt sanction, approve. **sanzione** nf sanction.

sapere* (sa'pere) vt know. **sapere di** taste of. **sapiente** (sa'pjɛnte) adj wise. nm wise man. **sapienza** (sa'pjɛntsa) nf wisdom, learning.

sapone (sa'pone) nm soap. **saponata** nf lather. **saponetta** nf bar of soap. **saponiera** (sapo-'njɛra) nf soap dish.

sapore (sa'pore) nm taste, flavour. **saporito** adj 1 tasty. 2 witty. 3 expensive.

sappiamo (sap'pjamo) v see **sapere**.

saprò (sa'prɔ) v see **sapere**.

saracinesca (saratʃi'neska) nf roller blind.

sarcasmo (sar'kazmo) nm sarcasm. **sarcastico** (sar'kastiko) adj sarcastic.

sarchiare (sar'kjare) vt hoe, weed. **sarchio** nm hoe.

sarda ('sarda) nf pilchard. **sardina** nf sardine.

Sardegna (sar'deɲɲa) nf Sardinia. **sardo** adj,n Sardinian.

sardonico (sar'dɔniko) adj sardonic.

sarei (sa'rɛi) v see **essere**.

sarò (sa'rɔ) v see **essere**.

sarto ('sarto) nm tailor. **sarta** nf dressmaker. **sartoria** nf tailor's shop.

sasso ('sasso) nm stone. **sassoso** (sas'soso) adj stony.

sassofono (sas'sɔfono) nm saxophone.

Satana ('satana) nm Satan.

satellite (sa'tɛllite) nm satellite.

satira ('satira) nf satire. **satireggiare** vt satirize. **satirico** (sa'tiriko) adj satirical.

saturare (satu'rare) vt saturate. **saturazione** nf saturation.

Saturno (sa'turno) nm Saturn.

sauna ('sauna) nf sauna.

savio ('savjo) adj wise. nm sage.

saziare (sat'tsjare) vt satisfy, fill. **sazio** adj full, sated.

sbaccellare (zbattʃe'lare) vt shell (peas).

sbadataggine (zbada'taddʒine) nf carelessness. **sbadato** adj careless.

sbadigliare (zbadiʎ'ʎare) vi yawn. **sbadiglio** nm yawn.

sbagliare (zbaʎ'ʎare) vt 1 miscalculate. 2 mistake. vi make a mistake. **sbagliarsi** vr make a mistake, be mistaken. **sbagliato** adj wrong, mistaken. **sbaglio** nm mistake, error.

sballare (zbal'lare) vt unpack.

sballottare (zballot'tare) vt toss about.

sbalordire (zbalor'dire) vt amaze, stun. vi be amazed. **sbalordimento** nm amazement.

sbalzare (zbal'tsare) vt 1 throw, fling. 2 dismiss. vi bounce. **sbalzo** nm 1 bounce. 2 leap. **a sbalzi** by fits and starts.

sbandare (zban'dare) vt disband, disperse. vi mot skid. **sbandarsi** vr disperse.

sbandire (zban'dire) vt banish.

sbarazzare (zbarat'tsare) vt clear, rid. **sbarazzarsi di** vr get rid of.

sbarbare (zbar'bare) vt 1 uproot. 2 shave.

sbarcare (zbar'kare) vt put ashore, unload. vi go ashore, disembark. **sbarco** nm landing.

sbarrare (zbar'rare) vt block, bar. **sbarrare gli occhi** open one's eyes wide. **sbarra** nf 1 bar, barrier. 2 tiller.

sbatacchiare (zbatak'kjare) vt,vi bang, slam.

sbattere ('zbattere) vt 1 beat, shake. 2 bang, slam. vi slam. **sbattere fuori** throw out.

sbavare (zba'vare) vi dribble.

sbiadire (zbja'dire) vi fade.

sbieco ('zbjɛko) adj slanting, askew. **guardare di sbieco** look askance.

sbigottire (zbigot'tire) vt dismay. **sbigottirsi** vr be dismayed. **sbigottimento** nm dismay. **sbigottito** adj dismayed, amazed.

sbilenco (zbi'lɛnko) adj crooked.

sbirciare (zbir'tʃare) vt eye, gaze at.

sbirro ('zbirro) nm inf cop, policeman.

sboccare (zbok'kare) vi 1 flow. 2 lead, come out. **sbocco** nm outlet.

sborsare (zbor'sare) vt pay out.

sbottonare (zbotto'nare) vt unbutton.

sbozzare (zbot'tsare) vt sketch. **sbozzo** ('zbɔttso) nm sketch.

sbranare (zbra'nare) vt tear to pieces.

sbrattare (zbrat'tare) vt clean, clear.

sbriciolare (zbritʃoˈlare) *vt* crumble. **sbriciolarsi** *vr* crumble.

sbrigare (zbriˈgare) *vt* finish off, deal with. **sbrigarsi** *vr* hurry.

sbrodolare (zbrodoˈlare) *vt* stain, dirty.

sbronzo (ˈzbrontso) *adj inf* drunk.

sbucare (zbuˈkare) *vi* come out.

sbucciare (zbutˈtʃare) *vt* peel, skin. **sbucciarsi** *vr* graze. **sbucciapatate** *nm invar* potato peeler.

sbuffare (zbufˈfare) *vi* puff. **sbuffo** *nm* puff.

scabbia (ˈskabbja) *nf* scabies.

scabro (ˈskabro) *adj* rough.

scabroso (skaˈbroso) *adj* 1 rough. 2 difficult. 3 risqué.

scacchiera (skakˈkjɛra) *nf* chessboard.

scacciare (skatˈtʃare) *vt* chase or drive out.

scacco (ˈskakko) *nm* 1 square, check. 2 *pl* chess. **a scacchi** checked. **scacco matto** checkmate.

scadere* (skaˈdere) *vi* 1 decline, decrease. 2 expire, be due. **scadente** (skaˈdɛnte) *adj* of poor quality, shoddy. **scadenza** (skaˈdɛntsa) *nf* expiry.

scafandro (skaˈfandro) *nm* 1 diving suit. 2 spacesuit.

scaffale (skafˈfale) *nm* bookcase, bookshelf.

scafo (ˈskafo) *nm* hull.

scaglia (ˈskaʎʎa) *nf* 1 scale (of fish). 2 fragment. **scaglioso** (skaʎˈʎoso) *adj* scaly.

scagliare (skaʎˈʎare) *vt* throw, hurl.

scala (ˈskala) *nf* 1 stairs, staircase. 2 scale, proportion. **scala a piuoli** ladder. **scala mobile** escalator. **scalino** *nm* step, stair.

scalare (skaˈlare) *vt* scale. **scalatore** *nm* mountain climber.

scaldare (skalˈdare) *vt* warm up, heat. **scaldabagno** (skaldaˈbaɲɲo) *nm* water heater.

scalfire (skalˈfire) *vt* scratch.

scalo (ˈskalo) *nm* 1 wharf. 2 port of call. **volo senza scalo** *nm* non-stop flight.

scalogna (skaˈloɲɲa) *nf inf* bad luck.

scaloppa (skaˈloppa) *nf* escalope.

scalpello (skalˈpɛllo) *nm* chisel.

scalpore (skalˈpore) *nm* noise, row.

scaltro (ˈskaltro) *adj* shrewd, crafty. **scaltrezza** (skalˈtrettsa) *nf* cunning.

scalzare (skalˈtsare) *vt* take shoes and socks from. **scalzo** *adj* barefoot.

scambiare (skamˈbjare) *vt* 1 exchange. 2 mistake. **scambio** *nm* exchange.

scampanare (skampaˈnare) *vi* peal, chime. **scampanata** *nf* peal.

scampare (skamˈpare) *vt* save. *vi* escape. **scampo** *nm* refuge, safety. **non c'è scampo** there is no way out.

scampi (ˈskampi) *nm pl* scampi, prawns.

scampolo (ˈskampolo) *nm* remnant.

scanalare (skanaˈlare) *vt* groove. **scanalatura** *nf* groove.

scandalo (ˈskandalo) *nm* scandal. **scandalizzare** (skandalidˈdzare) *vt* shock. **scandalizzarsi** *vr* be shocked. **scandaloso** (skandaˈloso) *adj* scandalous, shocking.

scannare (skanˈnare) *vt* slaughter.

scanno (ˈskanno) *nm* seat, bench.

scansarsi (skanˈsare) *vt* avoid. **scansarsi** *vr* move aside.

scansia (skanˈsia) *nf* bookcase.

scapigliare (skapiʎˈʎare) *vt* ruffle, dishevel.

scapola (ˈskapola) *nf* shoulder-blade.

scapolo (ˈskapolo) *nm* bachelor.

scappare (skapˈpare) *vi* run away, flee. **scappata** *nf* 1 visit, call. 2 escapade.

scarabocchiare (skarabokˈkjare) *vt* scribble. **scarabocchio** (skaraˈbɔkkjo) *nm* scribble.

scarafaggio (skaraˈfaddʒo) *nm* cockroach.

scaramuccia (skaraˈmuttʃa) *nf* skirmish.

scaricare (skariˈkare) *vt* unload. **scaricarsi** *vr* 1 relax, unwind. 2 (of a clock) run down. **scarico** (ˈskariko) *adj* 1 unloaded. 2 (of a watch, etc.) run down. *nm* unloading. **tubo di scarico** *nm* exhaust pipe.

scarlatto (skarˈlatto) *adj,nm* scarlet. **scarlattina** *nf* scarlet fever.

scarno (ˈskarno) *adj* thin, scanty.

scarpa (ˈskarpa) *nf* shoe. **scarpino** *nm* dancing shoe.

scarso (ˈskarso) *adj* 1 scarce. 2 meagre. 3 lean, poor. **scarsità** *nf* scarcity.

scartabellare (skartabelˈlare) *vt* skim through (a book).

scartare (skarˈtare) *vt* 1 unwrap. 2 reject. *vi* swerve.

scassare (skasˈsare) *vt* break open. **scasso** *nm* housebreaking.

scassinatore (skassinaˈtore) *nm* burglar.

scatenare (skateˈnare) *vt* unleash. **scatenarsi** *vr* break out. **scatenato** *adj* wild.

scatola (ˈskatola) *nf* 1 box. 2 tin, can. **in scatola** tinned. **rompere le scatole** to annoy.

scattare (skatˈtare) *vi* 1 spring (up). 2 go off. *vt* take (a photo). **scatto** *nm* spring.

scaturire (skatu'rire) *vi* 1 gush. 2 spring.

scavare (ska'vare) *vt* 1 dig (up). 2 excavate. **scavo** *nm* excavation.

scegliere* (ʃeʎʎere) *vt* choose, pick.

sceicco (ʃe'ikko) *nm* sheik.

scelgo (ʃelgo) *v* see **scegliere.**

scellerato (ʃelle'rato) *adj* wicked. **scellera-tezza** (ʃellera'tettsa) *nf* wickedness.

scellino (ʃel'lino) *nm* shilling.

scelsi (ʃelsi) *v* see **scegliere.**

scelta (ʃelta) *nf* choice, selection.

scelto (ʃelto) *v* see **scegliere.** *adj* choice.

scemare (ʃe'mare) *vt,vi* diminish, reduce. **scemo**

scena (ʃena) *nf* 1 stage. 2 scene. **scenata** *nf* row, commotion.

scendere* (ʃendere) *vi* come or go down. 1 dismount. *vt* descend. **scendiletto** (ʃendi-'letto) *nm invar* bedside rug.

scenico (ʃɛniko) *adj* scenic.

sceriffo (ʃe'riffo) *nm* sheriff.

scesa (ʃesa) *nf* descent.

scesi (ʃesi) *v* see **scendere.**

sceso (ʃeso) *v* see **scendere.**

scettico (ʃettiko) *adj* sceptical. *nm* sceptic. **scetticismo** *nm* scepticism.

scettro (ʃettro) *nm* sceptre.

schedare (ske'dare) *vt* file. **scheda** (skɛda) *nf* 1 index card. 2 ballot paper, form. **schedario** *nm* 1 file. 2 filing cabinet.

scheggia (skeddʒa) *nf* chip, splinter.

scheletro (skɛletro) *nm* skeleton.

schema (skɛma) *nm* outline, plan.

schermire (sker'mire) *vi sport* fence. **scher-mirsi** *vr* defend oneself. **scherma** *nf* fencing.

schermo (skermo) *nm* screen.

schernire (sker'nire) *vt* sneer at. **scherno** *nm* scorn.

scherzare (sker'tsare) *vi* joke. **scherzo** *nm* joke. **per scherzo** as a joke. **scherzoso** *adj* playful.

schiacciare (skjat'tʃare) *vt* crush, squeeze. **schiaccianoci** *nm invar* nutcracker.

schiaffeggiare (skjaffed'dʒare) *vt* slap. **schiaf-fo** *nm* slap, smack.

schiamazzare (skjamat'tsare) *vi* 1 squawk. 2 cluck. **schiamazzo** *nm* 1 squawking. 2 din.

schiantare (skjan'tare) *vt* break. *vi* inf burst.

schiarire (skja'rire) *vt* clear up. *vi* become light.

schiavo (skjavo) *nm* slave. **schiavitù** (ʃ) *nf* slavery.

schidione (ski'djone) *nm cul* spit.

schiena (skjɛna) *nf* back, spine. **schienale** *nm* back (of a chair).

schierare (skje'rare) *vt* line up. **schierarsi** *vr* take sides. **schiera** (skjɛra) *nf* 1 rank. 2 formation.

schietto (skjɛtto) *adj* pure. **schiettezza** (skjet-'tettsa) *nf* 1 purity. 2 sincerity.

schifiltoso (skifil'toso) *adj* fussy.

schifo (skifo) *nm* disgust. **che schifo!** how disgusting! **schifoso** (ski'foso) *adj* disgusting, revolting.

schioccare (skjok'kare) *vt* 1 crack (a whip). 2 smack. **schiocco** (skjokko) *nm* 1 crack. 2 smack.

schioppo (skjɔppo) *nm* gun. **schioppettata** *nf* shot.

schiumare (skju'mare) *vt* skim. *vi* foam. **schiuma** *nf* froth, foam. **schiumoso** (skju-'moso) *adj* frothy.

schivare (ski'vare) *vt* avoid.

schizofrenia (skiddzofre'nia) *nf* schizophrenia.

schizzare (skit'tsare) *vi* 1 gush, squirt. *vt* 1 splash. 2 sketch. **schizzo** *nm* 1 squirt, splash. 2 sketch.

sci (ʃi) *nm invar* 1 ski. 2 skiing. **sci nautico** water-skiing.

scia (ʃia) *nf* wake, trail.

scià (ʃa) *nm* shah.

sciabola (ʃabola) *nf* sabre.

sciabordare (ʃabor'dare) *vt* (of water) lap. *vi* ripple.

sciacallo (ʃa'kallo) *nm* jackal.

sciacquare (ʃak'kware) *vt* rinse.

sciagura (ʃa'gura) *nf* misfortune. **sciagurato** *adj* unfortunate.

scialacquare (ʃalak'kware) *vt* dissipate.

scialbo (ʃalbo) *adj* pale.

scialle (ʃalle) *nm* shawl.

scialuppa (ʃa'luppa) *nf* sloop. **scialuppa di salvataggio** lifeboat.

sciamare (ʃa'mare) *vi* swarm. **sciame** *nm* swarm.

sciancato (ʃan'kato) *adj* 1 lame. 2 rickety. *nm* cripple.

sciare (ʃi'are) *vi* ski. **sciatore** *nm* skier.

sciarpa (ʃarpa) *nf* scarf.

sciatto (ʃatto) *adj* slovenly.

scientifico (ʃen'tifiko) *adj* scientific.

scienza (ʃentsa) *nf* 1 knowledge. 2 science. **scienziato** *nm* scientist.

scimmia (ʃimmja) *nf* monkey.

scimmiottare (ʃimmjot'tare) *vt* ape, imitate.

scimpanzè (ʃimpan'tse) nm chimpanzee.

scimunito (ʃimu'nito) adj silly. nm fool.

scintillare (ʃintil'lare) vi sparkle, glitter, twinkle. **scintilla** nf spark.

sciocco (ʃ'ɔkko) adj silly, foolish. nm fool. **sciocchezza** nf stupidity, foolishness.

sciogliere* (ʃ'ɔʎʎere) vt 1 untie, loosen. 2 melt, dissolve. 3 solve, resolve. **sciogliersi** vr 1 free oneself. 2 melt. **scioglilingua** nm invar tongue-twister.

sciolgo (ʃ'ɔlgo) v see **sciogliere.**

sciolsi (ʃ'ɔlsi) v see **sciogliere.**

sciolto (ʃ'ɔlto) v see **sciogliere**. adj 1 loose. 2 agile. 3 melted. **versi sciolti** nm pl blank verse.

scioperare (ʃope'rare) vi strike, go on strike. **scioperante** nm striker. **sciopero** (ʃ'ɔpero) nm strike.

sciorinare (ʃori'nare) vt hang out.

sciovinismo (ʃovi'nizmo) nm chauvinism.

scipito (ʃi'pito) adj tasteless.

scirocco (ʃi'rɔkko) nm sirocco.

sciroppo (ʃi'rɔppo) nm syrup. **sciroppato** adj in syrup.

sciupare (ʃu'pare) vt 1 waste. 2 spoil.

scivolare (ʃivo'lare) vi 1 slip, slide. 2 glide. **scivolo** (ʃ'ivolo) nm 1 slide, chute. 2 slipway.

scoccare (skok'kare) vt 1 shoot. 2 fling. 3 strike (hours). vi go off.

scocciare (skot'tʃare) vt inf annoy, bother.

scodella (sko'dɛlla) nf bowl, soup plate.

scodinzolare (skodintso'lare) vi (of a dog) wag its tail.

scoglio (sk'ɔʎʎo) nm 1 rock, cliff. 2 obstacle. **scogliera** (skoʎ'ʎɛra) nf reef. **scoglioso** (skoʎ'ʎoso) adj rocky.

scoiattolo (sko'jattolo) nm squirrel.

scolare (sko'lare) vt drain. vi drip. **scolo** nm drainage. **scolapiatti** nm invar draining rack.

scolaro (sko'laro) nm schoolboy, pupil.

scolastico (sko'lastiko) adj scholastic.

scollatura (skolla'tura) nf neckline.

scolorire (skolo'rire) vt discolour. vi fade, lose colour.

scolpare (skol'pare) vt excuse. **scolparsi** vr defend oneself.

scolpire (skol'pire) vt sculpt, carve.

scombro (sk'ombro) nm mackerel.

scommettere* (skom'mettere) vt bet. **scommessa** nf bet.

scomodare (skomo'dare) vt disturb, bother.

scomodarsi vr bother. **scomodo** (sk'ɔmodo) adj uncomfortable.

scomparire* (skompa'rire) vi disappear, vanish. **scomparsa** nf disappearance.

scompartire (skompar'tire) vt divide. **scompartimento** nm compartment.

scompigliare (skompiʎ'ʎare) vt 1 throw into disorder, upset. 2 ruffle. **scompiglio** nm disorder.

scomporre* (skom'porre) vt 1 break up. 2 disarrange. **scomporsi** vr lose composure.

scomunicare (skomuni'kare) vt excommunicate.

sconcertare (skontʃer'tare) vt disturb, disconcert.

sconcio (sk'ontʃo) adj indecent.

sconfessare (skonfes'sare) vt abjure, repudiate.

sconfitta (skon'fitta) nf defeat.

sconnettere* (skon'nettere) vt disconnect.

sconosciuto (skonoʃ'ʃuto) adj unknown.

sconquassare (skonkwas'sare) vt shatter.

sconsigliare (skonsiʎ'ʎare) vt dissuade.

sconsolato (skonso'lato) adj desolate.

scontare (skon'tare) vt 1 pay off. 2 pay for. **sconto** nm discount.

scontento (skon'tento) adj dissatisfied, displeased. **scontentezza** (skonten'tettsa) nf discontent.

scontrarsi (skon'trarsi) vr 1 meet. 2 clash. 3 collide. **scontro** nm 1 encounter, clash. 2 collision.

scontrino (skon'trino) nm 1 ticket. 2 token, voucher.

scontroso (skon'troso) adj sullen, touchy.

sconvolgere* (skon'vɔldʒere) vt upset, disturb. **sconvolto** (skon'volto) adj upset.

scopare (sko'pare) vt brush. **scopa** nf 1 broom. 2 Italian card game.

scoperta (sko'pɛrta) nf discovery.

scoperto (sko'pɛrto) adj uncovered.

scopo (sk'ɔpo) nm aim, purpose.

scoppiare (skop'pjare) vi 1 burst, explode. 2 break out. **scoppio** (sk'ɔppjo) nm 1 explosion, burst. 2 outburst. 3 outbreak.

scoppiettare (skoppjet'tare) vi crackle.

scoprire* (sko'prire) vt 1 uncover, disclose. 2 discover.

scoraggiare (skorad'dʒare) vt discourage. **scoraggiamento** nm discouragement.

scorciare (skor'tʃare) vt shorten. **scorciarsi** vr become shorter. **scorciatoia** nf short cut.

scordare[1] (skor'dare) *vt* forget. **scordarsi** *vr* forget.

scordare[2] (skor'dare) *vt* put out of tune. **scordarsi** *vr* go out of tune.

scorgere* ('skɔrdʒere) *vt* make out, discern.

scorpione (skor'pjone) *nm* 1 scorpion. 2 *cap* Scorpio.

scorrazzare (skorrat'tsare) *vi* wander.

scorrere* ('skorrere) *vi* 1 flow, run. 2 pass. *vt* scour. **scorreria** *nf* raid.

scorretto (skor'rɛtto) *adj* incorrect.

scorsa ('skorsa) *nf* glance.

scorso ('skorso) *adj* past, last. **l'anno scorso** last year.

scortare (skor'tare) *vt* escort. **scorta** ('skɔrta) *nf* 1 escort. 2 store, stock.

scortese (skor'teze) *adj* discourteous, impolite. **scortesia** *nf* rudeness.

scorticare (skorti'kare) *vt* skin, flay.

scorza ('skɔrdza) *nf* 1 *bot* bark. 2 rind, skin, peel.

scoscendere* (skoʃ'ʃendere) *vi* 1 crash down. 2 split.

scosceso (skoʃ'ʃeso) *adj* steep.

scossa ('skɔssa) *nf* shake, jolt. **scossa elettrica** electric shock.

scossi ('skɔssi) *v* see **scuotere.**

scosso ('skɔsso) *v* see **scuotere.**

scostare (skos'tare) *vt* shift, remove. **scostarsi** *vr* move away.

scostumato (skostu'mato) *adj* dissolute.

Scotch (skɔtʃ) *nm invar Tdmk* sellotape.

scottare (skot'tare) *vt* burn, scald. *vi* burn. **scottatura** *nf* burn.

scovare (sko'vare) *vt* 1 drive out. 2 discover.

Scozia ('skɔttsia) *nf* Scotland. **scozzese** (skot-'tsese) *adj* Scottish, Scots. *nm,f* Scot.

screditare (skredi'tare) *vt* discredit.

scremare (skre'mare) *vt* skim.

screpolare (skrepo'lare) *vi* crack. **screpolarsi** *vr* split. **screpolatura** *nf* crack.

scribacchiare (skribak'kjare) *vt,vi* scribble.

scricchiolare (skrikkjo'lare) *vi* creak, squeak. **scricciolo** ('skrittʃolo) *nm* wren.

scrigno ('skriɲɲo) *nm* casket.

scriminatura (skrimina'tura) *nf* parting (in the hair).

scrissi ('skrissi) *v* see **scrivere.**

scritta ('skritta) *nf* inscription.

scritto ('skritto) *v* see **scrivere.** *adj* written. *nm* writing. **scrittore** *nm* writer. **scrittura** *nf* 1 writing, handwriting. 2 contract.

scrivania (skriva'nia) *nf* writing desk.

scrivere* ('skrivere) *vt* write.

scroccare (skrok'kare) *vt* scrounge.

scrofa ('skrɔfa) *nf* sow.

scrollare (skrol'lare) *vt* shake, shrug.

scrosciare (skroʃ'ʃare) *vi* 1 pelt, pour. 2 roar. **scroscio** ('skroʃʃo) *nm* 1 roar, burst. 2 shower. **piovere a scroscio** pour.

scrupolo ('skrupolo) *nm* scruple. **scrupoloso** *adj* scrupulous.

scrutare (skru'tare) *vt* investigate, search.

scrutinio (skru'tinjo) *nm* counting, count (of votes). **scrutinio segreto** secret ballot.

scucire (sku'tʃire) *vt* unpick.

scuderia (skude'ria) *nf* stable.

scudiscio (sku'diʃʃo) *nm* riding whip.

scudo ('skudo) *nm* shield.

sculacciare (skulat'tʃare) *vt* spank. **sculacciata** *nf* spanking, spank.

scultura (skul'tura) *nf* sculpture. **scultore** *nm* sculptor.

scuola ('skwola) *nf* school.

scuotere* ('skwotere) *vt* shake.

scure ('skure) *nf* axe.

scuro ('skuro) *adj* 1 dark. 2 gloomy.

scusare (sku'zare) *vt* excuse, pardon. **scusarsi** *vr* 1 apologize. 2 find excuses. **scusa** *nf* 1 excuse. 2 pretext. **chiedere scusa** ask pardon. ~*interj* 1 I beg your pardon! 2 excuse me!

sdegnare (zdeɲ'ɲare) *vt* scorn, disdain. **sdegno** *nm* scorn. **sdegnoso** (zdeɲ'ɲoso) *adj* disdainful.

sdentato (zden'tato) *adj* toothless.

sdraia ('zdraja) *nf* deckchair.

sdraiare (zdra'jare) *vt* stretch out. **sdraiarsi** *vr* lie down.

sdraio ('zdrajo) **sedia a sdraio** *nf* deckchair.

sdrucciolare (zdruttʃo'lare) *vi* slip. **sdrucciolevole** (zdruttʃo'levole) *adj* slippery.

sdrucire (zdru'tʃire) *vt* tear.

se[1] (se) *conj* if, whether. **se mai** 1 if ever. 2 if anything.

se[2] (se) *pron 3rd pers m,f s,pl* form of **sé.**

sé (se) *pron 3rd pers m,f s,pl* oneself, itself, himself, herself, themselves. **se stessa** *pron 3rd pers fs* herself. **se stesse** *pron 3rd pers f pl* themselves. **se stesso** *3rd pers m s* himself. **se stessi** *pron 3rd pers m pl* themselves.

sebbene (seb'bɛne) *conj* although.

seccare (sek'kare) *vt* 1 dry. 2 bore. 3 annoy. **seccatore** *nm* bore.

secchia ('sekkja) nf bucket, pail. **secchiello** (sek'kjɛllo) nm pail.

secchio ('sekkjo) nm bucket, pail.

secco ('sekko) adj 1 dry. 2 lean.

secolare (seko'lare) adj 1 age-old. 2 secular, lay.

secolo ('sɛkolo) nm 1 century. 2 age.

secondario (sekon'darjo) adj secondary.

secondo[1] (se'kondo) adj second. nm 1 second. 2 main course. **seconda** nf second class.

secondo[2] (se'kondo) prep according to. **secondo me** in my opinion.

sedano ('sɛdano) nm celery.

sede ('sɛde) nf 1 seat. 2 head office.

sedere* (se'dere) vi sit, be seated. **sedersi** vr sit down. nm backside, bottom. **seduta** nf sitting, meeting.

sedia ('sɛdja) nf chair, seat. **sedia a dondolo** rocking chair.

sedici ('sedit∫i) adj sixteen. nm or f sixteen. **sedicesimo** adj sixteenth.

sedile (se'dile) nm seat, bench.

sedimento (sedi'mento) nm sediment, deposit.

sedurre* (se'durre) vt seduce.

seduzione (sedut'tsjone) nf seduction.

segale ('segale) nf rye.

segare (se'gare) vt saw. **sega** nf saw.

seggio ('sɛddzo) nm seat. **seggiovia** nf chair lift.

seggiola ('sɛddʒola) nf chair. **seggiolino** nm baby's chair.

segheria (sege'ria) nf sawmill.

seghettato (seget'tato) adj serrated.

segmento (seg'mento) nm segment.

segnalare (seɲɲa'lare) vt signal. **segnalarsi** vr distinguish oneself. **segnale** nm signal.

segnare (seɲ'ɲare) vt 1 mark, note. 2 indicate, show. 3 sport score. **segnarsi** vr make the sign of the cross. **segno** nm 1 mark, sign. 2 target. 3 limit, extent. **cogliere nel segno** hit the mark. **per filo e per segno** in detail. **segnalibro** (seɲɲa'libro) nm bookmark.

segregare (segre'gare) vt segregate, isolate. **segregazione** nf segregation.

segretaria (segre'tarja) nf secretary. **segreteria** nf 1 secretary's office. 2 secretariat.

segreto (se'greto) adj,nm secret. **segretezza** (segre'tettsa) nf secrecy.

segugio (se'gudʒo) nm bloodhound.

seguire (se'gwire) vt,vi follow. **seguace** nm follower. **seguente** adj next, following.

seguitare (segwi'tare) vi 1 continue. 2 follow.

seguito nm 1 suite. 2 following. 3 sequence, series. 4 continuation. **di seguito** uninterruptedly. **in seguito di** owing to.

sei[1] ('sɛi) adj six. nm or f six. **seicento** (sei't∫ɛnto) adj six hundred. nm 1 six hundred. 2 seventeenth century.

sei[2] ('sɛi) v see **essere**.

selce ('sɛlt∫e) nf flint.

selciare (sel't∫are) vt pave. **selciato** nm pavement.

selezionare (selettsjo'nare) vt select. **selezione** nf selection.

sella ('sɛlla) nf saddle. **sellino** nm saddle.

seltz ('sɛlts) nm soda-water.

selva ('selva) nf forest, wood.

selvaggio (sel'vaddʒo) adj wild, savage. nm savage. **selvaggina** nf (hunting) game.

selvatico (sel'vatiko) adj wild.

semaforo (se'maforo) nm 1 signal. 2 traffic light.

semantica (se'mantika) nf semantics. **semantico** (se'mantiko) adj semantic.

sembiante (sem'bjante) nm appearance. **sembianza** (sem'bjantsa) nf 1 appearance. 2 pl features.

sembrare (sem'brare) vi seem, appear.

seme ('seme) nm 1 seed. 2 game suit.

semicerchio (semi't∫erkjo) nm semicircle.

semifinale (semifi'nale) nf semifinal. **semifinalista** nm semifinalist.

seminare (semi'nare) vt sow.

seminario (semi'narjo) nm 1 seminary. 2 seminar.

semola ('semola) nf bran. **semolino** nm semolina.

semplice ('semplit∫e) adj simple, easy. **semplicità** nf simplicity. **semplificare** (semplifi'kare) vt simplify.

sempre ('sɛmpre) adv 1 always, all the time, ever. 2 still. **una volta per sempre** once and for all. **sempreverde** adj,nm evergreen.

senape ('sɛnape) nf mustard.

senato (se'nato) nm senate. **senatore** nm senator.

senile (se'nile) adj senile.

senno ('senno) nm judgment, commonsense.

seno ('seno) nm bosom, breast.

sensale (sen'sale) nm broker.

sensato (sen'sato) adj sensible.

sensazione (sensat'tsjone) nf sensation, feeling. **sensazionale** adj sensational.

sensibile (sen'sibile) adj 1 sensitive. 2 notable, considerable. **sensibilità** nf sensitivity.

sensitivo (sensi'tivo) adj sensitive. **sensitività** nf sensitivity.

senso ('sɛnso) nm 1 sense. 2 meaning. 3 direction, way. **senso unico** one way. **senso vietato** no entry. **sensuale** adj sensual, sensuous. **sensualità** nf sensuality.

sentenza (sen'tɛntsa) nf 1 sentence, judgment. 2 saying.

sentiero (sen'tjɛro) nm path, way.

sentimento (senti'mento) nm feeling, sentiment. **sentimentale** adj sentimental.

sentinella (senti'nɛlla) nf sentry, guard.

sentire (sen'tire) vt 1 feel. 2 hear, listen to. 3 smell. 4 taste. **sentirsi** vr feel. **sentirsela di** feel capable of.

sentore (sen'tore) nm 1 inkling. 2 feeling.

senza ('sɛntsa) prep without. **senz'altro!** of course! certainly!

separare (sepa'rare) vt separate, divide. **separarsi** vr separate. **separato** adj separate. **separazione** nf separation.

sepolcro (se'polkro) nm grave, tomb.

sepolto (se'polto) v see **seppellire.** adj buried.

sepoltura (sepol'tura) nf burial.

seppellire* (sepel'lire) vt bury.

seppi ('sɛppi) v see **sapere.**

seppia ('seppja) nf cuttlefish.

sequela (se'kwɛla) nf sequence.

sequenza (se'kwentsa) nf sequence.

sequestrare (sekwes'trare) vt 1 seize, confiscate. 2 kidnap. 3 confine. **sequestro** (se'kwɛstro) nm seizure.

sera ('sera) nf evening. **abito da sera** nm evening dress. **serata** nf evening.

serbare (ser'bare) vt keep. **serbo** ('sɛrbo) nm reserve. **mettere in serbo** store.

serbatoio (serba'tojo) nm 1 tank. 2 reservoir.

serenata (sere'nata) nf serenade.

sereno (se'reno) adj serene, calm. **serenità** nf serenity.

sergente (ser'dʒɛnte) nm sergeant.

serico ('srriko) adj silk, silky.

serie ('sɛrje) nf invar 1 series. 2 range.

serio ('sɛrjo) adj serious, grave. **poco serio** flighty. **sul serio** really. **serietà** nf gravity.

sermone (ser'mone) nm sermon.

serpe ('sɛrpe) nf snake.

serpeggiare (serped'dʒare) vi wind, meander.

serpente (ser'pɛnte) nm snake, serpent.

serra ('sɛrra) nf greenhouse, hothouse.

serraglio (ser'raʎʎo) nm menagerie.

serrare (ser'rare) vt 1 lock (up), close. 2 tighten. vi shut. **serrata** nf lockout. **serratura** nf lock.

servire (ser'vire) vt,vi serve. vi make use of. v imp need. **servirsi** vr 1 use. 2 help oneself.

servizio (ser'vittsjo) nm 1 service. 2 favour. **donna di servizio** nf domestic help. **essere di servizio** be on duty. **fare servizio** operate, be open. **servizio da caffè** coffee set.

servo ('sɛrvo) nm servant. **serva** ('sɛrva) nf maid, servant. **servile** adj servile. **servitore** nm servant. **servitù** nf 1 servitude, slavery. 2 servants.

sesamo ('sɛzamo) nm sesame.

sessanta (ses'santa) adj,nm sixty. **sessantesimo** adj sixtieth.

sessione (ses'sjone) nf session.

sesso ('sɛsso) nm sex. **sessuale** adj sexual. **sessualità** nf sexuality.

sesto ('sɛsto) adj sixth.

seta ('seta) nf silk.

sete ('sete) nf 1 thirst. 2 desire, longing. **avere sete** be thirsty.

setola ('setola) nf bristle.

setta ('sɛtta) nf sect.

settanta (set'tanta) adj,nm seventy. **settantesimo** adj seventieth.

sette ('sɛtte) adj seven. nm or f seven. **settecento** (sette'tʃɛnto) adj seven hundred. nm 1 seven hundred. 2 eighteenth century. **settimo** ('sɛttimo) adj seventh.

settembre (set'tɛmbre) nm September.

settentrione (setten'trjone) nm north. **settentrionale** adj northern.

settico ('sɛttiko) adj septic.

settimana (setti'mana) nf week. **settimanale** adj weekly. nm weekly magazine.

settore (set'tore) nm sector.

severo (se'vɛro) adj 1 severe, harsh. 2 austere. **severità** nf rigour, severity.

sezionare (settsjo'nare) vt dissect. **sezione** nf 1 part, section. 2 department.

sfaccendare (sfattʃen'dare) vi be busy. **sfaccendato** adj idle.

sfacciato (sfat'tʃato) adj impudent.

sfacelo (sfa'tʃɛlo) nm ruin, collapse.

sfaldare (sfal'dare) vt flake. **sfaldarsi** vr flake off.

sfarzo ('sfartso) nm pomp. **sfarzoso** (sfar'tsoso) adj showy.

sfasciare (sfaʃˈʃare) *vt* smash. **sfasciarsi** *vr* **1** collapse. **2** crash.

sfavillare (sfavilˈlare) *vi* sparkle, glitter.

sfavorevole (sfavoˈrevole) *adj* unfavourable.

sfera (ˈsfɛra) *nf* sphere. **sferico** (ˈsfɛriko) *adj* spherical.

sferrare (sferˈrare) *vt* **1** land, hit (a blow). **2** launch (an attack).

sferza (ˈsfɛrtsa) *nf* whip, lash. **sferzare** *vt* whip.

sfiatato (sfjaˈtato) *adj* breathless.

sfidare (sfiˈdare) *vt* challenge. **sfida** *nf* challenge.

sfiducia (sfiˈdutʃa) *nf* distrust.

sfigurare (sfiguˈrare) *vt* disfigure.

sfilacciare (sfilatˈtʃare) *vi* fray.

sfilare (sfiˈlare) *vt* **1** unthread. **2** take off. *vi* march past. **sfilata** *nf* **1** procession, line. **2** march-past.

sfinge (ˈsfindʒe) *nf* sphinx.

sfinito (sfiˈnito) *adj* exhausted.

sfiorare (sfjoˈrare) *vt* **1** graze, skim, brush. **2** touch upon.

sfiorire (sfjoˈrire) *vi* fade, wither.

sfocato (sfoˈkato) *adj* out of focus.

sfogare (sfoˈgare) *vt* vent, let out. **sfogarsi** *vr* pour out one's feelings. **sfogo** *nm* **1** outlet. **2** vent, free rein.

sfoggiare (sfodˈdʒare) *vt,vi* show off. **sfoggio** (ˈsfɔddʒo) *nm* parade, display.

sfoglia (ˈsfɔʎʎa) *nf* rolled pastry. **pasta sfoglia** *nf* puff pastry.

sfogliare (sfoʎˈʎare) *vt* leaf through, turn the pages of (of book).

sfolgorare (sfolgoˈrare) *vi* flash, blaze.

sfollare (sfolˈlare) *vi* **1** empty, disperse. **2** evacuate. **sfollato** *nm* evacuee.

sfondo (ˈsfondo) *nm* background.

sformare (sforˈmare) *vt* deform.

sfortuna (sforˈtuna) *nf* bad luck, misfortune. **sfortunato** *adj* unfortunate, unlucky.

sforzare (sforˈtsare) *vt* force. **sforzarsi** *vr* do one's best. **sforzo** *nm* effort.

sfrattare (sfratˈtare) *vt* **1** expel. **2** evict. **sfratto** *nm* eviction.

sfregare (sfreˈgare) *vt* rub.

sfregiare (sfreˈdʒare) *vt* deface. **sfregio** *nm* gash, scar.

sfrenare (sfreˈnare) *vt* let loose. **sfrenato** *adj* unbridled.

sfrontato (sfronˈtato) *adj* shameless.

sfruttare (sfrutˈtare) *vt* exploit. **sfruttamento** *nm* exploitation.

sfuggire (sfudˈdʒire) *vt* avoid. *vi* escape, elude. **di sfuggita** *adv* in passing.

sfumatura (sfumaˈtura) *nf* **1** gradation, shade. **2** nuance.

sgabello (zgaˈbɛllo) *nm* stool.

sgambettare (zgambetˈtare) *vi* scurry.

sganciare (zganˈtʃare) *vt* unhook.

sgangherare (zgangeˈrare) *vt* unhinge. **sgangherato** *adj* **1** awkward. **2** ramshackle. **3** coarse.

sgarbo (ˈzgarbo) *nm* rudeness. **sgarbatezza** (zgarbaˈtettsa) *nf* rudeness. **sgarbato** *adj* rude, impolite.

sgattaiolare (zgattajoˈlare) *vi* slip away.

sgelare (zdʒeˈlare) *vt,vi* thaw. **sgelarsi** *vr* thaw. **sgelo** (ˈzdʒɛlo) *nm* thaw.

sghembo (ˈzgembo) *adj* slanting, askew.

sghignazzare (zgiɲɲatˈtsare) *vi* guffaw.

sgobbare (zgobˈbare) *vi* *inf* **1** work hard. **2** swot.

sgocciolare (zgottʃoˈlare) *vi* drip.

sgombrare (zgomˈbrare) *vt* **1** clear. **2** remove. *vi* move house.

sgombro [1] (ˈzgombro) *nm* removal.

sgombro [2] (ˈzgombro) *nm* mackerel.

sgomentare (zgomenˈtare) *vt* terrify, frighten. **sgomento** *nm* dismay.

sgomitolare (zgomitoˈlare) *vt* unwind.

sgonfiare (zgonˈfjare) *vt* deflate. **sgonfiarsi** *vr* go down. **sgonfio** *adj* deflated, flat.

sgorbiare (zgorˈbjare) *vt* **1** scribble. **2** blot. **sgorbio** (ˈzgɔrbjo) *nm* **1** scribble. **2** blot.

sgorgare (zgorˈgare) *vi* gush, pour.

sgradevole (zgraˈdevole) *adj* unpleasant.

sgradito (zgraˈdito) *adj* unwelcome.

sgranare (zgraˈnare) *vt* **1** shell, husk. **2** devour. **sgranare gli occhi** open one's eyes wide.

sgranchire (zgranˈkire) *vt* stretch. **sgranchirsi** *vr* stretch.

sgravare (zgraˈvare) *vt* unburden.

sgraziato (zgratˈtsjato) *adj* clumsy.

sgretolare (zgretoˈlare) *vt* grind. **sgretolarsi** *vr* crumble.

sgridare (zgriˈdare) *vt* scold, rebuke. **sgridata** *nf* scolding.

squainare (zgwaiˈnare) *vt* unsheathe.

squalcire (zgwalˈtʃire) *vt* crease, wrinkle.

sguardo (ˈzgwardo) *nm* look, glance. **al primo sguardo** at first sight.

squazzare (zgwatˈtsare) *vi* **1** splash about. **2** wallow.

sgusciare (zguʃ'ʃare) vt shell, husk. vi slip away.

si (si) pron 1 himself, herself, oneself, itself, themselves. 2 one. 3 one, people, they. 3 one another, each other. **si fa così** it is done this way.

sì (si) adv yes.

sia ('sia) v see **essere**. **sia...sia** both...and.

siamo ('sjamo) v see **essere**.

sibilare (sibi'lare) vi whistle. **sibilo** ('sibilo) nm hiss, whistle.

sicché (sik'ke) conj so that, so.

siccità (sittʃi'ta) nf drought.

siccome (sik'kome) conj since, as.

Sicilia (si'tʃilja) nf Sicily. **siciliano** adj,n Sicilian.

sicomoro (siko'mɔro) nm sycamore.

sicuro (si'kuro) adj 1 safe, secure. 2 sure, certain. 3 reliable. **di sicuro** certainly. **mettere al sicuro** put in a safe place. **sicurezza** (siku'rettsa) nf 1 security, safety. 2 certainty.

sidro ('sidro) nm cider.

siedo ('sjɛdo) v see **sedere**.

siepe ('sjɛpe) nf hedge.

siesta ('sjɛsta) nf siesta, nap.

siete ('sjɛte) v see **essere**.

sifilide (si'filide) nf syphilis.

sifone (si'fone) nm siphon.

sigaretta (siga'retta) nf cigarette.

sigaro ('sigaro) nm cigar.

sigillare (sidʒil'lare) vt seal. **sigillo** nm seal.

sigla ('sigla) nf 1 initials. 2 abbreviation. **sigla musicale** signature tune.

significare (siɲɲifi'kare) vt mean, signify. **significante** adj significant. **significativo** adj significant. **significato** nm meaning, sense.

signora (siɲ'ɲora) nf 1 lady, woman. 2 (title of address) Mrs. **signorina** nf 1 young lady. 2 (title of address) Miss.

signore (siɲ'ɲore) nm 1 man, gentleman. 2 (title of address) Mr. **signorile** adj refined.

signoreggiare (siɲɲored'dʒare) vt dominate. **signoria** nf domination.

silenzio (si'lɛntsjo) nm silence. **silenzioso** (silen'tsjoso) adj silent, quiet.

sillaba ('sillaba) nf syllable.

siluro (si'luro) nm torpedo.

simbolo ('simbolo) nm symbol. **simboleggiare** vt symbolize. **simbolico** (sim'bɔliko) adj symbolic.

simile ('simile) adj like, alike, similar.

simmetria (simme'tria) nf symmetry.

simpatia (simpa'tia) nf liking, fondness. **simpatico** (sim'patiko) adj likeable, nice. **simpatizzare** vi take a liking.

simultaneo (simul'taneo) adj simultaneous.

sinagoga (sina'gɔga) nf synagogue.

sincero (sin'tʃero) adj sincere. **sincerità** nf sincerity.

sindacato (sinda'kato) nm trade union. **sindacalista** nm trade unionist.

sindaco ('sindako) nm mayor.

sinfonia (sinfo'nia) nf symphony.

singhiozzare (singjot'tsare) vi 1 hiccup. 2 sob. **singhiozzo** (sin'gjottso) nm 1 hiccup. 2 sob.

singolare (singo'lare) adj 1 singular. 2 peculiar.

singolo ('singolo) adj single, individual.

sinistro (si'nistro) adj 1 left. 2 sinister. nm misfortune. **sinistra** nf 1 left hand. 2 left-hand side. 3 pol Left Wing.

sino ('sino) prep until, up to. **sin da** since.

sinonimo (si'nɔnimo) adj synonymous. nm synonym.

sintassi (sin'tassi) nf invar syntax.

sintesi ('sintɛzi) nf invar synthesis. **sintetico** (sin'tɛtiko) adj synthetic.

sintomo ('sintomo) nm symptom.

sinuoso (sinu'oso) adj winding.

sionismo (sio'nizmo) nm Zionism. **sionista** nm Zionist.

sipario (si'parjo) nm curtain.

sirena (si'rena) nf 1 mermaid. 2 siren.

siringa (si'ringa) nf syringe.

sistemare (siste'mare) vt put in order, arrange, settle. **sistemarsi** vr settle down. **sistema** nm system, method.

sito ('sito) nm site, place.

situare (situ'are) vt place. **situazione** nf situation.

slacciare (zlat'tʃare) vt undo, untie.

slanciare (zlan'tʃare) vt throw. **slanciarsi** vr hurl oneself. **slancio** nm 1 rush. 2 impulse, burst.

sleale (zle'ale) adj disloyal, unfaithful. **slealtà** nf disloyalty.

slegare (zle'gare) vt untie.

slittare (zlit'tare) vi 1 slide. 2 skid. **slitta** nf sledge, sleigh.

slogare (zlo'gare) vt dislocate.

sloggiare (zlod'dʒare) vt dislodge. vi move out.

smacchiare (zmak'kjare) vt clean.

smagliarsi (zmaʎ'ʎarsi) vr (of stockings) rip,

ladder. **smagliatura** nf (in a stocking) rip, ladder.

smalto ('zmalto) nm 1 enamel. 2 nail varnish.

smania ('zmanja) nf longing, desire.

smantellare (zmantel'lare) vt dismantle.

smargiasso (zmar'dʒasso) nm boaster.

smarrire (zmar'rire) vt lose, mislay. **smarrirsi** vr 1 lose one's way. 2 become confused.

smentire (zmen'tire) vt 1 deny. 2 contradict.

smeraldo (zme'raldo) nm emerald.

smettere* ('zmettere) vt stop, give up.

smilzo ('zmiltso) adj thin, lean.

sminuzzare (zminut'tsare) vt crumble.

smisurato (zmizu'rato) adj immense, huge.

smoccolare (zmokko'lare) vt 1 snuff (a candle). vi swear.

smodato (zmo'dato) adj excessive.

smoking ('smɔkiŋ) nm invar dinner jacket.

smontare (zmon'tare) vt 1 dismantle, take to pieces. 2 dishearten. vi dismount, get off.

smorfia ('zmɔrfja) nf grimace.

smorto ('zmɔrto) adj wan, pale.

smorzare (zmor'tsare) vt 1 dim, lower. 2 quench (thirst). 3 put out.

smuovere* ('zmwɔvere) vt move, shift.

snello ('znɛllo) adj 1 slim, slender. 2 agile.

snob (znɔb) nm invar snob. adj trendy.

snocciolare (znottʃo'lare) vt 1 stone (fruit). 2 pay out.

snodare (zno'dare) vt untie, loosen.

so (sɔ) v see **sapere.**

soave (so'ave) adj soft, gentle.

sobbalzare (sobbal'tsare) vi 1 jolt, jerk. 2 start, jump. **sobbalzo** nm 1 jolt. 2 jump, start.

sobborgo (sob'borgo) nm suburb.

sobrio ('sɔbrjo) adj sober.

socchiudere (sok'kjudere) vt half-close.

soccombere (sok'kombere) vi give way.

soccorrere* (sok'korrere) vt assist, help. **soccorso** (sok'korso) nm help, assistance.

sociale (so'tʃale) adj social. **socialismo** nm socialism. **socialista** nm socialist.

società (sotʃe'ta) nf 1 society. 2 company, firm.

socievole (so'tʃevole) adj sociable.

socio (so'tʃo) nm 1 member. 2 partner.

sociologia (sotʃolo'dʒia) nf sociology. **sociologo** (so'ʃɔlogo) nm sociologist.

soda ('sɔda) nf 1 soda. 2 soda-water.

soddisfare* (soddis'fare) vt,vi satify, fulfil. **soddisfacente** (soddisfa'tʃɛnte) adj satisfactory. **soddisfazione** nf satisfaction.

sodo ('sɔdo) adj hard, firm. adv 1 hard. 2 deeply, intensely.

sofà (so'fa) nm invar sofa, settee.

sofferente (soffe'rɛnte) adj suffering.

sofferenza (soffe'rɛntsa) nf suffering.

soffiare (sof'fiare) vt,vi 1 blow. 2 puff.

soffice ('sɔffitʃe) adj soft.

soffietto (sof'fjetto) nm bellows.

soffio ('sɔffjo) nm puff, whiff, breath.

soffitta (sof'fitta) nf attic, garret.

soffitto (sof'fitto) nm ceiling.

soffocare (soffo'kare) vt 1 suffocate, choke, strangle. 2 stifle. **soffocazione** nf suffocation.

soffrire* (sof'frire) vt 1 suffer. 2 endure, put up with, bear. vi suffer.

soggetto (sod'dʒetto) adj,nm subject. **recitare a soggetto** improvise. **soggettivo** adj subjective. **soggezione** nf 1 subjection. 2 embarrassment.

sogghignare (soggiɲ'ɲare) vi sneer.

soggiorno (sod'dʒorno) nm 1 stay. 2 living room.

soggiungere* (sod'dʒundʒere) vt add.

soglia ('sɔʎʎa) nf 1 doorstep. 2 threshold.

soglio ('sɔʎʎo) v see **solere.**

sogliola ('sɔʎʎola) nf zool sole.

sognare (soɲ'ɲare) vt,vi dream. **sogno** nm dream.

soia ('sɔja) nf soya.

solaio (so'lajo) nm attic.

solcare (sol'kare) vt plough, furrow. **solco** nm 1 furrow. 2 rut, track.

soldato (sol'dato) nm soldier. **soldatino** nm toy soldier.

soldo ('sɔldo) nm 1 penny. 2 pl money.

sole ('sole) nm sun. **solare** adj solar.

solenne (so'lɛnne) adj solemn, grave.

solere* (so'lere) vi be in the habit of.

soletta (so'letta) nf 1 sole (of a sock). 2 insole.

solido ('sɔlido) adj,nm solid. **solidificare** vt solidify. **solidificarsi** vr solidify.

solitario (soli'tarjo) adj 1 lonely, solitary.

solito ('sɔlito) v see **solere.** adj usual, habitual. **di solito** usually.

solitudine (soli'tudine) nf solitude.

sollecitare (solletʃi'tare) vt urge. **sollecito** (sol'letʃito) adj prompt.

solleticare (solleti'kare) vt tickle. **solletico** (sol'letiko) nm tickle. **fare il solletico a** tickle.

sollevare (solle'vare) vt 1 lift, raise. 2 comfort. **sollevarsi** vr rise.

sollievo (sol'ljɛvo) nm relief.

solo ('solo) adj 1 alone. 2 only. 3 one, single. **una sola volta** once only. ~adv only. **da solo** by oneself, on one's own. **solamente** adv only. **solista** nm soloist.

solstizio (sol'stittsjo) nm solstice.

soltanto (sol'tanto) adv only.

solubile (so'lubile) adj soluble.

soluzione (solut'tsjone) nf solution.

soma ('soma) nf load. **bestia da soma** nf beast of burden.

somaro (so'maro) nm ass, donkey.

somigliare (somiʎ'ʎare) vt,vi resemble, be like. **somigliarsi** vr resemble one another. **somiglianza** (somiʎ'ʎantsa) nf resemblance.

sommare (som'mare) vt add up. **somma** nf 1 sum, total. 2 sum of money. **in somma** in a word. **sommario** adj,nm summary.

sommergere* (som'mɛrdʒere) vt submerge, flood. **sommergibile** (sommer'dʒibile) nm submarine.

sommesso (som'messo) adj 1 docile. 2 soft.

somministrare (somminis'trare) vt administer.

sommissione (sommis'sjone) nf submission.

sommo ('sommo) adj highest, supreme. nm summit. **sommità** nf summit.

sommozzatore (sommottsa'tore) nm frogman, deep-sea diver.

sonaglio (so'naʎʎo) nm bell. **serpente a sonagli** nm rattlesnake.

sonare (so'nare) also **suonare** vt,vi 1 ring, sound. 2 mus play. **sonata** nf sonata. **sonatore** nm player.

sondare (son'dare) vt sound, test. **sondaggio** nm opinion poll, survey.

sonetto (so'netto) nm sonnet.

sonico ('sɔniko) adj sonic. **barriera sonica** nf sound barrier.

sonnambulo (son'nambulo) nm sleepwalker.

sonnecchiare (sonnek'kjare) vi doze.

sonnifero (son'nifero) nm sleeping pill.

sonno ('sonno) nm sleep. **avere sonno** be sleepy.

sono ('sono) v see **essere**.

sonoro (so'nɔro) adj resonant. **onda sonora** nf soundwave.

sontuoso (sontu'oso) adj sumptuous.

soppiatto (sop'pjatto) **di soppiatto** adv secretly.

sopportare (soppor'tare) vt endure, bear, tolerate, stand.

sopprimere* (sop'primere) vt 1 suppress. 2 abolish.

sopra ('sopra) prep 1 above, over. 2 upon. **al di sopra di** above. **di sopra** 1 upstairs. 2 above.

soprabito (so'prabito) nm overcoat.

sopracciglio (soprat'tʃiʎʎo) nm eyebrow.

sopraccoperta (soprakko'pɛrta) nf 1 bed-spread. 2 dust jacket (of a book).

sopraffare* (sopraf'fare) vt overcome.

sopraggiungere* (soprad'dʒundʒere) vi 1 arrive. 2 occur.

soprannaturale (soprannatu'rale) adj,nm super-natural.

soprannome (sopran'nome) nm nickname.

soprano (so'prano) nm soprano.

soprappiù (soprap'pju) nm extra.

soprascarpa (sopras'karpa) nf overshoe, galosh.

soprattassa (soprat'tassa) nf surtax.

soprattutto (soprat'tutto) adv above all.

sopravvenire* (sopravve'nire) vi 1 arrive. 2 occur.

sopravvivere* (soprav'vivere) vi survive. **sopravvissuto** nm survivor.

soprintendere* (soprin'tɛndere) vi supervise.

soqquadro (sok'kwadro) nm disorder, men.

sorbire (sor'bire) vt sip.

sorcio ('sɔrtʃo) nm mouse.

sordido ('sordido) adj sordid.

sordo ('sordo) adj 1 deaf. 2 dull, low. **sordità** nf deafness. **sordomuto** (sordo'muto) nm deaf-mute.

sorella (so'rɛlla) nf sister. **sorellastra** nf half-sister.

sorgere* ('sɔrdʒere) vi rise. **sorgente** (sor'dʒɛnte) nf 1 spring, fountain. 2 source.

sormontare (sormon'tare) vt surmount.

sornione (sor'njone) adj cunning, sly.

sorpassare (sorpas'sare) vt 1 overtake. 2 exceed. **sorpassato** adj out-of-date. **sorpasso** nm overtaking.

sorprendere* (sor'prɛndere) vt 1 surprise. 2 catch. **sorprendente** (sorpren'dɛnte) adj sur-prising. **sorpresa** (sor'presa) nf surprise.

sorreggere* (sor'reddʒere) vt support.

sorridere* (sor'ridere) vi smile. **sorriso** (sor-'riso) nm smile.

sorseggiare (sorsed'dʒare) vt sip. **sorso** nm sip.

sorsi ('sorsi) v see **sorgere**.

sorta ('sɔrta) nf kind, sort.

sorte ('sɔrte) nf fate, destiny. **tirare a sorte** draw lots.

sorteggio (sor'teddʒo) nm draw.

sortilegio (sorti'lɛdʒo) nm witchcraft.

sortire[1] (sor'tire) vt 1 get, receive. 2 draw.

sortire[2] (sor'tire) vi 1 come out, emerge. 2 happen.

sorto ('sorto) v see **sorgere**.

sorvegliare (sorveʎ'ʎare) vt watch over, supervise. **sorvegliante** nm keeper, watchman. **sorveglianza** nf supervision.

sorvolare (sorvo'lare) vt 1 fly over. 2 skip over.

sosia ('sɔzja) nm invar double (of a person).

sospendere* (sos'pɛndere) vt 1 hang (up). 2 suspend. **sospensione** nf suspension.

sospettare (sospet'tare) vt 1 suspect. 2 distrust. **sospetto** (sos'petto) vi be suspicious. adj suspect. nm suspicion. **sospettoso** (sospet'toso) adj suspicious.

sospirare (sospi'rare) vi sigh. **sospiro** nm sigh.

sosta ('sɔsta) nf halt, stop. **divieto di sosta** no parking.

sostanza (sos'tantsa) nf substance.

sostegno (sos'teɲɲo) nm support.

sostenere* (soste'nere) vt 1 support, maintain. 2 uphold, defend. 3 affirm.

sostentare (sosten'tare) vt support.

sostituire (sostitu'ire) vt 1 replace, substitute. 2 take the place of. **sostituto** nm substitute.

sottaceti (sotta'tʃeti) nm pl pickles.

sottana (sot'tana) nf 1 petticoat. 2 skirt.

sotterraneo (sotter'raneo) adj underground. nm cave.

sotterrare (sotter'rare) vt 1 bury. 2 hide.

sottile (sot'tile) adj 1 fine, thin. 2 slim, slender. 3 subtle.

sottintendere* (sottin'tɛndere) vt 1 understand. 2 imply.

sotto ('sotto) prep under, below. **sott'acqua** adv underwater. **sott'olio** in oil. ~adv below. **di sotto** below.

sottocoppa (sotto'kɔppa) nf saucer.

sottolineare (sottoline'are) vt underline.

sottomettere* (sotto'mettere) vt subdue, subject. vr submit.

sottopassaggio (sottopas'saddʒo) nm underground passage.

sottoporre* (sotto'porre) vt subject, submit. **sottoporsi** vr submit.

sottoscrivere* (sottos'krivere) vt sign. vi assent.

sottosopra (sotto'sopra) adv 1 upside down. 2 topsy-turvy.

sottotitolo (sotto'titolo) nm subtitle.

sottoveste (sotto'vɛste) nf 1 petticoat. 2 waistcoat.

sottovoce (sotto'votʃe) adv in a quiet voice.

sottrarre (sot'trarre) vt 1 remove, steal. 2 subtract. 3 save. **sottrarsi** vr escape. **sottrazione** nf 1 subtraction. 2 theft.

sovraccaricare (sovrakkari'kare) vt overload.

sovrano (so'vrano) adj,nm sovereign.

sovrastare (sovras'tare) vi dominate.

sovvenzionare (sovventsjo'nare) vt subsidize. **sovvenzione** nf subsidy.

sovversivo (sovver'sivo) adj subversive.

sozzo ('sottso) adj filthy, dirty.

spaccare (spak'kare) vt break, split. **spaccarsi** vr split, crack. **spacco** nm split. **spaccamonti** (spakka'monti) nm invar boaster.

spacciare (spat'tʃare) vt 1 sell, sell off. 2 spread, circulate. **spacciarsi per** vr pass oneself off as. **spaccio** nm 1 selling. 2 shop.

spada ('spada) nf sword.

spaesato (spae'zato) adj lost.

spaghetti (spa'getti) nm pl long thin strips of pasta.

Spagna ('spaɲɲa) nf Spain. **spagnolo** adj Spanish. nm 1 Spaniard. 2 Spanish (language).

spago ('spago) nm string, twine.

spaiato (spa'jato) adj odd, unmatched.

spalancare (spalan'kare) vt open wide.

spalare (spa'lare) vt shovel.

spalla ('spalla) nf 1 shoulder. 2 pl anat back. **alzare le spalle** shrug one's shoulders. **spallata** nf shrug. **spalliera** (spal'ljɛra) nf 1 back (of a seat). 2 head or foot (of a bed). **spallina** nf epaulette.

spalmare (spal'mare) vt spread, smear.

spandere* ('spandere) vt 1 shed. 2 spread.

sparare (spa'rare) vt fire, shoot. **sparo** nm shot.

sparecchiare (sparek'kjare) vt clear (the table).

spargere* ('spardʒere) vt 1 spread, scatter. 2 shed. **spargersi** vr spread.

sparire (spa'rire) vi disappear, vanish.

sparpagliare (sparpaʎ'ʎare) vt scatter.

spartire (spar'tire) vt divide, share.

sparuto (spa'ruto) adj haggard.

spasimo ('spazimo) nm spasm.

spassarsi (spas'sarsi) vr also **spassarsela** (spas'sarsela) enjoy oneself. **spasso** nm enjoyment, amusement. **andare a spasso** go for a walk.

spaurire (spau'rire) vt frighten, terrify.

spaventare (spaven'tare) vt frighten, alarm. **spaventarsi** vr take fright. **spaventapasseri** (spaventa'passeri) nm invar scarescrow. **spavento** nm fear, terror. **spaventoso** (spaven-'toso) adj terrible.

spazio ('spattsjo) nm space. **spaziale** adj 1 spatial. 2 space. **volo spaziale** nm space flight. **spazioso** (spat'tsjoso) adj spacious.

spazzare (spat'tsare) vt sweep (away). **spazzacamino** (spattsaka'mino) nm chimneysweep. **spazzaneve** nm invar snowplough. **spazzatura** nf rubbish.

spazzola ('spattsola) nf brush. **spazzolare** vt brush. **spazzolino** nm toothbrush.

specchio ('spekkjo) nm mirror. **specchiarsi** (spek'kjarsi) vr 1 look at oneself (in a mirror). 2 be reflected.

speciale (spe't∫ale) adj special. **specialista** nm specialist. **specialità** nf speciality. **specializzarsi** (spet∫alid'dzarsi) vr specialize.

specie ('spet∫e) nf invar 1 species. 2 kind, type, sort. **(in) specie** especially.

specificare (spet∫ifi'kare) vt specify. **specifico** (spe't∫ifiko) adj specific.

speculare (speku'lare) vi speculate. **speculatore** nm speculator. **speculazione** nf speculation.

spedire (spe'dire) vt send, post. **spedizione** nf expedition.

spegnere* ('spennere) vt 1 put out, extinguish. 2 turn or switch off. **spegnersi** vr go out, be extinguished.

spellare (spel'lare) vt skin.

spelonca (spe'lonka) nf cavern.

spendere* ('spendere) vt spend.

spengo ('spengo) v see **spegnere.**

spennare (spen'nare) vt pluck.

spensi ('spensi) v see **spegnere.**

spensierato (spensje'rato) adj thoughtless.

spento ('spento) v see **spegnere.** adj 1 switched out or off. 2 extinct, dead.

sperare (spe'rare) vi hope. vt hope for. **speranza** (spe'rantsa) nf hope.

spergiurare (sperdʒu'rare) vi perjure oneself.

sperimentare (perimen'tare) vt 1 test, try. 2 experience. **sperimentale** adj experimental.

sperma ('sperma) nm sperm.

speronare (spero'nare) vt ram. **sperone** nm spur.

sperperare (sperpe'rare) vt squander.

spesa ('spesa) nf 1 expense, cost. 2 shopping. 3 purchase. **a spese di** at the expense of. **essere spesato** have all expenses paid.

spesi ('spesi) v see **spendere.**

speso ('speso) v see **spendere.**

spesso ('spesso) adj 1 thick. 2 frequent. adv often. **spessore** nm thickness.

spettacolo (spet'takolo) nm 1 sight. 2 show. **spettacolare** adj spectacular.

spettare (spet'tare) vi 1 be up to. 2 be the duty or right of.

spettatore (spetta'tore) nm 1 spectator. 2 pl audience.

spettro ('spettro) nm ghost, spectre. **spettrale** adj ghostly.

spezie ('spettsje) nf pl spices.

spezzare (spet'tsare) vt break, smash. **spezzarsi** vr 1 break. 2 get broken. **spezzatino** nm stew.

spiacere* (spja't∫ere) v imp displease. **spiacevole** (spja't∫evole) adj unpleasant.

spiaggia ('spjaddʒa) nf beach.

spianare (spja'nare) vt 1 smooth, flatten. 2 roll out (dough).

spiantare (spjan'tare) vt uproot.

spiare (spi'are) vt spy upon. **spia** nf spy.

spiccare (spik'kare) vt 1 pick. 2 cut off. 3 pronounce clearly. 4 issue. vi stand out. **spiccare il volo** take flight.

spicchio ('spikkjo) nm 1 segment, slice. 2 clove (of garlic).

spicciarsi (spit't∫arsi) vr hurry.

spiccioli ('spittʃoli) nm pl small change.

spiedo ('spjedo) nm cul spit.

spiegare (spje'gare) vt 1 explain. 2 unfold, spread out. **spiegazione** nf explanation.

spietato (spje'tato) adj pitiless, ruthless.

spiga ('spiga) nf ear (of corn, etc.).

spilla ('spilla) nf brooch. **spillo** nm pin.

spilorcio (spi'lort∫o) adj mean, stingy.

spina ('spina) nf 1 thorn. 2 electrical plug. **birra alla spina** nf draught beer. **spina dorsale** spine. **filo spinato** nm barbed wire. **spinoso** (spi'noso) adj thorny.

spinacio (spi'nat∫o) nm spinach.

spingere* ('spindʒere) vt 1 push, shove. 2 drive. 3 incite. **spingersi** vr 1 push forward. 2 dare.

spinsi ('spinsi) v see **spingere.**

spinta ('spinta) nf push, shove.

spinto ('spinto) v see **spingere.**

spionaggio (spio'naddʒo) nm espionage.

spira ('spira) nf coil. **spirale** adj,nf spiral.

spirare (spi'rare) vi **1** blow, breathe out. **2** breathe. **3** expire. vt exhale.

spirito ('spirito) nm **1** spirit. **2** ghost. **3** wit. **spiritoso** (spiri'toso) adj witty. **spirituale** adj spiritual.

splendere ('splɛndere) vi shine, gleam. **splendido** ('splɛndido) adj splendid, wonderful. **splendore** nm splendour.

spogliare (spoʎ'ʎare) vt **1** take off. **2** strip. **spogliarsi** vr undress. **spogliarello** (spoʎʎa-'rɛllo) nm striptease. **spogliatoio** nm changing room.

spoglio ('spɔʎʎo) nm **1** sorting out. **2** examination.

spoletta (spo'letta) nf fuse.

spolverare (spolve'rare) vt dust.

sponda ('sponda) nf **1** edge. **2** bank.

spontaneo (spon'taneo) adj spontaneous.

sporcare (spor'kare) vt dirty, soil. **sporco** ('sporko) adj dirty.

sporgere* (spor'dʒere) vi jut out. vt **1** put out. **2** stick out. **sporgersi** vr lean out.

sport (sport) nm invar sport. **sportivo** adj sporting.

sporta ('sporta) nf shopping basket.

sportello (spor'tɛllo) nm **1** door. **2** counter. **3** window. **4** shutter.

sposalizio (spoza'littsjo) nm wedding.

sposare (spo'zare) vt marry. **sposarsi** vr get married. **sposa** ('spoza) nf **1** bride. **2** wife. **sposo** ('spozo) nm **1** bridegroom. **2** husband.

spostare (spos'tare) vt move, shift.

sprangare (spran'gare) vt bolt. **spranga** nf bolt.

sprazzo ('sprattso) nm **1** spray. **2** flash.

sprecare (spre'kare) vt waste.

spremere ('sprɛmere) vt **1** squeeze. **2** wring. **spremuta** nf fruit squash.

sprimacciare (sprimat't fare) vt shake.

sprizzare (sprit'tsare) vt,vi squirt.

sprofondare (sprofon'dare) vi **1** collapse. **2** sink. **sprofondarsi** vr **1** collapse. **2** sink.

spronare (spro'nare) vt spur on. **sprone** nm spur.

sproporzionato (sproportsjo'nato) adj disproportionate.

sproposito (spro'pɔzito) nm blunder.

sprovvisto (sprov'visto) adj ill-prepared, lacking. **alla sprovvista** unawares.

spruzzare (sprut'tsare) vt squirt, spray, sprinkle. **spruzzo** nm spray, splash.

spugna ('spuɲɲa) nf **1** sponge. **2** towelling.

spumare (spu'mare) vi foam. **spuma** nf foam, froth. **spumante** nm sparkling wine.

spuntare (spun'tare) vt **1** blunt, break the point of. **2** check off. vi **1** appear, sprout. **2** (of the sun) rise. **spuntarsi** vr become blunt. **spuntino** nm snack.

sputare (spu'tare) vt,vi spit. **sputo** nm spit, spittle.

squadra ('skwadra) nf **1** squad, squadron. **2** team. **3** set square.

squadrare (skwa'drare) vt look squarely at.

squadriglia (skwa'driʎʎa) nf squadron.

squagliare (skwaʎ'ʎare) vt melt. **squagliarsi** vr melt.

squalificare (skwaʎifi'kare) vt disqualify. **squalifica** (skwa'lifika) nf disqualification.

squallido ('skwallido) adj **1** squalid. **2** bleak. **squallore** nm **1** squalor. **2** dreariness.

squalo ('skwalo) nm shark.

squama ('skwama) nf scale (of a fish).

squarciare (skwar't fare) vt tear, rip. **a squarciagola** adv at the top of one's voice. **squarcio** nm **1** tear. **2** gash.

squassare (skwas'sare) vt shake violently.

squattrinato (skwattri'nato) adj penniless.

squilibrare (skwili'brare) vt unbalance. **squilibrio** nm lack of balance.

squillare (skwil'lare) vi ring. **squilla** nf bell. **squillo** nm ring. **ragazza squillo** nf callgirl.

squisito (skwi'zito) adj **1** exquisite. **2** (of food) delicious.

squittire (skwit'tire) vi cheep, squeak.

sradicare (zradi'kare) vt uproot.

sregolato (zrego'lato) adj disordered.

stabile ('stabile) adj **1** stable, fixed. **2** permanent. **beni stabili** nm pl real estate. **stabilità** nf stability. **stabilizzare** (stabilid'dzare) vt stabilize.

stabilire (stabi'lire) vt establish, fix, determine. **stabilirsi** vr settle. **stabilimento** nm **1** factory. **2** establishment.

staccare (stak'kare) vt **1** remove, take off. **2** detach. vi stand out. **staccarsi** vr **1** come off. **2** leave.

stacciare (stat't fare) vt sieve. **staccio** nm sieve.

stadio ('stadjo) nm **1** stadium. **2** stage, phase.

staffa ('staffa) nf stirrup.

staffetta (staf'fetta) nf messenger. **corsa a staffetta** nf relay race.

staffile (staf'file) nm whip.

stagione (sta'dʒone) nf season. **stagionale** adj seasonal.

stagliare (staʎ'ʎare) vi stand out. **stagliarsi** vr stand out.

stagnare (staɲ'ɲare) vi stagnate. **stagnante** adj stagnant.

stagno [1] ('staɲɲo) nm pool.

stagno [2] ('staɲɲo) nm tin. **(carta) stagnola** nf 1 tinfoil. 2 silver paper.

staio ('stajo) nm bushel.

stalla ('stalla) nf stable.

stallo ('stallo) nm 1 seat. 2 game stalemate.

stallone (stal'lone) nm stallion.

stamattina (stamat'tina) adv also **stamani** this morning.

stamberga (stam'berga) nf hovel.

stambugio (stam'budʒo) nm small dark room.

stampare (stam'pare) vt 1 print. 2 publish. **stampa** nf 1 print, printing. 2 press. **stampatello** (stampa'tɛllo) nm block letters. **stamperia** nf printing works. **stampo** nm mould, form.

stancare (stan'kare) vt tire. **stancarsi** vr become tired. **stanchezza** (stan'kettsa) nf tiredness. **stanco** adj tired.

standardizzare (standardid'dzare) vt standardize.

stanga ('stanga) nf barrier, bar. **stangata** nf blow.

stanghetta (stan'getta) nf 1 bolt. 2 side (of spectacles).

stanotte (sta'nɔtte) adv 1 tonight. 2 last night.

stante ('stante) prep on account of.

stantio (stan'tio) adj stale.

stantuffo (stan'tuffo) nm piston.

stanza ('stantsa) nf room. **stanza da bagno** bathroom.

stanziare (stan'tsjare) vt assign.

stappare (stap'pare) vt uncork.

stare ('stare) vi 1 be. 2 stay, remain. 3 be situated. 4 live. **come stai?** how are you? **lasciar stare** leave alone. **starci** be in agreement. **stare bene** 1 be well. 2 suit. **stare in piedi** stand. **stare male** 1 be ill. 2 fit badly. **stare per** be on the point of. **stare seduto** be seated. **stiamo a vedere!** let's wait and see! **ti sta bene!** it serves you right!

starna ('starna) nf partridge.

starnutire (starnu'tire) vi sneeze. **starnuto** nm sneeze.

stasera (sta'sera) adv this evening, tonight.

statalizzare (statalid'dzare) vt nationalize. **statalizzazione** nf nationalization.

statico ('statiko) adj static.

statistica (sta'tistika) nf statistics. **statistico** adj statistical.

stato [1] ('stato) v see **essere.**

stato [2] ('stato) nm 1 state, condition. 2 status. 3 state, nation. **statale** adj state, of the state. **statista** nm statesman.

statua ('statua) nf statue.

statura (sta'tura) nf height, stature. **di alta/bassa statura** tall/short.

statuto (sta'tuto) nm statute.

stavolta (sta'vɔlta) adv nf this time.

stazionare (stattsjo'nare) vi park. **stazionamento** nm parking.

stazione (stat'tsjone) nf 1 station. 2 resort.

steccare (stek'kare) vt 1 fence in. 2 put in splints. **stecca** nf 1 small stick. 2 med splint. 3 rib (of an umbrella). 4 billiard cue. 5 false note. **steccato** nm fence. **stecco** nm twig. **stecchino** nm toothpick.

stella ('stella) nf star. **stellare** adj 1 stellar. 2 star-shaped.

stelo ('stɛlo) nm stem, stalk.

stemma ('stɛmma) nm coat of arms.

stemperare (stempe'rare) vt dissolve.

stempiato (stem'pjato) adj (of hair) thin at the temples.

stendardo (sten'dardo) nm standard, banner.

stendere * (sten'dere) vt 1 spread, spread out. 2 extend, stretch out. 3 hang out (washing). **stendersi** vr stretch out.

stenodattilografo (stenodatti'lɔgrafo) nm secretary, shorthand typist. **stenodattilografia** nf shorthand typing.

stenografia (stenogra'fia) nf shorthand.

stentare (sten'tare) vi 1 have difficulty. 2 be in want. **stentato** adj 1 stunted. 2 difficult. **stento** ('stɛnto) nm 1 need, hardship. 2 effort. **a stento** hardly.

sterco ('stɛrko) nm dung.

stereofonico (stereo'foniko) adj stereophonic.

stereotipato (stereoti'pato) adj stereotyped.

sterile ('stɛrile) adj 1 sterile. 2 barren. **sterilità** nf sterility. **sterilizzare** (sterilid'dzare) vt sterilize. **sterilizzazione** nf sterilization.

sterlina (ster'lina) nf pound (sterling).

sterminare (stermi'nare) vt exterminate, destroy. **sterminio** nm slaughter, extermination. **sterminato** adj immense.

sternutire (sternu'tire) vi sneeze.

sterpo ('sterpo) nm twig.

sterzare (ster'tsare) vt steer. **sterzo** ('stertso) nm steering wheel.

stesso ('stesso) adj 1 same. 2 very. **fa lo stesso** it's all the same.

stesura (ste'sura) nf 1 drawing up, drafting. 2 draft.

stetoscopio (stetos'kɔpjo) nm stethoscope.

stetti ('stetti) v see **stare**.

stia ('stia) nf hen coop.

stigma ('stigma) nm mark, stigma.

stile ('stile) nm style. **stilista** nm stylist. **stilistica** (sti'listika) nf stylistics. **stilistico** (sti'listiko) adj stylistic.

stillare (stil'lare) vi drip, ooze. **stilla** nf drop.

stilografico (stilo'grafiko) (**penna**) **stilografica** nf fountain pen.

stimare (sti'mare) vt 1 estimate. 2 esteem. 3 value. 4 consider. **stima** nf 1 estimate. 2 esteem.

stimolare (stimo'lare) vt stimulate. **stimolante** nm stimulant. **stimolo** ('stimolo) nm 1 stimulus. 2 incentive.

stinco ('stinko) nm inf shin.

stingere* ('stindʒere) vi fade. **stingersi** vr fade.

stipare (sti'pare) vt cram together.

stipendio (sti'pendjo) nm salary.

stipo ('stipo) nm cabinet.

stipulare (stipu'lare) vt draw up.

stiracchiare (stirak'kjare) vt stretch.

stirare (sti'rare) vt 1 stretch. 2 iron. **stirarsi** vr stretch.

stirpe ('stirpe) nf race, descent.

stitico ('stitiko) adj constipated. **stitichezza** (stiti'kettsa) nf constipation.

stiva ('stiva) nf naut hold.

stivale (sti'vale) nm boot.

stizzire (stit'tsire) vt make angry. vi get angry. **stizzirsi** vr get angry. **stizza** nf anger. **stizzoso** (stit'tsoso) adj irritable.

stocco ('stɔkko) nm rapier.

stoffa ('stɔffa) nf cloth, material.

stoico ('stɔiko) adj,n stoic.

stola ('stɔla) nf stole.

stolido ('stɔlido) adj 1 foolish. 2 dull.

stolto ('stɔlto) adj stupid, foolish. **stoltezza** (stol'tettsa) nf stupidity.

stomacare (stoma'kare) vt sicken. **stomachevole** (stoma'kevole) adj sickening.

stomaco ('stɔmako) nm stomach.

stonare (sto'nare) vi 1 be out of tune. 2 clash. **stonato** adj out of tune.

stoppia ('stoppja) nf stubble.

storcere* ('stɔrtʃere) vt twist. **storcersi** vr twist.

stordire (stor'dire) vt stun, daze. **stordito** adj stunned, amazed.

storia ('stɔrja) nf 1 history. 2 story, tale. **storico** ('stɔriko) adj historical. nm historian. **storiella** (sto'rjɛlla) nf 1 story. 2 fib.

storione (sto'rjone) nm sturgeon.

stormire (stor'mire) vi rustle. **stormo** nm 1 flock. 2 swarm.

stornare (stor'nare) vt 1 avert. 2 dissuade.

storno ('storno) nm starling.

storpiare (stor'pjare) vt 1 cripple. 2 maim. **storpio** ('stɔrpjo) adj 1 crippled. 2 maimed. nm cripple.

storta ('storta) nf twist, sprain.

storto ('stɔrto) adj twisted, bent.

stoviglie (sto'viʎʎe) nf pl crockery.

strabico ('strabiko) adj cross-eyed.

strabiliare (strabi'ljare) vi be amazed. **strabiliarsi** vr be amazed.

strabismo (stra'bizmo) nm squint.

stracarico (stra'kariko) adj overloaded.

straccare (strak'kare) vt tire out. **stracco** adj exhausted.

stracchino (strak'kino) nm type of cheese.

stracciare (strat'tʃare) vt tear. **stracciatella** (strattʃa'tella) nf soup with eggs and cheese.

straccio ('strattʃo) adj torn. nm rag. **carta straccia** nf wastepaper. **straccivendolo** (strattʃi'vendolo) nm ragman.

stracuocere* (stra'kwɔtʃere) vt overcook. **stracotto** (stra'kɔtto) adj overcooked. nm stew.

strada ('strada) nf 1 street, road. 2 way. **stradale** adj road. **lavori stradali** nm pl road works. **stradario** nm street plan.

strafare* (stra'fare) vi do too much, overwork. **strafatto** adj 1 overdone. 2 overripe.

strage ('stradʒe) nf slaughter, massacre.

stralunare (stralu'nare) vt roll (one's eyes).

strambo ('strambo) adj strange. **stramberia** nf oddity.

strame ('strame) nm fodder.

strampalato (strampa'lato) adj eccentric.

strangolare (strango'lare) vt strangle. **strangolamento** nm strangling. **strangolatore** nm strangler.

straniero (stra'njɛro) adj foreign. nm foreigner.

strano ('strano) adj strange, odd. **stranezza** (stra'nettsa) nf strangeness.

straordinario (straordi'narjo) *adj* extraordinary. *nm* overtime.

strapagare (strapa'gare) *vt* overpay.

strapazzare (strapat'tsare) *vt* ill-treat. **strapazzarsi** *vr* overdo things. **strapazzata** *nf* scolding. **strapazzato** *adj* ill-treated.

strapieno (stra'pjɛno) *adj* full up.

strapiombare (strapjom'bare) *vi* lean over.

strappare (strap'pare) *vt* 1 tear, rip. 2 pull out. **strappata** *nf* tug. **strappo** *nm* 1 pull, tug. 2 tear.

straripare (strari'pare) *vi* (of a river) overflow its banks.

strascicare (straʃʃi'kare) *vt also* **strascinare** drag. **strascico** ('straʃʃiko) *nm* train (of a dress).

stratagemma (strata'dʒɛmma) *nm* stratagem.

strategia (strate'dʒia) *nf* strategy. **strategico** (stra'tɛdʒiko) *adj* strategic.

strato ('strato) *nm* 1 layer, coat (of paint). 2 stratum.

stravagante (strava'gante) *adj* strange, odd, eccentric. **stravaganza** (strava'gantsa) *nf* eccentricity.

stravecchio (stra'vɛkkjo) *adj* very old.

stravizio (stra'vittsjo) *nm* excess.

stravolgere (stra'voldʒere) *vt* twist. **stravolto** (stra'volto) *adj* troubled.

straziare (strat'tsjare) *vt* torture, torment. **strazio** ('strattsjo) *nm* torment, torture.

stregare (stre'gare) *vt* bewitch. **strega** *nf* witch. **stregone** *nm* wizard. **stregoneria** *nf* witchcraft.

stregua ('stregwa) *nf* measure.

stremare (stre'mare) *vt* exhaust.

strenna ('strɛnna) *nf* Christmas present.

strepitare (strepi'tare) *vi* make a loud noise.

strepito ('strɛpito) *nm* din, noise. **strepitoso** (strepi'toso) *adj* noisy.

stretto[1] ('stretto) *v see* **stringere**. *adj* 1 narrow. 2 tight. 3 strict. 4 precise. 5 close, intimate. **a denti stretti** with clenched teeth. **stretta di mano** handshake. **stretta di mano** grasp. **stretta di mano** handshake. **strettezza** (stret'tettsa) *nf* narrowness.

stretto[2] ('stretto) *nm* strait.

stria ('stria) *nf* stripe. **striato** *adj* striped.

stridere ('stridere) *vi* 1 screech. 2 (of colours) clash. **strido** *nm* screech, shriek. **stridore** *nm* screeching. **stridulo** ('stridulo) *adj* shrill.

strillare (stril'lare) *vi* scream. **strillo** *nm* scream.

strimpellare (strimpel'lare) *vt* strum.

strinare (stri'nare) *vt* singe.

stringa ('stringa) *nf* lace, shoelace.

stringere[*] ('strindʒere) *vt* 1 tighten. 2 squeeze. 3 clasp, grasp. 4 conclude. 5 take in (a dress). *vi* be urgent.

strinsi ('strinsi) *v see* **stringere.**

striscia ('striʃʃa) *nf* 1 strip. 2 stripe.

strisciare (striʃ'ʃare) *vt* 1 drag. 2 graze. *vi* creep, crawl.

stritolare (strito'lare) *vt* crush.

strizzare (strit'tsare) *vt* 1 squeeze. 2 wring (clothes). **strizzare l'occhio** wink. **strizzata** *nf* squeeze. **strizzata d'occhio** wink.

strofe ('strofe) *nf also* **strofa** (strofa) stanza.

strofinaccio (strofi'nattʃo) *nm* rag, duster, cloth. **strofinare** *vt* rub.

stroncare (stron'kare) *vt* 1 break off. 2 destroy.

stropicciare (stropit'tʃare) *vt* rub.

strozzare (strot'tsare) *vt* strangle, choke.

struggere[*] ('struddʒere) *vt* 1 melt. 2 consume. **struggersi** *vr* 1 melt. 2 torment oneself. **struggimento** *nm* torment.

strumento (stru'mento) *nm* 1 instrument. 2 tool. **strumentale** *adj* instrumental.

strusciare (struʃ'ʃare) *vt* rub.

strutto ('strutto) *nm* lard.

struttura (strut'tura) *nf* structure. **strutturale** *adj* structural. **strutturalismo** *nm* structuralism.

struzzo ('struttso) *nm* ostrich.

stuccare[1] (stuk'kare) *vt* putty, plaster, stucco. **stucco** *nm* plaster, putty.

stuccare[2] (stuk'kare) *vt* 1 sicken, nauseate. 2 annoy. **stuccarsi** *vr* be bored.

studente (stu'dɛnte) *nm* student. **studentesco** *adj* student. **studentessa** *nf* student.

studiare (stu'djare) *vt* study.

studio ('studjo) *nm* 1 study. 2 study, office. 3 studio. **borsa di studio** *nf* grant. **studioso** (stu'djoso) *adj* studious. *nm* scholar.

stufa ('stufa) *nf* 1 stove. 2 heater.

stufare (stu'fare) *vt* 1 stew. 2 *inf* bore. **stufato** *nm* stew. **stufo** *adj inf* fed up.

stuoia ('stwoja) *nf* mat.

stuolo ('stwolo) *nm* crowd.

stupefare (stupe'fare) *vt* amaze. **stupefacente** (stupefa't ʃɛnte) *nm* drug.

stupido ('stupido) *adj* stupid, foolish. **stupidaggine** (stupi'daddʒine) *nf* 1 stupid act. 2 nonsense. **stupidità** *nf* stupidity.

stupire (stu'pire) *vt* amaze. *vi* be amazed. **stupirsi** *vr* be amazed. **stupendo** (stu'pɛndo) *adj* marvellous, wonderful. **stupore** *nm* astonishment.

stuprare (stu'prare) *vt* rape. **stupro** *nm* rape.

sturare (stu'rare) *vt* uncork. **sturabottiglie** *nm invar* corkscrew.

stuzzicare (stuttsi'kare) *vt* **1** poke, prod. **2** provoke. **3** arouse. **stuzzicadenti** (stuttsika-'dɛnti) *nm invar* toothpick. **stuzzicante** *adj* appetizing.

su (su) *adv* up. *prep* **1** up, upon. **2** over. **3** about. **4** towards. **in su** upwards. **su due piedi** at once. **su per** up. **su per giù** roughly. ~*interj* come on!

sua ('sua) *poss adj, poss pron* see **suo.**

subacqueo (su'bakkweo) *adj* underwater.

subaffittare (subaffit'tare) *vt* sublet.

subappaltare (subappal'tare) *vt* subcontract.

subbuglio (su'buʎʎo) *nm* confusion.

subcosciente (subkoʃ'ʃɛnte) *adj,nm* subconscious.

subentrare (suben'trare) *vi* replace.

subire (su'bire) *vt* undergo, suffer.

subitaneo (subi'taneo) *adj* sudden.

subito ('subito) *adv* immediately, at once.

sublime (su'blime) *adj* sublime.

subordinare (subordi'nare) *vt* subordinate. **subordinato** *adj,n* subordinate.

suburbio (su'burbjo) *nm* suburb. **suburbano** *adj* suburban.

succedere* (sut'tʃɛdere) *vi* **1** succeed, follow. **2** happen, occur. **succedersi** *vr* follow one another. **successione** *nf* succession. **successivo** *adj* following. **successo** (sut'tʃɛsso) *nm* **1** outcome. **2** success. **successore** *nm* successor.

succhiare (suk'kjare) *vt* suck, suck up.

succinto (sut'tʃinto) *adj* succinct.

succo ('sukko) *nm* **1** juice. **2** sap. **succoso** *adj* juicy. **succulento** (sukku'lɛnto) *adj* succulent.

succursale (sukkur'sale) *nf* branch (office).

sud (sud) *nm* south. *adj invar* south, southern. **del sud 1** southern. **2** southerly. **verso sud** southwards. **sud-est** *nm* south-east. *adj invar* south-east, south-eastern. **del sud-est 1** south-eastern. **2** south-easterly. **sud-ovest** *nm* south-west. *adj invar* south-west, south-western. **del sud-ovest 1** south-western. **2** south-westerly.

sudare (su'dare) *vi* sweat, perspire. **sudato** *adj* covered in sweat. **sudore** *nm* sweat, perspiration.

sudario (su'darjo) *nm* shroud.

suddetto (sud'detto) *adj* above-mentioned.

suddito ('suddito) *nm* subject, citizen.

suddividere* (suddi'videre) *vt* subdivide. **suddivisione** *nf* subdivision.

sudicio ('suditʃo) *adj* dirty, filthy. *nm* dirt. **sudicieria** *nf* filthiness. **sudiciume** *nm* dirt, filth.

sue ('sue) *poss adj, poss pron* see **suo.**

sufficiente (suffi'tʃɛnte) *adj* sufficient, enough. **sufficienza** (suffi'tʃɛntsa) *nf* sufficiency.

suffisso (suf'fisso) *nm* suffix.

suffragio (suf'fradʒo) *nm* vote, suffrage. **suffragista** *nf* suffragette.

suffumicare (suffumi'kare) *vt* fumigate.

suga ('suga) **carta suga** or **cartasuga** *nf* blotting paper.

suggellare (suddʒel'lare) *vt* seal. **suggello** *nm* seal.

suggerire (suddʒe'rire) *vt* suggest. **suggerimento** *nm* suggestion. **suggeritore** *nm* prompter.

suggestionare (suddʒestjo'nare) *vt* influence. **suggestione** *nf* instigation. **suggestivo** *adj* **1** evocative. **2** picturesque.

sughero ('sugero) *nm* cork.

sugli ('suʎʎi) contraction of **su gli.**

sugna ('suɲɲa) *nf* **1** fat. **2** grease.

sugo ('sugo) *nm* **1** juice. **2** gravy. **3** sauce. **4** essence, gist. **sugoso** (su'goso) *adj* juicy.

sui ('sui) contraction of **su i.**

suicidarsi (suitʃi'darsi) *vr* commit suicide. **suicida** *nm* one who has committed suicide. **suicidio** *nm* suicide.

suino (su'ino) *nm* **1** pig. **2** *pl* swine. **carne suina** *nf* pork.

sul (sul) contraction of **su il.**

sull' (sul) contraction of **su l'.**

sulla ('sulla) contraction of **su la.**

sulle ('sulle) contraction of **su le.**

sullo ('sullo) contraction of **su lo.**

sultanina (sulta'nina) *nf* (fruit) sultana.

sultano (sul'tano) *nm* sultan.

sunto ('sunto) *nm* summary.

suntuoso (suntu'oso) *adj* sumptuous.

suo, sua, suoi, sue ('suo, 'sua, 'swɔi, 'sue) *poss adj* **1** *3rd pers s* his, her, its. **2** *2nd pers s fml* your. *poss pron* **1** *3rd pers s* his, hers, its. **2** *2nd pers s fml* yours.

suocera ('swɔtʃera) *nf* mother-in-law.

suocero ('swɔtʃero) *nm* father-in-law.

suoi ('swɔi) *poss adj, poss pron* see **suo.**

suola ('swɔla) *nf* sole (of a shoe).

suoli ('swɔli) v see **solere.**

suolo ('swɔlo) nm 1 ground. 2 soil. 3 layer.

suonare (swo'nare) vt,vi 1 ring, sound. 2 mus play. **suono** ('swɔno) nm sound.

suora ('swɔra) nf nun, sister.

superare (supe'rare) vt 1 exceed, surpass. 2 overcome, get over. **superato** adj out-of-date.

superbo (su'pɛrbo) adj proud, arrogant. **superbia** (su'pɛrbja) nf pride.

superficiale (superfi't∫ale) adj superficial. **superficialità** nf superficiality.

superficie (super'fit∫e) nf, pl **superfici** or **superficie** surface.

superfluo (su'pɛrfluo) adj superfluous. nm surplus.

superiore (supe'rjore) adj 1 higher, upper. 2 superior. nm superior. **superiorità** nf superiority.

superlativo (superla'tivo) adj,nm superlative.

supermercato (supermer'kato) nm supermarket.

supersonico (super'sɔniko) adj supersonic.

superstite (su'pɛrstite) adj surviving. nm survivor.

superstizione (superstit'tsjone) nf superstition. **superstizioso** (superstit'tsjoso) adj superstitious.

supino (su'pino) adj supine. **cadere supino** fall on one's back.

suppellettile (suppel'lɛttile) nf furnishings, fittings.

suppergiù (supper'dʒu) adv inf roughly, approximately.

supplemento (supple'mento) nm supplement. **supplementare** adj supplementary, extra.

supplicare (suppli'kare) vt beg, implore. **supplica** ('supplika) nf petition.

supplire (sup'plire) vt take the place of. vi 1 make up (for). 2 take the place (of). **supplente** (sup'plɛnte) adj,n substitute.

supplizio (sup'plittsjo) nm torture.

supporre* (sup'porre) vt suppose, imagine. **supposizione** nf supposition. **supposto** (sup'posto) adj supposed. **supposto che** supposing.

supposta (sup'posta) nf suppository.

suppurare (suppu'rare) vi fester.

supremo (su'prɛmo) adj supreme. **supremazia** (supremat'tsia) nf supremacy.

surclassare (surklas'sare) vt outclass.

surgelare (surdʒe'lare) vt freeze. **surgelato** adj frozen. **surgelati** nm pl frozen foods.

surrealismo (surrea'lizmo) nm surrealism. **surrealista** adj surrealist.

surrogare (surro'gare) vt take the place of, replace. **surrogato** nm substitute.

suscettibile (su∫∫et'tibile) adj susceptible.

suscitare (su∫∫i'tare) vt 1 arouse. 2 provoke, cause.

susina (su'sina) nf plum. **susino** nm plum tree.

susseguire (susse'gwire) vi follow.

sussidiare (sussi'djare) vt 1 subsidize. 2 support. **sussidiario** adj subsidiary. nm primary schoolbook. **sussidio** nm 1 aid, help. 2 subsidy.

sussiego (sus'sjɛgo) nm haughtiness.

sussistere (sus'sistere) vi 1 exist. 2 be valid.

sussultare (sussul'tare) vi start. **sussulto** nm start, jump.

sussurrare (sussur'rare) vt,vi whisper, murmur. **sussurro** nm murmur.

svagare (zva'gare) vt amuse. **svagarsi** vr enjoy oneself. **svago** nm amusement.

svaligiare (zvali'dʒare) vt rob, ransack.

svalutare (zvalu'tare) vt devalue. **svalutazione** nf devaluation.

svampare (zvam'pare) vi die down, calm down.

svanire (zva'nire) vi disappear, vanish.

svantaggio (zvan'taddʒo) nm disadvantage. **svantaggioso** (zvantad'dʒoso) adj unfavourable.

svariare (zva'rjare) vt vary.

svedese (zve'dese) adj Swedish. nm 1 Swede. 2 Swedish (language).

svegliare (zveʎ'ʎare) vt awaken, wake up. **svegliarsi** vr wake up. **sveglia** nf alarm clock. **sveglio** adj 1 awake. 2 quick-witted.

svelare (zve'lare) vt reveal.

svelto ('zvɛlto) adj 1 quick. 2 quick-witted. 3 slim.

svendita ('zvendita) nf (clearance) sale.

svenire* (zve'nire) vi faint. **svenimento** nm faint, fainting fit.

sventolare (zvento'lare) vt,vi flutter.

sventrare (zven'trare) vt disembowel.

sventura (zven'tura) nf misfortune, bad luck. **sventurato** adj unlucky.

svergognato (zvergoɲ'ɲato) adj shameless.

svernare (zver'nare) vi spend the winter.

svestire (zves'tire) vt undress.

Svezia ('zvɛtsja) nf Sweden.

sviare (zvi'are) vt 1 divert. 2 lead astray. **sviarsi** vr go astray.

svignare (zviɲ'ɲare) vi slip away. **svignarsela** (zviɲ'ɲarsela) vr slip away.

sviluppare (zvilup'pare) vt,vi develop. **sviluppo** nm development.

svincolare (zvinko'lare) vt free.

svista ('zvista) nf oversight.

svitare (zvi'tare) vt unscrew.

Svizzera ('zvittsera) nf Switzerland. **svizzero** ('zvittsero) adj,n Swiss.

svogliato (zvoʎ'ʎato) adj unwilling.

svolazzare (zvolat'tsare) vi flutter.

svolgere ('zvoldʒere) vt 1 unwind. 2 develop. 3 carry out. **svolgersi** vr 1 take place. 2 unwind. **svolgimento** nm development.

svoltare (zvol'tare) vi turn. **svolta** ('zvolta) nf turn, bend.

svuotare (zvwo'tare) vt empty.

T

tabacco (ta'bakko) nm tobacco. **tabaccaio** nm tobacconist. **tabaccheria** nf tobacconist's shop.

tabella (ta'bɛlla) nf table, list.

tabernacolo (taber'nakolo) nm tabernacle.

tabù (ta'bu) adj,nm taboo.

tacca ('takka) nf notch, dent.

taccagno (tak'kaɲɲo) adj mean, miserly. nm miser.

taccheggiatore (takkeddʒa'tore) nm shoplifter.

tacchino (tak'kino) nm turkey.

taccio ('tattʃo) v see **tacere**.

tacco ('takko) nm heel.

taccuino (takku'ino) nm notebook.

tacere (ta'tʃere) vi be quiet or silent. vt keep secret. **far tacere** silence.

tachimetro (ta'kimetro) nm speedometer.

tacito ('tatʃito) adj 1 silent. 2 tacit. **taciturno** adj quiet, taciturn.

tacqui ('takkwi) v see **tacere**.

tafano (ta'fano) nm horsefly.

tafferuglio (taffe'ruʎʎo) nm brawl.

taffettà (taffe'ta) nm taffeta.

taglia ('taʎʎa) nf 1 reward. 2 ransom. 3 size.

tagliare (taʎ'ʎare) vt 1 cut. 2 cut off. vi cut across. **tagliacarte** (taʎʎa'karte) nm invar paperknife. **tagliando** nm voucher. **tagliente** adj cutting, sharp. **taglio** nm cut, cutting.

tagliatelle (taʎʎa'tɛlle) nf pl long flat strips of pasta.

tagliola (taʎ'ʎɔla) nf trap, snare.

tagliuzzare (taʎʎut'tsare) vt chop finely, shred.

talco ('talko) nm talcum.

tale ('tale) adj 1 such, such a. 2 so. pron someone. **il tal dei tali** so-and-so. **talchè** conj so that. **talmente** adv so. **talora** adv now and again. **taluno** adj,pron some. **talvolta** (tal'vɔlta) adv sometimes.

taleggio (ta'leddʒo) nm type of cheese.

talento (ta'lɛnto) nm talent.

tallone (tal'lone) nm anat heel.

talpa ('talpa) nf zool mole.

tamburo (tam'buro) nm drum. **tamburare** also **tamburellare** vt drum. **tamburello** (tambu-'rɛllo) nm tambourine.

Tamigi (ta'midʒi) nm Thames.

tamponare (tampo'nare) vt 1 plug, stop. 2 collide with, bump into. **tamponamento** nm collision. **tampone** nm pad.

tana ('tana) nf den, lair.

tanaglie (ta'naʎʎe) nf pl pincers, pliers.

tanfo ('tanfo) nm musty smell.

tangibile (tan'dʒibile) adj tangible.

tango ('tango) nm tango.

tanto ('tanto) adj 1 so much. 2 pl so many. pron 1 so much. 2 pl a lot of people. adv so, so much. **di tanto in tanto** from time to time. **ogni tanto** every now and then. **tanto quanto** as much as.

tappare (tap'pare) vt plug, stop up.

tappeto (tap'peto) nm carpet. **tappetino** nm rug.

tappezzare (tappet'tsare) vt 1 cover. 2 upholster. **tappezzeria** nf 1 tapestry. 2 upholstery. **fare tappezzeria** be a wallflower.

tappo ('tappo) nm stopper, cork.

tarantola (ta'rantola) nf tarantula.

tarchiato (tar'kjato) adj thickset, sturdy.

tardare (tar'dare) vi be late. vt delay. **tardi** adv late. **fare tardi** be late. **tardo** adj 1 slow. 2 late.

targa ('targa) nf 1 shield. 2 mot numberplate. 3 nameplate.

tariffa (ta'riffa) nf 1 price-list. 2 charge, rate, fare.

tarlo ('tarlo) nm woodworm.

tarma ('tarma) nf moth. **tarmato** adj moth-eaten.

tartagliare (tartaʎ'ʎare) vi stammer, stutter.

tartaro ('tartaro) nm tartar.

tartaruga (tarta'ruga) nf 1 tortoise. 2 turtle.

tartina (tar'tina) nf sandwich.

tartufo (tar'tufo) nm truffle.

127

tasca ('taska) nf pocket. **tascabile** (tas'kabile) adj pocket-sized. **tascapane** nm haversack.

tassare (tas'sare) vt tax. **tassa** nf tax. **tassazione** nf taxation.

tassi (tas'si) nm invar taxi. **tassista** nm taxi driver.

tasso[1] ('tasso) nm yew tree.

tasso[2] ('tasso) nm badger.

tastare (tas'tare) vt **1** touch. **2** feel. **tastiera** nf keyboard. **tasto** nm **1** key. **2** feel, touch. **tastoni** adv gropingly. **andare a tastoni** grope.

tattica ('tattika) nf tactics. **tattico** ('tattiko) adj tactical.

tatto ('tatto) nm **1** sense of touch, touch. **2** tact.

tatuaggio (tatu'addʒo) nm tattoo.

tautologia (tautolo'dʒia) nf tautology.

taverna (ta'vɛrna) nf inn, tavern.

tavola ('tavola) nf **1** table. **2** board, slab. **3** plate, illustration. **tavola calda** snack-bar. **tavolo** ('tavolo) nm table. **tavolino** nm table. **tavolino da notte** bedside table.

tazza ('tattsa) nf cup.

te (te) pron 2nd pers m,f s fam you. **da te** by yourself.

tè (tɛ) nm invar tea. **teiera** (te'jɛra) nf teapot.

teatro (te'atro) nm theatre. **teatrale** adj theatrical.

tecnica ('tɛknika) nf technique. **tecnico** ('tɛkniko) adj technical. nm technician. **tecnologia** nf technology.

tedesco (te'desko) adj,n German. nm German (language).

tedioso (te'djoso) adj tedious.

tegame (te'game) nm pan.

teglia ('teʎʎa) nf pan.

tegola ('tegola) nf tile.

tela ('tela) nf **1** cloth. **2** canvas, painting. **3** Th curtain.

telaio (te'lajo) nm loom, frame.

teleferica (tele'fɛrika) nf cableway.

telefonare (telefo'nare) vi,vt telephone. **telefonata** nf telephone call. **telefonata urbana/interurbana** local/long-distance call. **telefonico** (tele'fɔniko) adj telephonic. **cabina telefonica** nf telephone box. **telefonista** nm telephonist. **telefono** (te'lɛfono) nm telephone. **dare un colpo di telefono** ring.

telegiornale (teledʒor'nale) nm television news.

telegrafare (telegra'fare) vt wire, telegraph. **telegrafo** (te'lɛgrafo) nm telegraph.

telegramma (tele'gramma) nm telegram.

telepatia (telepa'tia) nf telepathy.

teleschermo (teles'kermo) nm television screen.

telescopio (teles'kɔpjo) nm telescope.

televisione (televi'zjone) nf television. **televisione a colori** colour television. **televisore** (televi'zore) nm television set.

telone (te'lone) nm tarpaulin.

tema ('tɛma) nm **1** theme, subject. **2** essay, composition. **tematico** (te'matiko) adj thematic.

temerario (teme'rarjo) adj rash, reckless. **temerarietà** nf boldness, recklessness.

temere (te'mere) vt **1** fear, be afraid of. **2** doubt. vi be afraid.

temperamento (tempera'mento) nm temperament.

temperare (tempe'rare) vt **1** moderate, mitigate, alleviate. **2** sharpen. **temperalapis** (tempera'lapis) nm also **temperamatite** nm invar pencil-sharpener. **temperato** adj moderate, temperate. **temperino** nm penknife.

temperatura (tempera'tura) nf temperature.

tempesta (tem'pɛsta) nf storm, tempest, hurricane. **tempestoso** (tempes'toso) adj **1** stormy. **2** agitated.

tempia ('tɛmpja) nf anat temple.

tempio ('tɛmpjo) nm **1** temple. **2** church.

tempo ('tɛmpo) nm **1** time, period. **2** weather. **3** tense. **4** sport half-time. **5** tempo, beat. **a tempo** in time. **tempo fa** some time ago.

temporale[1] (tempo'rale) nm storm, thunderstorm.

temporale[2] (tempo'rale) adj temporal, secular.

temporaneo (tempo'raneo) adj **1** temporary. **2** transient, transitory.

temprare (tem'prare) vt temper, strengthen.

tenace (te'natʃe) adj **1** tenacious. **2** stubborn. **tenacia** nf tenacity.

tenaglie (te'naʎʎe) nf pl pincers, pliers.

tenda ('tɛnda) nf **1** curtain. **2** awning. **3** tent. **tendina** nf curtain.

tendenza (ten'dɛntsa) nf **1** tendency. **2** trend. **3** inclination.

tendere* (te'tɛndere) vt **1** stretch. **2** hang or hold out. **3** tighten. **4** lay. vi **1** tend. **2** incline, be inclined. **tendere le orecchie** prick up one's ears.

tendine ('tɛndine) nm tendon, sinew.

tenebre ('tɛnebre) nf pl darkness, gloom. **tenebroso** (tene'broso) adj gloomy, dark.

tenente (te'nɛnte) nm lieutenant.

tenere* (te'nere) vt 1 hold. 2 have. 3 keep. 4 contain. 5 occupy. 6 consider. vi 1 resemble. 2 hold, stick. 3 (of a dye) be fast. **tenere conto di** keep in mind. **tenere la destra/sinistra** keep to the right/left. **tenere stretto** clasp, grip. **tenere un discorso** give a speech. **tenersi** vr 1 hold or keep oneself. 2 stand. 3 consider oneself. 4 restrain oneself. 5 avoid. 6 follow. **tenersi pronto** be on the alert.

tenero ('tɛnero) adj 1 tender. 2 affectionate. **tenerezza** (tene'rettsa) nf 1 tenderness. 2 affection.

tengo ('tɛngo) v see **tendere.**

tenni ('tenni) v see **tenere.**

tennis ('tɛnnis) nm tennis. **tennista** nm tennis player.

tenore (te'nore) nm tenor. **tenore di vita** standard of living.

tensione (ten'sjone) nf 1 tension, strain. 2 voltage.

tentacolo (ten'takolo) nm tentacle.

tentare (ten'tare) vt 1 try, attempt. 2 test. 3 tempt. **tentativo** nm attempt. **tentazione** nf temptation.

tentennare (tenten'nare) vi 1 waver. 2 stagger, totter. 3 hesitate. vt shake.

tenue ('tɛnue) adj 1 slender, slight. 2 soft.

tenuta (te'nuta) nf 1 capacity. 2 estate. 3 uniform. 4 dress. **a tenuta d'acqua** water-tight.

teologia (teolo'dʒia) nf theology. **teologo** (te'ɔlogo) nm theologian.

teorema (teo'rɛma) nm theorem.

teoria (teo'ria) nf theory, idea. **teorico** adj theoretical.

tepore (te'pore) nm mildness.

teppa ('teppa) nf mob, underworld.

terapia (tera'pia) nf therapy. **terapeutico** (tera-'pɛutiko) adj therapeutic.

tergicristallo (terdʒikris'tallo) nm windscreen-wiper.

tergiversare (terdʒiver'sare) vi beat about the bush.

terme ('tɛrme) nf pl hot springs, spa. **termale** adj also **termico** ('tɛrmiko) thermal.

terminare (termi'nare) vt,vi finish, end, terminate. **termine** ('tɛrmine) nm 1 limit, boundary. 2 term. 3 end, close.

termodinamica (termodi'namika) nf thermodynamics.

termometro (ter'mɔmetro) nm thermometer.

termonucleare (termonukle'are) adj thermonuclear.

termos ('tɛrmos) nm invar Thermos Tdmk.

termosifone (termosi'fone) nm radiator. **riscaldamento a termosifone** nm central heating.

termostato (ter'mɔstato) nm thermostat.

terra ('tɛrra) nf 1 earth. 2 land. 3 ground, floor. 4 soil. 5 clay. **per terra** on the ground. **terracotta** (terra'kɔtta) nf terracotta. **terremoto** (terre'mɔto) nm earthquake.

terrapieno (terra'pjɛno) nm embankment, earth-work.

terrazza (ter'rattsa) nf also **terrazzo** nm terrace.

terreno[1] (ter'reno) adj earthly.

terreno[2] (ter'reno) nm 1 ground, soil, land. 2 site.

terribile (ter'ribile) adj terrible, fearful.

territorio (terri'tɔrjo) nm territory. **territoriale** adj territorial.

terrò (ter'rɔ) v see **tenere.**

terrore (ter'rore) nm terror. **terrorismo** nm terrorism. **terrorista** nm terrorist.

terzo ('tɛrtso) adj third. nm 1 third. 2 third party. **terza** nf 1 third class. 2 third gear.

tesa ('tesa) nf brim (of a hat).

teschio ('tɛskjo) nm skull.

tesi[1] ('tɛzi) nf invar thesis.

tesi[2] ('tesi) v see **tendere.**

teso ('teso) v see **tendere.**

tesoro (te'zɔro) nm 1 treasure. 2 treasury. **tesoreria** nf treasury. **tesoriere** nm treasurer.

tessera ('tɛssera) nf pass, card.

tessere ('tɛssere) vt weave. **tessile** ('tɛssile) adj,nm textile. **tessuto** nm 1 cloth, material, fabric. 2 anat tissue.

testa ('tɛsta) nf head. **dare alla testa** go to one's head. **in testa** on one's head. **rompersi la testa** rack one's brains.

testamento (testa'mento) nm law will.

testardo (tes'tardo) adj 1 stubborn. 2 head-strong.

testicolo (tes'tikolo) nm testicle.

testimone (testi'mɔne) nm witness. **testimoniare** vt,vi testify. **testimonianza** (testimo-'njantsa) nf testimony. **testimonio** (testi'mɔn-jo) nm witness.

testo ('tɛsto) nm text. **libro di testo** nm textbook.

testone (tes'tone) nm obstinate person.

testuggine (tes'tuddʒine) nf tortoise.

tetro ('tɛtro) adj gloomy, sombre.

tetta ('tetta) nf inf 1 breast. 2 teat. **tettarella** (tetta'rɛlla) nf teat, dummy.

tetto ('tetto) nm roof. **tettoia** nf 1 shed. 2 roof.

Tevere ('tevere) nm Tiber.

ti (ti) pron 2nd pers m,f s fam you, to you.

tiara ('tjara) nf tiara.

tic (tik) nm invar 1 tic. 2 mannerism.

ticchettare (tikket'tare) vi tick.

ticchio ('tikkjo) nm 1 spasm. 2 whim.

tictac (tik'tak) nm tick, ticking.

tieni ('tjɛni) v see **tenere.**

tiepido ('tjɛpido) adj lukewarm.

tifo ('tifo) nm typhus.

tifone (ti'fone) nm typhoon.

tifoso (ti'foso) nm fan, supporter.

tiglio ('tiʎʎo) nm lime tree, linden.

tignuola (tiɲ'ɲɔla) nf moth.

tigre ('tigre) nf tiger.

timbrare (tim'brare) vt stamp. **timbro** nm 1 stamp. 2 timbre. **timbro di gomma** rubber stamp.

timido ('timido) adj shy, timid. **timidezza** (timi'dettsa) nf shyness.

timo ('timo) nm thyme.

timone (ti'mone) nm rudder. **timoniera** (timo'njɛre) nf wheelhouse.

timore (ti'more) nm fear. **timoroso** (timo'roso) adj timorous.

timpano ('timpano) nm 1 kettledrum. 2 eardrum. 3 arch gable.

tingere* ('tindʒere) vt dye, tint.

tino ('tino) nm vat.

tinta ('tinta) nf 1 dye. 2 colour, shade. **tintoria** nf 1 dry-cleaner's shop. 2 dyeworks.

tipo ('tipo) nm 1 type. 2 inf chap, fellow. **tipico** ('tipiko) adj typical.

tipografia (tipogra'fia) nf printing.

tiranneggiare (tiranned'dʒare) vt oppress.

tiranno (ti'ranno) nm tyrant. adj tyrannical. **tirannia** nf tyranny. **tirannico** (ti'ranniko) adj tyrannical.

tirare (ti'rare) vt 1 pull, drag, draw. 2 pull out, extract. 3 throw. 4 shoot. 5 print. 6 draw, trace. vi 1 pull. 2 aim, tend. 3 (of the wind) blow. 4 be tight. 5 shoot. **tirare avanti** struggle on. **tirare calci** kick. **tirare giù** jot down. **tirare su** 1 pull up. 2 bring up. **tirare vento** be windy. **tirarsi in là** vr move aside. **tirata** nf tug, pull. **tiratore** nm shooter. **tiratore scelto** marksman. **tiratura** nf 1 printing. 2 circulation. **tiro** nm 1 shooting, firing. 2 shot. 3 trick. **a tiro** within range.

tirchio ('tirkjo) adj mean, stingy.

tirocinio (tiro'tʃinjo) nm apprenticeship.

titolo ('titolo) nm 1 title. 2 headline. 3 security, share.

tizio ('tittsjo) nm 1 chap, fellow. 2 what's-his-name.

tizzo ('tittso) nm also **tizzone** 1 brand. 2 ember.

toboga (to'bɔga) nm invar toboggan.

toccare (tok'kare) vt touch, feel. vi 1 happen. 2 be the duty of. 3 concern. **a chi tocca? tocca a me** whose turn is it? it's my turn. **tocco** nm touch. **al tocco** at one o'clock.

toga ('tɔga) nf gown.

togliere* ('tɔʎʎere) vt 1 take (away). 2 remove, take off. **togliersi di mezzo** vr get out of the way.

toletta (to'lɛtta) nf 1 dressing-table. 2 toilet.

tolgo ('tɔlgo) v see **togliere.**

tollerare (tolle'rare) vt tolerate, bear. **tollerabile** (tolle'rabile) adj tolerable. **tolleranza** (tolle'rantsa) nf tolerance, toleration.

tolsi ('tɔlsi) v see **togliere.**

tolto ('tɔlto) v see **togliere.**

tomaia (to'maja) nf upper (of a shoe).

tomba ('tomba) nf tomb.

tomo ('tɔmo) nm tome, volume.

tonaca ('tɔnaka) nf 1 tunic. 2 habit.

tondo ('tondo) adj round.

tonfo ('tonfo) nm 1 thud. 2 splash.

tonico ('tɔniko) nm tonic.

tonnellata (tonnel'lata) nf ton.

tonno ('tonno) nm tuna fish.

tono ('tɔno) nm tone.

tonsilla (ton'silla) nf tonsil. **tonsillite** nf tonsillitis.

topazio (to'pattsjo) nm topaz.

topo ('tɔpo) nm 1 mouse. 2 rat. **topo di biblioteca** bookworm.

topografia (topogra'fia) nf topography.

toppa ('tɔppa) nf 1 patch. 2 lock.

torba ('torba) nf peat.

torbido ('torbido) adj 1 murky. 2 troubled.

torcere* ('tortʃere) vt 1 twist. 2 wring.

torchiare (tor'kjare) vt press. **torchio** ('tɔrkjo) nm press.

torcia ('tortʃa) nf torch.

tordo ('tordo) nm thrush.

Torino (to'rino) nf Turin.

torma ('torma) nf swarm, throng.

tormentare (tormen'tare) vt torment. **tormento** nm 1 torment. 2 agony.

tornare (tor'nare) vi 1 return, go or come back.

2 turn out, prove to be. 3 become again. **tornare a fare** do again.

torneo (tor'nɛo) nm tournament.

toro ('toro) nm 1 bull. 2 cap Taurus.

torpedine (tor'pedine) nf torpedo.

torpido ('torpido) adj torpid. **torpore** nm torpor, lethargy.

torre ('torre) nf 1 tower. 2 game rook. **torretta** nf turret.

torrefare (torre'fare) vt roast.

torrente (tor'rɛnte) nm torrent. **torrenziale** adj torrential.

torrido ('torrido) adj torrid.

torrone (tor'rone) nm nougat.

torsi ('torsi) v see **torcere.**

torso ('torso) nm trunk, torso.

torsolo ('torsolo) nm stump.

torta ('torta) nf cake.

tortellini (tortel'lini) nm pl stuffed rings of pasta.

torto[1] ('torto) v see **torcere.**

torto[2] ('torto) nm wrong. **a torto** wrongly. **avere torto** be wrong.

tortora ('tortora) nf dove.

tortuoso (tortu'oso) adj winding, curving.

torturare (tortu'rare) vt torture. **tortura** nf torture.

torvo ('torvo) adj surly.

tosare (to'zare) vt shear, clip. **tosatrice** nf lawn-mower.

Toscana (tos'kana) nf Tuscany. **toscano** adj,n Tuscan.

tossico ('tɔssiko) adj toxic. nm poison.

tossire (tos'sire) vi cough. **tosse** nf cough.

tostare (tos'tare) vt 1 roast. 2 toast. **tostapane** nm invar toaster.

totale (to'tale) adj total, complete. nm total.

totalitario (totali'tarjo) adj totalitarian.

totocalcio (toto'kaltʃo) nm football pools.

tovaglia (to'vaʎʎa) nf tablecloth. **tovagliolo** nm napkin.

tozzo ('tɔttso) nm piece, bit. adj stocky, squat.

tra (tra) prep 1 between. 2 among.

traballare (trabal'lare) vi stagger, totter.

traboccare (trabok'kare) vi overflow.

tracannare (trakan'nare) vt gulp down.

traccia ('trattʃa) nf 1 trace. 2 trail, track. 3 footprint. 4 outline. **tracciare** vt 1 outline. 2 trace.

trachea (tra'kɛa) nf windpipe.

tradire (tra'dire) vt 1 betray. 2 be unfaithful

to. **tradimento** nm 1 betrayal. 2 treachery. 3 treason. **traditore** nm traitor. adj treacherous.

tradizione (tradit'tsjone) nf tradition. **tradizionale** adj traditional.

tradurre* (tra'durre) vt translate. **traduttore** nm translator. **traduzione** nf translation.

trafficare (treffi'kare) vi trade, deal. vt trade in. **trafficante** nm dealer. **traffico** ('traffiko) nm 1 trade. 2 traffic. 3 bustle.

traforare (trafo'rare) vt pierce, bore.

tragedia (tra'dʒɛdja) nf tragedy. **tragico** ('tradʒiko) adj tragic. nm tragedian.

traggo ('traggo) v see **trarre.**

traghetto (tra'getto) nm 1 crossing. 2 ferryboat.

tragitto (tra'dʒitto) nm journey.

traguardo (tra'gwardo) nm winning post.

trai ('trai) v see **trarre.**

trainare (trai'nare) vt drag, haul.

tralasciare (tralaʃ'ʃare) vt 1 omit. 2 give up.

tralcio ('traltʃo) nm 1 bot shoot. 2 vine shoot.

traliccio (tra'littʃo) nm trellis.

tram (tram) nm invar tram.

trama ('trama) nf plot.

tramezzare (tramed'dzare) vt partition, separate. **tramezzo** (tra'mɛddzo) nm partition.

tramite ('tramite) nm way, means. prep by means of.

tramontana (tramon'tana) nf north wind.

tramontare (tramon'tare) vi 1 (of the sun) set, go down. 2 fade. **tramonto** nm sunset.

tramortire (tramor'tire) vi faint.

trampoli ('trampoli) nm pl stilts.

trampolino (trampo'lino) nm 1 springboard. 2 diving board.

tranello (tra'nɛllo) nm trap, plot.

tranguglare (trangu'dʒare) vt bolt, gulp down.

tranne ('tranne) prep except.

tranquillo (tran'kwillo) adj calm, peaceful, still. **tranquillità** nf calm, stillness.

transatlantico (transa'tlantiko) adj transatlantic. nm liner.

transitivo (transi'tivo) adj transitive.

transito ('transito) nm passage, transit.

transizione (transit'tsjone) nf transition.

tranvai (tran'vai) nm invar tram.

tranvia (tran'via) nf 1 tramway. 2 tram.

trapanare (trapa'nare) vt drill. **trapano** ('trapano) nm drill.

trapelare (trape'lare) vi 1 trickle. 2 leak out.

trapezio (tra'pɛttsjo) nm trapeze.

trapiantare (trapjan'tare) vt transplant. **trapianto** nm transplant.

131

trappola ('trappola) nf trap.

trarre* ('trarre) vt 1 drag, pull, draw. 2 throw. 3 obtain.

trasalire (trasa'lire) vi start, jump.

trasandare (trazan'dare) vt neglect. **trasandato** adj slovenly.

trascinare (traʃʃi'nare) vt drag, pull.

trascorrere* (tras'korrere) vt 1 spend, pass. 2 go through quickly (a book, etc.). vi pass.

trascurare (trasku'rare) vt 1 neglect. 2 ignore. **trascurato** adj 1 neglected. 2 careless.

trasferire (trasfe'rire) vt transfer, move. **trasferirsi** vr move. **trasferimento** nm transfer.

trasformare (trasfor'mare) vt change, transform. **trasformazione** nf transformation.

trasfusione (trasfu'zjone) nf transfusion.

trasgredire (trazgre'dire) vt infringe, violate.

traslocare (trazlo'kare) vt,vi move. **trasloco** (traz'lɔko) nm removal. **fare trasloco** move house.

trasmettere* (traz'mettere) vt 1 transmit. 2 send. **transmissione** nf 1 transmission. 2 programme, broadcast.

trasognato (trasoɲ'ɲato) adj dreamy.

trasparente (traspa'rɛnte) adj transparent.

traspirare (traspi'rare) vi 1 perspire. 2 leak out. **traspirazione** nf perspiration.

trasportare (traspor'tare) vt transport. **trasporto** (tras'pɔrto) nm transport.

trassi ('trassi) v see **trarre**.

trastullare (trastul'lare) vt amuse. **trastullo** nm toy.

trasudare (trasu'dare) vi sweat.

trattare (trat'tare) vt 1 treat. 2 deal with, discuss. vi deal with, be about. **trattarsi di** v imp be a matter of. **trattativa** nf negotiation. **trattato** nm 1 treatise. 2 treaty.

trattenere* (tratte'nere) vt 1 keep or hold back. 2 detain, keep waiting. 3 entertain. **trattenersi** vr 1 remain, stay. 2 restrain oneself.

tratto¹ ('tratto) v see **trarre**.

tratto² ('tratto) nm 1 line, stroke. 2 stretch, space. 3 passage (in a book). 4 feature. **a un tratto** all of a sudden.

trattore (trat'tore) nm tractor.

trattoria (tratto'ria) nf restaurant.

trauma ('trauma) nm trauma.

travagliare (travaʎ'ʎare) vt trouble. **travaglio** nm 1 toil. 2 suffering.

travasare (trava'zare) vt decant.

trave ('trave) nf beam, rafter.

traversare (traver'sare) vt cross. **traversa** nf crossbar. **traversata** nf crossing.

traverso (tra'vɛrso) adj oblique. **di traverso** 1 askance. 2 amiss, the wrong way.

travestire (traves'tire) vt disguise. **travestimento** nm disguise.

travisare (travi'zare) vt distort, falsify.

travolgere* (tra'vɔldʒere) vt 1 overturn, upset. 2 overthrow.

tre (tre) adj three. nm or f three. **trecento** (tre'tʃɛnto) adj three hundred. nm 1 three hundred. 2 fourteenth century.

trebbiare (treb'bjare) vt thresh.

treccia ('trettʃa) nf plait.

tredici ('treditʃi) adj thirteen. nm or f thirteen. **tredicesimo** adj thirteenth.

tregua ('tregwa) nf 1 truce. 2 respite.

tremare (tre'mare) vt 1 tremble, shake. 2 shiver.

tremendo (tre'mɛndo) adj awful, fearful.

trementina (tremen'tina) nf turpentine.

tremito ('tremito) nm shiver, shudder.

tremolare (tremo'lare) vi quiver.

tremore (tre'more) nm tremor.

treno ('trɛno) nm train. **treno di vita** way of life.

trenta ('trenta) adj,nm thirty. **trentesimo** adj thirtieth.

trespolo ('trespolo) nm trestle.

triangolo (tri'angolo) nm triangle. **triangolare** adj triangular.

tribolare (tribo'lare) vt torment.

tribordo (tri'bordo) nm starboard.

tribù (tri'bu) nf invar tribe. **tribale** adj tribal.

tribuna (tri'buna) nf 1 platform. 2 gallery. 3 sport stand. **tribunale** nm 1 court. 2 tribunal.

tricheco (tri'kɛko) nm walrus.

triciclo (tri'tʃiklo) nm tricycle.

trifoglio (tri'fɔʎʎo) nm 1 clover. 2 shamrock.

triglia ('triʎʎa) nf red mullet.

trillare (tril'lare) vi 1 trill. 2 vibrate. **trillo** nm 1 ring. 2 trill.

trilogia (trilo'dʒia) nf trilogy.

trimestre (tri'mɛstre) nm term.

trina ('trina) nf lace.

trincare (trin'kare) vt drink greedily.

trincea (trin'tʃea) nf trench.

trinciare (trin'tʃare) vt cut up, mince.

trinità (trini'ta) nf trinity.

trio ('trio) nm trio.

trionfare (trion'fare) vi triumph. **trionfale** adj triumphal. **trionfo** nm 1 triumph. 2 game trumps.

triplice ('triplitʃe) adj triple.

tripode ('tripode) nm tripod.

trippa ('trippa) nf tripe.

triregno (tri'reɲɲo) nm papal tiara.

triste ('triste) adj sad. **tristezza** (tris'tettsa) nf sadness.

tristo ('tristo) adj bad, evil.

tritare (tri'tare) vt mince. **tritacarne** nm invar mincer. **tritatutto** nm invar slicer and shredder.

trittico ('trittiko) nm triptych.

trivellare (trivel'lare) vt drill. **trivella** (tri'vɛlla) nf drill.

triviale (tri'vjale) adj low, vulgar.

trofeo (tro'fɛo) nm trophy.

trogolo ('trɔgolo) nm trough.

troia ('trɔja) nf sow.

tromba ('tromba) nf trumpet. **tromba d'aria** tornado. **trombone** nm trombone.

troncare (tron'kare) vt break or cut off, interrupt. **tronco** nm 1 trunk (of a tree or body). 2 section.

trono ('trɔno) nm throne.

tropico ('trɔpiko) nm tropic. **tropicale** adj tropical.

troppo ('trɔppo) adj 1 too much. 2 pl too many. adv too, too much. **di troppo** in the way.

trota ('trɔta) nf trout.

trottare (trot'tare) vi trot. **trotto** nm trot.

trotterellare (trotterel'lare) vi 1 trot along. 2 toddle.

trottola ('trɔttola) nf spinning top.

trovare (tro'vare) vt 1 find, discover. 2 meet. **andare a trovare** visit. **trovarsi** vr 1 be, be situated. 2 feel.

truccare (truk'kare) vt 1 disguise, make up. 2 cheat. **truccarsi** vr make oneself up. **trucco** nm 1 make-up. 2 trick.

truciolo ('trutʃolo) nm wood shaving.

truffare (truf'fare) vt swindle, cheat. **truffa** nf swindle, fraud. **truffatore** nm swindler.

truppa ('truppa) nf troop.

tu (tu) pron 2nd pers m,f s fam you. **dare del tu** use the familiar form of address. **tu stesso** 2nd pers s fam yourself.

tua ('tua) poss adj, poss pron see **tuo.**

tuba ('tuba) nf 1 tuba. 2 top-hat.

tubare (tu'bare) vi coo.

tubercolosi (tuberko'lɔzi) nf invar tuberculosis.

tubo ('tubo) nm 1 pipe. 2 tube. **tubatura** nf piping. **tubetto** nm tube.

tue ('tue) poss adj, poss pron see **tuo.**

tuffare (tuf'fare) vt plunge, dip. **tuffarsi** vr dive, plunge. **tuffatore** nm diver. **tuffo** nm dive, plunge.

tulipano (tuli'pano) nm tulip.

tumore (tu'more) nm tumour.

tumulto (tu'multo) nm uproar, tumult.

tunica ('tunika) nf tunic.

tuo, tua, tuoi, tue ('tuo, 'tua, 'twɔi, 'tue) poss adj 2nd pers s fam your. poss pron 2nd pers s fam yours.

tuoi ('twɔi) poss adj, poss pron see **tuo.**

tuono ('twono) nm thunder. **tuonare** vi thunder.

tuorlo ('twɔrlo) nm egg yolk.

turare (tu'rare) vt stop, plug, cork.

turba ('turba) nf mob, crowd.

turbante (tur'bante) nm turban.

turbare (tur'bare) vt trouble, worry, disturb. **turbarsi** vr become agitated. **turbamento** nm disturbance.

turbina (tur'bina) nf turbine.

turbine ('turbine) nm 1 whirlwind. 2 hurricane.

turchese (tur'kese) adj,nf turquoise.

Turchia (tur'kia) nf Turkey. **turco** adj Turkish. nm 1 Turk. 2 Turkish (language).

turchino (tur'kino) adj dark blue.

turismo (tu'rizmo) nm tourism. **turista** nm tourist. **turistico** (tu'ristiko) adj touristic.

turlupinare (turlupi'nare) vt cheat.

turno ('turno) nm turn. **di turno** on duty.

tuta ('tuta) nf overalls.

tutela (tu'tɛla) nf guardianship. **tutore** nm guardian.

tutto ('tutto) adj 1 all. 2 pl each, every. pron 1 all, everything. 2 pl all, everyone. **del tutto** completely. **innanzi tutto** 1 first of all. 2 above all. **tutt'al più** at very most. **tutt'altro!** on the contrary! **tutti e due** both. **tutto il giorno** the whole day. **tuttavia** conj yet, nevertheless.

U

ubbia (ub'bia) nf whim.

ubbidire (ubbi'dire) vt,vi obey. **ubbidiente** (ubbi'djɛnte) adj obedient. **ubbidienza** (ubbi'djɛntsa) nf obedience.

ubriacare (ubria'kare) vt intoxicate. **ubriacarsi** vr get drunk. **ubriachezza** (ubria'kettsa) nf drunkenness. **ubriaco** adj drunk. **ubriacone** nm drunkard.

uccello (ut'tʃello) *nm* bird. **uccelliera** (uttʃel-'ljɛra) *nf* aviary.

uccidere* (ut'tʃidere) *vt* kill.

uccisi (ut'tʃizi) *v* see **uccidere**.

ucciso (ut'tʃizo) *v* see **uccidere**. *adj* killed. *nm* victim. **uccisione** *nf* killing, murder. **uccisore** *nm* killer, murderer.

udire* (u'dire) *vt* hear. **udibile** (u'dibile) *adj* audible. **udienza** (u'djɛntsa) *nf* 1 hearing, sitting. 2 audience, interview. **udito** *nm* hearing. **uditore** *nm* listener. **uditorio** (udi'tɔrjo) *nm* audience.

uffa ('uffa) *interj* what a bore!

ufficio (uf'fitʃo) *nm* 1 office. 2 department. **ufficio postale** post office. **ufficiale** *adj* official. *nm* official, officer.

ufo ('ufo) **a ufo** *adv* free, for nothing.

uggia ('uddʒa) *nf* dislike.

uggiolare (uddʒo'lare) *vi* whine.

ugola ('ugola) *nf* uvula.

uguagliare (ugwaʎ'ʎare) *vt* make even or equal, equalize. **uguagliarsi** *vr* be equal. **uguaglianza** *nf* equality.

uguale (u'gwale) *adj* 1 equal. 2 alike, identical. **per me è uguale** it's all the same to me. **ugualmente** *adv* likewise.

ulcera ('ultʃera) *nf* ulcer.

uliva (u'liva) *nf* olive.

ulteriore (ulte'rjore) *adj* further, ulterior.

ultimo ('ultimo) *adj* last, final, latest. **ultimatum** *nm invar* ultimatum.

ultravioletto (ultravio'letto) *adj* ultraviolet.

ululare (ulu'lare) *vi* howl. **ululo** ('ululo) *nm* howl, howling.

umanesimo (uma'nezimo) *nm* humanism. **umanista** *nm* humanist.

umanitario (umani'tarjo) *adj* humanitarian.

umano (u'mano) *adj* 1 human. 2 humane. **umanista** *nm* humanist. **umanità** *nf* humanity.

umbilico (umbi'liko) *nm* navel.

umido ('umido) *adj* damp, wet. *nm* 1 dampness, damp. 2 stew. **umidità** *nf* dampness.

umile ('umile) *adj* humble. **umiltà** *nf* humility.

umiliare (umi'ljare) *vt* humiliate, humble. **umiliante** *adj* humiliating. **umiliazione** *nf* humiliation.

umore (u'more) *nm* mood, humour. **umorismo** *nm* humour. **umoristico** (umo'ristiko) *adj* funny, humorous.

un (un) see **uno**.

una ('una) see **uno**.

unanime (u'nanime) *adj* unanimous. **unanimità** *nf* unanimity.

uncino (un'tʃino) *nm* hook. **uncinetto** *nm* crochet hook. **lavorare all'uncinetto** crochet.

undici ('unditʃi) *adj* eleven. *nm* or *f* eleven. **undicesimo** *adj* eleventh.

ungere* ('undʒere) *vt* grease, oil. **ungere le ruote** grease someone's palm. **ungersi** *vr* dirty oneself with grease.

Ungheria (unge'ria) *nf* Hungary. **ungherese** (unge'rese) *adj,n* Hungarian. *nm* Hungarian (language).

unghia ('ungja) *nf* 1 nail. 2 claw, talon. **unghiata** *nf* scratch.

unguento (un'gwɛnto) *nm* ointment.

unico ('uniko) *adj* 1 sole, only. 2 unique. **unicamente** *adv* only.

unicorno (uni'kɔrno) *nm* unicorn.

unificare (unifi'kare) *vt* unify. **unificazione** *nf* unification.

uniforme (uni'forme) *adj* uniform, even. *nf* uniform. **uniformità** *nf* uniformity.

unire (u'nire) *vt* join, unite, connect. **unione** *nf* union. **unito** *adj* united.

unità (uni'ta) *nf* 1 unity. 2 unit.

università (universi'ta) *nf* university. **universitario** *adj* university. *nm* university student or teacher.

universo (uni'vɛrso) *nm* universe. **universale** *adj* universal.

uno, un, una ('uno, un, 'una) *adj* one. *indef art* a, an. *pron* one, someone. **a uno a uno** one by one. **l'un l'altro** one another.

unto ('unto) *adj* greasy, oily. *nm* grease. **untuoso** (untu'oso) *adj* greasy, oily.

uomo ('wɔmo) *nm, pl* **uomini** man.

uopo ('wɔpo) *nm* need.

uovo ('wɔvo) *nm, pl* **uova** *f* egg. **uova strapazzate** scrambled eggs. **uovo affogato** poached egg.

uragano (ura'gano) *nm* hurricane.

uranio (u'ranjo) *nm* uranium.

Urano (u'rano) *nm* Uranus.

urbano (ur'bano) *adj* 1 urban, city. 2 urbane. **urbanistica** (urba'nistika) *nf* town planning.

urgente (ur'dʒɛnte) *adj* urgent. **urgenza** (ur'dʒɛntsa) *nf* urgency. **d'urgenza** urgently.

urinare (uri'nare) *vi* urinate. **urina** *nf* urine.

urlare (ur'lare) *vi* howl. **urlata** *nf* howl. **urlo** *nm, pl* **urli** *m* or **urla** *f* howl.

urna ('urna) *nf* 1 urn. 2 ballot-box.

urrà (ur'ra) *interj* hurrah!

urtare (ur'tare) vt knock against, bump into. vi hit, run into. **urtarsi** vr 1 become annoyed. 2 collide. **urtata** nf shove. **urto** nm 1 collision, crash. 2 push. 3 clash.

usare (u'zare) vi 1 be accustomed. 2 be in fashion. vt use, employ. **usabile** (u'zabile) adj usable. **usanza** (u'zantsa) nf custom, habit. **usato** adj used, worn, second-hand. nm usual. **uso** nm 1 use. 2 custom. **usuale** adj usual.

uscio ('uʃʃo) nm door. **usciere** (uʃ'ʃɛre) nm usher.

uscire (uʃ'ʃire) vi 1 go or come out, leave. 2 appear, be published. **uscita** nf exit, way out. **uscita di sicurezza** emergency exit.

usignolo (uziɲ'ɲɔlo) nm nightingale.

ussaro ('ussaro) nm hussar.

ustionare (ustjo'nare) vt burn. **ustione** nf burn.

usura (u'zura) nf usury. **usuraio** nm usurer.

usurpare (uzur'pare) vt usurp.

utensile (uten'sile) nm utensil, tool.

utente (u'tɛnte) nm user.

utero ('utero) nm womb.

utile ('utile) adj useful. nm gain, profit. **utilità** nf usefulness. **utilitario** adj utilitarian. **utilizzare** (utilid'dzare) vt use, utilize.

uva ('uva) nf grape. **uva passa** raisin. **uva secca** currant. **uva spina** gooseberry.

V

va' (va) v imperative form of **andare**.

vacante (va'kante) adj vacant. **vacanza** (va'kantsa) nf 1 holiday. 2 vacancy. **andare in vacanza** go on holiday.

vacca ('vakka) nf cow.

vaccinare (vattʃi'nare) vt vaccinate. **vaccino** nm vaccine.

vacillare (vatʃil'lare) vi 1 stagger. 2 hesitate.

vacuo ('vakuo) adj empty.

vada ('vada) v imperative form of **andare**.

vadano ('vadano) v imperative form of **andare**.

vado ('vado) v see **andare**.

vagabondare (vagabon'dare) vi wander, roam. **vagabondaggio** nm vagrancy. **vagabondo** adj vagabond, wandering. nm tramp.

vagare (va'gare) vi wander.

vaghezza (va'gettsa) nf vagueness.

vagina (va'dʒina) nf vagina.

vagire (va'dʒire) vi (of a new-born baby) cry.

vaglia[1] ('vaʎʎa) nf worth.

vaglia[2] ('vaʎʎa) nm invar money order. **vaglia postale** postal order.

vagliare (vaʎ'ʎare) vt sift. **vaglio** nm sieve.

vago ('vago) adj vague.

vagone (va'gone) nm 1 wagon, truck. 2 carriage. **vagone letto** sleeping-car.

vai ('vai) v see **andare**.

vaiolo (va'jɔlo) nm smallpox.

valanga (va'langa) nf avalanche.

valere (va'lere) vi 1 be worth. 2 be equal or correspond to. **non vale!** it does not count! **vale a dire** that is to say. **valersi** vr make use of. **valevole** (va'levole) adj valid. **validità** nf validity. **valido** ('valido) adj valid.

valgo ('valgo) v see **valere**.

valicare (vali'kare) vt cross. **valico** ('valiko) nm pass.

valigia (va'lidʒa) nf suitcase. **fare le valigie** pack. **valigeria** nf leather goods shop.

valle ('valle) nf also **vallata** valley.

valletto (val'letto) nm valet.

valore (va'lore) nm 1 value, worth. 2 courage, valour. 3 valuables. 4 pl shares. **mettere in valore** bring out. **valorizzare** (valorid'dzare) vt make the most of, exploit. **valoroso** (valo-'roso) adj valiant.

valutare (valu'tare) vt 1 value. 2 estimate. **valuta** nf 1 currency, money. 2 value. **valutazione** nf estimate.

valvola ('valvola) nf 1 valve. 2 electric fuse.

valzer ('valtser) nm invar waltz.

vampa ('vampa) nf 1 blaze, flame. 2 flush.

vampiro (vam'piro) nm vampire.

vandalo ('vandalo) nm vandal. **vandalismo** nm vandalism.

vaneggiare (vaned'dʒare) vi rave.

vanesio (va'nɛzjo) adj vain.

vangare (van'gare) vt dig. **vanga** nf spade.

vangelo (van'dʒɛlo) nm gospel.

vaniglia (va'niʎʎa) nf vanilla.

vanno ('vanno) v see **andare**.

vano ('vano) adj 1 useless, vain. 2 vain, conceited. **vanità** nf vanity. **vanitoso** (vani'toso) adj vain.

vantaggio (van'taddʒo) nm advantage. **vantaggioso** (vantad'dʒoso) adj advantageous.

vantare (van'tare) vt boast of. **vantarsi** vr boast. **vantatore** nm boaster.

vapore (va'pore) nm 1 steam, vapour. 2 steamer. **vaporetto** nm steamboat. **vaporizzatore** (vaporiddza'tore) nm spray, atomizer.

varare (va'rare) vt launch. **varo** nm launching.

varcare (var'kare) vt go beyond, cross. **varco** nm way, passage.

variare (va'rjare) vt,vi vary, alter. **variabile** (va'rjabile) adj variable, changeable. **variante** nf variant. **variazione** nf variation. **varietà** nf variety.

varicella (vari'tʃɛlla) nf chickenpox.

varicoso (vari'koso) adj varicose.

vario ('varjo) adj various.

varrò (var'rɔ) v see **variare**.

vasca ('vaska) nf 1 basin. 2 tank, tub.

vascello (vaʃ'ʃɛllo) nm ship.

vasellame (vazel'lame) nm crockery, dishes.

vaso ('vazo) nm 1 vase. 2 jar. 3 pot.

vassoio (vas'sojo) nm tray.

vasto ('vasto) adj vast, spacious.

Vaticano (vati'kano) nm Vatican.

ve (ve) pron 2nd pers m,f pl fam you, to you. adv there.

vecchio ('vɛkkjo) adj old. **vecchiaia** nf old age. **vecchietto** nm old man.

vedere* (ve'dere) vt,vi see. **farsi vedere** appear. **non vedere l'ora di** look forward to. **vedersi** vr meet. **vedetta** nf look-out. **veduta** nf view.

vedova ('vedova) nf widow. **vedovo** ('vedovo) nm widower.

vedrò (ve'drɔ) v see **vedere**.

veemente (vee'mɛnte) adj vehement. **veemenza** (vee'mɛntsa) nf vehemence.

vegetare (vedʒe'tare) vi vegetate. **vegetariano** nm vegetarian. **vegetazione** nf vegetation.

vegliare (veʎ'ʎare) vi 1 stay awake. 2 attend, watch. **veglia** nf 1 vigil. 2 evening party. **veglione** nm masked ball.

veicolo (ve'ikolo) nm vehicle.

vela ('vela) nf sail. **veleggiare** vi sail. **veliero** (ve'ljɛro) nm sailing ship.

velare (ve'lare) vt 1 veil. 2 cover. **velo** nm veil.

veleno (ve'leno) nm poison. **velenoso** (vele-'noso) adj poisonous.

velino (ve'lino) adj vellum. **carta velina** nf tissue paper.

velivolo (ve'livolo) nm aircraft.

velleità (vellei'ta) nf empty wish.

vellicare (velli'kare) vt 1 tickle. 2 stimulate.

vello ('vɛllo) nm 1 fleece. 2 zool coat.

velluto (vel'luto) nm velvet. **vellutato** adj velvet.

veloce (ve'lotʃe) adj quick, rapid, fast. **velocità** nf speed.

velodromo (ve'lɔdromo) nm cycle track.

veltro ('vɛltro) nm greyhound.

vena ('vena) nf vein. **venato** adj veined.

vendemmiare (vendem'mjare) vt harvest (grapes). vi gather in the harvest. **vendemmia** nf wine harvest.

vendere ('vendere) vt sell. **venditore** nm seller.

vendetta (ven'detta) nf revenge.

vendicare (vendi'kare) vt revenge, avenge. **vendicativo** adj vindictive.

vendita ('vendita) nf sale. **in vendita** on sale.

venerare (vene'rare) vt worship, revere. **venerabile** (vene'rabile) adj venerable. **venerazione** nf veneration.

venerdì (vener'di) nm Friday. **venerdì santo** Good Friday.

Venere ('vɛnere) nf Venus.

Venezia (ve'nɛttsja) nf Venice. **veneziano** adj,n Venetian.

vengo ('vɛngo) v see **venire**.

veniale (ve'njale) adj venial.

venire* (ve'nire) vi 1 come, arrive. 2 happen. **fare venire** send for. **venire a prendere** fetch. **venire bene/male** turn out well/ badly. **venuta** nf coming, arrival.

venni ('venni) v see **venire**.

ventaglio (ven'taʎʎo) nm fan.

venti ('venti) adj twenty. nm or f twenty. **ventesimo** (ven'tezimo) adj twentieth.

ventilare (venti'lare) vt ventilate. **ventilazione** nf ventilation.

vento ('vɛnto) nm wind. **ventoso** adj windy.

ventosa (ven'tosa) nf sucker.

ventre ('vɛntre) nm stomach, belly.

ventricolo (ven'trikolo) nm ventricle.

ventriloquo (ven'trilokwo) nm ventriloquist.

ventura (ven'tura) nf chance, fortune.

venturo (ven'turo) adj next, coming.

venusto (ve'nusto) adj beautiful.

verace (ve'ratʃe) adj true, real.

veranda (ve'randa) nf veranda.

verbo ('verbo) nm 1 verb. 2 word. **verbale** adj verbal, oral. nm minutes.

verde ('verde) adj,nm green. **essere al verde** be broke. **verdeggiare** vi turn green. **verdura** nf vegetables.

verdetto (ver'detto) nm verdict.

verecondo (vere'kondo) adj modest.

verga ('verga) nf rod.

vergine ('verdʒine) nf virgin. **verginità** nf virginity.

vergogna (ver'goɲɲa) nf shame. **vergognarsi**

vr be ashamed. **vergognoso** (vergoɲ'ɲoso) adj **1** shameful. **2** bashful.

verificare (verifi'kare) vt verify, check. **verificarsi** vr happen. **verifica** (ve'rifika) nf check, inspection.

verme ('verme) nm worm. **vermicelli** (vermi'tʃɛlli) nm pl type of pasta.

vermiglio (ver'miʎʎo) adj,nm vermilion.

vermut ('vɛrmut) nm invar vermouth.

vernaccia (ver'nattʃa) nf type of white wine.

verniciare (verni'tʃare) vt varnish, paint. **vernice** nf paint, varnish.

vero ('vero) adj true, real. **verità** nf truth.

verosimile (vero'simile) adj probable.

verricello (verri'tʃɛllo) nm winch.

verro ('vɛrro) nm boar.

verrò (ver'rɔ) v see **venire**.

versare (ver'sare) vt **1** pour. **2** spill. **3** deposit. **versarsi** vr spill. **versamento** nm **1** deposit. **2** payment.

versatile (ver'satile) adj versatile. **versatilità** nf versatility.

versione (ver'sjone) nf **1** version. **2** translation.

verso[1] ('vɛrso) nm **1** verse. **2** line.

verso[2] ('vɛrso) nm reverse (of a coin, etc.).

verso[3] ('vɛrso) prep towards.

vertebrato (verte'brato) adj,nm vertebrate.

verticale (verti'kale) adj vertical.

vertice ('vɛrtitʃe) nm summit, top.

vertigine (ver'tidʒine) nf dizziness. **avere le vertigini** feel dizzy. **vertiginoso** (vertidʒi'noso) adj dizzy.

vescica (veʃ'ʃika) nf bladder.

vescovo ('veskovo) nm bishop.

vespa ('vɛspa) nf **1** wasp. **2** Tdmk scooter.

vestaglia (ves'taʎʎa) nf dressing-gown.

vestibolo (ves'tibolo) nm hall, foyer.

vestigio (ves'tidʒo) nm trace.

vestire (ves'tire) vt dress, clothe. **veste** ('vɛste) nf dress, clothing. **vestiario** (ves'tjarjo) nm clothing. **vestito** nm **1** dress. **2** suit. **3** pl clothes.

veterano (vete'rano) adj,nm veteran.

veterinario (veteri'narjo) nm veterinary surgeon, vet.

veto ('vɛto) nm veto.

vetro ('vetro) nm glass. **vetraio** nm glazier. **vetrata** nf glass door or window. **vetrina** nf **1** shopwindow. **2** glass case.

vetta ('vetta) nf summit.

vettovaglie (vetto'vaʎʎe) nf pl food supplies.

vettura (vet'tura) nf carriage, coach.

vezzeggiare (vettsed'dʒare) vt fondle. **vezzo** nm **1** habit. **2** affection. **3** pl charms. **vezzoso** (vet'tsoso) adj pretty.

vi (vi) pron 2nd pers m,f pl fam you, to you. adv there.

via[1] ('via) nf **1** street, road. **2** way. **per via aerea** airmail. **via di mezzo** middle course. **viale** nm avenue.

via[2] ('via) adv away.

viadotto (via'dotto) nm viaduct.

viaggiare (viad'dʒare) vi travel. **viaggiatore** nm traveller, passenger. **commesso viaggiatore** nm salesman. **viaggio** nm journey.

Via Lattia nf Milky Way.

viandante (vian'dante) nm wayfarer.

viavai (via'vai) nm invar bustle.

vibrare (vi'brare) vi vibrate, quiver. **vibrante** adj vibrant. **vibrazione** nf vibration.

vicario (vi'karjo) nm vicar.

viceconsole (vitʃe'kɔnsole) nm vice-consul.

vicedirettore (vitʃediret'tore) nm assistant manager.

vicenda (vi'tʃɛnda) nf event. **a vicenda** in turn.

vicepresidente (vitʃepresi'dɛnte) nm vice-president.

viceversa (vitʃe'vɛrsa) adv vice versa.

vicino (vi'tʃino) adj near, neighbouring. nm neighbour. adv close by. **vicino a** near. **vicinato** nm neighbourhood. **vicinanza** nf **1** vicinity. **2** pl neighbourhood.

vicolo ('vikolo) nm alley.

video ('video) nm video.

vidi ('vidi) v see **videre**.

vidimare (vidi'mare) vt stamp, authenticate.

vieni ('vjeni) v see **venire**.

vietare (vje'tare) vt forbid, prohibit.

vigilare (vidʒi'lare) vt watch over. **vigilante** adj watchful. **vigilanza** nf vigilance. **vigile** ('vidʒile) adj watchful. nm policeman. **vigile del fuoco** fireman. **vigilia** (vi'dʒilja) nf **1** eve. **2** vigil.

vigliacco (viʎ'ʎakko) adj cowardly. nm coward. **vigliaccheria** nf cowardice.

vigna ('viɲɲa) nf **1** vineyard. **2** vine. **vigneto** (viɲ'ɲeto) nm vineyard.

vignetta (viɲ'ɲetta) nf cartoon.

vigore (vi'gore) nm strength, force. **entrare in vigore** come into force. **vigoroso** (vigo'roso) adj vigorous.

vile ('vile) adj low, mean, base.

villa ('villa) nf villa, country house.

villaggio (vil'laddʒo) nm village.

villano (vil'lano) *adj* rude. *nm* **1** peasant. **2** boor.

villeggiare (villed'dʒare) *vi* go on holiday. **villeggiante** *nm* holiday-maker. **villeggiatura** *nf* holiday.

viltà (vil'ta) *nf* **1** cowardice. **2** meanness.

viluppo (vi'luppo) *nm* tangle.

vimini ('vimini) *nm pl* wicker.

vincere* ('vintʃere) *vt* **1** win. **2** conquer. **3** beat. *vi* win. **vincersi** *vr* keep one's self-control. **vincitore** *nm* winner.

vincolare (vinko'lare) *vt* bind. **vincolo** ('vinkolo) *nm* bond, tie.

vino ('vino) *nm* wine.

viola[1] (vi'ɔla) *nf bot* violet. *adj,nm* violet, mauve.

viola[2] (vi'ɔla) *nf* viola.

violare (vio'lare) *vt* violate.

violentare (violen'tare) *vt* **1** force. **2** violate, rape. **violento** (vio'lɛnto) *adj* violent. **violenza** (vio'lɛntsa) *nf* violence.

violetta (vio'letta) *nf* violet.

violino (vio'lino) *nm* violin.

violoncello (violon'tʃɛllo) *nm* cello.

viottolo (vi'ɔttolo) *nm* track, path.

vipera ('vipera) *nf* viper.

virgola ('virgola) *nf* comma. **virgolette** *nf pl* inverted commas.

virile (vi'rile) *adj* virile, manly. **virilità** *nf* virility, manhood.

virtù (vir'tu) *nf* virtue. **virtuoso** (virtu'oso) *adj* virtuous. *nm* virtuoso.

virulento (viru'lɛnto) *adj* virulent.

virus ('virus) *nm invar* virus.

viscere ('viʃʃere) *nm anat* organ. *nf pl* bowels.

vischio ('viskjo) *nm* mistletoe.

visconte (vis'konte) *nm* viscount.

viscoso (vis'koso) *adj* sticky, viscous.

visibile (vi'zibile) *adj* visible. **visibilità** *nf* visibility.

visiera (vi'zjɛra) *nf* visor.

visione (vi'zjone) *nf* vision.

visitare (vizi'tare) *vt* **1** visit. **2** *med* examine. **3** inspect. **visita** ('vizita) *nf* **1** visit. **2** examination. **visitatore** *nm* visitor.

visivo (vi'zivo) *adj* visual.

viso ('vizo) *nm* face.

vispo ('vispo) *adj* lively.

vissi ('vissi) *v* see **vivere**.

vissuto (vis'suto) *v* see **vivere**.

vista ('vista) *nf* **1** sight. **2** view.

visto ('visto) *v* see **videre**. *nm* visa.

vistoso (vis'toso) *adj* showy, striking.

visuale (vizu'ale) *adj* visual.

vita[1] ('vita) *nf* life. **vitale** *adj* vital. **vitalità** *nf* vitality.

vita[2] ('vita) *nf* waist.

vitamina (vita'mina) *nf* vitamin.

vite[1] ('vite) *nf* vine.

vite[2] ('vite) *nf* screw.

vitello (vi'tɛllo) *nm* **1** calf. **2** veal.

vittima ('vittima) *nf* victim.

vitto ('vitto) *nm* food. **vitto e alloggio** board and lodging.

vittoria (vit'tɔrja) *nf* victory. **vittorioso** (vitto'rjoso) *adj* victorious.

vituperare (vitupe'rare) *vt* insult, disgrace. **vituperio** (vitu'pɛrjo) *nm* **1** shame. **2** insult.

viva ('viva) *interj* hurrah! long live.

vivace (vi'vatʃe) *adj* **1** lively. **2** bright. **vivacità** *nf* liveliness.

vivaio (vi'vajo) *nm* **1** fish pond. **2** *bot* nursery.

vivanda (vi'vanda) *nf* food.

vivere* ('vivere) *vi,vt* live.

viveri (vi'veri) *nm pl* supplies, victuals.

vivido ('vivido) *adj* vivid.

vivisezione (viviset'tsjone) *nf* vivisection.

vivo ('vivo) *adj* **1** alive, living. **2** lively. **3** bright.

viziare (vit'tsjare) *vt* spoil. **viziato** *adj* spoilt.

vizio ('vittsjo) *nm* **1** bad habit, vice. **2** defect. **vizioso** (vit'tsjoso) *adj* **1** depraved. **2** defective. **circolo vizioso** *nm* vicious circle.

vizzo ('vittso) *adj* withered.

vocabolo (vo'kabolo) *nm* word. **vocabolario** *nm* **1** dictionary. **2** vocabulary.

vocale (vo'kale) *adj* vocal. *nf* vowel.

vocazione (vokat'tsjone) *nf* vocation.

voce ('votʃe) *nf* voice.

vociare (vo'tʃare) *vi* shout.

vodka ('vɔdka) *nf* vodka.

vogare (vo'gare) *vi* row. **voga** *nf* **1** rowing. **2** fashion, vogue. **vogatore** *nm* oarsman.

voglia ('vɔʎʎa) *nf* wish, desire. **di buona/mala voglia** willingly/unwillingly.

voglio ('vɔʎʎo) *v* see **volere**.

voi ('voi) *pron* 2nd pers *m,f pl fam* you. **voialtri** ('vojaltri) *pron* 2nd pers *m,f pl fam* you. **voi stesse** *pron* 2nd pers *pl fam* yourselves.

volano (vo'lano) *nm* shuttlecock.

volare (vo'lare) *vi* fly. **volante** *adj* flying. *nm* steering wheel. **volantino** *nm* leaflet. **volata** *nf* flight.

volatile (vo'latile) *adj* volatile.

volentieri (volen'tjɛri) *adv* willingly.

volere[*] (vo'lere) *vt* **1** want, wish. **2** demand, require. **voler bene** a love. **volerci** be necessary. **volere dire** mean. ~*nm* will.

volgare (vol'gare) *adj* vulgar, common. **volgarità** *nf* vulgarity.

volgere[*] ('voldʒere) *vt,vi* turn. **volgersi** *vr* turn round.

volgo ('volgo) *nm* common people.

volli ('volli) *v* see **volere.**

volo ('volo) *nm* flight.

volontà (volon'ta) *nf* will. **volontario** *adj* voluntary. *nm* volunteer. **volonteroso** (volonte'roso) *adj* willing.

volpe ('volpe) *nf* fox.

volsi ('volsi) *v* see **volgere.**

volta[1] ('volta) **1** time. **2** turn. **a volte** sometimes. **una volta** once.

volta[2] ('volta) *nf* arch vault.

voltaggio (vol'taddʒo) *nm* voltage.

voltare (vol'tare) *vt,vi* turn. **voltarsi** *vr* turn round. **voltata** *nf* turn, turning.

volteggiare (volted'dʒare) *vi* **1** fly about. **2** vault.

volto[1] ('volto) *v* see **volgere.**

volto[2] ('volto) *nm* face.

volubile (vo'lubile) *adj* fickle, changeable.

volume (vo'lume) *nm* volume. **voluminoso** (volumi'noso) *adj* bulky.

voluttuoso (voluttu'oso) *adj* voluptuous.

vomitare (vomi'tare) *vt,vi* vomit. **vomito** ('vomito) *nm* vomit.

vorace (vo'ratʃe) *adj* greedy, voracious. **voracità** *nf* greed.

voragine (vo'radʒine) *nf* chasm.

vorrò (vor'rɔ) *v* see **volere.**

vortice ('vortitʃe) *nm* whirl.

vostro ('vostro) *poss adj* 2nd pers pl fam your. *poss pron* 2nd pers pl fam yours.

votare (vo'tare) *vi* vote. **votante** *nm* voter. **votazione** *nf* voting, vote. **voto** *nm* **1** vow. **2** vote. **3** mark.

vulcano (vul'kano) *nm* volcano. **vulcanico** (vul'kaniko) *adj* volcanic.

vulnerabile (vulne'rabile) *adj* vulnerable.

vuoi ('vwoi) *v* see **volere.**

vuole ('vwole) *v* see **volere.**

vuotare (vwo'tare) *vt* empty. **vuoto** ('vwoto) *adj* empty. *nm* empty space, vacuum.

X

xenofobia (ksenofo'bia) *nf* xenophobia.

xeres ('ksɛres) *nm invar* sherry.

xerocopiare (kseroko'pjare) *vt* photocopy. **xerocopia** (ksero'kopja) *nf* photocopy.

xilofono (ksi'lofono) *nm* xylophone.

Y

yacht (jɔt) *nm invar* yacht.

yoga ('jɔga) *nm* yoga.

yoghurt ('jɔgurt) *nm* yoghurt.

Z

zabaione (dzaba'jone) *nm* dessert made of eggs and marsala.

zacchera ('tsakkera) *nf* splash of mud.

zaffare (tsaf'fare) *vt* plug, stop up.

zafferano (dzaffe'rano) *nm* saffron.

zaffiro (dzaf'firo) *nm* sapphire.

zagara ('dzagara) *nf* orange blossom.

zaino ('dzaino) *nm* rucksack.

zampa ('tsampa) *nf* paw, leg.

zampillare (tsampil'lare) *vi* gush, spring. **zampillo** *nm* spurt.

zampogna (tsam'poɲɲa) *nf* bagpipe.

zana ('tsana) *nf* cradle.

zangola ('tsangola) *nf* churn.

zanna ('tsanna) *nf* tusk, fang.

zanzara (dzan'dzara) *nf* mosquito. **zanzariera** (dzandza'rjɛra) *nf* mosquito net.

zappare (tsap'pare) *vt* hoe. **zappa** *nf* hoe.

zar (tsar) *nm* tsar. **zarina** *nf* tsarina.

zattera ('tsattera) *nf* raft.

zavorra (dza'vorra) *nf* ballast.

zazzera ('tsattsera) *nf* shock of hair.

zebra ('dzɛbra) *nf* zebra.

zecca ('tsekka) *nf* mint. **nuovo di zecca** *adj* brand-new.

zefiro ('dzɛfiro) *nm* zephyr.

zelo ('dzɛlo) *nm* zeal. **zelante** *adj* zealous.

zenit ('dzenit) *nm invar* zenith.

zenzero ('dzendzero) *nm* ginger.

zeppa ('tseppa) *nf* wedge.

zeppo ('tseppo) *adj* crammed, stuffed. **pieno zeppo** crammed full.

zerbino[1] (dzer'bino) *nm* dandy.

zerbino[2] (dzer'bino) *nm* doormat.

zero ('dzɛro) *nm* zero, nought.

zia ('tsia) *nf* aunt.

zibellino (dzibel'lino) *nm* sable.

zibetto (dzi'betto) *nm* civet.

zigomo ('dzigomo) *nm* cheekbone.

zigzag (dzig'dzag) *nm invar* zigzag. **camminare a zigzag** zigzag.

zimbello (tsim'bɛllo) *nm* 1 decoy bird. 2 laughingstock.

zinco ('tsiŋko) *nm* zinc.

zingaro ('tsingaro) *nm* gipsy. **zingaresco** *adj* gipsy.

zio ('tsio) *nm* uncle.

zirlare (dzir'lare) *vi* chirp.

zitella (tsi'tɛlla) *nf* spinster. **zitellona** *nf* old maid.

zittire (tsit'tire) *vt* silence.

zitto ('tsitto) *adj* quiet, silent. **stare zitto** be quiet.

zoccolo ('tsɔkkolo) *nm* 1 clog. 2 hoof.

zodiaco (dzo'diako) *nm* zodiac.

zolfo ('tsolfo) *nm* sulphur.

zolla ('dzolla) *nf* clod, tuft. **zolletta** *nf* sugar lump.

zona ('dzɔna) *nf* zone, area.

zonzo ('dzondzo) **andare a zonzo** *adv* wander about, stroll.

zoo ('dzɔo) *nm invar* zoo.

zoologia (dzoolo'dʒia) *nf* zoology. **zoologico** (dzoo'lɔdʒiko) *adj* zoological. **giardino zoologico** *nm* zoo. **zoologo** (dzo'ɔlogo) *nm* zoologist.

zoppicare (tsoppi'kare) *vi* 1 limp. 2 be shaky. **zoppicante** *adj* 1 lame. 2 unsteady. **zoppo** ('tsɔppo) *adj* 1 lame. 2 wobbly, unsteady.

zotico ('dzɔtiko) *adj* rough, uncouth.

zucca ('tsukka) *nf* pumpkin. **zuccone** *nm* fool.

zucchero ('tsukkero) *nm* sugar. **zuccheriera** (tsukke'rjɛre) *nf* sugar bowl.

zucchino (tsuk'kino) *nm* courgette.

zuccotto (tsuk'kɔtto) *nm* iced sweet made of cream and chocolate.

zuffa ('tsuffa) *nf* scuffle.

zufolo ('tsufolo) *nm* whistle.

zulù (dzu'lu) *nm invar* Zulu.

zuppa ('tsuppa) *nf* soup. **zuppa inglese** *nf* trifle. **zuppiera** (tsup'pjɛra) *nf* soup tureen.

A

a, an (ə, ən; *stressed* ei, æn) *indef art* un, uno *ms.* una, un' *fs.*

aback (ə'bæk) *adv* all'indietro. **taken aback** preso alla sprovvista.

abandon (ə'bændən) *vt* abbandonare, lasciare. *n* abbandono, trasporto *m.* **abandonment** *n* abbandono *m.* rinuncia *f.*

abashed (ə'bæʃt) *adj* intimidito, umiliato.

abate (ə'beit) *vt* mitigare, diminuire. *vi* calmarsi, indebolirsi.

abattoir ('æbətwɑ:) *n* mattatoio *m.*

abbess ('æbis) *n* badessa *f.*

abbey ('æbi) *n* abbazia *f.*

abbot ('æbət) *n* abate *m.*

abbreviate (ə'bri:vieit) *vt* abbreviare, accorciare. **abbreviation** *n* abbreviazione *f.*

abdicate ('æbdikeit) *vt* abdicare, rinunciare a. *vi* abdicare. **abdication** *n* abdicazione, rinuncia *f.*

abdomen ('æbdəmən) *n* addome *m.* **abdominal** *adj* addominale.

abduct (æb'dʌkt) *vt* rapire, portar via. **abduction** *n* rapimento, ratto *m.* **abductor** *n* rapitore *m.*

abet (ə'bet) *vt* incitare, istigare, favoreggiare.

abeyance (ə'beiəns) *n* sospensione *f.* **in abeyance** giacente.

abhor (əb'hɔ:) *vt* abborrire, detestare. **abhorrence** *n* avversione, ripugnanza *f.* **abhorrent** *adj* odioso, ripugnante.

abide (ə'baid) *vi* rimanere, dimorare. *vt* tollerare. **abide by** rispettare, tener fede a.

ability (ə'biliti) *n* abilità *f.* talento *m.*

abject ('æbdʒekt) *adj* abietto, vile, spregevole.

ablaze (ə'bleiz) *adj* in fiamme, risplendente.

able ('eibəl) *adj* 1 abile, esperto. 2 in grado di. **able-bodied** *adj* robusto, forte. **ably** *adv* abilmente.

abnormal (æb'nɔ:məl) *adj* anormale. **abnormality** *n* anormalità *f.*

aboard (ə'bɔ:d) *adv* a bordo. **go aboard** imbarcarsi. ~*prep* a bordo di.

abode (ə'boud) *n* dimora, residenza *f.*

abolish (ə'bɔliʃ) *vt* abolire, sopprimere. **abolition** *n* abolizione *f.*

abominable (ə'bɔminəbəl) *adj* abominevole, detestabile. **abomination** *n* 1 infamia *f.* 2 disgusto *m.*

Aborigine (æbə'ridʒini) *n* aborigeno *m.*

abort (ə'bɔ:t) *vi* 1 abortire. 2 fallire. **abortion** *n* aborto *m.* **abortive** *adj* 1 abortivo. 2 mancato.

abound (ə'baund) *vi* abbondare.

about (ə'baut) *prep* 1 circa, intorno a. 2 riguardo a. *adv* 1 circa, quasi. 2 presso.

above (ə'bʌv) *adv* in alto, lassù. *prep* sopra, più di, oltre. **above all** soprattutto. **above mentioned** suddetto. **aboveboard** *adv* lealmente, apertamente. *adj* leale.

abrasion (ə'breiʒən) *n* abrasione, escoriazione *f.* **abrasive** *adj,n* abrasivo *m.*

abreast (ə'brest) *adv* di fianco.

abridge (ə'bridʒ) *vt* abbreviare, ridurre. **abridgment** *n* sommario, riassunto *m.*

abroad (ə'brɔ:d) *adv* all'estero.

abrupt (ə'brʌpt) *adj* 1 brusco, improvviso. 2 ripido, scosceso.

abscess ('æbses) *n* ascesso *m.*

abscond (əb'skɔnd) *vi* nascondersi, rendersi latitante.

absent ('æbsənt) *adj* assente, mancante. **absent-minded** *adj* distratto. **absent-mindedness** *n* distrazione *f.* **absence** *n* assenza, mancanza *f.* **absentee** *n* persona abitualmente assente *f.* assente *m.*

absinthe ('æbsinθ) *n* assenzio *m.*

absolute ('æbsəlu:t) *adj* 1 assoluto. 2 completo, perfetto.

absolve (əb'zɔlv) *vt* assolvere. **absolution** *n* assoluzione *f.*

141

absorb (ab'zɔ:b) vt assorbire. **absorbent** adj assorbente. **absorption** n assorbimento m.

abstain (ab'stein) vi astenersi. **abstention** n astensione f. **abstinence** n astinenza f. digiuno m.

abstract (adj,n 'æbstrækt; v əb'strækt) adj astratto. n estratto, riassunto m. vt astrarre, rimuovere. **abstraction** n astrazione f.

absurd (ab'sɔ:d) adj assurdo, ridicolo. **absurdity** n assurdità f.

abundance (ə'bʌndəns) abbondanza f. **abundant** adj abbondante.

abuse (v ə'bju:z; n ə'bju:s) vt 1 abusare di. 2 insultare, maltrattare, ingiuriare. n 1 abuso, cattivo uso. 2 insulti m pl. **abusive** adj 1 ingiurioso. 2 abusivo.

abyss (ə'bis) n abisso m. **abysmal** adj abissale, profondo.

Abyssinia (æbə'siniə) n Abissinia f. **Abyssinian** adj,n abissino.

academy (ə'kædəmi) n accademia f. **academic** adj,n accademico, universitario m.

accelerate (ək'seləreit) vt accelerare. **acceleration** n accelerazione f. **accelerator** n acceleratore m.

accent ('æksənt) n accento m. **accentuate** vt accentuare, mettere in evidenza. **accentuation** n accentuazione f. enfasi f invar.

accept (ək'sept) vt accettare, accogliere, approvare. **acceptable** adj accettabile, ammissibile. **acceptance** n accettazione, approvazione f.

access ('ækses) n accesso, ingresso m. **accessible** adj accessibile.

accessory (ək'sesəri) adj accessorio. n 1 complice m. 2 accessorio m.

accident ('æksidnt) n 1 disgrazia f. incidente m. 2 accidente caso m. **by accident** per caso. **accidental** adj fortuito, casuale.

acclaim (ə'kleim) vt acclamare. **acclamation** n acclamazione f.

acclimatize (ə'klaimətaiz) vt acclimatare.

accommodate (ə'kɔmədeit) vt 1 ricevere, ospitare. 2 metter d'accordo, conciliare. 3 adattare, conformare. **accommodating** adj accomodante, compiacente. **accommodation** n alloggio m.

accompany (ə'kʌmpəni) vt accompagnare. **accompaniment** n accompagnamento m.

accomplice (ə'kʌmplis) n complice m,f.

accomplish (ə'kʌmpliʃ) vt compiere, terminare, realizzare. **accomplished** adj esperto. **ac-**

complishment n 1 compimento m. 2 talento m.

accord (ə'kɔ:d) n accordo, consenso m. **of one's own accord** spontaneamente. ~vt accordare, concedere. **accordance** n accordo m. conformità f. **accordingly** adv pertanto, di conseguenza, perciò, quindi. **according to** adv secondo, conformemente a.

accordion (ə'kɔ:diən) n fisarmonica f.

accost (ə'kɔst) vt indirizzarsi a, rivolgersi a.

account (ə'kaunt) n 1 conto, calcolo m. 2 versione f. resoconto m. **by all accounts** a quanto si dice. **on account of** a causa di. **on no account** per nessun motivo. ~vt considerare, riguardare. **account for** essere responsabile di, render conto di. **accountable** adj responsabile. **accountancy** n contabilità f. **accountant** n contabile m. **chartered accountant** ragioniere m.

accumulate (ə'kju:mjuleit) vt accumulare, ammassare. vi accumularsi. **accumulation** n accumulamento, ammasso m. **accumulative** adj accumulativo.

accurate ('ækjurət) adj accurato, preciso, esatto. **accuracy** n accuratezza, precisione f.

accuse (ə'kju:z) vt accusare, incolpare. **accusation** n accusa f. **accused** n accusato, imputato m.

accustom (ə'kʌstəm) vt abituare.

ace (eis) n 1 asso m. 2 inf campione m.

ache (eik) n dolore, male m. vi dolere, far male.

achieve (ə'tʃi:v) vt 1 compiere, portare a termine. 2 ottenere, raggiungere. **achievement** n 1 compimento m. 2 impresa f. successo m.

acid ('æsid) adj,n acido m. **acidity** n acidità f.

acknowledge (ək'nɔlidʒ) vt ammettere, riconoscere. **acknowledge receipt** accusare ricevuta. **acknowledgment** n 1 riconoscimento m. ammissione f. 2 ricevuta f.

acne ('ækni) n acne m.

acorn ('eikɔ:n) n ghianda f.

acoustic (ə'ku:stik) adj acustico. **acoustics** n acustica f.

acquaint (ə'kweint) vt informare, mettere al corrente. **be acquainted with** 1 conoscere. 2 essere al corrente di. **acquaintance** n conoscenza f.

acquiesce (ækwi'es) vi acconsentire, assentire. **acquiescence** n acquiescenza f. **acquiescent** adj acquiescente, docile.

acquire (ə'kwaiə) vt 1 acquistare, acquisire. 2

imparare. **acquisition** n acquisizione f. acquisto m. **acquisitive** adj avido di guadagno.

acquit (ə'kwit) vt 1 assolvere. 2 pagare. **acquit oneself well** comportarsi bene. **acquittal** n assoluzione f.

acre ('eikə) n acro m.

acrimony ('ækriməni) n acrimonia f. **acrimonious** adj acrimonioso.

acrobat ('ækrəbæt) n acrobata m. **acrobatic** adj acrobatico. **acrobatics** n acrobazia f.

across (ə'krɔs) prep attraverso, di là da. adv attraverso.

acrylic (ə'krilik) adj acrilico.

act (ækt) n 1 atto, decreto m. 2 azione f. gesto m. 3 Th atto m. vi agire, comportarsi. vt 1 fare. 2 Th recitare. **act as** fingere da. **acting** n recitazione f.

action ('ækʃən) n 1 azione f. fatto m. 2 effetto m. 3 processo m. **out of action** fuori servizio.

active ('æktiv) adj attivo. **activate** vt attivare. **activist** n attivista m. **activity** n attività, energia f.

actor ('æktə) n attore m.

actress ('æktris) n attrice f.

actual ('æktʃuəl) adj reale, vero, effettivo.

actuary ('æktʃuəri) n attuario m.

acupuncture ('ækjupʌŋktʃə) n agopuntura f.

acute (ə'kju:t) adj 1 acuto, aguzzo. 2 perspicace.

adamant ('ædəmənt) adj duro, inflessibile.

Adam's apple ('ædəmz) n pomo d'Adamo m.

adapt (ə'dæpt) vt adattare, modificare. **adaptable** adj adattabile. **adaptability** n adattabilità f. **adaptation** n adattamento m.

add (æd) vt 1 aggiungere. 2 sommare. **add to** aumentare. **add up** sommare. **adding machine** n addizionatrice, calcolatrice f. **addition** n 1 aggiunta f. 2 addizione f. **in addition to** oltre a. **additional** adj addizionale. **additive** adj,n additivo m.

addendum (ə'dendəm) n, pl **addenda** aggiunta, appendice f.

adder ('ædə) n vipera, aspide f.

addict (n 'ædikt; v ə'dikt) n tossicomane, drogato m. vt abbandonarsi a. **addiction** n inclinazione, dedizione f.

addled ('ædld) adj putrido.

address (ə'dres) n 1 indirizzo, recapito m. 2 discorso m. vt 1 indirizzare. 2 rivolgere la parola a. **address book** n rubrica f. **addressee** n destinatario m.

adenoids ('ædinɔidz) n pl adenoidi f pl.

adept ('ædept) adj perito, esperto, abile.

adequate ('ædikwət) adj adeguato, sufficiente.

adhere (əd'hiə) vi aderire, attaccarsi. **adherent** adj aderente. n partigiano, seguace m. **adhesion** n adesione f. **adhesive** adj adesivo, viscoso. **adhesive plaster** n cerotto m.

adjacent (ə'dʒeisənt) adj adiacente, attiguo.

adjective ('ædʒiktiv) n aggettivo m.

adjoining (ə'dʒɔiniŋ) adj contiguo, vicino.

adjourn (ə'dʒə:n) vt aggiornare, rinviare. vi trasferirsi. **adjournment** n rinvio, aggiornamento m.

adjudicate (ə'dʒu:dikeit) vi giudicare, decidere.

adjust (ə'dʒʌst) vt aggiustare, adattare, regolare. **adjustment** n adattamento m.

ad-lib (æd'lib) vt,vi improvvisare. n improvvisazione f. adj improvvisato.

administer (əd'ministə) vt 1 amministrare, gestire, governare. 2 somministrare. vi contribuire. **administration** n 1 amministrazione, gestione f. 2 somministrazione f. **administrative** adj amministrativo. **administrator** n amministratore m.

admiral ('ædmərəl) n ammiraglio m. **admiralty** n 1 ammiragliato m. 2 Ministero della Marina m.

admire (əd'maiə) vt ammirare. **admirable** adj ammirevole. **admiration** n ammirazione f. **admirer** n ammiratore, corteggiatore m.

admit (əd'mit) vt 1 ammettere, riconoscere. 2 lasciar entrare. **admission** n 1 ammissione, entrata f. ingresso m. 2 confessione f. **admittance** n accesso m. entrata f. **no admittance** vietato l'ingresso.

ado (ə'du:) n 1 fatica, difficoltà f. 2 rumore, trambusto m.

adolescence (ædə'lesəns) n adolescenza f. **adolescent** adj,n adolescente.

adopt (ə'dɔpt) vt adottare. **adoption** n adozione f.

adore (ə'dɔ:) vt adorare, venerare. **adorer** n adoratore m. adoratrice f.

adorn (ə'dɔ:n) vt adornare, abbellire.

adrenaline (ə'drenəlin) n adrenalina f.

Adriatic (eidri'ætik) adj adriatico. **Adriatic (Sea)** n (Mare) Adriatico m.

adrift (ə'drift) adv alla deriva.

adroit (ə'drɔit) adj abile, destro.

adulation (ædju'leiʃən) n adulazione f.

adult ('ædʌlt) adj,n adulto.

adulterate (ə'dʌltəreit) vt adulterare, falsificare.

adultery (ə'dʌltəri) n adulterio m. **adulterer** n adultero m. **adulteress** n adultera f.

advance (əd'vɑːns) n **1** avanzamento, progresso m. marcia in avanti f. **2** anticipo m. **make advances** fare degli approcci. ~vt **1** avanzare, promuovere. **2** anticipare. vi avanzare, progredire. **advancement** n **1** progresso m. **2** promozione f.

advantage (əd'vɑːntidʒ) n vantaggio, profitto m. **take advantage of** approfittare di. **advantageous** adj vantaggioso.

advent ('ædvent) n **1** avenuta f. **2** cap avvento m.

adventure (əd'ventʃə) n avventura, impresa f. **adventurous** adj avventuroso.

adverb ('ædvəːb) n avverbio m.

adverse ('ædvəːs) adj avverso, contrario. **adversity** n avversità f.

advertise ('ædvətaiz) vt annunziare, fare pubblicità a. vi mettere annunci. **advertisement** n annuncio m. inserzione f. **advertising** n pubblicità f.

advise (əd'vaiz) vt consigliare, raccomandare. **advice** n consigli m pl. avviso m. **advisable** adj consigliabile, opportuno. **advised** adj giudizioso, prudente. **ill-/well-advised** incanto/saggio.

advocate (n 'ædvəkət; v 'ædvəkeit) n difensore, avvocato m. vt difendere, sostenere.

Aegean (i'dʒiːən) adj egeo. **Aegean (Sea)** n (Mare) Egeo m.

aerate ('ɛəreit) vt aerare.

aerial ('ɛəriəl) adj aereo. n antenna f.

aerodynamics (ɛəroudai'næmiks) n aerodinamica f.

aeronautics (ɛərə'nɔːtiks) n aeronautica f. **aeronautical** adj aeronautico.

aeroplane ('ɛərəplein) n aeroplano m.

aerosol ('ɛərəsɔl) n aerosol m invar.

aesthetic (is'θetik) adj estetico. **aesthetics** n estetica f.

afar (ə'fɑː) adv lontano, in lontananza. **from afar** da lontano.

affable ('æfəbəl) adj affabile, cortese. **affability** n affabilità, cortesia f.

affair (ə'fɛə) n **1** affare m. **2** faccenda f. **3** relazione amorosa f.

affect[1] (ə'fekt) vt **1** concernere, riguardare. **2** commuovere.

affect[2] (ə'fekt) vt **1** affettare, ostentare. **2** fingere. **affectation** n affettazione, simulazione f. **affected** adj affettato, ricercato.

affection (ə'fekʃən) n affetto m. **affectionate** adj affettuoso, affezionato.

affiliate (ə'filieit) vt affiliare, associare. vi affiliarsi, unirsi.

affinity (ə'finiti) n affinità, parentela f.

affirm (ə'fəːm) vt affermare, confermare, asserire. **affirmation** n affermazione, asserzione f. **affirmative** adj affermativo. n affermativa f.

affix (ə'fiks) vt affiggere, apporre.

afflict (ə'flikt) vt affliggere, tormentare. **affliction** n afflizione f. dolore m.

affluence ('æfluəns) n abbondanza f. **affluent** adj ricco, opulente.

afford (ə'fɔːd) vt **1** concedere, offrire, dare. **2** permettere. **afford to** avere i mezzi di.

affront (ə'frʌnt) n affronto, insulto m. vt offendere, insultare.

Afghanistan (æf'gænistɑːn, -stæn) n Afganistan m. **Afghan** adj,n afghano.

afield (ə'fiːld) adv lontano. **far afield** adv molto lontano.

afloat (ə'flout) adv a galla, in mare.

afoot (ə'fut) adv in movimento.

aforesaid (ə'fɔːsed) adj suddetto, predetto.

afraid (ə'freid) adj spaventato, pauroso. **be afraid** aver paura.

afresh (ə'freʃ) adv da capo, di nuovo.

Africa ('æfrikə) n Africa f. **African** adj,n africano.

aft (ɑːft) adv a poppa.

after ('ɑːftə) prep **1** dopo, in seguito a. **2** secondo. adv dopo, poi. conj dopo che. **after-care** n assistenza postoperatoria f. **after-effect** n conseguenza f. risultato m. **afterlife** n vita dell'ai di là f. **aftermath** n conseguenze f pl. frutti m pl. **afternoon** n pomeriggio m. **afterthought** n ripensamento m. riflessione f. **afterwards** adv dopo, in seguito.

again (ə'gen) adv ancora, di nuovo. **again and again** ripetutamente. **as much again** altrettanto. **now and again** di tanto in tanto.

against (ə'genst) prep contro, in opposizione a.

age (eidʒ) n **1** età f. **2** periodo, secolo m. **be of age** essere maggiorenne. **be under age** essere minorenne. ~vi invecchiare, invecchiarsi. **aged** adj vecchio, stagionato. **age-group** n persone pressapoco della stessa età f pl.

agency ('eidʒənsi) n agenzia, succursale f.

agenda (ə'dʒendə) n ordine del giorno m.

agent ('eidʒənt) n agente, rappresentante m.

aggravate ('ægreveit) vt aggravare.

aggregate (adj,n 'ægrigit; v 'ægrigeit) adj,n aggregato m. vt aggregare.

aggression (ə'greʃən) n aggressione f. **aggressive** adj aggressivo, offensivo. **aggressor** n aggressore m.

aggrieved (ə'gri:vd) adj addolorato.

aghast (ə'gɑ:st) adj atterrito, costernato.

agile ('ædʒail) adj agile.

agitate ('ædʒiteit) vt **1** agitare, scuotere. **2** turbare. **agitation** n agitazione f.

aglow (ə'glou) adj ardente.

agnostic (æg'nɔstik) adj,n agnostico.

ago (ə'gou) adv fa, passato. **long ago** molto tempo fa.

agog (ə'gɔg) adv,adj in ansia, bramoso.

agony ('ægəni) n agonia, angoscia f. dolore m. **agonize** vi agonizzare. **agonizing** adj angoscioso, lancinante.

agrarian (ə'greəriən) adj agrario, agricolo.

agree (ə'gri:) vi **1** accordarsi, convenire, andare d'accordo. **2** acconsentire. **agreeable** adj **1** piacevole. **2** disposto. **agreement** n **1** accordo m. **2** contratto, patto m.

agriculture ('ægrikʌltʃə) n agricoltura f. **agricultural** adj agricolo.

aground (ə'graund) adv a secco. **run aground** arenarsi, incagliarsi.

ahead (ə'hed) adv (in) avanti.

aid (eid) n **1** aiuto, soccorso m. sussidi m pl. **2** aiutante m. vt soccorrere, assistere.

ailment ('eilmənt) n indisposizione, malattia f.

aim (eim) n **1** mira f. **2** proposito, scopo m. vt **1** puntare. **2** dirigere. vi **1** mirare. **2** aspirare.

air (ɛə) n **1** aria, atmosfera f. **2** aspetto m. **in the open air** all'aperto. ~vt ventilare.

airborne ('ɛəbɔ:n) adj **1** sostenuto dall'aria. **2** aviotrasportato.

air-conditioning n aria condizionata f.

aircraft ('ɛəkrɑ:ft) n aereo, velivolo m.

aircraft carrier n portaerei f invar.

airfield ('ɛəfi:ld) n campo d'aviazione m.

airforce ('ɛəfɔ:s) n aviazione, aeronautica f.

air-hostess n hostess f. assistente di volo f.

air lift n ponte aereo m. vt mandare per aereo.

airline ('ɛəlain) n linea aerea f.

airmail ('ɛəmeil) n posta aerea f. **by air mail** per via aerea.

airman ('ɛəmən) n aviatore m.

airport ('ɛəpɔ:t) n aeroporto m.

air-raid n incursione aerea f.

airtight ('ɛətait) adj a tenuta d'aria, ermetico.

airy ('ɛəri) adj aerato, arioso, leggero.

aisle (ail) n navata f.

ajar (ə'dʒɑ:) adj,adv socchiuso.

alabaster ('æləbɑ:stə) n alabastro m.

alarm (ə'lɑ:m) n **1** allarme m. **2** (electrical) suoneria elettrica f. vt allarmare, spaventare. **alarm clock** n sveglia f. **alarming** adj allarmante.

alas (ə'læs) interj ahimè!

Albania (æl'beiniə) n Albania f. **Albanian** adj,n albanese.

albatross ('ælbətrɔs) n albatro m.

albeit (ɔ:l'bi:it) conj quantunque.

album ('ælbəm) n album m invar.

alchemy ('ælkəmi) n alchimia f.

alcohol ('ælkəhɔl) n alcool m invar. spirito m. **alcoholic** adj alcoolico. n alcolizzato m.

alcove ('ælkouv) n alcova f.

alderman ('ɔ:ldəmən) n assessore municipale m.

ale (eil) n birra f. **brown ale** n birra scura f. **pale ale** n birra chiara f.

alert (ə'lə:t) adj vigilante. n allarme m. **on the alert** all'erta.

algebra ('ældʒibrə) n algebra f.

Algeria (æl'dʒiəriə) n Algeria f. **Algerian** adj,n algerino.

alias ('eiliəs) adv altrimenti detto, alias.

alibi ('ælibai) n alibi m invar.

alien ('eiliən) adj alieno, straniero, estraneo. n straniero, forestiero m. **alienate** vt alienare, estraniare. **alienation** n alienazione f.

alight[1] (ə'lait) adj in fiamme, illuminato. **set alight** dar fuoco a.

alight[2] (ə'lait) vi discendere, smontare, atterrare.

align (ə'lain) vt allineare. vi allinearsi. **alignment** n allineamento m.

alike (ə'laik) adj simile, somigliante. **be alike** assomigliarsi. ~adv similmente.

alimentary (æli'mentəri) adj alimentare, alimentario.

alimony ('æliməni) n alimenti m pl.

alive (ə'laiv) adj vivo, vivente.

alkali ('ælkəlai) n, pl -is or -ies alcale f.

all (ɔ:l) adj tutto, intero. adv completamente.. **all right** va bene. ~pron tutto.

allay (ə'lei) vt calmare, mitigare.

allege (ə'ledʒ) vt allegare, asserire.

allegiance (ə'li:dʒəns) n fedeltà, obbedienza f.

allegory ('æligəri) n allegoria f. **allegorical** adj allegorico.

allergy ('ælədʒi) n allergia f. **allergic** adj allergico.

alleviate (ə'li:vieit) vt alleviare, lenire, attenuare.

alley ('æli) n vicolo m.

alliance (ə'laiəns) n alleanza f.

allied (ə'laid, 'ælaid) adj alleato, connesso.

alligator ('æligeitə) n alligatore m.

alliteration (əlitə'reifən) n allitterazione f.

allocate ('æləkeit) vt assegnare, distribuire. **allocation** n assegnamento, stanziamento m.

allot (ə'lɔt) vt assegnare, spartire.

allow (ə'lau) vt permettere, lasciare, concedere. **allow for** tener conto di. **allowance** n 1 assegno m. pensione f. 2 riduzione f.

alloy (ə'lɔi) n lega metallica. vt amalgamare.

All Saint's Day n Ognissanti m pl.

allude (ə'lu:d) vi alludere. **allusion** n allusione f.

allure (ə'luə) vt adescare, allettare. **alluring** adj seducente, attraente.

ally (n 'ælai; v ə'lai) n alleato m. vt unire, alleare. vi allearsi.

almanac ('ɔ:lmənæk) n almanacco, calendario m.

almighty (ɔ:l'maiti) adj onnipotente.

almond ('a:mənd) n mandorla f. **almond tree** n mandorlo m.

almost ('ɔ:lmoust) adv quasi.

alms (a:mz) n pl invar elemosina f. **almshouse** n ospizio di carità m.

aloft (ə'lɔft) adv in alto, in aria.

alone (ə'loun) adj solo, solitario. adv solamente.

along (ə'lɔŋ) prep lungo. adv avanti. **all along** sempre. **along with** insieme a. **alongside** prep accanto a, al fianco di. adv a fianco.

aloof (ə'lu:f) adj riservato. adv a distanza.

aloud (ə'laud) adv a voce alta or forte.

alphabet ('ælfəbet) n alfabeto m. **alphabetical** adj alfabetico.

alpine ('ælpain) adj alpino.

Alps (ælps) n pl Alpi f pl.

already (ɔ:l'redi) adv già.

Alsatian (æl'seifən) n cane-lupo m.

also ('ɔ:lsou) adv anche, inoltre, pure.

altar ('ɔ:ltə) n altare m. **altarpiece** n pala d'altare f. **altar rail** n balaustra f.

alter ('ɔ:ltə) vt alterare, cambiare. vi cambiarsi. **alteration** n alterazione, modifica f.

alternate (adj ɔ:l'tə:nit; v 'ɔ:ltəneit) adj alterno, alternato. vt alternare. vi alternarsi. **alternative** adj n alternativa f.

although (ɔ:l'ðou) conj sebbene, benchè, quantunque.

altitude ('æltitju:d) n altitudine, altezza f.

alto ('æltou) n contralto m.

altogether (ɔ:ltə'geðə) adv interamente, complessivamente.

aluminium (ælju'miniəm) n alluminio m.

always ('ɔ:lweiz) adv sempre.

am (əm; stressed æm) v see **be**.

amalgamate (ə'mælgəmeit) vt amalgamare. vi amalgamarsi. **amalgamation** n amalgamazione f.

amass (ə'mæs) vt accumulare, ammassare.

amateur ('æmətə) n dilettante m,f.

amaze (ə'meiz) vt meravigliare, stupire. **amazed** adj stupito, sorpreso. **amazing** adj straordinario, sbalorditivo.

ambassador (æm'bæsədə) n ambasciatore m.

amber ('æmbə) n ambra f.

ambidextrous (æmbi'dekstrəs) adj ambidestro.

ambiguous (æm'bigjuəs) adj ambiguo.

ambition (æm'bifən) n ambizione f. **ambitious** adj ambizioso.

ambivalent (æm'bivələnt) adj ambivalente.

amble ('æmbəl) vi camminare lentamente.

ambulance ('æmbjuləns) n ambulanza f.

ambush ('æmbuʃ) n imboscata f. agguato m. vt tendere un imboscata a.

amenable (ə'mi:nəbəl) adj malleabile, trattabile.

amend (ə'mend) vt emendare, migliorare. vi migliorarsi. **amendment** n emendamento m. **amends** n pl compenso m. riparazione f. **make amends** fare ammenda.

amenity (ə'mi:niti) n amenità f.

America (ə'merikə) n America f. **American** adj,n americano.

amethyst ('æmiθist) n ametista f.

amiable ('eimiəbəl) adj amabile.

amicable ('æmikəbəl) adj amichevole.

amid (ə'mid) prep also **amidst** fra, tra, in mezzo a.

amiss (ə'mis) adv male, erroneamente.

ammonia (ə'mouniə) n ammoniaca f.

ammunition (æmju'niʃən) n munizioni f pl.

amnesty ('æmnəsti) n amnistia f.

amoeba (ə'mi:bə) n, pl **-bae** or **-bas** ameba f.

among (ə'mʌŋ) prep also **amongst** tra, fra, in mezzo a.

amoral (ei'mɔrəl) adj amorale.

amorous ('æmərəs) adj amoroso, erotico.

amorphous (ə'mɔ:fəs) adj amorfo.

amount (ə'maunt) n ammontare, totale m. somma f. vi ammontare, equivalere.

ampere ('æmpɛə) n ampère m.

amphetamine (æm'fetəmi:n) n anfetamina f.

amphibian (æm'fibiən) *adj,n* anfibio *m.* **amphibious** *adj* anfibio.

amphitheatre ('æmfiθiətə) *n* anfiteatro *m.*

ample ('æmpəl) *adj* ampio, abbondante.

amplify ('æmplifai) *vt* amplificare, ampliare. **amplification** *n* amplificazione *f.* **amplifier** *n* amplificatore *m.*

amputate ('æmpjuteit) *vt* amputare.

amuse (ə'mju:z) *vt* divertire, dilettare. **amusement** *n* divertimento *m.* **amusing** *adj* divertente.

an (ən; *stressed* æn) *indef art see* **a.**

anachronism (ə'nækrənizəm) *n* anacronismo *m.*

anaemia (ə'ni:miə) *n* anemia *f.* **anaemic** *adj* anemico.

anaesthetic (ænis'θetik) *adj,n* anestetico *m.* **anaesthetist** *n* anestesista *m.* **anaesthetize** *vt* anestetizzare.

anagram ('ænəgræm) *n* anagramma *m.*

anal ('einl) *adj* anale.

analogy (ə'nælədʒi) *n* analogia *f.* **analogous** (ə'næləgəs) *adj* analogo.

analysis (ə'nælisis) *n, pl* **-ses** analisi *f invar.* **analyse** *vt* analizzare. **analyst** *n* analista *m.*

anarchy ('ænəki) *n* anarchia *f.* **anarchist** *n* anarchico *m.*

anatomy (ə'nætəmi) *n* anatomia *f.* **anatomical** *adj* anatomico.

ancestor ('ænsəstə) *n* antenato *m.*

anchor ('æŋkə) *n* ancora *f. vt* ancorare. *vi* ancorarsi.

anchovy ('æntʃəvi) *n* acciuga *f.*

ancient ('einʃənt) *adj* antico, vecchio.

ancillary (æn'siləri) *adj* sussidiario, ausiliario.

and (ən, ənd; *stressed* ænd) *conj* e, ed. **and so forth** e così via.

anecdote ('ænikdout) *n* aneddoto *m.*

anemone (ə'neməni) *n* anemone *m.*

anew (ə'nju:) *adv* di nuovo, da capo.

angel ('eindʒəl) *n* angelo *m.* **angelic** *adj* angelico.

angelica (æn'dʒelikə) *n* angelica *f.*

anger ('æŋgə) *n* ira, collera *f. vt* adirare, far andare in collera.

angle[1] ('æŋgəl) *n* **1** *math* angolo *m.* **2** punto di vista *m.* prospettiva *f.*

angle[2] ('æŋgəl) *vi* **1** pescare. **2** *inf* adescare. **angler** *n* pescatore *m.* **angling** *n* pesca con l'amo.

Anglican ('æŋglikən) *adj,n* anglicano.

angry ('æŋgri) *adj* arrabbiato, adirato, stizzito. **get angry** arrabbiarsi, adirarsi.

anguish ('æŋgwiʃ) *n* angoscia *f.*

angular ('æŋgjulə) *adj* angolare.

animal ('æniməl) *adj,n* animale *m.*

animate (*adj* 'ænimət; *v* 'ænimeit) *adj* animato, vivente. *vt* animare. **animation** *n* animazione, vivacità *f.*

aniseed ('ænisi:d) *n* semi di anice *m pl.*

ankle ('æŋkəl) *n* caviglia *f.*

annals ('ænlz) *n pl* annali *m pl.*

annex (ə'neks) *vt* annettere, unire. **annexe** *n* annesso, edificio secondario *m.*

annihilate (ə'naiəleit) *vt* annientare. **annihilation** *n* annientamento *m.*

anniversary (æni'və:səri) *n* anniversario *m.*

annotate ('ænəteit) *vt* annotare.

announce (ə'nauns) *vt* annunciare, render noto. **announcement** *n* annuncio *m.* dichiarazione *f.* **announcer** *n* annunciatore *m.*

annoy (ə'nɔi) *vt* disturbare, irritare. **annoying** *adj* seccante, fastidioso.

annual ('ænjuəl) *adj* annuale, annuo. *n* annuario *m.*

annuity (ə'nju:iti) *n* pensione annuale *f.*

annul (ə'nʌl) *vt* annullare.

anode ('ænoud) *n* anodo *m.*

anoint (ə'nɔint) *vt* consacrare, ungere.

anomaly (ə'nɔməli) *n* anomalia *f.*

anonymous (ə'nɔniməs) *adj* anonimo.

another (ə'nʌðə) *adj,pron* altro. **one another** l'un l'altro, si.

answer ('a:nsə) *n* risposta *f. vt* rispondere a.

ant (ænt) *n* formica *f.*

antagonize (æn'tægənaiz) *vt* opporsi, provocare. **antagonism** *n* antagonismo *m.*

Antarctic (æn'ta:ktik) *adj,n* antartico *m.*

antelope ('æntiloup) *n* antilope *f.*

antenatal (ænti'neitl) *adj* prenatale.

antenna (æn'tenə) *n,pl* **-tennae** antenna *f.*

anthem ('ænθəm) *n* inno *m.* antifona *f.*

anthology (æn'θɔlədʒi) *n* antologia *f.*

anthropology (ænθrə'pɔlədʒi) *n* antropologia *f.*

anti-aircraft *adj* antiaereo, contraereo.

antibiotic (æntibai'ɔtik) *adj,n* antibiotico *m.*

antibody ('æntibɔdi) *n* anticorpo *m.*

anticipate (æn'tisipeit) *vt* anticipare, aspettarsi, prevenire. **anticipation** *n* anticipazione *f.* anticipo *m.*

anticlimax (ænti'klaimæks) *n* conclusione banale *f.*

anticlockwise (ænti'klɔkwaiz) *adj,adv* in senso antiorario.

antics ('æntiks) *n pl* buffoneria, stramberia *f.*

anticyclone (ˌæntiˈsaikloun) n anticiclone m.

antidote (ˈæntidout) n antidoto m.

antifreeze (ˈæntifriːz) n anticongelante m.

antique (ænˈtiːk) n oggetto antico m. adj antico, arcaico. **antique dealer** n antiquario m. **antiquated** adj antiquato. **antiquity** n 1 antichità f. 2 pl ruderi m.

anti-Semitic adj antisemita.

antiseptic (ˌæntiˈseptik) adj,n antisettico m.

antisocial (ˌæntiˈsouʃəl) adj antisociale.

antithesis (ænˈtiθəsis) n, pl **-ses** antitesi f invar.

antler (ˈæntlə) n corno m, pl corna m.

antonym (ˈæntənim) n opposto m.

anus (ˈeinəs) n ano m.

anvil (ˈænvil) n incudine f.

anxious (ˈæŋkʃəs) adj ansioso, apprensivo. **anxiety** n ansietà, apprensione f.

any (ˈeni) adj 1 del, qualche. 2 ogni, qualsiasi, qualunque. pron 1 alcuno. 2 ne. **in any case** comunque. **anybody** pron also **anyone** 1 qualcuno, alcuno. 2 chiunque. **anyhow** adv in ogni caso, comunque, tuttavia. **anything** pron 1 qualche cosa. 2 qualunque cosa. **anyway** adv in ogni modo, in tutti i casi. **anywhere** adv dovunque, in qualunque luogo. **anywhere else** in qualsiasi altro luogo.

apart (əˈpɑːt) adv a parte, in disparte. **come apart** dividersi, sfasciarsi.

apartheid (əˈpɑːtait) n segregazione razziale f.

apartment (əˈpɑːtmənt) n 1 stanza, camera f. 2 appartamento m.

apathy (ˈæpəθi) n apatia f. **apathetic** adj apatico.

ape (eip) n scimmia f. vt scimmiottare, imitare.

aperitif (əˈperitif) n aperitivo m.

aperture (ˈæpətʃə) n apertura f.

apex (ˈeipeks) n, pl **apexes** or **apices** apice, vertice m.

apiece (əˈpiːs) adv a testa, per ciascuno.

apology (əˈpɔlədʒi) n scusa, giustificazione f. **apologetic** adj spiacente, pieno di scuse. **apologize** vi scusarsi.

apostle (əˈpɔsəl) n apostolo m.

apostrophe (əˈpɔstrəfi) n apostrofo m.

appal (əˈpɔːl) vt spaventare, inorridire. **appalling** adj terribile, spaventoso.

apparatus (ˌæpəˈreitəs) n, pl **-tus** or **-tuses** apparato, apparecchio m.

apparent (əˈpærənt) adj apparente, visibile, chiaro.

appeal (əˈpiːl) vi 1 appellarsi, fare appello a. 2 ricorrere in appello. 3 attrarre. n appello m. attrazione f.

appear (əˈpiə) vi 1 apparire, comparire. 2 sembrare. **appearance** n 1 apparenza f. aspetto m. 2 apparizione f.

appease (əˈpiːz) vt pacificare, calmare, placare.

appendix (əˈpendiks) n pl **-ixes** or **-ices** appendice f. **appendicitis** n appendicite f.

appetite (ˈæpətait) n appetito m. **appetizing** adj appetitoso.

applaud (əˈplɔːd) vt,vi applaudire. **applause** n applauso m.

apple (ˈæpəl) n mela f. **apple tree** n melo m.

apply (əˈplai) vt applicare. vi 1 applicarsi, riferirsi. 2 rivolgersi. **apply oneself** dedicarsi. **appliance** n apparecchio, dispositivo m. **applicable** adj applicabile. **applicant** n candidato m. richiedente m,f. **application** n 1 applicazione. 2 domanda, richiesta f.

appoint (əˈpɔint) vt 1 fissare, stabilire. 2 nominare. **appointment** n 1 appuntamento. impegno m. 2 nomina f.

appraise (əˈpreiz) vt stimare, valutare.

appreciate (əˈpriːʃieit) vt apprezzare, rendersi conto di. **appreciable** adj apprezzabile. **appreciation** n apprezzamento, giudizio m.

apprehend (ˌæpriˈhend) vt 1 arrestare. 2 cogliere, afferrare. **apprehension** n 1 timore m. 2 arresto m. **apprehensive** adj timoroso.

apprentice (əˈprentis) n apprendista m. vt mettere a far pratica. **apprenticeship** n apprendistato m.

approach (əˈproutʃ) vt avvicinare, avvicinarsi a. vi avvicinarsi. n 1 accostamento m. 2 accesso m.

appropriate (adj əˈprouprit; v əˈprouprieit) adj appropriate, adatto. vt 1 appropriarsi di. 2 assegnare.

approve (əˈpruːv) vt approvare, sanzionare. **approval** n approvazione f. **on approval** in prova, in visione.

approximate (adj əˈprɔksimət; v əˈprɔksimeit) adj approssimativo. vt approssimare.

apricot (ˈeiprikɔt) n albicocca f. **apricot tree** n albicocco m.

April (ˈeiprəl) n aprile m. **April Fool** n pesce d'aprile m.

apron (ˈeiprən) n grembiule, grembiale m.

apse (æps) n abside f.

apt (æpt) adj adatto, idoneo.

aptitude (ˈæptitjuːd) n abilità, attitudine f.

aquarium (ə'kwɛəriəm) n acquario m.

Aquarius (ə'kwɛəriəs) n Aquario m.

aquatic (ə'kwætik) adj acquatico.

aqueduct ('ækwədʌkt) n acquedotto m.

Arabia (ə'reibiə) n Arabia f. **Arab** adj,n arabo. **Arabic** adj arabico. **Arabic** (language) n arabo m.

arable ('ærəbəl) adj arabile.

arbitrary ('a:bitrəri) adj arbitrario.

arbitrate ('a:bitreit) vt,vi arbitrare. **arbitration** n arbitraggio, arbitrato m. **arbitrator** n arbitro m.

arc (a:k) n arco m.

arcade (a:'keid) n galleria f. portico m.

arch (a:tʃ) n arco m. arcata, volta f. vt arcuare, curvare. vi arcuarsi.

archaeology (a:ki'ɔlədʒi) n archeologia f. **archaeologist** n archeologo m.

archaic (a:'keiik) adj arcaico.

archangel (a:keindʒəl) n arcangelo m.

archbishop (a:tʃ'biʃəp) n arcivescovo m.

archduke (a:tʃ'dju:k) n arciduca m.

archery ('a:tʃəri) n tiro all'arco m.

archetype ('a:kitaip) n archetipo m. **archetypal** adj archetipo.

archipelago (a:ki'peləgou) n, pl **-gos** or **-goes** arcipelago m.

architect ('a:kitekt) n architetto m. **architecture** n architettura f. **architectural** adj architettonico.

archives ('a:kaivz) n pl archivio m.

archway ('a:tʃwei) n passaggio a volta m.

arctic ('a:ktik) adj,n artico m.

ardent ('a:dnt) adj ardente, fervente.

ardour ('a:də) n ardore, fervore m.

arduous ('a:djuəs) adj arduo, difficile.

are (ə; stressed a:) v see **be**.

area ('ɛəriə) n area, zona f.

arena (ə'ri:nə) n arena f.

Argentina (a:dʒən'ti:nə) n Argentina f. **Argentinian** adj,n Argentino.

argue ('a:gju:) vi argomentare, discutere, disputare. **arguable** adj discutibile. **argument** n discussione, disputa f. **argumentative** adj polemico.

arid ('ærid) adj arido.

Aries ('ɛəri:z) n Ariete m.

arise (ə'raiz) vi 1 alzarsi, sorgere. 2 derivare.

aristocrat ('æristəkræt) n aristocratico m. **aristocracy** n aristocrazia f.

arithmetic (ə'riθmətik) n aritmetica f.

arm[1] (a:m) n 1 braccio m,pl braccia f. or bracci

m. 2 (of a chair, etc.) bracciuolo m. **arm in arm** a braccetto. **armchair** n poltrona f. **armful** n bracciata f. **armhole** n giro della manica m. **armpit** n ascella f.

arm[2] (a:m) vt armare. vi armarsi.

armour ('a:mə) n armatura, corazza f. **armour-plated** adj corazzato. **armoury** n arsenale m.

arms (a:mz) n pl armi f pl. **in arms** armato.

army ('a:mi) n esercito m. armata f. **be in the army** prestare servizio militare.

aroma (ə'roumə) n aroma m.

arose (ə'rouz) v see **arise**.

around (ə'raund) adv intorno, all'intorno. prep intorno a.

arouse (ə'rauz) vt 1 destare, risvegliare. 2 eccitare.

arrange (ə'reindʒ) vt 1 accomodare, disporre, combinare. 2 mus adattare. **arrangement** n 1 accomodamento, ordinamento m. 2 mus arrangiamento m. **make arrangements** fare i preparativi.

array (ə'rei) vt 1 ornare. 2 mil schierare. n schiera f.

arrears (ə'riəz) n pl arretrati m pl.

arrest (ə'rest) n 1 arresto m 2 sospensione f. vt 1 arrestare. 2 fermare, sospendere.

arrive (ə'raiv) vi arrivare, giungere. **arrival** n arrivo m. venuta f.

arrogant ('ærəgənt) adj arrogante. **arrogance** n arroganza f.

arrow ('ærou) n freccia f. **arrowroot** n fecola dell'arundinacca f.

arsenic ('a:snik) n arsenico m.

arson ('a:sən) n incendio doloso m.

art (a:t) n arte f. **art gallery** n galleria d'arte f. **art school** n scuola d'arte f. **artful** adj subdolo, astuto.

artery ('a:təri) n arteria f. **arterial** adj arterioso, arteriale.

arthritis (a:'θraitis) n artrite f.

artichoke ('a:titʃouk) n carciofo m.

article ('a:tikəl) n articolo m. vt collocare come apprendista.

articulate (adj a:'tikjulət; v a:'tikjuleit) adj articolato, distinto. vt,vi articolare.

artificial (a:ti'fiʃəl) adj artificiale, artificioso.

artillery (a:'tiləri) n artiglieria f.

artist ('a:tist) n artista, pittore m. pittrice f. **artistic** adj artistico.

as (əz; stressed æz) conj 1 come. 2 poiché. 3 mentre. **as far as** sin dove. **as if** come se. **as long as** finché. **as for me** per quanto mi riguarda. **as soon as** non appena. **as it were** per così dire. ~*adv* così, come, tanto, quanto. *pron* che.

asbestos (æs'bestəs) *n* amianto *m*.

ascend (ə'send) *vi* ascendere, salire. *vt* salire. **ascension** *n* ascensione *f*.

ascertain (æsə'tein) *vt* assicurarsi di, accertarsi di.

ash[1] (æʃ) *n* cenere *f*. **ashtray** *n* portacenere *m*.

ash[2] (æʃ) *n bot* frassino *m*.

ashamed (ə'ʃeimd) *adj* vergognoso. **be ashamed** vergognarsi.

ashore (ə'ʃɔː) *adv* a *or* sulla riva.

Ash Wednesday *n* le Ceneri *f pl*.

Asia ('eiʃə) *n* Asia *f*. **Asian** *adj,n* asiatico.

aside (ə'said) *adv* da parte, in disparte. *n* parole dette a parte *f pl*.

ask (ɑːsk) *vt* **1** domandare, chiedere. **2** invitare. *vi* informarsi. **ask a question** rivolgere una domanda.

askew (ə'skjuː) *adv* di traverso. *adj* obliquo, storto.

asleep (ə'sliːp) *adv,adj* addormentato. **fall asleep** addormentarsi.

asparagus (ə'spærəgəs) *n* asparago *m*, *pl* asparagi *m*.

aspect ('æspekt) *n* aspetto *m*. apparenza *f*.

asphalt ('æsfælt) *n* asfalto *m*.

aspire (ə'spaiə) *vi* aspirare. **aspiring** *adj* ambizioso.

aspirin ('æsprin) *n* aspirina *f*.

ass (æs) *n* asino *m*.

assassin (ə'sæsin) *n* assassino *m*. **assassinate** *vt* assassinare. **assassination** *n* assassinio *m*.

assault (ə'sɔːlt) *n* assalto, attacco *m*. *vt* assalire, aggredire.

assemble (ə'sembəl) *vt* riunire. *vi* riunirsi. **assembly** *n* **1** assemblea *f*. **2** montaggio *m*. **assembly hall** *n* sala di riunioni *f*. **assembly line** *n* catena di montaggio *f*.

assent (ə'sent) *n* consenso *m*. sanzione *f*. *vi* acconsentire, approvare.

assert (ə'sɜːt) *vt* asserire, sostenere. **assert oneself** farsi valere. **assertion** *n* asserzione *f*.

assess (ə'ses) *vt* valutare, stimare. **assessment** *n* valutazione *f*.

asset ('æset) *n* **1** bene, vantaggio *m*. **2** *pl comm* attività *f pl*.

assign (ə'sain) *vt* assegnare, attribuire. **assignment** *n* **1** assegnazione *f*. **2** incarico *m*.

assimilate (ə'simileit) *vt* assimilare.

assist (ə'sist) *vt* assistere, aiutare. **assistance** *n* assistenza *f*.

assizes (ə'saiziz) *n pl* corte d'assise *f*.

associate (*v* ə'souʃieit; *n* ə'souʃiit) *vt* associare. *vi* associarsi. **associate with** frequentare. ~*n* collega *m*. **association** *n* associazione *f*.

assort (ə'sɔːt) *vt* assortire, raggruppare. **assortment** *n* assortimento *m*.

assume (ə'sjuːm) *vt* assumere, fingere, presumere.

assure (ə'ʃuə) *vt* assicurare, rassicurare. **assurance** *n* assicurazione, certezza *f*.

asterisk ('æstərisk) *n* asterisco *m*.

asthma ('æsmə) *n* asma *f*.

astonish (ə'stɔniʃ) *vt* stupire, meravigliare. **astonishment** *n* sorpresa *f*. stupore *m*.

astound (ə'staund) *vt* stupefare.

astray (ə'strei) *adv* fuori strada. **go astray** smarrirsi, traviarsi. **lead astray** sviare, traviare.

astride (ə'straid) *adv* a cavalcioni.

astrology (ə'strɔlədʒi) *n* astrologia *f*. **astrologer** *n* astrologo *m*. **astrological** *adj* astrologico.

astronaut ('æstrənɔːt) *n* astronauta *m*.

astronomy (ə'strɔnəmi) *n* astronomia *f*. **astronomer** *n* astronomo *m*. **astronomical** *adj* astronomico.

astute (ə'stjuːt) *adj* furbo, astuto.

asunder (ə'sʌndə) *adv* separatamente, a pezzi.

asylum (ə'sailəm) *n* asilo, rifugio *m*. **lunatic asylum** *n* manicomio *m*.

at (ət; *stressed* æt) *prep* **1** a, in. **2** da.

ate (eit) *v* see **eat.**

atheism ('eiθiizəm) *n* ateismo *m*. **atheist** *n* ateo *m*.

Athens ('æθinz) *n* Atene *f*.

athlete ('æθliːt) *n* atleta *m*. **athletic** *adj* atletico. **athletics** *n* atletica *f*.

Atlantic (ət'læntik) *adj* atlantico. **Atlantic (Ocean)** *n* (Oceano) Atlantico *m*.

atlas ('ætləs) *n* atlante *m*.

atmosphere ('ætməsfiə) *n* atmosfera *f*. **atmospheric** *adj* atmosferico. **atmospherics** *n pl* disturbi atmosferici *m pl*.

atom ('ætəm) *n* atomo *m*. **atom bomb** *n* bomba atomica *f*. **atomic** *adj* atomico.

atone (ə'toun) *vi* espiare, fare ammenda. **atonement** *n* espiazione, riparazione *f*.

atrocious (ə'trouʃəs) *adj* atroce. **atrocity** *n* atrocità *f*.

attach (ə'tætʃ) *vt* **1** attaccare. **2** attribuire. *vi* attaccarsi. **attachment** n attaccamento, affetto m.

attaché (ə'tæʃei) n addetto diplomatico m. **attaché case** n borsa per documenti f.

attack (ə'tæk) n **1** attacco m. offensiva f. **2** med accesso m. vt assalire, attaccare.

attain (ə'tein) vt raggiungere, ottenere. **attainment** n conseguimento m.

attempt (ə'tempt) n tentativo, attentato m. vt tentare, provare, attentare a.

attend (ə'tend) vt frequentare, assistere a. vi prestare attenzione. **attendance** n **1** servizio m. **2** frequenza f. **3** pubblico m. **attendant** n inserviente, accompagnatore m. adj presente. **attention** n attenzione, premura f. **pay attention** fare attenzione. **attentive** adj attento, premuroso.

attic ('ætik) n attico m. soffitta f.

attire (ə'taiə) vt vestire. n vestiti m pl.

attitude ('ætitju:d) n posa f. atteggiamento m.

attorney (ə'tə:ni) n procuratore m. **attorney general** n procuratore generale m.

attract (ə'trækt) vt attrarre. **attraction** n attrazione f. **attractive** adj attraente.

attribute (n 'ætribju:t; v ə'tribju:t) n attributo m. qualità f. vt attribuire, ascrivere.

aubergine ('oubəʒi:n) n melanzana f.

auburn ('ɔ:bən) adj color di rame, ramato.

auction ('ɔ:kʃən) n asta f. vt vendere all'asta. **auctioneer** n banditore m.

audacious (ɔ:'deiʃəs) adj audace.

audible ('ɔ:dibəl) adj udibile, intelligibile.

audience ('ɔ:diəns) n pubblico m. udienza f.

audiovisual (ɔ:diou'viʒuəl) adj audiovisivo.

audit ('ɔ:dit) n controllo m. verifica dei conti f. vt verificare. **auditor** n revisore, sindaco m.

audition (ɔ:'diʃən) n audizione f. vt ascoltare in audizione.

auditorium (ɔdi'tɔ:riəm) n auditorio m. sala per concerti f.

August ('ɔ:gəst) n agosto m.

aunt (ɑ:nt) n zia f.

au pair (ou 'pɛə) adj,adv alla pari. n ragazza alla pari f.

aura ('ɔ:rə) n atmosfera, aria f.

austere (ɔ:'stiə) adj austero. **austerity** n austerità f.

Australia (ɔ'streiliə) n Australia f. **Australian** adj,n australiano.

Austria ('ɔstriə) n Austria f. **Austrian** adj,n austriaco.

authentic (ɔ:'θentik) adj autentico.

author ('ɔ:θə) n autore m. autrice f.

authority (ɔ:'θɔriti) n autorità f. **on good authority** da fonte autorevole. **authoritarian** adj autoritario, assolutista. **authoritative** adj autoritario, autorevole.

authorize ('ɔ:θəraiz) vt autorizzare. **authorization** n autorizzazione f.

autistic (ɔ:'tistik) adj autistico.

autobiography (ɔ:təbai'ɔgrafi) n autobiografia f. **autobiographical** adj autobiografico.

autograph ('ɔ:təgra:f) n autografo m. firma f. vt autografare.

automatic (ɔ:tə'mætik) adj automatico.

automation (ɔ:tə'meiʃən) n automazione f.

autonomous (ɔ:'tɔnəməs) adj autonomo.

autumn ('ɔ:təm) n autunno m.

auxiliary (ɔ:g'ziliəri) adj,n ausiliario, ausiliare.

available (ə'veiləbəl) adj disponibile, libero.

avalanche ('ævəla:nʃ) n valanga f.

avenge (ə'vendʒ) vt vendicare.

avenue ('ævənju:) n viale m.

average ('ævridʒ) n media f. adj medio. vt fare la media di.

aversion (ə'və:ʃən) n avversione, antipatia f.

aviary ('eiviəri) n uccelliera f.

aviation (eivi'eiʃən) n aviazione f.

avid ('ævid) adj avido.

avocado (ævə'ka:dou) n avocado m.

avoid (ə'vɔid) vt evitare, schivare.

await (ə'weit) vt aspettare.

awake * (ə'weik) vt svegliare. vi svegliarsi. adj sveglio. **awaken** vt risvegliare. vi risvegliarsi. **awakening** n risveglio m.

award (ə'wɔ:d) n ricompensa f. vt giudicare, conferire.

aware (ə'wɛə) adj conscio, consapevole. **awareness** n consapevolezza f.

away (ə'wei) adv lontano, via.

awe (ɔ:) n timore reverenziale m. **awe-inspiring** adj maestoso. **awe-struck** adj in preda a timore.

awful ('ɔ:fəl) adj terribile, spaventoso. **awfully** adv **1** terribilmente, notevolmente. **2** inf molto.

awkward ('ɔ:kwəd) adj goffo, difficile.

awoke (ə'wouk) v see **awake.**

axe (æks) n ascia f.

axis ('æksis) n, pl **axes** asse m.

axle ('æksəl) n asse, assale m.

azalea (ə'zeiliə) n azalea f.

B

babble ('bæbəl) vt balbettare. vi ciarlare, far pettegolezzi. n 1 balbettio m. 2 chiacchiera f.

baboon (bə'bu:n) n babbuino m.

baby ('beibi) n bimbo m. **babyhood** n prima infanzia f. **baby-sit** vi far da baby-sitter.

baccarat ('bækərɑ:) n baccarà m.

bachelor ('bætʃələ) n 1 celibe, scapolo m. 2 educ laureato m. **Bachelor of Arts/Science** laureato in lettere/scienze.

back (bæk) n 1 anat dorso m. schiena f. 2 schienale m. parte posteriore f. adj 1 posteriore. 2 arretrato. adv 1 dietro, indietro. 2 di ritorno. **be back** essere di ritorno. ~vt 1 sostenere, aiutare. 2 scommettere (su). **back out** ritirarsi.

backache ('bækeik) n mal di schiena m.

backbone ('bækboun) n 1 spina dorsale f. 2 fermezza f.

backbreaking ('bækbreikiŋ) adj massacrante, faticosissimo.

backchat ('bæktʃæt) n rimbecco m.

backcloth ('bækklɔθ) n fondale m.

backdate ('bækdeit) vt retrodatare.

backdoor ('bækdɔ:) n porta di servizio f. adj segreto.

backfire ('bækfaiə) vi 1 far ritorno di fiamma. 2 fallire. n ritorno di fiamma m.

backgammon ('bækgæmən) n tavola reale f.

background ('bækgraund) n 1 sfondo m. 2 precedenti m pl. **background** n retroscena m.

backhand ('bækhænd) adj di rovescio.

backlash ('bæklæʃ) n reazione sfavorevole f.

backlog ('bæklɔg) n arretrati m pl.

backstage (bæk'steidʒ) adj,adv dietro le quinte.

backstroke ('bækstrouk) n nuoto sul dorso m.

backward ('bækwəd) adj arretrato, tardivo. **backwards** adv indietro, all'indietro.

backwater ('bækwɔ:tə) n acqua stagnante f.

bacon ('beikən) n lardo affumicato m. pancetta f.

bacteria (bæk'tiəriə) n pl batteri m pl.

bad (bæd) adj cattivo, malvagio, nocivo. **from bad to worse** di male in peggio. **not too bad** non c'è male. **bad-tempered** adj irascibile.

bade (beid) v see **bid**.

badge (bædʒ) n distintivo, emblema m.

badger ('bædʒə) n tasso m. vt tormentare.

badminton ('bædmintən) n badminton, volano m.

baffle ('bæfəl) vt eludere, confondere.

bag (bæg) n 1 sacco m. 2 borsa, borsetta f. vt insaccare. **baggage** n bagaglio m. **baggy** adj rigonfio. **bagpipes** n pl cornamusa f.

bail (beil) n cauzione, garanzia f. **go bail for** rendersi garante per. ~vt prestare cauzione.

bailiff ('beilif) n 1 ufficiale fiscale m. 2 fattore m.

bait (beit) n esca f. vt 1 adescare. 2 tormentare.

baize (beiz) n panno di lana m.

bake (beik) vt cuocere al forno. vi cuocersi. **baker** n fornaio m. **bakery** n forno, panificio m.

balance ('bæləns) n 1 bilancia f. 2 comm bilancio m. 3 equilibrio m. armonia f. **lose one's balance** perdere l'equilibrio. ~vt 1 bilanciare 2 pareggiare. vi bilanciarsi. **balance sheet** n bilancio di esercizio m.

balcony ('bælkəni) n 1 balcone m. 2 Th balconata f.

bald (bɔ:ld) adj 1 calvo. 2 nudo, disadorno. **baldness** n 1 calvizie f. 2 semplicità f.

bale[1] (beil) n balla f. vt (straw, etc.) imballare.

bale[2] (beil) vt vuotare, aggottare. **bale out** lanciarsi col paracadute.

ball[1] (bɔ:l) n 1 palla f. pallone m. 2 sfera f. **ball-bearing** n cuscinetto a sfere m.

ball[2] (bɔ:l) n (dance) ballo m. **ballroom** n sala da ballo f.

ballad ('bæləd) n ballata f.

ballast ('bæləst) n zavorra f.

ballet ('bælei) n balletto m. **ballet-dancer** n ballerino m.

ballistic (bə'listik) adj balistico. **ballistics** n balistica f.

balloon (bə'lu:n) n aerostato, pallone m.

ballot ('bælət) n 1 scheda f. 2 voto m. vi votare a scrutinio segreto. **ballot-box** n urna elettorale f.

Baltic ('bɔ:ltik) adj baltico. **Baltic (Sea)** n (Mare) Baltico m.

bamboo (bæm'bu:) n bambù m.

ban (bæn) vt bandire, proibire. n bando m. interdizione f.

banal (bə'nɑ:l) adj banale.

banana (bə'nɑ:nə) n banana f. **banana tree** n banano m.

band[1] (bænd) n 1 comitiva f. 2 mus banda, orchestrina f.

band[2] (bænd) n (strip) benda, striscia, fascia f. **bandage** n benda f. vt bendare, fasciare.

bandit ('bændit) n bandito m.

bandy ('bændi) vt **1** gettare, lanciare. **2** scambiare. adj arcato, curvo, storto.

bang (bæŋ) n **1** fracasso, colpo rumoroso m. **2** esplosione f. vt,vi sbattere, rimbombare.

bangle ('bæŋgəl) n braccialetto m.

banish ('bæniʃ) vt bandire, esiliare. **banishment** n esilio, bando m.

banister ('bænistə) n ringhiera f.

banjo ('bændʒou) n banjo m.

bank[1] (bæŋk) n altura, sponda, riva f.

bank[2] (bæŋk) n comm banca f. vt,vi depositare in banca. **bank on** contare su. **bank account** n conto in banco m. **bankbook** n libretto di deposito m. **banker** n banchiere m. **banker's card** n carta di credito f. **bank holiday** n festività legale f. **banking** n operazione bancaria f. adj di banca. **banknote** n banconota f.

bankrupt ('bæŋkrʌpt) adj,n fallito. **go bankrupt** fallire. ~vt far fallire, rovinare. **bankruptcy** n bancarotta f.

banner ('bænə) n stendardo m. insegna f.

banquet ('bæŋkwit) n banchetto m.

baptize (bæp'taiz) vt battezzare. **baptism** n battesimo m. **baptismal** adj battesimale.

bar (ba:) n **1** sbarra, spranga f. **2** barriera f. **3** bar m invar. **4** law tribunale m. **5** (of chocolate, etc.) tavoletta f. vt **1** impedire, sbarrare. **2** escludere. **barmaid** n cameriera (al banco) f. **barman** n barista m.

barbarian (ba:'bɛəriən) adj,n barbaro. **barbaric** adj barbarico, incolto. **barbarity** n barbarie f invar. **barbarous** adj barbaro.

barbecue (ba:bikju:) n festino all'aperto m.

barbed wire ('ba:bd) n filo spinato m.

barber ('ba:bə) n barbiere m.

barbiturate (ba:'bitjurət) n barbiturico m.

bare (bɛə) adj **1** nudo, scoperto, brullo. **2** vuoto. vt denudare, smascherare. **barefoot** adj scalzo. adv a piedi scalzi. **barely** adv appena, a mala pena.

bargain ('ba:gin) n affare m. occasione f. **into the bargain** in aggiunta. ~vi contrattare, pattuire.

barge (ba:dʒ) n chiatta f. barcone m. v **barge into** urtare contro.

baritone ('bæritoun) n baritono m.

bark[1] (ba:k) n (of a dog) abbaio, latrato m. vi abbaiare, latrare.

bark[2] (ba:k) n bot scorza, corteccia f.

barley ('ba:li) n orzo m. **barley sugar** n zucchero d'orzo m.

barn (ba:n) n granaio m.

barometer (bə'rɔmitə) n barometro m.

baron ('bærən) n barone m. **baronet** n baronetto m.

barracks ('bærəks) n pl caserma f.

barrel ('bærəl) n **1** barile m. botte f. **2** (of a gun) canna f.

barren ('bærən) adj desolato, nudo, sterile.

barricade ('bærikeid) n barricata f. vt barricare.

barrier ('bæriə) n barriera f.

barrister ('bæristə) n avvocato m.

barrow ('bærou) n carretta, carriola f.

barter ('ba:tə) vt barattare, scambiare. n baratto, cambio m.

base[1] (beis) n base f. fondamento m. vt basare, fondare. **baseball** n base-ball m. **basement** n sottosuolo m.

base[2] (beis) adj vile, indegno. **baseness** n bassezza f.

bash (bæʃ) vt inf fracassare, colpire violentemente. n colpo m.

bashful ('bæʃfəl) adj timido, vergognoso.

basic ('beisik) adj basilare, fondamentale.

basil ('bæzəl) n basilico m.

basin ('beisən) n **1** bacino m. **2** lavabo m. catinella f.

basis ('beisis) n, pl **bases** base f. fondamento m.

bask (ba:sk) vi scaldarsi, bearsi.

basket ('ba:skit) n canestro, cesto m. **basketball** n pallacanestro f.

bass[1] (beis) adj,n mus basso m.

bass[2] (bæs) n zool pesce persico m.

bassoon (bə'su:n) n fagotto m.

bastard ('ba:stəd) adj,n bastardo.

baste (beist) vt cul spruzzare.

bat[1] (bæt) n **1** mazza f. **2** racchetta f. vi battere. **batsman** n battitore m.

bat[2] (bæt) n zool pipistrello m.

batch (bætʃ) n **1** lotto m. partita f. **2** (of loaves) infornata f.

bath (ba:θ) n bagno m. **have a bath** fare un bagno. **bathrobe** n accappatoio m. **bathroom** n stanza da bagno f.

bathe (beið) vt bagnare. vi farsi il bagno. n bagno m. **bathing costume** n costume da bagno m. **bathing trunks** n pl calzoncini da bagno m pl.

153

baton ('bætɔn) n 1 bastone (di comando) m. 2 bacchetta f.

battalion (bə'tæliən) n battaglione m.

batter¹ ('bætə) vt colpire, battere.

batter² ('bætə) n pastella f.

battery ('bætəri) n 1 pila, batteria f. 2 also **storage battery** accumulatore m.

battle ('bæt‖) n battaglia f. combattimento m. vi combattere, lottare. **battlefield** n campo di battaglia m. **battleship** n nave da battaglia f.

bawl (bɔːl) vi urlare, schiamazzare. n schiamazzo m.

bay¹ (bei) n geog baia, insenatura del mare f.

bay² (bei) n arch vano m. **bay window** n finestra sporgente f.

bay³ (bei) vi abbaiare, latrare. **at bay** adv a bada.

bay⁴ (bei) n bot lauro m. **bay leaf** n foglia d'alloro f.

bay⁵ (bei) adj baio. n cavallo baio m.

bayonet ('beiənit) n baionetta f.

be* (biː) vi 1 essere. 2 esistere, vivere. 3 stare. 4 fare. v aux essere. **be about to** stare per. **be cold** 1 (of a person) aver freddo. 2 (of the weather) far freddo. **be warm** 1 (of a person) aver caldo. 2 (of the weather) far caldo.

beach (biːtʃ) n spiaggia f. lido m. **beachcomber** n vagabondo m.

beacon ('biːkən) n faro m. segnalazione luminosa f.

bead (biːd) n 1 perlina f. grano m. 2 goccia f. 3 pl rosario m.

beak (biːk) n becco, rostro m.

beaker ('biːkə) n coppa f.

beam (biːm) n 1 trave f. 2 raggio m. 3 sorriso m. vi 1 irradiare. 2 sorridere.

bean (biːn) n fagiolo m. fava f. **full of beans** pieno d'energia.

bear¹ (bɛə) vt 1 sopportare, tollerare. 2 portare. 3 partorire. **bear a grudge** portare rancore. **bearable** adj sopportabile. **bearing** n 1 condotta f. 2 portamento m. 3 rientamanto m. 4 tech cuscinetto m.

bear² (bɛə) n orso m.

beard (biəd) n barba f. **bearded** adj barbuto.

beast (biːst) n bestia f. animale m.

beat* (biːt) vt battere, bastonare. vi battere, palpitare. **beat about the bush** menare il can per l'aia. ~n 1 battito, palpito m. 2 ronda f.

beauty ('bjuːti) n bellezza f. **beauty queen** n regina di bellezza f. **beautiful** adj bello.

beaver ('biːvə) n castoro m.

became (bi'keim) v see **become.**

because (bi'kɔːz) conj poichè, perchè. **because of** a causa di.

beckon ('bekən) vt,vi accennare.

become* (bi'kʌm) vi diventare, divenire. vt addirsi a, star bene a. **becoming** adj adatto.

bed (bed) n 1 letto m. 2 (of a river) alveo m. **bedclothes** n pl coperte f pl. **bedding** n coperte per letto f pl. **bedridden** adj costretto a letto. **bedroom** n camera da letto f. **bedside** n capezzale m. **bed-sitter** n monocamera f. **bedspread** n copriletto m.

bedraggled (bi'drægəld) adj inzaccherato, infangato.

bee (biː) n ape f. **beehive** n alveare m.

beech (biːtʃ) n faggio m.

beef (biːf) n manzo m.

been (bin) v see **be.**

beer (biə) n birra f.

beet (biːt) n barbabietola f. **beetroot** n barbabietola f.

beetle ('biːt‖) n scarafaggio m.

befall* (bi'fɔːl) vi accadere, succedere.

before (bi'fɔː) adv prima, precedentemente. prep 1 davanti a. 2 prima di. conj prima che. **beforehand** adv in anticipo.

befriend (bi'frend) vt 1 aiutare, sostenere. 2 mostrarsi amico a.

beg (beg) vt implorare, pregare. vi elemosinare. **beggar** n mendicante m.

begin* (bi'gin) vt,vi cominciare, iniziare. **to begin with** innanzi tutto. **beginner** n principiante m,f. **beginning** n 1 inizio, esordio m. 2 origine f.

begrudge (bi'grʌdʒ) vt 1 invidiare. 2 lesinare.

behalf (bi'hɑːf) n vantaggio m. **on behalf of** a nome di, a favore di.

behave (bi'heiv) vi comportarsi. **behave oneself** comportarsi bene. **behaviour** n comportamento m. condotta f.

behind (bi'haind) prep dietro a. adv indietro, in ritardo. **behindhand** adv in arretrato, in ritardo.

behold* (bi'hould) vt scorgere, vedere.

beige (beiʒ) adj,nm beige.

being ('biːiŋ) n 1 creatura f. 2 essere m. esistenza f. **for the time being** per il momento.

belch (beltʃ) vi ruttare.

belfry ('belfri) n campanile m.

Belgium ('beldʒəm) n Belgio m. **Belgian** adj,n belga.

believe (bi'li:v) vt **1** credere, aver fede in. **2** pensare, supporre. vi credere. **belief** n credenza, fede, convinzione f. **believer** n credente, fedele m,f.

bell (bel) n campana f. campanello m. **bell-ringer** n campanaro m.

bellow ('belou) vt,vi muggire, rombare, tuonare. n muggito m.

bellows ('belouz) n pl mantice m.

belly ('beli) n pancia f. ventre m.

belong (bi'lɔŋ) vi appartenere, spettare, far parte di. **belongings** n pl effetti personali m pl. roba f.

below (bi'lou) prep sotto, al di sotto di. adv al di sotto, giù.

belt (belt) n **1** cintura f. **2** zona, regione f.

bench (bentʃ) n **1** panca f. sedile, seggio m. **2** banco di lavoro m. **3** law ufficio di magistrato m.

bend* (bend) vt curvare, piegare, torcere. vi piegarsi, chinarsi, adattarsi. n **1** curva, curvatura f. **2** inclinazione f.

beneath (bi'ni:θ) prep sotto, al di sotto di. adv sotto, in basso.

benefit ('benifit) n beneficio, vantaggio m. utilità f. vt giovare a, beneficare. vi profittare, avvantaggiarsi. **beneficial** adj utile, vantaggioso.

benevolent (bi'nevələnt) adj benevolo, caritatevole.

bent (bent) v see **bend.** adj **1** curvato. **2** risoluto. n tendenza f.

bereave* (bi'ri:v) vt privare, spogliare.

berry ('beri) n bacca f. chicco m.

berth (bə:θ) n **1** cuccetta f. **2** naut ormeggio m. vt ancorare.

beside (bi'said) prep accanto a, di fianco a, presso. **be beside oneself** essere fuori di sè. **besides** adv d'altronde, inoltre. prep oltre a.

besiege (bi'si:dʒ) vt assediare.

best (best) adj il migliore. adv nel modo migliore. n meglio, migliore m. **best man** n testimone dello sposo m. **best-seller** n libro di gran successo m.

bestow (bi'stou) vt elargire, conferire, dare.

bet* (bet) vt,vi scommettere. n scommessa, puntata f.

betray (bi'trei) vt tradire, svelare. **betrayal** n tradimento m.

better ('betə) adj migliore, meglio. **all the better** tanto meglio. **be better** star meglio.

~adv meglio. **better and better** di bene in meglio. **get the better of** avere la meglio su.

between (bi'twi:n) prep tra, fra, in mezzo a. adv in mezzo.

beverage ('bevridʒ) n bevanda f.

beware* (bi'wɛə) vi guardarsi, stare attento.

bewilder (bi'wildə) vt disorientare, confondere. **bewildering** adj sconcertante, sbalorditivo. **bewilderment** n confusione f. smarrimento m.

beyond (bi'jɔnd) adv oltre. prep al di là di, oltre.

bias ('baiəs) n inclinazione f. pregiudizio m. vt influenzare.

bib (bib) n bavaglino m.

Bible ('baibəl) n Bibbia f. **biblical** adj biblico.

bibliography (bibli'ɔgrəfi) n bibliografia f. **bibliographical** adj bibliografico.

biceps ('baiseps) n bicipite m.

bicker ('bikə) vi bisticciare, litigare. **bickering** n litigio m.

bicycle ('baisikəl) n bicicletta f.

bid* (bid) vt **1** comandare, ordinare. **2** offrire. **3** invitare. n offerta, proposta f. **bidder** n offerente m,f.

biennial (bai'eniəl) adj biennale.

big (big) adj **1** grosso, grande. **2** ampio. **3** importante.

bigamy ('bigəmi) n bigamia f. **bigamist** n bigamo m.

bigoted ('bigətid) adj bigotto, fanatico.

bikini (bi'ki:ni) n bikini m.

bilingual (bai'liŋgwəl) adj bilingue.

bilious ('biliəs) adj biliare.

bill¹ (bil) n **1** conto m. fattura f. **2** pol progetto di legge m. **3** affisso m.

bill² (bil) n zool becco m.

billiards ('biliədz) n biliardo m.

billion ('biliən) n **1** bilione m. **2** US miliardo m.

bin (bin) n bidone m. deposito m.

binary ('bainəri) adj binario.

bind* (baind) vt **1** attaccare, legare. **2** rilegare. **3** obbligare. **be bound to** dovere. **binding** adj obbligatorio, impegnativo. n **1** legame m. **2** rilegatura f.

binoculars (bi'nɔkjuləz) n pl binocolo m.

biography (bai'ɔgrəfi) n biografia f. **biographical** adj biografico.

biology (bai'ɔlədʒi) n biologia f. **biological** adj biologico. **biologist** n biologo m.

birch (bə:tʃ) n betulla f.

bird (bə:d) n uccello m. **birdcage** n gabbia per uccelli f.

birth (bə:θ) n **1** nascita f. **2** origine f. **3** discendenza f. **give birth to 1** partorire. **2** dar luogo a. **birth certificate** n certificato di nascita m. **birth control** n limitazione delle nascite f. **birthday** n compleanno m. **birthmark** n voglia f. **birth rate** n natalità f.

biscuit ('biskit) n biscotto m.

bishop ('biʃəp) n **1** vescovo m. **2** game alfiere m.

bit n **1** pezzetto m. briciola f. **2** tozzo, boccone m. **a bit more** un po'di più. **bit by bit** a poco a poco. **not to care a bit** infischiarsene.

bitch (bitʃ) n cagna f.

bite* (bait) vt mordere, pungere. n **1** morso, boccone m. **2** puntura f.

bitter ('bitə) adj **1** amaro. **2** aspro. **3** accanito. **bitterness** n **1** amarezza f. **2** rancore m.

bizarre (bi'za:) adj bizzarro, strano.

black (blæk) adj nero, oscuro, sporco. n **1** nero. **2** cap negro m. **blacken** vt annerire. vi diventar nero. **blackness** n nerezza f.

blackberry ('blækbəri) n mora f. **blackberry bush** n rovo m.

blackbird ('blækbə:d) n merlo m.

blackboard ('blækbɔ:d) n lavagna f.

blackcurrant (blæk'kʌrənt) n ribes nero m.

black eye n occhio nero m.

blackleg ('blæklɛg) n truffatore, crumiro m.

blackmail ('blækmeil) n ricatto m. vt ricattare.

black market n mercato nero m.

blackout ('blækaut) n **1** oscuramento m. **2** perdita momentanea della conoscenza f.

black pudding n sanguinaccio m.

blacksmith ('blæksmiθ) n fabbro m.

bladder ('blædə) n vescica f.

blade (bleid) n **1** lama f. **2** (of grass) filo m.

blame (bleim) n biasimo m. colpa f. vt biasimare, rimproverare. **blameless** adj innocente.

blancmange (blə'mɔnʒ) n biancomangiare m.

blank (blæŋk) adj **1** in bianco. **2** confuso. n **1** spazio vuoto m. lacuna f. **2** mil cartuccia a salve f.

blanket ('blæŋkit) n coperta di lana f.

blare (blɛə) vi squillare. n squillo m.

blaspheme (blæs'fi:m) vi bestemmiare. **blasphemous** adj blasfemo, empio.

blast (bla:st) n esplosione, raffica f. squillo m. vt fare esplodere, rovinare.

blatant ('bleitnt) adj evidente.

blaze (bleiz) n fiamma, vampata f. vi ardere, fiammeggiare. **blazer** n giacca sportiva f.

bleach (bli:tʃ) n candeggina f. vt imbiancare, scolorire. vi scolorirsi.

bleak (bli:k) adj squallido, deserto, desolato. **bleakness** n desolazione, freddezza f.

bleat (bli:t) vi belare. n belato m.

bleed* (bli:d) vi sanguinare. **bleeding** n **1** emorragia f. **2** salasso m.

blemish ('blemiʃ) n macchia f. difetto m. vt macchiare, sfigurare.

blend (blend) vt mescolare. vi fondersi. n miscela f. miscuglio m.

bless (bles) vt benedire, consacrare. **bless you!** interj salute! **blessing** n benedizione f.

blew (blu:) v see **blow²**.

blind (blaind) adj **1** cieco. **2** senza apertura f. persiana f. **2** pretesto m. vt. **1** accecare. **2** ingannare. **blind alley** n vicolo cieco m. **blindfold** adv ad occhi bendati. vt bendare gli occhi a. **blind person** n cieco m.

blink (bliŋk) vi battere le palpebre, ammiccare. n occhiata f. **blinkers** n pl paraocchi m pl.

bliss (blis) n beatitudine f. **blissful** adj beato.

blister ('blistə) n bolla, vescica f.

blizzard ('blizəd) n tormenta f.

blob (blɔb) n macchia f.

bloc (blɔk) n blocco m.

block (blɔk) n **1** blocco, ceppo m. **2** (of houses) gruppo m. **3** ostacolo m. vt bloccare, ostacolare.

blockade (blɔ'keid) n blocco m. vt bloccare.

blond (blɔnd) adj,n biondo.

blood (blʌd) n **1** sangue m. **2** stirpe, parentela f. **bloodcurdling** adj raccapricciante. **blood pressure** n pressione del sangue f. **bloodstream** n corrente sanguigna f. **bloodthirsty** adj assetato di sangue. **bloody** adj **1** sanguinoso, cruento. **2** sl maledetto.

bloom (blu:m) n **1** fiore m. fioritura f. **2** freschezza f. **blooming** adj **1** fiorente. **2** prosperoso.

blossom ('blɔsəm) n fiore m. fioritura f. vi fiorire, essere in fiore.

blot (blɔt) n **1** macchia f. **2** cancellatura f. **3** colpa f. vt **1** macchiare. **2** asciugare. **blotting paper** n carta assorbente f.

blotch (blɔtʃ) n macchia f. scarabocchio m.

blouse (blauz) n camicetta, blusa f.

blow¹ (blou) n colpo m.

blow*² (blou) vt **1** soffiare. **2** suonare. vi buffare. **blow one's nose** soffiarsi il naso. **blow up** (far) saltare per aria.

blubber ('blʌbə) n grasso di balena m.

blue (blu:) adj azzurro, celeste, blu. n blu m. **bluebell** n giacinto selvatico m.

bluff (blʌf) vi bluffare, ingannare.

blunder ('blʌndə) n errore, sbaglio m. papera f. vi commettere un errore grossolano.

blunt (blʌnt) adj 1 ottuso, spuntato. 2 sgarbato. vt ottundere, smussare. **bluntly** adv bruscamente.

blur (blə:) vt offuscare, confondere. n offuscamento m. macchia f.

blush (blʌʃ) n rossore m. vi arrossire.

boar (bɔ:) n cinghiale m.

board (bɔ:d) n 1 asse m. tavola f. 2 pensione f. 3 commissione f. ministero m. **on board** a bordo. ~vi alloggiare. vt imbarcarsi. **boarder** n pensionante m,f. **boarding house** n pensione f. **boarding school** n collegio m.

boast (boust) vi gloriarsi, vantarsi. n vanto m.

boat (bout) n barca f. battello m. imbarcazione f.

bob (bɔb) n inchino m. vi 1 oscillare. 2 inchinarsi. **bob up** venire a galla.

bodice ('bɔdis) n corpetto m.

body ('bɔdi) n 1 corpo. 2 tronco, cadavere m. 3 gruppo m. 4 mot carrozzeria f. **bodyguard** n guardia del corpo f.

bog (bɔg) n palude f. pantano m.

bohemian (bə'hi:miən) adj 1 boemo. 2 di artista.

boil¹ (bɔil) vi bollire. vt far bollire, lessare. **boil down** condensare, ridursi. **boiler** n caldaia f. **boiling point** n punto d'ebollizione m.

boil² (bɔil) n vescica f. foruncolo m.

boisterous ('bɔistərəs) adj impetuoso, turbolento.

bold (bould) adj audace, temerario, impudente. **boldness** n audacia, spavalderia f.

bolster ('boulstə) n cuscinetto m.

bolt (boult) n 1 tech bullone m. 2 catenaccio m. vt 1 sprangare. 2 imbullonare. vi scappare.

bomb (bɔm) n bomba f. vt bombardare. **bombard** vt bombardare.

bond (bɔnd) n 1 legame, vincolo m. 2 titolo m. 3 cauzione f.

bone (boun) n osso m, pl ossa f. **bony** adj ossuto.

bonfire ('bɔnfaiə) n falò m.

bonnet ('bɔnit) n 1 berretto, cappellino da donna m. 2 mot cofano m.

bonus ('bounəs) n gratifica, indennità f.

booby trap ('bu:bi) n mina nascosta f. tranello m.

book (buk) n 1 libro m. 2 registro m. vt 1 prenotare. 2 registrare, mettere in lista. **bookcase** n scaffale m. **booking office** n biglietteria f. ufficio prenotazioni m. **bookkeeping** n contabilità f. **booklet** n libretto, opuscolo m. **bookmaker** n allibratore m. **bookshop** n libreria f. **bookstall** n edicola f.

boom (bu:m) vi 1 rimbombare. 2 essere in periodo di sviluppo. n 1 rimbombo m. 2 comm aumento improvviso, boom m.

boost (bu:st) n spinta, pressione f. vt 1 alzare. 2 aumentare.

boot (bu:t) n 1 stivale m. 2 mot portabagagli m invar.

booth (bu:θ) n baracca, cabina f.

booze (bu:z) n inf bevande alcoliche f pl. vi inf sbronzarsi.

border ('bɔ:də) n 1 confine, margine m. 2 bordo m. vt orlare. **border on** confinare con. **borderline** n linea di demarcazione f. adj marginale.

bore¹ (bɔ:) n 1 buco m. 2 (of a gun) calibro m. vt forare, trapanare.

bore² (bɔ:) vt annoiare, infastidire. n 1 seccatura, noia f. 2 seccatore m.

bore³ (bɔ:) v see **bear**¹.

born (bɔ:n) adj nato, generato. **be born** nascere.

borough ('bʌrə) n borgo, capoluogo, comune m.

borrow ('bɔrou) vt farsi prestare, prendere a prestito.

bosom ('buzəm) n petto, seno m. adj intimo, del cuore.

boss (bɔs) n inf capo, direttore m. vt spadroneggiare. **bossy** adj autoritario, dispotico.

botany ('bɔtəni) n botanica f. **botanical** adj botanico. **botanist** n botanico m.

both (bouθ) adj,pron ambedue, entrambi. **both of them** tutti e due. **both...and** tanto ...quanto. ~adv insieme.

bother ('bɔðə) vt infastidire, seccare. vi preoccuparsi. n noia, seccatura f.

bottle ('bɔtl) n bottiglia f. vt imbottigliare. **bottleneck** n ingorgo m.

bottom ('bɔtəm) adj ultimo, inferiore. n 1 fondo m. base f. 2 inf sedere m.

bough (bau) n ramo m.

bought (bɔ:t) v see **buy**.

boulder ('bouldə) n macigno m. raccia f.

bounce (bauns) vi rimbalzare. vt far rimbalzare. n balzo, salto m.

bound[1] (baund) v see **bind**. adj 1 legato. 2 rilegato. 3 obbligato.

bound[2] (baund) n (jump) salto, balzo m. vi saltare.

bound[3] (baund) n confine, limite m. **boundary** n limite m. frontiera f.

bound[4] (baund) adj diretto, con destinazione. **be bound for** essere diretto a.

boundary ('baundri) n limite m. frontiera f.

bouquet (bu'kei) n mazzo di fiori m.

bourgeois ('buəʒwa:) adj,n borghese.

bout (baut) n 1 periodo d'attività m. 2 med accesso m. 3 sport turno m. ripresa f.

bow[1] (bau) vt piegare. vi chinarsi, sottomettersi. n saluto, inchino m.

bow[2] (bou) n 1 arco m. 2 mus archetto m. **bow-legged** adj dalle gambe arcuate.

bow[3] (bau) n naut prua f.

bowels ('bauəlz) n pl intestini m pl. viscere f pl.

bowl[1] (boul) n ciotola, vaschetta f. recipiente m.

bowl[2] (boul) n boccia f. vt far rotolare. vi servire la palla.

box[1] (bɔks) n 1 scatola f. 2 cassetta f. 3 law banco dei testimoni m. 4 Th palco m. **box number** n casella postale f. **box office** n Th botteghino m.

box[2] (bɔks) vi fare del pugilato. vt schiaffeggiare. n ceffone, pugno m. **boxing** n pugilato m.

Boxing Day n giorno di San Stefano m.

boy (bɔi) n ragazzo m. **boyfriend** n amico, ragazzo m. **boyhood** n adolescenza f. **boyish** adj fanciullesco, giovanile.

boycott ('bɔikɔt) vt boicottare. n boicottaggio m.

bra (bra:) n inf reggipetto m.

brace (breis) n 1 supporto m. 2 pl bretelle f pl. 3 coppia f. vt assicurare, fortificare.

bracelet ('breislət) n braccialetto m.

bracket ('brækit) n 1 mensola f. 2 parentesi f invar. vt 1 munire di supporto. 2 mettere tra parentesi.

brag (bræg) vi vantarsi.

braid (breid) n gallone m. vt intrecciare, legare con un nastro.

braille (breil) n braille m.

brain (brein) n 1 cervello m. 2 pl intelligenza f. senno m. **rack one's brains** lambiccarsi il

cervello. **brainwash** vt fare il lavaggio del cervello a. **brainwave** n buona idea f.

braise (breiz) vt brasare, cuocere a stufato.

brake (breik) n freno m. vi frenare.

branch (bra:ntʃ) n 1 ramo m. 2 comm filiale f. vi diramarsi. **branch off** biforcarsi.

brand (brænd) n 1 tizzone m. 2 marchio m. 3 marca f. 4 qualità f. vt 1 marchiare. 2 stigmatizzare. **brand-new** adj nuovo fiammante.

brandish ('brændiʃ) vt brandire.

brandy ('brændi) n acquavite f.

brass (bra:s) n 1 ottone m. 2 sl moneta f. adj di ottone. **brass band** n banda f.

brassiere ('bræziə) n reggipetto m.

brave (breiv) adj coraggioso, ardito. vt sfidare, affrontare.

brawl (brɔ:l) n zuffa, disputa f. vi rissare, azzuffarsi.

bray (brei) vi ragliare. n raglio m.

brazen ('breizən) adj 1 impudente. 2 di ottone.

Brazil (brə'zil) n Brasile m. **Brazilian** adj,n brasiliano.

breach (bri:tʃ) n 1 breccia f. 2 rottura f. 3 violazione f. vt far breccia in.

bread (bred) n pane m. **breadcrumb** n mollica, briciola f. **breadknife** n coltello da pane m. **breadwinner** n sostegno della famiglia m.

breadth (bredθ) n 1 larghezza, ampiezza f. altezza f.

break* (breik) vt 1 rompere. 2 infrangere. 3 interrompere. vi rompersi. **break away** fuggire, distaccarsi. **break down** avere una panna. **breakdown** n 1 collasso, esaurimento nervoso m. 2 mot panna f. **break out** scoppiare. **break up** sciogliere. ~n 1 rottura f. 2 interruzione f. 3 pausa f. **breakthrough** n innovazione, conquista f.

breakfast ('brekfəst) n prima colazione f.

breast (brest) n petto, seno m. **breaststroke** n nuoto a rana m.

breath (breθ) n respiro, fiato, soffio m. **out of breath** ansimante. **breathtaking** adj sorprendente, affascinante.

breathe (bri:ð) vi respirare, soffiare, sussurrare. **breathe a sigh** sospirare. **breathing** n respirazione f.

breed* (bri:d) vt 1 generare. 2 allevare. vi nascere. n razza, stirpe, covata f. **breeding** n allevamento m.

breeze (bri:z) n brezza f.

brew (bru:) vt mescolare, fare fermentare. n mistura f. **brewery** n fabbrica di birra f.

bribe (braib) vt corrompere, allettare. n offerta a scopo di corruzione, bustarella f. **bribery** n corruzione f.

brick (brik) n mattone m.

bride (braid) n sposa f. **bridegroom** n sposo m. **bridesmaid** n damigella d'onore f.

bridge[1] (bridʒ) n ponte m. vt congiungere.

bridge[2] (bridʒ) n game bridge m.

bridle ('braidl) n briglia f. freno m. **bridlepath** n pista f.

brief (bri:f) adj breve, conciso. n riassunto m. istruzioni f pl. vt impartire istruzioni a. **briefcase** n cartella f. borsa d'avvocato f.

brigade (bri'geid) n brigata f. **brigadier** n generale di brigata m.

bright (brait) adj 1 risplendente, luminoso, chiaro. 2 allegro. 3 intelligente. **brighten** vt 1 rendere più brillante. 2 rallegrare. vi illuminarsi, schiarirsi.

brilliant ('briliant) adj 1 brillante, splendido. 2 di talento.

brim (brim) n orlo, bordo m. 2 (of a hat) tesa f.

bring* (briŋ) vt 1 portare, recare. 2 produrre, provocare. **bring about** far accadere. **bring up** educare.

brink (briŋk) n orlo, limite estremo m.

brisk (brisk) adj vivace, arzillo.

bristle ('brisal) n setola f. vi rizzarsi.

Britain ('britn) n Gran Bretagna f. **British** adj britannico. **Briton** n inglese m,f.

brittle ('britl) adj fragile.

broad (brɔ:d) adj 1 largo, ampio. 2 generale. 3 marcato. **broad bean** n fava f. **broaden** vt allargare. vi allargarsi. **broad-minded** adj di larghe vedute.

broadcast* ('brɔ:dka:st) n trasmissione radiofonica f. vt trasmettere per radio, diffondere.

broccoli ('brɔkəli) n broccoli m pl.

brochure ('brouʃə) n opuscolo m.

broke (brouk) v see **break**. adj inf rovinato, al verde.

broken ('broukən) v see **break**. adj rotto, sconnesso, affranto.

broker ('broukə) n mediatore, sensale, agente di cambio m.

bronchitis (brɔŋ'kaitis) n bronchite f.

bronze (brɔnz) n bronzo m. adj di bronzo.

brooch (broutʃ) n spilla f.

brood (bru:d) n covata f. vi 1 covare. 2 meditare.

brook (bruk) n ruscello m.

broom (bru:m) n 1 scopa f. 2 bot ginestra f.

brothel ('brɔθəl) n bordello m. casa di tolleranza f.

brother ('brʌðə) n fratello m. **brotherhood** n fratellanza, fraternità f. **brother-in-law** n cognato m. **brotherly** adj fraterno.

brought (brɔ:t) v see **bring**.

brow (brau) n sopracciglio m. fronte f.

brown (braun) adj marrone, castano. n bruno m. vt 1 brunire. 2 cul rosolare. vi diventare bruno.

browse (brauz) vi scartabellare.

bruise (bru:z) n contusione f. livido m. vt ammaccare. vi ammaccarsi.

brunette (bru:'net) adj bruna, brunetta f.

brush (brʌʃ) n 1 pennello m. 2 spazzola f. vt spazzolare. **brush against** sfiorare. **brush up** ripassare.

brusque (bru:sk) adj brusco, rude.

Brussels ('brʌsəlz) n Bruxelles f. **Brussels sprout** n cavolino di Bruxelles m.

brute (bru:t) n bruto m. adj brutale, selvaggio. **brutal** adj brutale.

bubble ('bʌbəl) n bolla f. vi formare bolle.

buck[1] (bʌk) vi impennarsi.

buck[2] (bʌk) n zool daino, caprone m.

bucket ('bʌkit) n secchio m.

buckle ('bʌkəl) n fibbia f. vt affibbiare, allacciare. vi affibbiarsi.

bud (bʌd) n germoglio, bocciolo m.

Buddhism ('budizəm) n buddismo m. **Buddhist** adj,n buddista.

budget ('bʌdʒit) n bilancio preventivo m. vi fare un bilancio preventivo.

buffalo ('bʌfəlou) n, pl **-loes** or **-los** bufalo m.

buffer ('bʌfə) n respingente, cuscinetto m.

buffet[1] ('bufit) n schiaffo m. vt schiaffeggiare.

buffet[2] ('bʌfei) n ristorante m. tavola calda f.

bug (bʌg) n 1 zool cimice f. 2 inf virus m.

bugle ('bju:gəl) n tromba f.

build* (bild) vt 1 costruire, fabbricare, edificare. n corporatura f. **building** n fabbricato, edificio m. **building society** n credito edilizio m.

bulb (bʌlb) n 1 bot bulbo m. 2 (electric) lampadina f.

Bulgaria (bʌl'gɛəriə) n Bulgaria f. **Bulgarian** adj,n bulgaro. **Bulgarian** (language) n bulgaro m.

bulge (bʌldʒ) n gonfiore m. protuberanza f. vi gonfiare, gonfiarsi.

bulk (bʌlk) n massa f. volume m. **bulky** adj ingombrante, voluminoso.

bull (bul) *n* toro *m*. **bulldog** *n* mastino *m*. **bulldozer** *n* livellatrice *f*. **bullfight** *n* corrida *f*.

bullet ('bulit) *n* pallottola *f*. **bullet-proof** *adj* a prova di pallottola, corazzato.

bulletin ('bulǝtin) *n* bollettino *m*.

bully ('buli) *n* gradasso, prepotente *m*. *vt* maltrattare, tiranneggiare.

bump (bʌmp) *vt* battere, urtare. *vi* sbattere. *n* colpo, bernoccolo *m*. **bumper** *n* paraurti *m invar. adj inf* abbondante.

bun (bʌn) *n* 1 *cul* focaccia *f*. 2 crocchia *f*.

bunch (bʌntʃ) *n* fascio, mazzo, grappolo *m*. *vt* riunire, raggruppare.

bundle ('bʌndl) *n* fagotto, involto *m*. *vt* fare un involto di.

bungalow ('bʌŋgǝlou) *n* casa ad un piano *f*.

bungle ('bʌŋgǝl) *vt* guastare. *n* lavoro malfatto *m*.

bunk (bʌŋk) *n* cuccetta *f*.

bunker ('bʌŋkǝ) *n* 1 carbomile *m*. 2 *sport* ostacolo *m*.

buoy (bɔi) *n* boa *f*. **buoyant** *adj* 1 galleggiante. 2 allegro, esuberante.

burden ('bǝ:dn) *n* fardello, carico, onere *m*. *vt* caricare, opprimere.

bureau ('bjuǝrou) *n, pl* **-eaus** *or* **-eaux** 1 ufficio *m*. 2 scrittoio *m*.

bureaucracy (bju'rɔkrǝsi) *n* burocrazia *f*. **bureaucrat** *n* burocrate *m*.

burglar ('bǝ:glǝ) *n* 1 ladro, scassinatore *m*. **burglar alarm** *n* campanello antifurto *m*. **burglary** *n* furto con scasso *m*. **burgle** *vt* svaligiare, scassinare.

burn* (bǝ:n) *vt* bruciare, incendiare. *vi* 1 bruciare, essere in fiamme. 2 scottare. *n* ustione, scottatura *f*.

burrow ('bʌrou) *n* tana *f*. *vi* fare una tana, nascondersi.

burst* (bǝ:st) *vt* far esplodere. *vi* scoppiare. *n* scoppio *m*. esplosione *f*.

bury ('beri) *vt* seppellire, sotterrare. **burial** *n* sepoltura *f*.

bus (bʌs) *n* autobus *m invar*. **bus-stop** *n* fermata dell'autobus *f*.

bush (buʃ) *n* 1 cespuglio *m*. 2 macchia *f*. **bushy** *adj* folto, cespuglioso.

business ('biznis) *n* affari *m pl*. commercio *m*. occupazione *f*. **business-like** *adj* pratico, sbrigativo. **businessman** *n* uomo d'affari *m*.

bust¹ (bʌst) *n* busto *m*.

bust² (bʌst) *inf vt* far saltare. *vi* andare in malora.

bustle ('bʌsǝl) *n* attività disordinata *f*. trambusto *m*. *vi* muoversi, agitarsi.

busy ('bizi) *adj* indaffarato, occupato.

but (bǝt; *stressed* bʌt) *conj* ma. *adv* solo, soltanto. *prep* tranne, eccetto.

butcher ('butʃǝ) *n* macellaio *m*. *vt* massacrare, macellare. **butcher's shop** *n* macelleria *f*.

butler ('bʌtlǝ) *n* maggiordomo *m*.

butt¹ (bʌt) *n* 1 mozzicone *m*. 2 (of a gun) calcio *m*.

butt² (bʌt) *n* (person or object) bersaglio *m*. meta *f*.

butt³ (bʌt) *n* cornata *f*. *vt* dar cornate a, cozzare.

butter ('bʌtǝ) *n* burro *m*. **buttercup** *n* ranuncolo *m*. **butterfly** *n* farfalla *f*. **butterscotch** *n* tipo di caramella *m*.

buttocks ('bʌtǝks) *n* natiche *f pl*.

button ('bʌtn) *n* bottone *m*. *vt* abbottonare. **button up** abbottonarsi. **buttonhole** *n* occhiello *m*. *vt* inchiodare.

buttress ('bʌtrǝs) *n* contrafforte *f*. sperone *m*.

buy* (bai) *vt* comprare, acquistare. *n* acquisto *m*. **buyer** *n* acquirente, compratore *m*.

buzz (bʌz) *n* 1 ronzio *m*. 2 *inf* telefonata *f*. *vi* ronzare, mormorare.

by (bai) *prep* 1 da, di, a, per, in, con. 2 vicino a. 3 entro, durante. *adv* 1 vicino. 2 da parte. **by the way** a proposito. **by-election** *n* elezione straordinaria *f*. **bylaw** *n* legge locale *f*. regolamento *m*. **bypass** *n* circonvallazione *f*. *vt* girare intorno a.

Byzantine (bi'zæntain, bai-) *adj,n* bizantino.

C

cab (kæb) *n* tassì *m invar*. vettura pubblica *f*.

cabaret ('kæbǝrei) *n* caffè concerto *m*.

cabbage ('kæbidʒ) *n* cavolo *m*.

cabin ('kæbin) *n* cabina *f*. capanna *f*. **cabin cruiser** *n* cabinato *m*.

cabinet ('kæbinǝt) *n* 1 armadietto *m*. 2 *pol* gabinetto *m*. **cabinet-maker** *n* ebanista *m*.

cable ('keibǝl) *n* 1 cavo *m*. 2 cablogramma *m*. *vt* mandare un cablogramma a. **cable car** *n* funivia *f*.

cackle ('kækǝl) *vi* schiamazzare, ridacchiare. *n* 1 verso della gallina *m*. 2 chiaccherio *m*.

cactus ('kæktǝs) *n, pl* **-ti** *or* **-tuses** cactus *m*.

cadence ('keidns) *n* cadenza *f*.

cadet (kə'det) n cadetto m.

cafe ('kæfei) n caffè m invar. ristorante m.

cafeteria (kæfi'tiəriə) n bar-ristorante m.

caffeine ('kæfi:n) n caffeina f.

cage (keidʒ) n gabbia f.

cake (keik) n torta, focaccia f. vt incrostare. vi incrostarsi, indurirsi.

calamity (kə'læməti) n calamità f.

calcium ('kælsiəm) n calcio m.

calculate ('kælkjuleit) vt calcolare, valutare. **calculation** n calcolo m. **calculator** n calcolatore m. macchina calcolatrice f.

calendar ('kælində) n calendario m.

calf[1] (kɑ:f) n, pl **calves** anat polpaccio m.

calf[2] (kɑ:f) n, pl **calves** zool vitello m.

calibre ('kælibə) n calibro m.

call (kɔ:l) vt 1 chiamare. 2 richiamare. 3 svegliare. vi 1 gridare. 2 fare scalo. 3 visitare. **call on** visitare. **call up** 1 convocare. 2 richiamare. ~n 1 chiamata f. appello, grido m. 2 visita f. 3 vocazione f. **callbox** n cabina telefonica f.

callous ('kæləs) adj calloso, insensibile, spietato.

calm (kɑ:m) adj calmo, sereno. n calma, quiete f. vt calmare. **calm down** calmarsi.

calorie ('kæləri) n caloria f.

Cambodia (kæm'boudiə) n Cambogia f. **Cambodian** adj,n cambogiano f.

came (keim) v see **come.**

camel ('kæməl) n cammello m. **camelhair** n pelo di cammello m.

camera ('kæmrə) n macchina fotografica f. **cameraman** n operatore m.

camouflage ('kæməflɑ:ʒ) n mimetizzazione f. camuffamento m. vt 1 mascherare. 2 mil mimetizzare.

camp[1] (kæmp) n accampamento, campo m. vi accampare, accamparsi. **camp bed** n brandina f. **camping** n campeggio m. **camping site** n luogo per campeggio m.

camp[2] (kæmp) adj effeminato.

campaign (kæm'pein) n campagna f. vi fare una campagna.

campus ('kæmpəs) n città universitaria f.

can[1] (kæn) n recipiente, bidone, barattolo m. vt mettere in scatola.

can[2] (kæn) v mod aux 1 potere, essere in grado di. 2 sapere.

Canada ('kænədə) n Canadà m. **Canadian** adj,n canadese.

canal (kə'næl) n canale m.

canary (kə'nɛəri) n canarino m.

Canary Islands n pl Isole Canarie f pl.

cancel ('kænsəl) vt annullare, cancellare, sopprimere. **cancellation** n cancellazione f. annullamento m.

cancer ('kænsə) n 1 cancro m. 2 cap Capro m.

candid ('kændid) adj franco, sincero.

candidate ('kændidət) n candidato m.

candle ('kændl) n candela f. **candlelight** n lume di candela m. **candlestick** n candelabro, candeliere m.

candour ('kændə) n franchezza f.

cane (kein) n 1 canna f. 2 bastone da passeggio m. vt bastonare.

canine ('keinain) adj canino.

cannabis ('kænəbis) n ascisc m.

cannibal ('kænəbəl) n cannibale m.

cannon ('kænən) n cannone m.

cannot ('kænət) contraction of **can not.**

canoe (kə'nu:) n canoa f.

canon[1] ('kænən) n canone m. regola, disciplina f.

canon[2] ('kænən) n rel canonico m. **canonize** vt canonizzare.

canopy ('kænəpi) n baldacchino m. volta f.

canteen (kæn'ti:n) n mensa aziendale, cantina f.

canter ('kæntə) n piccolo galoppo m. vi andare al piccolo galoppo.

canton ('kæntən) n cantone m.

canvas ('kænvəs) n canovaccio m. tela, vela f.

canvass ('kænvəs) vt sollecitare.

canyon ('kænjən) n burrone m.

cap (kæp) n 1 berretto m. cuffia f. 2 tech cappuccio m.

capable ('keipəbəl) adj capace, abile.

capacity (kə'pæsiti) n 1 capacità, abilità f. 2 tech potenza f.

cape[1] (keip) n cappa, mantellina f.

cape[2] (keip) n geog capo, promontorio m.

caper ('keipə) n cappero m.

capital ('kæpitl) n 1 geog capitale f. 2 comm capitale m. 3 (letter) maiuscola f. adj 1 capitale, eccellente. 2 maiuscolo. **capitalism** n capitalismo m. **capitalist** n capitalista m, f. **capitalize** vt capitalizzare.

capricious (kə'priʃəs) adj capriccioso, volubile.

Capricorn ('kæprikɔ:n) n Capricorno m.

capsicum ('kæpsikəm) n peperone, pimento m.

capsize ('kæpsaiz) vi capovolgersi. vt rovesciare.

capsule ('kæpsju:l) n capsula f.

captain ('kæptin) n capitano, comandante m.

caption ('kæpʃən) n 1 intestazione f. 2 (cinema) didascalia f.

captivate ('kæptiveit) vt attrarre, sedurre.

captive ('kæptiv) adj,n prigioniero, schiavo m.

capture ('kæptʃə) vt catturare, far prigioniero. n cattura f. arresto m.

car (kɑː) n 1 automobile, macchina f. 2 (railway) carro m. **car park** n posteggio m.

caramel ('kærəməl) n caramella f.

carat ('kærət) n carato m.

caravan ('kærəvæn) n carovana f.

caraway ('kærəwei) n cumino m.

carbohydrate (kɑːbou'haidreit) n carboidrato m.

carbon ('kɑːbən) n 1 sci carbonio m. 2 tech carbone m. **carbon paper** n carta carbone f. **carbon dioxide** n anidride carbonica f.

carburettor (kɑːbju'retə) n carburatore m.

carcass ('kɑːkəs) n carcassa f.

card (kɑːd) n carta f. **cardboard** n cartone m.

cardigan ('kɑːdigən) n giacchetta di lana f.

cardinal ('kɑːdinl) adj cardinale, principale. n cardinale m.

care (kɛə) n 1 ansietà f. 2 cura, premura, sollecitudine f. 3 custodia f. **care of** presso. ~vi curarsi, preoccuparsi. **care for 1** voler bene a. **2** curare. **carefree** adj spensierato. **careful** adj attento, accurato. **careless** adj trascurato, negligente. **caretaker** n custode, guardiano m.

career (kə'riə) n carriera f.

caress (kə'res) n carezza f. vt accarezzare.

cargo ('kɑːgou) n, pl **-goes** carico m.

Caribbean (kæri'biən) adj dei caraibi. **Caribbean (Sea)** n Mare dei Caraibi m.

caricature ('kærikətjuə) n caricatura f. vt far la caricatura di.

carnal ('kɑːnl) adj carnale, sensuale.

carnation (kɑː'neiʃən) n garofano m.

carnival ('kɑːnivəl) n carnevale m.

carnivorous (kɑː'nivərəs) adj carnivoro.

carol ('kærəl) n canto, inno natalizio m.

carpenter ('kɑːpintə) n carpentiere, falegname m.

carpet ('kɑːpit) n tappeto m.

carriage ('kæridʒ) n 1 carro m. vettura f. 2 (railway) vagone m. 3 trasporto m. 4 portamento m. **carriageway** n strada rotabile f.

carrier ('kæriə) n trasportatore m. **carrier bag** n sacchetto di carta m.

carrot ('kærət) n carota f.

carry ('kæri) vt,vi portare. **carry away** trasportare. **carry on** proseguire. **carry out** effettuare. **carrycot** n culla portabile f.

cart (kɑːt) n carro, calesse m. **carthorse** n cavallo da traino m. **cartwheel** n ruota di carro f.

cartilage ('kɑːtilidʒ) n cartilagine f.

carton ('kɑːtn) n 1 scatola di cartone f. 2 (of cigarettes) stecca f.

cartoon (kɑː'tuːn) n cartone m. **cartoonist** n disegnatore, vignettista m.

cartridge ('kɑːtridʒ) n cartuccia f.

carve (kɑːv) vt 1 Art intagliare, incidere. 2 tagliare. **carving** n intaglio m. **carving-knife** n trinciante m.

cascade (kæ'skeid) n cascata f.

case¹ (keis) n 1 caso, avvenimento m. 2 law causa f. processo m.

case² (keis) n 1 scatola, custodia f. 2 (for glasses, etc.) astuddio m.

cash (kæʃ) n cassa f. denaro m. contanti m pl. vt incassare, riscuotere. **cash desk** n cassa f.

cashier¹ (kæ'ʃiə) n cassiere m.

cashier² (kæ'ʃiə) vt destituire.

cashmere (kæʃ'miə) n cachemire m.

casino (kə'siːnou) n casinò m.

casket ('kɑːskit) n cofanetto, scrigno m.

casserole ('kæsəroul) n teglia, casseruola f.

cassette (kə'set) n cassetta f.

cassock ('kæsək) n tonaca, veste f.

cast* (kɑːst) vt 1 gettare, lanciare. 2 reluttare. 3 fondere. n 1 lancio, getto, stampo m. 2 Th complesso m.

castanets (kæstə'nets) n pl nacchere f pl.

caste (kɑːst) n casta f.

castle ('kɑːsəl) n castello m.

castrate (kæ'streit) vt castrare.

casual ('kæʒuəl) adj 1 accidentale, casuale, fortuito. 2 sportivo, semplice. **casualty** n 1 vittima m. 2 incidente, sinistro m.

cat (kæt) n gatto m. **cat's eye** n mot catarifrangente m.

catalogue ('kætələg) n catalogo m. vt catalogare.

catamaran (kætəmə'ræn) n catamarano m.

catapult ('kætəpʌlt) n catapulta, fionda f.

cataract ('kætərækt) n cateratta f.

catarrh (kə'tɑː) n catarro m.

catastrophe (kə'tæstrəfi) n catastrofe f.

catch* (kætʃ) vt 1 prendere, afferrare. 2 sorprendere. vi attaccarsi. n 1 cattura, preda f. 2 trucco m.

catechism ('kætikizəm) n catechismo m.

category ('kætigəri) n categoria f. **categorical** adj categorico. **categorize** vt classificare, giudicare.

cater ('keitə) vi provvedere cibo. **cater for** provvedere. **caterer** n fornitore, negoziante m.

caterpillar ('kætəpilə) n bruco m.

cathedral (kə'θi:drəl) n cattedrale f.

cathode ('kæθoud) n catodo m.

Catholic ('kæθəlik) adj,n cattolico. **Catholicism** n cattolicesimo m.

catkin ('kætkin) n amento m.

cattle ('kætl) n pl bestiame m.

caught (kɔ:t) v see **catch**.

cauliflower ('kɔliflauə) n cavolfiore m.

cause (kɔ:z) n ragione, causa f. motivo m. vt causare, provocare.

causeway ('kɔ:zwei) n strada rialzata f.

caustic ('kɔ:stik) adj caustico, mordente.

caution ('kɔ:ʃən) n 1 cautela, prudenza f. 2 avvertimento m. vt ammonire, mettere in guardia.

cavalry ('kævəlri) n cavalleria f.

cave (keiv) n caverna, tana f.

caviar ('kævia:) n caviale m.

cavity ('kæviti) n cavità f.

cayenne (kei'en) n pepe di Caienna f.

cease (si:s) vt,vi cessare, finire. **cease-fire** n cessato il fuoco m. tregua f. **ceaseless** adj incessante.

cedar ('si:də) n cedro m.

ceiling ('si:liŋ) n soffitto m.

celebrate ('seləbreit) vt celebrare, onorare. vi far festa. **celebration** n celebrazione f.

celebrity (si'lebriti) n celebrità f.

celery ('seləri) n sedano m.

celestial (si'lestiəl) adj celestiale.

celibate ('selibət) adj,n celibe m.

cell (sel) n 1 cella f. 2 sci cellula f.

cellar ('selə) n cantina f. sottosuolo m.

cello ('tʃelou) n violoncello m.

Cellophane ('seləfein) n Tdmk Cellophane m.

Celt (kelt) n Celta m. **Celtic** adj celtico.

cement (si'ment) n cemento m. vt cementare.

cemetery ('semətri) n cimitero m.

censor ('sensə) n censore m. vt censurare. **censorship** n censura f.

censure ('senʃə) n censura, critica f. vt criticare, biasimare.

census ('sensəs) n censimento m.

cent (sent) n 1 centesimo m. 2 soldo m.

centenary (sen'ti:nəri) adj,n centenario m.

centigrade ('sentigreid) adj centigrado.

centimetre ('sentimi:tə) n centimetro m.

centipede ('sentipi:d) n millepiedi m invar.

centre ('sentə) n centro m. vt centrare, concentrare. vi concentrarsi. **centre-forward** n centravanti m. **centre-half** n centromediano m. **central** adj centrale. **central heating** n riscaldamento centrale m. **centralize** vt centralizzare. **centralization** n centralizzazione f.

century ('sentʃəri) n secolo m.

ceramic (si'ræmik) adj di ceramica. **ceramics** n ceramica f.

cereal ('siəriəl) n cereale m.

ceremony ('serəməni) n cerimonia f. **stand on ceremony** far complimenti. **ceremonial** adj da cerimonia. n cerimonia f. **ceremonious** adj cerimonioso.

certain ('sə:tn) adj certo, sicuro. **certainty** n certezza f.

certify ('sə:tifai) vt attestare, certificare. **certificate** n certificato m.

Ceylon (si'lɔn) n Ceylon m. **Ceylonese** adj,n cingalese.

chaffinch ('tʃæfintʃ) n fringuello m.

chain (tʃein) n catena f. vt incatenare. **chain-smoke** vi fumare ininterrottamente. **chain-reaction** n reazione a catena f. **chain-store** n negozio a catena m.

chair (tʃeə) n 1 sedia f. seggio m. 2 educ cattedra f. **chair lift** n seggiovia f. **chairman** n presidente m.

chalet ('ʃælei) n chalet m.

chalk (tʃɔ:k) n gesso m.

challenge ('tʃæləndʒ) n sfida, provocazione f. vt sfidare, provocare. **challenging** adj stimolante.

chamber ('tʃeimbə) n camera, sala f. **chambermaid** n cameriera f. **chamber music** n musica da camera f.

chamberlain ('tʃeimbəlin) n ciambellano m.

chameleon (kə'mi:liən) n camaleonte m.

chamois ('ʃæmi) n invar pelle di camoscio f.

champagne (ʃæm'pein) n sciampagna m.

champion ('tʃæmpiən) n campione m. vt difendere, sostenere. **championship** n campionato m.

chance (tʃa:ns) n fortuna f. caso m. **by chance** per caso. ~vt arrischiare. vi accadere. adj fortuito, casuale.

chancellor ('tʃa:nsələ) n cancelliere m.

chandelier (ʃændə'liə) n lampadario m.

change (tʃeindʒ) vt cambiare. vi mutarsi. n 1 cambio m. alterazione f. 2 (of money) moneta. **changeable** adj mutevole.

channel ('tʃænl) n canale m. vt incanalare.

Channel Islands n pl Isole Normanne f pl.

chant (tʃɑːnt) n canto monotono m. cantilena f. vi cantare, salmodiare.

chaos ('keiɔs) n caos m.

chap[1] (tʃæp) vt screpolare. vi screpolarsi. n screpolatura f.

chap[2] (tʃæp) n inf tipo, individuo, ragazzo m.

chapel ('tʃæpəl) n cappella f.

chaperon ('ʃæpəroun) n compagna f. vt accompagnare.

chaplain ('tʃæplin) n cappellano m.

chapter ('tʃæptə) n capitolo m.

char[1] (tʃɑː) vt carbonizzare. vi carbonizzarsi.

char[2] (tʃɑː) n inf domestica a ore f. vi lavorare a giornata.

character ('kæriktə) n 1 carattere m. indole f. 2 personalità f. 3 personaggio m. **characteristic** adj caratteristico. n caratteristica f.

charcoal ('tʃɑːkoul) n carbonella f.

charge (tʃɑːdʒ) vt 1 far pagare. 2 incaricare. 3 caricare. n 1 spesa f. costo m. 2 incarico m. sorveglianza f. 3 accusa f. 4 mil carica f.

chariot ('tʃæriət) n cocchio m.

charisma (kə'rizmə) n carisma m.

charity ('tʃæriti) n carità, elemosina f. **charitable** adj caritatevole.

charm (tʃɑːm) n 1 fascino m. 2 incantesimo m. 3 amuleto m. vt affascinare, incantare, stregare. **charming** adj attraente, grazioso.

chart (tʃɑːt) n 1 carta nautica f. 2 grafico m. 3 cartella clinica f. vt fare la carta idrografica di, tracciare.

charter ('tʃɑːtə) n carta f. documento m. **charter flight** n volo speciale or charter m. ~vt 1 noleggiare. 2 concedere statuto.

chase (tʃeis) vt cacciare, inseguire, rincorrere. n caccia f. inseguimento m.

chasm ('kæzəm) n abisso m.

chassis ('ʃæsi) n invar telaio m.

chaste (tʃeist) adj casto, virtuoso, severo.

chastise (tʃæ'staiz) vt castigare, punire. **chastisement** n castigo m. punizione f.

chat (tʃæt) n chiacchierata f. vi chiacchierare. **chatty** adj chiacchierone, ciarliero.

chatter ('tʃætə) n chiacchiera f. **chatterbox** n chiacchierone m. vi 1 chiacchierare. 2 battere i denti.

chauffeur ('ʃoufə) n autista m.

chauvinism ('ʃouvinizəm) n sciovinismo m. **chauvinist** n sciovinista m.

cheap (tʃiːp) adj 1 a buon mercato. 2 di scarso valore, spregevole.

cheat (tʃiːt) n 1 inganno m. 2 (person) imbroglione m. vt,vi ingannare, truffare.

check (tʃek) n 1 arresto, impedimento m. 2 controllo m. 3 (on material) quadretto m. 4 game scacco m. vt 1 controllare. 2 fermare. 3 tenere in scacco. **checkmate** n scacco matto m. vt dar scacco matto a. **checkpoint** n punto di controllo m. **check up** n 1 revisione f. 2 visita medica f.

cheek (tʃiːk) n 1 guancia, gota f. 2 inf sfrontatezza f. **cheekbone** n zigomo m. **cheeky** adj insolente.

cheer (tʃiə) n applauso m. vt rallegrare, incoraggiare. vi applaudire. **cheer up** rallegrarsi. **cheerful** adj allegro.

cheese (tʃiːz) n formaggio m. **cheesecake** n torta di formaggio f.

cheetah ('tʃiːtə) n ghepardo m.

chef (ʃef) n capocuoco m.

chemical ('kemikəl) adj chimico. n prodotto chimico m.

chemist ('kemist) n 1 chimico m. 2 med farmacista m. **chemist's shop** n farmacia f.

chemistry ('kemistri) n chimica f.

cheque (tʃek) n assegno m. **chequebook** n libretto degli assegni m. **cheque card** n carta bancaria f.

cherish ('tʃeriʃ) vt 1 tener caro, amare. 2 nutrire.

cherry ('tʃeri) n ciliegia f. **cherry tree** n ciliegio m.

cherub ('tʃerəb) n cherubino m.

chess (tʃes) n scacchi m pl. **chessboard** n scacchiera f. **chessman** n pezzo degli scacchi m.

chest (tʃest) n 1 anat petto, torace m. 2 cassa f. **chest of drawers** n cassettone m.

chestnut ('tʃesnʌt) n castagna f. **chestnut tree** n castagno m.

chew (tʃuː) vt,vi masticare. **chew over** meditare. **chewing gum** n gomma da masticare f.

chick (tʃik) n pulcino m.

chicken ('tʃikən) n pollo, pollastro m. **chickenpox** n varicella f.

chicory ('tʃikəri) n cicoria f.

chief (tʃiːf) adj principale. n capo, comandante m.

chilblain ('tʃilblein) n gelone m.

child (tʃaild) n, pl **children** 1 bambino m. 2 figlio m. **childbirth** n parto m. **childhood** n infanzia f. **childish** adj puerile, infantile. **childlike** adj da bambino, infantile.

chill (tʃil) n 1 med raffredore m. 2 brivido m. vt raffreddare. adj freddo. **chilly** adj 1 freddoloso, frescolino. 2 senza cordialità.

chilli ('tʃili) n pepe di Caienna m.

chime (tʃaim) n scampanio m. vi risuonare, scampanare. vt suonare, battere.

chimney ('tʃimni) n camino, fumaiolo m. **chimneypot** n comignolo m. **chimneysweep** n spazzacamino m.

chimpanzee (tʃimpæn'zi:) n scimpanzè m.

chin (tʃin) n mento m.

china ('tʃainə) n porcellana f.

China ('tʃainə) n Cina f. **Chinese** adj,n cinese. **Chinese** (language) n cinese m.

chink[1] (tʃiŋk) n fessura, crepa f.

chink[2] (tʃiŋk) vt far tintinnare. vi tintinnare. n tintinnio m.

chip (tʃip) n 1 frammento m. scheggia f. 2 cul patatina fritta f. vt rompere. vi scheggiarsi.

chiropody (ki'rɔpədi) n arte del pedicure f. **chiropodist** n chiropodista m.

chirp (tʃə:p) n cinguettio, canto m. vi cinguettare, pigolare.

chisel ('tʃizəl) n scalpello, cesello m. vt cesellare, scalpellare.

chivalry ('ʃivəlri) n galanteria f.

chives (tʃaivz) n erba cipollina f.

chlorine ('klɔːriːn) n cloro m.

chlorophyll ('klɔrəfil) n clorofilla f.

chocolate ('tʃɔklit) n 1 cioccolato m. cioccolata f. 2 (sweet) cioccolatino m. adj di cioccolato.

choice (tʃɔis) n scelta f. assortimento m. adj scelto, di prima qualità.

choir (kwaiə) n coro m. **choirboy** n ragazzo cantore m. **choirmaster** n maestro di cappella m.

choke (tʃouk) vt soffocare, asfissiare. vi soffocarsi, ostruirsi.

cholera ('kɔlərə) n colera m.

choose* (tʃuːz) vt,vi scegliere.

chop[1] (tʃɔp) vt tagliare, spaccare. n 1 colpo m. 2 cul braciola f. **chopper** n accetta f.

chop[2] (tʃɔp) vi mutare.

chopsticks ('tʃɔpstiks) n pl bastoncini m pl.

chord (kɔːd) n 1 corda f. 2 mus accordo m.

chore (tʃɔː) n 1 lavoro m. 2 pl lavori in casa.

choreography (kɔri'ɔɡrəfi) n coreografia f. **choreographer** n coreografo m.

chorus ('kɔːrəs) n coro m. **choral** adj corale.

chose (tʃouz) v see **choose**.

chosen ('tʃouzən) v see **choose**.

Christ (kraist) n Cristo m.

christen ('krisən) vt battezzare. **christening** n battesimo m.

Christian ('kristʃən) adj,n cristiano. **Christian name** n nome di battesimo m. **Christianity** n cristianesimo m.

Christmas ('krisməs) n Natale m. **Christmas tree** n albero di Natale m.

chromatic (krə'mætik) adj cromatico.

chrome (kroum) n cromo m.

chromium ('kroumiəm) n cromo m.

chromosome ('krouməsoum) n cromosomo m.

chronic ('krɔnik) adj cronico.

chronicle ('krɔnikəl) n cronaca f. vt narrare.

chronological (krɔnə'lɔdʒikəl) adj cronologico.

chrysalis ('krisəlis) n crisalide f.

chrysanthemum (kri'zænθiməm) n crisantemo m.

chubby ('tʃʌbi) adj paffuto, pienotto.

chuck (tʃʌk) vt lanciare. **chuck out** scacciare.

chuckle ('tʃʌkəl) n riso soffocato m. vi ridacchiare.

chunk (tʃʌŋk) n grosso pezzo m.

church (tʃə:tʃ) n chiesa f. **churchyard** n cimitero m.

churn (tʃə:n) n zangola f.

chute (ʃuːt) n 1 cascata d'acqua f. 2 scivolo m.

chutney ('tʃʌtni) n salsa indiana f.

cicada (si'kɑːdə) n cicala f.

cider ('saidə) n sidro m.

cigar (si'ɡɑː) n sigaro m. **cigarette** n sigaretta f. **cigarette lighter** n accendino m.

cinder ('sində) 1 brace f. tizzone m. 2 pl cenere f.

cinecamera ('sinikæmrə) n macchina da presa f.

cinema ('sinəmə) n cinema m.

cinnamon ('sinəmən) n cannella f.

circle ('sə:kəl) n 1 cerchio, circolo m. 2 Th galleria. 3 gruppo m. vt circondare, aggirare. vi volteggiare. **circular** adj circolare. **circulation** n 1 circolazione f. 2 tiratura f. **circulate** vi circolare. vt mettere in circolazione.

circuit ('sə:kit) n circuito, giro m.

circumcise ('sə:kəmsaiz) vt circoncidere. **circumcision** n circoncisione f.

circumference (sə'kʌmfərəns) n circonferenza f.

circumscribe ('sɔ:kəmskraib) vt circoscrivere.

circumstance ('sɔ:kəmstæns) n circostanza, condizione f.

circus ('sɔ:kəs) n circo m.

cistern ('sistən) n cisterna f. serbatoio m.

cite (sait) vt citare.

citizen ('sitizən) n cittadino m. **citizenship** n cittadinanza f.

citrus ('sitrəs) n agrume m. **citrus fruits** agrumi m pl.

city ('siti) n città f.

civic ('sivik) adj civico.

civil ('sivəl) adj 1 civile. 2 cortese, educato. **civil engineering** n ingegneria civile f. **civil servant** n funzionario dello stato m. **civil service** n amministrazione statale f. **civil war** n guerra civile f.

civilian (si'viliən) adj,n borghese m.

civilization (sivilai'zeiʃən) n civiltà, civilizzazione f. **civilize** vt incivilire, civilizzare. **civilized** adj civile, civilizzato.

clad (klæd) adj vestito, rivestito.

claim (kleim) n 1 richiesta, pretesa, rivendicazione f. 2 diritto m. vt 1 chiedere, reclamare, rivendicare. 2 asserire.

clam (klæm) n mollusco m.

clamber ('klæmbə) vi arrampicarsi.

clammy ('klæmi) adj vischioso, viscido.

clamour ('klæmə) n clamore, schiamazzo m. vi gridare a gran voce, richiedere rumorosamente. **clamour for** strepitare per.

clamp (klæmp) n morsa, tenaglia f. vt stringere, incastrare.

clan (klæn) n tribù f.

clandestine (klæn'destin) adj clandestino.

clang (klæŋ) vt far risuonare. vi risuonare. n suono metallico m.

clank (klæŋk) vt,vi risuonare. n rumore metallico m.

clap (klæp) n 1 colpo, scoppio m. 2 battimano m. vt,vi applaudire. vt battere.

claret ('klærət) n chiaretto m.

clarify ('klærifai) vt chiarificare. vi chiarificarsi. **clarity** n 1 chiarezza f. 2 lucidità di mente f.

clarinet (klæri'net) n clarinetto m.

clash (klæʃ) n urto, conflitto m. vi 1 urtare, urtarsi. 2 (of colours) stonare. vt far cozzare.

clasp (klɑ:sp) vt abbracciare, stringere, afferrare. n 1 fermaglio m. 2 abbraccio m. presa f.

class (klɑ:s) n 1 classe, categoria f. 2 lezione f.

vt classificare. **classroom** n aula f. **classify** vt classificare.

classic ('klæsik) adj,n classico m. **classical** adj classico.

clatter ('klætə) vi far fracasso. vt far risuonare. n fracasso, schiamazzo m.

clause (klɔ:z) n 1 clausola f. 2 gram proposizione f.

claustrophobia (klɔstrə'foubiə) n claustrofobia f.

claw (klɔ:) n 1 artiglio m. 2 grinfia, chela f. vt artigliare, graffiare.

clay (klei) n argilla, creta f.

clean (kli:n) adj pulito, netto. vt pulire, purificare.

cleanse (klenz) vt pulire, depurare. **cleanser** n detersivo m.

clear (kliə) adj 1 chiaro, evidente. 2 libero. 3 limpido. vt 1 chiarire, schiarire. 2 assolvere. vi schiarirsi. **clear away** 1 portar via. 2 dissiparsi. **clear off** andarsene. **clear up** 1 rassettare. 2 rasserenarsi. **clearance** n 1 chiarificazione f. 2 sgombero m. 3 comm liquidazione f. **clearing** n 1 schiarimento m. 2 radura f.

clef (klef) n chiave f.

clench (klentʃ) vt stringere, serrarsi.

clergy ('klɔ:dʒi) n clero m. **clergyman** n ecclesiastico, pastore evangelico m.

clerical ('klerikəl) adj 1 clericale. 2 impiegatizio.

clerk (klɑ:k) n impiegato, commesso m.

clever ('klevə) adj intelligente, abile, ingegnoso.

cliché ('kli:ʃei) n luogo comune m.

click (klik) n suono secco, schiocco m. vt fare schioccare. vi produrre un suono breve e secco.

client ('klaiənt) n cliente m,f. **clientele** n clientela f.

cliff (klif) n scogliera, rupe f.

climate ('klaimit) n clima m.

climax ('klaimæks) n apice, punto culminante m.

climb (klaim) vt salire, scalare. vi arrampicarsi. n ascesa f.

cling (kliŋ) vi aggrapparsi, aderire, attaccarsi.

clinic ('klinik) n clinica f. **clinical** adj clinico.

clip[1] (klip) vt tosare, tagliare. n tosatura f. taglio m.

clip[2] (klip) n molletta f. fermaglio m.

clitoris ('klitəris) n clitoride m.

cloak (klouk) n 1 mantello m. 2 pretesto m. **cloakroom** n guardaroba m.

clock (klɔk) n orologio m. pendola f. **clock-tower** n campanile m. **clockwise** adj,adv in senso orario. **clockwork** n meccanismo d'orologeria m.

clog (klɔg) n 1 (shoe) zoccolo m. 2 impedimento m. vt impedire, impacciare, intasare.

cloister ('klɔistə) n convento, monastero m.

close vt,vi (klouz) 1 chiudere. 2 terminare, finire. **close down** chiudere. adj (klous) 1 chiuso. 2 stretto. 3 intimo. 4 pesante. adv (klous) vicino, presso. n 1 (klouz) fine, conclusione f. 2 (klous) recinto, spazio, cintato m. **closeness** n 1 prossimità f. 2 afa f.

closet ('klɔzit) n gabinetto m. vt chiudere, rinchiudere.

clot (klɔt) n grumo, coagulo m. vi raggrumare, coagularsi.

cloth (klɔθ) n 1 stoffa, tela f. panno m. 2 tovaglia f.

clothe (klouð) vt vestire, abbigliare. **clothes** n pl indumenti, vestiti m pl. **clothes brush** n spazzola per vestiti f. **clothes line** n corda per stendere il bucato f. **clothes peg** n molletta per biancheria f. **clothing** n invar vestiario m. abiti m pl.

cloud (klaud) n nuvola f. **cloudburst** n raffica di pioggia f. **cloudy** adj 1 nuvoloso. 2 oscuro.

clove¹ (klouv) n chiodo di garofano m.

clove² (klouv) n (of garlic) spicchio m.

clover ('klouvə) n trifoglio m.

clown (klaun) n pagliaccio, buffone m.

club (klʌb) n 1 bastone m. 2 circolo m. associazione f. 3 game fiore m. v **club together** riunirsi.

clue (klu:) n indizio m. traccia f.

clump (klʌmp) n gruppo, cespo m.

clumsy ('klʌmzi) adj goffo, maldestro.

clung (klʌŋ) v see **cling.**

cluster ('klʌstə) n 1 grappolo m. 2 gruppo, sciame m.

clutch (klʌtʃ) n 1 stretta, presa f. 2 mot frizione f. vt afferrare, aggrapparsi a.

clutter ('klʌtə) n trambusto m. confusione f. vt scompigliare.

coach (koutʃ) n 1 mot corriera f. pullman m. 2 istruttore, allenatore m. vt allenare.

coal (koul) n carbone m. **coalmine** n miniera di carbone f.

coalition (kouə'liʃən) n coalizione f.

coarse (kɔ:s) adj 1 grezzo. 2 ruvido, volgare, grossolano.

coast (koust) n costa f. litorale m. **coastguard**

n guardia costiera f. **coastline** n costa f. litorale m.

coat (kout) n 1 cappotto, soprabito m. 2 (of an animal) pelliccia f. 3 rivestimento, strato m. vt spalmare, rivestire. **coat-hanger** n attaccapanni m invar. stampella f. **coat of arms** n insegna nobiliare f.

coax (kouks) vt persuadere.

cobble ('kɔbəl) n ciottolo m. **cobblestone** n ciottolo m.

cobbler ('kɔblə) n calzolaio m.

cobra ('koubrə) n cobra m.

cobweb ('kɔbweb) n ragnatela f.

cock¹ (kɔk) n 1 gallo m. 2 maschio di uccelli m.

cock² (kɔk) n 1 drizzare. 2 (a gun) armare.

cockle ('kɔkəl) n 1 zool cardio m. 2 bot loglio m.

cockpit ('kɔkpit) n 1 aviat carlinga f. 2 naut castello di poppa m.

cockroach ('kɔkroutʃ) n scarafaggio m.

cocktail ('kɔkteil) n cocktail m.

cocky ('kɔki) adj arrogante.

cocoa ('koukou) n cacao m.

coconut ('koukənʌt) n noce di cocco f.

cocoon (kə'ku:n) n bozzolo m.

cod (kɔd) n merluzzo m.

code (koud) n codice, cifrario m. vt codificare, cifrare.

codeine ('koudi:n) n codeina f.

co-education (kouedju'keiʃən) n istruzione in scuola mista f.

coerce (kou'ə:s) vt costringere.

coexist (kouig'zist) vi coesistere.

coffee ('kɔfi) n caffè m invar. **coffee bar** n caffè f. **coffee bean** n chicco di caffè m. **coffee table** n tavolo da caffè m.

coffin ('kɔfin) n bara f.

cog (kɔg) n dente m.

cognac ('kɔnjæk) n cognac m.

cohabit (kou'hæbit) vi coabitare.

cohere (kou'hiə) vi aderire. **coherence** n coerenza f. **coherent** adj coerente.

coil (kɔil) n 1 matassa f. rotolo m. 2 (of a snake) spira f. 3 tech bobina f. vt avvolgere.

coin (kɔin) n moneta f. vt 1 coniare. 2 inventare.

coincide (kouin'said) vi coincidere. **coincidence** n coincidenza f.

colander ('kʌləndə) n colino m.

cold (kould) adj freddo. **be cold 1** (of a person) aver freddo. 2 (of the weather) fare freddo. ~n 1 freddo m. 2 med raffreddore m. **catch a cold** prendersi un raffreddore.

collaborate (kə'læbəreit) vi collaborare.

collapse (kə'læps) n crollo m. caduta f. vi 1 crollare, sprofondare. 2 accasciarsi.

collar ('kɔlə) n colletto, bavero, collare m. **collarbone** n clavicola f.

colleague ('kɔli:g) n collega m.

collect (kə'lekt) vt 1 fare collezione di, raccogliere. vi radunarsi, ammassarsi. **collection** n 1 collezione, raccolta f. 2 colletta f. **collective** adj collettivo.

college ('kɔlidʒ) n collegio m.

collide (kə'laid) vi scontrarsi, urtarsi. **collision** n urto, scontro m.

colloquial (kə'loukwiəl) adj familiare. **colloquialism** n espressione familiare f.

colon ('koulən) n gram due punti m pl.

colonel ('kə:nl) n colonnello m.

colony ('kɔləni) n colonia f. **colonial** adj coloniale.

colossal (kə'lɔsəl) adj colossale.

colour ('kʌlə) n 1 colore m. tinta f. 2 colorito m. 3 pl bandiera f. vt colorire, dipingere. vi arrossire, colorirsi. **colour-bar** n discriminazione razziale f. **colour-blind** adj daltonico. **coloured person** n persona di colore f.

colt (koult) n puledro m.

column ('kɔləm) n colonna f.

columnist ('kɔləmnist) n giornalista, cronista m.

coma ('koumə) n coma m.

comb (koum) n 1 pettine m. 2 (of a cock) cresta f. vt 1 pettinare, strigliare. 2 perlustrare.

combat (n 'kɔmbæt; v kəm'bæt) n combattimento m. lotta f. vt combattere, lottare.

combine (v kəm'bain; n 'kɔmbain) vt combinare, unire. vi unirsi. n associazione f.

combustion (kəm'bʌstʃən) n combustione f.

come * (kʌm) vi 1 venire, arrivare. 2 avvenire. 3 derivare. **come about** accadere. **come across** incontrare per caso. **come back** ritornare. **comeback** n ritorno m. **come round** riprendere i sensi.

comedy ('kɔmədi) n commedia f. **comedian** n comico m. **comic** adj comico, buffo. n giornale a fumetti m.

comet ('kɔmit) n cometa f.

comfort ('kʌmfət) n 1 agio, benessere m. comodità f. 2 sollievo m. vt confortare, consolare. **comfortable** adj confortevole, agiato.

comma ('kɔmə) n virgola f.

command (kə'mɑ:nd) vt comandare, ordinare, controllare. n 1 comando, ordine m. 2 padro-

nanza f. **commandment** n comandamento m.

commemorate (kə'meməreit) vt commemorare, celebrare.

commence (kə'mens) vt cominciare. vi esordire. **commencement** n inizio, principio m.

commend (kə'mend) vt raccomandare, lodare. **commendable** adj lodevole.

comment ('kɔment) n commento m. critica f. vi commentare, fare note critiche. **commentary** n commentario m. **commentator** n commentatore, radiocronista m.

commerce ('kɔmə:s) n commercio, scambio m. **commercial** adj commerciale. n pubblicità f. **commercial vehicle** n utilitaria f.

commission (kə'miʃən) n 1 commissione f. comitato m. 2 incarico m. 3 provvigione f. vt 1 incaricare. 2 mil dare una carica a. **commissioner** n commissario m.

commit (kə'mit) vt 1 commettere. 2 affidare, consegnare. **commit oneself** impegnarsi. **committed** adj impegnato.

committee (kə'miti) n comitato m. commissione f.

commodity (kə'mɔditi) n merce f.

common ('kɔmən) adj 1 comune, ordinario. 2 pubblico. 3 vulgare. n terreno demaniale m. **commonplace** adj banale, comune. n luogo comune m. banalità f. **commonsense** n buon senso m. **commonwealth** n confederazione f.

Common Market n Mercato Comune m.

commotion (kə'mouʃən) n agitazione f. tumulto m.

communal ('kɔmju:nl) adj della comunità, comunale.

commune [1] (kə'mju:n) vi comunicare, discutere.

commune [2] ('kɔmju:n) n comune m.

communicant (kə'mju:nikənt) n comunicando m.

communicate (kə'mju:nikeit) vt comunicare, far conoscere. vi fare la comunione. **communication** n comunicazione, informazione f.

communion (kə'mju:niən) n 1 comunione f. 2 rel santa comunione f.

communism ('kɔmjunizəm) n comunismo m. **communist** adj,n comunista.

community (kə'mju:niti) n comunità f.

commute (kə'mju:t) vt commutare. vi viaggiare con abbonamento, fare il pendolare. **commuter** n pendolare m.

compact[1] (*adj* kəm'pækt; *n* 'kɔmpækt) *adj* compatto, unito. *n* cipria compatta *f.*

compact[2] ('kɔmpækt) *n* accordo, trattato *m.*

companion (kəm'pæniən) *n* compagno, socio *m.* **companionship** *n* amicizia *f.* cameratismo *m.*

company ('kʌmpəni) *n* **1** compagnia. **2** *comm* società. **3** comitiva *f.*

compare (kəm'pɛə) *vt* comparare, confrontare. *vi* reggere al confronto. **comparable** *adj* paragonabile. **comparative** *adj* comparativo, comparato. **comparison** *n* paragone, confronto *m.*

compartment (kəm'pɑ:tmənt) *n* scompartimento *m.*

compass ('kʌmpəs) *n* **1** bussola *f.* **2** circonferenza *f.* spazio *m.* **3** *pl* compasso *m.*

compassion (kəm'pæʃən) *n* compassione, pietà *f.* **compassionate** *adj* compassionevole.

compatible (kəm'pætibəl) *adj* compatibile.

compel (kəm'pel) *vt* costringere, obbligare.

compensate ('kɔmpənseit) *vt* compensare, ricompensare. *vi* compensarsi. **compensation** *n* compenso *m.*

compete (kəm'pi:t) *vi* competere, concorrere. **competition** *n* competizione, gara *f.* concorso *m.* **competitive** *adj* di correnza, di competizione, competitivo, agonistico.

competent ('kɔmpitənt) *adj* competente, abile.

compile (kəm'pail) *vt* compilare.

complacent (kəm'pleisənt) *adj* compiacente, soddisfatto.

complain (kəm'plein) *vi* lagnarsi, lamentarsi. **complaint** *n* **1** lamentela *f.* **2** *med* malattia *f.*

complement (*n* 'kɔmplimənt; *v* 'kɔmpliment) *n* complemento *m.* *vt* completare. **complementary** *adj* complementare.

complete (kəm'pli:t) *adj* **1** completo, finito. **2** intero. *vt* completare, terminare.

complex ('kɔmpleks) *adj* complesso, intricato. *n* complesso *m.*

complexion (kəm'plekʃən) *n* carnagione *f.* colorito *m.*

complicate ('kɔmplikeit) *vt* complicare.

compliment (*n* 'kɔmplimənt; *v* 'kɔmpliment) *n* complimento *m.* *vt* congratularsi con. **complimentary** *adj* **1** lusinghiero. **2** di favore.

comply (kəm'plai) *vi* accondiscendere, prestare osservanza.

component (kəm'pounənt) *adj,n* componente *m.*

compose (kəm'pouz) *vt* comporre. **compose**

oneself calmarsi. **composed** *adj* calmo, composto. **composition** *n* composizione *f.* **composure** *n* calma, imperturbabilità *f.*

compound[1] (*adj,n* 'kɔmpaund; *v* kəm'paund) *adj* composto. *n* miscela *f.* composto *m.* *vt* mescolare, comporre.

compound[2] ('kɔmpaund) *n* cinta *f.*

comprehend (kɔmpri'hend) *vt* comprendere. **comprehension** *n* comprensione *f.* **comprehensive** *adj* comprensivo, inclusivo, esauriente. **comprehensive school** *n* scuola secondaria *f.*

compress (*v* kəm'pres; *n* 'kɔmpres) *vt* comprimere. *n* compressa *f.*

comprise (kəm'praiz) *vt* comprendere, includere.

compromise ('kɔmprəmaiz) *n* compromesso *m.* *vi* venire a un compromesso, compromettere.

compulsion (kəm'pʌlʃən) *n* costrizione *f.* **compulsive** *adj* coercitivo.

compulsory (kəm'pʌlsəri) *adj* obbligatorio, irresistibile.

computer (kəm'pju:tə) *n* calcolatore *m.*

comrade ('kɔmrəd, -reid) *n* compagno *m.*

concave ('kɔŋkeiv) *adj* concavo, a volta.

conceal (kən'si:l) *vt* nascondere, dissimulare.

concede (kən'si:d) *vt* ammettere, riconoscere.

conceit (kən'si:t) *n* **1** presunzione *f.* **2** idea ricercata *f.* **conceited** *adj* presuntuoso.

conceive (kən'si:v) *vt* **1** concepire. **2** immaginare.

concentrate ('kɔnsəntreit) *vt* concentrare. *vi* concentrarsi. **concentration camp** *n* campo di concentramento *m.*

concentric (kən'sentrik) *adj* concentrico.

concept ('kɔnsept) *n* concetto *m.*

conception (kən'sepʃən) *n* **1** concezione *f.* **2** idea *f.*

concern (kən'sə:n) *vt* **1** concernere, riguardare. **2** toccare. *n* **1** interesse *m.* faccenda *f.* **2** ansietà *f.* **3** azienda *f.* **concerning** *prep* riguardo a, circa.

concert (*n* 'kɔnsət; *v* kən'sə:t) *n* concerto *m.* *vt* concertare. **concerted** *adj* concertato, convenuto.

concertina (kɔnsə'ti:nə) *n* piccola fisarmonica *f.*

concerto (kən'tʃɛətou) *n* concerto *m.*

concession (kən'seʃən) *n* concessione *f.*

concise (kən'sais) *adj* conciso, breve.

conclude (kən'klu:d) *vt* **1** concludere. **2** dedurre. *vi* terminare. **conclusion** *n* **1** conclusione *f.* **2** decisione *f.*

concoct (kən'kɔkt) vt 1 mescolare. 2 preparare, tramare. **concoction** n 1 intruglio m. 2 storia inventata f.

concrete ('kɔŋkri:t) adj concreto. n cemento m.

concussion (kən'kʌʃən) n 1 trauma m. commozione cerebrale f.

condemn (kən'dem) vt condannare, biasimare. **condemnation** n condanna f.

condense (kən'dens) vt condensare. **condensation** n condensazione f.

condescend (kɔndi'send) vi accondiscendere. **condescending** adj condiscendente.

condition (kən'diʃən) n 1 condizione f. 2 patto m. **conditional** adj condizionale.

condolence (kən'douləns) n condoglianza f.

condone (kən'doun) vt condonare, perdonare.

conduct (n 'kɔndʌkt; v kən'dʌkt) n 1 condotta f. comportamento m. vt 1 condurre. 2 mus dirigere. **conductor** n 1 mus direttore d'orchestra. 2 bigliettaio, capotreno m.

cone (koun) n 1 cono m. 2 bot pigna f.

confectioner (kən'fekʃənə) n pasticciere m. **confectioner's shop** n pasticceria f.

confederate (adj,n kən'fedərət; v kən'fedəreit) adj,n confederato, alleato m. vi associarsi.

confer (kən'fə:) vi conferire, consultarsi. vt conferire. **conference** n conferenza f. congresso m.

confess (kən'fes) vt,vi confessare. **confession** n confessione f.

confetti (kən'feti) n pl coriandoli m pl.

confide (kən'faid) vt confidare. **confide in** confidarsi con, fare affidamento su. **confidence** n fiducia, confidenza f. **confident** adj 1 fiducioso, sicuro. 2 baldanzoso. **confidential** adj confidenziale, riservato.

confine (kən'fain) vt relegare, confinare. limitare. **confinement** n 1 imprigionamento m. reclusione f. 2 parto m.

confirm (kən'fə:m) vt 1 confermare, convalidare. 2 rel cresimare. **confirmation** n 1 conferma f. 2 rel cresima f. **confirmed** adj convinto.

confiscate ('kɔnfiskeit) vt confiscare.

conflict (v kən'flikt; n 'kɔnflikt) vi essere in conflitto, lottare. n conflitto m. lotta, guerra f.

conform (kən'fə:m) vt conformare. vi uniformarsi.

confound (kən'faund) vt 1 confondere, 2 turbare.

confront (kən'frʌnt) vt affrontare, mettere a confronto.

confuse (kən'fju:z) vt confondere, disorientare. **confusion** n 1 confusione f. 2 tumulto m.

congeal (kən'dʒi:l) vt congelare. vi coagularsi.

congenial (kən'dʒi:niəl) adj congeniale, affine.

congested (kən'dʒestid) adj congestionato, sovrappopolato.

congratulate (kən'grætjuleit) vt congratularsi con, rallegrarsi con. **congratulation** n felicitazione f.

congregate ('kɔŋgrigeit) vt radunare. vi unirsi. **congregation** n congregazione f. insieme dei fedeli m.

congress ('kɔŋgres) n congresso m.

conical ('kɔnikəl) adj conico.

conifer ('kɔnifə) n conifera f.

conjugal ('kɔndʒugəl) adj coniugale.

conjugate ('kɔndʒugeit) vt coniugare.

conjunction (kən'dʒʌŋkʃən) n 1 gram congiunzione. 2 unione f.

conjure ('kʌndʒə) vi fare giochi di prestigio. vt scongiurare. **conjure up** evocare. **conjurer** n prestigiatore m.

connect (kə'nekt) vt 1 connettere, collegare. n 1 connessione o collegarsi. **connection** n 1 connessione, attinenza f. 2 parentela f. 3 (of trains, buses, etc.) coincidenza f.

connoisseur (kɔnə'sə:) n conoscitore, intenditore m.

connotation (kɔnə'teiʃən) n significato implicito m. connotazione f.

conquer ('kɔŋkə) vt conquistare, vincere. **conqueror** n conquistatore m.

conquest ('kɔŋkwest) n conquista f.

conscience ('kɔnʃəns) n coscienza f. **conscientious** adj coscienzioso.

conscious ('kɔnʃəs) adj conscio, consapevole, cosciente.

conscript ('kɔnskript) n conscritto m.

consecrate ('kɔnsikreit) vt consacrare.

consecutive (kən'sekjutiv) adj consecutivo.

consent (kən'sent) n accordo, consenso m. vi acconsentire, aderire.

consequence ('kɔnsikwəns) n 1 conseguenza f. risultato m. 2 importanza f.

conservative (kən'sə:vətiv) adj,n conservatore.

conservatory (kən'sə:vətri) n serra f. conservatorio m.

conserve (kən'sə:v) vt conservare. n conserva f.

consider (kən'sidə) vt considerare. vi pensare. **considerable** adj considerevole, notevole. **considerably** adv assai. **considerate** adj gentile, riguardoso. **consideration** n 1 considerazione, riflessione f. 2 riguardo m.

consign (kənˈsain) vt consegnare, affidare. **consignment** n 1 consegna f. 2 partita di merci f.

consist (kənˈsist) vi consistere, essere composto. **consistency** n consistenza, densità f. **consistent** adj coerente, logico.

console (kənˈsoul) vt consolare.

consolidate (kənˈsɔlideit) vt consolidare. vi consolidarsi.

consonant (ˈkɔnsənənt) n consonante f.

conspicuous (kənˈspikjuəs) adj cospicuo, evidente.

conspire (kənˈspaiə) vi cospirare, congiurare.

constable (ˈkɔnstəbəl) n poliziotto m. guardia f.

Constance, Lake n Lago di Costanza m.

constant (ˈkɔnstənt) adj invariabile, costante, fedele. n math costante f.

constellation (kɔnstəˈleiʃən) n costellazione f.

constipation (kɔnstiˈpeiʃən) n stitichezza f.

constituency (kənˈstitjuənsi) n circoscrizione elettorale f.

constituent (kənˈstitjuənt) adj costituente. n 1 costituente m. 2 elettore m.

constitute (ˈkɔnstitjuːt) vt costituire, fondare. **constitution** n costituzione f. statuto m.

constraint (kənˈstreint) n 1 repressione, costrizione f. 2 imbarazzo m.

constrict (kənˈstrikt) vt costringere, comprimere.

construct (kənˈstrʌkt) vt costruire. **construction** n costruzione f.

consul (ˈkɔnsəl) n console m.

consulate (ˈkɔnsjulət) n consolato m.

consult (kəˈsʌlt) vt consultare. **consultant** n consulente, esperto m.

consume (kənˈsjuːm) vt consumare.

contact (ˈkɔntækt) n contatto m. vt mettere in contatto. vi mettersi in contatto. **contact lenses** n pl lenti a contatto f pl.

contagious (kənˈteidʒəs) adj contagioso.

contain (kənˈtein) vt 1 contenere. 2 reprimere. **container** n recipiente m.

contaminate (kənˈtæmineit) vt contaminare.

contemplate (ˈkɔntəmpleit) vt contemplare, meditare. vi proporsi.

contemporary (kənˈtempərəri) adj,n contemporaneo.

contempt (kənˈtempt) n disprezzo m. **contemptuous** adj sprezzante.

content[1] (ˈkɔntent) n contenuto m. dose f.

content[2] (kənˈtent) adj contento, soddisfatto. vt accontentare.

contest (n ˈkɔntest; v kənˈtest) n contesa, gara f. vt,vi contestare, disputare. **contestant** n concorrente m,f.

context (ˈkɔntekst) n contesto m.

continent (ˈkɔntinənt) n continente m. adj 1 moderato. 2 casto. **continental** adj,n continentale.

contingency (kənˈtindʒənsi) n contingenza f.

continue (kənˈtinjuː) vt,vi continuare. **continual** adj continuo. **continuity** n continuità f. **continuous** adj continuo.

contour (ˈkɔntuə) n contorno m.

contraband (ˈkɔntrəbænd) n contrabbando m. adj di contrabbando.

contraception (kɔntrəˈsepʃən) n pratiche antifecondative f pl. **contraceptive** adj,n antifecondativo, anticoncezionale m.

contract (n ˈkɔntrækt; v kənˈtrækt) n 1 contratto m. 2 appalto m. vt contrarre. vi contrarsi, contrattare. **contraction** n contrazione f.

contradict (kɔntrəˈdikt) vt contraddire. **contradiction** n contraddizione f.

contralto (kənˈtræltou) n contralto f.

contraption (kənˈtræpʃən) n aggeggio m.

contrary (ˈkɔntrəri) adj contrario, opposto, sfavorevole. n contrario m. **on the contrary** al contrario.

contrast (v kənˈtrɑːst; n ˈkɔntrɑːst) vt mettere in contrasto. vi far contrasto. n contrasto m.

contravene (kɔntrəˈviːn) vt contravvenire a.

contribute (kənˈtribjuːt) vt contribuire. vi contribuire a. **contribution** n 1 contributo m. 2 lit collaborazione f.

contrive (kənˈtraiv) vt 1 escogitare. 2 inventare.

control (kənˈtroul) n 1 autorità f. 2 controllo m. sorveglianza f. 3 freno m. 4 pl comandi m pl. vt 1 regolare, dirigere. 2 dominare.

controversy (ˈkɔntrəvəːsi, kənˈtrɔvəsi) n polemica, controversia f. **controversial** adj polemico, controverso.

convalesce (kɔnvəˈles) vi essere in convalescenza. **convalescence** n convalescenza f.

convenience (kənˈviːniəns) n convenienza, comodità f. comodo m. **convenient** adj conveniente, adatto.

convent (ˈkɔnvənt) n convento m.

convention (kənˈvenʃən) n convenzione f. **conventional** adj tradizionale, convenzionale.

converge (kənˈvəːdʒ) vi convergere.

converse[1] (kən'vəːs) vi conversare. **conversation** n conversazione f.

converse[2] ('kɔnvəːs) adj,n contrario, opposto m.

convert (v kən'vəːt; n 'kɔnvəːt) vt convertire, trasformare. n convertito m. **conversion** n conversione f. **convertible** adj 1 trasformabile. 2 mot decappottabile.

convex ('kɔnveks) adj convesso.

convey (kən'vei) vt 1 trasportare. 2 esprimere. **conveyor belt** n nastro trasportatore m.

convict (v kən'vikt; n 'kɔnvikt) vt condannare. n forzato, ergastolano m.

conviction (kən'vikʃən) n 1 law condanna f. 2 convinzione f.

convince (kən'vins) vt convincere.

convoy ('kɔnvɔi) n convoglio m. scorta f. vt convogliare, scortare.

cook (kuk) n cuoco m. vt 1 fare cuocere, cucinare. 2 inf falsificare. vi cuocersi. **cookery** n arte culinaria f. **cookery book** n libro di cucina m.

cool (kuːl) adj 1 fresco. 2 calmo. 3 disinvolto, senza entusiasmo. n fresco m. vt rinfrescare. vi raffreddarsi.

coop (kuːp) n stia f. v **coop up** rinchiudere.

cooperate (kou'ɔpəreit) vi cooperare. **cooperation** n cooperazione f. **cooperative** adj cooperativo.

coordinate (adj, n kou'ɔːdnət; v kou'ɔːdineit) adj coordinato. n math coordinata f. vt coordinare.

cope[1] (koup) vi far fronte, riuscire.

cope[2] (koup) n cappa di ecclesiastico f.

copious adj abbondante.

copper[1] ('kɔpə) n rame m. adj di rame.

copper[2] ('kɔpə) n inf poliziotto m.

copy ('kɔpi) n 1 copia, trascrizione f. 2 (of a book) esemplare m. vt 1 copiare. 2 imitare. **copyright** n diritto d'autore m.

coral ('kɔrəl) n corallo m. adj di corallo.

cord (kɔːd) n corda f. spago m.

cordial ('kɔːdiəl) adj,n cordiale f.

cordon ('kɔːdn) n cordone m.

corduroy ('kɔːdərɔi) n velluto a coste m.

core (kɔː) n 1 (of fruit) torsolo m. 2 centro m.

cork (kɔːk) n 1 sughero m. 2 (of a bottle) tappo m. vt tappare. **corkscrew** n cavatappi m invar.

corn[1] (kɔːn) n grano, granoturco m. cereali m pl. **cornflakes** n pl fiocchi di granturco m pl. **cornflour** n farina di granturco f. **cornflower** n fiordaliso m.

corn[2] (kɔːn) n med callo m.

corner ('kɔːnə) n angolo m. vt 1 mettere alle strette. 2 comm accaparrare.

cornet ('kɔːnit) n 1 mus cornetta f. 2 cartoccio, cono m.

coronary ('kɔrənəri) adj coronario.

coronation (kɔrə'neiʃən) n incoronazione f.

corporal[1] ('kɔːprəl) adj corporale, corporeo.

corporal[2] ('kɔːprəl) n mil corporale m.

corporation (kɔːpə'reiʃən) n corporazione f.

corps (kɔː) n invar corpo m.

corpse (kɔːps) n cadavere m.

correct (kə'rekt) adj corretto, esatto. vt correggere. **correction** n correzione f.

correlate ('kɔrəleit) vt mettere in correlazione. vi essere in correlazione.

correspond (kɔri'spɔnd) vi corrispondere, rispondere. **correspondence** n corrispondenza f. **correspondent** adj,n corrispondente.

corridor ('kɔridɔː) n corridoio m.

corrode (kə'roud) vt corrodere. vi corrodersi. **corrosion** n corrosione f.

corrupt (kə'rʌpt) adj corrotto, guasto. vt corrompere. **corruption** n corruzione, decomposizione f.

corset ('kɔːsit) n corsetto, busto m.

Corsica ('kɔːsikə) n Corsica f. **Corsican** adj,n corso.

cosmetic (kɔz'metik) adj,n cosmetico m.

cosmopolitan (kɔzmə'pɔlitən) adj,n cosmopolita.

cosmos ('kɔzmɔs) n cosmos m. **cosmic** adj cosmico.

cost* (kɔst) n costo, prezzo m. spesa f. vi,vt costare.

costume ('kɔstjuːm) n costume, abito m.

cosy ('kouzi) adj comodo, intimo.

cot (kɔt) n lettino per bambini m. culla f.

cottage ('kɔtidʒ) n villino m. casetta f. **cottage cheese** n specie di ricotta f.

cotton ('kɔtn) n cotone m. **cottonwool** n cotone idrofilo m.

couch (kautʃ) n divano m.

cough (kɔf) n tosse f. vi tossire.

could (kud; unstressed kəd) v see **can.**

council ('kaunsəl) n consiglio m. **councillor** n consigliere m.

counsel ('kaunsəl) n 1 consiglio, parere m. 2 law avvocato m. vt raccomandare.

count[1] (kaunt) vt 1 contare, calcolare. 2 considerare. *vi* avere importanza, contare. *n* conto, calcolo *m*. **countdown** *n* conto alla rovescia *m*.

count[2] (kaunt) *n* (title) conte *m*.

counter[1] ('kauntə) *n* **1** banco *m*. cassa *f*. **2** game gettone *m*.

counter[2] ('kauntə) *adj* contrario, opposto. *adv* contrariamente. *vt* contraddire, opporsi a.

counterattack ('kauntərətæk) *n* contrattacco *m*.

counterfeit ('kauntəfit) *adj* contraffatto. *n* contraffazione, falsificazione *f*. *vt* contraffare, falsificare.

counterfoil ('kauntəfɔil) *n* matrice *f*.

counterpart ('kauntəpɑːt) *n* **1** sostituto *m*. **2** sosia *m*. **3** complemento *m*.

countess (kauntis) *n* contessa *f*.

country ('kʌntri) *n* **1** paese *m*. nazione *f*. **2** campagna *f*. **countryside** *n* campagna *f*.

county ('kaunti) *n* contea *f*.

coup (kuː) *n* colpo audace *m*. **coup de grâce** *n* colpo di grazia *m*. **coup d'état** *n* colpo di stato *m*.

couple ('kʌpəl) *n* coppia *f*. paio *m*, *pl* paia *f*. *vt* accoppiare, agganciare.

coupon ('kuːpɔn) *n* tagliando, scontrino *m*.

courage ('kʌridʒ) *n* coraggio *m*. **courageous** *adj* coraggioso.

courgette (kuəˈʒet) *n* zucchina *f*.

courier ('kuriə) *n* corriere, messaggero *m*.

course (kɔːs) *n* **1** corso *m*. direzione *f*. **2** *cul* portata *f*. **in due course** a tempo debito. **of course** naturalmente.

court (kɔːt) *n* **1** corte *f*. **2** law tribunale *m*. **3** sport campo *m*. *vt* corteggiare. **court martial** *n* corte marziale *f*. **court-martial** *vt* processare davanti alla corte marziale. **courtyard** *n* cortile *m*.

courteous ('kɔːtiəs) *adj* cortese. **courtesy** *n* cortesia *f*.

cousin ('kʌzən) *n* cugino *m*.

cove (kouv) *n* grotta, insenatura *f*.

covenant ('kʌvənənt) *n* patto, contratto *m*.

cover ('kʌvə) *vt* **1** coprire. **2** nascondere. *n* **1** coperto *m*. copertura *f*. **2** (of a book) copertina *f*. **3** riparo *m*.

cow (kau) *n* vacca *f*. **cowboy** *n* bovaro, cowboy *m*. **cowhand** *n* vaccaro *m*. **cowshed** *n* stalla *f*.

coward ('kauəd) *n* vigliacco, codardo *m*. **cowardly** *adj* codardo, vile.

cower ('kauə) *vi* acquattarsi, accasciarsi.

coy (kɔi) *adj* timido, modesto.

crab (kræb) *n* granchio *m*.

crack (kræk) *vt* **1** incrinare. **2** schiantare. **3** (a joke) fare. *vi* **1** spaccarsi. *n* **1** spaccatura, screpolatura *f*. **2** schianto *m*. *adj* di prim'ordine.

cracker ('krækə) *n* petardo *m*. galletta *f*.

crackle ('krækəl) *n* crepitio *m*. *vi* crepitare.

cradle ('kreidl) *n* culla *f*.

craft (krɑːft) *n* **1** mestiere *m*. arte *f*. **2** naut imbarcazione *f*. **craftsman** *n* artigiano *m*. **craftsmanship** *n* artigianato *m*. abilità d'esecuzione *f*. **crafty** *adj* astuto, abile.

cram (kræm) *vt* stipare, rimpinzare. *vi* imbottirsi di nozioni.

cramp[1] (kræmp) *n* crampo *m*. *vt* paralizzare, causare crampi a.

cramp[2] (kræmp) *n* tech morsetto *m*.

crane (krein) *n* gru *f invar*.

crash (kræʃ) *vt* fracassare. *vi* **1** fracassarsi. **2** aviat precipitare. *n* **1** tonfo *m*. **2** comm crollo *m*. *adj* intenso. **crash-helmet** *n* casco paraurti *m*.

crate (kreit) *n* gabbia d'imballaggio *f*.

crater ('kreitə) *n* cratere *m*.

crave (kreiv) *vt* desiderare ardentemente. **crave for** bramare.

crawl (krɔːl) *vi* **1** strisciare, trascinarsi. **2** brulicare. *n* **1** movimento strisciante *m*. **2** (swimming) crawl *m*.

crayfish ('kreifiʃ) *n* gambero *m*.

crayon ('kreiən) *n* pastello per disegno *m*.

craze (kreiz) *n* pazzia, mania *f*. **crazy** *adj* pazzo, instabile.

creak (kriːk) *n* cigolio *m*. *vi* scricchiolare, cigolare.

cream (kriːm) *n* crema, panna *f*. **creamy** *adj* cremoso.

crease (kriːs) *n* grinza, piegatura *f*. *vt* increspare. *vi* fare pieghe, sgualcirsi. **crease-resistant** *adj* antipiega.

create (kriˈeit) *vt* creare. **creation** *n* creazione *f*. creato *m*. **creative** *adj* creativo.

creature ('kriːtʃə) *n* creatura *f*.

creche (kreʃ) *n* nido, asilo infantile *m*.

credentials (kriˈdenʃəlz) *n pl* credenziali *f pl*.

credible ('kredibəl) *adj* credibile.

credit ('kredit) *n* **1** credito *m*. **2** fiducia *f*. **3** merito *m*. *vt* **1** credere, attribuire. **2** comm accreditare. **credit card** *n* carta di credito *f*.

creep* (kriːp) *vi* **1** insinuarsi, strisciare. **2** bot arrampicarsi.

cremate (kri'meit) vt cremare. **crematorium** n crematorio m.

creosote ('kri:əsout) n creosoto m.

crept (krept) v see **creep**.

crescent ('kresənt) adj crescente. n mezzaluna f.

cress (kres) n crescione m.

crest (krest) n 1 cresta f. ciuffo m. 2 pennacchio m. **crestfallen** adj abbattuto.

crevice ('krevis) n fessura, crepa f.

crew (kru:) n 1 naut equipaggio m. 2 squadra f.

crib (krib) n presepio, letto da bambino m.

cricket[1] ('krikit) n zool grillo m.

cricket[2] ('krikit) n sport cricket m.

crime (kraim) n crimine, delitto m. **criminal** adj criminale. n criminale, delinquente m,f.

crimson ('krimzən) adj,n cremisi m.

cringe (krindʒ) vi 1 acquattarsi. 2 sottomettersi.

crinkle ('kriŋkəl) n crespa, ruga f. vi increspare, raggrinzirsi.

cripple ('kripəl) n invalido, storpio m. vt storpiare, menomare.

crisis ('kraisis) n, pl **-ses** crisi f invar.

crisp (krisp) adj 1 croccante. 2 crespo. 3 frizzante. n patatina f.

criterion (krai'tiəriən) n, pl **-teria** or **-terions** criterio m.

criticize ('kritisaiz) vt criticare, censurare. **critic** n critico m. **critical** adj critico. **criticism** n critica f.

croak (krouk) vi gracchiare, gracidare, brontolare. n gracchio m.

crochet ('krouʃei) n lavoro all'uncinetto m. vt lavorare all'uncinetto.

crockery ('krokəri) n vasellame m.

crocodile ('krokədail) n coccodrillo m.

crocus ('kroukəs) n croco m.

crook (kruk) n 1 curva f. 2 inf imbroglione m.

crooked ('krukid) adj 1 storto, piegato. 2 inf disonesto.

crop (krɔp) n 1 raccolto m. 2 (of a bird) gozzo m. vt 1 mietere, falciare. 2 brucare. **crop up** capitare.

croquet ('kroukei) n croquet m.

cross (krɔs) n croce f. adj 1 trasversale. 2 imbronciato, contrario. vt 1 attraversare. 2 incrociare. 3 ostacolare. vi accoppiarsi. **cross-examine** vt sottoporre ad interrogatorio. **cross-eyed** adj strabico. **crossing** n 1 incrocio m. 2 traversata f. **cross-question** vt esaminare attentamente, sottoporre ad interrogatorio. **cross-reference** n riferimento m. **crossroads** n incrocio, crocevia m. **crossword** n parole incrociate f pl. **crossword puzzle** n cruciverba m.

crotchet ('krɔtʃit) n mus semiminima f.

crouch (krautʃ) vi rannicchiarsi.

crow[1] (krou) n zool corvo m. cornacchia f.

crow[2] (krou) vi 1 cantare. 2 esultare. n canto del gallo m.

crowd (kraud) n folla, massa f. vt affollare. vi accalcarsi.

crown (kraun) n 1 corona f. 2 cima, sommità f. vt 1 incoronare. 2 sormontare. **crowning** adj supremo, finale. n coronamento m. incoronazione f.

crucial ('kru:ʃəl) adj cruciale, critico.

crucify ('kru:sifai) vt crocifiggere. **crucifix** n crocifisso m. **crucifixion** n crocifissione f.

crude (kru:d) adj 1 grezzo, rozzo. 2 volgare. **crude oil** n petrolio grezzo m.

cruel ('kruəl) adj crudele. **cruelty** n crudeltà f.

cruise (kru:z) n crociera f. **cruiser** n incrociatore m.

crumb (krʌm) n mollica, briciola f.

crumble ('krʌmbəl) vi 1 sbriciolarsi, sgretolarsi. 2 crollare. vt sbriciolare.

crumple ('krʌmpəl) vt sgualcire. vi spiegazzarsi, sgualcirsi.

crunch (krʌntʃ) n sgretolio m. vt sgranocchiare.

crusade (kru:'seid) n crociata f.

crush (krʌʃ) n calca f. affollamento m. vt 1 sgualcire. 2 frantumare, annientare.

crust (krʌst) n crosta f.

crustacean (krʌs'teiʃən) adj,n crostaceo m.

crutch (krʌtʃ) n gruccia, stampella f.

cry (krai) n grido, richiamo, lamento m. vt,vi gridare. vi piangere.

crypt (kript) n cripta f. **cryptic** adj occulto, misterioso.

crystal ('kristl) n cristallo m. adj di cristallo. **crystallize** vt cristallizzare. vi fossilizzarsi.

cub (kʌb) n cucciolo m.

cube (kju:b) n cubo m. **cubic** adj cubico. **cubicle** n cubicolo m.

cuckoo ('kuku:) n cuculo m.

cucumber ('kju:kʌmbə) n cetriolo m.

cuddle ('kʌdl) vt abbracciare affettuosamente. n abbraccio affettuoso m.

cue[1] (kju:) n spunto m. indicazione f.

cue[2] (kju:) n sport stecca f.

cuff[1] (kʌf) n polsino m. **cufflinks** n pl gemelli da camicia m pl.

cuff[2] (kʌf) vt schiaffeggiare, picchiare. n pugno, schiaffo m.

culinary ('kʌlinri) adj culinario.

culprit ('kʌlprit) n accusato, colpevole m.

cult (kʌlt) n culto m.

cultivate ('kʌltiveit) vt coltivare.

culture ('kʌltʃə) n **1** cultura f. **2** coltivazione f. **cultural** adj culturale. **cultured** adj colto.

cumbersome ('kʌmbəsəm) adj ingombrante, scomodo.

cunning ('kʌniŋ) n furbizia, accortezza f. adj astuto, furbo.

cup (kʌp) n **1** tazza f. **2** sport coppa f. **cupful** n tazza piena f.

cupboard ('kʌbəd) n credenza f.

curate ('kjuərit) n curato m.

curator ('kjuə'reitə) n sovrintendente m,f.

curb (kə:b) n freno m. vt frenare, reprimere.

curdle ('kə:dl) vt agghiacciare. vi rapprendersi, coagularsi.

cure (kjuə) n cura f. rimedio m. vt **1** guarire, sanare. **2** cul salare.

curfew ('kə:fju:) n coprifuoco m.

curious ('kjuəriəs) adj curioso. **curiosity** n curiosità f.

curl (kə:l) n ricciolo m. vt arricciare. vi arrotolarsi. **curly** adj ricciuto.

currant ('kʌrənt) n **1** ribes m. **2** (dried) uva sultanina f.

current ('kʌrənt) n corrente f. adj attuale, in corso. **current account** n conto corrente m. **currency** n valuta, moneta legale f.

curry ('kʌri) n pietanza indiana f. v **curry favour with** cercare di avere il favore di. **curry powder** n curry, polvere di radice di curcuma f.

curse (kə:s) n maledizione, bestemmia f. vt maledire, imprecare. vi bestemmiare.

curt (kə:t) adj brusco, sbrigativo.

curtail (kə:'teil) vt accorciare, restringere.

curtain ('kə:tn) n **1** cortina, tendina f. **2** Th sipario m.

curtsy ('kə:tsi) n inchino m. riverenza f. vi inchinarsi, fare la riverenza.

curve (kə:v) n curva f. diagramma m. vt curvare. vi piegarsi, svoltare.

cushion ('kuʃən) n cuscino m. vt imbottire, ammortizzare.

custard ('kʌstəd) n crema f.

custody ('kʌstədi) n custodia, detenzione f.

custom ('kʌstəm) n **1** usanza, abitudine f. **2**

comm clientela f. **3** pl dogana f. **customs officer** n doganiere m.

customer ('kʌstəmə) n cliente m,f. avventore m.

cut* (kʌt) n **1** taglio m. incisione f. **2** riduzione f. **3** (of clothes) linea f. vt,vi tagliare. vt alzare. **cut down 1** abbattere. **2** ridurre. **cut off** tagliar fuori. **cut out** ritagliare. **cut-price** adj a prezzo ridotto. **cutting** adj **1** tagliente. **2** mordace. n **1** taglio m. **2** ritaglio. m.

cute (kju:t) adj **1** svelto, ingegnoso. **2** grazioso.

cuticle ('kju:tikəl) n cuticola f.

cutlery ('kʌtləri) n posate f pl.

cutlet ('kʌtlit) n cotoletta f.

cycle ('saikəl) n **1** ciclo m. **2** bicicletta f. vi andare in bicicletta.

cyclone ('saikloun) n ciclone m.

cygnet ('signit) n giovane cigno m.

cylinder ('silində) n cilindro m.

cymbal ('simbəl) n cembalo m.

cynic ('sinik) n cinico m. **cynical** adj cinico.

cypress ('saiprəs) n cipresso m.

Cyprus ('saiprəs) n Cipro f. **Cypriot** adj,n cipriota.

czar (zɑ:) n zar m.

Czechoslovakia (tʃekəslə'vækiə) n Cecoslovacchia f. **Czech** adj,n ceco. **Czech** (language) n ceco m.

D

dab (dæb) n colpetto m. macchia f. vt toccare leggermente, cospargere.

dabble ('dæbəl) vt inumidire. vi sguazzare. **dabble in** dilettarsi in.

daddy (dæd) n inf also **dad** babbo, babbino m.

daffodil ('dæfədil) n narciso selvatico m.

daft (dɑ:ft) adj sciocco, matto.

dagger ('dægə) n stiletto, pugnale m.

dahlia ('deiliə) n dalia f.

daily ('deili) adj quotidiano, giornaliero. adv ogni giorno. n giornale, quotidiano m.

dainty ('deinti) adj raffinato, prelibato, grazioso.

dairy ('dɛəri) n latteria f. caseificio m. **dairy farm** n fattoria con cascina f.

daisy ('deizi) n margherita f.

dam (dæm) n diga f. argine m. vt arginare, sbarrare.

damage ('dæmidʒ) n danno, guasto m. vt danneggiare, avariare.

damn (dæm) vt dannare. n un bel niente m. **I**

don't give a damn! non m'importa un fico!
damnable adj 1 maledetto, dannabile. 2
detestabile. **damnation** n dannazione f.

damp (dæmp) adj umido, bagnato. n umidità f.
vapore m. **dampen 1** inumidire. 2 soffocare,
deprimere.

damson ('dæmzən) n prugna damaschina
f. **damson tree** n prugno di Damasco m.

dance (dɑːns) n 1 danza f. 2 ballo m. vi ballare.

dandelion ('dændilaiən) n dente di leone m.

dandruff ('dændrʌf) n forfora f.

Dane (dein) n danese m,f. **Danish** adj danese.
Danish (language) n danese m.

danger ('deindʒə) n pericolo m. **dangerous** adj
pericoloso.

dangle ('dæŋgəl) vt far ciondolare. vi penzolare.

dare (dɛə) vi osare. vt sfidare. **daring** adj
audace, temerario.

dark (dɑːk) adj buio, cupo, scuro. n oscurità f.
buio m. tenebre f pl. **darken** vt scurire,
turbare. vi rabbuiarsi.

darling ('dɑːliŋ) adj caro, amatissimo. n tesoro
m.

darn (dɑːn) vt rammendare. n rammendo m.

dart (dɑːt) 1 dardo m. 2 movimento improvviso
m. vi scagliare, balzare, slanciarsi. **dartboard**
n tirassegno per frecciette m.

dash (dæʃ) n 1 slancio m. 2 spruzzo m. 3
trattino m. vt 1 cozzare. 2 spruzzare. vi 1
slanciarsi. 2 sbattere violentemente. **dashboard** n cruscotto m.

data ('deitə) n pl dati, elementi m pl. **data
processing** n elaborazione di dati f.

date[1] (deit) n 1 data f. 2 inf appuntamento
m. **be up to date 1** essere al corrente. 2
essere aggiornato. **out of date** antiquato.
~vt datare, mettere la data a. **date from**
risalire a.

date[2] (deit) n bot dattero m.

daughter ('dɔːtə) n figlia f. **daughter-in-law** n
nuora f.

dawdle ('dɔːdl) vi bighellonare, oziare.

dawn (dɔːn) n aurora, alba f. vi albeggiare.

day (dei) n giorno m. giornata f. **by day** di
giorno. **day after tomorrow** dopodomani.
day before yesterday l'altroieri. **one day** un
bel giorno. **daybreak** n spuntar del giorno
m. **daydream** n fantasticheria f. sogno ad
occhi aperti m. vi sognare ad occhi aperti.
daylight n luce del giorno f.

daze (deiz) n stupore, sbalordimento m. vt
sbalordire, stupefare.

dazzle ('dæzəl) vt abbagliare. n abbagliamento
m.

dead (ded) adj 1 morto, estinto. 2 spento. 3
sordo. adv assolutamente. **deaden** vt attutire,
affievolire. **deadline** n data di scadenza
f. **deadlock** n punto morto m.

deaf (def) adj sordo. **deaf-aid** n apparecchio
acustico m. **deafen** vt assordare. **deafmute**
n sordomuto m.

deal[*] (diːl) vt 1 trattare. 2 occuparsi. 3 negoziare. vt distribuire. n 1 quantità f. 2 comm
affare m. 3 accordo m. 4 game mano f.

dean (diːn) n 1 educ preside m. 2 rel decano m.

dear (diə) adj 1 caro. 2 costoso.

death (deθ) n morte f. **death certificate** n
certificato di morte m. **death duty** n tana di
successione m. **death rate** n (indice di) mortalità f.

debase (di'beis) vt abbassare, degradare, svalutare.

debate (di'beit) n dibattito m. disputa f. vt,vi
discutere, deliberare.

debit ('debit) n debito m. vt addebitare.

debris ('deibri) n detriti m pl.

debt (det) n debito m. **debtor** n debitore m.

decade ('dekeid) n decennio m.

decadent ('dekədənt) adj decadente.

decant (di'kænt) vt travasare. **decanter** n
caraffa f.

decay (di'kei) n 1 rovina f. deperimento m. 2
putrefazione f. vi decadere, andare in rovina,
deperire.

decease (di'siːs) n decesso m. **deceased** adj,n
defunto.

deceit (di'siːt) n inganno m. frode f. **deceitful**
adj ingannevole, falso.

deceive (di'siːv) vt ingannare. **deceive oneself**
illudersi.

December (di'sembə) n dicembre m.

decent ('diːsənt) adj 1 decente, modesto. 2
onesto.

deceptive (di'septiv) adj ingannevole.

decibel ('desibel) n decibel m.

decide (di'said) vi decidersi. vt decidere.
decided adj deciso, risoluto.

deciduous (di'sidjuəs) adj caduco.

decimal ('desiməl) adj,n decimale f.

decipher (di'saifə) vt decifrare.

decision (di'siʒən) n decisione f. **decisive** adj
decisivo, fermo.

deck (dek) n ponte m. coperta f. vt coprire,
adornare. **deckchair** n sedia a sdraio f.

declare (di'klɛə) vt dichiarare, proclamare. **declaration** n dichiarazione f.

decline (di'klain) vt 1 declinare. 2 rifiutare. vi deperire. n 1 declino m. 2 deperimento m. 3 decadenza f. **declension** n declinazione f.

decorate ('dekəreit) vt decorare, abbellire. **decoration** n decorazione f. ornamento m.

decoy (n 'di:kɔi; v di'kɔi) n 1 trappola f. 2 uccello da richiamo m. vt adescare, abbindolare.

decrease (di'kri:s) n diminuzione f. vt,vi diminuire.

decree (di'kri:) n decreto m.

decrepit (di'krepit) adj decrepito.

dedicate ('dedikeit) vt dedicare. **dedicated** adj dedicato, scrupoloso.

deduce (di'dju:s) vt dedurre.

deduct (di'dʌkt) vt dedurre, sottrarre. **deduction** n sottrazione, deduzione f.

deed (di:d) n 1 atto m. 2 azione f. 3 impresa f.

deep (di:p) adj profondo, alto. n abisso m. adv profondamente. **deepen** vt approfondire. vi approfondirsi. **deep-freeze** n congelatore m. vt surgelare. **deep-seated** adj radicato.

deer (diə) n invar cervo, daino m.

deface (di'feis) vt sfigurare, deturpare, cancellare.

default (di'fɔ:lt) n 1 mancanza f. 2 law contumacia f.

defeat (di'fi:t) n sconfitta, disfatta f. vt sconfiggere.

defect (n 'di:fekt; v di'fekt) n difetto m. mancanza f. vi disertare, defezionare. **defection** n defezione f. abbandono m. **defective** adj difettoso, anormale.

defence (di'fens) n difesa f. **defenceless** adj indifeso. **defend** vt difendere. **defendant** n imputato m.

defer (di'fə:) vt differire, rimandare. **deference** n deferenza f. riguardo m. **deferential** adj deferente.

defiant (di'faiənt) adj ardito, provocante.

deficient (di'fiʃənt) adj deficiente, insufficiente.

deficit ('defisit) n deficit, disavanzo m.

define (di'fain) vt definire, determinare. **definition** n definizione f.

definite ('defənit) adj determinato, preciso. **definitely** adv definitivamente, senz'altro.

deflate (di'fleit) vt 1 sgonfiare. 2 comm deflazionare. vi sgonfiarsi. **deflation** n 1 sgonfiamento m. 2 comm deflazione m.

deform (di'fɔ:m) vt deformare.

defraud (di'frɔ:d) vt defraudare, privare.

defrost (di'frɔst) vt disgelare, sbrinare.

deft (deft) adj abile, destro.

defunct (di'fʌŋkt) adj defunto.

defy (di'fai) vt sfidare. **defiance** n sfida f.

degenerate (v di'dʒenəreit; adj,n di'dʒenərit) vi degenerare. adj,n degenerato.

degrade (di'greid) vt degradare. **degrading** adj avvilente.

degree (di'gri:) n 1 grado, punto m. 2 educ laurea f.

dehydrate (di'haidreit) vt disidratare.

deity ('deiiti) n divinità f.

dejected (di'dʒektid) adj scoraggiato, abbattuto.

delay (di'lei) n ritardo, indugio, rinvio m. vt ritardare. vi indugiare.

delegate (n 'deligət; v 'deligeit) n delegato m. vt delegare.

delete (di'li:t) vt cancellare.

deliberate (adj di'libərət; v di'libəreit) adj ponderato, intenzionale. vt,vi deliberare, riflettere.

delicate ('delikət) adj delicato, sensibile. **delicacy** n 1 delicatezza f. 2 leccornia f.

delicatessen (delikə'tesən) n pizzicheria f.

delicious (di'liʃəs) adj delizioso.

delight (di'lait) n gioia f. entusiasmo m. vt dilettare. **delightful** adj piacevole, simpatico.

delinquency (di'liŋkwənsi) n delinquenza f. delinquente m.

deliver (di'livə) vt 1 distribuire, consegnare. 2 liberare. 3 partorire. 4 (a speech) pronunciare. **delivery** n 1 consegna, distribuzione f. 2 med parto m. 3 dizione f.

delta ('deltə) n delta m.

delude (di'lu:d) vt deludere, illudere.

delve (delv) vi scavare, far ricerche.

demand (di'mɑ:nd) n 1 domanda f. 2 esigenza f. vt 1 richiedere, domandare. 2 esigere.

democracy (di'mɔkrəsi) n democrazia f. **democrat** n democratico m. **democratic** adj democratico.

demolish (di'mɔliʃ) vt demolire. **demolition** n demolizione f.

demon ('di:mən) n demonio m.

demonstrate ('demənstreit) vt dimostrare. vi fare una dimostrazione. **demonstration** n 1 dimostrazione f. 2 pol manifestazione f.

demoralize (di'mɔrəlaiz) vt demoralizzare.

demure (di'mjuə) adj modesto, pudico.

den (den) n covo m. tana f.

denial (di'naiəl) n rifiuto, diniego m.

denim ('denim) n 1 tessuto di cotone m. 2 pl pantaloni, blue-jeans m pl.

Denmark ('denmɑːk) n Danimarca f.

denomination (dinɔmi'neiʃən) n 1 denominazione f. 2 confessione f. 3 comm taglio m. **denominator** n denominatore m.

denote (di'nout) vt denotare, indicare.

denounce (di'nauns) vi denunciare.

dense (dens) adj 1 denso, fitto. 2 inf stupido. **density** n densità f.

dent (dent) n incavo m. ammaccatura f. vt ammaccare, intaccare.

dental ('dentl) adj dentale. **dentist** n dentista m. **dentistry** n odontoiatria f. **denture** n dentiera f.

deny (di'nai) vt negare, smentire.

deodorant (di'oudərənt) n deodorante m.

depart (di'pɑːt) vi 1 partire. 2 deviare. **departure** n partenza f.

department (di'pɑːtmənt) n dipartimento, reparto m. **department store** n grande magazzino m.

depend (di'pend) vi 1 dipendere. 2 fare assegnamento. **dependable** adj fidato, sicuro. **dependant** n dipendente m,f. **dependence** n dipendenza f. **dependent** adj dipendente.

depict (di'pikt) vt descrivere, rappresentare.

deplete (di'pliːt) vt vuotare, esaurire.

deplore (di'plɔː) vt deplorare.

deport (di'pɔːt) vt deportare, esiliare. **deportment** n comportamento m.

depose (di'pouz) vt deporre.

deposit (di'pɔzit) n deposito m. vt depositare, posare.

depot ('depou) n magazzino m.

deprave (di'preiv) vt depravare.

depreciate (di'priːʃieit) vi deprezzarsi.

depress (di'pres) vt deprimere. **depression** n 1 depressione f. avvilimento m. 2 comm depressione f. crisi f invar.

deprive (di'praiv) vt privare.

depth (depθ) n profondità, altezza f.

deputize ('depjutaiz) vi fungere da delegato. **deputation** n deputazione f. **deputy** n deputato, delegato m.

derail (di'reil) vi deragliare. vt far deragliare. **derailment** n deragliamento m.

derelict ('derəlikt) adj derelitto, abbandonato.

deride (di'raid) vt deridere.

derive (di'raiv) vt,vi derivare. vi provenire.

derogatory (di'rɔgətri) adj calunnioso, sprezzante.

178

descend (di'send) vt,vi discendere, scendere. **descendant** n discendente m,f. **descent** n 1 discesa f. 2 discendenza f.

describe (di'skraib) vt descrivere. **description** n descrizione f.

desert[1] ('dezət) n deserto m.

desert[2] (di'zəːt) vt,vi disertare. **deserter** n disertore m. **desertion** n diserzione f. abbandono m.

desert[3] (di'zəːt) n merito m.

deserve (di'zəːv) vt meritare.

design (di'zain) n 1 progetto, disegno m. 2 intento m. vt progettare.

designate ('dezigneit) vt designare.

desire (di'zaiə) n desiderio m. passione f. vt desiderare, augurare.

desk (desk) n scrivania f.

desolate ('desələt) adj desolato, deserto.

despair (di'spɛə) n disperazione f. vi disperare.

desperate ('desprət) adj disperato, accanito.

despise (di'spaiz) vt disprezzare.

despite (di'spait) prep malgrado.

despondent (di'spɔndənt) adj scoraggiato, depresso.

dessert (di'zəːt) n frutta f. dolce m. **dessertspoon** n cucchiaio da dessert m.

destine ('destin) vt destinare. **destination** n destinazione f. **destiny** n destino m.

destitute ('destitjuːt) adj indigente.

destroy (di'strɔi) vt distruggere, abbattere. **destroyer** n naut cacciatorpediniere m.

detach (di'tætʃ) vt staccare, isolare. **detachable** adj staccabile. **detachment** n 1 distacco m. indifferenza f. 2 mil distaccamento m.

detail ('diːteil) n dettaglio, particolare m. vt specificare, dettagliare.

detain (di'tein) vt trattenere, detenere. **detainee** n confinato m.

detect (di'tekt) vt scoprire, scovare, percepire. **detective** n investigatore m. adj poliziesco.

detention (di'tenʃən) n detenzione f. arresto m.

deter (di'təː) vt trattenere, dissuadere. **deterrent** n arma f. freno m.

detergent (di'təːdʒənt) n detergente, detersivo m.

deteriorate (di'tiəriəreit) vi deteriorare, deteriorarsi.

determine (di'təːmin) vt determinare, stabilire. vi decidersi. **determination** n determinazione, risolutezza f.

detest (di'test) *vt* detestare. **detestable** *adj* odioso.

detonate ('detǝneit) *vt,vi* detonare, esplodere.

detour ('di:tuǝ) *n* deviazione, digressione *f*.

detract (di'trækt) *vt* detrarre.

devalue (di'vælju:) *vt* svalutare. **devaluation** *n* svalutazione *f*.

devastate ('devǝsteit) *vt* devastare, rovinare.

develop (di'velǝp) *vt* sviluppare, ampliare. *vi* svilupparsi. **development** *n* sviluppo *m*. crescita *f*.

deviate ('di:vieit) *vi,vt* deviare. **devious** *adj* tortuoso, remoto.

device (di'vais) *n* **1** congegno, dispositivo *m*. **2** mezzo, stratagemma *m*.

devil ('devǝl) *n* diavolo, demonio *m*.

devise (di'vaiz) *vt* escogitare, progettare.

devoid (di'vɔid) *adj* privo.

devote (di'vout) *vt* dedicare, consacrare. **devotee** *n* devoto, fanatico *m*. **devotion** *n* devozione *f*. affetto *m*.

devour (di'vauǝ) *vt* divorare.

devout (di'vaut) *adj* devoto, fervente.

dew (dju:) *n* rugiada *f*.

dexterous ('dekstrǝs) *adj* abile, capace.

diabetes (daiǝ'bi:tiz) *n* diabete *m*.

diagonal (dai'agǝnl) *adj,n* diagonale *m*.

diagram ('daiǝgræm) *n* diagramma *m*.

dial (dail) *n* **1** (of a clock) quadrante *m*. **2** (of a telephone) disco combinatore *m*. *vt* comporre.

dialect ('daiǝlekt) *n* dialetto *m*.

dialogue ('daiǝlog) *n* dialogo *m*.

diameter (dai'æmitǝ) *n* diametro *m*.

diamond ('daiǝmǝnd) *n* diamante *m*.

diaphragm ('daiǝfræm) *n* diaframma *m*.

diarrhoea (daiǝ'riǝ) *n* diarrea *f*.

diary ('daiǝri) *n* diario *m*.

dice (dais) *n pl* dadi *m pl*. *vt* tagliare a cubetti.

dictate (dik'teit) *vt,vi* dettare. **dictation** *n* dettato *m*. **dictator** *n* dittatore *m*. **dictatorship** *n* dittatura *f*.

dictionary ('dikʃǝnri) *n* dizionario *m*.

did (did) *v* see **do**.

die (dai) *vi* morire.

diesel ('di:zǝl) *n* diesel *m*.

diet ('daiǝt) *n* **1** dieta *f*. **2** alimentazione *f*. *vi* essere a dieta.

differ ('difǝ) *vi* **1** dissentire. **2** essere diverso.

difference ('difrǝns) *n* **1** differenza *f*. **2** divergenza *f*. **different** *adj* differente. **differential** *adj,n* differenziale *m*. **differentiate** *vt* differenziare.

difficult ('difikǝlt) *adj* difficile. **difficulty** *n* difficoltà *f*.

dig* (dig) *vt,vi* scavare. *n* **1** vangata *f*. **2** urto *m*. **3** scavi *m pl*. **4** *pl* camera, ammobiliata *f*.

digest (dai'dʒest) *vt,vi* digerire. **digestible** *adj* digeribile. **digestion** *n* digestione *f*.

digit ('didʒit) *n* numero semplice *m*. cifra *f*. **digital** *adj* digitale.

dignity ('digniti) *n* dignità *f*. **dignified** *adj* dignitoso, nobile.

dilapidated (di'læpideitid) *adj* decrepito, in rovina.

dilemma (di'lemǝ) *n* dilemma *m*.

diligent ('dilidʒǝnt) *adj* diligente.

dilute (dai'lu:t) *vt* diluire.

dim (dim) *adj* pallido, vago, ottuso. *vt* smorzare, offuscare. *vi* oscurarsi, indebolirsi.

dimension (di'menʃǝn) *n* dimensione *f*.

diminish (di'miniʃ) *vt* diminuire, ridurre. *vi* ridursi.

diminutive (di'minjutiv) *adj,n* diminutivo *m*.

dimple ('dimpǝl) *n* fossetta *f*.

din (din) *n* rumore assordante, fracasso *m*.

dine (dain) *vi* pranzare. **dining car** *n* carrozza ristorante *f*. **dining room** *n* sala da pranzo *f*.

dinghy ('dingi) *n* lancia, barchetta *f*.

dingy ('dindʒi) *adj* scuro, sbiadito, sporco.

dinner ('dinǝ) *n* pranzo, desinare *m*. cena *f*. **dinner jacket** *n* smoking *m*.

dinosaur ('dainɔsɔ:) *n* dinosauro *m*.

diocese ('daiǝsis) *n* diocesi *f invar*.

dip (dip) *vt* **1** immergere, intingere, tuffare. **2** abbassare. *vi* **1** immergersi. **2** abbassarsi. *n* **1** immersione *f*. tuffo *m*. **2** pendenza *f*.

diphthong ('difθɔŋ) *n* dittongo *m*.

diploma (di'ploumǝ) *n* diploma *m*.

diplomacy (di'ploumǝsi) *n* diplomazia *f*. **diplomat** ('diplǝmæt) *n* diplomatico *m*. **diplomatic** *adj* diplomatico.

direct (di'rekt) *vt* **1** dirigere. **2** indirizzare. **3** ordinare. *adj*. **1** diretto. **2** sincero. **direction** *n* **1** direzione *f*. senso *m*. **2** istruzione *f*. **director** *n* **1** direttore *m*. **2** *Th* regista *m*. **directory** *n* elenco telefonico *m*. guida *f*.

dirt (dǝ:t) *n* sporcizia, immondizia *f*. **dirty** *adj* sporco, sudicio. *vt* insudiciare, sporcare.

disability (disǝ'biliti) *n* incapacità, impotenza *f*. **disabled** *adj* invalido *m*.

disadvantage (disǝd'va:ntidʒ) *n* svantaggio *m*. **disadvantageous** *adj* svantaggioso.

disagree (disǝ'gri:) *vi* **1** non andar d'accordo.

differire. **2** far male. **disagreeable** adj sgradevole.

disappear (disə'piə) vi sparire. **disappearance** n scomparsa f.

disappoint ('disə'pɔint) vt deludere. **disappointment** n delusione f.

disapprove (disə'pru:v) vt,vi disapprovare. **disapproval** n disapprovazione f.

disarm (dis'ɑ:m) vt disarmare. **disarmament** n disarmo m.

disaster (di'zɑ:stə) n disastro m. catastrofe f. **disastrous** adj disastroso.

disc (disk) n disco m. **disc jockey** n presentatore radiofonico di dischi m.

discard (di'skɑ:d) vt scartare, abbandonare.

discern (di'sə:n) vt percepire, scorgere. **discernment** n discernimento, acume m.

discharge (dis'tʃɑ:dʒ) vt **1** scaricare. **2** congedare. **3** assolvere, liberare. n **1** scarico m. **2** mil congedo m. **3** law assoluzione f.

disciple (di'saipəl) n discepolo m.

discipline ('disəplin) n disciplina f.

disclose (dis'klouz) vt rivelare, svelare.

discomfort (dis'kʌmfət) n disagio m. vt mettere a disagio.

disconnect (diskə'nekt) vt **1** sconnettere. **2** tech disinnestare.

disconsolate (dis'kɔnsələt) adj sconsolato.

discontinue (diskən'tinju:) vt,vi cessare.

discord ('diskɔ:d) n discordia, disarmonia f.

discotheque ('diskətek) n discoteca f.

discount (n 'diskaunt; v dis'kaunt) n sconto m. riduzione f. vt scontare, ribassare.

discourage (dis'kʌridʒ) vt scoraggiare, dissuadere. **discouragement** n scoraggiamento m.

discover (dis'kʌvə) vt scoprire. **discovery** n scoperta f.

discredit (dis'kredit) vt screditare.

discreet (dis'kri:t) adj prudente, riservato.

discrepancy (dis'krepənsi) n contraddizione f. divario m. **discretion** n discrezione f. discernimento m.

discrete (dis'kri:t) adj separato, distinto.

discriminate (dis'krimineit) vt,vi discriminare, distinguere. **discrimination** n **1** discriminazione f. **2** discernimento m.

discus ('diskəs) n, pl **discuses** disco m.

discuss (dis'kʌs) vt discutere. **discussion** n discussione f.

disease (di'zi:z) n malattia f.

disembark (disim'bɑ:k) vi sbarcare.

disengage (disin'geidʒ) vt disimpegnare, disinnestare.

disfigure (dis'figə) vt deturpare, sfigurare.

disgrace (dis'greis) n disonore m. vergogna f. disonorare, destituire.

disgruntled (dis'grʌntəld) adj di cattivo umore, scontento.

disguise (dis'gaiz) vt travestire, dissimulare. n **1** travestimento m. **2** finzione f.

disgust (dis'gʌst) n disgusto m. nausea f. vt disgustare.

dish (diʃ) n **1** piatto m. **2** cul pietanza f. vt scodellare, servire. **dishcloth** n strofinaccio per i piatti m.

dishearten (dis'hɑ:tn) vt scoraggiare.

dishevelled (di'ʃevəld) adj arruffato.

dishonest (dis'ɔnist) adj disonesto. **dishonesty** n disonestà f.

dishonour (dis'ɔnə) n disonore m. vt disonorare.

disillusion (disi'lu:ʒən) n disinganno m. vt disilludere.

disinfect (disin'fekt) vt disinfettare. **disinfectant** adj,n disinfettante m.

disinherit (disin'herit) vt diseredare.

disintegrate (dis'intigreit) vt disintegrare. vi disgregarsi.

disinterested (dis'intrəstid) adj disinteressato.

disjointed (dis'dʒɔintid) adj disgiunto, sconnesso.

dislike (dis'laik) vt non piacere. n antipatia, avversione f.

dislocate ('disləkeit) vt slogare, spostare.

dislodge (dis'lɔdʒ) vt sloggiare, scacciare.

disloyal (dis'lɔiəl) adj sleale.

dismal ('dizməl) adj tetro, cupo, lugubre.

dismantle (dis'mæntl) vt smantellare, demolire.

dismay (dismei) n sgomento m. vt costernare, spaventare.

dismiss (dis'mis) vt **1** licenziare, mandar via. **2** respingere. **dismissal** n **1** licenziamento m. **2** congedo m.

dismount (dis'maunt) vi scendere. vt smontare.

disobey (disə'bei) vt disubbidire a. **disobedient** adj disubbidiente. **disobedience** n disubbidienza f.

disorder (dis'ɔ:də) n **1** disordine m. **2** med disturbo m.

disorganized (dis'ɔ:gənaizd) adj disorganizzato.

disown (dis'oun) vt smentire, rinnegare.

disparage (dis'pæridʒ) vt sottovalutare, disprezzare. **disparaging** adj sprezzante, spregiativo.

dispassionate (dis'pæ∫ənət) adj calmo, spassionato.

dispatch (dis'pæt∫) vt spedire, inviare, sbrigare. n 1 spedizione f. 2 dispaccio m. 3 prontezza f.

dispel (dis'pel) vt dissipare, disperdere.

dispense (dis'pens) vt dispensare, distribuire. **dispense with** fare a meno di. **dispensary** n dispensario m.

disperse (dis'pə:s) vt disperdere, sparpagliare. vi disperdersi.

displace (dis'pleis) vt spostare, soppiantare. **displacement** n 1 spostamento m. 2 naut dislocamento m.

display (dis'plei) n 1 mostra f. 2 ostentazione f. vt mostrare, ostentare, rivelare.

displease (dis'pli:z) vt dispiacere a, offendere.

dispose (dis'pouz) vt disporre. **dispose of** liberarsi di, eliminare. **disposal** n disposizione f. **disposition** n disposizione f. carattere m.

disprove (dis'pru:v) vt confutare, contraddire.

dispute (dis'pju:t) n disputa, vertenza f. vt contestare. vi discutere.

disqualify (dis'kwɔlifai) vt sport squalificare. **disqualification** n squalifica f.

disregard (disri'gɑ:d) n noncuranza f. disprezzo m. vt ignorare, trascurare.

disreputable (dis'repjutəbəl) adj indecoroso, di cattiva fama.

disrespect (disri'spekt) n mancanza di rispetto f.

disrupt (dis'rʌpt) vt 1 mettere in confusione. 2 rompere, spaccare. **disruption** n disordine m.

dissatisfy (di'sætisfai) vt scontentare, deludere. **dissatisfaction** n scontento m.

dissect (di'sekt) vt sezionare, analizzare. **dissection** n sezionamento m.

dissent (di'sent) n dissenso m. vi dissentire.

dissimilar (di'similə) adj diverso.

dissociate (di'souʃieit) vt dissociare, separare.

dissolve (di'zɔlv) vt dissolvere. vi sciogliersi.

dissuade (di'sweid) vt dissuadere.

distance (distəns) n distanza f.

distant ('distnt) adj 1 distante, lontano. 2 vago, riservato.

distaste (dis'teist) n ripugnanza f.

distil (dis'til) vt stillare, distillare.

distinct (dis'tiŋkt) adj 1 distinto, chiaro. 2 diverso. **distinction** n distinzione f. **distinctive** adj caratteristico.

distinguish (dis'tiŋgwiʃ) vt distinguere. **distinguished** adj distinto, illustre.

distort (dis'tɔ:t) vt distorcere, alterare.

distract (dis'trækt) vt 1 distrarre. 2 turbare. **distraction** n 1 distrazione f. 2 svago m. 3 follia f.

distraught (dis'trɔ:t) adj turbato, pazzo.

distress (dis'tres) n 1 dolore m. angoscia f. 2 miseria f. vt affliggere, tormentare.

distribute (dis'tribju:t) vt distribuire. **distribution** n distribuzione f.

district ('distrikt) n distretto, quartiere m.

distrust (dis'trʌst) n diffidenza f. sospetto m. vt non aver fiducia in.

disturb (dis'tə:b) vt disturbare. **disturbance** n perturbazione f. tumulto m.

ditch (ditʃ) n fossato m. vt inf piantare in asso.

ditto ('ditou) n idem, lo stesso m.

divan (di'væn) n divano m.

dive (daiv) n tuffo m. immersione f. vi tuffarsi, immergersi. **diving board** n trampolino m.

diverge (dai'və:dʒ) vi divergere.

diverse (dai'və:s) adj 1 differente. 2 vario.

diversify (di'və:rsifai) vt differenziare.

divert (dai'və:t) vt 1 deviare, sviare. 2 divertire. **diversion** n 1 diversione f. 2 diversivo m.

divide (di'vaid) vt dividere. vi separarsi. **divisible** adj divisibile. **division** n divisione f.

dividend ('dividend) n dividendo m.

divine (di'vain) adj divino. **divinity** n divinità f.

divorce (di'vɔ:s) n divorzio m. vt 1 divorziare. 2 separare.

divulge (di'vʌldʒ) vt divulgare.

dizzy ('dizi) adj 1 stordito, che ha il capogiro. **dizziness** n vertigine f.

do* (du:) vt fare, compiere. vi 1 bastare. 2 andare bene. 3 agire. **do one's utmost** fare tutto il possibile. **do up** abbottonare. **do without** fare a meno.

docile ('dousail) adj docile.

dock[1] (dɔk) n naut molo, bacino, portuario m. vi attraccare. **dockyard** n arsenale m.

dock[2] (dɔk) n (tail) troncone m. vt mozzare, ridurre.

dock[3] (dɔk) n law banco degli imputati m.

doctor ('dɔktə) n dottore, medico m.

doctrine ('dɔktrin) n dottrina f.

document ('dɔkjumənt) n documento m. vt documentare. **documentary** adj,n documentario m.

dodge (dɔdʒ) vt schivare, eludere. vi scansarsi. n 1 sotterfugio m. 2 schivata f.

dog (dɔg) n cane m. vt pedinare. **dog-collar** n 1 collare per cani m. 2 inf collarino m. **dogged** adj ostinato.

dogma ('dɔgmə) n dogma m. **dogmatic** adj dogmatico.

dole (doul) n sussidio m. distribuzione f. **go on the dole** ricevere il sussidio per disoccupati. v **dole out** distribuire.

doll (dɔl) n bambola f.

dollar ('dɔlə) n dollaro m.

Dolomites ('dɔləmaits) n pl Dolomiti f pl.

dolphin ('dɔlfin) n delfino m.

domain (də'mein) n dominio m. proprietà f.

dome (doum) n cupola f.

domestic (də'mestik) adj domestico, casalingo. **domesticate** vt addomesticare.

dominate ('dɔmineit) vt,vi dominare. **dominant** adj dominante. **domineer** vi tiranneggiare.

dominion (də'miniən) n dominio m.

donate (dou'neit) vt donare. **donation** n 1 dono m. 2 pl carità f.

done (dʌn) v see **do**.

donkey ('dɔŋki) n asino m.

donor ('dounə) n donatore m. donatrice f.

doom (du:m) n destino m. sorte, distruzione, morte f. **doomsday** n giorno del giudizio m.

door (dɔ:) n porta f. **doorbell** n campanello m. **doorhandle** n maniglia della porta f. **doorknob** n pomo della porta m. **doorknocker** n battente m. **doormat** n zerbino m. **doorstep** n gradino della porta m. **doorway** n soglia, entrata f.

dope (doup) n sl stupefacente m. vt sl narcotizzare, drogare.

dormant ('dɔ:mənt) adj dormiente, sopito, latente.

dormitory ('dɔ:mitri) n dormitorio m.

dormouse ('dɔ:maus) n ghiro m.

dose (dous) n dose f. vt somministrare a dosi, dosare. **dosage** n dosaggio m.

dot (dɔt) n punto, puntino m. **on the dot** in punto. ~vt mettere il punto su, punteggiare.

dote (dout) vi **dote on** essere infatuato di.

double ('dʌbəl) adj doppio. n 1 doppio m. 2 sosia m,f invar. adv due volte tanto, in coppia. vt raddoppiare, doppiare. vi piegarsi. **double bass** n contrabbasso m. **double-cross** vt tradire. **double-decker bus** n autobus a due piani m invar. **double-dutch** n lingua incomprensibile f. **double glazing** n vetro doppio m.

doubt (daut) n dubbio m. incertezza f. vt dubitare di. vi dubitare. **doubtful** adj ambiguo, incerto.

dough (dou) n pasta f. **doughnut** n ciambella f.

dove (dʌv) n colomba f. **dovecote** n colombaia f.

dowdy ('daudi) adj sciatto, vestito male.

down[1] (daun) adv giù, in basso, di sotto. adj abbattuto, depresso. prep giù per. vt 1 abbattere. 2 inf tracannare.

down[2] (daun) n (soft fur etc.) lanugine f.

downcast ('daunka:st) adj scoraggiato, abbattuto.

downfall ('daunfɔ:l) n caduta, rovina f.

downhearted (daun'ha:tid) adj depresso.

downhill ('daunhil) adj discendente. adv in pendio.

downpour ('daunpɔ:) n acquazzone m.

downright ('daunrait) adj vero, sincero. adv assolutamente.

downstairs (daun'stɛəz) adj di sotto. adv dabbasso. n pianterreno m.

downstream (daun'stri:m) adv seguendo la corrente.

downtrodden ('dauntrɔdn) adj calpestato, oppresso.

downward ('daunwəd) adj discendente. **downwards** adv dall'alto al basso, verso il basso.

dowry ('dauəri) n dote f.

doze (douz) n sonnellino m. vi sonnecchiare. **doze off** assopirsi.

dozen ('dʌzən) n dozzina f.

drab (dræb) adj sbiadito, scialbo.

draft (dra:ft) n 1 abbozzo m. 2 comm assegno m. 3 mil leva f. vt 1 redigere. 2 mil arruolare.

drag (dræg) vt 1 trascinare. 2 naut dragare. vi trascinarsi. **drag on** prolungarsi.

dragon ('drægən) n drago m. **dragonfly** n libellula f.

drain (drein) n canale, tubo di scarico m. vt prosciugare, drenare. vi defluire, prosciugarsi. **drainage** n fognatura f. drenaggio m. **draining board** n scolatoio m. **drainpipe** n tubo di scarico m.

drake (dreik) n anitra maschio m.

dram (dræm) n 1 (weight) dramma f. 2 sorso m.

drama ('dra:mə) n dramma m. arte drammatica f. **dramatic** adj drammatico. **dramatist** n drammaturgo m. **dramatize** vt drammatizzare, mettere in forma drammatica.

drank (dræŋk) v see **drink**.

drape (dreip) vt drappeggiare.

draper ('dreipə) n' negoziante di tessuti m. **drapery** n tendaggio m. tessuti m pl.

drastic ('dræstik) adj drastico.

draught (dra:ft) n **1** corrente d'aria f. **2** sorso m. **draughtsman** n disegnatore m.

draw* (drɔ:) vt **1** tirare, attirare, estrarre. **2** disegnare. **draw near** avvicinarsi. ~n **1** tirata f. **2** sport pareggio m. **3** estrazione f. **4** attrazione f. **drawback** n inconveniente, ostacolo m. **drawbridge** n ponte levatoio m. **drawer** n cassetto m. **drawing** n disegno m. **drawing pin** n puntina da disegno f. **drawing room** n salotto m.

drawl (drɔ:l) vt,vi strascicare.

dread (dred) n timore m. adj terribile. vt temere, aver paura di. **dreadful** adj spaventoso, terribile.

dream* (dri:m) n sogno m. vt,vi sognare.

dreary ('driəri) adj triste, cupo.

dredge (dredʒ) vt dragare. **dredger** n draga f.

dregs (dregz) n pl feccia f. scorie f pl.

drench (drentʃ) vt inzuppare, bagnare.

dress (dres) vt **1** vestire. **2** med bendare. **3** cul condire. vi abbigliarsi. **1** abito m. **2** vestito m. **dress circle** n Th prima galleria f. **dressmaker** n sarta da donna f. **dress rehearsal** n prova generale f. **dressing** n **1** med medicazione, benda f. **2** cul condimento m. **dressing-gown** n vestaglia f. **dressing-room** n spogliatoio, camerino m. **dressing-table** n tavola da toletta f.

dresser[1] ('dresə) n Th guardarobiere m.

dresser[2] ('dresə) n credenza f.

drew (dru:) v see **draw**.

dribble ('dribəl) n gocciolamento m. vi gocciolare, sbavare.

drier ('draiə) n essiccatore m.

drift (drift) n **1** spinta f. **2** corrente f. **3** deriva f. **4** (of snow) monticello m. vi andare alla deriva.

drill (dril) n **1** tech trapano m. **2** mil esercitazione f. vt **1** tech trapanare. **2** mil addestrare.

drink* (driŋk) vt,vi bere. n bevanda f. **drinking water** n acqua potabile f.

drip (drip) n gocciolare. n sgocciolio m. **drip-dry** adj che s'asciuga rapidamente e non si stira. **dripping** adj gocciolante. n **1** cul grasso colato m. **2** sgocciolio m.

drive* (draiv) n **1** corsa f. **2** viale m. **3** impulso m. vt,vi **1** guidare, condurre. **2** spingere. vi guidare. **drive away** scacciare. **drive mad**

far impazzire. **drive off** partire. **driver** n guidatore, autista m. **driving licence** n patente automobilistica f. **driving school** n scuola guida f. **driving test** n esame di guida m.

drivel ('drivəl) vi **1** sbavare. **2** dire sciocchezze. n **1** bava f. **2** stupidaggini f pl.

drizzle ('drizəl) vi piovigginare. n pioggerella f.

dromedary ('drʌmədəri) n dromedario m.

drone[1] (droun) n zool fuco m.

drone[2] (droun) vi ronzare. n ronzio m.

droop (dru:p) vi curvarsi, languire, afflosciarsi. **drooping** adj pendente, abbattuto.

drop (drɔp) n **1** goccio m. goccia f. **2** dislivello m. **3** abbassamento m. **4** pastiglia f. vt lasciar cadere. vi **1** cadere. **2** diminuire. **drop out** sparire, ritirarsi. **drop-out** n persona emarginata dalla società f.

drought (draut) n siccità f.

drove[1] (drouv) v see **drive**.

drove[2] (drouv) n mandria f. gregge m.

drown (draun) vt,vi annegare, affogare.

drowsy (drauzi) adj sonnolento.

drudge (drʌdʒ) n sgobbone, schiavo m. vi sfacchinare. **drudgery** n lavoro faticoso e monotono m.

drug (drʌg) n **1** droga f. stupefacente m. **2** prodotto chimico m. vt narcotizzare, drogare. **drug addict** n morfinomane m,f.

drum (drʌm) n **1** tamburo m. **2** tech rullo m. **3** anat timpano m. vi suonare il tamburo. vt tamburellare.

drunk (drʌŋk) v see **drink**. adj,n ubriaco. **drunken** adj ebbro, ubriaco.

dry (drai) adj **1** secco, arido. **2** monotono. vt seccare. vi asciugarsi. **dry-clean** vt lavare a secco. **dry-cleaning** n lavaggio a secco m.

dual ('djuəl) adj doppio, duplice. **dual carriageway** n strada a doppia carreggiata f.

dubious ('dju:biəs) adj dubbio, esitante.

duchess ('dʌtʃis) n duchessa f.

duck[1] (dʌk) n anitra f. **duckling** n anatroccolo m.

duck[2] (dʌk) n **1** tuffo m. immersione f. **2** colpo m. vi **1** immergersi. **2** chinarsi di colpo. vt **1** tuffare. **2** chinare.

duct (dʌkt) n **1** condotto, canale m. **2** anat vaso m.

dud (dʌd) adj inutile, falso. n proiettile che non esplode m.

due (dju:) adj **1** dovuto, adatto. **2** scaduto. **3**

atteso. **be due to** essere causato da. ~n spettanza f. debito m.

duel ('djuəl) n duello m.

duet (dju'et) n duetto m.

dug (dʌg) v see **dig.**

duke (dju:k) n duca m.

dulcimer ('dʌlsimə) n salterio m.

dull (dʌl) adj 1 tardo, lento. 2 sordo. 3 monotono. 4 cupo. vt 1 istupidire, intorpidire. 2 smussare. 3 offuscare. **dullness** n 1 stupidità, lentezza f. 2 monotonia f.

dumb (dʌm) adj 1 muto, reticente. 2 sciocco. **dumbfound** vt sbalordire, confondere.

dummy ('dʌmi) adj muto, falso. n 1 fantoccio m. 2 game morto m.

dump (dʌmp) n 1 mucchio, deposito m. 2 luogo di scarico m. vt scaricare, ammassare.

dumpling ('dʌmpliŋ) n gnocco m.

dunce (dʌns) n inf ignorante m,f. asino m.

dune (dju:n) n duna f.

dung (dʌŋ) n sterco, letame m.

dungeon ('dʌndʒən) n cella sotterranea f.

duplicate (adj,n 'dju:plikət; v 'dju:plikeit) adj doppio. n duplicato m. vt duplicare.

durable ('djuərəbəl) adj durevole.

duration (djuə'reiʃən) n durata f.

during ('djuəriŋ) prep durante.

dusk (dʌsk) n crepuscolo m.

dust (dʌst) n polvere f. vt 1 impolverare. 2 spolverare. **dustbin** n pattumiera f. **duster** n spolverino m. **dustman** n netturbino m. **dustpan** n paletta per la spazzatura f.

Dutch (dʌtʃ) adj olandese. **go Dutch** pagare alla romana. **Dutch** (language) n olandese m. **Dutchman** n olandese m.

duty ('dju:ti) n 1 dovere, obbligo m. 2 comm dazio m. imposta f. **be on/off duty** essere in/fuori servizio. **duty-free** adj esente da dogana. **dutiful** adj rispettoso, obbediente.

duvet ('du:vei) n coperta imbottita con piume f.

dwarf (dwɔ:f) n nano m. vt rimpicciolire.

dwell* (dwel) vi 1 dimorare. 2 soffermarsi, restare. **dwelling** n abitazione, dimora f.

dwindle ('dwindl) vi diminuire, consumarsi.

dye (dai) n tintura f. colorante m. vt tingere. vi tingersi.

dyke (daik) n diga f. argine m.

dynamic (dai'næmik) adj dinamico. **dynamics** n dinamica f.

dynamite ('dainəmait) n dinamite f.

dynasty ('dinəsti) n dinastia f.

dysentery ('disəntri) n dissenteria f.

dyslexia (dis'leksiə) n dislessia f.

E

each (i:tʃ) adj ogni, ciascuno. pron ognuno. **each other** l'un l'altro, reciprocamente.

eager ('i:gə) adj ardente, avido, impaziente. **eagerness** n brama, impazienza f.

eagle ('i:gəl) n aquila f.

ear [1] (iə) n anat orecchio m. **turn a deaf ear** fare orecchi da mercante. **earache** n mal d'orecchi m. **eardrum** n timpano m. **earmark** n marchio di riconoscimento m. vt assegnare. **earring** n orecchino m.

ear [2] (iə) n bot spiga f.

earl (ə:l) n conte m. **earldom** n contea f.

early ('ə:li) adv presto, di buon'ora. adj 1 primo. 2 mattiniero. 3 precoce.

earn (ə:n) vt guadagnare, meritarsi. **earnings** n pl guadagni m pl. stipendio m.

earnest ('ə:nist) adj serio, zelante. **in earnest** sul serio.

earth (ə:θ) n 1 terra f. mondo m. 2 terreno m. **earthenware** n terraglia f. **earthly** adj terrestre, terreno. **earthquake** n terremoto m. **earthworm** n lombrico m.

earwig ('iəwig) n forfecchia f.

ease (i:z) n 1 agio, comodo m. 2 riposo m. vt alleviare, calmare. vi attenuarsi. **easy** adj 1 facile, agevole. 2 disinvolto. adv facilmente, piano. **easygoing** adj facilone, poco esigente.

easel ('i:zəl) n cavalletto m.

east (i:st) n est, oriente m. adj d'est, orientale. **easterly** adj d'est, orientale. **eastern** adj orientale.

Easter ('i:stə) n Pasqua f.

eat* (i:t) vt,vi 1 mangiare. 2 corrodere.

eavesdrop ('i:vzdrɔp) vi origliare.

ebb (eb) n 1 riflusso m. 2 declino m. vi rifluire, abbassarsi.

ebony ('ebəni) n ebano m. adj d'ebano, nero.

eccentric (ik'sentrik) adj,n eccentrico.

ecclesiastical (ikli:zi'æstikəl) adj ecclesiastico.

echo ('ekou) n, pl **echoes** eco f, pl echi m. vi echeggiare. vt ripetere.

eclair (ei'klɛə) n bignè m. pasta al cioccolato f.

eclipse (i'klips) n eclissi f. vt eclissare.

ecology (i:'kɔlədʒi) n ecologia f.

economy (i'kɔnəmi) n economia f. **economic** adj economico. **economics** n scienze economiche f pl. economia f. **economical** adj economico, parsimonioso. **economize** vi economizzare.

ecstasy ('ekstəsi) n ectasi f invar.

eczema ('eksimə) n eczema m.

edge (edʒ) n 1 orlo, margine m. 2 (of a blade) filo m. 3 sponda f. **be on edge** avere i nervi tesi. ~vt bordare, rasentare. **edge one's way** farsi strada.

edible ('edibəl) adj commestibile.

Edinburgh ('edinbərə) n Edimburgo f.

edit ('edit) vt 1 redigere, corare. 2 dirigere. **editor** n redattore, direttore m. **editorial** adj editoriale. n articolo di fondo m.

edition (i'diʃən) n edizione f.

educate ('edjukeit) vt educare, istruire. **educated** adj istruito, colto. **education** n istruzione, pedagogia f. **educational** adj pedagogico, della scuola.

eel (i:l) n anguilla f.

eerie ('iəri) adj strano, misterioso.

effect (i'fekt) n 1 risultato m. consequenza f. 2 pl effetti personali m pl. vt compiere, eseguire. **effective** adj efficace.

effeminate (i'feminət) adj effeminato.

effervesce (efə'ves) vi essere effervescente.

efficient (i'fiʃənt) adj efficiente, abile.

effigy ('efidʒi) n effigie f.

effort ('efət) n sforzo m. **effortless** adj senza sforzo.

egg[1] (eg) n 1 uovo m, pl uova f. **eggcup** n portauovo m. **eggshell** n guscio d'uovo m. **eggwhisk** n frullino m.

egg[2] (eg) vt **egg on** incitare, istigare.

ego ('i:gou) n ego m. **egocentric** adj egocentrico. **egoism** n egoismo m. **egotism** n egotismo m.

Egypt ('i:dʒipt) n Egitto m. **Egyptian** adj,n egiziano.

eiderdown ('aidədaun) n piumino m.

eight (eit) adj,n otto m. **eighth** adj ottavo.

eighteen (ei'ti:n) adj,n diciotto.m or f. **eighteenth** adj diciottesimo.

eighty ('eiti) adj. ottanta m. **eightieth** adj ottantesimo.

either ('aiðə) adj,pron 1 l'uno o l'altro. 2 tutti e due. adv nemmeno. **either...or** o...o.

ejaculate (i'dʒækjuleit) vt 1 esclamare. 2 eiaculare. **ejaculation** n 1 esclamazione f. 2 emissione f.

eject (i'dʒekt) vt espellere, emettere. **ejection** n 1 espulsione f. 2 tech eiezione f.

eke (i:k) vt **eke out** aggiungere a, accrescere.

elaborate (adj i'læbrət; v i'læbəreit) adj elaborato, minuzioso. vt elaborare.

elapse (i'læps) vi trascorrere.

elastic (i'læstik) adj,n elastico m. **elastic band** n elastico m.

elated (i'leitid) adj esaltato, esultante.

elbow ('elbou) n gomito m.

elder[1] ('eldə) adj maggiore, più vecchio. n maggiore m,f. **elderly** adj anziano.

elder[2] ('eldə) n bot sambuco m. **elderberry** n bacca del sambuco f.

eldest ('eldist) adj primogenito, maggiore.

elect (i'lekt) vt eleggere, designare, scegliere. adj scelto, eletto. **election** n elezione f. **electorate** n elettorato m.

electricity (ilek'trisiti) n elettricità f. **electric** adj elettrico. **electrician** n elettricista m. **electrify** vt 1 elettrificare. 2 elettrizzare. **electrocute** vt fulminare con l'elettricità. **electrode** n elettrodo m. **electron** n elettrone m. **electronic** adj elettronico. **electronics** n elettronica f.

elegant ('eligənt) adj elegante. **elegance** n eleganza f.

element ('eləmənt) n elemento, fattore m. **elemental** adj degli elementi, essenziale. **elementary** adj elementare, schematico.

elephant ('eləfənt) n elefante m.

elevate ('eləveit) vt innalzare, esaltare. **elevation** n elevazione, altezza f. **elevator** n ascensore, elevatore m.

eleven (i'levən) adj,n undici m or f. **eleventh** adj undicesimo.

elf (elf) n folletto m.

eligible ('elidʒəbəl) adj eleggibile, accettabile.

eliminate (i'limineit) vt 1 eliminare. 2 scartare.

elite (ei'li:t) n elite f. fior fiore della società m.

ellipse (i'lips) n ellisse f.

elm (elm) n olmo m.

elocution (elə'kju:ʃən) n elocuzione f.

elope (i'loup) vi fuggire. **elopement** n fuga f.

eloquent ('eləkwənt) adj eloquente.

else (els) adv 1 altro. 2 altrimenti, oppure. **elsewhere** adv altrove.

elucidate (i'lu:sideit) vt spiegare, chiarire.

elude (i'lu:d) vt eludere, schivare.

emaciate (i'meisieit) vt emaciare. **emaciated** adj emaciato.

emanate ('eməneit) vi emanare, provenire.

emancipate (i'mænsipeit) vt emancipare. **emancipation** n emancipazione f.

embalm (im'ba:m) vt imbalsamare.

embankment (im'bæŋkmənt) *n* argine *m*.

embargo (im'bɑːgou) *n*, *pl* **-goes** embargo *m*. proibizione *f*.

embark (im'bɑːk) *vt* imbarcare. *vi* imbarcarsi.

embarrass (im'bærəs) *vt* mettere in imbarazzo. **embarrassing** *adj* imbarazzante. **embarrassment** *n* imbarazzo *m*.

embassy ('embəsi) *n* ambasciata *f*.

embellish (im'beliʃ) *vt* abbellire, ornare.

ember ('embə) *n* 1 tizzone *m*. 2 *pl* brace *f*.

embezzle (im'bezəl) *vt* appropriarsi indebitamente di. **embezzlement** *n* appropriazione fraudolenta *f*.

embitter (im'bitə) *vt* amareggiare.

emblem ('embləm) *n* emblema *m*.

embody (im'bɔdi) *vt* 1 incarnare, personificare. 2 includere.

emboss (im'bɔs) *vt* scolpire in rilievo.

embrace (im'breis) *vt* abbracciare. *vi* abbracciarsi. *n* abbraccio *m*.

embroider (im'brɔidə) *vt* ricamare. **embroidery** *n* ricamo *m*.

embryo ('embriou) *n* embrione *m*.

emerald ('emrəld) *n* smeraldo *m*.

emerge (i'məːdʒ) *vi* emergere, affiorare.

emergency (i'məːdʒənsi) *n* emergenza *f*. **emergency exit** *n* uscita di sicurezza *f*.

emigrate ('emigreit) *vi* emigrare.

eminent ('eminənt) *adj* eminente.

emit (i'mit) *vt* emettere, emanare.

emotion (i'mouʃən) *n* emozione *f*. sentimento *m*. **emotional** *adj* emotivo, commovente.

empathy ('empəθi) *n* empatia *f*.

emperor ('empərə) *n* imperatore *m*.

emphasis ('emfəsis) *n*, *pl* **-ses** rilievo *m*. evidenza *f*. enfasi *f invar*. **emphasize** *vt* accentuare, mettere in evidenza. **emphatic** *adj* enfatico, espressivo.

empire ('empaiə) *n* impero *m*.

empirical (im'pirikəl) *adj* empirico.

employ (im'plɔi) *vt* 1 impiegare, servirsi di. 2 dare impiego a. **employee** *n* impiegato *m*. **employer** *n* datore di lavoro *m*. **employment** *n* impiego *m*. occupazione *f*. **employment exchange** *n* ufficio collocamento *m*.

empower (im'pauə) *vt* autorizzare.

empress ('emprəs) *n* imperatrice *f*.

empty ('empti) *adj* 1 vuoto. 2 vano. *vt* vuotare. *vi* vuotarsi. **empty-handed** *adj* a mani vuote. **empty headed** *adj* scervellato.

emu ('iːmjuː) *n* emu *m*.

emulate ('emjuleit) *vt* emulare.

emulsion (i'mʌlʃən) *n* emulsione *f*.

enable (i'neibəl) *vt* mettere in grado di.

enact (i'nækt) *vi* 1 *law* decretare. 2 *Th* rappresentare.

enamel (i'næməl) *n* smalto *m*. *vt* smaltare.

enchant (in'tʃɑːnt) *vt* incantare. **enchantment** *n* incantesimo *m*.

encircle (in'səːkəl) *vt* circondare, cingere.

enclose (in'klouz) *vt* 1 racchiudere. 2 includere.

encore ('ɔŋkɔː) *n* *Th* bis *m*.

encounter (in'kauntə) *n* 1 incontro *m*. 2 lotta *f*. *vt* 1 incontrare. 2 affrontare.

encourage (in'kʌridʒ) *vt* incoraggiare. **encouragement** *n* incoraggiamento *m*.

encroach (in'kroutʃ) *vi* usurpare, abusare, intromettersi.

encumber (in'kʌmbə) *vt* ingombrare, ostacolare, opprimere.

encyclopedia (insaiklə'piːdiə) *n* enciclopedia *f*.

end (end) *n* 1 fine *f*. termine *m*. 2 scopo, fine *m*. 3 morte *f*. **make ends meet** sbarcare il lunario. ~*vt,vi* finire, concludere. **endless** *adj* senza fine, interminabile.

endanger (in'deindʒə) *vt* mettere in pericolo.

endeavour (in'devə) *n* sforzo, tentativo *m*. *vi* tentare, sforzarsi.

endemic (en'demik) *adj* endemico.

endive ('endaiv) *n* indivia *f*.

endorse (in'dɔːs) *vt* 1 *comm* girare, firmare. 2 approvare. **endorsement** *n* 1 *comm* girata *f*. 2 altergato *m*.

endow (in'dau) *vt* dotare. **endowment** *n* dotazione *f*.

endure (in'djuə) *vt* 1 sopportare. 2 durare. *vi* durare.

enemy ('enəmi) *adj,n* nemico, *pl* nemici *m*.

energy ('enədʒi) *n* energia *f*. **energetic** *adj* energico.

enfold (in'fould) *vt* avvolgere.

enforce (in'fɔːs) *vt* imporre, far rispettare. **enforcement** *n* 1 imposizione *f*. 2 *law* applicazione *f*.

engage (in'geidʒ) *vt* 1 impegnare, occupare. 2 *mot* ingranare. *vi* impegnarsi. **engaged** 1 fidanzato. 2 occupato. **engagement** *n* 1 impegno, appuntamento *m*. 2 fidanzamento *m*.

engine ('endʒin) *n* motore *m*.

engineer (endʒi'niə) *n* 1 ingegnere *m*. 2 meccanico *m*. *vt* costruire, ideare. **engineering** *n* ingegneria *f*.

England ('iŋglənd) *n* Inghilterra *f*. **English** *adj*

186

inglese. **English** (language) n inglese m. **English Channel** n Manica f. **Englishman** n inglese m.

engrave (in'greiv) vt intagliare, incidere. **engraving** n incisione f.

engross (in'grous) vt assorbire.

engulf (in'gʌlf) vt inghiottire, inabissare.

enhance (in'hɑːns) vt **1** migliorare. **2** accrescere.

enigma (i'nigmə) n enigma m. **enigmatic** adj enigmatico.

enjoy (in'dʒɔi) vt **1** godere. **2** apprezzare. **enjoy oneself** divertirsi. **enjoyment** n divertimento, piacere m.

enlarge (in'lɑːdʒ) vt espandere, ingrandire.

enlighten (in'laitn) vt illuminare. **enlightenment** n **1** spiegazione f. **2** cap Illuminismo m.

enlist (in'list) vt arruolare. vi arruolarsi.

enormous (i'nɔːməs) adj enorme, immenso.

enough (i'nʌf) adj abbastanza. adv sufficientemente, abbastanza. **be enough** bastare.

enquire (in'kwaiə) vi chiedere, domandare, informarsi. vt chiedere, domandare. **enquiry** n **1** domanda f. **2** law inchiesta f. **enquiry office** n ufficio informazioni m.

enrage (in'reidʒ) vt far arrabbiare.

enrich (in'ritʃ) vt arricchire.

enrol (in'roul) vt arruolare, iscrivere. **enrolment** n arruolamento m.

ensign (i'ensain) n bandiera, insegna f.

enslave (in'sleiv) vt assoggettare, asservire.

ensure (in'ʃuə) vt assicurare, garantire.

entail (in'teil) vt implicare.

entangle (in'tæŋgəl) vt impigliare, coinvolgere. **entanglement** n groviglio, imbroglio m.

enter ('entə) vt **1** entrare in. **2** iscrivere. vi entrare.

enterprise ('entəpraiz) n impresa, iniziativa f. **enterprising** adj intraprendente.

entertain (entə'tein) vt **1** intrattenere, divertire. **2** ricevere. **3** accarezzare. **entertaining** adj divertente. **entertainment** n festa f. spettacolo m.

enthral (in'θrɔːl) vt affascinare, incantare.

enthusiasm (in'θjuːziæzəm) n entusiasmo m. **enthusiast** n entusiasta m. **enthusiastic** adj entusiastico.

entice (in'tais) vt **1** sedurre. **2** allettare.

entire (in'taiə) adj intero, completo.

entitle (in'taitl) vt intitolare, dare diritto a.

entity ('entiti) n entità f.

entrails ('entreilz) n pl viscere f pl. intestini m pl.

entrance[1] ('entrəns) n **1** entrata f. ingresso m. **2** ammissione f. **entrance fee** n tassa d'iscrizione f.

entrance[2] (in'trɑːns) vt mandare in estasi.

entreat (in'triːt) vt supplicare. **entreaty** n supplica f.

entrench (in'trentʃ) vt trincerare.

entrepreneur (ɔntrəprə'nəː) n impresario, imprenditore m.

entrust (in'trʌst) vt affidare, consegnare.

entry ('entri) n **1** entrata f. ingresso m. **2** registrazione f.

entwine (in'twain) vt intrecciare.

enunciate (i'nʌnsieit) vt enunciare.

envelop (in'veləp) vt avviluppare.

envelope ('envəloup) n busta f.

environment (in'vairənmənt) n ambiente m.

envisage (in'vizidʒ) vt considerare, immaginare.

envoy ('envɔi) n inviato m.

envy ('envi) n invidia, gelosia f. vt invidiare.

enzyme ('enzaim) n enzima m.

epaulet ('epəlet) n spallina f.

ephemeral (i'femərəl) adj effimero.

epic ('epik) adj epico. n epica f.

epidemic (epi'demik) n epidemia f. adj epidemico.

epilepsy ('epilepsi) n epilessia f. **epileptic** adj,n epilettico.

epilogue ('epilɔg) n epilogo m.

Epiphany (i'pifəni) n Epifania f.

episcopal (i'piskəpəl) adj episcopale.

episode ('episoud) n episodio m.

epitaph ('epitɑːf) n epitaffio m.

epitome (i'pitəmi) n epitome f.

epoch ('iːpɔk) n epoca f.

equable ('ekwəbəl) adj uniforme, costante.

equal ('iːkwəl) adj uguale, simile, pari. n pari m invar. vt uguagliare. **equalize** vt uguagliare. vt,vi sport pareggiare.

equate (i'kweit) vt uguagliare, paragonare. **equation** n equazione f. **equator** n equatore m.

equestrian (i'kwestriən) adj equestre.

equilateral (iːkwi'lætərəl) adj equilatero.

equilibrium (iːkwi'libriəm) n equilibrio m.

equinox ('iːkwinɔks) n equinozio m.

equip (i'kwip) vt **1** equipaggiare. **2** fornire. **equipment** n **1** equipaggiamento m. **2** attrezzatura f.

equity ('ekwiti) n giustizia f.

equivalent (i'kwivələnt) *adj* equivalente.

era ('iərə) *n* era, epoca *f*.

eradicate (i'rædikeit) *vt* sradicare.

erase (i'reiz) *vt* cancellare, raschiare.

erect (i'rekt) *adj* eretto, elevato. *vt* erigere, rizzare. **erection** *n* costruzione, erezione *f*.

ermine ('ə:min) *n* ermellino *m*.

erode (i'roud) *vt* erodere, corrodere. **erosion** *n* erosione *f*.

erotic (i'rɔtik) *adj* erotico.

err (ə:) *vi* sbagliare.

errand ('erənd) *n* commissione *f*. **errand boy** *n* fattorino *m*.

erratic (i'rætik) *adj* erratico, irregolare.

error ('erə) *n* **1** errore *m*. **2** torto *m*.

erupt (i'rʌpt) *vi* erompere, eruttare. **eruption** *n* eruzione *f*.

escalate ('eskəleit) *vt* aumentare, accrescere. **escalator** *n* scala mobile *f*.

escalope (i'skæləp) *n* scaloppa *f*.

escape (i'skeip) *vi* fuggire, evadere, sfuggire. *vt* **1** evitare. **2** sfuggire. *n* **1** fuga *f*. **2** salvezza *f*.

escort (*n* 'eskɔ:t; *v* is'kɔ:t) *n* scorta *f*. *vt* scortare, accompagnare.

Eskimo ('eskimou) *adj,n* eschimese.

esoteric (esə'terik) *adj* esoterico.

especial (i'speʃəl) *adj* speciale. **especially** *adv* soprattutto, specialmente.

espionage ('espiəna:ʒ) *n* spionaggio *m*.

esplanade ('espləneid) *n* spianata, passeggiata lungo mare *f*.

essay ('esei) *n* saggio *m*.

essence ('esəns) *n* essenza *f*. **essential** *adj* essenziale.

establish (i'stæbliʃ) *vt* **1** affermare. **2** fondare, stabilire. **establishment** *n* **1** fondazione *f*. **2** stabilimento *m*.

estate (i'steit) *n* proprietà *f*. patrimonio *m*. **estate agent** *n* mediatore *m*. **estate car** *n* giardiniera *f*.

esteem (i'sti:m) *vt* stimare, rispettare. *n* stima, considerazione *f*.

estimate (*n* 'estimət; *v* 'estimeit) *n* valutazione *f*. preventivo *m*. *vt* valutare, preventivare..

estuary ('estʃuəri) *n* estuario *m*.

etching ('etʃiŋ) *n* incisione *f*, acquaforte *f*.

eternal (i'tə:nl) *adj* eterno. **eternity** *n* eternità *f*.

ether ('i:θə) *n* etere *m*.

ethereal (i'θiəriəl) *adj* etereo, leggero.

ethical ('eθikəl) *adj* etico, morale. **ethics** *n pl* etica *f*.

Ethiopia (i:θi'oupiə) *n* Etiopia *f*. **Ethiopian** *adj,n* etiope.

ethnic ('eθnik) *adj* etnico.

etiquette ('etikit) *n* etichetta *f*. cerimoniale *m*.

etymology (eti'mɔlədʒi) *n* etimologia *f*.

eucalyptus (ju:kə'liptəs) *n* eucalipto *m*.

Eucharist ('ju:kərist) *n* Eucarestia *f*.

eunuch ('ju:nək) *n* eunuco *m*.

euphemism ('ju:fəmizəm) *n* eufemismo *m*.

euphoria (ju:'fɔ:riə) *n* euforia *f*.

Europe ('juərəp) *n* Europa *f*. **European** *adj,n* europeo.

European Economic Community *n* Mercato Comune Europeo *m*.

euthanasia (ju:θə'neiziə) *n* eutanasia *f*.

evacuate (i'vækjueit) *vt* evacuare, sfollare. **evacuation** *n* evacuazione *f*.

evade (i'veid) *vt* evitare, eludere. **evasion** *n* evasione *f*. **evasive** *adj* evasivo.

evaluate (i'væljueit) *vt* valutare.

evangelical (i:væn'dʒelikəl) *adj* evangelico. **evangelist** *n* evangelista *m*.

evaporate (i'væpəreit) *vi* evaporare. *vt* far evaporare.

eve (i:v) *n* vigilia *f*.

even ('i:vən) *adj* **1** uguale, costante. **2** pari. **3** piano. *adv* perfino, anche. *vt* appianare, livellare. **even-tempered** *adj* di umore costante.

evening ('i:vəniŋ) *n* sera, serata *f*. **evening dress** *n* abito da sera *m*.

event (i'vent) *n* **1** avvenimento *m*. **2** eventualità *f*. **3** *sport* prova *f*. **eventual** *adj* eventuale, finale. **eventually** *adv* alla fine.

ever ('evə) *adv* **1** mai. **2** sempre. **for ever** per sempre. **evergreen** *adj,n* sempreverde *m*. **everlasting** *adj* eterno, perenne. **evermore** *adv* sempre.

every ('evri) *adj* ogni, ciascuno. **every now and then** di tanto in tanto. **everybody** *pron* ognuno, tutti. **everyday** *adj* di tutti i giorni. **everyone** *pron* ognuno, tutti. **everything** *pron* tutto, ogni cosa. **everywhere** *adv* dovunque.

evict (i'vikt) *vt* sfrattare. **eviction** *n* sfratto *m*.

evidence ('evidəns) *n* **1** evidenza, prova *f*. **2** *law* deposizione *f*. **evident** *adj* evidente, ovvio.

evil ('i:vəl) *adj* cattivo, malvagio. *n* male *m*.

evoke (i'vouk) *vt* evocare.

evolve (i'vɔlv) *vt* evolvere. *vi* svilupparsi. **evolution** *n* evoluzione *f*. sviluppo *m*.

ewe (ju:) *n* pecora *f*.

exact (ig'zækt) *adj* esatto, giusto. *vt* esigere, richiedere. **exacting** *adj* esigente, impegnativo.

exaggerate (ig'zædʒəreit) *vt,vi* esagerare. **exaggeration** *n* esagerazione *f*.

exalt (ig'zɔːlt) *vt* esaltare, innalzare. **exaltation** *n* esaltazione *f*.

examine (ig'zæmin) *vt* esaminare, verificare. **examination** *n* esame *m*. **examiner** *n* ispettore, esaminatore *m*.

example (ig'zaːmpəl) *n* esempio *m*.

exasperate (ig'zaːspəreit) *vt* esasperare, inasprire.

excavate ('ekskəveit) *vt* scavare. **excavation** *n* scavo *m*.

exceed (ik'siːd) *vt* eccedere, superare.

excel (ik'sel) *vi* eccellere. *vt* battere.

Excellency ('eksələnsi) *n* (title) Eccellenza *f*.

excellent ('eksələnt) *adj* eccellente, ottimo.

except (ik'sept) *prep* eccetto, tranne, all'infuori di. **excepting** *prep* tranne. **exception** *n* eccezione *f*. **with the exception of** eccetto. **exceptional** *adj* eccezionale.

excerpt ('eksəːpt) *n* brano *m*.

excess (ik'ses) *n* eccesso *m*. **excessive** *adj* eccessivo.

exchange (iks'tʃeindʒ) *n* **1** scambio *m*. **2** *comm* cambio *m*. **3** (telephone) centralino *m*. *vt* cambiare, scambiare.

exchequer (iks'tʃekə) *n* tesoro *m*.

excise ('eksaiz) *n* imposta indiretta *f*.

excite (ik'sait) *vt* **1** eccitare. **2** provocare, suscitare. **excitement** *n* agitazione *f*.

exclaim (ik'skleim) *vt,vi* esclamare, gridare. **exclamation** *n* esclamazione *f*. **exclamation mark** *n* punto esclamativo *m*.

exclude (ik'skluːd) *vt* escludere, interdire. **exclusion** *n* esclusione *f*. **exclusive** *adj* scelto, esclusivo, unico.

excommunicate (ekskə'mjuːnikeit) *vt* scomunicare.

excruciating (ik'skruːʃieitiŋ) *adj* straziante, tormentoso.

excursion (ik'skəːʒən) *n* gita *f*.

excuse (*v* ik'skjuːz; *n* ik'skjuːs) *vt* scusare, esentare. *n* scusa *f*. pretesto *m*.

execute ('eksikjuːt) *vt* **1** eseguire. **2** giustiziare. **execution** *n* esecuzione *f*. **executioner** *n* boia *m invar*.

executive (ig'zekjutiv) *adj* esecutivo. *n* **1** *pol* potere esecutivo *m*. **2** *comm* dirigente *m*.

exempt (ig'zempt) *adj* esente. *vt* esentare, esonerare.

exercise ('eksəsaiz) *n* **1** esercizio *m*. **2** *mil* esercitazione *f*. **exercise book** *n* quaderno *m*.

exert (ig'zəːt) *vt* esercitare, fare uso di. **exert oneself** sforzarsi.

exhale (eks'heil) *vt* esalare, emanare.

exhaust (ig'zɔːst) *vt* esaurire. *n* scarico, scappamento *m*. **exhaust pipe** *n* tubo di scappamento *m*. **exhausted** *adj* esaurito, sfinito.

exhibit (ig'zibit) *vt* esibre, esporre. *n* oggetto per mostra *m*. **exhibition** *n* mostra, esibizione *f*. **exhibitionism** *n* esibizionismo *m*.

exhilarate (ig'ziləreit) *vt* rallegrare, esilarare.

exile ('egzail) *n* **1** esilio *m*. **2** esule *m,f*. *vt* esiliare, bandire.

exist (ig'zist) *vi* esistere. **existence** *n* esistenza *f*. **existent** *adj* esistente. **existentialism** *n* esistenzialismo *m*.

exit ('eksit) *n* uscita *f*.

exorbitant (ig'zɔːbitənt) *adj* esorbitante.

exorcize ('eksɔːsaiz) *vt* esorcizzare.

exotic (ig'zɔtik) *adj* esotico.

expand (ik'spænd) *vt* espandere. *vi* dilatarsi. **expansion** *n* espansione *f*.

expanse (ik'spæns) *n* spazio *m*. estensione *f*.

expatriate (*adj,n* eks'pætriit; *v* eks'pætrieit) *adj,n* espatriato. *vt* **1** esiliare, espatriare. **expatriation** *n* espatrio *m*.

expect (ik'spekt) *vt* **1** aspettare, aspettarsi. **2** pensare. **expectation** *n* aspettativa *f*. **2** attesa *f*. **3** speranza *f*.

expedient (ik'spiːdiənt) *adj* conveniente. *n* espediente, mezzo *m*.

expedition (ekspi'diʃən) *n* spedizione *f*.

expel (ik'spel) *vt* espellere.

expenditure (ik'spenditʃə) *n* spesa *f*.

expense (ik'spens) *n* **1** spesa *f*. **2** *pl* spese *f pl*. indennità *f*. **expensive** *adj* costoso, caro.

experience (ik'spiəriəns) *n* esperienza *f*. *vt* provare, subire.

experiment (ik'sperimənt) *n* esperimento *m*. *vi* fare esperimenti. **experimental** *adj* sperimentale.

expert ('ekspəːt) *adj* esperto, competente. *n* esperto, perito *m*. **expertise** *n* abilità *f*.

expire (ik'spaiə) *vi* **1** scadere. **2** morire.

explain (ik'splein) *vt* spiegare. **explanation** *n* spiegazione *f*.

expletive (ik'spliːtiv) *n* bestemmia *f*.

explicit (ik'splisit) *adj* esplicito.

explode (ik'sploud) *vt* **1** far esplodere. **2** demolire. *vi* esplodere, scoppiare. **explosive** *adj,n* esplosivo *m*.

exploit[1] (ik'sploit) *vt* sfruttare, utilizzare. **exploitation** *n* sfruttamento *m*. utilizzazione *f*.

exploit[2] ('eksploit) *n* impresa eroica *f*.

explore (ik'splo:) *vt* esplorare.

exponent (ik'spounant) *n* esponente *m*.

export (*v* ik'spo:t, 'ekspo:t; *n* 'ekspo:t) *vt* esportare. *n* esportazione *f*.

expose (ik'spouz) *vt* esporre, scoprire, svelare. **exposure** *n* 1 esposizione *f*. 2 smascheramento *m*. 3 *phot* posa *f*.

express (ik'spres) *adj* 1 espresso. 2 preciso. *vt* esprimere. **expression** *n* 1 espressione *f*. 2 manifestazione *f*. **express train** *n* direttissimo *m*.

exquisite (ek'skwizit) *adj* squisito, fine.

extend (ik'stend) *vt* estendere, prolungare. *vi* estendersi. **extension** *n* estensione, proroga *f*. **extensive** *adj* esteso, vasto.

extent (ik'stent) *n* limite, grado, punto *m*.

exterior (ek'stiaria) *adj* esteriore. *n* esterno *m*.

exterminate (ik'stə:mineit) *vt* distruggere, sterminare.

external (ek'stə:nl) *adj* esterno.

extinct (ik'stiŋkt) *adj* estinto, spento.

extinguish (ik'stiŋgwiʃ) *vt* estinguere, spegnere.

extra ('ekstrə) *adj* extra, straordinario. *n* 1 supplemento *m*. 2 edizione straordinaria *f*. 3 *Th* comparsa *f*. *adv* in più.

extract (ik'strækt) *n* estratto *m*. citazione *f*. *vt* estrarre. **extraction** *n* 1 estrazione *f*. 2 origine *f*.

extramural (ekstra'mjuaral) *adj* fuori dell'università.

extraordinary (ik'stro:danri) *adj* straordinario.

extravagant (ik'strævagant) *adj* stravagante, eccessivo.

extreme (ik'stri:m) *adj* estremo, grave. *n* estremo *m*. **extremist** *n* estremista *m*. **extremity** *n* estremità *f*.

extricate ('ekstrikeit) *vt* districare, liberare.

extrovert ('ekstrəvə:t) *n* estroverso *m*.

exuberant (ig'zju:bərənt) *adj* esuberante.

eye (ai) *n* 1 occhio *m*. 2 (of needle) cruna *f*. *vt* 1 guardare. 2 sbirciare.

eyeball ('aibo:l) *n* bulbo oculare *m*.

eyebrow ('aibrau) *n* sopracciglio *m,pl* sopracciglia *f*.

eye-catching *adj* che salta all'occhio.

eyelash ('ailæʃ) *n* ciglio *m*, *pl* ciglia *f*.

eyelid ('ailid) *n* palpebra *f*.

eye-opener *n* fatto sorprendente *m*.

eye shadow *n* ombretto *m*.

eyesight ('aisait) *n* vista *f*.

eye-witness *n* testimone oculare *m,f*.

F

fable ('feibəl) *n* favola *f*.

fabric ('fæbrik) *n* 1 tessuto *m*. stoffa *f*. 2 struttura *f*. **fabricate** *vt* inventare, falsificare.

fabulous ('fæbjuləs) *adj* favoloso, leggendario.

façade (fə'sa:d) *n* 1 *arch* facciata *f*. 2 apparenza *f*.

face (feis) *n* 1 faccia *f*. volto *m*. 2 (of a clock) quadrante *m*. **lose face** perdere prestigio. ~*vt* fronteggiare, essere esposto a. **facecloth** *n* telo per lavarsi il volto *m*. **facecream** *n* crema per il viso *f*. **facelift** *n* plastica facciale *f*. **face-pack** *n* maschera di bellezza *f*. **face value** *n* valore nominale *m*.

facet ('fæsit) *n* 1 faccetta *f*. 2 aspetto *m*.

facetious (fə'si:ʃəs) *adj* gioviale, scherzoso.

facile ('fæsail) *adj* 1 facile. 2 superficiale. **facilitate** *vt* facilitare. **facility** *n* 1 facilità, destrezza *f*. 2 *pl* attrezzatura *f*.

facing ('feisiŋ) *n* rivestimento *m*.

facsimile (fæk'simali) *n* facsimile *m*.

fact (fækt) *n* fatto *m*. **as a matter of fact** effettivamente. **in fact** infatti. **factual** *adj* effettivo, reale.

faction ('fækʃən) *n* 1 fazione *f*. 2 discordia *f*.

factor ('fæktə) *n* 1 fattore *m*. 2 agente *m*.

factory ('fæktəri) *n* fabbrica, officina, azienda *f*.

faculty ('fækəlti) *n* facoltà *f*.

fad (fæd) *n* capriccio *m*. ubbia *f*.

fade (feid) *vi* 1 appassire. 2 scolorirsi. *vt* far sbiadire. **faded** *adj* sbiadito.

fag (fæg) *n* 1 lavoro pesante *m*. 2 *sl* sigaretta *f*. **fagged out** *adj* stanco morto.

Fahrenheit ('færənhait) *adj* Fahrenheit.

fail (feil) *vi* 1 venire a mancare. 2 diminuire. 3 *comm* fallire. *vt* 1 bocciare. 2 abbandonare. **without fail** *adv* senza fallo. **failing** *n* difetto *m*. debolezza *f*. *adj* debole. *prep* in mancanza di. **failure** *n* 1 insuccesso *m*. 2 indebolimento *m*. 3 fallimento *m*.

faint (feint) *vi* svenire. *adj* fiacco, incerto, tenue. *n* svenimento *m*. **faint-hearted** *adj* timido, pusillanime.

fair[1] (fɛə) *adj* 1 giusto, onesto. 2 chiaro, biondo.

3 bello. adv giustamente, lealmente. **fair play** n comportamento leale m. **fairly** adv abbastanza, giustamente.

fair² (fɛə) n mercato m. fiera f. **fairground** n spazio per la fiera m.

fairy ('fɛəri) n fata f. **fairytale** n fiaba f.

faith (feiθ) n fede, fiducia f. **faith-healing** n guarigione ottenuta con preghiere f. **faithful** adj fedele.

fake (feik) vt contraffare, fingere. n trucco m. adj falso.

falcon ('fɔ:lkən) n falcone m.

fall¹ (fɔ:l) n 1 caduta f. 2 crollo m. 3 ribasso m. vi cadere. **fall down** prostrarsi. **fall off** staccarsi. **fall through** fallire.

fallacy ('fæləsi) n errore, sofisma f. **fallacious** adj fallace.

fallible ('fæləbəl) adj fallibile.

fallow ('fælou) adj fulvo, incolto.

false (fɔ:ls) adj falso. adv falsamente. **false alarm** n falso allarme m. **falsehood** n menzogna, bugia f. **false pretences** n pl millantato credito m. **false teeth** n pl dentiera f. **falsify** vt falsificare.

falter ('fɔ:ltə) vi barcollare, indugiare. vi balbettare.

fame (feim) n fama, rinomanza f.

familiar (fə'miliə) adj familiare, usuale. **familiarize** vt familiarizzare.

family ('fæmili) n famiglia f.

famine ('fæmin) n carestia f. **famished** adj affamato.

famous ('feiməs) adj famoso.

fan¹ (fæn) n 1 ventaglio m. 2 ventilatore m. vt far vento a, ventilare. **fanbelt** n cinghia del ventilatore f.

fan² (fæn) n tifoso, appassionato m. **fan club** n circolo di ammiratori m.

fanatic (fə'nætik) adj,n fanatico.

fanciful ('fænsifəl) adj fantasioso, bizzarro.

fancy ('fænsi) adj elaborato. n 1 immaginazione f. 2 capriccio m. 3 illusione f. vt 1 credere 2 desiderare. 3 immaginare. **fancy dress** n costume m.

fanfare ('fænfɛə) n fanfara f.

fang (fæŋ) n zanna f.

fantasy ('fæntəsi) n fantasia f.

fantastic (fæn'tæstik) adj fantastico.

far (fɑ:) adj lontano, distante. adv 1 lontano. 2 molto, assai. **far-fetched** adj improbabile, inverosimile. **far-off** lontano. **far-reaching** adj di grande portata.

farce (fɑ:s) n farsa f.

fare (fɛə) n prezzo m. tariffa f.

Far East n Estremo Oriente m.

farewell (fɛə'wel) n addio, congedo m.

farm (fɑ:m) n fattoria f. podere m. vt coltivare. vi fare l'agricoltore. **farmer** n coltivatore m. **farmhouse** n casa colonica f. **farmland** n terreno da coltivare m. **farmyard** n aia f.

farther ('fɑ:ðə) adj,adv più lontano. **farthest** adj il più lontano.

fascinate ('fæsineit) vt affascinare. **fascination** n fascino m.

fascism ('fæʃizəm) n fascismo m. **fascist** n fascista m.

fashion ('fæʃən) n 1 moda f. 2 maniera f. vt foggiare, adattare. **fashionable** adj elegante, di moda.

fast¹ (fɑ:st) adj 1 veloce. 2 saldo, costante. 3 inf dissoluto. adv 1 velocemente. 2 saldamente.

fast² (fɑ:st) vi digiunare. n digiuno m.

fasten ('fɑ:sən) vt attaccare, fissare. vi chiudersi. **fastener** n chiusura f. fermaglio m.

fastidious (fə'stidiəs) adj meticoloso, schizzinoso.

fat (fæt) adj 1 untuoso. 2 grasso. n grasso m.

fatal ('feitl) adj fatale, mortale. **fatality** n fatalità f.

fate (feit) n fato m. sorte f.

father ('fɑ:ðə) n padre m. **father-in-law** n suocero m. **fatherland** n patria f. **fatherly** adj paterno.

fathom ('fæðəm) n naut braccio m, pl braccia f. vt capire. **fathomless** adj impenetrabile.

fatigue (fə'ti:g) n stanchezza f. vt affaticare.

fatten ('fætn) vt,vi ingrassare.

fatuous ('fætjuəs) adj fatuo.

fault (fɔ:lt) n 1 errore m. 2 colpa f. 3 difetto m. **faulty** adj difettoso.

fauna ('fɔ:nə) n fauna f.

favour ('feivə) n 1 favore m. 2 parzialità f. vt favorire, preferire. **favourable** adj propizio, favorevole. **favourite** adj preferito. n favorito m.

fawn¹ (fɔ:n) n 1 zool cerbiatto m. 2 fulvo m. adj fulvo.

fawn² (fɔ:n) vi **fawn on** adulare.

fear (fiə) n paura f. vt temere, aver paura di. **fearless** adj ardimentoso.

feasible ('fi:zibəl) adj probabile, realizzabile.

feast (fi:st) n 1 festa f. 2 banchetto m. vi fare festa, banchettare.

feat (fi:t) n azione, impresa f.

feather ('feðə) n piuma, penna f. **featherbed** n letto di piume m. **featherweight** n peso piuma m.

feature ('fi:tʃə) n 1 fattezza f. 2 pl fisionomia f. 3 caratteristica f. 4 articolo speciale m. vt 1 caratterizzare. 2 mettere in risalto.

February ('februəri) n febbraio m.

feckless ('fekləs) adj debole, inetto.

fed (fed) v see **feed.**

federal ('fedərəl) adj federale. **federate** vt imfederare. vi confederarsi. adj confederato. **federation** n federazione f.

fee (fi:) n 1 onorario m. 2 tassa f.

feeble ('fi:bəl) adj debole.

feed* (fi:d) vt nutrire. vi nutrirsi. **be fed up** essere stufo. ~n alimentazione, pastura f. **feedback** n reazione f.

feel* (fi:l) vt 1 sentire, percepire. 2 ritenere. vi sentirsi. **feel one's way** procedere a tastoni. ~n tatto m. **feeler** n 1 tentacolo m. 2 sondaggio m. **feeling** n sentimento m. sensazione f.

feign (fein) vt fingere, simulare.

feint[1] (feint) n finta f. vi fare una finta.

feint[2] (feint) adj rigato leggermente.

feline ('fi:lain) adj felino.

fell[1] (fel) v see **fall.**

fell[2] (fel) vt abbattere.

fellow ('felou) n 1 compagno, collega m. 2 individuo m. 3 educ docente m. **fellowship** n 1 associazione f. 2 borsa di studio f.

felon ('felən) n criminale m,f. **felony** n crimine m.

felt[1] (felt) v see **feel.**

felt[2] (felt) n feltro m.

female ('fi:meil) adj femminile, di sesso femminile. n donna, femmina f.

feminine ('feminin) adj femminile, femminino. **feminism** n femminismo m.

fence (fens) n recinto m. palizzata f. vt recintare. vi tirar di scherma. **fencing** n 1 sport scherma f. 2 recinto m.

fend (fend) vt **fend for oneself** provvedere a se stesso. **fend off** parare, schivare. **fender** n paraurti m invar.

fennel ('fenl) n finocchio m.

ferment (fə'ment) vi fermentare. vt fare fermentare. **fermentation** n fermentazione f.

fern (fə:n) n felce f.

ferocious (fə'rouʃəs) adj feroce.

ferret ('ferit) n furetto m. vi frugare. **ferret out** scoprire.

ferry ('feri) n traghetto m. **ferryboat** n nave traghetto f.

fertile ('fə:tail) adj fertile. **fertilize** vt fertilizzare.

fervent ('fə:vənt) adj fervente, ardente.

fervour ('fə:və) n fervore m.

fester ('festə) vi suppurare.

festival ('festivəl) n festival m. celebrazione f. **festivity** n festa f.

festoon (fes'tu:n) vt decorare con festoni. n festone m.

fetch (fetʃ) vt 1 andare a prendere, andare a chiamare. 2 dare. **fetching** adj attraente.

fete (feit) n festa f.

fetid ('fetid) adj fetido.

fetish ('fetiʃ) n feticcio m.

fetlock ('fetlɔk) n barbetta f.

fetter ('fetə) n catena f. vt incatenare.

feud (fju:d) n feudo m. **feudal** adj feudale.

fever ('fi:və) n febbre f. **feverish** adj febbricitante, eccitato.

few (fju:) adj,pron pochi, alcuni. adj qualche. **a few** alcuni. **quite a few** un numero considerevole.

fiancé (fi'ãsei) n fidanzato m. **fiancée** n fidanzata f.

fiasco (fi'æskou) n fiasco, insuccesso m.

fib (fib) n frottola, bugia f. vi raccontare frottole.

fibre ('faibə) n fibra f. **fibreglass** n lana di vetro f.

fickle ('fikəl) adj volubile.

fiction ('fikʃən) n 1 novellistica f. 2 finzione f. **fictitious** adj falso.

fiddle ('fidl) n 1 violino m. 2 inf imbroglio m. vt inf imbrogliare.

fidelity (fi'deliti) n fedeltà f.

fidget ('fidʒit) vi agitarsi, essere irrequieto.

field (fi:ld) n 1 campo m. 2 settore m. **fieldwork** n fortificazione f.

fiend (fi:nd) n demonio m. **fiendish** adj diabolico.

fierce (fiəs) adj 1 fiero, selvaggio. 2 ardente.

fiery ('faiəri) adj impetuoso.

fifteen (fif'ti:n) adj,n quindici m or f. **fifteenth** adj quindicesimo.

fifth (fifθ) adj quinto.

fifty ('fifti) adj,n cinquanta m. **fiftieth** adj cinquantesimo.

fig (fig) n fico m.

fight* (fait) vt,vi combattere. n combattimento m. lotta f.

figment ('figmənt) n finzione, invenzione f.

figure ('figǝ) n **1** figura f. **2** math cifra f. **3** linea f. vt figurarsi, immaginare. vi apparire. **figure out** calcolare. **figurative** adj figurativo, simbolico. **figurehead** n uomo di paglia m.

filament ('filǝmǝnt) n filamento m.

file[1] (fail) n schedario, archivio m. vt ordinare, archiviare. **filing cabinet** n casellario m.

file[2] (fail) n lima f. vt limare.

filial ('filiǝl) adj filiale.

fill (fil) vt **1** riempire. **2** (a tooth) otturare. **3** ricoprire. vi riempirsi. **fill in** compilare. **fill up** mot fare il pieno. ~n sazietà, sufficienza f. **filling** n **1** otturazione f. **2** cul ripieno m. **filling station** stazione di rifornimento f.

fillet ('filit) n filetto m.

filly ('fili) n puledra f.

film (film) n **1** pellicola f. velo m. **2** film m. vt filmare. **film star** n diva, stella del cinema f.

filter ('filtǝ) n filtro m. vt filtrare.

filth (filθ) n sudiciume m. **filthy** adj sudicio, sporco, sordido.

fin (fin) n pinna f.

final ('fainl) adj ultimo, decisivo. n **1** sport finale f. **2** pl esami finali m pl. **finalize** vt mettere a punto, concludere.

finance ('fainæns) n finanza f. vt finanziare. **financial** adj finanziario. **financier** n finanziere m.

finch (fintʃ) n fringuello m.

find* (faind) vt trovare, scoprire. **find out** scoprire. n scoperta f.

fine[1] (fain) adj bello, buono, raffinato. adv bene. **fine arts** n pl belle arti f pl. **finery** n abiti delle feste m pl.

fine[2] (fain) n multa f. vt multare.

finesse (fi'nes) n delicatezza, sottigliezza f.

finger ('fiŋgǝ) n dito m,pl dita f. vt toccare con le dita. **fingermark** n ditata f. **fingernail** n unghia f. **fingerprint** n impronta digitale f. **fingertip** n punta delle dita f.

finish ('finiʃ) vt,vi finire. n **1** fine, conclusione f. **2** rifinitura f.

finite ('fainait) adj limitato, circoscritto.

Finland ('finlǝnd) n Finlandia f. **Finn** n finlandese m,f. **Finnish** adj finnico, finlandese. **Finnish** (language) n finlandese m.

fiord (fjɔ:d) n fiordo m.

fir (fǝ:) n abete m. **fir cone** n pigna f.

fire (faiǝ) n **1** fuoco m. **2** incendio m. **catch fire** prendere fuoco. ~vt **1** incendiare. **2** (a gun, etc.) sparare. **3** inf licenziare. vi **1** incendiarsi. **2** sparare.

fire alarm n allarme d'incendio m.

fire brigade n pompieri m pl.

fire drill n esercitazione di pompieri f.

fire-engine n pompa antincendio f.

fire-escape n uscita di sicurezza f.

fireguard ('faiǝga:d) n parafuoco m.

firelight ('faiǝlait) n luce del focolare f.

fireman ('faiǝmǝn) n pompiere m.

fireplace ('faiǝpleis) n caminetto m.

fireside ('faiǝsaid) n angolo del focolare m.

fire station n caserma dei pompieri f.

firework ('faiǝwǝ:k) n fuoco d'artificio m.

firm[1] (fǝ:m) adj **1** solido. **2** risoluto. **firmly** adv fermamente.

firm[2] (fǝ:m) n ditta, società f.

first (fǝ:st) adj primo. adv prima di tutto. **first aid** n pronto soccorso m. **first-class** adj di prima qualità. **first-hand** adj,adv di prima mano. **first person** n prima persona f. **first-rate** adj ottimo.

fiscal ('fiskǝl) adj fiscale.

fish (fiʃ) n, pl **fishes** or **fish** pesce m. vi pescare. **fisherman** n pescatore m. **fish finger** n bastoncino di pesce m. **fishing** n pesca f. adj da pesca. **fishing rod** n canna da pesca f. **fishmonger** n pescivendolo m. **fish-slice** n paletta per il pesce f. **fishy** adj inf losco, ambiguo.

fission ('fiʃǝn) n fissione f.

fist (fist) n pugno m.

fit[1] (fit) adj **1** adatto. **2** sano, in forma. n misura f. vt **1** adattare. **2** convenire a. vi **1** andare bene. **2** convenire. **fitting** adj adatto, opportuno. n **1** prova f. **2** pl mobili m pl.

fit[2] (fit) n med convulsione f. accesso m. **fitful** adj spasmodico, incostante.

five (faiv) adj,n cinque m.

fix (fiks) vt **1** assicurare, sistemare. **2** riparare. n inf difficoltà f. **fixation** n fissazione f. **fixture** n **1** infisso m. **2** avvenimento sportivo m.

fizz (fiz) vi frizzare. **fizzy** adj effervescente, frizzante. **fizzle** vi frizzare. **fizzle out** fare fiasco.

flabbergast ('flæbǝga:st) vt inf sbalordire.

flabby ('flæbi) adj floscio, molle.

flag[1] (flæg) n bandiera f. **flagpole** n asta della bandiera f.

flag[2] (flæg) vi pendere, avvizzire, indebolirsi.

flagon ('flægǝn) n flacone, bottiglione m.

flagrant ('fleigrǝnt) adj flagrante.

flair ('fleǝ) n istinto m. attitudine f.

flake (fleik) *n* **1** fiocco *m.* **2** scaglia *f.* *vt* sfaldare. *vi* squamarsi. **flaky** *adj* a scaglie.

flamboyant (flæm'bɔiənt) *adj* sgargiante, vistoso.

flame (fleim) *n* fiamma *f.*

flamingo (flə'miŋgou) *n* fenicottero *m.*

flan (flæn) *n* sformato *m.*

flank (flæŋk) *n* fianco, lato *m.* *vt* fiancheggiare.

flannel ('flænl) *n* flanella *f.* *adj* di flanella.

flap (flæp) *n* **1** lembo *m.* **2** colpo leggero *m.* **3** *tech* deflettore *m.* **be in a flap** essere agitato. ~*vt* **1** agitare. **2** (*wings*) battere. *vi* sbattere.

flare (fleə) *n* **1** bagliore *m.* fiammata *f.* **2** razzo *m.* *vi* splendere, avvampare. **flare up** infiammarsi.

flash (flæʃ) *n* lampo, sprazzo *m.* *vi* lampeggiare, balenare. *vt* dirigere. **flashback** *n* scena retrospettiva *f.* **flashbulb** *n* lampada per fotolampo *f.* **flashlight** *n* fotolampo *f.*

flask (flɑ:sk) *n* borraccia *f.* fiasco *m.*

flat[1] (flæt) *adj* **1** piatto. **2** insipido. **3** deciso. **flatfish** *n* sogliola *f.* **flat-footed** *adj* con i piedi piatti. **flatten** *vt* appiatire.

flat[2] (flæt) *n* appartamento *m.*

flatter ('flætə) *vt* adulare, lusingare. **flattering** *adj* lusinghiero. **flattery** *n* adulazione *f.*

flaunt (flɔ:nt) *vt* ostentare. *vi* pavoneggiarsi.

flautist ('flɔ:tist) *n* flautista *m.*

flavour ('fleivə) *n* gusto, sapore *m.* *vt* aromatizzare.

flaw (flɔ:) *n* difetto *m.*

flax (flæks) *n* lino *m.*

flea (fli:) *n* pulce *f.*

fleck (flek) *n* chiazza *f.*

fled (fled) *v* see **flee.**

flee* (fli:) *vt* fuggire, abbandonare. *vi* fuggire.

fleece (fli:s) *n* vello *m.* *vt* **1** tosare. **2** *sl* derubare.

fleet (fli:t) *n* flotta *f.*

fleeting ('fli:tiŋ) *adj* fuggevole.

Fleming ('flemiŋ) *n* fiammingo *m.*

Flemish ('flemiʃ) *adj* fiammingo. **Flemish** (language) *n* fiammingo *m.*

flesh (fleʃ) *n* **1** carne *f.* **2** polpa *f.*

flew (flu:) *v* see **fly.**

flex (fleks) *n* filo *m.* **flexible** *adj* flessibile, arrendevole.

flick (flik) *n* colpo, buffetto *m.* *vt* far saltare con un colpetto.

flicker ('flikə) *n* barlume, guizzo *m.* *vi* tremolare.

flight[1] (flait) *n* **1** (of a bird, plane, etc.) volo *m.* **2** slancio *m.* **3** (of stairs) rampa *f.*

flight[2] (flait) *n* (departure) fuga *f.*

flimsy ('flimzi) *adj* **1** sottile, fragile. **2** inconsistente.

flinch (flintʃ) *vi* ritrarsi, sottrarsi.

fling* (fliŋ) *vt* gettare, lanciare. *n* lancio *m.*

flint (flint) *n* **1** selce *f.* **2** pietra focaia *f.*

flip (flip) *n* colpetto, buffetto *m.* *vt* dare un buffetto a. **flipper** *n* pinna *f.*

flippant ('flipənt) *adj* impertinente, leggero.

flirt (flə:t) *vi* civetta *f.* *vi* civettare, flirtare.

flit (flit) *vi* **1** svolazzare. **2** andarsene.

float (flout) *n* **1** carro *m.* **2** galleggiante *m.* **3** *comm* riserva di cassa. *vi* **1** galleggiare. **2** fluttuare.

flock[1] (flɔk) *n* **1** gregge *m.* **2** folla *f.* *vi* affollarsi.

flock[2] (flɔk) *n* (of wool, etc.) fiocco di lana *m.*

flog (flɔg) *vt* frustare.

flood (flʌd) *n* **1** diluvio *m.* inondazione, piena *f.* **2** (of tears) torrente *m.* *vt* allagare, inondare. **floodlight** *n* riflettore *m.*

floor (flɔ:) *n* **1** pavimento *m.* **2** piano *m.* **floorboard** *n* tavola di pavimento *f.*

flop (flɔp) *vi* fallire. **flop down** cadere. ~*n* **1** tonfo *m.* **2** *inf* fiasco *m.*

flora ('flɔ:rə) *n* flora *f.*

floral ('flɔ:rəl) *adj* floreale. **florist** *n* fiorista *m,f.*

Florence ('flɔrəns) *n* Firenze *f.* **Florentine** *adj,n* fiorentino.

flounce[1] (flauns) *n* gesto rapido *m.* *vi* sussultare, agitarsi.

flounce[2] (flauns) *n* falpalà *m.*

flounder[1] ('flaundə) *vi* dibattersi.

flounder[2] ('flaundə) *n* *zool* passera *f.*

flour (flauə) *n* farina *f.*

flourish ('flʌriʃ) *vi* prosperare, fiorire. *vt* agitare. *n* **1** ornamento *m.* **2** squillo di tromba *m.*

flout (flaut) *vt* sprezzare.

flow (flou) *n* **1** flusso *m.* **2** corrente *f.* *vi* **1** scorrere. **2** circolare.

flown (floun) *v* see **fly.**

flower ('flauə) *n* fiore *m.* *vi* fiorire. **flowerbed** *n* aiuola *f.* **flowerpot** *n* vaso da fiori *m.*

fluctuate ('flʌktʃueit) *vi* fluttuare, oscillare. **fluctuation** *n* fluttuazione *f.*

flue (flu:) *n* canna del camino *f.*

fluent ('flu:ənt) *adj* scorrevole. **fluently** *adv* correntemente.

fluff (flʌf) *n* lanugine, peluria *f.*

fluid ('flu:id) *adj,n* fluido *m.*

flung (flʌŋ) *v* see **fling.**

fluorescent (flu'resənt) *adj* fluorescente.

fluoride ('fluəraid) *n* fluoruro *m.*

flush[1] (flʌʃ) n 1 rossore m. 2 violento flusso d'acqua m. 3 game colore m. vi arrossire. vt sciacquare. **flushed** adj accaldato.

flush[2] (flʌʃ) adj 1 a livello, rasente. 2 abbondante.

fluster ('flʌstə) n agitazione f. vt stordire, eccitare.

flute (flu:t) n flauto m.

flutter ('flʌtə) n 1 battito m. 2 agitazione f. vt 1 battere. 2 innervosire. vi sventolare.

flux (flʌks) n flusso m.

fly[1] (flai) vi volare, slanciarsi. vt far volare. **flyover** n cavalcavia m.

fly[2] (flai) n mosca f.

foal (foul) n puledro m.

foam (foum) n schiuma, bava f. vi spumeggiare, far bava.

focus ('foukəs) n 1 fuoco m. 2 centro vt 1 mettere a fuoco. 2 concentrare. vi convergere.

fodder ('fɔdə) n foraggio m.

foe (fou) n nemico, pl nemici, avversario m.

foetus ('fi:təs) n feto m.

fog (fɔg) n nebbia f. **foghorn** n sirena da nebbia f. **foggy** adj nebbioso.

foible ('fɔibəl) n punto debole m.

foil[1] (fɔil) vt frustrare, sventare.

foil[2] (fɔil) n 1 lamina di metallo f. 2 carta stagnola f.

foil[3] (fɔil) n sport fioretto m.

foist (fɔist) vt rifilare, introdurre di soppiatto.

fold[1] (fould) n piega, ripiegatura f. vt 1 piegare. 2 (one's arms) incrociare. **folder** n cartella f.

fold[2] (fould) n (for sheep) ovile m.

foliage ('fouliidʒ) n fogliame m.

folk (fouk) n gente f. popolo m. **folkdance** n ballo popolare m. **folklore** n folclore m. **folksong** n canzone popolare f. **folktale** n racconto m. leggenda popolare f.

follicle ('fɔlikəl) n follicolo m.

follow ('fɔlou) vt 1 seguire. 2 imitare. vi seguire, risultare. **follower** n seguace m,f.

folly ('fɔli) n pazzia, follia f.

fond (fɔnd) adj amante, affezionato. **be fond of** 1 voler bene a. 2 amare.

fondant ('fɔndənt) adj,n fondente m.

fondle ('fɔndl) vt accarezzare, vezzeggiare.

font (fɔnt) n fonte battesimale f.

food (fu:d) n cibo, nutrimento m.

fool (fu:l) n 1 sciocco, stupido, buffone m. **make a fool of oneself** rendersi ridicolo. ~vt ingannare. **foolish** adj stolto, insensato.

foolscap ('fu:lzkæp) n carta protocollo f.

foot (fut) n, pl **feet** 1 anat piede m. 2 base f. 3 (measure) piede m. v **foot the bill** pagare il conto. **football** n 1 (game) calcio m. 2 pallone m. **footbridge** n passerella f. **foothold** n punto d'appoggio m. **footing** n 1 punto d'appoggio m. 2 posizione f. **footnote** n nota in calce f. **footprint** n orma f. **footstep** n passo, rumore di passi m. **footwear** n calzatura f.

for (fə; stressed fɔ:) prep per, adatto a, di. **for sale** in vendita. ~conj poichè, perchè.

forage ('fɔridʒ) n foraggio m.

forbear[1] (fə'bɛə) vt astenersi da. vi astenersi.

forbid[*] (fə'bid) vt proibire, impedire. **forbidding** adj severo, minaccioso.

force (fɔ:s) n 1 forza f. vigore m. 2 validità f. 3 pl forze armate f pl. vt forzare, costringere. **forcible** adj forte.

forceps ('fɔ:seps) n pl forcipe m.

ford (fɔ:d) n guado m.

fore (fɔ:) adj anteriore. n naut prua f.

forearm[1] (fɔ:'rɑ:m) n avambraccio m.

forearm[2] (fɔ:'rɑ:m) vt premunire.

forecast ('fɔ:kɑ:st) vt prevedere, predire. n pronostico m. previsione f.

forecourt ('fɔ:kɔ:t) n cortile m.

forefather ('fɔ:fɑ:ðə) n avo, antenato m.

forefinger ('fɔ:fiŋgə) n dito indice m.

forefront ('fɔ:frʌnt) n prima linea f.

foreground ('fɔ:graund) n primo piano m.

forehand ('fɔ:hænd) n 1 posizione superiore f. 2 sport colpo diritto m.

forehead ('fɔrid) n fronte f.

foreign ('fɔrin) adj straniero, estraneo. **foreigner** n straniero m.

foreleg ('fɔ:leg) n zampa anteriore f.

forelock ('fɔ:lɔk) n ciuffo m.

foreman ('fɔ:mən) n caposquadra, capo-operaio m.

foremost ('fɔ:moust) adj primo, principale. adv in testa.

forensic (fə'rensik) adj forense.

forerunner ('fɔ:rʌnə) n precursore m.

foresee[*] (fɔ:'si:) vt prevedere.

foresight ('fɔ:sait) n previsione, prudenza f.

forest ('fɔrist) n foresta f.

forestall (fɔ:'stɔ:l) vt prevenire, anticipare.

foretaste ('fɔ:teist) n pregustazione f.

foretell (fɔ:'tel) vt predire.

forethought ('fɔ:θɔ:t) n premeditazione, previdenza f.

forfeit ('fɔːfit) n multa, pena, perdita f. vt perdere.

forge[1] (fɔːdʒ) n fucina f. vt 1 forgiare. 2 contraffarre, falsificare. **forgery** n 1 contraffazione f. 2 documento falso m. 3 falsificazione f.

forge[2] (fɔːdʒ) vi **forge ahead** avanzare gradatamente.

forget* (fə'get) vt dimenticare. **forgetful** adj smemorato, immemore.

forgive* (fə'giv) vt perdonare. **forgiving** adj indulgente.

forgo* (fɔː'gou) vt rinunziare a, fare senza di.

fork (fɔːk) n 1 cul forchetta f. 2 forca f. 3 (in a road) biforcazione f. vi biforcarsi.

forlorn (fə'lɔːn) adj sperduto, desolato.

form (fɔːm) n 1 forma f. 2 modulo m. 3 classe f. 4 formalità f. vt formare. **formal** adj formale. **formality** n 1 formalità f. 2 convenzionalismo m. **formation** n formazione f. **formative** adj formativo.

former ('fɔːmə) adj precedente, anteriore. **formerly** adv in passato, già.

formidable ('fɔːmidəbəl) adj spaventoso, temibile.

formula ('fɔːmjulə) n, pl **-las** or **-lae** formula f. **formulate** vt formulare.

forsake* (fə'seik) vt abbandonare.

fort (fɔːt) n forte m.

forte ('fɔːtei) n forte m.

forth (fɔːθ) adv avanti. **and so forth** e così via. **forthcoming** adj prossimo, imminente.

fortify ('fɔːtifai) vt 1 mil fortificare. 2 rinvigorire, incoraggiare.

fortnight ('fɔːtnait) n due settimane f pl. quindicina f.

fortress ('fɔːtrəs) n fortezza f.

fortune ('fɔːtʃən) n 1 fortuna, sorte f. 2 ricchezza f. **fortune-teller** n chiromante m,f. **fortunate** adj fortunato.

forty ('fɔːti) adj,n quaranta m. **fortieth** adj quarantesimo.

forum ('fɔːrəm) n foro m.

forward ('fɔːwəd) adj 1 avanzato, precoce. 2 sfrontato. adv avanti. n sport attaccante m. vt 1 promuovere, agevolare, inoltrare. 2 rispedire. **forwards** adv avanti, in poi.

fossil ('fɔsəl) n fossile m.

foster ('fɔstə) vt 1 allevare. 2 favorire, incoraggiare. **fosterchild** n figlio adottivo m. **fostermother** n madre adottiva f.

fought (fɔːt) v see **fight**.

foul (faul) adj 1 sporco, infetto, osceno. 2 (of weather) cattivo. n sport fallo m. vt 1 sporcare. 2 sport commettere un fallo su. **foul play** n giuoco scorretto m.

found[1] (faund) v see **find**.

found[2] (faund) vt fondare, istituire. **foundation** n 1 istituzione f. 2 base f. 3 pl fondamenta f pl.

founder[1] ('faundə) n fondatore m.

founder[2] ('faundə) vi affondare, sprofondarsi.

foundry ('faundri) n fonderia f.

fountain ('fauntin) n fontana, sorgente f.

four (fɔː) adj,n quattro m or f. **on all fours** carponi. **four-poster** n letto a quattro colonne m. **foursome** n quartetto m. **fourth** adj quarto.

fourteen (fɔː'tiːn) adj,n quattordici m or f. **fourteenth** adj quattordicesimo.

fowl (faul) n pollo, uccello m.

fox (fɔks) n volpe f. **foxglove** n digitale m. **foxhound** n cane per caccia alla volpe m. **foxhunting** n caccia alla volpe f.

foyer ('fɔiei) n ridotto m.

fraction ('frækʃən) n frazione f.

fracture ('fræktʃə) n frattura f. vt spaccare. vi fratturarsi.

fragile ('frædʒail) adj fragile.

fragment ('frægmənt) n frammento, brano m.

fragrant ('freigrənt) adj fragrante.

frail (freil) adj debole, fragile.

frame (freim) n 1 struttura f. 2 telaio m. 3 cornice f. 4 inquadratura f. **frame of mind** stato d'animo m. ~vt 1 costruire. 2 incorniciare. **framework** n struttura f. scheletro m.

franc (fræŋk) n franco m.

France (frɑːns) n Francia f.

franchise ('fræntʃaiz) n 1 diritto di voto m. 2 franchigia f.

frank (fræŋk) adj sincero, schietto.

frankfurter ('fræŋkfəːtə) n salsiccia tedesca f.

frantic ('fræntik) adj frenetico.

fraternal (frə'təːnl) adj fraterno. **fraternity** n fraternità, confraternità f. **fraternize** vi fraternizzare.

fraud (frɔːd) n frode f.

fraught (frɔːt) adj carico.

fray[1] (frei) n lotta f. conflitto m.

fray[2] (frei) vt consumare. vi logorarsi.

freak (friːk) n 1 capriccio m. 2 anomalia della natura f.

freckle ('frekəl) n lentiggine f.

free (friː) adj 1 libero. 2 esente. 3 gratuito. adv

liberamente, gratuitamente. *vt* liberare. **freedom** *n* libertà f. **freehold** *n* proprietà fondiaria assoluta f. **freelance** *adj* a ore, indipendente. *n* giornalista indipendente *m*. **free will** *n* libero arbitrio *m*.

freeze* (fri:z) *vt* congelare, gelare. *vi* gelare. **freezing point** *n* punto di congelamento *m*.

freight (freit) *n* 1 carico mercantile *m*. 2 trasporto *m*. *vt* trasportare. **freight train** *n* treno merci *m*.

French (frentʃ) *adj* francese. **French** (language) *n* francese *m*. **French bean** *n* fagiolino verde *m*. **French dressing** *n* condimento alla francese *m*. **French horn** *n* corno da caccia *m*. **Frenchman** *n* francese *m*. **French window** *n* porta-finestra *f*.

frenzy ('frenzi) *n* frenesia f.

frequency ('fri:kwənsi) *n* frequenza f. **frequent** *adj* frequente, diffuso.

fresco ('freskou) *n*, *pl* -**oes** *or* -**os** affresco *m*.

fresh (freʃ) *adj* 1 fresco, nuovo. 2 vigoroso. **freshwater** *adj* d'acqua dolce.

fret[1] (fret) *vi* logorarsi, affliggersi.

fret[2] (fret) *n* arch fregio m. **fretwork** *n* lavoro di traforo *m*.

friar ('fraiə) *n* frate *m*.

friction ('frikʃən) *n* frizione f.

Friday ('fraidi) *n* venerdì m.

fridge (fridʒ) *n* frigorifero *m*.

friend (frend) *n* amico, *pl* amici *m*. **friendly** *adj* amichevole, affabile. **friendship** *n* amicizia f.

frieze (fri:z) *n* fregio m.

fright (frait) *n* spavento m. paura f. **frighten** *vt* spaventare. **frightful** *adj* spaventoso, terribile. **frightfully** *adv* straordinariamente.

frigid ('fridʒid) *adj* frigido, freddo.

frill (fril) *n* fronzolo m.

fringe (frindʒ) *n* 1 frangia f. orlo m. 2 periferia f. *vt* ornare con frangia, orlare.

frisk (frisk) *vt* perquisire. *vi* saltellare.

fritter[1] ('fritə) *vt* sperperare, sciupare.

fritter[2] ('fritə) *n* frittella f.

frivolity (fri'vɔliti) *n* leggerezza, vanità f. **frivolous** *adj* leggero, frivolo.

frizz (friz) *vt* arricciare. *n* ricciolo m. **frizzy** *adj* ricciuto.

frizzle[1] ('frizl) *vt* arricciare. *vi* arricciarsi.

frizzle[2] ('frizəl) *cul* *vt* friggere. *vi* sfrigolare.

fro (fro) **to and fro** *adv* avanti e indietro.

frock (frɔk) *n* abito m.

frog (frɔg) *n* rana f. **frogman** *n* sommozzatore *m*.

frolic ('frɔlik) *vi* divertirsi. *n* scherzo *m*. **frolicsome** *adj* allegro, vivace.

from (frəm; *stressed* frɔm) *prep* 1 da. 2 da parte di. 3 per.

front (frʌnt) *adj* di fronte, anteriore. *n* 1 arch facciata f. 2 fronte m. 3 lungomare m. **in front of** davanti a.

frontier ('frʌntiə) *n* frontiera f. confine m.

frost (frɔst) *n* gelo m. brina f. **frostbite** *n* congelamento m. **frosty** *adj* gelato, congelato.

froth (frɔθ) *n* schiuma, spuma f. *vi* schiumare.

frown (fraun) *n* cipiglio m. *vi* aggrottare le ciglia.

froze (frouz) *v* see **freeze.**

frozen ('frouzn) *v* see **freeze.**

frugal ('fru:gəl) *adj* frugale, sobrio.

fruit (fru:t) *n* 1 frutta *f* *invar*. 2 frutto m. **fruit salad** *n* macedonia di frutta f. **fruitful** *adj* fertile, vantaggioso. **fruition** *n* realizzazione f. **fruitless** *adj* infruttuoso, vano.

frustrate (frʌs'treit) *vt* frustrare, deludere.

fry (frai) *vt,vi* friggere. **frying pan** *n* padella f.

fuchsia ('fju:ʃə) *n* fucsia m.

fuck (fʌk) *tab* *vt* chiavare. **fuck off!** va' fan culo!

fudge (fʌdʒ) *n* dolce caramellato con cioccolata *m*.

fuel ('fju:əl) *n* carburante m.

fugitive ('fju:dʒitiv) *adj* fuggente. *n* fuggiasco *m*.

fulcrum ('fʌlkrəm) *n* fulcro m.

fulfil (ful'fil) *vt* soddisfare, esaudire, completare. **fulfilment** *n* adempimento m. realizzazione f.

full (ful) *adj* pieno, completo, colmo, abbondante. **full-length** *adj* in tutta la lunghezza. **full moon** *n* luna piena f. **full stop** *n* punto *m*. **full-time** *adj,adv* orario completo m.

fumble ('fʌmbəl) *vi* 1 annaspare. 2 andare a tastoni.

fume (fju:m) *n* esalazione f. *vi*.1 esalare fumo. 2 irritarsi.

fun (fʌn) *n* allegria f. divertimento m. **make fun of** prendere in giro. **funfair** *n* parco dei divertimenti m.

function ('fʌŋkʃən) *n* 1 funzione f. 2 cerimonia f. *vi* funzionare.

fund (fʌnd) *n* fondo m. riserva f.

fundamental (fʌndə'mentl) *adj* fondamentale.

funeral ('fju:nərəl) *n* funerale m. *adj* funebre, funereo.

fungus ('fʌŋgəs) *n. pl* **fungi** or **funguses** *bot* fungo *m.*

funnel ('fʌnl) *n* 1 imbuto *m.* 2 *naut* ciminiera *f.*

funny ('fʌni) *adj* 1 divertente. 2 strano.

fur (fə:) *n* 1 pelo, pelame *m.* 2 pelliccia *f.*

furious ('fjuəriəs) *adj* furibondo, furioso.

furnace ('fə:nis) *n* fornace *f.*

furnish ('fə:niʃ) *vt* ammobiliare, fornire.

furniture ('fə:nitʃə) *n* mobilio *m.*

furrow ('fʌrou) *n* solco *m.* scia *f.*

further ('fə:θə) *adj* più lontano, ulteriore. *adv* oltre, inoltre. *vt* favorire, promuovere. **furthest** *adj* il più lontano, estremo.

furtive ('fə:tiv) *adj* furtivo.

fury ('fjuəri) *n* furia, violenza *f.*

fuse[1] (fju:z) *n* 1 *tech* fusibile *m.* valvola *f.* 2 *mil* spoletta, miccia *f.* *vi* saltare.

fuse[2] (fju:z) *vt* fondere. *vi* fondersi.

fuselage ('fju:zəla:ʒ) *n* fusoliera *f.*

fusion ('fju:ʒən) *n* fusione *f.*

fuss (fʌs) *n* trambusto *m.* agitazione *f.* *vi* affaccendarsi, preoccuparsi per nulla. **fussy** *adj* pignolo, meticoloso.

futile ('fju:tail) *adj* inutile, vano.

future ('fju:tʃə) *n* futuro *m.*

fuzz (fʌz) *n* 1 lanuggine *f.* 2 *sl* polizia *f.* **fuzzy** *adj* 1 increspato. 2 confuso.

G

gabble ('gæbəl) *n* borbottio *m.* *vt* borbottare. *vi* parlare in modo confuso.

gable ('geibəl) *n* frontone *m.*

gadget ('gædʒit) *n* congegno, gingillo *m.*

gag[1] (gæg) *n* bavaglio *m.* *vt* imbavagliare.

gag[2] (gæg) *n* battuta comica *f.*

gaiety ('geiəti) *n* allegria *f.*

gaily ('geili) *adv* gaiamente.

gain (gein) *n* 1 guadagno, profitto *m.* 2 miglioramento *m* *vt* guadagnare. *vi* profittare.

gait (geit) *n* andatura *f.*

gala ('ga:lə) *n* gala *f.*

galaxy ('gæləksi) *n* galassia *f.*

gale (geil) *n* burrasca *f.*

gall (gɔ:l) *n* bile *f.* fiele *m.*

gallant ('gælənt) *adj* valoroso, cortese.

galleon ('gæliən) *n* galeone *m.*

gallery ('gæləri) *n* galleria *f.* loggione *m.*

galley ('gæli) *n* 1 galera, galea *f.* 2 cambusa *f.*

gallon ('gælən) *n* gallone *m.*

gallop ('gæləp) *n* galoppo *m.* *vi* galoppare.

gallows ('gælouz) *n pl* forca *f.* patibolo *m.*

galore (gə'lɔ:) *adv* in quantità.

galvanize ('gælvənaiz) *vt* galvanizzare.

gamble ('gæmbəl) *n* gioco d'azzardo *m.* *vi* giocare d'azzardo. *vt* 1 giocare. 2 rischiare. **gambler** *n* giocatore d'azzardo *m.*

game (geim) *n* 1 gioco *m.* 2 partita *f.* 3 (hunting) selvaggina *f.* *adj* 1 coraggioso. 2 pronto. **gamekeeper** *n* guardiacaccia *m.*

gammon ('gæmən) *n* prosciutto affumicato *m.*

gander ('gændə) *n* papero *m.*

gang (gæŋ) *n* squadra, banda *f.* *v* **gang up** allearsi. **gangster** *n* bandito *m.* **gangway** *n* corridoio, passaggio *m.* passerella *f.*

gangrene ('gæŋgri:n) *n* cancrena *f.*

gap (gæp) *n* breccia, apertura, fessura, lacuna *f.*

gape (geip) *vi* 1 sbadigliare. 2 restare a bocca aperta. *n* sbadiglio *m.*

garage ('gæra:ʒ) *n* garage *m.* autorimessa *f.*

garbage ('ga:bidʒ) *n* 1 rifiuti *m pl.* 2 cosa spregevole *f.*

garble ('ga:bəl) *vt* alterare.

garden ('ga:dn) *n* giardino *m.* *vi* fare del giardinaggio. **gardener** *n* giardiniere *m.* **gardening** *n* giardinaggio *m.*

gargle ('ga:gəl) *vi* fare gargarismi. *n* liquido per gargarismi.

gargoyle ('ga:gɔil) *n* mascherone da grondaia *m.*

garland ('ga:lənd) *n* ghirlanda *f.*

garlic ('ga:lik) *n* aglio *m.*

garment ('ga:mənt) *n* indumento *m.*

garnish ('ga:niʃ) *vt* guarnire, ornare. *n* guarnizione *f.* contorno *m.*

garrison ('gærisən) *n* presidio *m.* guarnigione *f.* *vt* presidiare.

garter ('ga:tə) *n* giarrettiera *f.*

gas (gæs) *n* gas *m invar.* *vt* asfissiare con il gas. **gas cooker** *n* fornello a gas *m.* **gas fire** *n* stufa a gas *f.* **gasworks** *n pl* officina del gas *f.*

gash (gæʃ) *n* ferita *f.* squarcio *m.* *vt* sfregiare, tagliare.

gasket ('gæskit) *n* guarnizione *f.*

gasp (ga:sp) *n* rantolo *m.* *vi* boccheggiare, ansimare.

gastric ('gæstrik) *adj* gastrico. **gastronomic** *adj* gastronomico.

gate (geit) *n* cancello *m.* porta *f.* **gatecrash** *vt* entrare senza invito a.

gateau ('gætou) *n, pl* **-teaux** pasticcino *m.*

gather ('gæðə) vt **1** riunire. **2** raccogliere. **3** dedurre. vi radunarsi. **gathering** n riunione f.

gauche (gouʃ) adj maldestro.

gaudy ('gɔ:di) adj vistoso, di gusto pesante.

gauge (geidʒ) n **1** misura f. **2** calibro m. vt misurare, stimare.

gaunt (gɔ:nt) adj magro, scarno.

gauze (gɔ:z) n garza f. velo m.

gave (geiv) v see **give.**

gay (gei) adj allegro, vivace.

gaze (geiz) n sguardo fisso m. vi guardare fissamente.

gazelle (gə'zel) n gazzella f.

gear (giə) n **1** meccanismo m. **2** mot marcia f. **3** utensili m pl. vt adattare. **gearbox** n scatola del cambio f. **gear lever** n leva del cambio f.

gelatine ('dʒeləti:n) n gelatina f.

gelignite ('dʒelignait) n nitroglicerina f.

gem (dʒem) n gemma f. gioiello m.

Gemini ('dʒeminai) n pl Gemelli m pl.

gender ('dʒendə) n genere m.

gene (dʒi:n) n gene m.

genealogy (dʒini'ælədʒi) n genealogia f.

general ('dʒenərəl) adj generale, comune. **general election** n elezioni generali f pl. **general practitioner** n medico generico m. **generally** adv in generale, generalmente. **generalize** vt, vi generalizzare.

generate ('dʒenəreit) vt generare, produrre. **generation** n generazione f.

generic (dʒi'nerik) adj generico.

generous ('dʒenərəs) adj generoso, abbondante.

genetic (dʒi'netik) adj genetico. **genetics** n genetica f.

genial ('dʒi:niəl) adj cordiale, amabile.

genital ('dʒenitl) adj genitale. **genitals** n pl organi genitali m pl.

genius ('dʒi:niəs) n **1** genio m. **2** talento m.

genteel (dʒen'ti:l) adj garbato, compito.

gentian ('dʒenʃən) n genziana f.

gentile ('dʒentail) adj pagano. n gentile, pagano m.

gentle ('dʒentl) adj mite, nobile, cortese. **gentleman** n, pl **gentlemen** signore m.

genuflect ('dʒenjuflekt) vi genuflettersi.

genuine ('dʒenjuin) adj **1** genuino. **2** sincero. **3** puro.

genus ('dʒi:nəs) n, pl **genera** classe, specie f.

geography (dʒi'ɔgrəfi) n geografia f. **geographical** adj geografico.

geology (dʒi'ɔlədʒi) n geologia f. **geological** adj geologico.

geometry (dʒi'ɔmətri) n geometria f. **geometric** adj also **geometrical** geometrico.

geranium (dʒə'reiniəm) n geranio m.

geriatric (dʒeri'ætrik) adj geriatrico. **geriatrics** n geriatria, gerontologia f.

germ (dʒə:m) n germe m.

Germany ('dʒə:məni) n Germania f. **German** adj, n tedesco. **German (language)** n tedesco m. **German measles** n rosolia f. **Germanic** adj germanico.

germinate ('dʒə:mineit) vi germinare. **germination** n germinazione f.

gerund ('dʒerənd) n gerundio m.

gesticulate (dʒis'tikuleit) vi gesticolare.

gesture ('dʒestʃə) n gesto m.

get (get) vt **1** ottenere, guadagnare. **2** prendere, afferrare. vi **1** divenire. **2** arrivare. **3** fare, farsi. **4** persuadere. **get off** scendere. **get on** montare. **get over** superare. **get up** alzarsi.

geyser ('gi:zə) n **1** geog geyser m. **2** scaldabagno m.

ghastly ('ga:stli) adj orrendo, spettrale.

gherkin ('gə:kin) n cetriolo m.

ghetto ('getou) n, pl **-os** or **-oes** ghetto m.

ghost (goust) n spirito, fantasma m.

giant ('dʒaiənt) n gigante m. adj gigantesco.

giddy ('gidi) adj stordito, vertiginoso. **giddiness** n vertigine f.

gift (gift) n regalo, dono m. **gifted** adj dotato, fornito di talento.

gigantic (dʒai'gæntik) adj gigantesco.

giggle n risatina sciocca f. vi far risatine.

gild (gild) vt dorare.

gill (gil) n zool branchia f.

gilt (gilt) adj dorato. n doratura f.

gimmick ('gimik) n trucco, stratagemma m.

gin (dʒin) n gin m.

ginger ('dʒindʒə) n zenzero m. adj fulvo. **ginger beer** n bibita allo zenzero f. **gingerbread** n pan di zenzero m.

gingham ('giŋəm) n percallina f.

Gipsy ('dʒipsi) n gitano, zingaro m.

giraffe (dʒi'ra:f) n giraffa f.

girder ('gə:də) n putrella f.

girdle ('gə:dl) n cintura f. busto m. vt cingere, fasciare.

girl (gə:l) n ragazza, fanciulla f.

Giro ('dʒairou) n sistema bancario m.

girth (gə:θ) n **1** giro m. circonferenza f. **2** sottopancia f.

give[*] (giv) vt 1 dare. 2 consegnare. vi cedere. **give away** 1 rivelare, tradire. 2 regalare. **give back** restituire. **give in** cedere. **give up** 1 smettere. 2 arrendersi.

glacier ('glæsiə) n ghiacciaio m.

glad (glæd) adj contento, allegro. **gladly** adv con piacere.

glamour ('glæmə) n fascino, incantesimo m. **glamorous** adj affascinante. **glamorize** vt rendere attraente, valorizzare.

glance (gla:ns) n occhiata f. sguardo m. vi dare un'occhiata, guardare di sfuggita.

gland (glænd) n ghiandola f.

glare (gleə) n 1 riverbero m. 2 sguardo penetrante m. vi guardare con astio.

glass (gla:s) n 1 vetro m. 2 bicchiere m. 3 pl occhiali m pl. adj di vetro.

glaze (gleiz) n smalto m. vernice f. vt 1 fornire di vetro. 2 smaltare.

gleam (gli:m) n barlume m. vi scintillare, brillare.

glean (gli:n) vt 1 spigolare. 2 raccogliere.

glee (gli:) n allegria, gioia f.

glib (glib) adj scorrevole, loquace.

glide (glaid) n 1 scivolata f. 2 mus legamento m. 3 aviat volo libero m. vi 1 scorrere. 2 scivolare. 3 planare. **glider** n aliante m.

glimmer ('glimə) n barlume, luccichio m. vi brillare, luccicare.

glimpse (glimps) n visione f. colpo d'occhio m. **catch a glimpse of** vedere di sfuggita.

glint (glint) n scintillio m. vi scintillare.

glisten ('glisən) vi brillare.

glitter ('glitə) n scintillio m. lucentezza f. vi brillare, rifulgere.

gloat (glout) vi gongolare (malignamente).

globe (gloub) n 1 globo m. sfera f. 2 mappamondo m.

gloom[1] (glu:m) n oscurità f. buio m. **gloomy** adj annuvolato.

gloom[2] (glu:m) n malinconia, tristezza f. **gloomy** adj cupo, triste.

glory ('glɔ:ri) n gloria f. splendore m. **glorify** vt glorificare. **glorious** adj maestoso, splendido.

gloss[1] (glɔs) n lucentezza f. vt 1 lucidare. 2 rendere plausibile.

gloss[2] (glɔs) n chiosa f. commento m. vt interpretare, commentare.

glossary ('glɔsəri) n glossario, lessico m.

glove (glʌv) n guanto m.

glow (glou) n ardore m. incandescenza f. vi ardere, essere incandescente. **glow-worm** n lucciola f.

glower ('glauə) vi guardare con occhi torvi.

glucose ('glu:kous) n glucosio m.

glue (glu:) n colla f. vt incollare.

glum (glʌm) adj tetro, accigliato.

glut (glʌt) n sovrabbondanza. vt satollare, rimpinzare.

glutton ('glʌtn) n ghiottone, goloso m. **gluttony** n ghiottoneria f.

gnarled (nɑ:ld) adj nodoso, rugoso.

gnash (næʃ) vt digrignare.

gnat (næt) n moscerino m. zanzara f.

gnaw (nɔ:) vt rodere, tormentare.

gnome (noum) n gnomo m.

go[*] (gou) vi 1 andare, partire. 2 funzionare. 3 divenire. **go about** occuparsi di. **go back** ritornare. **go down** 1 discendere. 2 affondare. **go into** entrare. **go on** continuare. **go out** 1 uscire. 2 spegnersi. **go up** salire. ~n 1 vigore m. 2 tentativo m.

goad (goud) n pungolo m. vt stimolare, incitare.

goal (goul) n 1 traguardo, scopo m. 2 sport rete, porta f. **goalkeeper** n portiere m. **goalpost** n palo della porta m.

goat (gout) n capra f.

gobble ('gɔbəl) vt inghiottire, tranguiare.

goblin ('gɔblin) n folletto m.

god (gɔd) n 1 idolo m. divinità f. 2 cap Dio m. **goddaughter** n figlioccia f. **godfather** n padrino m. **godmother** n madrina f. **godson** n figlioccio m. **goddess** n dea f.

goggles ('gɔgəlz) n pl occhiali di protezione m pl.

going ('gouiŋ) n 1 landare m. andatura f. 2 sport terreno. adj attivo.

gold (gould) n oro m. adj d'oro. **goldfish** n pesce rosso m. **goldmine** n 1 miniera d'oro f. 2 fonte di ricchezza f. **gold rush** n febbre dell'oro f. **goldsmith** n orefice m. **golden** adj d'oro, aureo. **golden syrup** n melassa f.

golf (gɔlf) n golf m. **golfball** n palla da golf f. **golf club** n 1 mazza da golf f. 2 circolo del golf m. **golfcourse** n campo di golf m.

gondola ('gɔndələ) n gondola f. **gondolier** n gondoliere m.

gone (gɔn) v see **go**.

gong (gɔŋ) n gong m.

good (gud) adj 1 buono, onesto. 2 valido. n bene, vantaggio m. **for good** per sempre. **it is no good** è inutile.

good afternoon interj buon giorno!

goodbye (gud'bai) *interj* addio! arrivederci!

good evening *interj* buona sera!

Good Friday *n* Venerdì Santo *m.*

good-humoured *adj* di buon umore.

good-looking *adj* di bell'aspetto.

good morning *interj* buon giorno!

good night *interj* buona notte!

goods train *n* treno merci *m.*

good will *n* buona volontà *f.*

goose (gu:s) *n, pl* **geese** *n* oca *f.* **gooseberry** *n* uva spina *f.*

gore[1] (gɔ:) *n* sangue *m.*

gore[2] (gɔ:) *vt* trafiggere con le corna.

gorge (gɔ:dʒ) *n* gola *f. vt* satollare.

gorgeous ('gɔ:dʒəs) *adj* magnifico, splendido.

gorilla (gə'rilə) *n* gorilla *m.*

gorse (gɔ:s) *n* ginestra spinosa *f.*

gory ('gɔ:ri) *adj* insanguinato.

gosh (gɔʃ) *interj* perbacco!

gosling ('gɔzliŋ) *n* papero *m.*

gospel ('gɔspəl) *n* vangelo *m.*

gossip ('gɔsip) *n* 1 chiacchiera *f.* pettegolezzo *m.* 2 pettegolo *m. vi* far pettegolezzi.

got (gɔt) *v see* **get.**

Gothic ('gɔθik) *adj* gotico.

goulash ('gu:læʃ) *n* gulash *m.*

gourd (guəd) *n* zucca *f.*

gourmet (guə'mei) *n* buongustaio *m.*

govern ('gʌvən) *vt* governare, influenzare, controllare. **government** *n* governo *m.* **governmental** *adj* governativo. **governor** *n* 1 governatore *m.* 2 *sl* capo, principale *m.*

gown (gaun) *n* 1 veste *f.* 2 toga *f.*

grab (græb) *vt* afferrare, arraffare. *n* presa, stretta *f.*

grace (greis) *n* grazia *f.* **His/Your Grace** Sua/Vostra Grazia. **graceful** *adj* grazioso, leggiadro. **gracious** *adj* clemente, benigno.

grade (greid) *n* grado, rango *m. vt* graduare, classificare. **gradient** *n* pendenza *f.* gradiente *m.* **gradual** *adj* graduale. **graduate** *n* laureato *m. vi* laurearsi.

graffiti (grə'fi:ti) *n pl* graffiti *m pl.*

graft (grɑ:ft) *vt* 1 innestare. 2 trapiantare. *n* 1 *bot* innesto *m.* 2 *med* trapianto *m.*

grain (grein) *n* 1 grano *m.* 2 chicco *m.* 3 granello *m.*

gram (græm) *n* grammo *m.*

grammar ('græmə) *n* grammatica *f.* **grammar school** *n* scuola secondaria *f.* **grammatical** *adj* grammaticale.

gramophone ('græməfoun) *n* grammofono *m.*

granary ('grænəri) *n* granaio *m.*

grand (grænd) *adj* grandioso, imponente. **grandeur** *n* grandiosità *f.* splendore *m.*

grandad ('grændæd) *n inf also* **grandpa** nonno *m.*

grandchild ('græntʃaild) *n* nipote *m,f.*

granddaughter ('grændɔ:tə) *n* nipote, nipotina *f.*

grandfather ('grænfɑ:ðə) *n* nonno *m.*

grandma ('grænmɑ:) *n inf also* **granny** nonnina *f.*

grandmother ('grænmʌðə) *n* nonna *f.*

grandparent ('grænpɛərənt) *n* nonno *m.*

grand piano *n* piano a coda *m.*

grandson ('grænsʌn) *n* nipote, nipotino *m.*

grandstand ('grændstænd) *n* tribuna d'onore *f.*

granite ('grænit) *n* granito *m.*

grant (grɑ:nt) *vt* concedere, ammettere. **take for granted** dare per scontato. *n* 1 concessione *f.* 2 *educ* borsa di studio *f.*

grape (greip) *n* 1 acino *m.* 2 *pl* uva *f.* **grapefruit** *n* pompelmo *m.* **grapevine** *n* vite *f.*

graph (græf) *n* grafico *m.* curva *f.* **graphic** *adj* grafico.

grapple ('græpəl) *vi* venire alle prese.

grasp (grɑ:sp) *vt* afferrare, capire. *n* 1 stretta *f.* 2 comprensione *f.*

grass (grɑ:s) *n* erba *f.* prato *m.*

grate[1] (greit) *n* griglia, graticola *f.*

grate[2] (greit) *vt* grattugiare. *vi* stridere.

grateful ('greitfəl) *adj* grato, riconoscente. **gratify** *vt* ricompensare, soddisfare.

gratitude ('grætitju:d) *n* gratitudine *f.*

grave[1] (greiv) *n* fossa, tomba *f.* **gravestone** *n* lapide *f.* **graveyard** *n* cimitero *m.*

grave[2] (greiv) *adj* serio, solenne, grave.

gravel ('grævəl) *n* ghiaia *f.*

gravity ('græviti) *n* gravità, serietà *f.*

gravy ('greivi) *n* sugo di carne *m.*

graze[1] (greiz) *vi* pascolare.

graze[2] (greiz) *vt med* sfiorare, scalfire. *n* scalfittura *f.*

grease (gri:s) *n* unto, grasso *m. vt* ungere, ingrassare. **greaseproof** *adj* deato.

great (greit) *adj* 1 grande. 2 celebre. **a great deal** molto.

Great Britain *n* Gran Bretagna *f.*

Greece (gri:s) *n* Grecia *f.* **Grecian** *adj* greco, *pl* greci. **Greek** *adj,n* greco, *pl* greci. **Greek** (language) *n* greco *m.*

greed (gri:d) *n* avidità, ingordigia *f.* **greedy** *adj* avido, goloso.

201

green (gri:n) *adj* 1 verde. 2 inesperto. *n* 1 prato *m.* 2 (colour) verde *m.* 3 *pl* verdura *f.* **greenery** *n* vegetazione *f.* **greenfly** *n* pidocchio delle piante *m.* **greengage** *n* prugna *f.* **greengrocer** *n* erbivendolo *m.* **greenhouse** *n* serra *f.*

Greenland ('gri:nlənd) *n* Groenlandia *f.* **Greenlander** *n* groenlandese *m,f.*

greet (gri:t) *vt* salutare. **greeting** *n* saluto *m.*

gregarious (gri'gɛəriəs) *adj* socievole, gregario.

grenade (gri'neid) *n* granata *f.*

grew (gru:) *v* see **grow.**

grey (grei) *adj,n* grigio *m.* **greyhound** *n* levriero *m.*

grid (grid) *n* griglia *f.*

grief (gri:f) *n* dolore *m.* angoscia *f.*

grieve (gri:v) *vt* affliggere. *vi* affliggersi. **grievance** *n* 1 lamentela *f.* 2 ingiustizia *f.*

grill (gril) *n* graticola *f.* *vt* cuocere ai ferri.

grille (gril) *n* griglia, inferriata *f.*

grim (grim) *adj* torvo, sinistro.

grimace ('grimis) *n* smorfia *f.* *vi* fare smorfie.

grime (graim) *n* sporcizia *f.* **grimy** *adj* sporco.

grin (grin) *n* sogghigno *m.* *vi* sogghignare.

grind* (graind) *vt* 1 macinare. 2 affilare. 3 (teeth) digrignare. *vi* sgobbare. *n* lavoro arduo *m.*

grip (grip) *vt* 1 afferrare. 2 attirare. *vi* afferrare. *n* stretta *f.*

gripe (graip) *n* colica *f.*

gristle ('grisəl) *n* cartilagine *f.*

grit (grit) *n* 1 sabbia *f.* pulviscolo *m.* 2 *inf* forza di carattere *f.* *vt* digrignare.

groan (groun) *n* gemito *m.* *vi* lamentarsi.

grocer ('grousə) *n* droghiere *m.* **grocer's shop** *n* drogheria *f.*

groin (grɔin) *n* inguine *m.*

groom (gru:m) *n* 1 palafreniere *m.* 2 sposo *m.* *vt* strigliare, riordinare.

groove (gru:v) *n* scanalatura *f.* canale *m.* *vt* scanalare.

grope (group) *vi* brancolare, andare a tastoni.

gross (grous) *adj* 1 volgare, grossolano. 2 *comm* lordo. *n* massa *f.*

grotesque (grou'tesk) *adj* grottesco.

grotto ('grɔtou) *n, pl* **-toes** *or* **-tos** grotta *f.*

ground[1] (graund) *n* 1 terra *f.* terreno *m.* 2 motivo *m.* base *f.* 3 campo, fondo *m.* *vt* 1 basare. 2 trattenere a terra. *vi* incagliarsi. **ground floor** *n* pianterreno *m.* **groundsheet** *n* telone impermeabile *m.* **groundsman** *n*

addetto in un campo sportivo *m.* **groundwork** *n* base *f.* fondamento *m.*

ground[2] (graund) *v* see **grind.** *adj* macinato, levigato.

group (gru:p) *n* gruppo *m.* *vt* raggruppare.

grouse[1] (graus) *n* gallo cedrone *m.*

grouse[2] (graus) *vi* brontolare.

grove (grouv) *n* boschetto *m.*

grovel ('grɔvəl) *vi* umiliarsi.

grow* (grou) *vi* 1 crescere, aumentare. 2 diventare. *vt* coltivare. **grow up** crescere. **growth** *n* 1 crescita *f.* aumento *m.* 2 *med* escrescenza *f.*

growl (graul) *n* brontolio, ringhio *m.* *vi* borbottare, ringhiare.

grub (grʌb) *n* 1 verme, lombrico *m.* 2 *sl* cibo *m.* **grubby** *adj* sporco.

grudge (grʌdʒ) *n* rancore, risentimento *m.* **bear a grudge** avere del risentimento. ~*vt* lesinare, concedere a malincuore.

gruelling ('gru:əliŋ) *adj* estenuante.

gruesome ('gru:səm) *adj* macabro.

gruff (grʌf) *adj* burbero, arcigno.

grumble ('grʌmbəl) *vi* borbottare, lamentarsi. *n* lagnanza *f.*

grumpy ('grʌmpi) *adj* bisbetico, irritabile.

grunt (grʌnt) *vi* grugnire, brontolare. *n* grugnito, borbottio *m.*

guarantee (gærən'ti:) *n* 1 garanzia *f.* 2 garante *m.* *vt* garantire, assicurare, rendersi garante di. **guarantor** *n* garante *m.*

guard (gɑ:d) *vt,vi* guardare. *n* 1 guardia *f.* 2 (railway) capotreno *m.* 3 protezione *f.* **guard's van** *n* carro di servizio *m.* **guardian** *n* guardiano *m.* **guardian angel** *n* angelo custode *m.*

guerrilla (gə'rilə) *n* guerrigliero *m.*

guess (ges) *n* congettura, supposizione *f.* *vt,vi* supporre, indovinare. **guesswork** *n* congettura *f.*

guest (gest) *n* ospite *m,f.* invitato *m.* **guesthouse** *n* pensione *f.*

guide (gaid) *n* guida *f.* cicerone *m.* *vt* dirigere, guidare. **guidance** *n* guida, direzione *f.* **guidebook** *n* guida *f.* manuale *m.* **guide-dog** *n* cane guida *m.*

guild (gild) *n* corporazione *f.*

guillotine ('gilə'ti:n) *n* ghigliottina *f.* *vt* ghigliottinare.

guilt (gilt) *n* colpa *f.* **guilty** *adj* colpevole.

guinea ('gini) *n* ghinea *f.* **guinea pig** *n* porcellino d'India *m.* cavia *f.*

guitar (gi'tɑ:) n chitarra f.

gulf (gʌlf) n 1 geog golfo m. 2 abisso m.

gull (gʌl) n gabbiano m.

gullet ('gʌlit) n gola f. esofago m.

gulp (gʌlp) n boccone, sorso m. vt inghiottire, tranguiare.

gum[1] (gʌm) n gengiva f.

gum[2] (gʌm) n gomma f. vt ingommare.

gun (gʌn) n 1 cannone m. 2 rivoltella f. fucile m. **gunman** n bandito, terrorista m. **gunpowder** n polvere da sparo f. **gunrunning** n contrabbando d'armi m. **gunshot** n colpo d'arma da fuoco m.

gurgle ('gə:gəl) n gorgoglio m. vi gorgogliare, mormorare.

gush (gʌʃ) n 1 sgorgo, zampillo m. 2 effusione f. vi 1 sgorgare. 2 abbandonarsi ad effusioni.

gust (gʌst) n raffica f.

gut (gʌt) n 1 budello m, pl budella f. 2 pl sl coraggio m. vt sventrare.

gutter ('gʌtə) n grondaia f. rigagnolo m.

guy[1] (gai) n 1 inf individuo, tipo m. 2 spauracchio m.

guy[2] (gai) n (rope) tirante di fissaggio m.

gymnasium (dʒim'neiziəm) n palestra f. **gymnast** n ginnasta m. **gymnastic** adj ginnastico. **gymnastics** n pl ginnastica f.

gynaecology (gaini'kɔlədʒi) n ginecologia f. **gynaecologist** n ginecologo m.

gypsum ('dʒipsəm) n pietra da gesso f.

H

haberdasher ('hæbədæʃə) n merciaio m. **haberdashery** n merceria f.

habit ('hæbit) n abitudine f. **habitable** adj abitabile. **habitual** adj abituale.

hack[1] (hæk) vt tagliare, troncare. n tacca f. taglio m. **hacksaw** n seghetto m.

hack[2] (hæk) n 1 (horse) ronzino m. 2 scribacchino m.

hackneyed ('hæknid) adj trito, banale.

had (hæd) v see **have.**

haddock ('hædək) n merluzzo m.

haemorrhage ('heməridʒ) n emorragia f.

hag (hæg) n strega, vecchiaccia f.

haggard ('hægəd) adj smunto, sparuto.

haggle ('hægl) vi mercanteggiare.

Hague, The (heig) n L'Aia f.

hail[1] (heil) n grandine f. vi grandinare.

hailstone n chicco di grandine m. **hailstorm** n grandinata f.

hail[2] (heil) vt salutare, chiamare. n saluto m.

hair (hɛə) n 1 capelli m pl. 2 pelo m. 3 pelame m. **split hairs** cercare il pelo nell'uovo. **hairbrush** ('hɛəbrʌʃ) n spazzola per capelli f. **haircut** ('hɛəkʌt) n taglio dei capelli m. **hairdo** ('hɛədu:) n acconciatura f. **hairdresser** ('hɛədresə) n parrucchiere m. parrucchiera f. **hairdressing** n mestiere del parrucchiere m. **hairdryer** ('hɛədraiə) n asciugacapelli m invar. **hairgrip** ('hɛəgrip) n forcina per capelli f. **hairnet** ('hɛənet) n retina per capelli f. **hairpiece** ('hɛəpi:s) n toupet m.

hair-raising adj raccapricciante, che fa rizzare i capelli.

hairstyle ('hɛəstail) n pettinatura f.

hairy ('hɛəri) adj peloso.

half (hɑ:f) n, pl **halves** metà f. mezzo m. **go halves** fare a metà. ~adj mezzo. adv a mezzo.

half-a-dozen adj,n mezza dozzina f.

half-and-half adj,adv mezzo e mezzo.

half-back n mediano m.

half-baked adj 1 non completamente cotto. 2 incompleto.

half-breed n meticcio m.

half-brother n fratellastro m.

half-caste n mulatto m.

half-hearted adj esitante, abulico.

half-hour n mezz'ora f.

half-mast adv **at half-mast** a mezz'asta.

halfpenny ('heipni) n moneta da mezzo penny f.

half-pint n mezza pinta f.

half-sister n sorellastra f.

half-term n vacanza di metà trimestre f.

half-time n intervallo m.

halftone ('hɑ:ftoun) n mezzatinta f.

halfway (hɑ:f'wei) adj,adv a mezza strada.

halfwit ('hɑ:fwit) n tonto, stupido m.

halibut ('hælibət) n, pl **-buts** or **-but** sogliola atlantica f. halibut m invar.

hall (hɔ:l) n sala f. salone m.

hallelujah (hæli'lu:jə) interj n alleluia m.

hallmark ('hɔ:lmɑ:k) n marchio m.

hallo (hə'lou) interj salve m.

hallowed ('hæloud) adj benedetto, santo.

Hallowe'en (hælou'i:n) n vigilia dell'Ognissanti f.

hallucination (həlu:si'neiʃən) n allucinazione f.

halo

halo (ˈheilou) *n, pl* **-loes** *or* **-los** aureola *f.* alone *m.*

halt (hɔ:lt) *n* fermata, sosta *f.* *vt* fermare. *vi* trattenersi.

halter (ˈhɔ:ltə) *n* cavezza *f.* capestro *m.*

halve (hɑ:v) *vt* dimezzare.

ham (hæm) *n* prosciutto *m.*

hamburger (ˈhæmbə:gə) *n* 1 polpetta di carne *f.* 2 panino con polpetta *m.*

hammer (ˈhæmə) *n* martello *m.* *vt* martellare.

hammock (ˈhæmək) *n* amaca *f.*

hamper[1] (ˈhæmpə) *vt* ostacolare, impedire.

hamper[2] (ˈhæmpə) *n* paniere *m.*

hamster (ˈhæmstə) *n* criceto *m.*

hand (hænd) *n* 1 mano *f, pl* mani. 2 operaio *m.* 3 lato *m.* 4 calligrafia *f.* 5 (of a clock) lancetta *f.* **at hand** a portata di mano. **on the other hand** d'altra parte. ~*vt* porgere, consegnare, dare.

handbag (ˈhændbæg) *n* borsa, borsetta *f.*

handbook (ˈhændbuk) *n* manuale *m.*

handbrake (ˈhændbreik) *n* freno a mano *m.*

handcart (ˈhændkɑ:t) *n* carretto a mano *m.*

handcuff (ˈhændkʌf) *n* manetta *f.* *vt* mettere le manette a.

handful (ˈhændful) *n* 1 manata, manciata *f.* 2 piccolo numero *m.*

hand grenade *n* granata *or* bomba a mano *f.*

handicap (ˈhændikæp) *n* 1 svantaggio, ostacolo *m.* 2 *sport* handicap *m.* *vt* 1 impedire, intralciare. 2 regolare un handicap. **handicapped** *adj* mutilato, menomato.

handicraft (ˈhændikrɑ:ft) *n* 1 artigianato *m.* 2 arte *f.*

handiwork (ˈhændiwə:k) *n* lavoro a mano *m.*

handkerchief (ˈhæŋkətʃif) *n* fazzoletto *m.*

handle (ˈhændl) *n* 1 manico *m.* 2 maniglia *f.* 3 manubrio *m.* *vt* maneggiare, trattare. **handlebar** *n* manubrio *m.*

handmade (ˈhændˈmeid) *adj* fatto a mano.

hand-pick *vt* scegliere singolarmente, cogliere a mano.

handrail (ˈhændreil) *n* corrimano *m* ringhiera *f.*

handshake (ˈhændʃeik) *n* stretta di mano *f.*

handsome (ˈhænsəm) *adj* 1 bello, ben fatto. 2 considerevole, generoso.

handstand (ˈhændstænd) *n* posata verticale sulle mani *f.*

handwriting (ˈhændraitiŋ) *n* calligrafia *f.*

handy (ˈhændi) *adj* 1 abile. 2 utile, a portata di mano.

hang [*] (hæŋ) *vt* 1 appendere. 2 impiccare. 3

attaccare. *vi* pendere. **hang back** esitare. **hang on** 1 persistere. 2 rimanere attaccato. **hang out** stendere. **hang up** 1 appendere. 2 riattaccare. **hanger** *n* gancio *m.* stampella *f.* **hangman** *n* boia *m invar.* **hangover** *n* malessere *m.* postumi di sbornia *m pl.*

hanker (ˈhæŋkə) *vi* agognare, bramare.

haphazard (hæpˈhæzəd) *adj* casuale.

happen (ˈhæpən) *vi* avvenire, accadere. **happening** *n* avvenimento *m.*

happy (ˈhæpi) *adj* felice, contento. **happy-go-lucky** *adj* spensierato.

harass (ˈhærəs) *vt* molestare, tormentare. **harassment** *n* molestia *f.* tormento *m.*

harbour (ˈhɑ:bə) *n* 1 porto *m.* 2 rifugio *m.* *vt* 1 dar rifugio a. 2 albergare.

hard (hɑ:d) *adj* 1 duro. 2 difficile, faticoso. *adv* 1 energicamente. 2 molto. **hardback** *n* libro con la copertina dura *m.* **hardboard** *n* pannello di fibra di legno *m.* **hard-boiled** *adj* sodo. **hard-headed** *adj* ostinato. **hard-hearted** *adj* insensibile, senza cuore. **hardship** *n* disagio, stento *m.* privazione *f.* **hardware** *n* ferramenta *f pl.* **harden** *vt* indurire. *vi* indurirsi.

hardly (ˈhɑ:dli) *adv* 1 appena, a stento. 2 quasi.

hardy (ˈhɑ:di) *adj* coraggioso, resistente.

hare (hɛə) *n* lepre *f.*

haricot (ˈhærikou) *n* fagiolino *m.*

hark (hɑ:k) *vi* ascoltare.

harm (hɑ:m) *n* 1 torto, danno *m.* *vt* nuocere a, danneggiare.

harmonic (hɑ:ˈmɔnik) *adj* armonioso, armonico. **harmonica** *n* armonica *f.* **harmonize** *vt* armonizzare. *vi* andare d'accordo. **harmony** *n* armonia *f.*

harness (ˈhɑ:nis) *n* finimenti *m pl.* *vt* bardare, imbrigliare.

harp (hɑ:p) *n* arpa *f.*

harpoon (hɑ:ˈpu:n) *n* fiocina *f.* *vt* fiocinare.

harpsichord (ˈhɑ:psikɔ:d) *n* clavicembalo *m.*

harrow (ˈhærou) *n* erpice *m.* *vt* 1 erpicare. 2 straziare.

harsh (hɑ:ʃ) *adj* ruvido, aspro, severo. **harshness** *n* durezza, severità *f.*

harvest (ˈhɑ:vist) *n* raccolto *m.* *vt* mietere, raccogliere.

has (hæz) *v see* **have.**

hashish (ˈhæʃiʃ) *n* hascisc *m.*

haste (heist) *n* fretta *f.* **hasten** *vt* affrettare. *vi* affrettarsi.

hat (hæt) *n* cappello *m.* **bowler hat** bombetta *f.*

hatch[1] (hætʃ) vt covare. vi nascere. n covata f.

hatch[2] (hætʃ) naut portello, boccaporto m.

hatchet ('hætʃit) n scure, accetta f.

hate (heit) vt odiare, detestare. n odio m. **hateful** adj odioso.

haughty ('hɔːti) adj superbo, altezzoso.

haul (hɔːl) vt tirare, trainare. n bottino m. retata f.

haunch (hɔːntʃ) n anca f. fianco m.

haunt (hɔːnt) vt 1 frequentare. 2 perseguitare. n ritrovo m. tana f. **haunted** adj 1 perseguitato. 2 infestato da apparizioni.

have* (hæv) vt 1 avere. 2 possedere. 3 dovere. v aux avere. **have done** or **made** far fare.

haven ('heivən) n 1 porto m. 2 rifugio m.

haversack ('hævəsæk) n zaino m.

havoc ('hævək) n rovina, devastazione f.

hawk (hɔːk) n falco, sparviero m.

hawthorn ('hɔːθɔːn) n biancospino m.

hay (hei) n fieno m. **hayfever** n febbre da fieno f. **haystack** n mucchio di fieno m. **haywire** adj pazzo. **go haywire** eccitarsi.

hazard ('hæzəd) n rischio, azzardo m. vt arrischiare. **hazardous** adj rischioso.

haze (heiz) n 1 nebbia f. 2 confusione f.

hazel ('heizəl) n nocciuolo m. **hazelnut** n nocciuola f.

he (hiː) pron 3rd pers s 1 egli m. 2 lui m. 3 colui m.

head (hed) n 1 anat testa f. 2 dirigente m,f. 3 capezzale m. 4 schiuma f. vt 1 colpire con la testa. 2 intestare. 3 dirigere. **head for** dirigersi verso.

headache ('hedeik) n mal di testa m.

heading ('hediŋ) n intestazione f.

headlight ('hedlait) n faro m.

headline ('hedlain) n titolo di prima pagina m.

headlong ('hedlɔŋ) adv a capofitto.

headmaster (hed'mɑːstə) n direttore, preside m.

headphone ('hedfoun) n cuffia f.

headquarters ('hedkwɔːtəz) n pl 1 mil quartiere generale m. 2 centro m.

headscarf ('hedskɑːf) n fazzoletto da testa m.

headstrong ('hedstrɔŋ) adj testardo.

headway ('hedwei) n progresso m.

heal (hiːl) vt,vi guarire.

health (helθ) n salute f. **healthy** adj sano, salubre.

heap (hiːp) n mucchio, cumulo m. vt ammucchiare, accumulare.

hear* (hiə) vt 1 udire, ascoltare. 2 apprendere. vi udire, sentire. **hear about** avere notizie di.

hearing n 1 udito m. 2 udienza f. **hearing aid** n apparecchio acustico m.

hearse (hɔːs) n carro funebre m.

heart (hɑːt) n 1 cuore m. 2 coraggio m. 3 centro m. **by heart** a memoria. **heart attack** n attacco cardiaco m. **heartbeat** n pulsazione f. **heartbroken** adj affranto, angosciato. **heartless** adj spietato, senza cuore. **hearty** adj cordiale, vigoroso.

hearth (hɑːθ) n focolare m.

heat (hiːt) n 1 caldo m. 2 ardore m. 3 sport prova singola f. **heater** n radiatore m. stufetta f. **heatwave** n ondata di caldo f.

heath (hiːθ) n brughiera f.

heathen ('hiːðən) adj,n pagano.

heather ('heðə) n erica f.

heave (hiːv) n 1 sollevamento m. vt sollevare, issare. vi gonfiarsi.

heaven ('hevən) n cielo, paradiso m.

heavy ('hevi) adj pesante. **heavyweight** n sport peso massimo m.

Hebrew ('hiːbruː) adj ebreo, ebraico. n ebreo m. **Hebrew** (language) n ebraico m.

heckle ('hekəl) vt tempestare di domande.

hectare ('hektɛə) n ettaro m.

hectic ('hektik) adj movimentato.

hedge (hedʒ) n siepe f. vt circondare con siepe. vi evitare di dare una risposta diretta. **hedgehog** n porcospino m.

heed (hiːd) n attenzione f. vt fare attenzione a, badare a.

heel (hiːl) n 1 calcagno m, pl calcagna f or calcagni m. 2 tacco m.

hefty ('hefti) adj 1 forte. 2 vigoroso.

height (hait) n 1 altezza f. 2 colmo m. 3 altura f. **heighten** vt 1 intensificare. 2 innalzare. vi accentuarsi.

heir (ɛə) n erede m,f. **heirloom** n cimelio di famiglia m.

held (held) v see **hold.**

helicopter ('helikɔptə) n elicottero m.

helium ('hiːliəm) n elio m.

hell (hel) n inferno m. **hellish** adj infernale.

hello (hə'lou) interj 1 salve! ciao! 2 (on the telephone) pronto!

helm (helm) n timone m.

helmet ('helmit) n casco, elmetto m.

help (help) n 1 aiuto m. assistenza f. 2 rimedio m. vt aiutare, assistere. **helpful** adj utile, vantaggioso. **helpless** adj indifeso, debole.

hem (hem) n orlo m. vt orlare.

205

hemisphere ('hemisfiə) *n* emisfero *m*.

hemp (hemp) *n* canapa *f*.

hen (hen) *n* **1** gallina *f*. **2** femmina *f*.

hence (hens) *adv* **1** di qui. **2** perciò. **henceforth** *adv* d'ora in avanti.

henna ('henə) *n* alcanna *f*.

her (hə:) *pron 3rd pers s* la, lei, le *f*. *poss adj 3rd pers s* (il) suo, (la) sua, (i) suoi, (le) sue.

herald ('herəld) *n* araldo, messaggero *m*. *vt* annunziare.

herb (hə:b) *n* erba aromatica *f*.

herd (hə:d) *n* gregge *m*. mandria *f*.

here (hiə) *adv* qui, qua. **hereafter** *adv* in futuro.

hereditary (hi'reditri) *adj* ereditario.

heredity (hi'rediti) *n* ereditarietà *f*.

heresy ('herəsi) *n* eresia *f*.

heritage ('heritidʒ) *n* eredità *f*.

hermit ('hə:mit) *n* eremita *m*.

hero ('hiərou) *n, pl* **-oes** *n* **1** eroe *m*. **2** protagonista *m*.

heroin ('herouin) *n* eroina *f*.

heroine ('herouin) *n* **1** eroina *f*. **2** protagonista *f*.

heron ('herən) *n* airone *m*.

herring ('heriŋ) *n, pl* **herrings** *or* **herring** aringa *f*.

hers (hə:z) *pron 3rd pers s* il suo, la sua, i suoi, le sue, di lei. **herself** *pron 3rd pers s* **1** ella o lei stessa. **2** si, sè.

hesitate ('heziteit) *vi* esitare. **hesitation** *n* esitazione *f*.

heterosexual (hetərə'sekʃuəl) *adj* eterosessuale.

hexagon ('heksəgən) *n* esagono *m*. **hexagonal** *adj* esagonale.

hibernate ('haibəneit) *vi* svernare, essere in letargo. **hibernation** *n* ibernazione *f*.

hiccup ('hikʌp) *n* singhiozzo *m*. *vi* avere il singhiozzo.

hide[*1] (haid) *vt* nascondere. *vi* celarsi. **hide-and-seek** *n* nascondino *m*.

hide[2] (haid) *n* cuoio *m*. pelle *f*.

hideous ('hidiəs) *adj* orrendo, mostruoso.

hiding[1] ('haidiŋ) *n* nascondiglio *m*.

hiding[2] ('haidiŋ) *n inf* bastonatura, sculacciata *f*.

hierarchy ('haiərɑ:ki) *n* gerarchia *f*.

high (hai) *adj* **1** alto, elevato. **2** importante. **3** *cul* alterato. *adv* **1** in alto. **2** fortemente. **highbrow** *adj* intellettuale. **high-fidelity** *n* alta fedeltà *f*. **high-frequency** *adj* ad alta frequenza *f*. **highland** *n* altopiano *m*. regione montuosa *f*. **highlight** *n* momento culminante *m*. *vt* **1** mettere in risalto. **2** proiettare un fascio di luce su. **highpitched** *adj* stridulo, acuto. **high tide** *n* alta marea *f*. **highway** *n* strada maestra *f*.

Highness ('hainis) *n* Altezza *f*.

hijack ('haidʒæk) *vt* **1** sequestrare. **2** costringere a cambiar rotta. **hijacker** *n* pirata *m*.

hike (haik) *n* escursione a piedi *f*.

hilarious (hi'leəriəs) *adj* allegro, esilarante.

hill (hil) *n* colle *m*. collina *f*. **hillside** *n* pendio *m*. **hilltop** *n* sommità della collina *f*.

him (him) *pers pron 3rd pers s* lo, lui, gli *m*. **himself** *pron 3rd pers s* **1** egli *or* lui stesso. **2** si, sè.

hind (haind) *adj* posteriore. **hindleg** *n* gamba posteriore *f*. **hindsight** *n* senno di poi *m*.

hinder ('hində) *vt* impedire, ostacolare. **hindrance** *n* impedimento, ostacolo *m*.

Hindu ('hindu:) *adj,n* indù.

hinge (hindʒ) *n* perno, cardine *m*. cerniera *f*.

hint (hint) *n* **1** accenno *m*. allusione *f*. **2** consiglio *m*. *vi* accennare, insinuare, alludere. **take the hint** capire al volo.

hip (hip) *n* anat anca *f*. fianco *m*.

hippopotamus (hipə'pɔtəməs) *n, pl* **-muses** *or* **-mi** ippopotamo *m*.

hire (haiə) *vt* affittare, noleggiare. *n* affitto *m*. **for hire** a nolo.

his (hiz) *pron 3rd pers s* il suo, la sua, i suoi, le sue, di lui. *poss adj 3rd pers s* (il) suo, (la) sua, (i) suoi, (le) sue.

hiss (his) *vi* sibilare, fischiare. *n* sibilo, fischio *m*.

history ('histri) *n* storia *f*. **historian** *n* storico *m*. **historic** *adj* storico.

hit[*] (hit) *vt* **1** colpire. **2** urtare. **3** toccare. *n* **1** colpo *m*. **2** successo *m*.

hitch (hitʃ) *vt* agganciare. *vi* fare l'autostop. *n* difficoltà *f*. **hitch-hike** *vi* fare l'autostop.

hive (haiv) *n* alveare *m*.

hoard (hɔ:d) *n* cumulo, tesoro *m*. *vt* ammassare.

hoarding ('hɔ:diŋ) *n* **1** recinto provvisorio *m*. **2** tabellone *m*.

hoarse (hɔ:s) *adj* rauco. **hoarseness** *n* raucedine *f*.

hoax (houks) *n* inganno, scherzo *m*.

hobble ('hɔbəl) *vi* zoppicare.

hobby ('hɔbi) *n* passatempo svago *m*.

hock[1] (hɔk) *n* (of a horse) garetto *m*.

hock[2] (hɔk) *n* vino bianco del Reno *m*.

hockey ('hɔki) *n* hockey *m*.

hoe (hou) *n* zappa *f*. *vt* zappare.

hoist (hɔist) n montacarichi m. vt alzare, sollevare.

hold¹ (hould) vt **1** tenere. **2** contenere. **3** trattenere. vi tenere. **hold back** trattenersi, esitare. **hold up 1** (traffic, etc.) fermare. **2** rapinare. ~n **1** presa f. **2** sostegno m. **holdall** n borsa da viaggio f. **holder** n **1** possessore m. **2** astuccio m.

hold² (hould) n naut stiva f.

hole (houl) n **1** buco m. buca f. **2** tana f.

holiday ('hɔlidi) n vacanza, festa f. **holiday-maker** n villeggiante m,f.

Holland ('hɔlənd) n Olanda f.

hollow ('hɔlou) n cavità f. fosso m. adj **1** cavo, vuoto. **2** falso. vt scavare.

holly ('hɔli) n agrifoglio m. **hollyhock** n altea rosata f.

holster ('houlstə) n fondina f.

holy ('houli) adj santo, sacro.

homage ('hɔmidʒ) n omaggio m.

home (houm) n **1** casa f. focolare domestico m. **2** patria f. **3** rifugio m. adj **1** familiare, domestico. **2** nazionale adv **1** a casa, di ritorno. **2** a segno. **homecoming** n ritorno alla propria casa f. **homeland** n patria f. **homesick** adj nostalgico. **homesickness** n nostalgia f. **homework** n compiti m pl.

homosexual (houmə'sekʃuəl) adj,n omosessuale m.

honest ('ɔnist) adj onesto, leale, genuino. **honestly** adv veramente. **honesty** n onestà f.

honey ('hʌni) n miele m. **honeycomb** n favo m. **honeymoon** n luna di miele f. **honeysuckle** n caprifoglio m.

honour ('ɔnə) n **1** onore m. **2** reputazione f. **His/Your Honour** Sua/Vostra Eccellenza. ~vt onorare, rispettare. **honorary** adj onorario, onorifico. **honourable** adj stimato, onorevole.

hood (hud) n **1** cappuccio m. **2** mot mantice m. vt incappucciare. **hoodwink** vt ingannare.

hoof (hu:f) n, pl **hoofs** or **hooves** zoccolo m.

hook (huk) n **1** gancio, uncino m. **2** amo m. **by hook or by crook** a qualunque costo. ~vt agganciare.

hooligan ('hu:ligən) n teppista m. **hooliganism** n teppismo m.

hoop (hu:p) n cerchio m. vt cerchiare.

hoot (hu:t) n grido m. vi **1** urlare. **2** mot suonare.

Hoover ('hu:və) n Tdmk aspirapolvere m.

hop¹ (hɔp) n balzo, salto m. vi saltellare.

hop² (hɔp) n bot luppolo m.

hope (houp) n speranza f. vt,vi sperare. **hopeful** adj fiducioso, promettente. **hopeless** adj disperato, irrimediabile.

horde (hɔ:d) n orda f.

horizon (hə'raizn) n orizzonte m. **horizontal** adj orizzontale.

hormone ('hɔ:moun) n ormone m.

horn (hɔ:n) n **1** corno m, pl corna f. or corni m. **2** mot clacson m.

hornet ('hɔ:nit) n calabrone m.

horoscope ('hɔrəskoup) n oroscopo m.

horrible ('hɔrəbl) adj orrendo, orribile.

horrid ('hɔrid) adj **1** spaventoso. **2** inf spiacevole.

horrify ('hɔrifai) vt atterrire, far inorridire.

horror ('hɔrə) n orrore m.

hors d'oeuvres (ɔ: 'də:vs) n pl antipasto m.

horse (hɔ:s) n cavallo m. **on horseback** adv a cavallo. **horse chestnut** n ippocastano m. **horsefly** n mosca cavallina f. **horsehair** n crine di cavallo m. **horseman** n cavaliere m. **horsepower** n cavallo vapore m. **horseradish** n rafano m. **horseshoe** n ferro di cavallo m.

horticulture ('hɔ:tikʌltʃə) n orticultura f.

hose (houz) n tubo flessibile m.

hosiery ('houziəri) n maglieria f.

hospitable ('hɔspitəbəl) adj ospitale.

hospital ('hɔspitl) n ospedale m.

hospitality (hɔspi'tæliti) n ospitalità f.

host¹ (houst) n ospite m.

host² (houst) n (crowd) moltitudine, schiera f.

hostage ('hɔstidʒ) n ostaggio m.

hostel ('hɔstl) n locanda f. ostello m.

hostess ('houstis) n ospite f.

hostile ('hɔstail) adj nemico, ostile.

hot (hɔt) adj **1** caldo, bollente, ardente. **2** piccante. **3** pericoloso. **hot-blooded** adj ardente, dal sangue caldo. **hot dog** n panino imbottito con salsiccia m. **hothouse** n serra f. **hotplate** n fornello m. piastra riscaldante f. **hot-tempered** adj dal temperamento focoso. **hot-water bottle** n borsa dell'acqua calda f.

hotel (hou'tel) n albergo m.

hound (haund) n cane da caccia m. vt inseguire.

hour (auə) n ora f.

house (n haus; v hauz) n **1** case f. **2** dinastia f. **3** ditta f. **4** Th sala f. vt alloggiare.

houseboat ('hausbout) n casa galleggiante f.

housebound ('hausbaund) adj costretto a casa.

household ('haushould) n famiglia f.
housekeeper ('hauski:pə) n governante, massaia f.
housemaid ('hausmeid) n cameriera f.
House of Commons n Camera dei Comuni f.
House of Lords n Camera dei Pari f.
houseproud ('hauspraud) adj orgoglioso della propria casa.
housewife ('hauswaif) n casalinga, donna di casa f.
housework ('hauswə:k) n faccende domestiche f pl.
housing ('hauziŋ) n alloggio m. **housing estate** n zona residenziale f.
hover ('hɔvə) vi librarsi sulle ali, ondeggiare, sorvolare. **hovercraft** n veicolo a cuscino pneumatico m. hovercraft m invar.
how (hau) adv 1 come, in che modo. 2 quanto. **how are you?** come stai? **how long** quanto tempo. **however** conj tuttavia. adv 1 comunque. 2 per quanto.
howl (haul) n ululato m. vi lamentarsi, ululare.
hub (hʌb) n 1 mot mozzo m. 2 centro m.
huddle ('hʌdl) n calca, folla f. vt metter insieme alla rinfusa. vi affollarsi.
huff (hʌf) n collera f.
hug (hʌg) n abbraccio m. vt abbracciare. vi abbracciarsi.
huge (hju:dʒ) adj enorme, vasto.
hulk (hʌlk) n carcassa f.
hull[1] (hʌl) n bot baccello, guscio m. vt sgusciare.
hull[2] (hʌl) n naut scafo m.
hullo (hə'lou) interj see **hello**.
hum (hʌm) vi ronzare, mormorare. vt cantare a bocca chiusa. n ronzio m.
human ('hju:mən) adj umano. n essere umano m. **human nature** n natura umana f. **humane** adj umano, compassionevole. **humanism** n umanesimo m. **humanitarian** adj filantropico. n filantropo m. **humanity** n umanità, benevolenza f.
humble ('hʌmbəl) adj umile, modesto. vt umiliare.
humdrum ('hʌmdrʌm) adj monotono.
humid ('hju:mid) adj umido.
humiliate (hju:'milieit) vt umiliare. **humiliation** n umiliazione f.
humility (hju:'militi) n umiltà f.
humour ('hju:mə) n 1 umore m. 2 capriccio m. vt assecondare, compiacere. **humorist** n umorista m. **humorous** adj umoristico, comico.

hump (hʌmp) n gobba f.
hunch (hʌntʃ) n 1 gobba f. 2 inf sospetto, presentimento m. vt curvare. **hunchback** n gobbo m.
hundred ('hʌndrəd) adj,n cento m. n centinaio m, pl centinaia f. **hundredth** adj centesimo. **hundredweight** n misura di peso di 112 libbre f.
hung (hʌŋ) v see **hang**.
Hungary ('hʌŋgəri) n Ungheria f. **Hungarian** adj,n ungherese. **Hungarian** (language) n ungherese m.
hunger ('hʌŋgə) n fame f. vi bramare. **hunger-strike** n sciopero della fame m. **hungry** adj affamato. **be hungry** avere fame.
hunt (hʌnt) n 1 caccia f. 2 inseguimento m. vt 1 cacciare. 2 inseguire. **hunting** n caccia f. **huntsman** n cacciatore m.
hurdle ('hə:dl) n 1 ostácolo m. 2 barriera f.
hurl (hə:l) vt scagliare.
hurrah (hu'rɑ:) interj urrà! evviva!
hurricane ('hʌrikein) n uragano, ciclone m.
hurry ('hʌri) n fretta, urgenza f. vt affrettare. vi precipitarsi.
hurt* (hə:t) vt 1 far male a. 2 offendere. 3 danneggiare. vi dolere.
husband ('hʌzbənd) n marito m.
hush (hʌʃ) n silenzio m. interj zitto! vi tacere. vt far tacere.
husk (hʌsk) n guscio, baccello m.
husky ('hʌski) adj rugoso, rauco.
hustle ('hʌsəl) vt spingere. vi affrettarsi. n spinta, fretta f.
hut (hʌt) n capanna, baracca f.
hutch (hʌtʃ) n conigliera f.
hyacinth ('haiəsinθ) n giacinto m.
hybrid ('haibrid) adj,n ibrido m.
hydraulic (hai'drɔ:lik) adj idraulico.
hydro-electric (haidroui'lektrik) adj idroelettrico.
hydrogen ('haidrədʒən) n idrogeno m. **hydrogen bomb** n bomba all'idrogeno f.
hyena (hai'i:nə) n iena f.
hygiene ('haidʒi:n) n igiene f. **hygienic** adj igienico.
hymn (him) n inno m. **hymnbook** n libro di inni m.
hyphen ('haifən) n trattino m. lineetta di congiunzione f. **hyphenate** vt mettere un trattino a.
hypnosis (hip'nousis) n, pl **-ses** ipnosi f. **hypnotism** n ipnotismo m.

hypochondria (haipə'kɔndriə) n ipocondria f. **hypochondriac** n ipocondriaco.

hypocrisy (hi'pɔkrəsi) n ipocrisia f. **hypocrite** n ipocrita m. **hypocritical** adj ipocrito.

hypodermic (haipə'də:mik) adj ipodermico.

hypothesis (hai'pɔθəsis) n, pl **-ses** ipotesi f invar. **hypothetical** adj ipotetico.

hysterectomy (histə'rektəmi) n isterectomia f.

hysteria (his'tiəriə) n isterismo m. **hysterical** adj isterico. **hysterics** n pl attacco d'isteria m.

I

I (ai) pron 1st pers s io m,f.

ice (ais) n ghiaccio m. vt **1** ghiacciare. **2** cul glassare. **iceberg** n massa di ghiaccio galleggiante f. **ice-cream** n gelato m. **ice-cube** n cubetto di ghiaccio m. **ice hockey** n hockey su ghiaccio m. **ice rink** n pista di pattinaggio f. **icicle** n ghiacciolo m. **icing** n glassa f. **icy** adj gelido, ghiacciato.

Iceland ('aislənd) n Islanda f. **Icelandic** adj islandese. **Icelandic** (language) n islandese m. **Icelander** n islandese m,f.

icon ('aikɔn) n icona f.

idea (ai'diə) n idea f. concetto m.

ideal (ai'diəl) adj,n ideale m. **idealistic** adj idealistico. **idealize** vt idealizzare.

identify (ai'dentifai) vt identificare. **identification** n identificazione f.

identity (ai'dentiti) n identità f. **identity card** n carta d'identità f. **identical** adj identico. **identical twins** n pl gemelli monozigotici m pl.

ideology (aidi'ɔlədʒi) n ideologia f.

idiom ('idiəm) n idioma, dialetto m. **idiomatic** adj idiomatico.

idiosyncrasy (idiə'siŋkrəsi) n idiosincrasia f.

idiot ('idiət) n idiota m. **idiotic** adj idiota, ebete.

idle ('aidl) adj pigro, inutile, vano. vi oziare. **idleness** n pigrizia, indolenza f.

idol ('aidl) n idolo m. **idolatry** n idolatria f. **idolize** vt idolatrare.

idyllic (i'dilik) adj idillico.

if (if) conj se. **if anything** se mai.

igloo ('iglu:) n igloo m.

ignite (ig'nait) vt accendere. vi accendersi. **ignition** n ignizione, accensione f.

ignorant ('ignərənt) adj ignorante.

ignore (ig'nɔ:) vt ignorare, far finta di non vedere or sentire.

ill (il) adj **1** ammalato. **2** cattivo. n male, danno m. adv male. **ill-bred** adj maleducato. **illness** n malattia f. **ill-treat** vt maltrattare. **ill will** n cattiva volontà f.

illegal (i'li:gəl) adj illegale.

illegible (i'ledʒəbl) adj illeggibile.

illegitimate (ili'dʒitimət) adj illegittimo.

illicit (i'lisit) adj illecito.

illiterate (i'litərət) adj analfabeta.

illogical (i'lɔdʒikəl) adj illogico.

illuminate (i'lu:mineit) vt rischiarare, illuminare. **illumination** n illuminazione f.

illusion (i'lu:ʒən) n illusione f.

illustrate ('iləstreit) vt spiegare, illustrare. **illustration** n illustrazione f.

illustrious (i'lʌstriəs) adj illustre, celebre.

image ('imidʒ) n immagine f. **imagery** n linguaggio figurato m.

imagine (i'mædʒin) vt immaginare, farsi un' idea di. **imaginary** adj immaginario. **imagination** n fantasia, immaginazione f. **imaginative** adj fantasioso.

imbecile ('imbisi:l) adj,n imbecille.

imitate ('imiteit) vt imitare. **imitation** n imitazione f. adj contraffatto, artificiale.

immaculate (i'mækjulət) adj immacolato.

immature (imə'tjuə) adj immaturo.

immediate (i'mi:diət) adj immediato, istantaneo. **immediately** adv subito, d'un tratto.

immense (i'mens) adj immenso. **immensely** adv moltissimo.

immerse (i'mə:s) vt immergere, tuffare.

immigrate ('imigreit) vi immigrare. **immigrant** n immigrante m,f. **immigration** n immigrazione f.

imminent ('iminənt) adj imminente.

immobile (i'moubail) adj immobile. **immobilize** vt immobilizzare.

immoral (i'mɔrəl) adj immorale.

immortal (i'mɔ:tl) adj immortale. **immortality** n immortalità f.

immovable (i'mu:vəbəl) adj inamovibile.

immune (i'mju:n) adj immune, esente. **immunize** vt immunizzare.

imp (imp) n diavoletto m.

impact ('impækt) n **1** urto m. **2** impressione f.

impair (im'pɛə) vt indebolire, menomare.

impart (im'pa:t) vt impartire, dare.

impartial (im'pa:ʃəl) adj imparziale, giusto. **impartiality** n imparzialità f.

impatient (im'peiʃənt) adj impaziente. **impatience** n impazienza f.

impeach (im'pi:tʃ) vt imputare, incriminare. **impeachment** n accusa, incriminazione f.

impeccable (im'pekəbəl) adj impeccabile.

impediment (im'pedimənt) n ostacolo, impedimento m.

impel (im'pel) vt incitare, stimolare.

imperative (im'perativ) adj imperativo, urgente. n imperativo m.

imperfect (im'pə:fikt) adj imperfetto.

imperial (im'piəriəl) adj imperiale.

impersonal (im'pə:sənl) adj impersonale.

impersonate (im'pə:səneit) vt impersonare, imitare.

impertinent (im'pə:tinənt) adj impertinente.

impetuous (im'petʃuəs) adj impetuoso.

impetus ('impitəs) n impeto, slancio m.

impinge (im'pindʒ) vi **impinge on 1** urtare contro. **2** violare.

implement (n 'impləmənt; v 'impləmənt) n **1** utensile m. **2** pl attrezzi m pl. vt compiere, attuare.

implicit (im'plisit) adj implicito.

implore (im'plɔ:) vt implorare.

imply (im'plai) vt implicare, insinuare, significare.

import (v im'pɔ:t; n 'impɔ:t) vt **1** comm importare. **2** significare. n **1** comm importazione f. **2** portata f. significato m.

importance (im'pɔ:tns) n importanza f. **important** adj importante.

impose (im'pouz) vt imporre. vi imporsi. **impose on** abusare di. **imposing** adj imponente, grandioso.

impossible (im'posəbəl) adj impossibile.

impostor (im'postə) n impostore, imbroglione m.

impotent ('impətənt) adj impotente, debole.

impound (im'paund) vt sequestrare, confiscare.

impoverish (im'povəriʃ) vt impoverire.

impress (im'pres) vt **1** fare buona impressione su. **2** inculcare. **3** stampare. **impression** n **1** impressione f. **2** ristampa f. **impressive** adj impressionante.

imprint (n 'imprint; v im'print) n impronta f. vt stampare.

improbable (im'probəbəl) adj improbabile.

impromptu (im'promptju:) adj improvvisato. adv all'improvviso, a prima vista.

improper (im'propə) adj erroneo, sconveniente.

improve (im'pru:v) vt,vi migliorare. **improvement** n miglioramento, progresso m.

improvise ('imprəvaiz) vt improvvisare. **improvisation** n improvvisazione f.

impudent ('impjudənt) adj sfrontato. **impudence** n impudenza f.

impulse ('impʌls) n impeto, stimolo m. **impulsive** adj impulsivo.

impure (im'pjuə) adj impuro, contaminato. **impurity** n impurità f.

in (in) prep **1** a, in. **2** entro, tra. **3** durante. **4** di. adv dentro, a casa.

inability (inə'biliti) n incapacità f.

inaccurate (in'ækjurət) adj impreciso, sbagliato. **inaccuracy** n inesattezza f.

inadequate (in'ædikwit) adj insufficiente.

inadvertent (inəd'və:tnt) adj sbadato, involontario.

inane (i'nein) adj vuoto, insensato.

inarticulate (ina:'tikjulət) adj inarticolato, indistinto.

inasmuch (inəz'mʌtʃ) conj **inasmuch as** in quanto che.

inaugurate (i'nɔ:gjureit) vt inaugurare.

incapable (in'keipəbəl) adj incapace, inetto.

incendiary (in'sendiəri) adj,n incendiario m.

incense[1] ('insens) n incenso m.

incense[2] (in'sens) vt provocare, irritare.

incessant (in'sesənt) adj continuo.

incest ('insest) n incesto m. **incestuous** adj incestuoso.

inch (intʃ) n pollice m. **inch by inch** gradatamente.

incident ('insidənt) n **1** caso m. **2** episodio m. **incidental** adj fortuito, accidentale.

incite (in'sait) vt spronare, incitare.

incline (in'klain) vt inclinare. vi propendere. n pendio m. **inclined** adj propenso.

include (in'klu:d) vt includere, comprendere. **inclusion** n inclusione f. **inclusive** adj compreso.

incognito (inkɔg'ni:tou) adj incognito. adv in incognito.

incoherent (inkou'hiərənt) adj incoerente.

income ('inkʌm) n reddito m. entrata f. **income tax** n tassa sul reddito f.

incompatible (inkəm'pætibəl) adj incompatibile.

incompetent (in'kompətənt) adj incompetente, incapace.

incongruous (in'kɔngruəs) adj incongruo, assurdo.

inconsiderate (inkən'sidərit) adj sconsiderato, senza riguardi.

inconsistent (inkən'sistənt) *adj* inconsistente, incompatibile.

inconvenient (inkən'vi:niənt) *adj* scomodo, inopportuno. **inconvenience** *n* inconveniente, incomodo *m*. *vt* incomodare, disturbare.

incorporate (in'kɔ:pəreit) *vt* incorporare. *vi* unirsi.

incorrect (inkə'rekt) *adj* inesatto, scorretto.

increase (*v* in'kri:s; *n* 'inkri:s) *n* aumento *m*. aggiunta *f*. *vt* accrescere. *vi* ingrandirsi.

incredible (in'kredəbl) *adj* incredibile.

incubate ('inkjubeit) *vt,vi* covare. **incubator** *n* incubatrice *f*.

incur (in'kə:) *vt* incorrere in, esporsi a.

incurable (in'kjuərəbəl) *adj* incurabile.

indecent (in'di:sənt) *adj* indecente.

indeed (in'di:d) *adv* veramente, infatti, proprio, anzi.

indefinite (in'definət) *adj* indefinito.

indent (in'dent) *vt* **1** dentellare. **2** iniziare a distanza dal margine.

independent (indi'pendənt) *adj* indipendente. **independence** *n* indipendenza *f*.

index ('indeks) *n, pl* **-exes** *or* **-ices** indice *m*. rubrica *f*. *vt* **1** corredare d'indice. **2** mettere in ordine alfabetico. **index finger** *n* dito indice *m*.

India ('indiə) *n* India *f*. **Indian** *adj,n* indiano.

indicate ('indikeit) *vt* indicare. **indicator** *n* indicatore *m*.

indifferent (in'difrənt) *adj* indifferente, mediocre.

indigestion (indi'dʒestʃən) *n* indigestione *f*.

indignant (in'dignənt) *adj* indignato.

indirect (indi'rekt) *adj* indiretto, secondario.

indispensable (indi'spensəbəl) *adj* indispensabile.

individual (indi'vidʒuəl) *adj* singolo, particolare. *n* individuo *m*.

indoctrinate (in'dɔktrineit) *vt* addottrinare.

indolent ('indələnt) *adj* indolente.

Indonesia (ində'ni:ziə) *n* Indonesia *f*. **Indonesian** *adj,n* indonesiano.

indoor ('indɔ:) *adj* interno, da casa. **indoors** *adv* al coperto, all'interno.

induce (in'dju:s) *vt* indurre, produrre.

indulge (in'dʌldʒ) *vt* essere indulgente con. **indulge in** permettersi di. **indulgent** *adj* indulgente, condiscendente, benevolo.

industry ('indəstri) *n* **1** industria *f*. **2** diligenza *f*. **industrial** *adj* industriale. **industrious** *adj* operoso, attivo.

inefficient (ini'fiʃənt) *adj* inefficiente.

inept (i'nept) *adj* incapace, sciocco.

inequality (ini'kwɔliti) *n* ineguaglianza *f*.

inert (i'nə:t) *adj* inerte, apatico. **inertia** *n* inerzia, apatia *f*.

inevitable (in'evitəbəl) *adj* inevitabile.

infallible (in'fæləbəl) *adj* infallibile.

infamous ('infəməs) *adj* infame.

infant ('infənt) *n* neonato, bambino *m*. **infancy** *n* infanzia *f*. **infantile** *adj* infantile, puerile.

infantry ('infəntri) *n* fanteria *f*.

infatuate (in'fætʃueit) *vt* infatuare. **infatuation** *n* infatuazione *f*.

infect (in'fekt) *vt* infettare. **infection** *n* infezione *f*. contagio *m*.

infer (in'fə:) *vt* dedurre, arguire.

inferior (in'fiəriə) *adj,n* inferiore. **inferiority** *n* inferiorità *f*.

infernal (in'fə:nl) *adj* infernale.

infest (in'fest) *vt* infestare.

infidelity (infi'deliti) *n* infedeltà *f*.

infiltrate ('infiltreit) *vt* infiltrare. *vi* infiltrarsi.

infinite ('infinit) *adj* infinito, immenso. *n* infinito *m*. **infinity** *n* infinità *f*.

infinitive (in'finitiv) *adj,n* infinito *m*.

infirm (in'fə:m) *adj* infermo, malaticcio.

inflame (in'fleim) *vt* infiammare. *vi* ardere, infiammarsi. **inflammable** *adj* infiammabile.

inflate (in'fleit) *vt* gonfiare. *vi* gonfiarsi. **inflation** *n* **1** gonfiatura *f*. **2** *comm* inflazione *f*.

inflection (in'flekʃən) *n* inflessione *f*.

inflict (in'flikt) *vt* infliggere.

influence ('influəns) *n* ascendenza, influenza *f*. *vt* influenzare.

influenza (influ'enzə) *n* influenza *f*.

influx ('inflʌks) *n* affluenza *f*.

inform (in'fɔ:m) *vt* informare. **informant** *n* informatore *m*. **information** *n* **1** informazioni *f pl*. **2** *law* accusa *f*.

informal (in'fɔ:məl) *adj* non ufficiale, semplice.

infringe (in'frindʒ) *vt* violare. **infringe upon** trasgredire. **infringement** *n* violazione, infrazione *f*.

infuriate (in'fjuərieit) *vt* far infuriare.

ingenious (in'dʒi:niəs) *adj* ingegnoso.

ingredient (in'gri:diənt) *n* ingrediente *m*.

inhabit (in'hæbit) *vt* abitare. **inhabitant** *n* abitante *m,f*.

inhale (in'heil) *vt* inalare, aspirare.

inherent (in'hiərənt) *adj* inerente, intrinsico.

inherit (in'herit) *vt,vi* ereditare. **inheritance** *n* eredità *f.*

inhibit (in'hibit) *vt* inibire, reprimere. **inhibition** *n* inibizione *f.*

inhuman (in'hju:mən) *adj* inumano, brutale.

initial (i'niʃəl) *adj,n* iniziale *f.* *vt* siglare.

initiate (i'niʃieit) *vt* **1** cominciare. **2** iniziare a. **initiative** *n* iniziativa *f.*

inject (in'dʒekt) *vt* iniettare. **injection** *n* iniezione *f.*

injure ('indʒə) *vt* **1** danneggiare, ferire. **2** offendere. **injury** *n* **1** male *m.* ferita *f.* **2** offesa *f.*

injustice (in'dʒʌstis) *n* ingiustizia *f.*

ink (iŋk) *n* inchiostro *m.* *vt* imbrattare d'inchiostro.

inkling ('iŋkliŋ) *n* indizio, sentore *m.*

inland ('inlənd) *adv* interno. *n* retroterra *m.*

Inland Revenue *n* fisco *m.*

inmate ('inmeit) *n* **1** inquilino *m.* **2** ricoverato *m.*

inn (in) *n* osteria, locanda *f.*

innate (i'neit) *adj* istintivo, innato.

inner ('inə) *adj* interiore, intimo. **innermost** *adj* il più profondo.

innocent ('inəsənt) *adj* innocente, innocuo.

innocuous (i'nɔkjuəs) *adj* innocuo.

innovation (inə'veiʃən) *n* innovazione *f.*

innuendo (inju'endou) *n* insinuazione, allusione *f.*

innumerable (i'nju:mərəbəl) *adj* innumerevole.

inoculate (i'nɔkjuleit) *vt* inoculare.

input ('input) *n* *tech* potenza, entrata *f.* input *m* invar.

inquest ('inkwest) *n* inchiesta, indagine *f.*

inquire (in'kwaiə) *vt* domandare. *vi* **1** informarsi. **2** indagare. **inquiry** *n* **1** domanda *f.* **2** indagine *f.* **3** *law* inchiesta *f.*

inquisition (inkwi'ziʃən) *n* **1** inchiesta *f.* **2** *cap* Inquisizione *f.*

inquisitive (in'kwizitiv) *adj* curioso, indagatore.

insane (in'sein) *adj* pazzo, insensato.

insatiable (in'seiʃəbəl) *adj* insaziabile.

inscribe (in'skraib) *vt* incidere, iscrivere. **inscription** *n* iscrizione *f.*

insect ('insekt) *n* insetto *m.* **insecticide** *n* insetticida *m.*

insecure (insi'kjuə) *adj* malsicuro, instabile.

inseminate (in'semineit) *vt* fecondare.

insert (in'sə:t) *vt* inserire, introdurre. *n* inserzione *f.* allegato *m.* **insertion** *n* inserzione, aggiunta *f.*

inside (in'said) *prep* entro. *adv* **1** internamente. **2** dentro. *adj,n* interno *m.*

insidious (in'sidiəs) *adj* insidioso.

insight ('insait) *n* perspicacia *f.* intuito *m.*

insinuate (in'sinjueit) *vt* **1** insinuare. **2** introdurre.

insist (in'sist) *vi* insistere. **insistence** *n* insistenza *f.* **insistent** *adj* insistente.

insolent ('insələnt) *adj* insolente.

insomnia (in'sɔmniə) *n* insonnia *f.*

inspect (in'spekt) *vt* ispezionare, sorvegliare. **inspection** *n* ispezione *f.* **inspector** *n* ispettore *m.*

inspire (in'spaiə) *vt* ispirare, infondere. **inspiration** *n* ispirazione *f.*

instability (instə'biliti) *n* instabilità *f.*

install (in'stɔ:l) *vt* installare. **installation** *n* impianto *m.* installazione *f.*

instalment (in'stɔ:lmənt) *n* **1** *comm* rata *f.* **2** puntata *f.*

instance ('instəns) *n* esempio, caso *m.* **instant** *adj* istantaneo. *n* istante, momento *m.* **instantaneous** *adj* istantaneo.

instead (in'sted) *adv* invece.

instep ('instep) *n* collo del piede *m.*

instigate ('instigeit) *vt* istigare, incitare.

instil (in'stil) *vt* infondere, instillare.

instinct ('instiŋkt) *n* istinto *m.* **instinctive** *adj* istintivo, impulsivo.

institute ('institju:t) *n* istituto *m.* istituzione *f.* *vt* istituire, fondare. **institution** *n* istituzione *f.* ente *m.*

instruct (in'strʌkt) *vt* istruire, dare istruzioni a. **instruction** *n* **1** istruzione *f.* **2** *pl* disposizioni *f pl.*

instrument ('instrumənt) *n* strumento *m.* **instrumental** *adj* strumentale.

insubordinate (insə'bɔ:dinət) *adj* insubordinato.

insufferable (in'sʌfərəbəl) *adj* insopportabile.

insular ('insjulə) *adj* insulare.

insulate ('insjuleit) *vt* isolare. **insulation** *n* isolamento *f.*

insulin ('insjulin) *n* insulina *f.*

insult (*v* in'sʌlt; *n* 'insʌlt) *vt* insultare. *n* insulto *m.*

insure (in'ʃuə) *vt* assicurare, garantire. **insurance** *n* assicurazione *f.* **insurance company** *n* compagnia d'assicurazione *f.*

intact (in'tækt) *adj* intatto, integro.

intake ('inteik) *n* **1** *tech* presa *f.* **2** entrata *f.*

integral ('intigrəl) *adj* integrale, completo.

integrate ('intigreit) *vt* integrare, completare.

integrity (in'tegriti) *n* integrità *f.*

intellect ('intəlekt) n intelletto m. **intellectual** adj,n intellettuale.

intelligent (in'telidʒənt) adj intelligente. **intelligence** n 1 intelligenza f. 2 informazioni f pl. **intelligence service** n servizio segreto m. **intelligible** adj intelligibile, chiaro.

intend (in'tend) vt 1 intendere, proporsi. 2 destinare.

intense (in'tens) adj intenso, profondo. **intensify** vt intensificare. vi rafforzarsi. **intensity** n intensità f. vigore m. **intensive** adj intensivo. **intensive course** n corso accelerato m.

intent[1] (in'tent) n scopo, proposito m.

intent[2] (in'tent) adj intento, assorto.

intention (in'tenʃən) n intenzione f. proposito m.

inter (in'tə:) vt seppellire.

interact (intə'rækt) vi esercitare un'azione reciproca.

intercept (intə'sept) vt intercettare. **interception** n intercettamento m.

interchange (v intə'tʃeindʒ; n 'intətʃeindʒ) vt scambiare. vi scambiarsi. n scambio reciproco m.

intercourse ('intəkɔ:s) n relazione f. rapporto m.

interest ('intrəst) vt interessare. n 1 interesse m. 2 interessamento m. **interesting** adj interessante.

interfere (intə'fiə) vi interferire, intromettersi. **interfere with** ostacolare. **interference** n 1 ingerenza f. 2 tech interferenza f.

interim ('intərim) adj 1 provvisorio. 2 pol interino. n interim, intervallo m.

interior (in'tiəriə) adj,n interno m.

interjection (intə'dʒekʃn) n interiezione f.

interlude ('intəlu:d) n 1 intervallo m. 2 mus intermezzo m.

intermediate (intə'mi:diət) adj intermedio. **intermediary** adj,n intermediario m.

interminable (in'tə:minəbəl) adj interminabile.

intermission (intə'miʃən) n pausa f. intervallo m.

intermittent (intə'mitnt) adj intermittente.

intern (in'tə:n) vt internare. **internee** n internato m.

internal (in'tə:nl) adj interno.

international (intə'næʃənl) adj internazionale.

interpose (intə'pouz) vt interporre. vi interferire.

interpret (in'tə:prit) vt interpretare. vi fare l'interprete. **interpretation** n interpretazione f. **interpreter** n interprete m,f.

interrogate (in'terəgeit) vt interrogare. **interrogation** n interrogazione f. **interrogative** adj interrogativo.

interrupt (intə'rʌpt) vt interrompere. **interruption** n interruzione f.

intersect (intə'sekt) vt intersecare. vi incrociarsi. **intersection** n intersecazione f.

interval ('intəvəl) n intervallo m.

intervene (intə'vi:n) vi 1 intervenire. 2 accadere.

interview ('intəvju:) n intervista f. colloquio m. vt intervistare.

intestine (in'testin) n intestino m.

intimate[1] ('intimit) adj intimo.

intimate[2] ('intimeit) vt intimare, accennare a.

intimidate (in'timideit) vt intimidire.

into ('intə; stressed 'intu:) prep in, dentro, entro.

intolerable (in'tɔlərəbəl) adj insopportabile, intollerabile. **intolerance** n intolleranza f. **intolerant** adj intollerante.

intonation (intə'neiʃən) n intonazione f. accento m.

intoxicate (in'tɔksikeit) vt ubriacare, inebriare.

intransitive (in'trænsitiv) adj intransitivo.

intricate ('intrikət) adj intricato, complicato.

intrigue (in'tri:g) vt incuriosire. vi intrigare. n intrigo m.

intrinsic (in'trinsik) adj intrinseco.

introduce (intrə'dju:s) vt 1 introdurre. 2 presentare. **introduction** n 1 introduzione f. 2 presentazione f.

introspective (intrə'spektiv) adj introspettivo.

introvert ('intrəvə:t) adj introverso, introvertito. n introvertito m.

intrude (in'tru:d) vi intromettersi. **intrusion** n intrusione f.

intuition (intju'iʃən) n intuito m. intuizione f. **intuitive** adj intuitivo.

inundate ('inʌndeit) vt inondare.

invade (in'veid) vt invadere, assalire. **invasion** n invasione f.

invalid[1] ('invəli:d) adj,n invalido.

invalid[2] (in'vælid) adj non valevole, nullo.

invaluable (in'væljubəl) adj inestimabile.

invariable (in'vɛəriəbəl) adj invariabile, costante.

invent (in'vent) vt inventare. **invention** n invenzione f.

inventory ('invəntəri) n inventario m.

invert (in'və:t) vt invertire. **inverted** adj rovesciato, capovolto. **inverted commas** n pl virgolette f pl.

213

invertebrate (in'və:təbreit) *adj,n* invertebrato *m.*

invest (in'vest) *vt* investire. **investment** *n* investimento *m.*

investigate (in'vestigeit) *vt* investigare, indagare. **investigation** *n* investigazione *f.*

invincible (in'vinsəbəl) *adj* invincibile.

invisible (in'vizəbəl) *adj* invisibile.

invite (in'vait) *vt* 1 invitare. 2 provocare. **invitation** *n* invito *m.*

invoice ('invɔis) *n* fattura *f. vt* fatturare.

invoke (in'vouk) *vt* invocare.

involve (in'vɔlv) *vt* 1 implicare, avvolgere, coinvolgere. 2 richiedere, comportare. **get involved** impegnarsi. **involvement** *n* implicazione *f.*

inward ('inwəd) *adj* interno, intimo. **inwards** *adv* internamente, verso l'interno.

iodine ('aiədi:n) *n* iodio *m.*

ion ('aiən) *n* ione *m.*

Iran (i'rɑ:n) *n* Iran *m.* **Iranian** *adj,n* persiano.

Iraq (i'rɑ:k) *n* Iraq *m.* **Iraqi** *adj,n* iracheno.

Ireland ('aiələnd) *n* Irlanda *f.* **Irish** *adj* irlandese. **Irishman** *n* irlandese *m.*

iris ('airis) *n* 1 *anat* iride *f.* 2 *bot* giaggiolo *m.*

iron ('aiən) *n* 1 ferro *m.* 2 *dom* ferro da stiro *m. adj* di ferro. *vt* stirare. **ironing board** *n* tavola da stiro *f.* **ironmonger** *n* negoziante in ferramenta *m.* **Iron Curtain** *n* Cortina di ferro *f.*

irony ('airəni) *n* ironia *f.* **ironic** *adj* ironico.

irrational (i'ræʃnl) *adj* irrazionale, assurdo.

irregular (i'regjulə) *adj* irregolare.

irrelevant (i'reləvənt) *adj* non pertinente.

irresistible (iri'zistəbəl) *adj* irresistibile.

irrespective (iri'spektiv) *adj* noncurante.

irresponsible (iri'spɔnsəbəl) *adj* irresponsabile.

irrevocable (i'revəkəbəl) *adj* irrevocabile.

irrigate ('irigeit) *vt* irrigare. **irrigation** *n* irrigazione *f.*

irritate ('iriteit) *vt* irritare.

is (iz) *v see* **be.**

Islam ('izlɑ:m) *n* islamismo *m.* **Islamic** *adj* islamico, maomettano.

island ('ailənd) *n* isola *f.*

isle (ail) *n* isola *f.*

isolate ('aisəleit) *vt* isolare, separare. **isolation** *n* isolamento *f.*

Israel ('izreiəl) *n* Israele *m.* **Israeli** *adj,n* israeliano.

issue ('iʃu:) *n* 1 edizione *f.* numero *m.* 2 risultato *m.* 3 problema *m.* 4 prole *f. vt* 1 emettere. 2 pubblicare. 3 rilasciare. *vi* uscire.

it (it) *pron 3rd pers s* 1 esso *m.* essa *f.* 2 lo *m.* la *f.* 3 gli *m.* le *f.* 4 ci *m,f.* 5 ne, sè *m,f.* **its** *poss adj* (il) suo, (la) sua, (i) suoi, (le) sue. **itself** *pron 3rd pers s* 1 se stesso or esso stesso. 2 si, sè. sue.

italic (i'tælik) *adj* italico. **italics** *n pl* corsivi *m pl.*

Italy ('itəli) *n* Italia *f.* **Italian** *adj,n* italiano. **Italian** (language) *n* italiano *m.*

itch (itʃ) *n* prurito *m. vi* prudere.

item ('aitəm) *n* 1 *comm* voce *f.* capo *m.* 2 articolo *m.*

itinerary (ai'tinərəri) *n* itinerario *m.*

ivory ('aivəri) *n* avorio *m. adj* d'avorio.

ivy ('aivi) *n* edera *f.*

J

jab (dʒæb) *vt* colpire, dare un colpo secco a. *n* colpo *m.* stoccata *f.*

jack (dʒæk) *n* 1 *mot* cricco *m.* 2 *game* fante *m. v* **jack up** levare.

jackal ('dʒækəl) *n* sciacallo *m.*

jackdaw ('dʒækdɔ:) *n* cornacchia *f.*

jacket ('dʒækit) *n* 1 giacca, giubba *f.* 2 *cul* buccia *f.* 3 (of a book) copertina *f.*

jackpot ('dʒækpɔt) *n* vincita *f.*

jade (dʒeid) *n* giada *f.*

jaded ('dʒeidid) *adj* stanco, sfinito.

jagged ('dʒægid) *adj* frastagliato, dentellato.

jaguar ('dʒægjuə) *n* giaguaro *m.*

jail (dʒeil) *n* carcere *m. vt* incarcerare.

jam [1] (dʒæm) *n* conserva di frutta, marmellata *f.* **jam-jar** *n* barattolo per marmellata *m.*

jam [2] (dʒæm) *vt* 1 pigiare. 2 bloccare. *vi* bloccarsi. *n* ingorgo *m.*

Jamaica (dʒə'meikə) *n* Giamaica *f.* **Jamaican** *adj,n* giamaicano.

jangle ('dʒæŋgəl) *n* suono stonato *m. vi* far rumori discordanti.

January ('dʒænjuəri) *n* gennaio *m.*

Japan (dʒə'pæn) *n* Giappone *m.* **Japanese** *adj,n* giapponese. **Japanese** (language) *n* giapponese *m.*

jar [1] (dʒɑ:) *n* barattolo *m.* brocca *f.*

jar [2] (dʒɑ:) *vi* discordare, stridere. *n* discordanza *f.* stridio *m.*

jargon ('dʒɑ:gən) *n* gergo *m.*

jasmine ('dʒæzmin) *n* gelsomino *m.*

jaundice ('dʒɔ:ndis) *n* itterizia *f.*

jaunt (dʒɔːnt) n gita f.

javelin ('dʒævlin) n giavellotto m.

jaw (dʒɔː) n mascella, mandibola f. **jawbone** n osso mascellare m. mascella f.

jazz (dʒæz) n jazz m.

jealous ('dʒeləs) adj geloso, invidioso. **jealousy** n gelosia f.

jeans (dʒiːnz) n pl blue-jeans, calzoni all'americana m pl.

jeep (dʒiːp) n jeep, camionetta f.

jeer (dʒiə) vi schernire. n scherno m. derisione f.

jelly ('dʒeli) n gelatina f. **jellyfish** n medusa f.

jeopardize ('dʒepədaiz) vt mettere in pericolo.

jerk (dʒəːk) n 1 strattone m. 2 sussulto m. vt dare uno strattone a. vi sobbalzare.

jersey ('dʒəːzi) n maglia f.

Jersey ('dʒəːzi) n Jersey f.

jest (dʒest) n scherzo m. burla f. vi scherzare.

Jesus ('dʒiːzəs) n Gesù m.

jet[1] (dʒet) n 1 spruzzo, zampillo m. 2 aviat aviogetto m.

jet[2] (dʒet) n min giavazzo m. ambra nera f. adj 1 d'ambra nera. 2 nero lucido.

jetty ('dʒeti) n gettata f. molo m.

Jew (dʒuː) n ebreo, giudeo m. **Jewish** adj ebreo, giudeo.

jewel ('dʒuːəl) n gioiello m. **jeweller** n gioielliere, orefice m.

jig[1] (dʒig) n tech maschera di montaggio f.

jig[2] (dʒig) n giga f.

jiggle ('dʒigəl) vi muoversi a scatti.

jigsaw ('dʒigsɔː) n (puzzle) gioco di pazienza m.

jilt (dʒilt) vt piantare in asso.

jingle ('dʒingəl) n tintinnio m. vi tintinnare.

job (dʒɔb) n impiego, lavoro, affare m. impresa f.

jockey ('dʒɔki) n fantino m.

jodhpurs ('dʒɔdpəz) n pl calzoni da cavallerizzo m pl.

jog (dʒɔg) vt spingere, urtare. vi muoversi a rilento. n 1 spinta, gomitata f. 2 andatura lenta f.

join (dʒɔin) vt 1 unire, congiungere. 2 partecipare a. vi unirsi. **join up** arruolarsi. ~n giuntura f. **joiner** n falegname m. **joint** n 1 giuntura f. 2 cul pezzo di carne m. 3 anat articolazione f. adj comune, collettivo.

joist (dʒɔist) n travetto m.

joke (dʒouk) n scherzo m. burla f. **crack a joke** dire una battuta. ~vi burlare, celiare.

jolly ('dʒɔli) adj gaio, vivace. adv inf molto.

jolt (dʒoult) n scossa f. sobbalzo m. vt spingere, urtare. vi sobbalzare.

Jordan ('dʒɔːdn) n Giordania f. (**River**) **Jordan** n (fiume) Giordano m. **Jordanian** adj,n giordano.

jostle ('dʒɔsəl) n urto m. gomitata f. vt spingere, urtare col gomito. vi urtarsi.

journal ('dʒəːnl) n 1 giornale m. 2 diario m. **journalism** n giornalismo m. **journalist** n giornalista m.

journey ('dʒəːni) n viaggio m.

jovial ('dʒouviəl) adj allegro, gioviale.

joy (dʒɔi) n gioia, allegria f. **joyful** adj gioioso.

jubilee ('dʒuːbiliː) n giubileo m.

Judaism ('dʒuːdeiizəm) n giudaismo m.

judge (dʒʌdʒ) n giudice m. vt,vi giudicare. **judgment** n 1 giudizio m. 2 sentenza f.

judicial (dʒuː'diʃəl) adj giuridico, giudiziario. **judicious** adj giudizioso.

judo ('dʒuːdou) n giudò m.

jug (dʒʌg) n caraffa f. boccale m.

juggernaut ('dʒʌgənɔːt) n gran camion m.

juggle ('dʒʌgəl) vt 1 giocare. 2 ingannare. vi fare giochi di prestigio. **juggler** n giocoliere m.

juice (dʒuːs) n succo m. **juicy** adj succoso, sostanzioso.

jukebox ('dʒuːkbɔks) n grammofono automatico a gettoni, jukebox m.

July (dʒu'lai) n luglio m.

jumble ('dʒʌmbəl) n miscuglio m. confusione f. vt mescolare, gettare alla rinfusa. **jumble sale** n vendita di merci varie per beneficenza f.

jump (dʒʌmp) n salto, balzo, sussulto m. vi 1 saltare, trasalire. 2 (of prices, etc.) rincarare. vt saltare.

jumper ('dʒʌmpə) n 1 maglione m. 2 casacchina f.

junction ('dʒʌŋkʃən) n 1 cogiunzione f. 2 (railway) nodo ferroviario m.

June (dʒuːn) n giugno m.

jungle ('dʒʌŋgəl) n giungla f.

junior ('dʒuːniə) adj minore, cadetto. n minore, cadetto m.

juniper ('dʒuːnipə) n ginepro m.

junk (dʒʌŋk) n cianfrusaglie f pl.

junta ('dʒʌntə) n giunta f.

Jupiter ('dʒuːpitə) n Giove m.

jurisdiction (dʒuəris'dikʃən) n giurisdizione f.

jury ('dʒuəri) n giuria f. **juror** n giurato m.

just (dʒʌst) adj giusto, retto, dovuto. adv 1 proprio, appunto. 2 soltanto. 3 appena.

justice ('dʒʌstis) n giustizia f. **justice of the peace** n giudice conciliatore m.

justify ('dʒʌstifai) vt giustificare, assolvere.

jut (dʒʌt) vi **jut out** sporgersi, protendersi.

jute (dʒu:t) n iuta f.

juvenile ('dʒu:vənail) adj giovane, immaturo. n giovane, ragazzo m. **juvenile delinquency** n delinquenza minorile f.

juxtapose (dʒʌkstə'pouz) vt affiancare.

K

kaftan ('kæftn) n caffettano m.

kaleidoscope (kə'laidəskoup) n caleidoscopio m.

kangaroo (kæŋgə'ru:) n canguro m.

karate (kə'rɑ:ti) n karatè m.

kebab (kə'bæb) n carne marinata cotta allo spiedo f.

keel (ki:l) n chiglia f. v **keel over** capovolgere, rovesciarsi.

keen (ki:n) adj 1 aguzzo, acuto, perspicace. 2 appassionato.

keep* (ki:p) vt 1 tenere. 2 mantenere, conservare. 3 trattenere. vi 1 continuare. 2 mantenersi, restare. 3 durare. **keep on** continuare. **keep up** mantenere. **keeper** n guardiano m. custode m,f. **keepsake** n ricordo, pegno m.

keg (keg) n barilotto m.

kennel ('kenl) n canile m.

Kenya ('kenjə) n Kenia m. **Kenyan** adj,n keniano.

kept (kept) v see **keep.**

kerb (kə:b) n bordo del marciapiede m.

kernel ('kə:nl) n 1 mandorla f. 2 seme m. 3 nucleo m.

kettle ('ketl) n bollitore m. **kettledrum** n timpano m.

key (ki:) n 1 chiave f. 2 (of a piano, typewriter, etc.) tasto m. 3 mus tono m. **keyboard** n tastiera f. **keyhole** n buco della serratura m. **keyring** n portachiavi m invar.

khaki ('kɑ:ki) adj,n cachi m.

kibbutz (ki'buts) n kibbutz m. comunità agricola israeliana f.

kick (kik) n calcio m. pedata f. tirar pedate a. vi calciare. **kick off** dare il calcio d'inizio. **kick-off** n calcio d'inizio m.

kid[1] (kid) n 1 capretto m. 2 sl bambino m.

kid[2] (kid) vt inf burlare, prendere in giro.

kidnap ('kidnæp) vt rapire. **kidnapper** n rapitore m. rapitrice f.

kidney ('kidni) n 1 anat rene m. 2 cul rognone m. **kidney bean** n fagiolo m.

kill (kil) vt 1 uccidere. 2 distruggere. **killer** n assassino, uccisore m.

kiln (kiln) n fornace f.

kilo ('ki:lou) n chilo m.

kilogram ('kiləgræm) n chilogrammo m.

kilometre (ki'lɔmitə) n chilometro m.

kilowatt ('kiləwɔt) n chilowatt m.

kilt (kilt) n gonnellino scozzese m.

kimono (ki'mounou) n chimono m.

kin (kin) n parenti m pl.

kind[1] (kaind) adj buono, gentile. **kindness** n bontà, gentilezza f.

kind[2] (kaind) n specie, natura f. genere m.

kindergarten ('kindəgɑ:tn) n asilo, giardino d'infanzia m.

kindle ('kindl) vt 1 accendere. 2 eccitare. vi infiammarsi.

kinetic (ki'netik) adj cinetico. **kinetics** n cinetica f.

king (kiŋ) n re m invar. monarca m. **kingdom** n reame, regno m. **kingfisher** n martin pescatore m.

kink (kiŋk) n 1 nodo m. 2 ghiribizzo m. vt attorcigliare. vi attorcigliarsi.

kiosk ('ki:ɔsk) n edicola f. chiosco m.

kipper ('kipə) n aringa affumicata f.

kiss (kis) n bacio m. vt baciare.

kit (kit) n equipaggiamento m. attrezzi m pl.

kitchen ('kitʃin) n cucina f.

kite (kait) n 1 aquilone m. 2 zool nibbio m.

kitten ('kitn) n gattino m.

kitty ('kiti) n fondi comuni m pl.

kiwi ('ki:wi) n kiwi m.

kleptomania (kleptə'meiniə) n cleptomania f. **kleptomaniac** n cleptomane m,f.

knack (næk) n abilità, facoltà f.

knave (neiv) n 1 furfante m. 2 game fante m.

knead (ni:d) vt impastare, massaggiare.

knee (ni:) n ginocchio m. pl ginocchi m. or ginocchia f. **kneecap** n rotula f.

kneel* (ni:l) vi inginocchiarsi.

knew (nu:) v see **know.**

knickers ('nikəz) n pl mutandine f pl.

knife (naif) n. pl **knives** coltello m. vt pugnalare, accoltellare.

knight (nait) n cavaliere m.

knit* (nit) vt 1 lavorare a maglia. 2 (one's brows) aggrottare. vi 1 lavorare a maglia. 2

(one's bones) saldarsi. **knitting** n lavoro a maglia m. **knitting needle** n ferro da calza m. **knitwear** n maglieria f.

knob (nɔb) n 1 pomo m. manopola f. 2 protuberanza f. **knobbly** adj nodoso, bitorzoluto.

knock (nɔk) n colpo m. vt urtare, colpire, battere. vi bussare. **knock down** abbattere. **knock out** mettere fuori combattimento.

knot (nɔt) n nodo m. vt annodare.

know* (nou) vt 1 conoscere. 2 sapere. 3 riconoscere. **knowing** adj intelligente, accorto. **knowledge** n conoscenza f. sapere m. **known** adj noto.

knuckle ('nʌkəl) n nocca delle dita, giuntura f.

Korea (kə'riə) n Corea f. **Korean** adj,n coreano.

kosher ('kouʃə) adj puro, lecito. n cibo permesso dalla religione ebraica m.

Kuwait (ku'weit) n Kuwait m. **Kuwaiti** adj,n kuwaitiano.

L

label ('leibəl) n etichetta f. cartellino m. vt 1 mettere le etichette a. 2 classificare.

laboratory (lə'bɔrətri) n laboratorio m.

labour ('leibə) n 1 lavoro m. fatica f. 2 manodopera f. 3 med doglie f pl. vi lavorare, affaticarsi. **labour-saving** adj che fa risparmiare lavoro. **laborious** adj laborioso. **Labour Party** n partito laburista m.

laburnum (lə'bə:nəm) n laburno m.

labyrinth ('læbərinθ) n labirinto m.

lace (leis) n 1 (of shoes) laccio m. 2 merletto m. vt allacciare.

lack (læk) n mancanza f. vt mancare di. vi mancare.

lacquer ('lækə) n lacca f. vt laccare.

lad (læd) n inf ragazzo m.

ladder ('lædə) n 1 scala f. 2 (in a stocking) smagliatura f. vi smagliarsi.

laden ('leidn) adj carico.

ladle ('leidl) n mestolo m. vt versare.

lady ('leidi) n signora f. **ladybird** n coccinella f.

lag¹ (læg) vi ritardare. n ritardo m.

lag² (læg) vt rivestire con materiale isolante.

lager ('lɑːgə) n birra chiara f.

laid (leid) v see **lay**.

lain (lein) v see **lie**.

lair (leiə) n tana f.

laity ('leiəti) n laici m pl.

lake (leik) n lago m.

lamb (læm) n agnello m.

lame (leim) adj zoppo. vt storpiare.

lament (lə'ment) n lamento m. vi lamentarsi, dolersi. vt lamentare.

lamp (læmp) n lampada f. lume m. **lamppost** n lampione m. **lampshade** n paralume m.

lance (lɑːns) n lancia f.

land (lænd) n 1 terra f. 2 paese m. 3 terreno m. proprietà f. vi 1 sbarcare. 2 approdare. 3 aviat atterrare. vt 1 ottenere. 2 allungare. **land on one's feet** cadere in piedi. **landing** n 1 pianerottolo m. 2 atterraggio m. 3 sbarco m. **landlady** n padrona di casa, affittacamere f. **landlord** n padrone di casa, affittacamere, proprietario m. **landmark** n punto di riferimento m. **landscape** n paesaggio m.

lane (lein) n 1 viottolo m. 2 mot corsia f.

language ('læŋgwidʒ) n lingua f. linguaggio m. **language laboratory** n laboratorio linguistico m.

lanky ('læŋki) adj allampanato.

lantern ('læntən) n lanterna f.

lap¹ (læp) n grembo, seno m.

lap² (læp) n sport giro di pista m.

lap³ (læp) vt bere avidamente. vi lambire.

lapel (lə'pel) n risvolto m.

Lapland ('læplænd) n Lapponia f. **Lapp** n lappone m,f.

lapse (læps) n 1 errore m. 2 intervallo m. vi 1 sbagliare. 2 trascorrere. 3 scadere.

larceny ('lɑːsəni) n furto m.

larch (lɑːtʃ) n larice m.

lard (lɑːd) n lardo, strutto m. vt ungere con lardo.

larder ('lɑːdə) n dispensa f.

large (lɑːdʒ) adj grande, spazioso.

lark¹ (lɑːk) n zool allodola f.

lark² (lɑːk) n burla f.

larva ('lɑːvə) n, pl **larvae** larva f.

larynx ('læriŋks) n laringe f. **laryngitis** n laringite f.

laser ('leizə) n laser m.

lash (læʃ) n 1 frustata f. 2 (of an eye) ciglio m, pl cigli m. or ciglia f. vt frustare.

lass (læs) n ragazza, fanciulla f.

lasso (læ'suː) n lasso, laccio m.

last¹ (lɑːst) adj ultimo, scorso, finale. n 1 fine f. 2 ultimo m. adv per ultimo, l'ultima volta. **at last** finalmente. **to the last** fino all'ultimo.

last² (lɑːst) vi durare, resistere.

latch (lætʃ) n chiavistello m.

late (leit) adj 1 tardi, tardivo. 2 recente. 3

defunto. adv tardi, in ritardo. **be late** essere in ritardo. **latecomer** n ritardatario m. **lately** adj ultimamente, recentemente.

latent ('leitnt) adj latente, nascosto.

lateral ('lætərəl) adj laterale.

latest ('leitist) adj ultimo. **at the latest** al più tardi.

lathe (leið) n tornio m.

lather ('lɑːðə) n schiuma f. vt insaponare. vi schiumare.

Latin ('lætin) adj,n latino m.

latitude ('lætitjuːd) n latitudine f.

latter ('lætə) adj ultimo. **2** posteriore.

lattice ('lætis) n grata, inferriata f.

laugh (lɑːf) vi ridere. **laugh at** farsi beffe di. ~n risata f.

launch[1] (lɔːntʃ) n naut lancia, scialuppa f.

launch[2] (lɔːntʃ) vt **1** aviat lanciare. **2** naut varare. **launching pad** n piattaforma di lancio f.

launder ('lɔːndə) vt lavare e stirare. **laundry** n **1** (place) lavanderia f. **2** bucato m.

laurel ('lɔrəl) n lauro, alloro m.

lava ('lɑːvə) n lava f.

lavatory ('lævətri) n gabinetto m.

lavender ('lævində) n lavanda f.

lavish ('læviʃ) adj prodigo, generoso. vt prodigare, elargire.

law (lɔː) n legge f. diritto m. **law-abiding** adj osservante della legge. **lawful** adj legale, consentito. **lawyer** n avvocato m.

lawn (lɔːn) n prato m. **lawn-mower** n falciatrice per prati f.

lax (læks) adj **1** trascurato. **2** rilasciato.

laxative ('læksətiv) adj,n lassativo m.

lay[1] (lei) vt posare, collocare, adagiare. vi fare le uova. **lay aside** mettere da parte. **lay out** esporre, distendere. **layer** n strato m.

lay[2] (lei) v see **lie**.

lay[3] (lei) adj laico. **layman** n secolare m.

laze (leiz) vi oziare, fare il pigro. **lazy** adj pigro, indolente. **laziness** n pigrizia f.

lead*[1] (liːd) vt **1** condurre, dirigere. **2** indurre. vi cominciare. **lead astray** traviare, sviare. ~n **1** comando m. **2** guida f. **3** guinzaglio m. **be in the lead** essere in testa. **leader** n **1** capo m. guida f. **2** articolo di fondo m. **leadership** n comando m. direzione f.

lead[2] (led) n piombo m.

leaf (liːf) n, pl **leaves 1** bot foglia f. **2** pagina f. **3** battente m. **leaflet** n volantino, manifestino

league (liːg) n lega, società f.

leak (liːk) n **1** naut falla f. **2** (of gas) fuga f. **3** fessura f. vi perdere, colare. **leak out** trapelare.

lean*[1] (liːn) vi **1** pendere, inclinare. **2** appoggiarsi. vt appoggiare. **lean out** sporgersi.

lean[2] (liːn) adj magro, esile.

leap* (liːp) vi balzare, lanciarsi. n salto, balzo m. **leapfrog** n cavalletta f. **leap year** n anno bisestile m.

learn* (ləːn) vt,vi imparare, studiare. **learned** adj colto, istruito.

lease (liːs) n contratto d'affitto m. vt affittare. **leasehold** n proprietà in affitto f.

leash (liːʃ) n guinzaglio m.

least (liːst) adj minimo. n meno m. **at least** almeno. **not in the least** per niente. ~adv (il) meno, minimamente.

leather ('leðə) n pelle f. cuoio m.

leave*[1] (liːv) vt abbandonare, lasciare. vi partire. **leave alone** lasciare in pace. **leave off** smettere.

leave[2] (liːv) n **1** permesso m. **2** congedo m.

Lebanon ('lebənən) n Libano m. **Lebanese** adj,n libanese.

lecherous ('letʃərəs) adj lascivo, vizioso.

lectern ('lektən) n leggio m.

lecture ('lektʃə) n **1** conferenza, lezione f. **2** inf ramanzina f. vi tenere delle lezioni. vt ammonire. **lecturer** n insegnante universitario m.

led (led) v see **lead**[1].

ledge (ledʒ) n sporgenza f.

ledger ('ledʒə) n libro mastro m.

lee (liː) n **1** riparo m. **2** sottovento m. adj sottovento. **leeward** adj,adv sottovento.

leech (liːtʃ) n sanguisuga f.

leek (liːk) n porro m.

leer (liə) n occhiata tendenziosa f. vi guardare di traverso o biecamente.

left[1] (left) adj sinistro. n sinistra f. adv a sinistra. **left hand** n mano sinistra f. **left-handed** adj mancino. **left-wing** adj sinistro. **left-luggage office** n deposito bagagli m.

left[2] (left) v see **leave**.

leg (leg) n **1** anat gamba f. **2** (of furniture) piede m. **3** zool zampa f. **pull someone's leg** prendere in giro qualcuno.

legacy ('legəsi) n lascito m. eredità f.

legal ('liːgəl) adj legale. **legalize** vt legalizzare.

legend ('ledʒənd) n leggenda f.

legible ('ledʒibl) adj leggibile.

legion ('li:dʒən) n legione f.

legislate ('ledʒisleit) vi promulgare leggi. **legislation** n legislazione f.

legitimate (li'dʒitimət) adj legittimo.

leisure ('leʒə) n 1 agio m. 2 tempo a disposizione m.

lemon ('lemən) n limone m. **lemon tree** n limone m. **lemonade** n limonata f.

lend° (lend) vt prestare, imprestare.

length (leŋθ) n 1 lunghezza f. 2 durata f. 3 (of material, etc.) taglio m.

lenient ('li:niənt) adj indulgente, benevolo.

lens (lenz) n lente f.

lent (lent) v see **lend**.

Lent (lent) n Quaresima f.

lentil ('lentl) n lenticchia f.

Leo ('li:ou) n Leone m.

leopard ('lepəd) n leopardo, gattopardo m.

leper ('lepə) n lebbroso m. **leprosy** n lebbra f.

lesbian ('lezbiən) adj lesbico. n lesbica f.

less (les) adj minore, meno. n meno m. adv,prep meno. **lessen** vt,vi diminuire.

lesson ('lesən) n lezione f.

lest (lest) conj per paura che.

let° (let) vt 1 permettere, lasciare. 2 affittare. **let down** 1 piantare in asso. 2 allungare. **let know** far sapere. **let loose** sciogliere, scatenare.

lethal ('li:θəl) adj letale.

lethargy ('leθədʒi) n letargo m. **lethargic** adj letargico.

letter ('letə) n lettera f. **letterbox** n buca delle lettere f. **lettering** n iscrizione f.

lettuce ('letis) n lattuga f.

leukaemia (lu:'ki:miə) n leucemia f.

level ('levəl) adj 1 uniforme. 2 a livello. n livello m. **on the level** onesto. ~vt 1 livellare, spianare. 2 (a gun) puntare. **level crossing** n passaggio a livello m. **level-headed** adj equilibrato.

lever ('li:və) n leva f. manubrio m.

levy ('levi) n 1 imposta f. 2 mil leva f. vt 1 imporre. 2 mil arruolare.

lewd (lu:d) adj lascivo, osceno.

liable ('laiəbl) adj 1 soggetto. 2 responsabile. **liability** n 1 obbligo m. 2 responsabilità f. 3 tendenza f. 4 pl comm passività f. debiti m pl.

liaison (li'eizən) n 1 legame m. 2 mil collegamento m.

liar ('laiə) n bugiardo m.

libel ('laibəl) n calunnia f.

liberal ('libərəl) adj liberale, generoso. n liberale m,f.

liberate ('libəreit) vt liberare.

liberty ('libəti) n libertà f.

Libra ('li:brə) n Libra f.

library ('laibrəri) n biblioteca f. **librarian** n bibliotecario m.

libretto (li'bretou) n libretto d'opera m.

Libya ('libiə) n Libia f. **Libyan** adj,n libico.

licence ('laisəns) n 1 mot patente f. 2 licenza f. **license** vt permettere, autorizzare. **licensee** n colui che possiede un'autorizzazione m.

lichen ('laikən) n lichene m.

lick (lik) vt leccare. n leccata f.

lid (lid) n coperchio m.

lie¹ (lai) n bugia, menzogna f. vi mentire.

lie² (lai) vi 1 giacere. 2 trovarsi. 3 consistere. **lie down** coricarsi.

lieutenant (lef'tenənt) n tenente m. **lieutenant colonel** n tenente colonnello m.

life (laif) n, pl **lives** vita f. **lifebelt** n cintura di salvataggio f. **lifeboat** n scialuppa di salvataggio f. **lifebuoy** n salvagente m. **lifeguard** n bagnino m. **lifeline** n sagola di salvataggio f. **lifetime** n durata della vita f.

lift (lift) vt alzare, sollevare. vi 1 levarsi. 2 dissiparsi. n 1 ascensore m. 2 passaggio m.

light¹ (lait) adj chiaro, luminoso. n 1 luce f. lume m. 2 fuoco, fiammifero m. vt 1 accendere. 2 illuminare. **light up** illuminarsi. **lighter** n accendisigari m invar. **lighthouse** n faro m. **lighting** n illuminazione f.

light² (lait) adj 1 leggero. 2 semplice, frivolo. **light-headed** adj scervellato, frivolo. **light-hearted** adj allegro, gaio. **lightweight** n peso leggero m.

light³ (lait) vi scendere, smontare.

lighten¹ ('laitn) vt illuminare. vi 1 illuminarsi. 2 rischiararsi.

lighten² ('laitn) vt alleggerire. vi alleggerirsi.

lightning ('laitniŋ) n fulmine, lampo m.

like¹ (laik) prep come, alla maniera di. adj 1 simile, uguale. 2 tipico di. n simile, uguale m. **feel like** aver voglia di. **likelihood** n probabilità f. **likely** adj verosimile. adv probabilmente. **like-minded** adj dello stesso parere. **likeness** n 1 somiglianza f. 2 ritratto m. **likewise** adv similmente, lo stesso. **liking** n simpatia f.

like² (laik) vt 1 gradire, piacere a. 2 amare, preferire. vi desiderare, volere, piacere.

lilac ('lailək) n bot lilla f.

lily ('lili) n giglio m. **lily-of-the-valley** n mughetto m.

limb (lim) n **1** arto m. membro m, pl membra f. **2** bot ramo m.

limbo ('limbou) n limbo m.

lime[1] (laim) n calce, calcina f. **limelight** n luci della ribalta f pl. **limestone** n calcare m.

lime[2] (laim) n bot cedro m. **limejuice** n succo di cedro m. **lime tree** n tiglio m.

limerick ('limərik) n piccola poesia umoristica f.

limit ('limit) n **1** limite m. **2** inf colmo m. vt limitare. **limitation** n limitazione f.

limp[1] (limp) vi zoppicare. n andatura zoppicante f.

limp[2] (limp) adj molle, debole, floscio.

limpet ('limpit) n patella f.

linden ('lindən) n tiglio m.

line[1] (lain) n **1** linea, riga f. **2** corda f. **3** limite m. **4** campo d'attività m. **5** tipo m. vt legare, segnare. **lineage** n lignaggio m. stirpe f. **linear** adj lineare.

line[2] (lain) vt (clothes, etc.) foderare. **lining** n fodera f.

linen ('linin) n **1** tela di lino f. **2** biancheria f invar. adj di lino. **linen basket** n cesto dei panni m.

liner ('lainə) n transatlantico m.

linger ('lingə) vi indugiare, soffermarsi.

lingerie ('lonʒəri:) n biancheria per signora f.

linguist ('lingwist) n linguista m. **linguistic** adj linguistico. **linguistics** n linguistica f.

link (link) n **1** anello m. **2** legame m. **3** collegamento m. vt collegare. vi congiungersi.

linoleum (li'nouliəm) n linoleum m. **lino** n linoleum m.

linseed ('linsi:d) n semi di lino m pl.

lion ('laiən) n leone m. **lioness** n leonessa f.

lip (lip) n **1** labbro m, pl labbra f. **2** orlo m. **lip-read** vt capire dal movimento delle labbra. **lipstick** n rossetto m.

liqueur (li'kjuə) n liquore m.

liquid ('likwid) adj,n liquido m. **liquidate** vt liquidare. **liquidation** n liquidazione f. **liquidize** vt rendere liquido.

liquor ('likə) n bevanda alcoolica f.

liquorice ('likəris) n liquirizia f.

lira ('liərə) n lira f.

lisp (lisp) n blesità f. vi parlare bleso.

list (list) n lista f. elenco, listino m. vt elencare.

listen ('lisən) vi ascoltare. **listener** n ascoltatore m.

listless ('listləs) adj svogliato, apatico, languido.

lit (lit) v see **light.**

litany ('litəni) n litania f.

literal ('litərəl) adj letterale, alla lettera.

literary ('litərəri) adj letterario.

literate ('litərət) adj che sa leggere e scrivere.

literature ('litərətʃə) n letteratura f.

litre ('li:tə) n litro m.

litter ('litə) n **1** rifiuti m pl. cartacce f pl. **2** (of animals) figliata f. vt mettere in disordine. **litter-bin** n cestino dei rifiuti m.

little ('litl) adj **1** piccolo. **2** poco. **3** breve. adv poco, un po'. **little by little** a poco a poco. ~n poco, po' m. **little finger** n (dito) mignolo m. **little toe** n mignolo (del piede) m.

liturgy ('litədʒi) n liturgia f.

live[1] (liv) vt,vi vivere, abitare. **live on** nutrirsi di. **live up to** mettere in pratica, non venir meno a.

live[2] (laiv) adj **1** vivo, vivente. **2** ardente. **3** (of electricity) sottotensione. **livestock** n bestiame m.

livelihood ('laivlihud) n vita f.

lively ('laivli) adj vivace. **liveliness** n vivacità f.

liver ('livə) n fegato m.

livery ('livəri) n livrea f.

livid ('livid) adj **1** livido, cereo. **2** furioso.

living ('livin) adj vivo, in esistenza. n **1** vita, sussistenza f. **2** rel benefizio m. **living room** n stanza di soggiorno m.

lizard ('lizəd) n lucertola f.

llama ('lɑ:mə) n lama m invar.

load (loud) n carico, fardello m. vt caricare.

loaf[1] (louf) n, pl **loaves** pagnotta f. pane carré m.

loaf[2] (louf) vi oziare, vagabondare, bighellonare.

loan (loun) n prestito m. vt prestare.

loathe (louð) vt detestare, provare ripugnanza per. **loathing** n ripugnanza f. **loathsome** adj ripugnante.

lob (lɔb) vt tirare alto. n pallonetto m.

lobby ('lɔbi) n **1** atrio m. **2** pol corridoio m. vi sollecitar voti.

lobe (loub) n lobo m.

lobster ('lɔbstə) n aragosta f.

local ('loukəl) adj locale. n **1** inf pub m invar. **2** pl gente del luogo f. **locality** n località f. **localize** vt circoscrivere. **locate** vt **1** individuare, localizzare. **2** situare. **location** n luogo, sito m.

loch (lɔx) n lago m.

lock[1] (lɔk) n **1** (of a door, etc.) serratura f. **2**

naut chiusa *f.* *vt* chiudere a chiave, sprangare. **lock in** chiudere dentro a chiave. **lock up** mettere sotto chiave, chiudere.

lock ² (lɔk) *n* (of hair) riccio *m.* crocca *f.*

locker ('lɔkə) *n* armadietto *m.*

locket ('lɔkit) *n* medaglione *m.*

locomotive (loukə'moutiv) *n* locomotiva *f.* *adj* locomotivo. **locomotion** *n* locomozione *f.*

locust ('loukəst) *n* locusta *f.*

lodge (lɔdʒ) *n* 1 villetta, dipendenza *f.* 2 portineria *f.* *vt* 1 alloggiare. 2 piazzare. 3 presentare. *vi* alloggiare. **lodger** *n* pensionante *m,f.* **lodgings** *n pl* camera d'affitto *f.*

loft (lɔft) *n* soffitta *f.* solaio *m.*

log (lɔg) *n* 1 tronco, ciocco *m.* 2 *naut* giornale di bordo *m.* **logbook** *n mot* libretto di circolazione *m.*

logarithm ('lɔgəriðəm) *n* logaritmo *m.*

logic ('lɔdʒik) *n* logica *f.* **logical** *adj* logico.

loins (lɔinz) *n pl* fianchi *m pl.*

loiter ('lɔitə) *vi* bighellonare.

lollipop ('lɔlipɔp) *n* lecca lecca *m invar.*

London ('lʌndən) *n* Londra *f.*

lonely ('lounli) *adj* solitario, solo. **loneliness** *n* solitudine *f.*

long ¹ (lɔŋ) *adj* 1 lungo. 2 lento. **a long time ago** molto tempo fa. **in the long run** a lungo andare. ~*adv* a lungo. **all day long** tutto il giorno. **as long as I want** finchè voglio. **as long as** purchè. **long-distance** *adj* interurbano. **long-playing** *adj* a lunga durata. **long-range** *adj* a lunga scadenza, a lunga portata. **long-sighted** *adj* 1 presbite. 2 previdente. **longstanding** *adj* di vecchia data, di lunga data. **long wave** *n* onda lunga *f.* **longwinded** *adj* 1 prolisso. 2 noioso.

long ² (lɔŋ) *vi* struggersi per, desiderare ardentemente. **long to** non veder l'ora di.

longevity (lɔn'dʒeviti) *n* longevità *f.*

longitude ('lɔndʒitjuːd) *n* longitudine *f.*

loo (luː) *n inf* gabinetto *m.*

look (luk) *n* 1 sguardo *m.* occhiata *f.* 2 apparenza *f.* *vi* 1 guardare. 2 sembrare, parere. **look after** prendersi cura di. **look at** guardare. **look for** cercare. **look on to** dare su. **look out** fare attenzione.

loom ¹ (luːm) *n* telaio *m.*

loom ² (luːm) *vi* intravedersi, apparire.

loop (luːp) *n* cappio *m.* *vi* descrivere una curva. **loophole** ('luːphoul) *n* scappatoia *f.*

loose (luːs) *adj* 1 sciolto, libero. 2 allentato. 3 sfrenato, dissoluto. 4 vago, libero. **at a loose**

end senza nulla da fare. ~*vt* sciogliere. **loosen** *vt* 1 allentare. 2 sciogliere.

loot (luːt) *n* bottino *m.* *vt* saccheggiare. **looting** *n* saccheggio *m.*

lop (lɔp) *vt* 1 mozzare. 2 *bot* potare.

lopsided (lɔp'saidid) *adj* storto, pencolante.

lord (lɔːd) *n* 1 sovrano, signore *m.* 2 *cap* Pari *m invar.* **lordship** *n* potere *m.* signoria *f.* **Your Lordship** Vostra Signoria, Vostra Eccellenza.

lorry ('lɔri) *n* camion *m invar.* autocarro *m.*

lose * (luːz) *vt* perdere, smarrire. *vi* 1 rimetterci. 2 (of a watch) ritardare. **lose one's temper** arrabbiarsi. **lose one's way** smarrirsi. **loser** *n* perdente *m.*

loss (lɔs) *n* perdita *f.*

lost (lɔst) *v* see **lose.**

lot (lɔt) *n* 1 sorte, ventura *f.* destino *m.* 2 *comm* partita *f.* 3 quantità *f.*

lotion ('louʃən) *n* lozione *f.*

lottery ('lɔtəri) *n* lotteria *f.* lotto *m.*

lotus ('loutəs) *n* loto *m.*

loud (laud) *adj* 1 forte, alto, rumoroso. 2 (of colours) vistoso. *adv* alto, forte. **loud-mouthed** *adj* sguaiato, vociferatore. **loudness** *n* sonorità *f.* **loudspeaker** *n* altoparlante *m.*

lounge (laundʒ) *n* 1 salotto *m.* 2 sala di ritrovo *f.* *vi* poltrire, oziare.

louse (laus) *n, pl* **lice** pidocchio *m.* **lousy** *adj* 1 pidocchioso. 2 *inf* sordido, pessimo.

love (lʌv) *n* 1 amore *m.* 2 *sport* zero *m.* **fall in love with** innamorarsi di. ~*vt* 1 amare. 2 voler bene a. **lovely** *adj* bello, carino, piacevole. **lover** *n* amante *m,f.* **lovesick** *adj* malato d'amore.

low ¹ (lou) *adj* 1 basso. 2 volgare. *adv* 1 basso. 2 sottovoce. **lowbrow** *adj* incolto, di bassa levatura. **low frequency** *n* bassa frequenza *f.* **low-grade** *adj* inferiore, di qualità inferiore. **lowland** *n* pianura *f.* bassopiano *m.* *adj* di pianura. **low-necked** *adj* scollato. **low-pitched** *adj* basso. **low tide** *n* bassa marea *f.*

low ² (lou) *vi* muggire.

lower ('louə) *vt* abbassare. *vt,vi* calare, diminuire. *adj* minuscolo. **lower classes** classi inferiori *f pl.*

loyal ('lɔiəl) *adj* fedele, leale. **loyalty** *n* fedeltà, lealtà *f.*

lozenge ('lɔzindʒ) *n* pastiglia *f.*

LSD *n* LSD *f.*

lubricate ('luːbrikeit) *vt* lubrificare. **lubrication** *n* lubrificazione *f.*

lucid ('lu:sid) adj **1** chiaro, limpido. **2** lucido.

luck (lʌk) n fortuna f. **good luck!** auguri! **lucky** adj fortunato.

lucrative ('lu:krətiv) adj lucroso, lucrativo.

ludicrous ('lu:dikrəs) adj ridicolo, irrisorio.

lug (lʌg) vt trascinare.

luggage ('lʌgidʒ) n bagaglio m.

lukewarm (lu:k'wɔ:m) adj tiepido.

lull (lʌl) n pausa, calma f. **lullaby** n ninna-nanna f.

lumbago (lʌm'beigou) n lombaggine f.

lumber[1] ('lʌmbə) n legname m. **lumberjack** n boscaiolo, taglialegna m.

lumber[2] ('lʌmbə) vi muoversi goffamente.

luminous ('lu:minəs) adj luminoso.

lump (lʌmp) n **1** massa f. pezzo m. **2** gonfiore m. vt ammassare.

lunacy ('lu:nəsi) n pazzia f.

lunar ('lu:nə) adj lunare.

lunatic ('lu:nətik) adj,n pazzo, matto m.

lunch (lʌntʃ) n colazione f. pranzo m. vi far colazione, pranzare.

lung (lʌŋ) n polmone m.

lunge (lʌndʒ) n affondo m. vi scagliarsi.

lurch[1] (lə:tʃ) n sbandata f. vi barcollare.

lurch[2] (lə:tʃ) n **leave in the lurch** piantare in asso.

lure (luə) vt allettare. n allettamento m.

lurid ('luərid) adj **1** spettrale. **2** raccapricciante.

lurk (lə:k) vi stare in agguato, essere nascosto.

luscious ('lʌʃəs) adj succulento.

lush (lʌʃ) adj lussureggiante.

lust (lʌst) n cupidigia, libidine f. v **lust for** or **after** bramare. **lustful** adj bramoso, avido.

lustre ('lʌstə) n lustro m.

lute (lu:t) n liuto m.

Luxembourg ('lʌksəmbə:g) n Lussemburgo m.

luxury ('lʌkʃəri) n lusso m. adj di lusso.

lynch (lintʃ) vt linciare.

lynx (liŋks) n lince f.

lyre ('laiə) n lira f.

lyrics ('liriks) n pl parole di una canzone f pl. **lyrical** adj lirico.

M

mac (mæk) n inf impermeabile m.

macabre (mə'ka:b) adj macabro.

macaroni (mækə'rouni) n maccheroni m pl.

mace[1] (meis) n mazza f.

mace[2] (meis) n bot macis m or f.

machine (mə'ʃi:n) n macchina f. **machine-gun** n mitragliatrice f. mitragliatore m. **machinery** n **1** macchinario m. **2** meccanismo m. **3** procedimento m. **machinist** n **1** macchinista m. **2** meccanico m. **3** lavorante m,f.

mackerel ('mækrəl) n sgombro m.

mackintosh ('mækintɔʃ) n impermeabile m.

mad (mæd) adj **1** matto, pazzo. **2** inf arrabbiato. **madness** n pazzia f.

madam ('mædəm) n signora f.

made (meid) v see **make**.

Madonna (mə'dɔnə) n Madonna f.

madrigal ('mædrigəl) n madrigale f.

magazine (mægə'zi:n) n **1** periodico, mensile m. **2** mil caricatore m.

Maggiore, Lake (mædʒi'ɔ:ri) n Lago Maggiore m.

maggot ('mægət) n larva f.

magic ('mædʒik) n magia f. adj magico. **magical** adj magico. **magician** n mago m.

magistrate ('mædʒistreit) n magistrato m.

magnanimous (mæg'næniməs) adj magnanimo.

magnate ('mægneit) n magnate m.

magnet ('mægnit) n calamita f. magnete m. **magnetic** adj magnetico. **magnetism** n magnetismo m. **magnetize** vt magnetizzare.

magnificent (mæg'nifisənt) adj magnifico.

magnify ('mægnifai) vt **1** ingrandire. **2** esagerare. **magnifying glass** n lente d'ingrandimento f.

magnitude ('mægnitju:d) n grandezza, magnitudine f.

magnolia (mæg'noulə) n magnolia f.

magpie ('mægpai) n gazza f.

mahogany (mə'hɔgəni) n mogano m. adj di mogano.

maid (meid) n domestica f. **maiden** adj inaugurale, primo. n fanciulla, signorina f. **maiden name** n cognome da ragazza m.

mail (meil) n posta f. vt imbucare, mandare per posta. **mailbag** n sacco postale m. **mailing list** n elenco di indirizzi per l'invio di materiale pubblicitario, etc. m. **mail order** n ordinazione per posta f.

maim (meim) vt ferire gravemente, mutilare.

main (mein) adj principale. **mainland** n terraferma f. **mainsail** n vela (di) maestra f. **mainspring** n **1** tech molla principale f. **2** agente principale m. **mainstream** n corrente principale f. **mains** n pl **1** fognatura f. **2** rete elettrica f.

maintain (mein'tein) vt **1** mantenere. **2** sostenere. **maintenance** n **1** manutenzione f. **2** mantenimento m.

maize (meiz) n granturco m.

majesty ('mædʒisti) n maestà f. **majestic** adj maestoso.

major ('meidʒə) adj maggiore, più importante. n maggiore m. **major general** n generale di divisione m. **majority** n **1** maggioranza f. **2** maggior età f.

make* (meik) vt **1** fare, costruire. **2** costringere a. vi fare. **make for** avviarsi verso. **make off** squagliarsela. **make out 1** scorgere. **2** riempire. **make up 1** completare. **2** inventare. **3** Th truccare. **make-up** n trucco m. **make up for** compensare. ~n **1** forma, fabbricazione f. **2** marca f. **make-believe** n finzione f. **make-shift** adj improvvisato.

maladjusted (mælə'dʒʌstid) adj incapace di adattarsi.

malaria (mə'lɛəriə) n malaria f.

Malaya (mə'leiə) n Malesia f. **Malay** adj,n malese. **Malay** (language) n malese m.

Malaysia (mə'leiziə) n Malaysia f. **Malaysian** adj,n malese.

male (meil) adj maschile. n maschio m.

malfunction (mæl'fʌŋkʃən) vi funzionare male. n funzionamento imperfetto m.

malice ('mælis) n malignità f.

malignant (mə'lignənt) adj maligno.

mallet ('mælət) n maglio m.

malnutrition (mælnju'triʃən) n malnutrizione f.

malt (mɔːlt) n malto m.

Malta ('mɔːltə) n Malta f. **Maltese** adj,n maltese.

maltreat (mæl'triːt) vt maltrattare.

mammal ('mæməl) n mammifero m.

mammoth ('mæməθ) adj immenso.

man (mæn) n, pl **men** uomo m, pl uomini. vt equipaggiare. **man-handle** vt malmenare. **manhole** n chiusino m. **man-made** adj artificiale. **manpower** n manodopera f. **manslaughter** n omicidio preterintenzionale m.

Man, Isle of n Isola di Man f.

manage ('mænidʒ) vt dirigere. vi cavarsela. **manage to** riuscire a. **manageable** adj docile. **management** n direzione f. **manager** n direttore m.

mandarin ('mændərin) n mandarino m.

mandate ('mændeit) n mandato m. **mandatory** adj obbligatorio.

mandolin ('mændəlin) n mandolino m.

mane (mein) n criniera f.

mange (meindʒ) n rogna f. **mangy** adj **1** rognoso. **2** inf squallido.

mangle[1] ('mæŋgəl) vt rovinare, deformare.

mangle[2] ('mæŋgəl) n mangano, strizzatoio m. vt manganare.

mango ('mæŋgou) n, pl **-goes** or **-gos** mango m.

mania ('meiniə) n mania f. **maniac** n maniaco m. **manic** adj maniaco.

manicure ('mænikjuə) n manicure, cosmesi delle mani f. vt fare la manicure. **manicurist** n manicure m,f.

manifest ('mænifest) adj evidente, palese, manifesto. vt dimostrare.

manifesto (mæni'festou) n manifesto m.

manifold ('mænifould) adj molteplice.

manipulate (mə'nipjuleit) vt **1** manipolare. **2** manovrare, maneggiare. **manipulation** n **1** manipolazione f. maneggio m.

mankind (mæn'kaind) n umanità f.

manner ('mænə) n maniera f. modo m. **mannerism** n manierismo m.

manoeuvre (mə'nuːvə) n manovra f. vt,vi manovrare.

manor ('mænə) n maniero m.

mansion ('mænʃən) n casa signorile f.

mantelpiece ('mæntəlpiːs) n mensola f.

mantilla (mæn'tilə) n mantiglia f.

mantle ('mæntl) n manto m.

manual ('mænjuəl) adj manuale.

manufacture (mænju'fæktʃə) n manifattura f. vt fabbricare. **manufacturer** n fabbricante m.

manure (mə'njuə) n letame m. vt concimare.

manuscript ('mænjuskript) n manoscritto m.

Manx (mæŋks) adj dell'isola di Man.

many ('meni) adj molti. **a good many** parecchi. **as many** altrettanti. **how many?** quanti? **many a** molti. **so many** tanti.

map (mæp) n **1** mappa, carta f. **2** (of a town) pianta f. vt fare la carta di. **map out** tracciare.

maple ('meipəl) n acero m.

mar (mɑː) vt guastare.

marathon ('mærəθən) n maratona f.

marble ('mɑːbəl) n **1** marmo m. **2** game billia, pallina f. adj di marmo, marmoreo.

march (mɑːtʃ) n marcia f. vi marciare.

March (mɑːtʃ) n marzo m.

marchioness ('mɑːʃənis) n marchesa f.

mare (mɛə) n cavalla f.

margarine (mɑːdʒə'riːn) n margarina f.

margin ('mɑ:dʒin) n margine m. **marginal** adj marginale.

marguerite (mɑ:gə'ri:t) n margherita f.

marigold ('mærigould) n calendola f.

marijuana (mæri'wɑ:nə) n marijuana f.

marinade (n mæri'neid) n marinata f. **marinate** vt marinare.

marine (mə'ri:n) adj marino. n soldato di marina m. **maritime** adj marittimo.

marital ('mærit|) adj maritale, coniugale.

marjoram ('mɑ:dʒərəm) n maggiorana f.

mark[1] (mɑ:k) n 1 segno, marchio m. impronta. f. 2 educ voto m. vt 1 segnare, marcare. 2 educ correggere. **mark out** tracciare. **marksman** n tiratore scelto m.

mark[2] (mɑ:k) n comm marco m.

market ('mɑ:kit) n 1 mercato m. 2 comm borsa f. vt mettere in vendita. **market garden** n orto m. **market research** n ricerca di mercato f.

marmalade ('mɑ:məleid) n marmellata f.

maroon[1] (mə'ru:n) adj,n marrone rossastro m.

maroon[2] (mə'ru:n) vt abbandonare.

marquee (mɑ:'ki:) n grande tenda f.

marquess ('mɑ:kwis) n marchese m.

marquise (mɑ:'ki:z) n marchesa f.

marrow ('mærou) n 1 midollo m. 2 bot zucca f. **marrowbone** n ossobuco m.

marry ('mæri) vt sposare. vi sposarsi. **marriage** n matrimonio m. **marriage certificate** n certificato di matrimonio m.

Mars (mɑ:z) n Marte m.

marsh (mɑ:ʃ) n palude f. **marshy** adj paludoso. **marshmallow** n 1 bot altea f. 2 specie di caramella f.

marshal ('mɑ:ʃəl) n maresciallo m. vt ordinare.

marsupial (mɑ:'sju:piəl) adj,n marsupiale m.

martial ('mɑ:ʃəl) adj marziale.

martin ('mæ:tin) n balestruccio m.

martini (mɑ:'ti:ni) n martini m invar.

martyr ('mɑ:tə) n martire m. **martyrdom** n martirio m.

marvel ('mɑ:vəl) n meraviglia f. vi meravigliarsi. **marvellous** adj meraviglioso.

Marxism ('mɑ:ksizəm) n marxismo m. **Marxist** adj,n marxista.

marzipan ('mɑ:zipæn) n marzapane m.

mascara (mæ'skɑ:rə) n mascara m.

mascot ('mæskət) n mascotte f, pl mascottes.

masculine ('mæskjulin) adj maschile, mascolino.

mash (mæʃ) vt schiacciare, pestare.

mask (mɑ:sk) n maschera f. vt mascherare.

masochism ('mæsəkizəm) n masochismo m. **masochist** n masochista m. **masochistic** adj masochistico.

mason ('meisən) n 1 muratore m. 2 massone m. **masonic** adj massonico. **masonry** n 1 muratura f. 2 massoneria f.

masquerade (mæskə'reid) n 1 ballo in maschera m. mascherata f. 2 finzione f. vi mascherarsi.

mass[1] (mæs) n massa f. **masses of** un sacco di. ~vt adunare, ammassare. **mass media** n mass media m pl. **mass-produce** vt produrre in massa.

mass[2] (mæs) n rel messa f.

massacre ('mæsəkə) n massacro m. vt massacrare.

massage ('mæsɑ:ʒ) vt massaggiare. n massaggio m.

massive ('mæsiv) adj massiccio.

mast (mɑ:st) n albero m.

master ('mɑ:stə) n 1 padrone m. 2 educ maestro, professore m. vt dominare. **masterful** adj imperioso. **mastermind** n cervello m. **masterpiece** n capolavoro m.

masturbate ('mæstəbeit) vi masturbarsi. **masturbation** n masturbazione f.

mat (mæt) n 1 stuoia f. 2 (table) sottovaso, sottopiatto m.

matador ('mætədɔ:) n matador m, pl matadores.

match[1] (mætʃ) n fiammifero m. **matchbox** n scatola da fiammiferi f. **matchstick** n fiammifero m.

match[2] (mætʃ) n 1 uguale m,f. pari m,f invar. 2 sport partita f. incontro m. 3 matrimonio m. vt 1 uguagliare. 2 andar bene con. 3 opporre. vi andar bene insieme.

mate (meit) n 1 inf compagno, amico m. 2 naut ufficiale in seconda m. vt accoppiare. vi accoppiarsi.

material (mə'tiəriəl) n 1 materiale m. 2 stoffa f. adj 1 materiale. 2 essenziale. **materialist** n materialista m. **materialistic** adj materialistico. **materialize** vi realizzarsi.

maternal (mə'tə:n|) adj materno. **maternity** n maternità f.

mathematics (mæθə'mætiks) n matematica f.

matins ('mætinz) n pl mattutino m.

matinee ('mætinei) n (rappresentazione) diurna f.

matriarchal ('meitriɑ:kəl) adj matriarcale.

matrimony ('mætrɪmənɪ) n matrimonio m.

matrix ('meɪtrɪks) n, pl **matrices** or **matrixes** matrice f.

matron ('meɪtrən) n **1** educ governante f. **2** med capoinfermiera f.

matter ('mætə) n **1** materia f. **2** contenuto m. **3** faccenda, questione f. **as a matter of fact** a dire il vero. **printed matter** n stampati m pl. **what's the matter?** che c'è? ~vi importare, aver importanza.

Matterhorn ('mætəhɔːn) n Cervino m.

mattress ('mætrəs) n materasso m.

mature (mə'tjuə) adj maturo. vt,vi maturare. **maturity** n maturità f.

maudlin ('mɔːdlɪn) adj piagnucoloso, sentimentale.

maul (mɔːl) vt dilaniare, straziare.

Maundy Thursday ('mɔːndɪ) n Giovedì Santo m.

mausoleum (mɔːsə'lɪəm) n mausoleo m.

mauve (mouv) adj,n malva m invar.

maxim ('mæksɪm) n massima f.

maximum ('mæksɪməm) adj,n massimo m. **maximize** vt rendere massimo.

may (meɪ) v mod aux potere. **it may be so** può darsi. **maybe** adv forse, può darsi che.

May (meɪ) n maggio m. **May Day** n primo maggio m. festa del lavoro f. **maypole** n albero di maggio m.

mayonnaise (meɪə'neɪz) n maionese f.

mayor ('mɛə) n sindaco m. **mayoress** n sindaca f.

maze (meɪz) n labirinto m.

me (miː) pers pron 1st pers s mi, me.

meadow ('medou) n prato m.

meagre ('miːgə) adj magro.

meal[1] (miːl) n cul pasto m.

meal[2] (miːl) n farina grossa f.

mean[1] (miːn) vt **1** significare, voler dire. **2** intendere. **3** destinare. **mean well** essere ben intenzionato.

mean[2] (miːn) adj **1** meschino, di basso conio. **2** gretto, tirchio, taccagno. **3** medio.

meander (mɪ'ændə) vi serpeggiare. n meandro m.

meaning ('miːnɪŋ) n significato m. **meaningful** adj significativo. **meaningless** adj privo di significato.

means (miːnz) n pl mezzo m. **by all means** certo, senz'altro. **by no means** non...affatto, niente affatto.

meantime ('miːntaɪm) adv intanto. **in the meantime** nel frattempo.

measles ('miːzəlz) n morbillo m.

measure ('meʒə) n misura f. **made to measure** confezionato su misura. ~vt,vi misurare. **measurement** n misura f.

meat (miːt) n carne f.

mechanic (mɪ'kænɪk) n meccanico m. **mechanical** adj meccanico. **mechanical engineering** n ingegneria meccanica f. **mechanism** n meccanismo m. **mechanize** vt meccanizzare.

medal ('medl) n medaglia f. **medallion** n medaglione m.

meddle ('medl) vi immischiarsi, intromettersi.

media ('miːdɪə) **mass media** n mezzi di comunicazione di massa m pl.

medial ('miːdɪəl) adj mediano, medio.

median ('miːdɪən) adj mediano. n mediana f.

mediate ('miːdɪeɪt) vt,vi mediare. **mediator** n mediatore m.

medical ('medɪkəl) adj medico. n esame medico m. **medication** n medicazione f. **medicine** n **1** medicina f. **2** farmaco m.

medieval (medɪ'iːvəl) adj medievale.

mediocre (miːdɪ'oukə) adj mediocre. **mediocrity** n mediocrità f.

meditate ('medɪteɪt) vt,vi meditare. **meditator** n meditatore m.

Mediterranean (medɪtə'reɪnɪən) adj mediterraneo. **Mediterranean (Sea)** n (Mare) Mediterraneo m.

medium ('miːdɪəm) n,pl **media** or **mediums** mezzo m. **happy medium** giusto mezzo. adj medio.

meek (miːk) adj remissivo, mite.

meet* (miːt) vt incontrare. vi **1** incontrarsi. **2** riunirsi. **meet with 1** imbattersi in. **2** subire. **meeting** n riunione, assemblea f.

megaphone ('megəfoun) n megafono m.

melancholy ('melənkəlɪ) n malinconia f. adj malinconico.

mellow ('melou) adj **1** maturo. **2** amabile. **3** addolcito. **4** morbido. vt far maturare, addolcire. vi maturare, addolcirsi.

melodrama ('melədrɑːmə) n melodramma m. **melodramatic** adj melodrammatico.

melody ('melədɪ) n melodia f.

melon ('melən) n melone m.

melt* (melt) vt squagliare, sciogliere, fondere. vi squagliarsi, sciogliersi, fondere. **melt down** fondere. **melting** n fusione f. **melting point** n punto di fusione m.

225

member (ˈmembə) n membro, socio m. **member of Parliament** n deputato m. **membership** n 1 appartenenza f. 2 totale dei membri m.

membrane (ˈmembrein) n membrana f.

memento (məˈmentou) n, pl **-os** or **-oes** ricordo m.

memo (ˈmemou) n inf memorandum m.

memoir (ˈmemwɑː) n 1 nota biografica f. 2 pl memorie f pl.

memorandum (meməˈrændəm) n, pl **-dums** or **-da** memorandum m.

memory (ˈmeməri) n 1 memoria f. 2 ricordo m. **memorable** adj memorabile. **memorial** n monumento m. adj commemorativo. **memorize** vt imparare a memoria.

menace (ˈmenəs) n minaccia f. vt minacciare. **menacing** adj minaccioso.

menagerie (məˈnædʒəri) n serraglio m.

mend (mend) vt 1 riparare, rammendare. 2 migliorare. vi rimettersi, migliorare. **mend one's ways** ravvedersi. n aggiustatura f. rammendo m. **mending** n 1 riparazione f. 2 roba da riparare f.

menial (ˈmiːniəl) adj umile, servile. n servo m.

menopause (ˈmenəpɔːz) n menopausa f.

menstrual (ˈmenstruəl) adj mestruale. **menstruate** vi mestruare.

mental (ˈmentl) adj mentale. **mental hospital** n manicomio m. **mentality** n mentalità f.

menthol (ˈmenθɔl) n mentolo m.

mention (ˈmenʃən) vt far menzione di, citare, menzionare. **don't mention it!** di nulla! ~n menzione, citazione f.

menu (ˈmenjuː) n menu m invar.

mercantile (ˈməːkəntail) adj mercantile.

mercenary (ˈməːsənəri) adj mercenario, venale. n mercenario m.

merchant (ˈməːtʃənt) n commerciante, mercante m. **merchant bank** n banca f. **merchant navy** n marina mercantile f. **merchandise** n merce, mercanzia f.

mercury (ˈməːkjuri) n mercurio m.

mercy (ˈməːsi) n misericordia, pietà, clemenza f.

mere (miə) adj puro, semplice, mero.

merge (məːdʒ) vt fondere, amalgamare. vi fondersi. **merger** n fusione f.

meridian (məˈridiən) n meridiano m.

meringue (məˈræŋ) n meringa f.

merit (ˈmerit) n merito m. vt meritare.

mermaid (ˈməːmeid) n sirena f.

merry (ˈmeri) adj 1 allegro, giocondo. 2 inf

brillo, alticcio. **merry-go-round** giostra f. carosello m.

mesh (meʃ) n maglia f.

mesmerize (ˈmezməraiz) vt ipnotizzare.

mess (mes) n 1 pasticcio m. confusione f. 2 mensa f. v **mess about** perdere tempo. **mess up** guastare.

message (ˈmesidʒ) n 1 messaggio m. 2 commissione f. **messenger** n messaggero, fattorino m.

met (met) v see **meet**.

metabolism (miˈtæbəlizəm) n metabolismo m.

metal (ˈmetl) n metallo m. adj di metallo, metallico. **metallic** adj metallico. **metallurgy** n metallurgia f.

metamorphosis (metəˈmɔːfəsis) n, pl **metamorphoses** metamorfosi f invar.

metaphor (ˈmetəfə) n metafora f. **metaphorical** adj metaforico.

metaphysics (metəˈfiziks) n metafisica f. **metaphysical** adj metafisico.

meteor (ˈmiːtiə) n meteora f. **meteorology** n meteorologia f.

meter (ˈmiːtə) n 1 contatore m. 2 mot parchimetro m.

methane (ˈmiːθein) n metano m.

method (ˈmeθəd) n metodo m. **methodical** adj metodico. **methodology** n metodologia f.

Methodist (ˈmeθədist) n metodista m.

meticulous (miˈtikjuləs) adj meticoloso.

metre (ˈmiːtə) n metro m. **metric** adj metrico.

metropolis (məˈtrɔpəlis) n metropoli f invar. **metropolitan** adj metropolitano.

Mexico (ˈmeksikou) n Messico m. **Mexican** adj messicano.

miaow (miˈau) n miagolio m. vi miagolare.

microbe (ˈmaikroub) n microbo m.

microphone (ˈmaikrəfoun) n microfono m.

microscope (ˈmaikrəskoup) n microscopio m.

mid (mid) adj 1 mezzo, di mezzo. 2 metà. 2 pieno. **midday** n mezzogiorno m. **midland** adj interno. **midmorning** n metà mattina f. **midnight** n mezzanotte f. **midstream** n centro della corrente m. **midsummer** n mezza estate f. **midway** adj,adv a metà strada. **midweek** n metà (della) settimana f.

middle (ˈmidl) n mezzo, centro m. metà f. adj di mezzo, medio. **middle finger** n (dito) medio m. **middle-aged** adj di mezz'età. **middle-class** adj borghese.

Middle Ages n pl medioevo m.

Middle East n Medio Oriente m.

midget ('midʒit) n nano m.

midst (midst) n mezzo, centro m.

midwife ('midwaif) n ostetrica f. **midwifery** n ostetricia f.

might[1] (mait) v see **may.**

might[2] (mait) n forza, potenza f.

migraine ('mi:grein) n emicrania f.

migrate (mai'greit) vi **1** zool migrare. **2** emigrare. **migration** n **1** migrazione f. **2** emigrazione f.

mike (maik) n inf microfono m.

Milan (mi'læn) n Milano f. **Milanese** adj,n milanese.

mild (maild) adj **1** mite, gentile. **2** dolce, leggero. **3** clemente. **mildly** adv gentilmente.

mildew ('mildju:) n muffa f.

mile (mail) n miglio m, pl miglia f. **mileage** n distanza percorsa in miglia f. chilometraggio m. **mileometer** n contamiglia, contachilometri m. **milestone** n pietra miliare f.

militant ('militənt) adj,n militante. **military** adj militare.

milk (milk) n latte m. vt mungere. **milkman** n lattaio m.

Milky Way n Via Lattea f.

mill (mil) n **1** mulino m. **2** fabbrica f. stabilimento m. **3** macinino m. **millstone** n macina f.

millennium (mi'leniəm) n, pl **-niums** or **-nia** millennio m.

milligram ('miligræm) n milligrammo m.

millilitre ('mililitə) n millilitro m.

millimetre ('milimi:tə) n millimetro m.

million ('miljən) n milione m. **millionaire** n milionario m. **millionth** adj milionesimo.

mime (maim) n mimo m. vt,vi mimare. **mimic** n mimo, imitatore m. vt imitare. **mimicry** n mimica f.

mimosa (mi'mouzə) n mimosa f.

minaret (minə'ret) n minareto m.

mince (mins) vt tritare, tagliuzzare. n carne tritata f. **mincer** n tritatutto m.

mind (maind) n **1** mente f. **2** memoria f. **make up one's mind** decidersi. ~vt **1** badare a, fare attenzione a. **2** occuparsi di. vi stare attento. **do you mind?** ti dispiace? **never mind!** non importa!

mine[1] (main) poss pron 1st pers s mio, il mio, mia, la mia, miei, i miei, mie, le mie.

mine[2] (main) n **1** miniera f. **2** mil mina f. vt **1** scavare, estrarre. **2** mil minare. **miner** n minatore m.

mineral ('minərəl) adj,n minerale m. **mineral water** n acqua minerale f.

minestrone (mini'strouni) n minestrone m.

mingle ('miŋgəl) vt mischiare. vi mescolarsi.

miniature ('miniətʃə) n miniatura f. adj in miniatura.

minim ('minim) n minima f. **minimize** vt minimizzare. **minimum** adj,n minimo m.

mining ('mainiŋ) n attività mineraria, estrazione f. adj minerario.

minister ('ministə) n **1** ministro m. **2** rel pastore m. **ministerial** adj ministeriale. **ministry** n **1** ministero m. **2** rel clero m.

mink (miŋk) n visone m.

minor ('mainə) adj minore, più piccolo, secondario. n minorenne m,f. **minority** n **1** minoranza f. **2** law qualità di minorenne f.

minstrel ('minstrəl) n menestrello m.

mint[1] (mint) n zool menta f.

mint[2] (mint) n zecca f. vt coniare.

minuet (minju'et) n minuetto m.

minus ('mainəs) adj,prep meno.

minute[1] ('minit) n **1** minuto m. **2** momento m. **3** pl verbale m.

minute[2] (mai'nju:t) adj **1** minuto. **2** particolareggiato.

miracle ('mirəkəl) n miracolo m. **miraculous** adj miracoloso.

mirage ('mira:ʒ) n miraggio m.

mirror ('mirə) n specchio m. vt rispecchiare.

mirth (mə:θ) n ilarità, allegria f. riso m, pl risa f.

misbehave (misbi'heiv) vi comportarsi male. **misbehaviour** n cattiva condotta f.

miscarriage (mis'kæridʒ) n **1** med aborto m. **2** insuccesso m. **miscarry** vi **1** abortire. **2** fare cilecca.

miscellaneous (misə'leiniəs) adj miscellaneo. **miscellany** n miscellanea f.

mischance (mis'tʃa:ns) n disavventura f.

mischief ('mistʃif) n **1** birichinata f. **2** danno m. **mischievous** adj birichino, dispettoso.

misconceive (miskən'si:v) vt fraintendere, farsi un'idea erronea di. **misconception** n malinteso m. idea erronea f.

misconduct (miskən'dʌkt) n **1** cattiva condotta f. **2** cattiva amministrazione f.

misdeed (mis'di:d) n misfatto m.

miser ('maizə) n avaro m. **miserly** adj avaro.

miserable ('mizərəbəl) adj **1** triste, infelice. **2** misero, miserabile.

misery ('mizəri) n depressione, sofferenza f.

misfire (mis'faiǝ) vi **1** incepparsi. **2** fare fiasco, mancare il bersaglio.

misfit ('misfit) n **1** spostato m. **2** vestito che non va bene m.

misfortune (mis'fɔ:tʃǝn) n sfortuna f.

misgiving (mis'giviŋ) n **1** dubbio, sospetto m. **2** diffidenza f.

misguided (mis'gaidid) adj sviato.

mishap ('mishæp) n infortunio m.

mislay (mis'lei) vt smarrire.

mislead (mis'li:d) vt **1** ingannare. **2** fuorviare. **misleading** adj fallace.

misprint (n 'misprint; v mis'print) n errore di stampa m. vt stampare male.

miss[1] (mis) vt **1** mancare, sbagliare. **2** sentire la mancanza di. **3** perdere. **4** evitare. vi mancare, sbagliare. **miss out** omettere. ∼n colpo mancato, sbaglio m. **missing** adj **1** mancante, smarrito. **2** mil disperso.

miss[2] (mis) n **1** signorina f. **2** cap (title of address) Signorina.

missile ('misail) n missile m.

mission ('miʃǝn) n missione f. **missionary** adj,n missionario m.

mist (mist) n foschia f. vi appannarsi. **misty** adj **1** fosco. **2** nebuloso.

mistake* (mis'teik) n sbaglio, errore m. vt **1** sbagliare. **2** fraintendere. **3** scambiare.

mister ('mistǝ) n signore m.

mistletoe ('misǝltou) n vischio m.

mistress ('mistrǝs) n **1** signora f. **2** padrona f. **3** professoressa f. **4** amante f.

mistrust (mis'trʌst) vt non fidarsi di. n diffidenza f. **mistrustful** adj diffidente.

misunderstand* (misʌndǝ'stænd) vt fraintendere. **misunderstanding** n equivoco m.

misuse (v mis'ju:z; n mis'ju:s) vt **1** far cattivo uso di, usare a sproposito. **2** maltrattare. n cattivo uso m.

mitre ('maitǝ) n mitra f.

mitten ('mitn) n manopola f.

mix (miks) vt mischiare, combinare, mettere insieme. vi mischiarsi, andar bene insieme. **mixture** n **1** misto m. mistura f. **2** miscela f.

moan (moun) n gemito, lamento m. vi gemere, lamentarsi. vt lamentare.

moat (mout) n fossato m.

mob (mɔb) n marmaglia f. popolaccio m. vt assalire.

mobile ('moubail) adj **1** mobile. **2** mutevole. **mobility** n mobilità f. **mobilize** vt mobilitare. vi mobilitarsi. **mobilization** n mobilitazione f.

mock (mɔk) vt deridere, prendere in giro. adj finto. **mockery** n derisione f.

mode (moud) n modo m.

model ('mɔdl) n **1** modello m. **2** Art modello m. **3** indossatrice f. adj essemplare, modello. vt modellare. vi fare l'indossatore.

moderate (adj,n 'mɔdǝrǝt; v 'mɔdǝreit) adj,n moderato. vt moderare. **moderation** n moderazione f.

modern ('mɔdǝn) adj moderno. **modernize** vt modernizzare.

modest ('mɔdist) adj modesto. **modesty** n modestia f.

modify ('mɔdifai) vt **1** modificare. **2** temperare. **modifier** n parola modificante f.

modulate ('mɔdjuleit) vt modulare.

module ('mɔdju:l) n modulo m.

mohair ('mouhɛǝ) n mohair m.

moist (mɔist) adj umido. **moisten** vt inumidire. vi inumidirsi. **moisture** n vapore condensato m. **moisturize** vt umidificare.

mole[1] (moul) n neo m.

mole[2] (moul) n zool talpa f.

molecule ('mɔlikju:l) n molecola f. **molecular** adj molecolare.

molest (mǝ'lest) vt molestare.

mollusc ('mɔlǝsk) n mollusco m.

molten ('moultǝn) adj fuso.

moment ('moumǝnt) n **1** momento m. **2** importanza f. **momentary** adj momentaneo. **momentous** adj grave, di grande importanza. **momentum** n **1** sci momento m. **2** slancio m.

monarch ('mɔnǝk) n monarca m. **monarchy** n monarchia f.

monastery ('mɔnǝstri) n monastero, convento m. **monastic** adj monastico.

Monday ('mʌndi) n lunedì m.

money ('mʌni) n quattrini, soldi m pl. denaro m. **moneybox** n salvadanaio m. **money order** n vaglia m invar. **monetary** adj monetario.

mongrel ('mʌŋgrǝl) adj,n bastardo m.

monitor ('mɔnitǝ) n **1** monitor m invar. **2** addetto all'ascolto di trasmissioni estere m. vt **1** controllare. **2** ascoltare.

monk (mʌŋk) n monaco, frate m.

monkey ('mʌŋki) n scimmia f.

monochrome ('mɔnǝkroum) adj monocromo. n monocromato m.

monogamy (mǝ'nɔgǝmi) n monogamia f.

monologue ('mɔnǝlɔg) n monologo m.

monopoly (məˈnɔpəli) n monopolio m. **monopolize** vt monopolizzare.

monosyllable (ˈmɔnəsiləbəl) n monosillabo m. **monosyllabic** adj monosillabico, monosillabo.

monotone (ˈmɔnətoun) n tono uniforme m. **monotonous** adj monotono. **monotony** n monotonia f.

monsoon (mɔnˈsuːn) n monsone m.

monster (ˈmɔnstə) n mostro m. **monstrous** adj mostruoso.

month (mʌnθ) n mese m. **monthly** adj mensile. adv mensilmente.

monument (ˈmɔnjumənt) n monumento m. **monumental** adj monumentale.

moo (muː) vi muggire. n muggito m.

mood[1] (muːd) n umore m. **moody** adj capriccioso.

mood[2] (muːd) n gram modo m.

moon (muːn) n luna f. **moonlight** n chiaro di luna m.

moor[1] (muə) n brughiera f. **moorhen** n gallinella d'acqua f. **moorland** n brughiera f.

moor[2] (muə) vt ormeggiare. **moorings** n pl ormeggio m.

Moor (muə) n moro, saraceno m. **Moorish** adj moresco.

mop (mɔp) n 1 strofinaccio m. 2 (of hair) zazzera f. vt 1 asciugare. 2 raccogliere. **mop up** pulire.

mope (moup) vi darsi alla malinconia, immusonirsi.

moped (ˈmouped) n ciclomotore m.

moral (ˈmɔrəl) adj morale. n 1 morale f. 2 pl morale f. **morale** n morale m. **morality** n moralità f. **moralize** vi moraleggiare. vt moralizzare.

morbid (ˈmɔːbid) adj morboso.

more (mɔː) adj più, di più, maggiore. adv 1 di più, più. 2 ancora. **more and more** sempre più. **once more** ancora una volta. **moreover** adj inoltre.

morgue (mɔːg) n obitorio m.

morning (ˈmɔːniŋ) n mattina, mattinata f. mattino m. **this morning** stamattina, stamane.

Morocco (məˈrɔkou) n Marocco m. **Moroccan** adj,n marocchino.

moron (ˈmɔːrɔn) n 1 med oligofrenico m. 2 inf idiota m.

morose (məˈrous) adj scontroso.

morphine (ˈmɔːfiːn) n morfina f.

morse code (mɔːs) n alfabeto Morse m.

mortal (ˈmɔːtl) adj,n mortale m. **mortality** n mortalità f.

mortar[1] (ˈmɔːtə) n mortaio m.

mortar[2] (ˈmɔːtə) n (for building) malta f.

mortgage (ˈmɔːgidʒ) n ipoteca f. vt ipotecare.

mortify (ˈmɔːtifai) vt mortificare.

mortuary (ˈmɔːtjuəri) n camera mortuaria f.

mosaic (mouˈzeiik) n mosaico m.

mosque (mɔsk) n moschea f.

mosquito (məˈskiːtou) n, pl -oes or -os zanzara f.

moss (mɔs) n muschio m.

most (moust) adj 1 il maggior numero di, la maggior quantità di, la maggior parte di. 2 più. n massimo, più m. **at the most** al massimo. **make the most of** usar bene, sfruttare. ~adv più, di più. **mostly** adv per lo più, per la maggior parte.

motel (mouˈtel) n motel m.

moth (mɔθ) n farfalla notturna f.

mother (ˈmʌðə) n madre, mamma f. **motherly** adj materno. **motherhood** n maternità f. **mother-in-law** n suocera f. **mother superior** n (madre) superiora f.

motion (ˈmouʃən) n 1 movimento, moto m. 2 pol mozione f. vt,vi far segno a. **motionless** adj immobile.

motive (ˈmoutiv) n motivo m. adj motore.

motor (ˈmoutə) n motore m. vi andare in macchina. **motor car** n automobile, macchina f. auto f invar. **motor cycle** n motocicletta f. **motorist** n automobilista m. **motorway** n autostrada f.

mottle (ˈmɔtl) vt chiazzare.

motto (ˈmɔtou) n, pl -oes or -os motto m.

mould[1] (mould) n stampo m. vt 1 formare, modellare. 2 plasmare.

mould[2] (mould) n muffa f. **mouldy** adj 1 ammuffito. 2 stantio.

moult (moult) vi fare la muda.

mound (maund) n 1 collinetta f. 2 mucchio m.

mount[1] (maunt) vt 1 montare, salire. 2 (jewels) incastonare. vi 1 salire, montare. 2 aumentare. n (of a picture, etc.) montatura f.

mount[2] (maunt) n monte m. montagna f.

mountain (ˈmauntin) n montagna f. **mountaineer** n alpinista m. **mountaineering** n alpinismo m. **mountainous** adj montuoso, montagnoso.

mourn (mɔːn) vi lamentarsi. vt lamentare, piangere, esser in lutto per. **mourning** n cordoglio, lutto m. lamentazione f.

mouse (maus) *n, pl* **mice** topo *m.* **mousetrap** *n* trappola per i topi *f.*

mousse (mu:s) *n* dolce di panna montata e aromi *m.*

moustache (məˈstɑːʃ) *n* baffi *m pl.*

mouth (mauθ) *n* 1 bocca *f.* 2 (of a river) foce *f.* **mouthful** *n* boccone *m.* **mouthpiece** *n* 1 bocchino *m.* 2 organo, portavoce *m.*

move (mu:v) *vi* 1 muoversi, spostarsi. 2 cambiar casa, traslocare. 3 far progressi. *vt* 1 muovere, spostare. 2 trasportare. 3 commuovere. 4 proporre. **move in** occupare. **move out** sgombrare. ~*n* 1 mossa *f.* 2 trasloco *m.* 3 manovra *f.* **movable** *adj* movibile, mobile. **movement** *n* movimento *m.* **moving** *adj* 1 commovente. 2 mobile. 3 in moto.

mow* (mou) *vt* falciare. **mow down** falciare, abbattere. **mower** *n* falciatrice *f.*

Mr (ˈmistə) (title of address) Signor.

Mrs (ˈmisiz) (title of address) Signora.

much (mʌtʃ) *adj,adv* molto, assai. **how much** quanto. **so much** tanto. **too much** troppo.

muck (mʌk) *n* 1 sterco *m.* 2 sudiciume *m.*

mud (mʌd) *n* fango *m.* **muddy** *adj* fangoso. **mudguard** *n* parafango *m.*

muddle (ˈmʌdl) *vt* 1 impasticciare. 2 confondere. *n* 1 pasticcio *m.* 2 confusione *f.*

muff (mʌf) *n* manicotto *m.*

muffle (ˈmʌfəl) *vt* 1 (sound) smorzare, attenuare. 2 imbaccucare, avvolgere.

mug (mʌg) *n* 1 boccale *m.* 2 *sl* muso, grugno *m.* *vt sl* assalire.

mulberry (ˈmʌlbəri) *n* mora *f.* **mulberry bush** *n* gelso *m.*

mule¹ (mju:l) *n zool* mulo *m.*

mule² (mju:l) *n* pianella *f.*

mullet (ˈmʌlit) *n* triglia *f.*

multiple (ˈmʌltipəl) *adj* molteplice. *n* multiplo *m.*

multiply (ˈmʌltiplai) *vt* moltiplicare. *vi* moltiplicarsi.

multitude (ˈmʌltitjuːd) *n* moltitudine *f.*

mum (mʌm) *n inf* mamma *f.*

mumble (ˈmʌmbəl) *vi* borbottare.

mummy¹ (ˈmʌmi) *n* mummia *f.*

mummy² (ˈmʌmi) *n inf* mamma *f.*

mumps (mʌmps) *n pl* orecchioni *m pl.*

munch (mʌntʃ) *vt* sgranocchiare. *vi* masticare rumorosamente.

mundane (ˈmʌndein) *adj* mondano.

municipal (mjuˈnisipəl) *adj* municipale, comunale. **municipality** *n* municipio, comune *m.*

mural (ˈmjuərəl) *adj* murale. *n* pittura murale *f.*

murder (ˈməːdə) *vt* assassinare. *n* assassinio *m.* **murderer** *n* assassino *m.* **murderous** *adj* 1 brutale. 2 micidiale.

murmur (ˈməːmə) *n* mormorio *m.* *vt,vi* mormorare.

muscle (ˈmʌsəl) *n* muscolo *m.*

muse (mju:z) *n* musa *f.* *vi* rimuginare, meditare.

museum (mju:ˈziəm) *n* museo *m.*

mushroom (ˈmʌʃrum) *n* fungo *m.*

music (ˈmuːzik) *n* musica *f.* **musical** *adj* musicale. **musician** *n* musicista *m.*

musk (mʌsk) *n* muschio *m.*

musket (ˈmʌskit) *n* moschetto *m.*

Muslim (ˈmuzlim) *adj,n* islamico, mussulmano.

muslin (ˈmʌzlin) *n* mussolina *f.*

mussel (ˈmʌsəl) *n* cozza *f.*

must* (mʌst) *v mod aux* dovere.

mustard (ˈmʌstəd) *n* senape, mostarda *f.*

mute (mju:t) *adj,n* muto.

mutilate (ˈmjuːtileit) *vt* mutilare. **mutilation** *n* mutilazione *f.*

mutiny (ˈmjuːtini) *n* ammutinamento *m.* *vi* ammutinarsi.

mutter (ˈmʌtə) *vt,vi* borbottare.

mutton (ˈmʌtn) *n* carne di montone *f.*

mutual (ˈmjuːtjuəl) *adj* mutuo, reciproco.

muzzle (ˈmʌzəl) *n* 1 muso *m.* 2 museruola *f.* 3 (of a gun) bocca *f.* *vt* mettere la museruola a.

my (mai) *poss adj* 1st pers s (il) mio, (la) mia, (il) miei, (le) mie. **myself** *pron* 1st pers s 1 io stesso. 2 me stesso, mi, me.

myrrh (məː) *n* mirra *f.*

myrtle (ˈməːtl) *n* mortella *f.*

mystery (ˈmistəri) *n* mistero *m.* **mysterious** *adj* misterioso.

mystic (ˈmistik) *adj,n* mistico *m.* **mysticism** *n* misticismo *m.* **mystify** *vt* sconcertare.

mystique (miˈstiːk) *n* mistica *f.*

myth (miθ) *n* mito *m.* **mythical** *adj* mitico. **mythology** *n* mitologia *f.* **mythological** *adj* mitologico.

N

nag¹ (næg) *vt* rimbrottare. *vi* brontolare.

nag² (næg) *n inf* ronzino *m.*

nail (neil) *n* 1 *anat* unghia *f.* 2 chiodo *m.* **hit the nail on the head** colpire nel segno. ~*vt* inchiodare. **nailbrush** *n* spazzolino per le unghie *m*. **nailfile** *n* lima per le unghie *f*. **nail varnish** *n* smalto *m*.

naive (nai'i:v) *adj* ingenuo.

naked ('neikid) *adj* nudo.

name (neim) *n* nome *m*. *vt* **1** chiamare. **2** nominare. **3** fissare. **nameless** *adj* senza nome, anonimo. **namely** *adv* vale a dire. **namesake** *n* omonimo *m*.

nanny ('næni) *n* governante, bambinaia *f*.

nap[1] (næp) *n* pisolino *m*.

nap[2] (næp) *n* (of material) pelo *m*.

napalm ('neipa:m) *n* napalm *m*.

napkin ('næpkin) *n* salvietta *f*. tovagliolo *m*.

Naples ('neiplz) *n* Napoli *f*.

nappy ('næpi) *n* pannolino *m*.

narcotic (na:'kɔtik) *adj,n* narcotico, stupefacente *m*.

narrate (nə'reit) *vt* narrare, raccontare. **narration** *n* narrazione *f*. racconto *m*. **narrative** *n* narrativa *f*. *adj* narrativo. **narrator** *n* narratore *m*.

narrow ('nærou) *adj* **1** stretto. **2** ristretto. *vt* **1** assottigliare. **2** restringere. *vi* **1** assottigliarsi. **2** restringersi. **narrowly** *adv* per un pelo. **narrow-minded** *adj* gretto.

nasal ('neizəl) *adj* nasale.

nasturtium (nə'stə:ʃəm) *n* nasturzio *m*.

nasty ('na:sti) *adj* **1** sgradevole, disgustoso. **2** cattivo. **nastily** *adv* con cattiveria. **nastiness** *n* cattiveria *f*.

nation ('neiʃən) *n* nazione *f*. popolo *m*. **national** *adj* nazionale. **national anthem** *n* inno nazionale *m*. **national insurance** *n* assicurazione sociale *f*. **national service** *n* servizio di leva *m*. leva *f*. **nationality** *n* nazionalità *f*. **nationalize** *vt* nazionalizzare. **nationalization** *n* nazionalizzazione *f*. **nationwide** *adj* nazionale.

native ('neitiv) *n* oriundo, indigeno, nativo *m*. *adj* **1** nativo, natio. **2** innato.

nativity (nə'tiviti) *n* natività *f*.

natural ('nætʃərəl) *adj* naturale. **natural gas** *n* metano *m*. **natural history** *n* storia naturale *f*. **natural science** *n* scienze naturali *f pl*. **naturalize** *vt* naturalizzare.

nature ('neitʃə) *n* natura *f*.

naughty ('nɔ:ti) *adj* **1** cattivo, birichino. **2** indecente.

nausea ('nɔ:siə, -ziə) *n* nausea *f*. **nauseate** *vt* nauseare.

nautical ('nɔ:tikəl) *adj* nautico.

naval ('neivəl) *adj* navale.

nave (neiv) *n* navata centrale *f*.

navel ('neivəl) *n* ombelico *m*.

navigate ('nævigeit) *vt* **1** pilotare, dirigere. **2** mantenere in rotta. *vi* navigare. **navigator** *n* **1** ufficiale di rotta *m*. **2** navigatore *m*.

navy ('neivi) *n* marina militare *f*. **navy blue** *adj,n* blu scuro *m*.

Neapolitan (niə'pɔlitn) *adj,n* napoletano.

near (niə) *adj* **1** vicino, prossimo. **2** intimo. **3** esalto. **4** stretto. *adv* **1** vicino. **2** quasi. **near at hand** a portata di mano. **near by** vicino. **~prep** vicino a, accanto a. *vt* avvicinarsi a. *vi* avvicinarsi. **nearby** *adj,adv* vicino. **nearly** *adv* quasi. **nearside** *n* lato a *or* di sinistra *m*.

Near East *n* Vicino Oriente *m*.

neat (ni:t) *adj* **1** nitido, accurato, ordinato. **2** elegante. **3** (of drinks) liscio.

nebulous ('nebjuləs) *adj* nebuloso, vago.

necessary ('nesəsəri) *adj* necessario. **necessity** *n* necessità *f*. bisogno *m*. **of necessity** necessariamente. **necessitate** *vt* necessitare.

neck (nek) *n* collo *m*. **neckband** *n* colletto *m*. **necklace** *n* collana *f*. **neckline** *n* scollatura *f*.

nectar ('nektə) *n* nettare *m*.

need (ni:d) *n* **1** bisogno *m*. necessità *f*. **2** povertà *f*. **if need be** all'occorrenza. **~vt 1** aver bisogno di. **2** dovere. **3** chiedere. *vi* occorrerre. **needless** *adj* superfluo. **needy** *adj* bisognoso.

needle ('ni:dl) *n* **1** ago *m*. **2** (knitting) ferro *m*. **3** *tech* puntina *f*. **needlework** *n* cucito, ricamo *m*.

negate (ni'geit) *vt* negare. **negative** *adj* negativo. *n* **1** negazione *f*. **2** *phot* negativa *f*.

neglect (ni'glekt) *vt* trascurare. *n* trascuratezza *f*. **negligent** *adj* negligente. **negligible** *adj* trascurabile.

negotiate (ni'gouʃieit) *vi* discutere, intavolare trattative. *vt* **1** negoziare. **2** superare. **negotiation** *n* trattiva *f*. **negotiator** *m* negoziatore *m*.

Negro ('ni:grou) *adj or n, pl* **-oes** negro *m*.

neigh (nei) *n* nitrito *m*. *vi* nitrire.

neighbour ('neibə) *n* vicino *m*. **neighbourhood** *n* vicinato *m*.

neither ('naiðə) *adj,pron* nessuno dei due, nè l'uno nè l'altro. *adv* nè. *conj* neppure, nemmeno. **neither...nor** nè...nè.

neon ('ni:ɔn) *n* neon *m*.

nephew ('nevju:) *n* nipote *m*.

nepotism ('nepətizəm) *n* nepotismo *m*.

231

Neptune ('neptju:n) n Nettuno m.

nerve (nə:v) n 1 nervo m. 2 nerbo m. 3 inf sfacciataggine f. **nerve-racking** adj esasperante. **nervous** adj 1 nervoso, timido. 2 vigoroso. **nervous breakdown** n esaurimento nervoso m. **nervous system** n sistema nervoso m.

nest (nest) n nido m. vi nidificare.

nestle ('nesəl) vi annidarsi.

net[1] (net) n rete f. vt prendere con la rete. **netball** n pallavolo f. **network** n rete f.

net[2] (net) adj netto. vt ricavare.

Netherlands ('neðələndz) n pl Paesi Bassi m pl.

nettle ('netl) n ortica f.

neurosis (njuə'rousis) n, pl -ses nevrosi f invar. **neurotic** adj nevrotico.

neuter ('nju:tə) adj 1 neutro. 2 castrato. n neutro m.

neutral ('nju:trəl) adj 1 neutrale. 2 tech neutro. 3 mot folle. **neutrality** n neutralità f. **neutralize** vt neutralizzare.

neutron ('nju:trɔn) n neutrone m.

never ('nevə) adv mai, non...mai. **never mind!** pazienza! **nevertheless** adv,conj nondimeno, tuttavia.

new (nju:) adj 1 nuovo. 2 fresco. **brand new** nuovo di zecca. **newcomer** n nuovo venuto m. **news** n 1 notizie f pl. novità f. 2 (on radio, etc.) notiziario m. informazioni f pl. **a piece of news** una notizia f. **newsagent** n giornalaio m. **newspaper** n giornale, quotidiano m. **newsreel** n cinegiornale m.

newt (nju:t) n tritone m.

New Testament n Nuovo Testamento m.

New Year n Anno Nuovo m. **Happy New Year!** Buon Anno!

New Zealand ('zi:lənd) n Nuova Zelanda f. adj della Nuova Zelanda. **New Zealander** n neozelandese m,f.

next (nekst) adj 1 prossimo. 2 vicino. 3 successivo, seguente. adv dopo, poi, in seguito. **next day** l'indomani. **next to nothing** quasi niente.

nib (nib) n pennino m.

nibble ('nibəl) vt,vi 1 mordicchiare. 2 sbocconcellare. 3 brucare.

nice (nais) adj 1 piacevole, buono, bello. 2 sottile, delicato. 3 fine, raffinato. **nicely** adv 1 molto bene, gradevolmente. 2 esattamente.

niche (nitʃ) n nicchia f.

nick (nik) n tacca f. vt 1 intaccare. 2 inf rubare.

nickel ('nikəl) n 1 nichel m. 2 comm nichelino m.

nickname ('nikneim) n soprannome, nomignolo m. vt soprannominare.

nicotine ('nikəti:n) n nicotina f.

niece (ni:s) n nipote f.

Nigeria (nai'dʒiəriə) n Nigeria f. **Nigerian** adj,n nigeriano.

nigger ('nigə) n derog negro m.

niggle ('nigəl) vi preoccuparsi d'inezie. **niggling** adj insignificante.

night (nait) n notte, nottata, sera f. **nightclub** n locale notturno m. **nightdress** n camicia da notte f. **nightmare** n incubo m. **night-time** n notte f. **night-watchman** n guardiano notturno m.

nightingale ('naitiŋgeil) n usignolo m.

nil (nil) n zero m.

Nile (nail) n Nilo m.

nimble ('nimbəl) adj agile, svelto.

nine (nain) adj,n nove m. **ninth** adj nono.

nineteen (nain'ti:n) adj,n diciannove m or f. **nineteenth** adj diciannovesimo.

ninety ('nainti) adj,n novanta m. **ninetieth** adj novantesimo.

nip[1] (nip) n pizzico, pizzicotto m. vt pizzicare.

nip[2] (nip) n (small amount) bicchierino m.

nipple ('nipəl) n capezzolo m.

nit (nit) n lendine m.

nitrogen ('naitrədʒən) n azoto m.

no[1] (nou) adv 1 no. 2 non. n, pl **noes** no m.

no[2] (nou) adj 1 nessun, nessuno. 2 non, niente.

noble ('noubəl) adj,n nobile m. **nobleman** n nobiluomo, nobile m. **nobility** n nobiltà f.

nobody ('noubədi) pron nessuno. n illustre sconosciuto m.

nocturnal (nɔk'tə:nl) adj notturno.

nod (nɔd) vi 1 inchinare la testa, fare un cenno col capo. 2 annuire. 3 addormentarsi, sonnecchiare. vt accennare col capo. n cenno m.

node (noud) n nodo m.

noise (nɔiz) n rumore, chiasso m. **noisy** adj rumoroso, chiassoso.

nomad ('noumæd) n nomade m,f. **nomadic** adj nomade.

nominal ('nɔminl) adj 1 nominale. 2 nominativo.

nominate ('nɔmineit) vt nominare, designare. **nomination** n nomina f.

nominative ('nɔminətiv) adj,n nominativo m.

non- pref non, non-.

nonchalant ('nɔnʃələnt) adj noncurante.

nondescript ('nɔndiskript) adj scadente.

none (nʌn) *pron* **1** nessuno. **2** niente. **none other than** nientedimeno che. ~*adj* nessuno. *adv* non...affatto, mica. **none the less** nondimeno.

nonentity (nɔn'entiti) *n* nullità *f*.

nonsense ('nɔnsəns) *n* **1** nonsenso *m*. insensatezza *f*. **2** sciocchezze *f pl*. **nonsensical** *adj* assurdo.

noodles ('nuːdlz) *n pl* pasta *f*.

noon (nuːn) *n* mezzogiorno *m*.

no-one *pron* nessuno.

noose (nuːs) *n* nodo scorsoio *m*.

nor (nɔː) *conj* né, e non, e neanche.

norm (nɔːm) *n* **1** norma *f*. **2** quota *f*. **normal** *adj* normale.

Norse (nɔːs) *adj,n* norvegese *m*. **Norse** (language) *n* norvegese *m*.

north (nɔːθ) *n* nord, settentrione *m*. *adj* del nord, settentrionale. **northerly** *adj* di, da, o a nord. **northern** *adj* settentrionale, del nord. **north-east** *n* nordest *m*. **north-easterly** *adj* di, da, *or* a nordest. **north-eastern** *adj* del *or* dal nordest. **north-west** *n* nordovest *m*. **north-westerly** *adj* di, da, *or* a nordovest. **north-western** *adj* del *or* dal nordovest.

North America *n* America del Nord *m*. **North American** *adj,n* nordamericano.

Northern Ireland *n* Irlanda del Nord *f*.

Norway ('nɔːwei) *n* Norvegia *f*. **Norwegian** *adj,n* norvegese. **Norwegian** (language) *n* norvegese *m*.

nose (nouz) *n* **1** naso *m*. **2** *aviat* muso *m*. **nosy** *adj* curioso.

nostalgia (nɔ'stældʒiə) *n* nostalgia *f*. **nostalgic** *adj* nostalgico.

nostril ('nɔstril) *n* narice *f*.

not (nɔt) *adv* non. **not at all!** di nulla!

notch (nɔtʃ) *n* tacca *f*. intaglio *m*. *vt* intaccare.

note (nout) *n* **1** nota *f*. appunto *m*. **2** biglietto *m*. **3** *mus* nota *f*. *vt* rilevare, fare attenzione a. **note down** prender nota di. **notable** *adj* notevole. **notation** *n* notazione *f*. **notebook** *n* taccuino *m*. **noted** *adj* celebre. **notepaper** *n* carta da lettere *f*. **noteworthy** *adj* degno di nota.

nothing ('nʌθiŋ) *n* nessuna cosa *f*. niente, nulla *m*. **for nothing** gratis. ~*adv* niente affatto. **nothingness** *n* nulla *m*.

notice ('noutis) *n* **1** annuncio, avviso *m*. **2** conoscenza, attenzione *f*. **3** recensione *f*. **4** preavviso *m*. **take no notice of** ignorare. **notice board** *n* quadro (degli) annunci *m*.

notify ('noutifai) *vt* informare, notificare a. **notification** *n* comunicazione, notifica *f*.

notion ('nouʃən) *n* idea, nozione *f*.

notorious (nou'tɔːriəs) *adj* famigerato, notorio. **notoriety** *n* notorietà *f*.

notwithstanding (nɔtwiθ'stændiŋ) *prep* nonostante. *adv* lo stesso.

nougat ('nuːgɑː) *n* torrone *m*.

nought (nɔːt) *n* zero *m*.

noun (naun) *n* sostantivo *m*.

nourish ('nʌriʃ) *vt* nutrire, alimentare. **nourishing** *adj* nutriente. **nourishment** *n* nutrimento, cibo *m*.

novel[1] ('nɔvəl) *n* romanzo *m*. **novelist** *n* romanziere *m*.

novel[2] ('nɔvəl) *adj* nuovo, insolito. **novelty** *n* novità *f*.

November (nou'vembə) *n* novembre *m*.

novice ('nɔvis) *n* novizio *m*.

now (nau) *adv* **1** adesso, ora. **2** dunque. *conj* ora che. **just now** appena adesso, proprio adesso. **now and then** di quando in quando. **nowadays** *adv* oggi, al giorno d'oggi.

nowhere ('nouweə) *adv* in nessun luogo.

noxious ('nɔkʃəs) *adj* nocivo, pericoloso.

nozzle ('nɔzəl) *n* becco *m*. imboccatura *f*.

nuance ('njuːɑːns) *n* sfumatura *f*.

nucleus ('njuːkliəs) *n* nucleo *m*. **nuclear** *adj* nucleare.

nude (njuːd) *adj,n* nudo *m*. **nudist** *n* nudista *m*. **nudity** *n* nudità *f*.

nudge (nʌdʒ) *n* gomitata *f*. *vt* dare una gomitata a.

nugget ('nʌgit) *n* pepita *f*.

nuisance ('njuːsəns) *n* **1** fastidio *m*. noia *f*. **2** (person) seccatore *m*.

null (nʌl) *adj* nullo. **null and void** annullato.

numb (nʌm) *adj* intorpidito. *vt* intorpidire. **numbness** *n* intorpidimento, torpore *m*.

number ('nʌmbə) *n* numero *m*. cifra *f*. *vt* numerare, contare. **a number of** parecchi. **numeral** *adj,n* numerale *m*. **numerate** *vt* enumerare, contare, numerare. **numerical** *adj* numerico. **numerous** *adj* numeroso.

nun (nʌn) *n* suora, religiosa, monaca *f*. **nunnery** *n* convento *m*.

nurse (nɔːs) *n* **1** infermiera *f*. **2** bambinaia *f*. *vt* **1** curare. **2** allattare. **3** covare. **nursery** *n* **1** stanza dei bambini *f*. **2** *bot* vivaio *m*. serra *f*. **nursery rhyme** *n* poesia per bambini *f*. **nursery school** *n* asilo *m*. **nursing home** *n* clinica *f*.

nurture ('nɔ:tʃə) vt allevare, nutrire.

nut (nʌt) n 1 noce f. 2 tech dado m. **nutcrackers** n schiaccianoci m. **nutmeg** n noce moscata f. **nutshell** n guscio di noce m. **in a nutshell** in poche parole.

nutrition (nju:'triʃən) n nutrizione f. **nutritious** adj nutriente, nutritivo.

nuzzle ('nʌzəl) vt annusare. vi annidarsi, accoccolarsi.

nylon ('nailən) n nailon m.

nymph (nimf) n ninfa f.

O

oak (ouk) n quercia f.

oar (ɔ:) n remo m. vi remare. **oarsman** n rematore m.

oasis (ou'eisis) n, pl **oases** oasi f invar.

oath (ouθ) n 1 (promise) giuramento m. 2 bestemmia f.

oats (outs) n pl avena f. **oatmeal** n farina d'avena f.

obedient (ə'bi:diənt) adj ubbidiente, obbediente. **obedience** n ubbidienza, obbedienza f.

obese (ou'bi:s) adj obeso, corpulento. **obesity** n obesità f.

obey (ə'bei) vt ubbidire, obbedire.

obituary (ə'bitjuəri) n necrologia f.

object (n 'ɔbdʒikt; v əb'dʒekt) n 1 oggetto m. 2 scopo, fine m. vi obiettare, protestare. **objection** n obiezione f. **objective** n obiettivo, scopo m. adj obiettivo.

oblige (ə'blaidʒ) vt 1 costringere, obbligare. 2 fare un favore a. **be obliged to 1** dovere. **2** essere riconoscente a. **obligation** n obbligazione f. dovere m. **obligatory** adj obbligatorio. **obliging** adj gentile, cortese.

oblique (ə'bli:k) adj obliquo.

obliterate (ə'blitəreit) vt cancellare, distruggere. **obliteration** n distruzione, obliterazione f.

oblivion (ə'bliviən) n oblio m. **oblivious** adj dimentico, immemore.

oblong ('ɔblɔŋ) adj oblungo. n rettangolo m.

obnoxious (əb'nɔkʃəs) adj odioso, offensivo.

oboe ('oubou) n oboe m.

obscene (əb'si:n) adj osceno, impudico. **obscenity** n oscenità f.

obscure (əb'skjuə) adj oscuro, sconosciuto. vt oscurare. **obscurity** n oscurità f.

observe (əb'zə:v) vt 1 osservare, notare. 2 celebrare. **observance** n osservanza f. rito m.

observant adj osservante, attento. **observation** n osservazione f. **observatory** n osservatorio m. **observer** n osservatore m.

obsess (əb'ses) vt ossessionare. **obsessed** adj ossesso. **obsession** n ossessione f.

obsolescent (ɔbsə'lesənt) adj che cade in disuso. **obsolescence** n disuso m.

obsolete ('ɔbsəli:t) adj caduto in disuso, disusato.

obstacle ('ɔbstəkəl) n ostacolo, impedimento m.

obstinate ('ɔbstinət) adj ostinato, inflessibile. **obstinacy** n ostinazione f.

obstruct (əb'strʌkt) vt impedire, ostruire. **obstruction** n ostacolo, impedimento m.

obtain (əb'tein) vt ottenere, raggiungere.

obtrusive (əb'tru:siv) adj importuno, indiscreto.

obtuse (əb'tju:s) adj 1 ottuso. 2 stupido.

obverse ('ɔbvə:s) n 1 faccia f. 2 (of a page) retto m.

obvious ('ɔbviəs) adj ovvio, evidente.

occasion (ə'keiʒən) n 1 occasione f. 2 causa f. motivo m. vt occasionare. **occasional** adj occasionale, raro. **occasionally** adv qualche volta.

Occident ('ɔksidənt) n occidente m.

occult (ɔ'kʌlt) adj occulto, misterioso, segreto.

occupy ('ɔkjupai) vt 1 occupare. 2 impiegare. 3 abitare in. **occupation** n 1 occupazione f. 2 lavoro m. professione f. **occupational** adj del lavoro. **occupier** n abitante m,f.

occur (ə'kə:) vi succedere, capitare, accadere. **occurrence** n avvenimento, caso m.

ocean ('ouʃən) n oceano m.

ochre ('oukə) n ocra f.

octagon ('ɔktəgən) n ottagono m. **octagonal** adj ottagonale.

octane ('ɔktein) n ottano m.

octave ('ɔktiv) n ottava f.

October (ɔk'toubə) n ottobre m.

octopus ('ɔktəpəs) n, pl **-puses** or **-pi** polipo m.

oculist ('ɔkjulist) n oculista m.

odd (ɔd) adj 1 dispari invar. 2 strano, bizzarro, eccentrico. **odds and ends** cianfrusaglie f pl. **oddity** n 1 bizzarria, stranezza f. 2 persona eccentrica f. **oddment** n articolo spaiato m. **odds** n pl 1 probabilità f. 2 differenza f. **odds and ends** avanzi m pl.

ode (oud) n ode f.

odious ('oudiəs) adj odioso.

odour ('oudə) n odore, profumo m. fragranza f.

oesophagus (i'sɔfəgəs) n esofago m.

oestrogen ('i:strədʒən) n estrogeno m.

oestrus ('i:strəs) n estro m.

of (əv; stressed ɔv) prep **1** di. **2** da. **3** a, in. **4** per. **of course** naturalmente.

off (ɔf) adv lontano, via. prep da. adj **1** più distante. **2** laterale. **3** esterno. **4** libero. **be well off** essere ricco.

offal ('ɔfəl) n frattaglie f pl.

offend (ə'fend) vt offendere. **offence** n **1** offesa, ingiuria f. **2** contravvenzione f. **3** delitto m. **offender** n offensore m. **offensive** adj offensivo, oltraggioso, spiacevole. n offensiva f.

offer ('ɔfə) vt offrire, porgere. n offerta, proposta f. **on offer** in vendita.

offhand (ɔf'hænd) adj indifferente, noncurante.

office ('ɔfis) n **1** ufficio m. **2** ministero m. **take office** entrare in carica. **officer** n ufficiale m. **official** n funzionario, impiegato m. adj ufficiale.

officious (ə'fiʃəs) adj ufficioso.

offing ('ɔfiŋ) **in the offing** adv in vista.

off-licence n negozio dove si vendono bevande alcoliche m.

off-peak adj non di punta.

off-putting adj dissuadente.

off-season adj fuori stagione.

offset ('ɔfset) vt controbilanciare.

offshore (ɔf'ʃɔ:) adv al largo. adj di terra.

offside (ɔf'said) adj,adv fuori gioco.

offspring ('ɔfspriŋ) n descendenti, figli m pl.

offstage (ɔf'steidʒ) adv,adj fuori scena.

often ('ɔfən) adv spesso, molte volte. **how often?** quante volte?

ogre ('ougə) n orco m.

oil (ɔil) n **1** olio m. **2** petrolio m. **3** gasolio m. vt lubrificare, ungere. **oilfield** n giacimento di petrolio, campo petrolifero m. **oilskin** n impermeabile m. **oily** adj oleoso.

ointment ('ɔintmənt) n unguento m.

old (ould) adj **1** vecchio. **2** antico. **old age** n vecchiaia f. **old-fashioned** adj fuori moda.

Old Testament n Antico Testamento m.

olive ('ɔliv) n oliva f. **olive oil** n olio d'oliva m. **olive tree** n olivo m.

omelette ('ɔmlət) n frittata f.

omen ('oumen) n presagio, augurio m.

ominous ('ɔminəs) adj sinistro, di cattivo augurio. **ominously** adv minaccevolmente.

omit (ə'mit) vt omettere, tralasciare. **omission** n omissione f.

omnibus ('ɔmnibəs) n autobus m invar.

omnipotent (ɔm'nipətənt) adj onnipotente.

on (ɔn) prep **1** su, sopra. **2** a, di. adv **1** avanti. **2** su, sopra. **and so on** e così via.

once (wʌns) adv una volta. **all at once** ad un tratto. **at once** subito.

one (wʌn) adj,n uno. adj unico, solo. pron **1** (l')uno m. (l')una f. **2** si, uno. **one and all** tutti quanti. **one by one** uno dopo l'altro. poss pron 3rd pers s il suo, la sua, i suoi, le sue. **oneself** pron 3rd pers s **1** se stesso. **2** sè. **one-sided** adj **1** unilaterale. **2** ingiusto. **one-way** adj a senso unico.

onion ('ʌniən) n cipolla f.

onlooker ('ɔnlukə) n spettatore m.

only ('ounli) adj solo, unico. adv soltanto, non...che. **if only** se almeno. **only just** appena.

onset ('ɔnset) n **1** inizio m. **2** attacco m.

onslaught ('ɔnslɔ:t) n assalto m.

onus ('ounəs) n onere m.

onward ('ɔnwəd) adv avanti. **onwards** adv avanti. **from now onwards** da ora in poi.

ooze (u:z) vi colare, trapelare.

opal ('oupəl) n opale m.

opaque (ou'peik) adj opaco.

open ('oupən) vt **1** aprire. **2** cominciare, iniziare. adj **1** aperto. **2** chiaro, franco. **wide open** spalancato. **in the open** all'aperto. **open-air** adj all'aria aperta. **open-ended** adj senza limiti. **open-handed** adj generoso. **open-hearted** adj franco, sincero. **open-minded** adj liberale, spregiudicato. **open-mouthed** adj,adv a bocca aperta. **open-plan** adj ambiente aperto. **opening** n **1** apertura f. **2** occasione f.

opera ('ɔprə) n opera f. **opera house** n teatro dell'opera m. **operetta** n operetta f.

operate ('ɔpəreit) vt **1** operare. **2** dirigere. vt,vi operare, agire. **operation** n **1** operazione f. **2** med intervento chirurgico m. **operative** adj operativo, attivo.

opinion (ə'piniən) n opinione f. parere m. **opinion poll** n scrutinio dell'opinione pubblica m.

opium ('oupiəm) n oppio m.

opponent (ə'pounənt) n avversario, opponente, rivale m.

opportune ('ɔpətju:n) adj opportuno.

opportunity (ɔpə'tju:niti) n occasione f.

oppose (ə'pouz) vt contrapporre, opporre, combattere. **opposed** adj contrario.

opposite ('ɔpəzit) adj contrario, opposto,

diverso. n contrario m. prep in faccia a, di fronte a. **opposition** n opposizione f.

oppress (ə'pres) vt opprimere. **oppression** n oppressione f. **oppressive** adj oppressivo. **oppressor** n oppressore, tiranno m.

opt (ɔpt) vi scegliere.

optical ('ɔptikəl) adj ottico. **optician** n ottico m. **optics** n pl ottica f.

optimism ('ɔptimizəm) n ottimismo m. **optimist** n ottimista m. **optimistic** adj ottimistico.

option ('ɔpʃən) n scelta, opzione f. **optional** adj facoltativo.

opulent ('ɔpjulənt) adj opulento. **opulence** n opulenza f.

or (ɔ:) conj o, oppure. **or else** altrimenti.

oral ('ɔ:rəl) adj orale.

orange ('ɔrindʒ) n **1** bot arancia f. **2** (colour) arancio m. adj arancione. **orange tree** n arancio m.

oration (ɔ'reiʃən) n orazione f. discorso m. **orator** n oratore m.

orbit ('ɔ:bit) n orbita f.

orchard ('ɔ:tʃəd) n frutteto m.

orchestra ('ɔ:kistrə) n orchestra f. **orchestrate** vt orchestrare. **orchestration** n orchestrazione f.

orchid ('ɔ:kid) n orchidea f.

ordain (ɔ:'dein) vt, **1** ordinare, decretare. **2** rel ordinare, consacrare.

ordeal (ɔ:'di:l) n prova f. travaglio m.

order ('ɔ:də) n **1** ordine m. **2** comm ordinazione f. **3** grado m. vt ordinare, comandare. **in order that** affinchè, perchè. **in order to** per. **orderly** adj ordinato, regolato. n attendente m.

ordinal ('ɔ:dinl) adj ordinale.

ordinary ('ɔ:dənri) adj ordinario, solito, normale, comune. **out of the ordinary** straordinario. **ordinarily** adv di solito.

ore (ɔ:) n minerale m.

oregano (ɔri'gɑ:nou) n origano m.

organ ('ɔ:gən) n organo m.

organism ('ɔ:gənizəm) n organismo m. **organic** adj organico.

organize ('ɔ:gənaiz) vt organizzare. **organization** n organizzazione f. **organizer** n organizzatore m.

orgasm ('ɔ:gæzəm) n orgasmo m.

orgy ('ɔ:dʒi) n orgia f.

Orient ('ɔ:riənt) n oriente, levante m. **oriental** adj orientale.

orientate ('ɔ:rienteit) vt orientare.

origin ('ɔridʒin) n origine f. **original** adj originale, nuovo. n originale m. **originality** n originalità f. **originate** vt originare, produrre. vi originarsi, derivare. **originate from** provenire da.

Orlon ('ɔ:lɔn) n Tdmk Orlon m.

ornament ('ɔ:nəmənt) n ornamento m. vt ornare, adornare, abbellire. **ornamental** adj decorativo.

ornate (ɔ:'neit) adj ornato.

ornithology (ɔ:ni'θɔlədʒi) n ornitologia f. **ornithologist** n ornitologo m.

orphan ('ɔ:fən) adj,n orfano. **orphanage** n orfanotrofio m.

orthodox ('ɔ:θədɔks) adj ortodosso.

orthography (ɔ:'θɔgrəfi) n ortografia f.

orthopaedic (ɔ:θə'pi:dik) adj ortopedico.

oscillate ('ɔsəleit) vi oscillare.

ostensible (ɔ'stensəbəl) adj ostensibile, preteso. **ostensibly** adv ostensibilmente.

ostentatious (ɔsten'teiʃəs) adj vanitoso, ostentato.

osteopath ('ɔstiəpæθ) n specialista di osteopatia m.

ostracize ('ɔstrəsaiz) vt ostracizzare.

ostrich ('ɔstritʃ) n struzzo m.

other ('ʌðə) adj altro, diverso. **every other day** ogni due giorni. **on the other hand** d'altra parte. ~pron l'altro. **each other** l'un l'altro. **otherwise** adv altrimenti.

otter ('ɔtə) n lontra f.

ought* (ɔ:t) v mod aux dovere.

ounce (auns) n oncia f.

our (auə) poss adj 1st pers pl (il) nostro, (la) nostra, (i) nostri, (le) nostre. **ours** poss pron 1st pers pl il nostro, la nostra, i nostri, le nostre. **ourselves** pron 1st pers pl **1** noi stessi. **2** ci.

oust (aust) vt espellere, cacciare.

out (aut) adv fuori, via. prep fuori di. adj **1** di fuori. **2** (of a fire, etc.) spento. **out of work** disoccupato. **out-of-date** adj fuori moda.

outboard ('autbɔ:d) adj fuoribordo.

outbreak ('autbreik) n **1** scoppio m. **2** med epidemia f.

outburst ('autbə:st) n **1** scoppio m. esplosione f. **2** tirata f.

outcast ('autkɑ:st) n proscritto m.

outcome ('autkʌm) n risultato, esito m.

outcry ('autkrai) n clamore, grido m.

outdo (aut'du:) vt superare, sorpassare.

outdoor ('autdɔ:) adj all'aperto, di fuori. **outdoors** adv fuori di casa, all'aria aperta.

outer ('auta) adj esterno, esteriore.

outfit ('autfit) n 1 abito, corredo m. 2 equipaggiamento m.

outgoing ('autgouiŋ) adj partente, uscente.

outgrow (aut'grou) vt diventare troppo grande per.

outhouse ('authaus) n tettoia f. edificio annesso m.

outing ('autiŋ) n gita, escursione f.

outlandish (aut'lændiʃ) adj strano, bizzarro.

outlaw ('autlɔ:) n bandito, fuorilegge m. vt bandire, proscrivere.

outlay ('autlei) n spesa f.

outlet ('autlet) n uscita f. sbocco m.

outline ('autlain) n 1 contorno m. 2 abbozzo m. vt abbozzare, delineare.

outlive (aut'liv) vt sopravvivere a.

outlook ('autluk) n prospetto m. veduta f.

outlying ('autlaiiŋ) adj remoto, lontano.

outnumber (aut'nʌmbə) vt superare in numero.

outpatient ('autpeiʃənt) n malato esterno m.

outpost ('autpoust) n avamposto m.

output ('autput) n produzione f.

outrage (aut'reidʒ) n oltraggio m. vt oltraggiare, violare. **outrageous** adj oltraggioso, esorbitante.

outright ('autrait) adv 1 subito, immediatamente. 2 apertamente. adj completo.

outside (aut'said) adj esterno, esteriore. adv fuori, all'aperto. prep fuori di. n esterno m. superficie f. **at the outside** al massimo. **outsider** n estraneo m.

outsize ('autsaiz) adj di taglia fuori misura.

outskirts ('autskə:ts) n pl periferia f. dintorni m pl.

outspoken (aut'spoukən) adj franco, esplicito.

outstanding (aut'stændiŋ) adj 1 prominente. 2 comm non pagato. 3 eminente.

outstrip (aut'strip) vt superare, sorpassare.

outward ('autwəd) adj esterno, esteriore. **outwards** adv fuori, esternamente.

outweigh (aut'wei) vt 1 sorpassare in importanza. 2 sorpassare in peso.

outwit (aut'wit) vt superare in furberia.

oval ('ouvəl) adj,n ovale m.

ovary ('ouvəri) n ovaia f.

ovation (ou'veiʃən) n ovazione f.

oven ('ʌvən) n forno m.

over ('ouvə) prep 1 sopra, su. 2 attraverso. 3 più di, oltre. **over here** da questa parte. **over**

there laggiù. ~adv 1 al di sopra. 2 oltre. **all over** dappertutto. **over and over again** continuamente.

overall ('ouvərɔ:l) n 1 (woman's) grembiule m. 2 (workman's) tuta f.

overbalance (ouvə'bæləns) vi perdere l'equilibrio.

overbearing (ouvə'bɛəriŋ) adj arrogante.

overboard ('ouvəbɔ:d) adv fuori bordo, in mare.

overcast ('ouvəka:st) adj coperto di nuvole.

overcharge (ouvə'tʃa:dʒ) vt far pagare troppo.

overcoat ('ouvəkout) n soprabito, cappotto m.

overcome (ouvə'kʌm) vt superare, vincere. adj commosso.

overdo (ouvə'du:) vt 1 esagerare. 2 cul cuocere troppo.

overdose ('ouvədous) n dose troppo forte f.

overdraft ('ouvədra:ft) n credito allo scoperto m.

overdraw*** (ouvə'drɔ:) vt trarre allo scoperto.

overdue (ouvə'dju:) adj in ritardo, non pagato in tempo.

overestimate (ouvər'estimeit) vt sopravalutare.

overfill (ouvə'fil) vt riempire troppo.

overflow (v ouvə'flou; n 'ouvəflou) vt inondare. vi 1 traboccare. 2 strairpare. n inondazione f.

overhang (v ouvə'hæŋ; n 'ouvəhæŋ) vt sovrastare a. n strapiombo m.

overhaul (ouvə'hɔ:l) vt esaminare, restaurare.

overhead (adv ouvə'hed; adj,n 'ouvəhed) adv in alto. adj di sopra. **overheads** n pl spese generali f pl.

overhear (ouvə'hiə) vt sentire per caso.

overheat (ouvə'hi:t) vt,vi riscaldare troppo.

overjoyed (ouvə'dʒɔid) adj molto felice, colmo di gioia.

overland (adv ouvə'lænd; adj 'ouvəlænd) adj, adv per terra.

overlap (v ouvə'læp; n 'ouvəlæp) vi 1 sovrapporsi. 2 coincidere. n sovrapposizione f.

overlay (v ouvə'lei; n 'ouvəlei) vt coprire. n copertura f.

overleaf (ouvə'li:f) adv al rovescio. **see overleaf** vedi retro.

overload (v ouvə'loud; n 'ouvəloud) vt sovraccaricare. n sovraccarico m.

overlook (ouvə'luk) vt passare sopra, trascurare.

overnight (adv ouvə'nait; adj 'ouvənait) adv durante la notte. adj 1 per una notta. 2 compiute durante la notte.

overpower (ouvə'pauə) vt soggiogare, vincere.

overrate (ouvə'reit) vt sopravalutare.

overreach (ouvə'ri:tʃ) vt oltrepassare.

overrule (ouvə'ru:l) vt annullare.

overrun (v ouvə'rʌn) vt invadere.

overseas (ouvə'si:z) adj d'oltremare. adv oltremare.

overshadow (ouvə'ʃædou) vt **1** ombreggiare. **2** oscurare.

overshoot (ouvə'ʃu:t) vt oltrepassare.

oversight ('ouvəsait) n svista f. sbaglio m.

oversleep (ouvə'sli:p) vi dormire oltre l'ora giusta.

overspend (ouvə'spend) vi spendere troppo.

overt ('ouvə:t) adj aperto, evidente.

overtake (ouvə'teik) vt sorpassare, raggiungere.

overthrow (v ouvə'θrou; n 'ouvəθrou) vt rovesciare, sconfiggere. n sconfitta f.

overtime ('ouvətaim) n ore straordinarie f pl.

overtone ('ouvətoun) n sfumatura f. sottinteso m.

overture ('ouvətʃə) n preludio m.

overturn (ouvə'tə:n) vt rovesciare, capovolgere.

overweight (adj ouvə'weit n 'ouvəweit) adj grasso, che pesa troppo. n eccesso di peso m.

overwhelm (ouvə'welm) vt opprimere, sconvolgere.

overwork (v ouvə'wə:k; n 'ouvəwə:k) vi lavorare troppo. vt far lavorare troppo. n eccesso di lavoro m.

overwrought (ouvə'rɔ:t) adj sovreccitato.

ovulate ('ɔvjuleit) vi ovulare.

owe (ou) vt dovere. **owing to** prep a causa di.

owl (aul) n gufo m.

own (oun) adj proprio. vt possedere. **own up** confessare. **owner** n proprietario, padrone m. **ownership** n possesso m. diritti di proprietà m pl.

ox (ɔks) n, pl **oxen** bue m, pl buoi. **oxtail** n coda di bue f.

oxygen ('ɔksidʒən) n ossigeno m.

oyster ('ɔistə) n ostrica f.

P

pace (peis) n **1** passo m. **2** velocità f. vt misurare con i passi. vi passeggiare, camminare lento.

Pacific (pə'sifik) adj pacifico. **Pacific (Ocean)** n (Ocean) Pacifico m.

pacify ('pæsifai) vt pacificare. **pacifism** n pacifismo m. **pacifist** n pacifista m.

pack (pæk) n **1** pacco m. **2** game mazzo m. **3** (of hounds) muta f. **4** (of thieves) banda f. vt imballare, impaccare. vi fare le valigie. **package** n pacco m. balla f. **packet** n pacchetto m. **packhorse** n cavallo da soma m.

pact (pækt) n patto m.

pad[1] (pæd) n **1** cuscinetto, tampone m. **2** blocco m. **3** zool zampa f. vt imbottire.

pad[2] (pæd) n passo m. vi camminare silenziosamente.

paddle[1] ('pædl) n (of a boat) pagaia f. remo m. vt pagaiare, remare.

paddle[2] ('pædl) vi sguazzare.

paddock ('pædək) n recinto per cavalli m.

paddyfield ('pædifi:ld) n risaia f.

padlock ('pædlɔk) n lucchetto m. vt chiudere col lucchetto.

paediatric (pi:di'ætrik) adj pediatrico. **paediatrics** n pediatria f.

pagan ('peigən) adj,n pagano.

page[1] (peidʒ) n (of a book) pagina f.

page[2] (peidʒ) n paggio, fattorino m.

pageant ('pædʒənt) n spettacolo storico m. **pageantry** n spettacolo sfarzoso m.

pagoda (pə'goudə) n pagoda f.

paid (peid) v see **pay.**

pain (pein) n dolore, male m. sofferenza f. **painful** adj doloroso. **painstaking** adj laborioso, diligente.

paint (peint) n colore m. vernice f. vt colorire, dipingere. **paintbrush** n pennello m. **painter** n **1** Art pittore m. **2** imbianchino m. **painting** n **1** pittura f. **2** quadro m.

pair (pɛə) n paio m, pl **paia** f. coppia f. vt appaiare, accoppiare. **pair off** andare in due, appaiare.

Pakistan (pɑ:ki'stɑ:n) n Pakistan m. **Pakistani** adj,n pachistano.

pal (pæl) n inf amico, compagno m.

palace ('pælis) n palazzo m.

palate ('pælət) n palato m. **palatable** adj appetitoso, gustoso.

pale (peil) adj pallido. **paleness** n pallidezza f.

Palestine ('pælistain) n Palestina f. adj,n palestinese.

palette ('pælit) n tavolozza f. **palette knife** n spatola f.

palm[1] (pɑ:m) n anat palmo m. **palmistry** n chiromanzia f.

palm[2] (pɑ:m) n bot palma f.

Palm Sunday n Domenica delle Palme f.

pamper ('pæmpə) vt accarezzare, viziare.

pamphlet ('pæmflət) n opuscolo, libretto m.

pan (pæn) n padella f. tegame m. **pancake** n frittella f.

Panama ('pænəmə:) n Panama m.

pancreas ('pæŋkriəs) n pancreas m.

panda ('pændə) n panda f.

pander ('pændə) n mezzano m. vi fare il mezzano.

pane (pein) n vetro m.

panel ('pænl) n 1 pannello m. 2 lista f. vt pannellare, rivestire di legno. **panelling** n rivestimento m.

pang (pæŋ) n dolore acuto, spasimo m.

panic* ('pænik) n panico m. vi essere colto dal panico.

pannier ('pæniə) n paniere, cesto m.

panorama (pænə'ra:mə) n panorama m. **panoramic** adj panoramico.

pansy ('pænzi) n viola del pensiero f.

pant (pænt) vi ansare, anelare. n anelito m.

panther ('pænθə) n pantera f.

pantomime ('pæntəmaim) n pantomima f.

pantry ('pæntri) n dispensa f.

pants (pænts) n mutande f pl.

papal ('peipəl) adj papale, pontificio.

paper ('peipə) n 1 carta f. 2 documento m. 3 giornale m. vt coprire di carta, tappezzare con carta. **paperback** n edizione economica f. **paperclip** n serracarte m. **paperwork** n amministrazione f.

papier-mâché (pæpiei'mæʃei) n cartapesta f.

papist ('peipist) n papista m.

paprika ('pæprikə) n paprica f.

par (pa:) n pari, parità f. **above/below par** sopra/sotto la pari. **on a par with** pari a.

parable ('pærəbl) n parabola f.

parachute ('pærəʃu:t) n paracadute m. **parachutist** n paracadutista m.

parade (pə'reid) n parata, mostra f. vt far mostra di. vi sfilare in parata.

paradise ('pærədais) n paradiso m.

paradox ('pærədɔks) n paradosso m. **paradoxical** adj paradossale.

paraffin ('pærəfin) n petrolio combustibile m.

paragraph ('pærəgra:f) n paragrafo m.

parallel ('pærəlel) adj 1 parallelo. 2 analogo. n 1 math parallela f. 2 geog parallelo m. vt paragonare.

paralyse ('pærəlaiz) vt paralizzare. **paralysis** n paralisi f.

paramount ('pærəmaunt) adj supremo, sommo.

paranoia (pærə'nɔiə) n paranoia f.

parapet ('pærəpit) n parapetto m.

paraphernalia (pærəfə'neiliə) n roba f. oggetti m pl.

paraphrase ('pærəfreiz) n parafrasi f. vt parafrasare.

parasite ('pærəsait) n parassita m.

paratrooper ('pærətru:pə) n soldato paracadutista m.

parcel ('pa:səl) n pacco, pacchetto m. vt impacchettare.

parch (pa:tʃ) vt arsicciare. vi diventare riarso. **parched** adj riarso.

parchment ('pa:tʃmənt) n pergamena f.

pardon ('pa:dn) n perdono m. grazia, amnistia f. vt perdonare. **pardon me!** mi scusi! **pardonable** adj scusabile.

pare (peə) vt sbucciare, pelare.

parent ('peərənt) n genitore m. **parenthood** n paternità, maternità f.

parenthesis (pə'renθəsis) n, pl **-ses** parentesi f.

parish ('pæriʃ) n 1 rel parrocchia f. 2 comune m. **parishioner** n parrocchiano m.

parity ('pæriti) n parità f.

park (pa:k) n parco m. vt posteggiare. **parking** n posteggio m. **parking meter** n parchimetro m.

parliament ('pa:ləmənt) n parlamento m. camera dei deputati f. **parliamentary** adj parlamentare.

parlour ('pa:lə) n salotto m.

parochial (pə'roukiəl) adj 1 comunale. 2 rel parrocchiale.

parody ('pærədi) n parodia f. vt parodiare.

parole (pə'roul) n parola d'onore f. **on parole** lasciato libero sulla parola.

parquet ('pa:kei) n pavimento di legno lucido m.

parrot ('pærət) n pappagallo m.

parry ('pæri) vt 1 parare. 2 evitare.

parsley ('pa:sli) n prezzemolo m.

parsnip ('pa:snip) n pastinaca f.

parson ('pa:sən) n parroco, prete m.

part (pa:t) n 1 parte f. 2 pezzo m. 3 regione f. **spare part** pezzo di ricambio. ~vt dividere, separare. vi dividersi, separarsi. **part with** disfare di. **parting** n 1 separazione, divisione f. 2 (in hair) scrimmatura f. **part-time** adj a mezza giornata.

partake (pa:'teik) vi partecipare, prendere parte.

partial ('pa:ʃəl) adj parziale. **be partial to** avere un debole per.

participate (pɑ:ˈtisipeit) vi partecipare. **participation** n partecipazione f.

participle (ˈpɑ:tikəpl) n participio m.

particle (ˈpɑ:tikəl) n particola, particella f.

particular (pəˈtikjulə) adj particolare, preciso. n particolare, dettaglio m.

partisan (pɑ:tiˈzæn) adj,n partigiano.

partition (pɑ:ˈtiʃən) n 1 partizione f. 2 (in a room) tramezzo m. vt 1 dividere. 2 tramezzare.

partner (ˈpɑ:tnə) n 1 compagno m. 2 comm socio m. vt fare da campagno di, ballare con. **partnership** n 1 società f. 2 associazione f.

partridge (ˈpɑ:tridʒ) n pernice f.

party (ˈpɑ:ti) n 1 ricevimento m. festa f. 2 pol partito m. 3 gruppo m.

pass (pɑ:s) vt 1 passare. 2 attraversare. 3 superare. vi 1 succedere. 2 accadere. n 1 lasciapassare m. 2 (through a mountain) passo m. **passer-by** n passante m. **password** n parola d'ordine f.

passage (ˈpæsidʒ) n 1 passaggio m. 2 corridoio m. 3 viaggio m.

passenger (ˈpæsindʒə) n viaggiatore m.

passion (ˈpæʃən) n passione f. **passionate** adj appassionato.

passive (ˈpæsiv) adj passivo.

passivity (pæˈsiviti) n passività f.

Passover (ˈpɑ:souvə) n Pasqua degli ebrei f.

passport (ˈpɑ:spɔ:t) n passaporto m.

past (pɑ:st) adj 1 passato, trascorso. 2 scorso. 3 ultimo. prep dopo, oltre. n passato m. **past participle** n participio passato m.

pasta (ˈpæstə) n pasta f.

paste (peist) n colla f. vt incollare.

pastel (ˈpæstəl) n pastello m.

pasteurize (ˈpæstəraiz) vt pastorizzare.

pastime (ˈpɑ:staim) n passatempo, svago m.

pastoral (ˈpæstərəl) adj pastorale.

pastry (ˈpeistri) n 1 pasticceria f. pasticcio m. 2 pasta f.

pasture (ˈpɑ:stʃə) n pascolo m. pastura f.

pasty[1] (ˈpeisti) adj pallido.

pasty[2] (ˈpæsti) n pasticcio m.

pat[1] (pæt) n 1 colpetto m. carezza f. 2 (of butter) panetto m. vt accarezzare.

pat[2] (pæt) adj pronto, opportuno. adv a proposito.

patch (pætʃ) n 1 toppa f. 2 (of land) pezzo m. vt raccomodare, rappezzare. **patchwork** n rappezzamento, mosaico m.

pâté (ˈpætei) n pasticcio m.

patent (ˈpeitnt) n brevetto m. adj aperto, evidente. vt prendere un brevetto per. **patent leather** n cuoio verniciato m.

paternal (pəˈtɑ:nl) adj paterno. **paternity** n paternità f.

path (pɑ:θ) n sentiero m. via, strada f.

pathetic (pəˈθetik) adj patetico, commovente.

pathology (pəˈθolədʒi) n patologia f.

patience (ˈpeiʃəns) n pazienza f. **patient** adj paziente. n paziente m,f. malato sotto cura m.

patio (ˈpætiou) n patio m.

patriarchal (peitriˈɑ:kəl) adj patriarcale.

patriot (ˈpeitriət) n patriota m. **patriotic** adj patriottico. **patriotism** n patriottismo m.

patrol (pəˈtroul) n pattuglia f. vi andare di pattuglia.

patron (ˈpeitrən) n 1 patrono, protettore m. 2 (customer) cliente m. **patronage** n patronato m. protezione f. **patronize** vt 1 proteggere. 2 frequentare. **patronizing** adj condiscendente.

patter[1] (ˈpætə) n (noise) picchiettio m. vi picchiettare.

patter[2] (ˈpætə) n (talk) cicalio m.

pattern (ˈpætən) n 1 modello, disegno m. 2 esempio m. vt modellare.

paunch (pɔ:ntʃ) n pancione m.

pauper (ˈpɔ:pə) n indigente, mendicante m.

pause (pɔ:z) n pausa, fermata f. vi far pausa, fermarsi.

pave (peiv) vt pavimentare. **pavement** n marciapiede m.

pavilion (pəˈviliən) n padiglione m. tenda f.

paw (pɔ:) n zampa f. vt zampare. **paw the ground** scalpitare.

pawn[1] (pɔ:n) vt impegnare. n pegno m. **pawnbroker** n prestatore su pegni m.

pawn[2] (pɔ:n) n game pedina f.

pay* (pei) vt 1 pagare. 2 fare. vi rendere. n paga f. stipendio, salario m. **payment** n pagamento m. **payroll** n distinta dei salarii f.

pea (pi:) n pisello m.

peace (pi:s) n pace, tranquillità f. **peaceful** adj tranquillo.

peach (pi:tʃ) n pesca f. **peach tree** n pesco m.

peacock (ˈpi:kɔk) n pavone m.

peak (pi:k) n 1 cima, vetta f. picco m. 2 (of a cap) visiera f.

peal (pi:l) n 1 scoppio, scroscio m. 2 (of bells) scampanio m. vi 1 scampanare, risonare. 2 (of thunder) tuonare.

peanut (ˈpi:nʌt) n arachide, nocciolina americana f.

pear (pɛə) n pera f. **pear tree** n pero m.

pearl ('pə:l) n perla f. **mother of pearl** n madreperla f.

peasant ('pezənt) n contadino m. adj contadinesco. **peasantry** n contadini m pl.

peat (pi:t) n torba f.

pebble ('pebəl) n ciottolo, sasso m.

peck (pek) vt,vi beccare. n 1 beccata f. 2 bacetto m.

peckish ('pekiʃ) adj che ha fame.

peculiar (pi'kju:liə) adj 1 particolare, speciale. 2 strano. **peculiarity** n particolarità, stranezza f.

pedal ('pedl) n pedale m. vi pedalare.

peddle ('pedl) vt vendere in piccola quantità. vi fare il venditore ambulante. **pedlar** n merciaiuolo ambulante m.

pedestal ('pedistəl) n piedestallo m.

pedestrian (pi'destriən) n pedone m. adj pedestre. **pedestrian crossing** n passaggio pedonale m.

pedigree ('pedigri:) n genealogia f. albero genealogico m. adj di razza pura.

peel (pi:l) n buccia, pelle f. vt sbucciare, pelare. **peelings** n pl bucce f pl.

peep (pi:p) n occhiata f. sguardo furtivo m. vi spiare, guardare furtivamente.

peer[1] (piə) n pari m invar. **peerage** n nobiltà f.

peer[2] (piə) vi guardare da vicino.

peevish ('pi:viʃ) adj irritabile, brontolone.

peg (peg) n 1 gancio m. 2 molletta f. appiglio m. vt fissare con mollette.

pejorative (pi'dʒɔrətiv) adj peggiorativo.

pelican ('pelikən) n pellicano m.

pellet ('pelit) n 1 pallina, pallottola f. 2 pillola f.

pelmet ('pelmit) n pendaglio sopra le tende m.

pelt[1] (pelt) vt,vi colpire, tirare.

pelt[2] (pelt) n pelliccia, pelle greggia f.

pelvis ('pelvis) n pelvi f. bacino m.

pen[1] (pen) n penna f. **fountain pen** n penna stilografica f. **penfriend** n amico per corrispondenza m. **penknife** n temperino m. **pen nib** n pennino m.

pen[2] (pen) n 1 recinto m. 2 (for sheep) ovile m. vt rinchiudere.

penal ('pi:nl) adj penale. **penalize** vt punire. **penalty** n pena, penalità f. **penalty kick** n calcio di rigore m.

penance ('penəns) n penitenza f.

pencil ('pensəl) n matita f. lapis m invar. **pencil-sharpener** n taglialapis m invar.

pendant ('pendənt) n pendente, pendaglio m.

pending ('pendiŋ) adj pendente. prep in attesa di.

pendulum ('pendjuləm) n pendolo m.

penetrate ('penitreit) vt penetrare. **penetration** n penetrazione f.

penguin ('peŋgwin) n pinguino m.

penicillin (peni'silin) n penicillina f.

peninsula (pə'ninsjulə) n penisola f. **peninsular** adj peninsulare.

penis ('pi:nis) n pene m.

penitent ('penitənt) adj penitente.

pennant ('penənt) n banderuola f. pennone m.

penny ('peni) n 1 pl **pennies** British unit of currency. 2 pl **pence** soldo m. **penniless** adj senza un soldo, povero, indigente.

pension ('penʃən) n pensione f. v **pension off** mettere in pensione. **pensioner** n pensionato m.

pensive ('pensiv) adj pensieroso.

pent (pent) adj rinchiuso. **pent-up** adj represso.

pentagon ('pentagon) n pentagono m.

Pentecost ('pentikɔst) n Pentecoste f.

penthouse ('penthaus) n tettoia f.

people ('pi:pəl) n 1 gente f. 2 (race) popolo m. nazione f. vt popolare.

pepper ('pepə) n pepe m. **peppercorn** n granello di pepe m. **peppermill** n macinino da pepe m. **peppermint** n 1 menta peperina f. 2 (sweet) caramella alla menta f.

per (pə:) prep per, per mezzo di.

perambulator (pə'ræmbjuleitə) n carrozzina f.

perceive (pə'si:v) vt 1 accorgersi di. 2 osservare. 3 capire. **perceptible** adj percettibile, visibile.

per cent (pə 'sent) prep per cento.

percentage (pə'sentidʒ) n percentuale f.

perception (pə'sepʃən) n percezione, nozione f. **perceptive** adj percettivo.

perch[1] (pə:tʃ) n zool pesce persico m.

perch[2] (pə:tʃ) n posatoio m. vi appollaiarsi, posarsi.

percolate ('pə:kəleit) vt,vi filtrare. **percolator** n filtro m.

percussion (pə'kʌʃən) n percussione f.

perennial (pə'reniəl) adj perenne, eterno.

perfect (adj,n 'pə:fikt; v pə'fekt) adj perfetto, completo. n gram tempo perfetto m. vt perfezionare. **perfection** n perfezione f.

perforate ('pə:fəreit) vt perforare. **perforation** n perforazione f. buco m.

perform (pə'fɔ:m) vt,vi 1 eseguire, compire. 2 Th rappresentare. **performance** n 1 esecuzione f. adempimento m. 2 Th rappresentazione f. spettacolo m.

perfume (n 'pə:fju:m; v pə'fju:m) n profumo m. fragranza f. vt profumare. **perfumery** n profumeria f.

perhaps (pə'hæps) adv forse.

peril ('perəl) n pericolo, rischio m. **perilous** adj pericoloso.

perimeter (pə'rimitə) n perimetro m.

period ('piəriəd) n **1** periodo m. **2** epoca f. **3** med mestruazioni f pl. **periodic** adj periodico. **periodical** n periodico, giornale m. rivista f.

peripheral (pə'rifərəl) adj periferico.

perish ('periʃ) vi **1** perire, morire. **2** guastarsi. **perishable** adj deperibile.

perjury ('pə:dʒəri) n spergiuro m.

perk (pə:k) vi **perk up** rianimarsi. **perky** adj impertinente, vivace.

permanent ('pə:mənənt) adj permanente, durevole.

permeate ('pə:mieit) vt permeare, penetrare.

permit (v pə'mit; n 'pə:mit) vt permettere, lasciare. n permesso, lasciapassare m. licenza f. **permission** n permesso m. licenza f. **permissive** adj permissivo.

permutation (pə:mju'teiʃən) n permutazione f.

peroxide (pə'rɔksaid) n perossido m.

perpendicular (pə:pən'dikjulə) adj,n perpendicolare f.

perpetual (pə'petʃuəl) adj perpetuo, continuo. **perpetuate** (pə'petʃueit) vt perpetuare.

perplex (pə'pleks) vt confondere, imbarazzare. **perplexed** adj perplesso. **perplexity** n perplessità f. imbarazzo m.

persecute ('pə:sikju:t) vt perseguitare, importunare. **persecution** n persecuzione f.

persevere (pə:si'viə) vi perseverare. **perseverance** n perseveranza f.

Persia ('pə:ʃə) n Persia f. **Persian** adj,n persiano. **Persian** (language) n persiano m.

persist (pə'sist) vi persistere, ostinarsi. **persist in** persistere a. **persistence** n persistenza f. **persistent** adj persistente, tenace.

person ('pə:sən) n persona f. **personage** n personaggio m. **personal** adj personale. **personality** n personalità f. **personify** vt personificare. **personnel** n personale m.

perspective (pə'spektiv) n prospettiva, vista f.

Perspex ('pə:speks) n Tdmk Perspex m.

perspire (pə'spaiə) vi sudare, traspirare. **perspiration** n sudore m.

persuade (pə'sweid) vt persuadere. **persuasion** n persuasione f. **persuasive** adj persuasivo.

pert (pə:t) adj **1** impertinente, sfrontato. **2** vivace.

pertain (pə'tein) vi appartenere. **pertinent** adj pertinente, relativo. **pertinence** n pertinenza f.

perturb (pə'tə:b) vt perturbare, confondere, agitare.

Peru (pə'ru:) n Perù m. **Peruvian** adj,n peruviano.

pervade (pə'veid) vt pervadere, permeare, diffondersi in. **pervasive** adj penetrante, diffuso.

perverse (pə'və:s) adj perverso, malvagio. **perversity** n perversità, malvagità f.

pervert (v pə'və:t; n 'pə:və:t) vt pervertire, corrompere. n pervertito m. **perversion** n perversione f.

pessimism ('pesimizəm) n pessimismo m. **pessimist** n pessimista m. **pessimistic** adj pessimistico.

pest (pest) n peste, pestilenza f. **pesticide** n pesticida f.

pester ('pestə) vt annoiare, tormentare.

pet (pet) n **1** favorito m. **2** animale favorito m. adj favorito, preferito. vt accarezzare. **pet name** n nomignolo m.

petal ('petl) n petalo m.

peter ('pi:tə) vi **peter out** diminuire, finire, morire.

petition (pi'tiʃən) n petizione, supplica f. vt **1** supplicare. **2** presentare una petizione a.

petrify ('petrifai) vt **1** pietrificare. **2** stupire, spaventare.

petroleum (pi'trouliəm) n petrolio m. **petrol** n benzina f.

petticoat ('petikout) n sottoveste f.

petty ('peti) adj insignificante, meschino, triviale. **petty cash** n spese minute f pl. **petty officer** n sottufficiale di marina m. **pettiness** n piccolezza, meschinità f.

petulant ('petjulənt) adj petulante, capriccioso, irritabile.

pew (pju:) n panca di chiesa f.

pewter ('pju:tə) n peltro m.

phantom ('fæntəm) n fantasma, spettro m. adj spettrale, irreale.

pharmacy ('fɑ:məsi) n farmacia f. **pharmacist** n farmacista m.

pharynx ('færiŋks) n faringe f.

phase (feiz) n fase f.

pheasant ('fezənt) n fagiano m.

phenomenon (fi'nɒminən) n, pl **-na** fenomeno m. **phenomenal** adj fenomenale.

philanthropy (fi'lænθrəpi) n filantropia f. **philanthropist** n filantropo m.

philately (fi'lætəli) n filatelia f. **philatelist** n filatelico m.

Philistine ('filistain) n filisteo m.

philosophy (fi'lɒsəfi) n filosofia f. **philosopher** n filosofo m. **philosophical** adj filosofico.

phlegm (flem) n flemma f.

phlegmatic (fleg'mætik) adj flemmatico, calmo.

phobia ('foubiə) n fobia f.

phoenix ('fi:niks) n fenice f.

phone (foun) inf n telefono m. vt,vi telefonare. **phone call** n inf telefonata f.

phonetic (fə'netik) adj fonetico. **phonetics** n fonetica f.

phoney ('founi) adj fasullo, falso, finto.

phosphate ('fɒsfeit) n fosfato m.

phosphorescence (fɒsfə'resəns) n fosforescenza f. **phosphorescent** adj fosforescente.

phosphorus ('fɒsfərəs) n fosforo m. **phosphorous** adj fosforoso.

photo ('foutou) n inf foto f invar.

photocopy ('foutoukɒpi) vt fotocopiare. n fotocopia f.

photogenic (foutə'dʒenik) adj fotogenico.

photograph ('foutəgrɑːf) n fotografia f. vt fotografare. **photographer** n fotografo m. **photographic** adj fotografico. **photography** n fotografia f.

phrase (freiz) n **1** frase f. **2** modo di dire m. vt esprimere, dire. **phrasebook** n libro di frasi m.

physical ('fizikəl) adj fisico. **physical education** n educazione fisica f.

physician (fi'ziʃən) n medico, dottore m.

physics ('fiziks) n fisica f. **physicist** n fisico m.

physiognomy (fizi'ɒnəmi) n fisionomia f.

physiology (fizi'ɒlədʒi) n fisiologia f. **physiological** adj fisiologico. **physiologist** n fisiologo m.

physiotherapy (fiziou'θerəpi) n fisioterapia f. **physiotherapist** n fisioterapista f.

physique (fi'zi:k) n fisico m. costituzione f.

piano (pi'ænou) n pianoforte m. **grand piano** pianoforte a coda. **pianist** n pianista m.

pick¹ (pik) n scelta f. vt **1** scegliere. **2** cogliere. **3** (a lock) aprire. **pick up** raccogliere. **picking** n raccolta f. **pickpocket** n borsaiolo m.

pick² (pik) n (tool) piccone m.

picket ('pikit) n picchetto, palo m. vt picchettare.

pickle ('pikəl) n **1** salamoia f. **2** pl sottaceti m pl. vt mettere sotto aceto, marinare. **pickled** adj in aceto.

picnic¹ ('piknik) n merenda all'aperto f. picnic m. vi mangiare all'aperto.

pictorial (pik'tɔ:riəl) adj pittorico, illustrato.

picture ('piktʃə) n **1** quadro m. pittura f. **2** immagine f. **3** pl cinema m. vt figurare, descrivere.

picturesque (piktʃə'resk) adj pittoresco.

pidgin ('pidʒən) n pidgin, gergo m.

pie (pai) n **1** (meat) pasticcio m. **2** (fruit) torta, crostata f.

piece (pi:s) n **1** pezzo m. parte f. **2** (of material) pezza f. **piecemeal** adv a spizzico, pezzo a pezzo. **piecework** n lavoro a cottimo m.

pied (paid) adj screziato, variegato.

pier (piə) n **1** molo m. banchina f. **2** arch pilone m.

pierce (piəs) vt penetrare, perforare. **piercing** adj penetrante, acuto.

piety ('paiəti) n pietà f.

pig (pig) n maiale, porco m. **pig-headed** adj ostinato, testardo. **pig-iron** n ghisa f. **piglet** n porcellino m. **pigskin** n pelle di cinghiale f. **pigsty** n porcile m. **pigtail** n treccia f.

pigeon ('pidʒən) n piccione m. colomba f. **pigeonhole** n casella f.

piggyback ('pigibæk) n cavalcata sul dorso f. adv sul dorso.

pigment ('pigmənt) n pigmento, colore m.

pike (paik) n picca f.

pilchard ('piltʃəd) n sardella f.

pile¹ (pail) n mucchio, ammasso m. vt ammucchiare, accumulare.

pile² (pail) n tech palo m. **piledriver** n battipalo m.

pile³ (pail) n (of material, etc.) pelo m.

piles (pailz) n pl emorroidi f pl.

pilfer ('pilfə) vt rubacchiare. **pilferer** n ladroncello m.

pilgrim ('pilgrim) n pellegrino m. **pilgrimage** n pellegrinaggio m.

pill (pil) n pillola, compressa f.

pillage ('pilidʒ) n saccheggio m. vt saccheggiare.

pillar ('pilə) n pilastro m. colonna f. **pillar-box** n buca delle lettere f.

pillion ('piliən) n sedile posteriore m.

243

pillow ('piləu) n guanciale, cuscino m. **pillow-case** n federa f.

pilot ('pailət) n pilota m. vt pilotare.

pimento (pi'mentəu) n pimento m.

pimple ('pimpəl) n pustoletta f. foruncolo m.

pin (pin) n spillo m. vt appuntare, fissare. **pins and needles** n formicolio m. **pincushion** n portaspilli m invar. **pinpoint** vt segnalare con precisione. **pinstripe** adj a striscie fine.

pinafore ('pinəfɔ:) n grembiule m.

pincers ('pinsəz) n pl tenaglie f pl.

pinch (pintʃ) vt **1** pizzicare, stringere. **2** sl rubare. n **1** pizzicotto m. **2** pizzico m. presa f.

pine[1] (pain) n pino m. **pine cone** n pigna f.

pine[2] (pain) vi languire, sospirare per, consumarsi.

pineapple ('painæpəl) n ananasso m. ananas m invar.

Ping-pong ('piŋpɔŋ) n Tdmk tennis da tavola m.

pinion ('piniən) n tech pignone m.

pink (piŋk) adj n rosa m invar.

pinnacle ('pinəkəl) n sommo, colmo m. cima f.

pint (paint) n pinta f.

pioneer (paiə'niə) n pioniere m. vt preparare la via a.

pious ('paiəs) adj pio, religioso.

pip[1] (pip) game macchia f.

pip[2] (pip) n bot granelle, seme m.

pipe (paip) n **1** tubo, condotto m. **2** (tobacco) pipa f. **3** mus piffero m. **pipedream** n progetto inattuabile m. **pipeline** n **1** condotto di petrolio m. **2** linea di comunicazione f. **pipette** n pipetta f.

piquant ('pi:kənt) adj piccante. **piquancy** n gusto piccante m.

pique (pi:k) n irritazione f. vt offendere, irritare.

pirate ('pairət) n pirata m. **piracy** n pirateria f.

pirouette (piru'et) n piroetta f. vi piroettare.

Pisces ('pisi:z) n pl Pesci m pl.

piss (pis) tab vi pisciare. **piss off!** va' via! n orina f.

pistachio (pis'tæʃiəu) n pistacchio m.

pistol ('pistəl) n pistola f.

piston ('pistən) n pistone m. stantuffo m.

pit (pit) n **1** fossa, buca f. pozzo m. **2** miniera f. **pitfall** n trappola f.

pitch[1] (pitʃ) n **1** punto, lancio m. **2** mus tono m. vt **1** lanciare, gettare. **2** fissare. vi beccheggiare. **pitchfork** n forcone m.

pitch[2] (pitʃ) n pece f.

pith (piθ) n midollo m.

pittance ('pitns) n piccola quantità f.

pituitary gland (pi'tjuətri) n pituitario m.

pity ('piti) n pietà, compassione f. vt avere pietà di. **pitiful** adj pietoso.

pivot ('pivət) n pernio m. asse f. vt imperniare.

pizza ('pi:tsə) n pizza f.

placard ('plækɑ:d) n affisso, cartellone m.

placate (plə'keit) vt placare, pacificare.

place (pleis) n luogo, posto m. **out of place** inopportuno. **take place** accadere, succedere, avere luogo. ~vt porre, mettere. **placename** n nome di località m.

placenta (plə'sentə) n placenta f.

placid ('plæsid) adj tranquillo, sereno.

plagiarize ('pleidʒəraiz) vt plagiare. **plagiarism** n plagio m. **plagiarist** n plagiario m.

plague (pleig) n **1** peste, pestilenza f. **2** flagello m. vt tormentare, importunare.

plaice (pleis) n passerino m.

plaid (plæd) n mantello scozzese m.

plain (plein) adj **1** semplice, ordinario. **2** evidente, chiaro. n pianura f. **plain-clothes** adj in borghese.

plaintiff ('pleintif) n attore m.

plaintive ('pleintiv) adj lamentoso, triste, querulo.

plait (plæt) n treccia f. vt intrecciare.

plan (plæn) n piano, disegno, progetto m. vt progettare, fissare. vi fare progetti.

plane[1] (plein) n **1** piano m. **2** aviat aereoplano m.

plane[2] (plein) n tech pialla f. vt piallare.

plane[3] (plein) n bot platano m.

planet ('plænit) n pianeta m.

plank (plæŋk) n asse, tavola f.

plankton ('plæŋktən) n plancton m.

plant (plɑ:nt) n **1** bot pianta f. **2** tech impianto m. attrezzi m pl. vt piantare. **plantation** n piantagione f.

plaque (plɑ:k) n placca, lastra f.

plasma ('plæzmə) n plasma m.

plaster ('plɑ:stə) n **1** med cerotto m. **2** gesso m. **3** stucco m. vt ingessare, intonacare. **plaster of Paris** n **1** gesso m. **2** med ingessatura f. **plasterer** n intonacatore m.

plastic ('plæstik) adj plastico. n plastica f. **plastic surgery** n chirurgia estetica f.

Plasticine ('plæstisi:n) n Tdmk Plastilina Tdmk f.

plate (pleit) n **1** cul piatto m. **2** placca, lamina f. **3** argenteria f. **4** illustrazione f. vt **1** placcare, laminare. **2** inargentare. **platelayer** n guardalinea m.

plateau ('plætou) n altipiano m.

platform ('plætfɔ:m) n **1** piattaforma f. **2** (railway) marciapiede, binario m. banchina f.

platinum ('plætnəm) n platino m.

platonic (pləʹtɔnik) adj platonico.

plausible ('plɔ:zəbl) adj plausibile.

play (plei) n **1** gioco, divertimento m. **2** Th dramma m. commedia f. vt **1** giocare a. **2** rappresentare. **3** suonare. vi scherzare. **playful** adj scherzoso. **playground** n cortile di ricreazione m. **playgroup** n asilo m. **playhouse** n teatro m. **playmate** n compagno di gioco m. **playschool** n asilo m. **playwright** n drammaturgo m. **playing card** n carta da gioco f. **playing field** n campo di gioco m.

plea (pli:) n **1** scusa f. pretesto m. **2** law causa, difesa f. **3** supplica f.

plead (pli:d) vt **1** perorare. **2** allegare. vi implorare, appellarsi.

pleasant ('plezənt) adj piacevole, gradevole, simpatico.

please (pli:z) vt,vi piacere, soddisfare. **pleased** adj contento, soddisfatto. **pleasing** adj piacevole, gradevole.

pleasure ('pleʒə) n piacere, favore m.

pleat (pli:t) n piega, ripiegatura f. vt piegare.

plectrum ('plektrəm) n, pl -**tra** or -**trums** plettro m.

pledge (pledʒ) n impegno m. promessa f. vt impegnare.

plenty ('plenti) n abbondanza f. **plenty of** tanto. **plentiful** adj abbondante.

pliable ('plaiəbl) adj **1** pieghevole, flessibile. **2** influenzato facilmente.

plight (plait) n condizione f. stato m.

plimsoll ('plimsəl) n scarpa da tennis f.

plod (plɔd) vi camminare a fatica. **plodder** n sgobbone m.

plonk (plɔŋk) vt buttare giù.

plot[1] (plɔt) n **1** complotto m. cospirazione f. **2** (of a book) intreccio m. vt **1** complottare. **2** fare un piano di. **plotter** n cospiratore m.

plot[2] (plɔt) n (of ground) pezzo di terreno m.

plough (plau) n aratro m. vt arare, solcare. **ploughing** n aratura f.

pluck (plʌk) vt **1** cogliere, tirare. **2** spennare. **pluck up courage** farsi coraggio. ~n **1** strappo m. **2** inf coraggio, fegato m. **plucky** adj coraggioso.

plug (plʌg) n **1** tappo, tampone, zaffo m. **2** tech

spina f. **3** mot candela f. vt tamponare, tappare, zaffare.

plum (plʌm) n prugna, susina f. **plum tree** n prugno, susino m.

plumage ('plu:midʒ) n piumaggio m. penne f pl.

plumb (plʌm) n piombo m. adj,adv a piombo. vt **1** piombare. **2** naut scandagliare. **plumber** n idraulico, tubista m. **plumbing** n piombatura f.

plume (plu:m) n penna, piuma f. pennacchio m.

plump[1] (plʌmp) adj grassoccio, paffuto.

plump[2] (plʌmp) vi cadere a piombo. **plump for** scegliere.

plunder ('plʌndə) n bottino, saccheggio m. vt rubare, saccheggiare.

plunge (plʌndʒ) n tuffo m. vt tuffare, immergere. vi **1** tuffarsi. **2** precipitare.

pluperfect (plu:ʹpə:fikt) n passato anteriore m.

plural ('pluərəl) adj,n plurale m.

plus (plʌs) prep più. adj in più.

plush (plʌʃ) n felpa f. adj lussuoso.

Pluto ('plu:tou) n Plutone m.

ply[1] (plai) vt **1** adoperare, usare. **2** applicare, manipolare.

ply[2] (plai) n spessore m. **plywood** n legno compensato m.

pneumatic (nju:ʹmætik) adj pneumatico. **pneumatic drill** n trapano pneumatico m.

pneumonia (nju:ʹmounia) n polmonite f.

poach[1] (poutʃ) vi andare a caccia di frodo. **poacher** n cacciatore di frodo m. **poaching** n caccia di frodo f.

poach[2] (poutʃ) vt cuocere. **poached egg** n uovo in camicia m.

pocket ('pɔkit) n tasca f. vt intascare, appropriarsi. **pocket-knife** n temperino m. **pocket-money** n pl soldi per le piccole spese m pl.

pod (pɔd) n baccello, guscio m.

poem ('pouim) n **1** poesia f. **2** (epic) poema m.

poet ('pouit) n poeta m. **poetic** adj poetico. **poetry** n poesia f.

poignant ('pɔinjənt) adj intenso, commovente. **poignancy** n acutezza, violenza f.

point (pɔint) n **1** punto m. **2** (of a pencil, etc.) punta f. **be on the point of** stare per. **to the point** a proposito. ~vt appuntare, puntare. **point out** additare, mostrare. **point-blank** adj diretto. adv a bruciapelo. **pointed** adj appuntato, acuto. **pointless** adj inutile.

poise (pɔiz) n 1 equilibrio m. 2 portamento m. vt equilibrare, bilanciare. vi equilibrarsi.

poison ('pɔizən) n veleno m. vt avvelenare, intossicare. **poisonous** adj velenoso.

poke (pouk) vt 1 colpire, dare una botta a. 2 (fire) attizzare. **poke fun at** deridere. ~n spinta, puntata f. **poky** adj piccolo.

poker[1] ('poukə) n attizzatoio m.

poker[2] ('poukə) n game poker m.

Poland ('poulənd) n Polonia f. **Pole** n polacco m.

polar ('poulə) adj polare. **polar bear** n orso bianco m. **polarization** n polarizzazione f. **polarize** vt polarizzare.

pole[1] (poul) n palo, polo m. **pole-vault** vi saltare all'asta.

pole[2] (poul) n geog polo m.

Pole Star n stella polare f.

polemic ('pɔ'lemik) n polemica f. adj polemico.

police (pə'li:s) n polizia f. **policeman** n poliziotto, carabiniere, vigile urbano m. **police station** n questura f. posto di polizia m.

policy[1] ('pɔlisi) n pol politica, linea di condotta f. sistema m.

policy[2] ('pɔlisi) n (insurance) polizza f.

polish ('pɔliʃ) n 1 lucido m. crema, vernice f. 2 raffinatezza f. vt 1 lustrare, lucidare. 2 raffinare. **polishing** n verniciatura f.

Polish ('pouliʃ) adj polacco. **Polish** (language) n polacco m.

polite (pə'lait) adj cortese, gentile. **politeness** n cortesia, gentilezza f.

politics ('pɔlitiks) n politica f. **political** adj politico. **politician** n politico m.

polka ('pɔlkə) n polca f.

poll (poul) n elezione, votazione f. scrutinio m. vt ottenere. **polling booth** n cabina elettorale f.

pollen ('pɔlən) n polline m. **pollinate** vt pollinare.

pollute (pə'lu:t) vt contaminare, corrompere. **pollution** n contaminazione, corruzione f. inquinamento m.

polygamy (pə'ligəmi) n poligamia f. **polygamist** n poligamo m. **polygamous** adj poligamo.

polygon ('pɔligən) n poligono m. **polygonal** adj poligonale.

Polynesia (pɔli'ni:ziə) n Polinesia f. **Polynesian** adj,n polinesiano.

polytechnic (pɔli'teknik) adj,n politecnico m.

polythene ('pɔliθi:n) n politene m.

pomegranate ('pɔmigrænət) n melagrana f.

pommel ('pʌməl) n pomo, pomolo m. vt battere, percuotere.

pomp (pɔmp) n pompa, ostentazione f. **pompous** adj pomposo, affettato.

pond (pɔnd) n stagno, laghetto m.

ponder ('pɔndə) vt,vi considerare, meditare.

pony ('pouni) n cavallino m.

poodle ('pu:dl) n cane barbone m.

pool[1] (pu:l) n (of water, etc.) stagno m. pozzanghera f.

pool[2] (pu:l) n 1 comm fondo comune m. 2 pl totocalcio m. vt mettere in comune.

poor (puə, pɔ:) adj 1 povero, indigente. 2 scarso, misero. **poorly** adv male. adj indisposto.

pop[1] (pɔp) n schiocco, scatto m. vt,vi schioccare, esplodere. **pop in** fare una breve visita. **pop out** uscire per un attimo. **popcorn** n pop-corn m. chicchi di granoturco arrostiti m pl.

pop[2] (pɔp) adj popolare. **pop music** n musica pop f.

pope (poup) n Papa m.

poplar ('pɔplə) n pioppo m.

poppy ('pɔpi) n papavero m.

popular ('pɔpjulə) adj 1 popolare, alla moda. 2 ben voluto. **popularity** n popolarità, voga f.

populate ('pɔpjuleit) vt popolare. **population** n popolazione f.

porcelain ('pɔ:slin) n porcellana f.

porch (pɔ:tʃ) n portico, vestibolo, atrio m.

porcupine ('pɔ:kjupain) n porcospino m.

pore[1] (pɔ:) vt **pore over** 1 studiare con diligenza. 2 meditare.

pore[2] (pɔ:) n poro m.

pork (pɔ:k) n carne di maiale f.

pornography (pɔ:'nɔgrəfi) n pornografia f. **pornographic** adj pornografico.

porous ('pɔ:rəs) adj poroso.

porpoise ('pɔ:pəs) n marsovino m.

porridge ('pɔridʒ) n pappa fatta con farina di avena f.

port[1] (pɔ:t) n (harbour) porto m.

port[2] (pɔ:t) n naut babordo m. sinistra f.

port[3] (pɔ:t) n (drink) vino di Oporto m.

portable ('pɔ:təbəl) adj portabile, portatile.

porter[1] ('pɔ:tə) n (of baggage) facchino, portabagagli m.

porter[2] ('pɔ:tə) n portinaio, portiere m.

portfolio (pɔ:t'fouliou) n 1 cartella f. 2 pol portafoglio m.

porthole ('pɔ:thoul) n bocca porto m.

portion ('pɔ:ʃən) n porzione, parte f.

portrait ('pɔ:trit) n ritratto m. **portrait painter** n ritrattista m.

portray (pɔ:'trei) vt **1** fare il ritratto a, dipingere. **2** descrivere.

Portugal ('pɔ:tjugəl) n Portogallo m. **Portuguese** adj,n portoghese. **Portuguese** (language) n portoghese m.

pose (pouz) vt proporre. vi atteggiarsi, posare. n posa f. atteggiamento m.

posh (pɔʃ) adj elegante.

position (pə'ziʃən) n **1** posizione, situazione f. **2** posto, impiego m. vt collocare.

positive ('pɔzitiv) adj positivo, sicuro, certo.

possess (pə'zes) vt possedere, avere. **possessed** adj possesso. **possession** n possesso, possedimento m. **possessive** adj possessivo. **possessor** n possessore m.

possible ('pɔsəbəl) adj possibile. **possibly** adv forse, può darsi.

post[1] (poust) n palo, pilastro m. vt affiggere. **poster** n affisso, avviso m.

post[2] (poust) n (job) posto, impiego m.

post[3] (poust) n (mail) posta f. vt imbucare. **postal** adj postale. **postal order** n vaglia m invar. **postage** n affrancatura, tariffa postale f. **postbox** n cassetta postale f. **postcard** n cartolina f. **postcode** n codice postale m. **postman** n postino m. **postmark** n timbro postale m. **post office** n ufficio postale m.

posterior (pɔs'tiəriə) adj posteriore.

posterity (pɔs'teriti) n posterità f.

postgraduate (poust'grædjuət) adj di perfezionamento. n perfezionando m.

posthumous ('pɔsthjuməs) adj postumo. **posthumously** adv dopo la morte.

post-mortem (poust'mɔ:təm) n autopsia f.

postpone (pəs'poun) vt posporre, rimandare, rinviare. **postponement** n rinvio m.

postscript ('pousskript) n poscritto m.

postulate ('pɔstjuleit) vt postulare, domandare.

posture ('pɔstʃə) n posizione f. atteggiamento m.

pot (pɔt) n **1** vaso m. **2** pentola f. vt piantare in vaso.

potassium (pə'tæsiəm) n potassio m.

potato (pə'teitou) n, pl **-toes** patata f.

potent ('poutnt) adj potente, forte. **potency** n potenza, forza f.

potential (pə'tenʃəl) adj,n potenziale m.

pothole ('pɔthoul) n **1** marmitta f. **2** (in a road) buca f.

potion ('pouʃən) n pozione, bevanda f.

potter ('pɔtə) vi gingillarsi.

pottery ('pɔtəri) n ceramica f. stoviglie f pl.

pouch (pautʃ) n borsa f. sacchetto m.

poultice ('poultis) n cataplasma m.

poultry ('poultri) n pollame m.

pounce (pauns) vi piombare. **pounce upon** gettarsi addosso a. ~n spolvero m.

pound[1] (paund) vt polverizzare, battere.

pound[2] (paund) n **1** (weight) libbra f. **2** (currency) sterlina f.

pour (pɔ:) vt versare, spargere. vi riversarsi.

pout (paut) vi fare il broncio. n broncio m.

poverty ('pɔvəti) n miseria, povertà f. **poverty-stricken** adj miserabile, indigente.

powder ('paudə) n **1** polvere f. **2** (face) cipria f. vt **1** spolverizzare. **2** incipriare. **powder room** n toilette f invar. **powdery** adj polveroso.

power ('pauə) n **1** potere m. potenza f. **2** energia f. **3** potestà f. **4** possibilità f. **powerful** adj potente. **powerless** adj senza potere, impotente.

practicable ('præktikəbəl) adj praticabile.

practical ('præktikəl) adj pratico. **practically** adv quasi.

practice ('præktis) n **1** pratica f. esercizio m. **2** clientela f. **3** abitudine f. **out of practice** fuori esercizio. **practise** vt esercitare, praticare. vi esercitarsi. **practised** adj pratico, esperto. **practising** adj praticante.

practitioner (præk'tiʃənə) n **1** professionista m. **2** medico m.

pragmatic (præg'mætik) adj prammatico.

prairie ('prɛəri) n prateria f.

praise (preiz) n lode f. elogio m. vt lodare, elogiare, vantare. **praiseworthy** adj lodevole.

pram (præm) n carrozzina f.

prance (prɑ:ns) vi **1** saltellare. **2** (of a horse) impennarsi.

prank (præŋk) n scherzo, tiro m. burla f.

prattle ('prætl) vi chiacchierare, cianciare. n chiacchierio m.

prawn (prɔ:n) n palemone m.

pray (prei) vt,vi pregare. **prayer** n preghiera, supplica f. **prayerbook** n libro di preghiere m.

preach (pri:tʃ) vt,vi predicare. **preacher** n predicatore m.

precarious (pri'kɛəriəs) adj precario, incerto.

precaution (pri'kɔ:ʃən) n precauzione f.

precede (pri'si:d) vt precedere. **precedence** n precedenza f. **precedent** n precedente m.

precinct ('pri:siŋkt) n **1** recinto m. **2** pl confini, limiti m pl.

precious ('preʃəs) adj **1** prezioso. **2** ricercato.

precipice ('presipis) n precipizio m.

precipitate (prə'sipiteit) vt precipitare. adj affrettato, precipitato.

precis ('preisi) n sunto m.

precise (pri'sais) adj preciso, esatto, scrupoloso. **precision** n precisione, esattezza f.

precocious (pri'kouʃəs) adj precoce.

preconceive (pri:kən'si:v) vt formare un'opinione di in anticipo. **preconceived** adj preconcetto. **preconception** n preconcetto, pregiudizio m.

predatory ('predətəri) adj predatorio, rapace.

predecessor ('pri:disesə) n predecessore m.

predestine (pri:'destin) vt predestinare. **predestination** n predestinazione f.

predicament (pri'dikəmənt) n imbroglio m. situazione difficile f.

predicate (n 'predikit; v 'predikeit) n predicato m. vt predicare.

predict (pri'dikt) vt predire. **prediction** n predizione f.

predominate (pri'domineit) vi predominare, prevalere. **predominance** n predominio m. **predominant** adj predominante.

pre-eminent adj preminente. **pre-eminence** n preminenza f.

preen (pri:n) vt pulire. **preen oneself** pavoneggiarsi.

prefabricate (pri'fæbrikeit) vt prefabbricare. **prefab** n casa prefabbricata f.

preface ('prefis) n prefazione f. vt premettere, scrivere la prefazione a.

prefect ('pri:fekt) n **1** prefetto m. **2** educ capoclasse, prefetto m.

prefer (pri'fə:) vt preferire. **preferable** adj preferibile. **preference** n preferenza f. **preferential** adj preferenziale.

prefix ('pri:fiks) n prefisso m. vt premettere.

pregnant ('pregnənt) adj **1** (of a woman) incinta. **2** (of an animal) gravida. **3** pregnante, fecondo. **pregnancy** n gravidanza f.

prehistoric (pri:his'tɔrik) adj preistorico.

prejudice ('predʒədis) n pregiudizio m. vt pregiudicare, compromettere. **prejudiced** adj prevenuto.

preliminary (pri'liminəri) adj,n preliminare m.

prelude ('prelju:d) n preludio m. vt,vi preludere, preannunziare.

premarital (pri:'mæritl) adj prematrimoniale.

premature ('prematʃə) adj prematuro, precoce.

premeditate (pri:'mediteit) vt premeditare. **premeditation** n premeditazione f.

premier ('premiə) adj primo. n primo ministro m.

premiere ('premiɛə) n Th prima f.

premise ('premis) n **1** premessa f. **2** pl locali m pl.

premium ('pri:miəm) n premio, aggio m. **premium bond** n titoli dello stato m pl.

preoccupied (pri:'ɔkjupaid) adj preoccupato.

prepare (pri'pɛə) vt **1** preparare. **2** apparecchiare. vi prepararsi. **be prepared to** essere pronto a. **preparation** n preparazione f. preparativo m. **preparatory** adj preparatorio.

preposition (prepə'ziʃən) n preposizione f.

preposterous (pri'pɔstərəs) adj assurdo.

prerogative (pri'rɔgətiv) n prerogativa f. privilegio m.

Presbyterian (prezbi'tiəriən) adj,n presbiteriano.

prescribe (pri'skraib) vt,vi **1** prescrivere. **2** med ordinare. **prescription** n ricetta medica f.

presence ('prezəns) n **1** presenza f. **2** aspetto m.

present[1] ('prezənt) adj attuale, presente. n presente m. **at present** adesso. **for the present** per il momento. **present participle** n participio presente m. **presently** adv fra poco.

present[2] (v pri'zent; n 'prezənt) vt **1** presentare. **2** regalare a. **3** Th rappresentare. n regalo m. **presentation** n presentazione f.

preserve (pri'zə:v) n **1** conserva, marmellata f. **2** (for animals) riserva f. vt conservare, preservare, salvare. **preservation** n **1** preservazione. **2** salvezza f.

preside (pri'zaid) vi presiedere.

president ('prezidənt) n presidente m. **presidential** adj presidenziale.

press (pres) vt **1** premere, comprimere, stringere. **2** stirare. n **1** stampa f. **2** tech torchio m. **3** calca f. **press conference** n conferenza stampa f. **press-stud** n automatico m. **press-up** n esercizio di ginnastica alzando il corpo con le braccia m. **pressing** adj urgente, incalzante.

pressure ('preʃə) n **1** pressione, costrizione f. **2** urgenza f. **pressure cooker** n pentola a pressione *f.* **pressurize** *vt* pressurizzare, costringere.

prestige (pres'ti:ʒ) *n* prestigio *m.*

presume (pri'zju:m) *vt* presumere, supporre. **presumption** *n* **1** presunzione, supposizione *f.* **2** arroganza *f.* **presumptuous** *adj* presuntuoso, arrogante.

pretend (pri'tend) *vt* fingere, far finta di. *vi* pretendere. **pretence** *n* pretesa, scusa *f.* pretesto *m.* **pretension** *n* pretesa *f.* **pretentious** *adj* prentenzioso, arrogante. **pretentiousness** *n* arroganza *f.*

pretext ('pri:tekst) *n* pretesto *m.* scusa *f.*

pretty ('priti) *adj* bellino, carino, grazioso. *adv* quasi, press'a poco, piuttosto.

prevail (pri'veil) *vi* prevalere, predominare. **prevalent** *adj* prevalente.

prevent (pri'vent) *vt* impedire. **prevention** *n* prevenzione *f.* **preventive** *adj* preventivo.

preview ('pri:vju:) *n* anteprima *f.*

previous ('pri:vias) *adj* precedente, anteriore. **previously** *adv* prima.

prey (prei) *n* preda *f.* *v* **prey on 1** predare. **2** consumare.

price (prais) *n* prezzo, costo *m.* *vt* valutare, fissare il prezzo di. **price-list** *n* listino dei prezzi *m.*

prick (prik) *n* pungolo *m.* puntura *f.* *vt* pungere, punzecchiare. **prick one's ears** drizzare gli orecchi. **prickle** *n* spina *f.* **prickly** *adj* spinoso, pungente.

pride (praid) *n* orgoglio *m.* superbia *f.* *v* **pride oneself on** vantarsi di.

priest (pri:st) *n* prete, sacerdote *m.* **priesthood** *n* sacerdozio *m.*

prim (prim) *adj* affettato, preciso.

primary ('praiməri) *adj* primario, elementare, fondamentale. **primary school** *n* scuola elementare *f.*

primate *n* **1** ('praimit) *rel* primate *m.* **2** ('praimeit) *pl* primati *m pl.*

prime (praim) *adj* primo, principale, fondamentale. *n* fiore, colmo *m.* *vt* **1** istruire. **2** caricare. **prime minister** *n* primo ministro *m.*

primitive ('primitiv) *adj* primitivo.

primrose ('primrouz) *n* primula *f.*

prince (prins) *n* principe *m.*

princess (prin'ses) *n* principessa *f.*

principal ('prinsəpəl) *adj* principale, primo. *n* capo, direttore, principale, padrone *m.*

principality (prinsi'pæliti) *n* principato *m.*

principle ('prinsəpəl) *n* principio *m.*

print (print) *n* **1** stampa, impressione *f.* **2** *phot* prova *f.* *vt* stampare, imprimere. **out of print** esaurito. **printer** *n* stampatore, tipografo *m.* **printing** *n* stampa, tiratura *f.*

prior ('praiə) *adj* antecedente, precedente. *adv* prima. **priority** *n* priorità *f.*

prise (praiz) *vt* far leva su. **prise open** forzare.

prism ('prizəm) *n* prisma *m.*

prison ('prizən) *n* prigione *f.* carcere *m.* **prisoner** *n* prigioniero, detenuto *m.*

private ('praivit) *adj* **1** privato, persolnale. **2** confidenziale. *n* soldato semplice *m.* **privacy** *n* solitudine, intimità *f.*

privet ('privit) *n* ligustro *m.*

privilege ('privilidʒ) *n* privilegio *m.*

prize[1] (praiz) *n* premio *m.* **prizewinner** *n* premiato, vincitore *m.*

prize[2] (praiz) *vt* valutare, apprezzare.

probable ('prɔbəbəl) *adj* probabile. **probability** *n* probabilità *f.* **probably** *adv* probabilmente.

probation (prə'beiʃən) *n* probazione, prova *f.* **on probation** in prova. **probation officer** *n* ufficiale-sorvegliante *m.* **probationary** *adj* probatorio.

probe (proub) *vt* **1** sondare. **2** esaminare a fondo. *n* sonda *f.*

problem ('prɔbləm) *n* problema *m.*

proceed (prə'si:d) *vi* **1** procedere, continuare. **2** derivare. **procedure** *n* procedura *f.* procedimento *m.* **proceeding** *n* **1** azione *f.* procedimento *m.* **2** *pl* atti *m pl.* **proceeds** *n pl* profitti *m pl.*

process ('prouses) *n* processo, corso *m.* *vt* processare, preparare.

procession (prə'seʃən) *n* processione *f.* corteo *m.*

proclaim (prə'kleim) *vt* proclamare, dichiarare. **proclamation** *n* proclamazione, dichiarazione *f.*

procreate ('proukrieit) *vt* procreare. **procreation** *n* procreazione *f.*

procure (prə'kjuə) *vt* procurare.

prod (prɔd) *vt* stimolare, pungere. *n* pungolo *m.*

prodigy ('prɔdidʒi) *n* prodigio, miracolo *m.*

produce (*v* prə'dju:s; *n* 'prɔdju:s) *vt* **1** produrre, fabbricare. **2** *Th* mettere in scena. *n* prodotto *m.* **producer** *n* **1** produttore *m.* **2** *Th* direttore *m.* **product** *n* prodotto, frutto *m.* **production** *n* **1** produzione *f.* **2** *Th* messa in scena *f.* **productive** *adj* produttivo, fertile. **productivity** *n* produttività *f.*

profane (prə'fein) *adj* profano. *vt* profanare.

profess (prə'fes) vt,vi professare, dichiarare. **profession** n professione f. mestiere m. **professional** adj professionale. n professionista m. **professor** n professore universitario m. **professorship** n cattedra f.

proficient (prə'fiʃənt) adj esperto, bravo. **proficiency** n abilità f.

profile ('proufail) n profilo m.

profit ('profit) n **1** profitto, guadagno m. **2** utile, vantaggio m. vi approfittare, trarre vantaggio. **profitable** adj utile, vantaggioso.

profound (prə'faund) adj profondo, intenso.

profuse (prə'fju:s) adj profuso, prodigo. **profusion** n profusione, prodigalità f.

programme ('prougræm) n programma m. **program** (in computers) n programma m. vt programmare.

progress (n 'prougres; v prə'gres) n progresso, corso, avanzamento m. vi progredire, procedere, avanzare. **progression** n progresso m. **progressive** adj progressivo.

prohibit (prə'hibit) vt proibire, vietare, interdire. **prohibition** n proibizione f. **prohibitive** adj proibitivo.

project (n 'prodʒekt; v prə'dʒekt) n progetto, disegno, piano m. vt **1** progettare. **2** proiettare. vi sporgere. **projectile** n proiettile m. **projection** n prominenza, sporgenza f. **projector** n **1** progettista m. **2** phot proiettore m.

proletariat (prouli'tɛəriət) n proletariato m. **proletarian** adj,n proletario.

proliferate (prə'lifəreit) vi prolificare.

prolific (prə'lifik) adj prolifico, fecondo.

prologue ('proulog) n prologo m.

prolong (prə'lɔŋ) vt prolungare, tirare in lungo.

promenade (promə'na:d) n **1** passeggiata f. **2** lungomare m.

prominent ('prominənt) adj **1** prominente. **2** eminente, importante. **3** notevole. **prominence** n prominenza, eminenza, importanza f.

promiscuous (prə'miskjuəs) adj promiscuo. **promiscuity** n promiscuità f.

promise ('promis) n promessa f. vt,vi promettere.

promote (prə'mout) vt promuovere, favorire. **promotion** n **1** promozione f. **2** comm lancio m.

prompt (prompt) adj pronto, rapido. vt **1** stimolare, ispirare. **2** Th suggerire. **prompter** n

suggeritore m. **prompting** n stimolo m. suggestione f. **promptness** n prontezza f.

prone (proun) adj incline, disposto, prono.

prong (prɔŋ) n rebbio m. punta f.

pronoun ('prounaun) n pronome m.

pronounce (prə'nauns) vt pronunciare, dire, dichiarare. **pronunciation** n pronuncia f.

proof (pru:f) n **1** prova f. **2** (of drink) grado m. vt rendere impermeabile. **proofreader** n correttore di bozze m.

prop[1] (prɔp) vt puntellare, sostenere. n appoggio, puntello, sostegno m.

prop[2] (prɔp) n Th oggetto teatrale m.

propaganda (propə'gændə) n propaganda f.

propagate ('propəgeit) vt propagare, spargere.

propel (prə'pel) vt spingere avanti, avviare. **propeller** n elica f.

proper ('propə) adj **1** proprio. **2** particolare. **3** adatto. **4** esatto, giusto, corretto. **proper noun** n nome proprio m. **properly** adv bene, giustamente.

property ('propəti) n proprietà f. possesso m. beni m pl.

prophecy ('profisi) n profezia f. **prophesy** vt,vi profetizzare, predire.

prophet ('profit) n profeta m. **prophetic** adj profetico.

proportion (prə'pɔ:ʃən) n proporzione, parte f. **out of proportion** fuori di misura.

propose (prə'pouz) vt **1** proporre, suggerire. **2** (a toast, etc.) fare. vi fare una proposta di matrimonio. **proposal** n proposta, offerta f. **proposition** n proposizione, proposta f. progetto m.

proprietor (prə'praiətə) n proprietario m.

propriety (prə'praiəti) n proprietà, convenienza f.

propulsion (prə'pʌlʃən) n propulsione f.

prose (prouz) n prosa f.

prosecute ('prosikju:t) vt processare. **prosecution** n processo m. **prosecutor** n accusatore m.

prospect ('prospekt) n **1** prospetto m. vista f. **2** prospettiva f. **3** speranza f. vi esplorare, fare ricerche. **prospective** adj prospettivo, aspettato, futuro. **prospectus** n prospetto, programma, manifesto m.

prosper ('prospə) vi prosperare, riuscire. **prosperity** n prosperità f. **prosperous** adj prospero, felice, fortunato.

prostitute ('prostitju:t) n prostituta, puttana f. vt prostituire. **prostitution** n prostituzione f.

prostrate (v prɔs'treit; adj 'prɔstreit) vt 1 prostrare. 2 abbattere. adj prostrato, abbattuto.

protagonist (prə'tægənist) n protagonista m.

protect (prə'tekt) vt proteggere, difendere. **protection** n protezione f. **protective** adj protettivo. **protectorate** n protettorato m.

protégé ('prɔtiʒei) n protetto m.

protein ('prouti:n) n proteina f.

protest (n 'proutest; v prə'test) n protesta f. **under protest** protestando. ~vt, vi protestare.

Protestant ('prɔtistənt) adj,n protestante.

protocol ('proutəkɔl) n protocollo m.

proton ('prouton) n protone m.

prototype ('proutətaip) n prototipo m.

protrude (prə'tru:d) vt,vi sporgere.

proud (praud) adj fiero, orgoglioso, superbo, arrogante.

prove (pru:v) vt provare, dimostrare. vi mostrarsi.

proverb ('prɔvə:b) n proverbio m. **proverbial** adj proverbiale.

provide (prə'vaid) vt provvedere, procurare, fornire. **provided** conj purché. **provision** n 1 provvedimento m. 2 provviste f pl. **provisional** adj provvisorio.

province ('prɔvins) n 1 provincia f. 2 competenza f. **provincial** adj,n provinciale.

proviso (prə'vaizou) n stipulazione f.

provoke (prə'vouk) vt provocare, irritare. **provocation** n provocazione f. **provocative** adj provocativo, provocatore.

prow (prau) n prua f.

prowess ('prauis) n bravura, prodezza f. valore m.

prowl (praul) vi vagare, gironzolare, vagolare. **prowler** n girellone, predone m.

proximity (prɔk'simiti) n prossimità, vicinanza f.

prude (pru:d) n persona di modestia affettata f.

prudent ('pru:dnt) adj prudente, cauto, giudizioso. **prudence** n prudenza f.

prune[1] (pru:n) n prugna secca f.

prune[2] (pru:n) vt potare, troncare. **pruning** n potatura f.

pry (prai) vi rovistare, ficcare il naso.

psalm (sɑ:m) n salmo m.

pseudonym ('sju:dənim) n pseudonimo m.

psychedelic (saiki'delik) adj psicodelico.

psychiatry (sai'kaiətri) n psichiatria f. **psychiatric** adj psichiatrico. **psychiatrist** n psichiatra m.

psychic ('saikik) adj psichico.

psychoanalysis (saikouə'nælisis) n psicoanalisi f. **psychoanalyst** n psicoanalista m.

psychology (sai'kɔlədʒi) n psicologia f. **psychological** adj psicologico. **psychologist** n psicologo m.

psychopath ('saikəpæθ) n psicopatico m **psychopathic** adj psicopatico.

psychosomatic (saikousə'mætik) adj psicosomatico.

pub (pʌb) n bar m invar. osteria, birreria f.

puberty ('pju:bəti) n pubertà f.

public ('pʌblik) adj,n pubblico m. **publican** n proprietario del bar m. **public holiday** n giorno di festa m. **public house** n bar m invar. osteria, birreria f. **public relations** n servizio di stampa e propaganda m. **public school** n scuola privata f.

publication (pʌbli'keiʃən) n pubblicazione f.

publicity (pʌb'lisiti) n pubblicità f.

publicize ('pʌblisaiz) vt pubblicare.

publish ('pʌbliʃ) vt pubblicare, promulgare. **publisher** n 1 editore m. 2 casa editrice f. **publishing** n pubblicazione f.

pucker ('pʌkə) vt raggrinzare, increspare, corrugare. vi raggrinzarsi, incresparsi. n grinza, crespa, riga f.

pudding ('pudiŋ) n budino, dolce m.

puddle ('pʌdl) n pozzanghera f.

puff (pʌf) n 1 sbuffo, soffio m. 2 piumino m. vt,vi soffiare, sbuffare. **puff pastry** n pasta sfoglia f.

pull (pul) n 1 tirata f. strappo, sforzo m. 2 sl influenza f. vt,vi 1 tirare, trascinare. 2 strappare. **pull down** demolire. **pull up** fermarsi. **pullover** n pullover m invar. maglione m.

pulley ('puli) n puleggia f.

pulp (pʌlp) n polpa f. vt ridurre in polpa.

pulpit ('pʌlpit) n pulpito m.

pulsate (pʌl'seit) vi pulsare, battere, palpitare.

pulse (pʌls) n polso m.

pulverize ('pʌlvəraiz) vt polverizzare.

pump (pʌmp) n pompa f. vt 1 pompare. 2 ottenere informazione da. **pump up** gonfiare.

pumpkin ('pʌmpkin) n zucca f.

pun (pʌn) n gioco di parole m.

punch[1] (pʌntʃ) n pugno m. vt dare pugni a.

punch[2] (pʌntʃ) n (tool) strumento per perforare. vt perforare.

punch[3] (pʌntʃ) n cul ponce m.

punctual ('pʌŋktʃuəl) adj puntuale. **punctuality** n puntualità f.

punctuate (ˈpʌŋktʃueit) vt punteggiare. **punctuation** n punteggiatura, puntuazione f.

puncture (ˈpʌŋktʃə) n 1 mot bucatura f. 2 med puntura f. vt forare, bucare.

pungent (ˈpʌndʒənt) adj acre, pungente, aspro.

punish (ˈpʌniʃ) vt punire, castigare. **punishment** n punizione, pena f. castigo m.

punt[1] (pʌnt) n naut chiatta f. vt spingere.

punt[2] (pʌnt) vi game scommettere.

pupil[1] (ˈpjuːpəl) n scolaro, alunno m.

pupil[2] (ˈpjuːpəl) n anat pupilla f.

puppet (ˈpʌpit) n marionetta f. burattino m.

puppy (ˈpʌpi) n cagnolino m.

purchase (ˈpəːtʃis) vt comprare, acquistare. n compera f. acquisto m. **purchaser** n compratore m.

pure (pjuə) adj puro, chiaro. **purity** n purità, purezza f.

purgatory (ˈpəːgətri) n purgatorio m.

purge (pəːdʒ) n 1 purga f. purgante m. 2 pol epurazione f. vt 1 purgare, purificare. 2 pol epurare.

purify (ˈpjuərifai) vt purificare. **purification** n purificazione f.

Puritan (ˈpjuəritən) n puritano m. **puritanical** adj puritano.

purl (pəːl) vt,vi smerlare.

purple (ˈpəːpəl) n porpora f. adj purpureo, violaceo.

purpose (ˈpəːpəs) n proposito, scopo, fine m. intenzione f. **on purpose** apposta.

purr (pəː) vi fare le fusa. n fusa f.

purse (pəːs) n borsellino m.

pursue (pəˈsjuː) vt 1 perseguire, incalzare. 2 cercare. **pursuer** n inseguitore m. **pursuit** n 1 inseguimento m. 2 ricerca f.

pus (pʌs) n pus m. marcia f.

push (puʃ) vt spingere, urtare, premere. **push on** avanzarsi. **push through** sbrigare. ~n spinta f. urto, impulso m. **pushchair** n carrozzino m.

pussy (ˈpusi) n inf micio m.

put* (put) vt 1 mettere, porre. 2 collocare, presentare. **put off** 1 rinviare. 2 dissuadere. **put on** indossare. **put up** aumentare. **put up with** sopportare.

putrid (ˈpjuːtrid) adj putrido, marcio, putrefatto.

putty (ˈpʌti) n stucco m.

puzzle (ˈpʌzəl) n enigma, indovinello m. vt confondere, sbalordire. **puzzled** adj perplesso.

PVC n PVC m.

Pygmy (ˈpigmi) adj,n pigmeo.

pyjamas (pəˈdʒɑːməz) n pl pigiama m.

pylon (ˈpailən) n pilone m.

pyramid (ˈpirəmid) n piramide f.

Pyrex (ˈpaireks) n Tdmk pirofila f.

python (ˈpaiθən) n pitone m.

Q

quack[1] (kwæk) n gracidio m. vi gracidare.

quack[2] (kwæk) n ciarlatano m.

quadrangle (ˈkwɔdræŋgəl) n quadrangolo m.

quadrant (ˈkwɔdrənt) n quadrante m.

quadrilateral (kwɔdriˈlætərəl) adj,n quadrilatero m.

quadruped (ˈkwɔdruped) adj,n quadrupede m.

quadruple (ˈkwɔdrupəl) adj,n quadruplo m. vt quadruplare. **quadruplet** n uno di quattri nati in un solo parto m.

quail[1] (kweil) n quaglia f.

quail[2] (kweil) vi tremare, avere paura.

quaint (kweint) adj 1 strano. 2 pittoresco.

quake (kweik) vi tremolare.

Quaker (ˈkweikə) n quacchero m.

qualify (ˈkwɔlifai) vt 1 qualificare, abilitare. 2 moderare, mitigare. vi abilitarsi. **qualification** n 1 titolo m. qualifica f. 2 condizione, riserva f. **qualified** adj qualificato, competente.

quality (ˈkwɔliti) n qualità f.

qualm (kwɑːm) n 1 scrupolo m. 2 nausea f. malessere m.

quandary (ˈkwɔndəri) n impaccio m. situazione difficile f.

quantify (ˈkwɔntifai) vt quantificare.

quantity (ˈkwɔntiti) n quantità f.

quarantine (ˈkwɔrəntiːn) n quarentena f.

quarrel (ˈkwɔrəl) n disputa, lite, contesa f. vi litigare, disputare. **quarrelsome** adj litigioso.

quarry[1] (ˈkwɔri) n cava, pietraia f. vt scavare.

quarry[2] (ˈkwɔri) n (prey) preda f.

quart (kwɔːt) n quarto di un gallone m.

quarter (ˈkwɔːtə) n 1 quarto m. 2 trimestre m. 3 quartiere m. località f. 4 pl mil quartieri m pl. **at close quarters** da vicino. ~vt dividere in quarti. **quarterly** adj trimestrale. **quarterdeck** n cassero m. **quartermaster** n commissario m.

quartet (kwɔːˈtet) n quartetto m.

quartz (kwɔːts) n quarzo m.

quash[1] (kwɔʃ) vt schiacciare.

quash[2] (kwɔʃ) vt law annullare, invalidare.

quaver (ˈkweivə) n mus croma f. vi tremolare, vibrare.

quay (kiː) n banchina f. molo m.

queasy (ˈkwiːzi) adj 1 nauseante. 2 delicato. **feel queasy** sentire la nausea.

queen (kwiːn) n 1 regina f. 2 game donna f. **beauty queen** reginetta f.

queer (kwiə) adj strano, bizzarro, curioso. n sl finocchio m.

quell (kwel) vt reprimere, domare, soffocare.

quench (kwentʃ) vt spegnere, estinguere. **quench one's thirst** dissetarsi.

query (ˈkwiəri) n domanda, questione f. vt 1 domandare. 2 mettere in dubbio.

quest (kwest) n ricerca f. **in quest of** in cerca di.

question (ˈkwestʃən) n 1 domanda, questione f. 2 dubbio m. 3 soggetto m. **ask a question** fare una domanda. **out of the question** impossibile. ~vt 1 interrogare. 2 mettere in dubbio. **question mark** n punto interrogativo m. **questionable** adj discutibile. **questionnaire** n questionario m.

queue (kjuː) n coda, fila f. vi far coda.

quibble (ˈkwibəl) vi cavillare, equivocare. n cavillo m. scappatoia f.

quick (kwik) adj 1 presto, rapido. 2 svelto, vivace. 3 intelligente. adv presto, subito. n vivo m. **quicken** vt affrettare. **quickness** n prontezza, rapidità f. **quicksand** n sabbia mobile f. **quicksilver** n mercurio m. argento vivo m. **quickstep** n quickstep m. **quick-tempered** adj irascibile. **quick-witted** adj acuto.

quid (kwid) n sl sterlina f.

quiet[1] (ˈkwaiət) n quiete, tranquillità f. silenzio m.

quiet[2] (ˈkwaiət) adj 1 quieto, tranquillo, placido. 2 modesto. **be quiet!** sta zitto! **on the quiet** quatto quatto. ~vt acquietare. vi acquietarsi. **quieten** vt calmare, quietare, pacificare. vi calmarsi.

quill (kwil) n 1 penna f. 2 (of a porcupine) spina f.

quilt (kwilt) n piumino m. vt trapuntare.

quinine (kwiˈniːn) n chinino m.

quintessence (kwinˈtesəns) n quintessenza f.

quintet (kwinˈtet) n quintetto m.

quirk (kwəːk) n vezzo, frizzo m.

quit* (kwit) vt lasciare, abbandonare. vi partire. **be quits** essere pari. **notice to quit** n disdetta f.

quite (kwait) adv tutto, affatto, proprio, completamente.

quiver[1] (ˈkwivə) vi tremare, vacillare. n brivido, tremito m.

quiver[2] (ˈkwivə) n sport faretra f.

quiz (kwiz) n, pl **quizzes** questionario m. quiz m invar. vt fare delle domande a.

quizzical (ˈkwizikəl) adj curioso.

quoit (kɔit) n anello (di ferro, etc.) m.

quota (ˈkwoutə) n quota, rata f.

quote (kwout) vt 1 citare. 2 comm quotare. **quotation** n 1 citazione f. brano m. 2 comm quotazione f. **quotation marks** n pl virgolette f pl.

R

rabbi (ˈræbai) n rabbino m.

rabbit (ˈræbit) n coniglio m.

rabble (ˈræbəl) n plebaglia f.

rabies (ˈreibiːz) n idrofobia, rabbia f. **rabid** adj 1 fanatico. 2 furioso. 3 med rabbioso, idrofobo.

race[1] (reis) n (competition) corsa, gara f. vt far correre in una corsa. vi correre. **racecourse** n campo di corsa m. pista f. **racehorse** n cavallo da corsa m.

race[2] (reis) n (people) razza, stirpe f. **race relations** n pl relazioni razziali f pl. **racial** adj razziale, di razza.

rack (ræk) n 1 rastrelliera f. 2 (for plates) scolapiatti m. 3 (for luggage, etc.) rete f. vt tormentare. **rack one's brains** stillarsi il cervello.

racket[1] (ˈrækit) n chiasso, rumore, fracasso m.

racket[2] (ˈrækit) n sport racchetta f.

radar (ˈreidaː) n radar m invar.

radial (ˈreidiəl) adj radiale.

radiant (ˈreidiənt) adj raggiante, irradiato, brillante. **radiance** n splendore m.

radiate (ˈreidieit) vt raggiare, diffondere, irradiare. **radiation** n irradiazione f. **radiator** n 1 termosifone m. 2 mot radiatore m.

radical (ˈrædikəl) adj,n radicale m.

radio (ˈreidiou) n radio f invar.

radioactive (reidiouˈæktiv) adj radioattivo. **radioactivity** n radioattività f.

radish (ˈrædiʃ) n ravanello m.

radium (ˈreidiəm) n radio m.

radius (ˈreidiəs) n, pl **-dii** or **-diuses** raggio m.

raffia (ˈræfiə) n rafia f.

raffle ('ræfəl) n lotteria privata f. vt vendere per mezzo di una lotteria.

raft (rɑːft) n zattera, chiatta f.

rafter ('rɑːftə) n trave f.

rag[1] (ræg) n straccio, cencio m. **ragged** adj 1 cencioso, stracciato. 2 aspro, ruvido.

rag[2] (ræg) vt prendere in giro.

rage (reidʒ) n 1 collera, furia f. 2 mania, passione f. **all the rage** di moda. ~vi infuriare.

raid (reid) n scorreria, incursione f. vt invadere, fare un'incursione in.

rail (reil) n 1 sbarra f. 2 (of banisters, etc.) ringhiera f. 3 (railway) rotaia f. **railing** n cancellata f. **railway** n ferrovia f. **railway line** n binario m.

rain (rein) n pioggia f. v imp piovere. **rainbow** n arcobaleno m. **raindrop** n goccia di pioggia f. **rainfall** n caduta di pioggia f.

raise (reiz) vt 1 alzare. 2 sollevare. 3 allevare. 4 innalzare, aumentare.

raisin ('reizən) n uva secca f.

rajah ('rɑːdʒə) n ragià m.

rake (reik) n rastrello m. vt rastrellare, raccogliere.

rally ('ræli) n 1 ripresa f. 2 riunione f. 3 mot rally m. vt raccogliere, riunire. vi rimettersi.

ram (ræm) n montone m. vt 1 ficcare. 2 naut speronare.

ramble ('ræmbəl) n passeggiata f. giro m. vi 1 vagare. 2 divagare.

ramp (ræmp) n rampa, salita f.

rampage ('ræmpeidʒ) n furia, condotta violenta f. vi smaniare, scalmanarsi.

rampant ('ræmpənt) adj 1 predominante. 2 violento.

rampart ('ræmpɑːt) n bastione m. difesa f.

ramshackle ('ræmʃækəl) adj sgangherato, rovinato.

ran (ræn) v see **run.**

ranch (rɑːntʃ) n podere m. fattoria f.

rancid ('rænsid) adj rancido.

rancour ('ræŋkə) n rancore, risentimento m. acrimonia f.

random ('rændəm) adj casuale, a caso. **at random** a casaccio.

rang (ræŋ) v see **ring.**

range (reindʒ) n 1 serie, portata f. 2 sport campo di tiro m. 3 geog catena f. vt ordinare, collocare. vi stendersi.

rank[1] (ræŋk) n 1 fila f. 2 classe, condizione f. 3 rango, grado m. **rank and file** n gregari m pl.

~vt 1 classificare. 2 ordinare. vi prendere posto.

rank[2] (ræŋk) adj rancido, schifoso, turpe.

rankle ('ræŋkəl) vi bruciare.

ransack ('rænsæk) vt frugare, saccheggiare.

ransom ('rænsəm) n riscatto m. vt riscattare.

rap (ræp) n colpo, colpetto m. picchiata f. vt battere, colpire, picchiare.

rape (reip) n violenza carnale f. vt violare.

rapid ('ræpid) adj rapido, veloce. n rapida f. **rapidity** n velocità, rapidità f.

rapier ('reipiə) n spada f.

rapture ('ræptʃə) n entusiasmo m. estasi f.

rare[1] (rɛə) adj 1 raro, scarso. 2 insolito. 3 prezioso. **rarity** n rarità f.

rare[2] (rɛə) adj cul poco cotto.

rascal ('rɑːskəl) n furfante, briccone m.

rash[1] (ræʃ) adj precipitoso, inconsiderato, avventato. **rashness** n imprudenza f.

rash[2] (ræʃ) n med eruzione f.

rasher ('ræʃə) n fetta di prosciutto f.

raspberry ('rɑːzbri) n lampone m. **raspberry cane** n lampone m.

rat (ræt) n ratto m.

rate (reit) n 1 prezzo m. tariffa f. 2 imposta f. 3 velocità f. 4 comm tasso m. **at any rate** comunque. ~vt 1 valutare. 2 stimare, considerare. **rate payer** n contribuente m.

rather ('rɑːðə) adv piuttosto, alquanto, abbastanza. interj certo!

ratio ('reiʃiou) n ragione, proporzione f.

ration ('ræʃən) n 1 razione f. 2 pl viveri m pl. vt razionare. **rationing** n razionamento m.

rational ('ræʃənəl) adj ragionevole, razionale. **rationalism** n razionalismo m. **rationalization** n razionalizzazione f. **rationalize** vt razionalizzare.

rattle ('rætl) n 1 (toy) sonaglio m. 2 rumore, fracasso, tintinnio m. vt risuonare. vi far rumore.

raucous ('rɔːkəs) adj rauco, aspro.

ravage ('rævidʒ) vt 1 devastare, rovinare. **ravages** n pl danni m pl. devastazione f.

rave (reiv) vi delirare. **rave about** andare pazzo per.

raven ('reivən) n corvo m. adj corvino. **ravenous** adj affamato, vorace.

ravine (rə'viːn) n burrone m. gola f.

ravioli (rævi'ouli) n pl ravioli m pl.

ravish ('ræviʃ) vt 1 violare, stuprare. 2 estasiare. **ravishing** adj incantevole.

raw (rɔ:) adj **1** crudo. **2** greggio. **3** inesperto. **raw materials** n pl materie prime f pl.

ray (rei) n raggio m.

rayon ('reiɔn) n raion m.

razor ('reizə) n rasoio m. **razor blade** n lametta f.

reach (ri:tʃ) vt arrivare a, giungere, raggiungere. vi stendersi. n portata, capacità f. **out of/within reach** fuori/alla mano.

react (ri'ækt) vi reagire. **reaction** n reazione f. **reactionary** adj,n reazionario.

read* (ri:d) vt **1** leggere. **2** studiare. **reading** n lettura f.

readjust (ri:ə'dʒʌst) vt raggiustare. **readjustment** n raggiustamento m.

ready ('redi) adj **1** pronto, preparato. **2** disposto. **get ready** prepararsi. **ready-made** adj confezionato. **ready money** n contanti m pl. **readiness** n prontezza f.

real (riəl) adj **1** reale. **2** vero, genuino. **real estate** n beni immobili m pl. **realism** n realismo m. **realist** n realista m. **realistic** adj realistico. **reality** n realtà f. **really** adv proprio. interj davvero!

realize ('riəlaiz) vt **1** accorgersi di, rendersi conto di. **2** realizzare. **realization** n realizzazione f.

realm (relm) n regno, dominio m.

reap (ri:p) vt mietere, raccogliere.

reappear (ri:ə'piə) vi riapparire. **reappearance** n ricomparsa f.

rear[1] (riə) n parte posteriore f. dietro m. **in the rear** al di dietro. ~adj posteriore. **rear admiral** n contrammiraglio m. **rearguard** n retroguardia f.

rear[2] (riə) vt allevare, coltivare. vi impennarsi. **rearing** n allevamento m.

rearrange (riə'reindʒ) vt riordinare, riarrangiare. **rearrangement** n riordinamento m.

reason ('ri:zən) n ragione, causa f. motivo m. vi ragionare, discorrere. **reasonable** adj ragionevole, giusto. **reasoning** n ragionamento m.

reassure (ri:ə'ʃuə) vt rassicurare.

rebate ('ri:beit) n sconto m. riduzione, restituzione f.

rebel (adj,n 'rebəl; v ri'bel) adj,n ribelle. vi ribellarsi. **rebellion** n ribellione, rivolta f. **rebellious** adj ribelle, disubbidiente.

rebound (v ri'baund; n 'ri:baund) vi rimbalzare. n **1** rimbalzo m. **2** reazione f.

rebuff (ri'bʌf) n rifiuto m. vt respingere, rifiutare.

rebuild (ri:'bild) vt ricostruire. **rebuilding** n ricostruzione f.

rebuke (ri'bju:k) n rimprovero, biasimo m. sgridata f. vt rimproverare, sgridare.

recall (ri'kɔ:l) vt richiamare, ricordare, rievocare.

recede (ri'si:d) vi recedere, ritirarsi.

receipt (ri'si:t) n ricevuta, quietanza f.

receive (ri'si:v) vt ricevere, accogliere. **receiver** n **1** (telephone) ricevitore m **2** destinatario m.

recent ('ri:sənt) adj recente, nuovo. **recently** adv di recente, in questi giorni.

receptacle (ri'septəkəl) n recipiente, ricettacolo m.

reception (ri'sepʃən) n **1** ricevimento m. accoglienza f. **2** tech ricezione f. **receptionist** n segretaria f. **receptive** adj recettivo.

recess (ri'ses) n **1** nicchia, alcova f. recesso m. **2** vacanze f pl.

recession (ri'seʃən) n recessione f.

recipe ('resipi) n ricetta f.

recipient (ri'sipiənt) n destinatario m. adj ricevente, ricettivo.

reciprocate (ri'siprəkeit) vt contraccambiare, reciprocare. **reciprocity** n reciprocità f. **reciprocal** adj reciproco.

recite (ri'sait) vt recitare, narrare, raccontare. **recital** n **1** racconto m. narrazione f. **2** mus concerto m.

reckless ('rekləs) adj temerario, imprudente. **recklessness** n temerità, imprudenza f.

reckon ('rekən) vt **1** contare, computare. **2** giudicare. **reckoning** n conto, calcolo m.

reclaim (ri'kleim) vt **1** redimere. **2** (land) bonificare. **reclamation** n **1** redenzione f. **2** bonifica f.

recline (ri'klain) vt appoggiare, reclinare. vi appoggiarsi, sdraiarsi.

recluse (ri'klu:s) n recluso, eremita m.

recognize ('rekəgnaiz) vt riconoscere. **recognition** n riconoscimento m.

recoil (ri'kɔil) vi rinculare, indietreggiare. n rinculo, indietreggiamento m.

recollect (rekə'lekt) vt ricordarsi di. **recollection** n ricordo m. memoria f.

recommence (ri:kə'mens) vt,vi ricominciare.

recommend (rekə'mend) vt raccomandare. **recommendation** n raccomandazione f.

recompense ('rekəmpens) n ricompensa, rimunerazione f. vt ricompensare, rimunerare.

reconcile ('rekənsail) vt riconciliare, comporre. **reconciliation** n riconciliazione f. **reconciliatory** adj riconciliatorio.

reconstruct (ri:kən'strʌkt) *vt* ricostruire. **reconstruction** *n* ricostruzione *f*.

record (*v* ri'kɔ:d; *n* 'rekɔ:d) *vt* registrare, notare. *n* 1 ricordo, registro *m*. 2 *sport* record, primato *m*. 3 *mus* disco *m*. **record player** *n* giradischi *m*.

recount (ri'kaunt) *vt* raccontare, narrare.

recover (ri'kʌvə) *vt* ricuperare, riprendere. *vi* rimettersi, guarire. **recovery** *n* 1 ricupero *m*. 2 *med* guarigione *f*.

recreation (rekri'eiʃən) *n* divertimento, passatempo *m*. ricreazione *f*.

recruit (ri'kru:t) *n* recluta *f*. *vt* reclutare. **recruitment** *n* reclutamento *m*.

rectangle ('rektæŋgəl) *n* rettangolo *m*. **rectangular** *adj* rettangolare.

rectify ('rektifai) *vt* correggere, rettificare.

recuperate (ri'kju:pəreit) *vt* ricuperare. *vi* ricuperarsi, rimettersi. **recuperation** *n* ricupero *m*.

recur (ri'kə:) *vi* ricorrere, ritornare. **recurrence** *n* 1 ricorrenza *f*. 2 *med* ripresa *f*. **recurrent** *adj* ricorrente, periodico.

red (red) *adj,n* rosso *m*. **turn red** arrossire. **redcurrant** *n* ribes *m*. **red-handed** *adj* in flagrante. **reddish** *adj* rossastro.

redeem (ri'di:m) *vt* redimere, riscattare, salvare. **redeeming** *adj* compensatore. **redemption** *n* redenzione *f*.

redevelop (ri:di'veləp) *vt* ricostruire. **redevelopment** *n* ricostruzione *f*.

Red Indian *n* pellerossa *m,f*.

redress (ri'dres) *n* riparazione *f*. rimedio *m*. *vt* riparare, correggere.

reduce (ri'dju:s) *vt* ridurre, diminuire. **reduction** *n* riduzione, diminuzione *f*.

redundant (ri'dʌndənt) *adj* ridondante. **redundancy** *n* ridondanza *f*.

reed (ri:d) *n* canna *f*.

reef (ri:f) *n* scoglio *m*. scogliera *f*.

reek (ri:k) *n* fumo, vapore, puzzo *m*. *vi* puzzare.

reel¹ (ri:l) *n* 1 aspo, rocchetto *m*. 2 *phot* rotolo *m*. *vt* aggomitolare.

reel² (ri:l) *vi* vacillare, girare.

re-establish (ri:i'stæbliʃ) *vt* ristabilire. **re-establishment** *n* ristabilimento *m*.

refectory (ri'fektəri) *n* refettorio *m*. mensa *f*.

refer (ri'fə:) *vt* 1 riferire, rimandare. 2 attribuire, ascrivere. *vi* 1 rivolgersi. 2 alludere. **referee** *n* arbitro *m*. *vt* arbitrare. **reference** *n* 1 riferimento *m*. allusione *f*. 2 referenza, raccomandazione *f*. **referendum** *n*, *pl* **-da** referendum *m*.

refill (*v* ri:'fil; *n* 'ri:fil) *vt* riempire, rifornire. *n* rifornimento *m*. refill *m* invar.

refine (ri'fain) *vt* raffinare, purificare. **refined** *adj* colto, elegante. **refinement** *n* raffinatezza, eleganza, sottigliezza *f*. **refinery** *n* raffineria *f*.

reflation (ri'fleiʃən) *n* inflazione controllata *f*.

reflect (ri'flekt) *vt* riflettere. *vi* riflettere, pensare, meditare. **reflection** *n* 1 riflessione *f*. 2 biasimo *m*. **reflective** *adj* riflessivo, pensieroso. **reflector** *n* riflettore *m*.

reflex ('ri:fleks) *adj,n* riflesso *m*. **reflexive** *adj* riflessivo.

reform (ri'fɔ:m) *n* riforma *f*. *vt* riformare, correggere. *vi* riformarsi, correggersi. **reformation** *n* riforma *f*. **reformer** *n* riformatore *m*.

refract (ri'frækt) *vt* rifrangere.

refrain¹ (ri'frein) *vi* frenarsi, trattenersi.

refrain² (ri'frein) *n* ripresa *f*.

refresh (ri'freʃ) *vt* rinfrescare, ristorare. **refreshments** *n pl* rinfreschi *m pl*.

refrigerate (ri'fridʒəreit) *vt* refrigerare. **refrigeration** *n* refrigerazione *f*. **refrigerator** *n* frigorifero *m*.

refuel (ri:'fju:əl) *vt* rifornire di carburante. *vi* rifornirsi di carburante.

refuge ('refju:dʒ) *n* rifugio, asilo *m*. **take refuge** rifugiarsi. **refugee** *n* rifugiato, esule, profugo *m*.

refund (*v* ri'fʌnd; *n* 'ri:fʌnd) *vt* rimborsare, restituire. *n* rimborso *m*.

refuse¹ (ri'fju:z) *vt* rifiutare, vietare. *vi* rifiutarsi. **refusal** *n* rifiuto *m*.

refuse² ('refju:s) *n* immondizie *f pl*. rifiuti *m pl*.

refute (ri'fju:t) *vt* confutare, ribattere.

regain (ri'gein) *vt* riprendere, riacquistare, ricuperare.

regal ('ri:gəl) *adj* regale, reale.

regard (ri'gɑ:d) *n* 1 rispetto *m*. 2 sguardo *m*. 3 considerazione, stima *f*. 4 *pl* saluti *m pl*. **with regard to** quanto a. ~*vt* considerare, stimare. **regardless** *adj* senza riguardo. **regardless of** indifferente a.

regatta (ri'gɑ:tə) *n* regata *f*.

regent ('ri:dʒənt) *n* reggente *m*. **regency** *n* reggenza *f*.

regime (rei'ʒi:m) *n* regime *m*.

regiment ('redʒimənt) *n* reggimento *m*. *vt* reggimentare. **regimental** *adj* reggimentale. **regimentation** *n* reggimentazione *f*.

region ('ri:dʒən) n regione f. **regional** adj regionale.

register ('redʒistə) n 1 registro m. 2 pol lista elettorale f. vt 1 registrare, indicare. 2 (post) raccomandare. vi iscriversi. **registrar** n segretario m. **registration** n registrazione f. **registry office** n ufficio dello stato civile m. anagrafe f.

regress (ri'gres) vi regredire. **regression** n regressione f. **regressive** adj regressivo.

regret (ri'gret) vt deplorare, rammaricarsi di. n dispiacere, rammarico, rincrescimento m. **regrettable** adj spiacevole.

regular ('regjulə) adj regolare, normale, ordinato. **regular soldier** n soldato di professione m. **regularity** n regolarità f.

regulate ('regjuleit) vt regolare, moderare. **regulation** n 1 regola, ordinanza f. 2 regolamento m. adj regolamentare. **regulator** n regolatore m.

rehabilitate (ri:ə'biliteit) vt riabilitare. **rehabilitation** n riabilitazione f.

rehearse (ri'hə:s) vt 1 ripetere, narrare. 2 Th provare. **rehearsal** n 1 ripetizione f. 2 Th prova f.

reheat (ri:'hi:t) vt riscaldare di nuovo.

reign (rein) n regno m. vi regnare.

reimburse (ri:im'bə:s) vt rimborsare, rifondere. **reimbursement** n rimborso m.

rein (rein) n 1 redine f 2 freno m.

reincarnation (ri:inka:'neiʃən) n rincarnazione f.

reindeer ('reindiə) n invar renna f.

reinforce (ri:in'fɔ:s) vt rinforzare, rafforzare. **reinforcement** n rinforzo m.

reinstate (ri:in'steit) vt ristabilire, reintegrare. **reinstatement** n ristabilimento m. reintegrazione f.

reinvest (ri:in'vest) vt rinvestire. **reinvestment** n rinvestimento m.

reissue (ri:'iʃu:) n 1 ristampa f. 2 comm nuova emissione f. vt 1 ristampare, ripubblicare. 2 comm emettere di nuovo.

reject (v ri'dʒekt; n 'ri:dʒekt) vt rifiutare, respingere. n rifiuto m. **rejection** n rifiuto m. ripulsa f.

rejoice (ri'dʒɔis) vi rallegrarsi, gioire, godere. **rejoicing** n allegrezza, gioia f.

rejuvenate (ri'dʒu:vəneit) vt ringiovanire. **rejuvenation** n ringiovanimento m.

relapse (ri'læps) n ricaduta f. vi ricadere.

relate (ri'leit) vt 1 raccontare, narrare. 2 riferire.

vi riferirsi, aver rapporto. **related** adj connesso, congiunto. **be related to** essere parente di. **relation** n 1 parente m,f. 2 narrazione f. 3 rapporto m. **relationship** n 1 parentela f. 2 rapporto m. **relative** n parente m,f. adj relativo, rispettivo. **relativity** n relatività f.

relax (ri'læks) vt rilassare, allentare, riposare. vi riposarsi, distrarsi. **relaxation** n 1 ricreazione f. riposo m. 2 rilassamento m. 3 svago m.

relay (n 'ri:lei; v ri'lei) n 1 muta f. 2 trasmissione f. vt 1 cambiare. 2 ritrasmettere. **relay race** n corsa a staffetta f.

release (ri'li:s) vt liberare, lasciar andare. n liberazione f.

relent (ri'lent) vi pentirsi, cedere. **relentless** adj inflessibile, severo.

relevant ('reləvənt) adj relativo, pertinente. **relevancy** n rapporto m.

reliable (ri'laiəbəl) adj fidato, sicuro. **reliability** n fidatezza, sicurezza f.

relic ('relik) n 1 reliquia f. 2 pl resti, avanzi m pl.

relief (ri'li:f) n 1 sollievo, soccorso m. 2 aiuto m. 3 rilievo m. 4 mil cambio m.

relieve (ri'li:v) vt 1 sollevare, mitigare. 2 soccorrere, aiutare.

religion (ri'lidʒən) n religione f. **religious** adj religioso, pio, devoto.

relinquish (ri'liŋkwiʃ) vt abbandonare, rinunziare a. **relinquishment** n abbandono m.

relish ('reliʃ) n 1 gusto m. 2 condimento m. vt gustare, godere.

relive (ri:'liv) vt,vi rivivere.

reluctant (ri'lʌktənt) adj riluttante, poco disposto a. **reluctance** n riluttanza, avversione f. **reluctantly** adv con riluttanza.

rely (ri'lai) vi contare, fidarsi. **reliance** n confidenza, fiducia f.

remain (ri'mein) vi rimanere, restare. **remainder** n 1 resto, rimanente m. 2 math avanzo m. **remains** n pl resti, avanzi m pl.

remand (ri'mɑ:nd) vt rimandare in carcere sotto processo.

remark (ri'mɑ:k) n osservazione f. commento m. vt osservare, notare. vi fare commenti. **remarkable** adj notevole, straordinario.

remarry (ri:'mæri) vt,vi risposarsi.

remedy ('remədi) n rimedio m. vt rimediare a.

remember (ri'membə) vt ricordarsi di, rimembrare. vi ricordarsi. **remembrance** n ricordo m. memoria, rimembranza f.

remind (ri'maind) vt ricordare, richiamare alla mente. **reminder** n ricordo m.

reminiscence (remi'nisəns) n reminiscenza f. **reminiscent** adj che fa ricordare.

remiss (ri'mis) adj negligente, trascurato. **remission** n remissione f. perdono m.

remit (ri'mit) vt 1 rimandare. 2 rimettere. 3 ridurre. vi mitigarsi. **remittance** n rimessa f.

remnant ('remnənt) n 1 resto, avanzo m. 2 (of material) scampolo m.

remorse (ri'mɔːs) n rimorso m.

remote (ri'mout) adj lontano, remoto.

remove (ri'muːv) vt 1 spostare, trasferire, rimuovere. 2 eliminare. vi sgombrare, trasferirsi. **removal** n spostamento, trasferimento m.

remunerate (ri'mjuːnəreit) vt rimunerare. **remuneration** n rimunerazione f. **remunerative** adj rimunerativo.

renaissance (ri'neisəns) n rinascimento m.

rename (riː'neim) vt rinominare.

render ('rendə) vt rendere, fare.

rendezvous ('rɒndivuː) n appuntamento m.

renew (ri'njuː) vt 1 rinnovare. 2 sostituire. **renewal** n 1 rinnovamento m. 2 ripresa f.

renounce (ri'nauns) vt rinunciare a, ripudiare. **renouncement** n rinuncia f. **renunciation** n rinunzia f.

renovate ('renəveit) vt rinnovare. **renovation** n rinnovamento m.

renown (ri'naun) n fama, rinomanza f. **renowned** adj famoso, celebre.

rent (rent) vt affittare, prendere in affitto, noleggiare. n affitto m. **rental** n affitto m.

reopen (riː'oupən) vt riaprire. vi riaprirsi. **reopening** n riapertura f.

reorganize (riː'ɔːgənaiz) vt riorganizzare. **reorganization** n riorganizzazione f.

repair (ri'pɛə) vt riparare, rifare, aggiustare. vi rifugiarsi, recarsi. n 1 riparazione f. 2 stato m.

repartee (repɑ'tiː) n riposta pronta f. rimbecco m.

repatriate (riː'pætrieit) vt rimpatriare. **repatriation** n rimpatrio m.

repay (ri'pei) vt 1 rimborsare, restituire. 2 ricompensare. **repayment** n 1 rimborso m. restituzione f. 2 ricompensa f.

repeal (ri'piːl) vt abrogare, revocare, annullare. n abrogazione f. annullamento m.

repeat (ri'piːt) vt ripetere, rifare. vi ripetersi. n ripetizione f. **repeatedly** adv ripetutamente.

repel (ri'pel) vt respingere. **repellent** adj repellente.

repent (ri'pent) vi pentirsi. **repentance** n penitenza f. **repentant** adj penitente, contrito.

repercussion (riːpə'kʌʃən) n ripercussione f.

repertoire ('repətwɑː) n repertorio m.

repertory ('repətri) n repertorio m.

repetition (repə'tiʃən) n ripetizione, copia f.

replace (ri'pleis) vt 1 rimettere a posto, restituire. 2 sostituire. **replacement** n restituzione, sostituzione f.

replay (v riː'plei; n 'riːplei) vt giocare di nuovo. n 1 partita ripetuta f. 2 ripetizione f.

replenish (ri'pleniʃ) vt riempire, rifornire.

replica ('replikə) n replica f. facsimile m.

reply (ri'plai) n risposta f. vi rispondere.

report (re'pɔːt) n 1 rapporto, resoconto m. 2 diceria f. 3 educ pagella f. vt 1 rapportare, raccontare. 2 fare la cronaca di. vi fare il cronista. **reporter** n giornalista, corrispondente m,f.

repose (ri'pouz) n riposo m. vi 1 riposarsi. 2 fondarsi.

represent (repri'zent) vt rappresentare. **representation** n rappresentazione f. **representative** n 1 rappresentante m,f. 2 deputato m. adj rappresentativo.

repress (ri'pres) vt reprimere, frenare. **repression** n repressione f. **repressive** adj repressivo.

reprieve (ri'priːv) n proroga, sospensione, grazia f. vt sospendere la sentenza di, graziare.

reprimand ('reprimɑːnd) n rimprovero m. sgridata f. vt rimproverare, sgridare.

reprint (v riː'print; n 'riːprint) vt ristampare. n ristampa f.

reprisal (ri'praizal) n rappresaglia f.

reproach (ri'proutʃ) vt rimproverare, biasimare. n rimprovero, biasimo m.

reproduce (riːprə'djuːs) vt riprodurre. vi riprodursi. **reproduction** n riproduzione f.

reptile ('reptail) n rettile m.

republic (ri'pʌblik) n repubblica f. **republican** adj,n repubblicano.

repudiate (ri'pjuːdieit) vt ripudiare, sconfessare. **repudiation** n ripustio m. sconfessione f.

repugnant (ri'pʌgnənt) adj ripugnante, spiacevole, contrario. **repugnance** n ripugnanza f. avversione f.

repulsion (ri'pʌlʃən) n ripulsione, ripulsa f. rifiuto m. **repulsive** adj ripulsivo, schifoso, ripugnante.

repute (ri'pju:t) n fama f. nome m. vt reputare, stimare, credere. **reputable** adj stimabile, reputato, onorevole. **reputation** n riputazione, fama f. onore m. **reputedly** adv secondo l'opinione generale.

request (ri'kwest) n richiesta, domanda f. vt chiedere, domandare, pregare.

requiem ('rekwiəm) n requiem m.

require (ri'kwaiə) vt 1 richiedere, esigere. 2 domandare. 3 aver bisogno di. **requirement** n 1 bisogno m. 2 esigenza f.

requisition (rekwi'ziʃən) n 1 richiesta, domanda f. 2 requisizione f. vt requisire.

re-read (ri:'ri:d) vt rileggere.

re-route (ri:'ru:t) vt deviare.

re-run (ri:'rʌn) vt ripetere. n ripetizione f.

resale ('ri:seil) n rivendita f.

rescue ('reskju:) n 1 soccorso, aiuto m. 2 liberazione f. vt 1 soccorrere, aiutare. 2 liberare.

research (ri'sə:tʃ) n 1 ricerca f. 2 studio m. vi far ricerche, ricercare. **researcher** n ricercatore, investigatore m.

resell (ri:'sel) vt rivendere.

resemble (ri'zembəl) vt somigliare a, assomigliare a. **resemblance** n somiglianza, rassomiglianza f.

resent (ri'zent) vt offendersi di, arrabbiarsi per. **resentful** adj acrimonioso, risentito. **resentment** n risentimento m.

reserve (ri'zə:v) vt riservare. n 1 riserva f. riserbo m. riservatezza f. **reservation** n 1 riserva f. 2 prenotazione f. **reserved** adj riservato.

reservoir ('rezəvwa:) n serbatoio m. cisterna f.

reside (ri'zaid) vi abitare, dimorare, stare. **residence** n abitazione, residenza, dimora f. **resident** n residente, abitante m,f. adj residente. **residential** adj residenziale.

residue ('rezidju:) n residuo, resto, avanzo m.

resign (ri'zain) vt rinunciare a. vi dimettersi. **resignation** n 1 dimissione f. 2 rassegnazione f. **resigned** adj rassegnato.

resilient (ri'ziliənt) adj 1 rimbalzante, elastico. 2 capace di ricupero. **resilience** n 1 elasticità f. 2 capacità di ricupero f.

resin ('rezin) n resina f. **resinous** adj resinoso.

resist (ri'zist) vt resistere a, opporsi a. vi resistere. **resistance** n resistenza f. **resistant** adj resistente.

resit (ri:'sit) vt rifare.

resolute ('rezalu:t) adj risoluto, deciso, determinato. **resolution** n 1 risoluzione f. 2 decisione f. 3 determinazione f.

resolve (ri'zɔlv) vt risolvere, decidere. vi risolversi, decidersi. n risoluzione, decisione f.

resonant ('rezənənt) adj risonante. **resonance** n risonanza f.

resort (ri'zɔ:t) vi ricorrere, recarsi. n 1 ricorso, ritrovo m. 2 stazione di villeggiatura f.

resound (ri'zaund) vi risuonare, echeggiare.

resource (ri'zɔ:s) n 1 risorsa f. 2 espediente, mezzo m. **resourceful** adj intraprendente.

respect (ri'spekt) n riguardo, rispetto m. stima f. vt stimare, rispettare. **respectable** adj rispettabile. **respectful** adj rispettoso. **respective** adj rispettivo.

respite ('respait) n 1 tregua f. 2 respiro, riposo m.

respond (ri'spɔnd) vi rispondere, reagire. **response** n risposta f. **responsibility** n responsabilità f. **responsible** adj responsabile. **responsive** adj responsivo.

rest[1] (rest) n riposo m. sosta f. vi 1 riposarsi. 2 appoggiarsi. 3 fermarsi, stare. vt far riposare. **restless** adj agitato, turbato, inquieto. **restlessness** n agitazione f.

rest[2] (rest) n 1 resto, rimanente m. 2 altri m pl.

restaurant ('restərɔnt) n ristorante m. trattoria f.

restore (ri'stɔ:) vt 1 restaurare. 2 ristabilire. 3 restituire. **restoration** n 1 restaurazione, restituzione f. 2 arch restauro m.

restrain (ri'strein) vt trattenere, frenare, reprimere. **restraint** n freno, ritegno m. restrizione f.

restrict (ri'strikt) vt restringere, limitare. **restriction** n restrizione f. **restrictive** adj restrittivo.

result (ri'zʌlt) n risultato, esito m. conseguenza f. vi risultare.

resume (ri'zju:m) vt 1 riprendere. 2 riassumere. **resumption** n ripresa f.

résumé ('rezumei) n sunto m.

resurrect (rezə'rekt) vt risuscitare. **resurrection** n risurrezione f.

retail ('ri:teil) n vendita al minuto or al dettaglio f. adj al minuto, al dettaglio. vt vendere al minuto or al dettaglio. **retailer** n venditore al minuto m.

retain (ri'tein) vt ritenere, mantenere, conservare.

retaliate (ri'tælieit) vt ricambiare insulto. vi rendere la pariglia, reagire. **retaliation** n rappresaglia, vendetta f.

retard (ri'tɑ:d) vt,vi ritardare.

reticent ('retisənt) adj reticente. **reticence** n reticenza f.

retina ('retinə) n retina f.

retire (ri'taiə) vi ritirarsi, andare in pensione. **retirement** n ritiro, riposo m.

retort[1] (ri'tɔ:t) n ritorsione, risposta aspra f. vt ribattere, rispondere aspramente. vi rimbeccare.

retort[2] (ri'tɔ:t) n sci storta f.

retrace (ri'treis) vt rintracciare. **retrace one's steps** rifare la strada.

retract (ri'trækt) vt ritirare, ritrarre, disdire. vi ritrattarsi.

retreat (ri'tri:t) n 1 ritiro, asilo m. 2 mil ritirata f. vi ritirarsi, andarsene.

retrieve (ri'tri:v) vt ricuperare, riprendere, riacquistare.

retrograde ('retrəgreid) adj retrogrado.

retrogressive (retrə'gresiv) adj regressivo.

retrospect ('retrəspekt) n sguardo retrospettivo m. **in retrospect** in retrospettivo.

return (ri'tə:n) vi tornare, ritornare. vt 1 rendere, restituire. 2 contraccambiare. n 1 ritorno m. 2 rinvio m. restituzione f. 3 comm rendiconto m. **return ticket** n biglietto di andata e ritorno m.

reunite (ri:ju:'nait) vt riunire. vi riunirsi. **reunion** n riunione f.

reveal (ri'vi:l) vt rivelare, manifestare. **revelation** n rivelazione f.

revel ('revəl) vi **revel in** divertirsi di.

revenge (ri'vendʒ) n vendetta f.

revenue ('revənju:) n 1 entrata f. reddito m. 2 fisco m.

reverberate (ri'və:bəreit) vi riverberare, risuonare. **reverberation** n riverberazione f. riverbero m.

reverence ('revərəns) n riverenza, venerazione f.

reverse (ri'və:s) n 1 contrario, opposto m. 2 rovescio m. 3 mot retromarcia f. adj 1 contrario. 2 rovescio. vt 1 rivoltare, capovolgere. 2 revocare. vi mot far retromarcia.

revert (ri'və:t) vi ritornare.

review (ri'vju:) n 1 rivista f. 2 recensione f. 3 revisione f. vt 1 rivedere, ripassare. 2 criticare, recensire.

revise (ri'vaiz) vt rivedere, correggere. **revision** n revisione, correzione f.

revive (ri'vaiv) vt ravvivare, rinnovare. vi riani-

marsi, rinascere. **revival** n rinascimento, risorgimento m.

revoke (ri'vouk) vt revocare, ritirare.

revolt (ri'voult) n rivolta, ribellione f. vi ribellarsi, rivoltarsi. vi disgustare. **revolting** adj ripugnante, disgustoso, nauseante. **revolution** n rivoluzione f. **revolutionary** adj,n rivoluzionario.

revolve (ri'vɔlv) vi girare. **revolving** adj girevole, rotante. **revolver** n revolver m invar.

revue (ri'vju:) n rivista f.

revulsion (ri'vʌlʃən) n ripugnanza, repulsione f.

reward (ri'wɔ:d) n ricompensa f. compenso m. vt ricompensare, retribuire, premiare.

rhetoric ('retərik) n retorica f. **rhetorical** adj retorico. **rhetorical question** n domanda retorica f.

rheumatism ('ru:mətizəm) n reumatismo m. **rheumatic** adj reumatico.

rhinoceros (rai'nɔsərəs) n rinoceronte m.

Rhodesia (rou'di:ʃə) n Rhodesia f. **Rhodesian** adj,n rhodesiano.

rhododendron (roudə'dendrən) n rododendro m.

rhubarb ('ru:bɑ:b) n rabarbaro m.

rhyme (raim) n rima, poesia f. vt mettere in rima. vi rimare.

rhythm ('riðəm) n ritmo m. **rhythmic** adj ritmico.

rib (rib) n 1 anat costola f. 2 stecca f.

ribbon ('ribən) n nastro m.

rice (rais) n riso m.

rich (ritʃ) adj ricco. **riches** n pl ricchezze f pl. **richness** n ricchezza, opulenza f.

rickety ('rikiti) adj zoppicante, sgangherato.

rid* (rid) vt liberare, sbarazzare. **get rid of** liberarsi di, sbarazzarsi di. **riddance** n liberazione f.

riddle[1] ('ridl) n indovinello, enigma m.

riddle[2] ('ridl) vt crivellare, vagliare.

ride* (raid) vt cavalcare. vi andare a cavallo. n 1 cavalcata f. 2 corsa f. giro m. **rider** n cavaliere m. **riding** n equitazione f.

ridge (ridʒ) n 1 geog cresta, cima f. 2 arch colmo, comignolo m. 3 solco m.

ridicule ('ridikju:l) n ridicolo m. vt mettere in ridicolo, canzonare. **ridiculous** adj ridicolo.

rife (raif) adj dominante, diffuso, generale. **be rife** imperversare.

rifle[1] ('raifəl) n fucile m. carabina f.

rifle[2] ('raifəl) vt svaligiare, saccheggiare, rubare.

rift (rift) n (of a friendship) spaccatura, rottura f.

rig (rig) n 1 arnese m. 2 naut impianto m. vt truccare. **rigging** n attrezzatura f.

right (rait) adj 1 destro. 2 giusto. 3 opportuno. adv 1 bene. 2 diritto. 3 a destra. n 1 diritto m 2 destra f. **on the right** a destra. ~vt 1 correggere. 2 raddrizzare. **right angle** n angolo retto m. **right hand** n mano destra f. **right-handed** adj destro. **right of way** n diritto di passaggio m. **right-wing** adj della destra.

righteous ('rait∫əs) adj giusto, retto, virtuoso. **righteousness** n giustizia f.

rigid ('ridʒid) adj rigido, inflessibile.

rigour ('rigə) n rigore m. severità f. **rigorous** adj rigoroso, rigido.

rim (rim) n orlo, bordo, margine m.

rind (raind) n 1 bot buccia f. 2 (of cheese) crosta f. 3 (of bacon) contenna f.

ring [1] (riŋ) n 1 anello m. 2 cerchio m. 3 sport recinto m. 4 comm sindacato m. vt circondare. **ringleader** n caporione m. **ring-road** n strada circolare f. **ringside** adj vicino all'arena.

ring [2] (riŋ) n 1 suono, squillo, tintinnio m. 2 risonanza f. vi suonare, squillare. vt 1 suonare. 2 chiamare. **ring up** telefonare.

rink (riŋk) n recinto di pattinaggio m. pista di pattinaggio f.

rinse (rins) vt risciacquare. n risciacquatura f.

riot ('raiət) n tumulto m. rivolta f. vi tumultuare, sollevarsi. **riotous** adj tumultuante, sedizioso.

rip (rip) n lacerazione f. squarcio, strappo m. vt squarciare, strappare.

ripe (raip) adj maturo. **ripen** vt,vi maturare. **ripeness** n maturità f.

ripple ('ripəl) n increspamento m. vi incresparsi.

rise [*] (raiz) vi 1 alzarsi, levarsi. 2 (of sun) sorgere. 3 salire, aumentare. n 1 geog salita, elevazione f. 2 comm aumento m.

risk (risk) n rischio, pericolo m. vt rischiare, azzardare.

rissole ('risoul) n crocchetta f.

rite (rait) n rito m.

ritual ('ritjuəl) adj,n rituale m.

rival ('raivəl) adj,n rivale. vt,vi rivaleggiare. **rivalry** n rivalità f.

river ('rivə) n fiume m. **down river** a valle. **up river** a monte. **river bank** n argine m. **riverbed** n letto del fiume m. **riverside** n riva del fiume f.

rivet ('rivit) n chiodo ribadito m. vt ribadire, fissare.

road (roud) n strada, via f. **roadblock** n blocco

stradale m. **roadside** n ciglio della strada m. **roadworthy** adj atto a prendere la strada.

roam (roum) vi girovagare, vagare, errare. vt percorrere.

roar (rɔ:) n 1 urlo, ruggito m. 2 muggito m. 3 (of laughter) scroscio m. vi 1 urlare, ruggire. 2 muggire. 3 scrosciare. 4 scoppiare.

roast (roust) n arrosto m. vt 1 arrostire. 2 (coffee) tostare. **roast beef** n arrosto di manzo m.

rob (rɔb) vt rubare, spogliare, svaligiare. **robber** n ladro m. **robbery** n furto m.

robe (roub) n vestito lungo. m toga f.

robin ('rɔbin) n pettirosso m.

robot ('roubɔt) n automa m.

robust (rou'bʌst) adj robusto, forte, vigoroso.

rock [1] (rɔk) n 1 roccia, rupe f. 2 sasso, scoglio m. **rock-bottom** adj bassissimo. **rock garden** n giardino alpino m. **rocky** adj roccioso, sassoso.

rock [2] (rɔk) vt cullare, dondolare. vi vacillare, oscillare, dondolarsi. **rocker** n asse ricurvo m. **rocking-chair** n sedia a dondolo f. **rocking-horse** n cavallo a dondolo m.

rocket ('rɔkit) n razzo m. vi rimbalzare.

rod (rɔd) n 1 bacchetta, verga f. 2 (fishing) canna per pescare f.

rode (roud) v see **ride**.

rodent ('roudnt) n roditore m.

roe (rou) n uova di pesce f pl.

rogue (roug) n 1 briccone, furfante m. 2 (child) biricchino m. **roguish** adj 1 furfante, furbo. 2 biricchino.

role (roul) n ruolo m.

roll (roul) n 1 rotolo m. 2 (bread) panino m. 3 elenco m. 4 rullo m. vt 1 arrotolare. 2 rullare. vi 1 rotolarsi. 2 rullare. **rollcall** n appello m. **roller** n cilindro, rullo m. **roller-skate** n pattino a rotelle m. **rolling pin** n matterello m.

Roman Catholic adj,n cattolico.

romance n ('roumæns) 1 romanzo m. favola f. 2 avventura amorosa f. vi (rə'mæns) favoleggiare. **romantic** adj 1 romantico. 2 romanzesco. **romanticism** n romanticismo m. **romanticize** vt rendere romantico.

Rome (roum) n Roma f. **Roman** adj,n romano.

romp (rɔmp) vi giocare con chiasso. n gioco chiassoso m. **rompers** n pl pagliaccetto da bambino m.

roof (ru:f) n tetto m. vt coprire con tetto.

rook[1] (ruk) n cornacchia f. **rookery** n cornacchiaia f.

rook[2] (ruk) n game torre f.

room (ru:m) n **1** stanza, sala, camera f. **2** posto, spazio m. **roomy** adj spazioso, ampio.

roost (ru:st) n posatoio m. pertica f. vi appollaiarsi.

root[1] (ru:t) n radice f. vi attecchire, radicarsi. vt **1** piantare. **2** fissare.

root[2] (ru:t) vi frugacchiare, sradicare.

rope (roup) n corda, fune f. filo m. vt legare, cingere.

rosary ('rouzəri) n rosario m.

rose (rouz) n rosa f. **rose bush** n rosaio m. **rosette** n rosetta f. nastrino m. **rosy** adj roseo, colore di rosa.

rosemary ('rouzməri) n rosmarino m.

rot (rɔt) vt putrefare, corrompere. vi marcire, guastarsi, imputridire. n **1** putrefazione, decadenza f. **2** sl sciocchezze f pl.

rota ('routə) n lista f. **rotary** adj rotatorio, rotante. **rotate** vt,vi rotare. **rotation** n rotazione, successione f.

rotten ('rɔtn) adj marcio, putrido, guasto.

rouble ('ru:bl) n rublo m.

rouge (ru:ʒ) n rossetto m.

rough (rʌf) adj **1** ruvido, rozzo. **2** grossolano, crudo. **3** agitato. **4** tempestoso. **5** approssimativo. **rough and ready** improvvisato. **roughness** n ruvidezza f.

roulette (ru:'let) n roulette f.

round (raund) n **1** tondo m. **2** cerchio m. **3** giro m. **4** sfera f. **5** sport ripresa f. adj **1** rotondo, circolare, sferico. **2** intero. **3** franco. adv in giro, all'intorno. prep intorno a. **roundabout** n rotatoria f. adj indiretto.

rouse (rauz) vt **1** svegliare. **2** provocare, incitare. **rousing** adj eccitante, travolgente.

route (ru:t) n via, strada f. itinerario m. vt avviare.

routine (ru:'ti:n) n **1** abitudine, usanza f. **2** uso m. adj abitudinario.

rove (rouv) vi errare, vagare.

row[1] (rou) n (line) fila, riga f. rango m.

row[2] (rou) vi,vt sport remare. **rower** n rematore, canottiere m. **rowing** n canottaggio m. **rowing boat** barca a remi f.

row[3] (rau) n **1** chiasso, rumore m. **2** lite f. vi litigare.

rowdy ('raudi) adj rumoroso, tumultuoso, litigioso.

royal ('rɔiəl) adj reale, regale. **royalist** n realista

m. **royalty** n **1** regalità f. reali m pl. **2** comm diritti d'autore m pl.

rub (rʌb) n **1** fregamento, strofinamento m. **2** med frizione f. vt **1** fregare, strofinare. **2** lucidare. vi fregarsi. **rub out** cancellare.

rubber ('rʌbə) n gomma f. **rubber band** n elastico m.

rubbish ('rʌbiʃ) n **1** immondizia f. rifiuti m pl. **2** sciocchezze f pl.

rubble ('rʌbəl) n macerie f pl.

ruby ('ru:bi) n rubino m. adj di rubino, vermiglio.

rucksack ('rʌksæk) n sacco da montagna m.

rudder ('rʌdə) n timone m.

rude (ru:d) adj grossolano, offensivo, sgarbato. **rudeness** n grossolanità, inciviltà f.

rudiment ('ru:dimənt) n **1** rudimento m. **2** pl elementi m pl. **rudimentary** adj rudimentale.

rueful ('ru:fəl) adj triste, malinconico.

ruff (rʌf) n gorgiera f.

ruffian ('rʌfiən) n furfante, scellerato m.

ruffle ('rʌfəl) vt **1** increspare. **2** arruffare. **3** agitare. **4** irritare.

rug (rʌg) n **1** tappeto, tappetino m. **2** coperta da viaggio f.

rugby ('rʌgbi) n rugby m.

rugged ('rʌgid) adj ruvido, rozzo, aspro. **ruggedness** n ruvidezza f.

ruin ('ru:in) n **1** rovina f. **2** disgrazia f. disastro m. vt rovinare. **ruinous** adj rovinoso, dannoso.

rule (ru:l) n **1** regola, legge f. **2** governo, dominio m. **as a rule** di solito. ~vt regolare, governare, dirigere. **ruler** n **1** sovrano, governatore m. **2** math regolo m. **ruling** adj dirigente. n decisione f.

rum (rʌm) n rum m.

rumble ('rʌmbəl) vi rimbombare, rumoreggiare. n rumorio m.

rummage ('rʌmidʒ) vt,vi rovistare. n ricerca f. rovistio m.

rumour ('ru:mə) n diceria, voce f. vt far correre voce.

rump (rʌmp) n **1** cul culatta f. **2** natiche f pl. **rump steak** n bistecca f.

run[1] (rʌn) vi,vt correre. vi **1** fluire. **2** (of colour) spandere. vt condurre. **run away** fuggire. **run out of** esaurire. **run over** (of a car, etc.) investire. ~n **1** corsa f. **2** serie f invar. **3** corso, recinto m. **4** gita f. **5** smagliatura f. **in the long run** a lungo andare. **runway** n pista di decollo f. **runner** n **1** fattorino, messaggero

m. 2 *sport* corridore m. **runner bean** n fagiolo rampicante m. **runner-up** n secondo in una gara m. **running** n 1 corsa f. 2 marcia f. funzionamento m. 3 direzione f. *adj* 1 corrente. 2 consecutivo.

rung[1] (rʌŋ) v see **ring**[2].

rung[2] (rʌŋ) n piolo m.

rupee (ru:'pi:) n rupia f.

rupture ('rʌptʃə) n 1 rottura f. 2 *med* ernia f. vt rompere.

rural ('ruərəl) *adj* rurale, campestre.

rush[1] (rʌʃ) vi precipitarsi, affrettarsi. vt prendere d'assalto. n 1 impeto m. 2 attacco m. 3 fretta, furia f. **rush hour** n ora di punta f.

rush[2] (rʌʃ) n *bot* giunco m.

Russia ('rʌʃə) n Russia f. **Russian** *adj,n* russo. **Russian (language)** n russo m.

rust (rʌst) n ruggine f. vt corrodere. vi arrugginirsi. **rusty** *adj* rugginoso.

rustic ('rʌstik) *adj* rustico, campagnolo, rurale.

rustle ('rʌsəl) n fruscio, mormorio m. vi frusciare, stormire.

rut (rʌt) n 1 rotaia f. solco m. 2 abitudine fissa f.

ruthless ('ru:θləs) *adj* spietato, crudele, inesorabile.

rye (rai) n segale f.

S

Sabbath ('sæbəθ) n domenica f.

sable ('seibəl) n zibellino m. *adj* di zibellino.

sabotage ('sæbətɑ:ʒ) n sabotaggio m. vt sabotare.

sabre ('seibə) n sciabola f.

saccharin ('sækərin) n saccarina f.

sachet ('sæʃei) n sacchetto m.

sack (sæk) n sacco m. **get the sack** essere licenziato. ~n *inf* congedare.

sacrament ('sækrəmənt) n sacramento m.

sacred ('seikrid) *adj* 1 sacro, consacrato. 2 santo.

sacrifice ('sækrifais) n sacrificio m. vt,vi sacrificare.

sacrilege ('sækrilidʒ) n sacrilegio m. **sacriligious** *adj* sacrilego.

sad (sæd) *adj* triste, addolorato, doloroso. **sadden** vt attristare, rattristare. **sadness** n tristezza f.

saddle ('sædl) n sella f. vt sellare. **saddle with** gravare di. **saddler** n sellaio m.

sadism ('seidizəm) n sadismo m. **sadist** n sadista m.

safari (sə'fɑ:ri) n safari m *invar.*

safe (seif) *adj* salvo, sicuro, sano, intatto. **safe and sound** sano e salvo. ~n 1 cassaforte f. 2 *cul* guardavivande m *invar.* **safeguard** n salvaguardia f. vt salvaguardare. **safely** *adv* in salvo. **safety** n sicurezza, salvezza f. **safety belt** n cintura di sicurezza f. **safety pin** n spillo di sicurezza m. **safety valve** n valvola di sicurezza f.

saffron ('sæfrən) n zafferano m.

sag (sæg) vi ripiegarsi, curvarsi. n depressione f.

saga ('sɑ:gə) n saga f.

sage[1] (seidʒ) n savio m. *adj* saggio, prudente.

sage[2] (seidʒ) n *bot* salvia f.

Sagittarius (sædʒi'tɛəriəs) n Sagittario m.

sago ('seigou) n sago m.

said (sed) v see **say.**

sail (seil) n 1 vela f. 2 viaggio sul mare m. 3 (of a windmill, etc.) ala f. vi navigare, veleggiare. vt navigare, percorrere. **sailing** n navigazione f. **sailor** n marinaio m.

saint (seint) n santo m. **saintly** *adj* santo, pio.

sake (seik) n ragione, causa f.

salad ('sæləd) n insalata f. **salad dressing** n condimento d'insalata m.

salamander ('sæləmændə) n salamandra f.

salami (sə'lɑ:mi) n salame m *pl.*

salary ('sæləri) n stipendio, salario m. paga f.

sale (seil) n 1 vendita f. 2 liquidazione f. 3 spaccio m. **for sale** da vendere. **on sale** in vendita. **salesman** n commesso, venditore m. **salesmanship** n arte commerciale f.

saliva (sə'laivə) n saliva f. **salivate** vi salivare.

sallow ('sælou) *adj* olivastro, pallido.

salmon ('sæmən) n salmone m.

salon ('sælɔn) n salone, negozio m.

saloon (sə'lu:n) n 1 sala f. salone m. 2 *mot* vettura salone f.

salt (sɔ:lt) n sale m. *adj* salato, salso. vt salare. **salt cellar** n saliera f.

salute (sə'lu:t) vt salutare. n 1 saluto m. 2 *mil* salva f.

salvage ('sælvidʒ) n salvataggio, ricupero m. vt salvare, ricuperare.

salvation (sæl'veiʃən) n salvazione, salvezza f.

same (seim) *adj* 1 stesso, medesimo. 2 monotono. *pron* stesso m. **all the same** nondimeno. **the same to you!** altrettanto!

sample ('sɑ:mpəl) n campione, modello, esemplare m. vt assaggiare.

sanatorium (sænəˈtɔːriəm) n sanatorio m. casa di salute f.

sanction (ˈsæŋkʃən) n 1 sanzione f. 2 autorizzazione f. permesso m. vt 1 sanzionare. 2 permettere, autorizzare.

sanctuary (ˈsæŋktʃuəri) n santuario, asilo m.

sand (sænd) n sabbia, rena f. vt coprire di sabbia. **sandpaper** n carta vetrata f. **sandpit** n cava di rena f. **sandy** adj sabbioso.

sandal (ˈsændl) n sandalo m.

sandwich (ˈsænwidʒ) n sandwich, panino imbottito m. tartina f. vt serrare in mezzo.

sane (sein) adj sano di mente, equilibrato.
sanity n sanità di mente f.

sang (sæŋ) v see **sing**.

sanitary (ˈsænitri) adj sanitario, igienico. **sanitary towel** n assorbente igienico m. **sanitation** n igiene f.

sank (sæŋk) v see **sink**.

sap (sæp) n bot succhio m. vt indebolire.

sapphire (ˈsæfaiə) n zaffiro m.

sarcasm (ˈsɑːkæzəm) n sarcasmo m. **sarcastic** adj sarcastico.

sardine (sɑːˈdiːn) n sardina f.

Sardinia (sɑːˈdiniə) n Sardegna f. **Sardinian** adj,n sardo.

sardonic (sɑːˈdɔnik) adj sardonico.

sari (ˈsɑːri) n sari m invar.

sash[1] (sæʃ) n cintura, sciarpa f.

sash[2] (sæʃ) n arch telaio m. **sash-window** n finestra all'inglese f.

sat (sæt) v see **sit**.

Satan (ˈseitn) n Satana m.

satchel (ˈsætʃəl) n cartella, borsa f.

satellite (ˈsætəlait) n satellite m.

satin (ˈsætin) n raso m.

satire (ˈsætaiə) n satira f. **satirical** adj satirico.

satisfy (ˈsætisfai) vt soddisfare, contentare. vi soddisfare, dare soddisfazione. **satisfaction** n soddisfazione, contentezza f. **satisfactory** adj soddisfacente.

saturate (ˈsætʃəreit) vt saturare. **saturation** n saturazione f.

Saturday (ˈsætədi) n sabato m.

Saturn (ˈsætən) n Saturno m.

sauce (sɔːs) n salsa f. condimento m. **saucepan** n pentola, casseruola f. tegame m. **saucer** n sottocoppa, piattino m. **saucy** adj insolente, impertinente.

Saudi Arabia (ˈsaudi) n Arabia Saudita f.

sauna (ˈsɔːnə) n sauna f.

saunter (ˈsɔːntə) vi gironzare, girovagare.

sausage (ˈsɔsidʒ) n 1 (fresh) salsiccia f. 2 (smoked) salame m.

savage (ˈsævidʒ) adj selvaggio, selvatico, feroce. n selvaggio, barbaro m. vt mordere.

save[1] (seiv) vt 1 salvare, preservare. 2 conservare. 3 risparmiare. vi economizzare. **savings** n pl risparmi m pl.

save[2] (seiv) prep eccetto, tranne, salvo.

saviour (ˈseiviə) n 1 salvatore m. 2 cap Redentore m.

savoury (ˈseivəri) adj saporoso, saporito, gustoso. n piatto saporito m.

saw[*1] (sɔː) n sega f. vt segare. **sawdust** n segatura f.

saw[2] (sɔː) v see **see**[1].

saxophone (ˈsæksəfoun) n sassofono m.

say[*] (sei) vt,vi dire, affermare. **have one's say** dire la sua. **saying** n adagio, proverbio m.

scab (skæb) n tigna, rogna f.

scaffold (ˈskæfəld) n palco, patibolo m. **scaffolding** n impalcatura f.

scald (skɔːld) vt scottare. n scottatura, scottata f.

scale[1] (skeil) n zool scaglia, squama f.

scale[2] (skeil) n 1 piatto della bilancia m. 2 pl bilancia f.

scale[3] (skeil) n 1 gradazione, scala f. 2 mus gamma f. vt 1 scalare, graduare. 2 scavalcare.

scallop (ˈskɔləp) n 1 zool pettine m. 2 smerlo m. dentellatura f. vt smerlare.

scalp (skælp) n cuoio capelluto m. vt scotennare.

scalpel (ˈskælpəl) n scalpello m.

scampi (ˈskæmpi) n pl scampi m pl.

scan (skæn) vt 1 scrutare, esaminare. 2 lit scandire.

scandal (ˈskændl) n 1 scandalo m. maldicenza f. 2 vergogna f. **scandalous** adj scandaloso.

Scandinavia (skændiˈneiviə) n Scandinavia f. **Scandinavian** adj,n scandinavo.

scant (skænt) adj scarso, insufficiente. **scanty** adj 1 scarso, scarso. 2 sommario.

scapegoat (ˈskeipgout) n capro espiatorio m.

scar (skɑː) n cicatrice f. sfregio, segno m. vt cicatrizzare, sfregiare. vi cicatrizzarsi.

scarce (skɛəs) adj raro, scarso. **scarcely** adv appena, quasi. **scarcity** n scarsezza f.

scare (skɛə) vt spaventare, impaurire. **be scared** aver paura. ~n spavento, panico m. paura f. **scarecrow** n spauracchio m.

scarf (skɑːf) n sciarpa, cravatta f.

scarlet ('skɑːlit) *adj,n* scarlatto *m*. **scarlet fever** *n* scarlattina *f*.

scathing ('skeiðiŋ) *adj* mordace, feroce.

scatter ('skætə) *vt* spargere, diffondere, disperdere. *vi* spargersi, disperdersi.

scavenge ('skævindʒ) *vt* spazzare. **scavenger** *n* spazzino *m*.

scene (siːn) *n* 1 scena, scenata *f*. 2 spettacolo *m*. **scenery** *n* 1 paesaggio, panorama *m*. 2 Th scenario *m*.

scent (sent) *n* 1 odore, profumo *m*. 2 (of an animal) fiuto *m*. *vt* profumare.

sceptic ('skeptik) *n* scettico *m*. **sceptical** *adj* scettico. **scepticism** *n* scetticismo *m*.

sceptre ('septə) *n* scettro *m*.

schedule ('ʃedjuːl) *n* orario, prospetto *m*. scheda *f*. *vt* schedare.

scheme (skiːm) *n* schema, progetto, piano *m*. *vt* progettare. *vi* far progetti, macchinare.

schizophrenia (skitsou'friːniə) *n* schizofrenia *f*. **schizophrenic** *adj* schizofrenico.

scholar ('skɔlə) *n* 1 erudito, letterato *m*. 2 (pupil) scolaro, alunno *m*. 3 borsista *m*. **scholarship** *n* 1 borsa di studio *f*. 2 erudizione *f*.

scholastic (skə'læstik) *adj* scolastico.

school[1] (skuːl) *n* educ scuola *f*. liceo, ginnasio, collegio *m*. *vt* istruire. **schoolboy** *n* scolaro *m*. **schoolgirl** *n* scolara *f*. **schoolmaster** *n* maestro, professore *m*. **schoolmistress** *n* maestra, professoressa *f*. **schoolteacher** *n* insegnante *m,f*.

school[2] (skuːl) *n* frotta *f*.

schooner ('skuːnə) *n* goletta *f*.

science ('saiəns) *n* scienza *f*. **science fiction** *n* fantascienza *f*. **scientific** *adj* scientifico. **scientist** *n* scienziato *m*.

scissors ('sizəz) *n pl* forbici *f pl*.

scoff[1] (skɔf) *n* derisione *f*. scherno *m*. *vi* beffare, schernire. **scoff at** beffarsi di, deridere.

scoff[2] (skɔf) *vt,vi* mangiare in fretta.

scold (skould) *vt* sgridare, rimproverare. *vi* brontolare.

scone (skoun) *n* focaccina *f*.

scoop (skuːp) *n* 1 paletta *f*. 2 ramaiolo *m*. 3 *inf* colpo *m*. *vt* scavare, vuotare. **scoop up** raccogliere.

scooter ('skuːtə) *n* motoretta *f*.

scope (skoup) *n* 1 portata *f*. 2 prospettiva *f*. campo *m*.

scorch (skɔːtʃ) *vt* bruciare, scottare. *n* scottatura *f*.

score (skɔː) *n* 1 *sport* punti *m pl*. 2 sconto *m*. 3 tacca *f*. 4 ventina *f*. 5 *mus* partitura *f*. *vt* 1 *sport* segnare. 2 intagliare. *vi* far punti. **scoreboard** *n* tabellone *m*.

scorn (skɔːn) *n* sdegno, disprezzo, spregio *m*. *vt* sdegnare, sprezzare. **scornful** *adj* sdegnoso, sprezzante.

Scorpio ('skɔːpiou) *n* Scorpione *m*.

scorpion ('skɔːpiən) *n* scorpione *m*.

Scot (skɔt) *n* scozzese *m,f*.

Scotch (skɔtʃ) *adj* scozzese. *n* whisky *m invar*.

Scotland ('skɔtlənd) *n* Scozia *f*.

Scots (skɔts) *adj* scozzese.

Scottish ('skɔtiʃ) *adj* scozzese.

scoundrel ('skaundrəl) *n* mascalzone, scellerato *m*.

scour[1] ('skauə) *vt* (clean) pulire, nettare, fregare.

scour[2] ('skauə) *vt* percorrere.

scout (skaut) *n* esploratore *m*. *vi* esplorare, perlustrare. *vt* respingere.

scowl (skaul) *n* sguardo torvo *m*. *vi* aggrottare le ciglia.

scramble ('skræmbəl) *n* parapiglia, confusione *f*. *vi* affrettarsi, sgambare, arrampicarsi. **scrambled eggs** *n pl* uova strapazzate *f pl*.

scrap (skræp) *n* pezzetto, frammento *m*. briciola *f*. *vt* rigettare, scartare. **scrapbook** *n* album *m invar*. **scrap iron** *n* ferraccio *m*.

scrape (skreip) *vt* raschiare, grattare, scrostare. *n* 1 raschiatura *f*. 2 imbroglio, impaccio *m*.

scratch (skrætʃ) *n* graffio *m*. graffiatura *f*. *vt* 1 graffiare, grattare. 2 *sport* ritirare.

scrawl (skrɔːl) *n* scarabocchio *m*. *vt,vi* scarabocchiare.

scream (skriːm) *vi* gridare, strillare, urlare. *n* grido, strillo *m*.

screech (skriːtʃ) *n* strillo *m*. *vt,vi* strillare.

screen (skriːn) *n* 1 riparo *m*. 2 parafuoco, paravento *m*. 3 (cinema, etc.) schermo *m*. *vt* nascondere, proteggere.

screw (skruː) *n* vite *f*. *vt* avvitare, torcere. **screwdriver** *n* cacciavite *m*.

scribble ('skribəl) *n* scarabocchio *m*. *vt,vi* scarabocchiare.

script (skript) *n* scritto *m*. scrittura *f*.

Scripture ('skriptʃə) *n* Sacra Scrittura *f*.

scroll (skroul) *n* rotolo *m*.

scrounge (skraundʒ) *vt,vi* mendicare, scroccare.

scrub[1] (skrʌb) vt strofinare, fregare. n strofinata f. **scrubbing brush** n spazzola dura f.

scrub[2] (skrʌb) n (bush) macchia, boscaglia f.

scruffy ('skrʌfi) adj scadente, trascurato, disordinato.

scruple ('skru:pəl) n scrupolo m. **scrupulous** adj scrupoloso.

scrutiny ('skru:tini) n esame, scrutinio m. **scrutinize** vt scrutinare, investigare.

scuffle ('skʌfəl) n baruffa, rissa, zuffa f.

scullery ('skʌləri) n retrocucina m.

sculpt (skʌlpt) vt scolpire. **sculptor** n scultore m. **sculpture** n scultura f.

scum (skʌm) n 1 spuma, schiuma f. 2 feccia f. vt schiumare.

scurf (skə:f) n forfora f.

scythe (saið) n falce f.

sea (si:) n mare m.

seabed ('si:bed) n letto del mare m.

seafaring ('si:fɛəriŋ) adj marinaro.

seafront ('si:frʌnt) n marina f.

seagull ('si:gʌl) n gabbiano m.

seahorse ('si:hɔ:s) n cavalluccio marino, ippocampo m.

seal[1] (si:l) n 1 sigillo, timbro, suggello m. 2 segno m. vt sigillare, bollare.

seal[2] (si:l) n zool foca f. **sealskin** n pelle di foca f.

sea-level n livello del mare m.

sea-lion n otaria f.

seam (si:m) n 1 cucitura, costura f. 2 geog vena f. giacimento m.

seaman ('si:mən) n marinaio m. **seamanship** n arte marinaresca f.

search (sə:tʃ) n ricerca, perquisizione, visita f. vt perquisire. vi cercare, ricercare. **searching** adj penetrante, scrutatore. **searchlight** n proiettore m.

seashore ('si:ʃɔ:) n spiaggia f.

seasick ('si:sik) adj che soffre il mal di mare. **seasickness** n mal di mare m.

seaside ('si:said) n marina, spiaggia f.

season ('si:zən) n 1 stagione f. 2 tempo m. vt condire. **season ticket** n tessera f. **seasoning** n cul condimento m.

seat (si:t) n 1 sedia f. posto m. 2 fondo m. 3 anat sedere m. 4 pol seggio m. 5 castello m. vt 1 far sedere. 2 installare. **seat belt** n cintura di sicurezza f.

seaweed ('si:wi:d) n alga f.

secluded (si'klu:did) adj ritirato, solitario. **seclusion** n solitudine f.

second[1] ('sekənd) adj secondo. vt secondare. **second-best** adj di seconda qualità, di riserva. **second-class** adj di seconda classe, inferiore. **second-hand** adj d'occasione. **second nature** n seconda natura f. **second-rate** adj inferiore, di secondo grado. **secondary** adj secondario. **secondary school** n scuola media f.

second[2] ('sekənd) n (of time) secondo m.

secret ('si:krət) adj segreto, nascosto, ritirato. n segreto m. **secretive** adj segreto, riservato.

secretary ('sekrətri) n 1 segretaria f. 2 pol ministro m.

secrete (si'kri:t) vt secernere.

sect (sekt) n setta f.

sectarian (sek'tɛəriən) adj,n settario. **sectarianism** n spirito settario m.

section ('sekʃən) n sezione, parte, divisione f.

sector ('sektə) n settore m.

secular ('sekjulə) adj 1 laico. 2 mondano. 3 secolare.

secure (si'kjuə) adj sicuro, certo, salvo. vt 1 ottenere. 2 assicurare. 3 chiudere. **security** n 1 sicurezza f. 2 law garanzia f. 3 pl titoli m pl.

sedate (si'deit) adj calmo, composto. vt rendere tranquillo. **sedation** n sedazione f. **sedative** adj,n sedativo, calmante m.

sediment ('sedimənt) n sedimento, deposito m.

seduce (si'dju:s) vt sedurre. **seduction** n seduzione f. **seductive** adj seducente.

see[*1] (si:) vt,vi 1 vedere. 2 capire. **see to** occuparsi di.

see[2] (si:) n rel sede f. diocesi f invar.

seed (si:d) n seme m. semenza f. **seedling** n pianticella f. **seedy** adj 1 trascurato, malconcio. 2 inf indisposto.

seek[*] (si:k) vt cercare.

seem (si:m) vi sembrare, parere. **seeming** adj apparente.

seep (si:p) vi gocciolare.

seesaw ('si:sɔ:) n altalena f.

seethe (si:ð) vi bollire, agitarsi.

segment ('segmənt) n 1 segmento m. 2 pezzo m. 3 spicchio m. porzione f.

segregate ('segrigeit) vt segregare. **segregation** n segregazione f.

seize (si:z) vt 1 afferrare, prendere. 2 confiscare, sequestrare. **seizure** n 1 afferramento f. confisca f. 2 med attacco m.

seldom ('seldəm) adv di rado, raramente.

select (si'lekt) vt 1 scegliere, 2 sport selezionare. adj scelto, eletto. **selection** n scelta, selezione f. **selective** adj selettivo.

self (self) n, pl **selves** persona f. io m. adj,pron stesso.
self-assured adj confidente.
self-aware adj conscio di sè.
self-centred adj egocentrico.
self-confident adj sicuro di sè. **self-confidence** n sicurezza di sè f.
self-conscious adj imbarazzato.
self-contained adj 1 indipendente. 2 riservato.
self-defence n difesa personale f.
self-discipline n autodisciplina f.
self-employed adj che lavora in proprio.
self-expression n espressione personale f.
self-government n autonomia f.
self-indulgent adj indulgente con sè stesso.
self-interest n interesse personale m.
selfish ('selfiʃ) adj egoista, egoistico.
self-made adj fatto da sè.
self-pity n autocommiserazione f.
self-portrait n autoritratto m.
self-respect n dignità f. amor proprio m.
self-righteous adj compiaciuto.
self-sacrifice n abnegazione f. sacrificio di sè m.
selfsame ('selfseim) adj proprio lo stesso.
self-satisfied adj soddisfatto di sè.
self-service adj,n self-service invar.
self-sufficient adj bastante a sè.
self-will n ostinazione f.
sell (sel) vt vendere, smerciare, spacciare. vi vendersi.
Sellotape ('seləteip) n Tdmk Scotch Tdmk m.
semantic (si'mæntik) adj semantico. **semantics** n semantica f.
semaphore ('seməfɔ:) n semaforo m.
semibreve ('semibri:v) n semibreve f.
semicircle ('semisə:kəl) n semicircolo m. **semicircular** adj semicircolare.
semicolon (semi'koulən) n punto e virgola m.
semidetached (semidi'tætʃt) adj gemello, accoppiato.
semifinal (semi'fainl) n semifinale f.
seminar ('seminɑ:) n seminario m.
semiprecious (semi'preʃəs) adj semiprezioso.
semiquaver (semi'kweivə) n semicroma f.
semivowel ('semivauəl) n semivocale f.
semolina (semɔli:nə) n semolino m.
senate ('senət) n senato m. **senator** n senatore m.
send (send) vt mandare, inviare, spedire. **send for** far venire.

Senegal (seni'gɔ:l) n Senegaglia f. **senegalese** adj,n senegalese.
senile ('si:nail) adj senile.
senior ('si:niə) adj 1 maggiore, più anziano. 2 principale. n seniore, maggiore m.
sensation (sen'seiʃən) n sensazione, impressione f. **sensational** adj sensazionale.
sense (sens) n 1 senso m. 2 facoltà f. **sense of humour** senso dell'umorismo. ~vt indovinare. **senseless** adj 1 assurdo, stupido. 2 senza conoscenza.
sensible ('sensəbəl) adj 1 ragionevole, saggio. 2 sensibile. **sensibility** n sensibilità f.
sensitive ('sensitiv) adj 1 sensibile, sensitivo. 2 impressionabile. **sensitivity** n sensitività f.
sensual ('senʃuəl) adj sensuale, carnale. **sensuality** n sensualità, voluttà f.
sensuous ('senʃuəs) adj sensuoso, sensuale.
sentence ('sentəns) n 1 gram frase f. 2 law sentenza, condanna f. vt condannare.
sentiment ('sentimənt) n 1 sentimento m. 2 idea, opinione f. **sentimental** adj sentimentale.
sentry ('sentri) n sentinella, guardia f.
separate (v 'sepəreit; adj 'seprit) vt separare, dividere. vi separarsi, dividersi. adj separato, diviso, distinto. **separation** n separazione, divisione f.
September (sep'tembə) n settembre m.
septet (sep'tet) n settimino m.
septic ('septik) adj settico.
sequel ('si:kwəl) n seguito m. conseguenza f.
sequence ('si:kwəns) n successione f. serie f. invar.
sequin ('si:kwin) n lustrino m.
serenade (serə'neid) n serenata f.
serene (si'ri:n) adj calmo, sereno, tranquillo. **serenity** n serenità, tranquillità f.
serf (sə:f) n servo della gleba, schiavo m.
sergeant ('sɑ:dʒənt) n sergente m. **sergeant major** n sergente maggiore m.
serial ('siəriəl) n romanzo or film a puntate m. **serialize** vt pubblicare a puntate.
series ('siəri:z) n 1 successione f. seguito m. 2 serie f invar.
serious ('siəriəs) adj grave, serio. **seriousness** n gravità f.
sermon ('sə:mən) n predica f. sermone m.
serpent ('sə:pənt) n serpente m.
serrated (sə'raitid) adj dentellato.
serve (sə:v) vt,vi 1 servire. 2 sport mandare. 3 portare. **servant** n domestico, servo m.

service ('sə:vis) n 1 servizio m. 2 impiego m. 3 utilità f. 4 servigio m. 5 rel ufficio divino. vt mettere in ordine, aggiustare. **service station** n stazione di servizio f.

serviette (sə:vi'et) n tovagliolo m.

servile ('sə:vail) adj servile.

session ('seʃən) n sessione, seduta f.

set* (set) vt 1 mettere, porre. 2 dare. 3 regolare. 4 ridurre. 5 stabilire. 6 montare. 7 assegnare. vi 1 rapprendersi. 2 (of the sun) tramontare. **set about** mettersi a. **set out** partire. ~n 1 collezione f. serie f invar. 2 (television, etc.) apparecchio m. 3 (of hair) messa in piega f. adj 1 fisso. 2 posto. 3 regolare. **setback** n 1 regresso m. 2 med ricaduta f. **setting** n 1 ambiente m. 2 (of the sun) tramonto m.

settee (se'ti:) n divano m.

settle ('setl) vt 1 accomodare, fissare. 2 stabilire. 3 decidere. 4 pagare. vi stabilirsi, fissarsi. **settlement** n 1 decisione f. 2 colonia f.

seven ('sevən) adj,n sette m or f. **seventh** adj settimo.

seventeen (sevən'ti:n) adj,n diciassette m or f. **seventeenth** adj diciassettesimo.

seventy ('sevənti) adj,n settanta m. **seventieth** adj settantesimo.

several ('sevrəl) adj 1 parecchi. 2 diversi. pron parecchi.

severe (si'viə) adj 1 severo, austero. 2 duro, rigido. **severity** n severità f.

sew* (sou) vt,vi cucire. **sewing** n cucito m. **sewing machine** n macchina da cucire f.

sewage ('su:idʒ) n fognatura, scolatura f.

sewer ('su:ə) n fogna, cloaca f.

sex (seks) n sesso m. **sexual** adj sessuale. **sexuality** n sessualità f. **sexy** adj sexy invar.

sextet (seks'tet) n sestetto m.

shabby ('ʃæbi) adj 1 trasandato, mal vestito. 2 malconcio. 3 meschino, gretto.

shack (ʃæk) n capanna f.

shade (ʃeid) n 1 ombra, oscurità f. 2 gradazione f. vt 1 ombreggiare, oscurare. 2 proteggere, parare. **shading** n sfumatura f.

shadow ('ʃædou) n ombra, riflessione f. vt 1 ombreggiare, oscurare. 2 sorvegliare, spiare. **shadow cabinet** n gruppo di ministri dell'opposizione m.

shaft (ʃɑ:ft) n 1 asta f. 2 raggio m. 3 tech asse m.

shaggy ('ʃægi) adj peloso, irsuto, ispido.

shake* (ʃeik) vt 1 scuotere, agitare. 2 scrollare.

3 stringere. vi tremolare, vacillare, agitarsi. n scossa f. urto, tremito m.

shall* (ʃəl; stressed ʃæl) v mod aux 1 dovere. 2 expressed by the future tense.

shallot (ʃə'lɔt) n scalogno m.

shallow ('ʃælou) adj 1 basso. 2 superficiale, leggero. n bassofondo m.

sham (ʃæm) n finzione, simulazione f. inganno m. adj finto, falso. vt fingere, simulare.

shame (ʃeim) n vergogna, ignominia, onta f. **what a shame!** che peccato! ~vt svergognare. **shamefaced** adj vergognoso, timido.

shampoo (ʃæm'pu:) n shampoo m invar.

shamrock ('ʃæmrɔk) n trifoglio d'Irlanda m.

shandy ('ʃændi) n bibita fatta di birra e di limonata f.

shanty¹ ('ʃænti) n capanna f.

shanty² ('ʃænti) n (song) canzone marinaresca f.

shape (ʃeip) n forma, figura f. vt 1 formare. 2 modellare. 3 dirigere, concepire. **shapeless** adj informe.

share (ʃeə) n 1 parte, porzione, quota f. 2 comm azione f. vt 1 dividere. 2 condividere. vi partecipare. **shareholder** n azionista m.

shark (ʃɑ:k) n zool pescecane m.

sharp (ʃɑ:p) adj 1 acuto, affilato. 2 penetrante, furbo. 3 piccante. 4 aspro, severo. adv pronto. n mus diesis m. **sharp-sighted** adj di vista acuta. **sharpen** vt 1 appuntare, affilare. 2 eccitare.

shatter ('ʃætə) vt 1 fracassare, spezzare. 2 distruggere.

shave (ʃeiv) vt fare la barba a. vi farsi la barba. n rasatura f.

shawl (ʃɔ:l) n scialle m.

she (ʃi:) pron 3rd pers s lei, ella f.

sheaf (ʃi:f) n, pl **sheaves** covone, fascio m.

shear (ʃiə) vt tosare. **shears** n pl cesoie f pl.

sheath (ʃi:θ) n guaina f. fodero, astuccio m. **sheathe** vt ringuainare, foderare.

shed¹ (ʃed) n rimessa, tettoia f. capannone m.

shed*² (ʃed) vt versare, spargere, perdere.

sheen (ʃi:n) n lustro, splendore m.

sheep (ʃi:p) n invar pecora f. **sheepdog** n cane pastore m. **sheepish** adj timido, goffo. **sheepskin** n pelle di pecora f.

sheer¹ (ʃiə) adj 1 puro, semplice. 2 a piombo invar. perpendicolare. 3 diafano. adv perpendicolarmente.

sheer² (ʃiə) vi cambiare rotta.

sheet (ʃiːt) *n* **1** lenzuolo *m*. **2** (of paper) foglio *m*. **3** (of metal, etc.) lastra *f*.

sheikh (ʃeik) *n* sceicco *m*.

shelf (ʃelf) *n*, *pl* **shelves** scaffale *m*. mensola *f*.

shell (ʃel) *n* **1** conchiglia *f*. guscio *m*. **2** involucro *m*. **3** *mil* proiettile, bossolo *m*. *vt* **1** sgusciare. **2** *mil* bombardare. **shellfish** *n* mollusco, crostaceo, frutto di mare *m*.

shelter (ˈʃeltə) *n* riparo, ricovero *m*. *vt* riparare.

shelve (ʃelv) *vt* **1** mettere su scaffali, archiviare. **2** mettere da parte, differire.

shepherd (ˈʃepəd) *n* pastore *m*. **shepherdess** *n* pastorella *f*.

sherbet (ˈʃəːbət) *n* sorbetto *m*.

sheriff (ˈʃerif) *n* sceriffo *m*.

sherry (ˈʃeri) *n* sherry, vino di Xeres *m*.

shield (ʃiːld) *n* **1** scudo *m*. **2** riparo *m*. *vt* riparare.

shift (ʃift) *n* **1** spostamento *m*. sostituzione *f*. **2** turno *m*. *vt* spostare. *vi* sostituirsi. **shifty** *adj* furtivo, equivoco.

shilling (ˈʃiliŋ) *n* scellino *m*.

shimmer (ˈʃimə) *n* luccichio *m*. *vi* luccicare.

shin (ʃin) *n* stinco *m*. tibia *f*.

shine (ʃain) *vt* lucidare. *vi* brillare, risplendere. *n* brillantezza, luce *f*.

ship (ʃip) *n* nave, imbarcazione *f*. *vt* **1** inviare, spedire. **2** imbarcare. **shipment** *n* **1** carico *m*. **2** consegna *f*. **shipshape** *adj,adv* a posto, in ordine. **shipwreck** *n* naufragio *m*. **shipyard** *n* cantiere navale *m*.

shirk (ʃəːk) *vt* evitare.

shirt (ʃəːt) *n* camicia *f*.

shit (ʃit) *n tab* merda *f*.

shiver (ˈʃivə) *n* tremolio, brivido *m*. *vi* tremare, rabbrividire.

shock[1] (ʃɔk) *n* **1** urto, impatto *m*. **2** spavento *m*. impressione *f*. *vt* spaventare, impressionare. **shock absorber** *n* ammortizzatore *m*. **shocking** *adj* terribile.

shock[2] (ʃɔk) *n* (of hair) zazzera *f*.

shoddy (ˈʃɔdi) *adj* scadente.

shoe (ʃuː) *n* scarpa, calzatura *f*. *vt* ferrare. **shoelace** *n* stringa *f*. **shoemaker** *n* calzolaio *m*. **shoeshop** *n* calzoleria *f*.

shone (ʃɔn) *v see* **shine.**

shook (ʃuk) *v see* **shake.**

shoot (ʃuːt) *vt* **1** lanciare, tirare. **2** fucilare. **3** (film) girare. *vi* **1** tirare. **2** cacciare. **3** crescere, germinare. *n* **1** *bot* rampollo *m*. **2** caccia *f*. **shooting** *n* **1** tiro *m*. **2** caccia *f*.

shop (ʃɔp) *n* negozio *m*. bottega *f*. *vi* fare gli acquisti. **shop assistant** *n* commesso *m*. **shop floor** *n* **1** fabbrica, officina *f*. **2** gli operai che lavorano nella fabbrica *m pl*. **shopkeeper** *n* negoziante *m*. **shoplifter** *n* taccheggiatore *m*. **shopping** *n* spesa *f*. **shop steward** *n* membro della commissione interna *m*. **shopwindow** *n* vetrina *f*.

shore[1] (ʃɔː) *n* riva, spiaggia, costa *f*.

shore[2] (ʃɔː) *vt* puntellare.

shorn (ʃɔːn) *v see* **shear.**

short (ʃɔːt) *adj* **1** breve, corto. **2** (in stature) basso. **3** privo. **4** brusco. *adv* corto. *vt,vi* mettere in corto circuito. **shortage** *n* mancanza, carenza *f*. **shorten** *vt* accorciare, ridurre. *vi* raccorciarsi. **shortly** *adv* fra poco. **shorts** *n pl* calzoncini *m pl*.

shortcoming (ˈʃɔːtkʌmiŋ) *n* difetto, ostacolo *m*.

short cut *n* scorciatoia *f*.

shorthand (ˈʃɔːthænd) *n* stenografia *f*. **shorthand typist** *n* stenodattilografo *m*.

short-handed *adj* a corto di manodopera.

shortlived (ˈʃɔːtlivd) *adj* di breve durata.

short-sighted *adj* miope.

short-tempered *adj* irritabile, brusco.

short-term *adj* a breve scadenza.

short wave *n* onda corta *f*.

shot[1] (ʃɔt) *n* **1** colpo, sparo *m*. **2** *phot* fotografia *f*. **shotgun** *n* fucile *m*.

shot[2] (ʃɔt) *v see* **shoot.**

should (ʃəd; *stressed* ʃud) *v see* **shall.**

shoulder (ˈʃouldə) *n* spalla *f*. **shoulder-blade** *n* scapola *f*.

shout (ʃaut) *vt,vi* gridare. **shout at** rimproverare. ~*n* grido *m*.

shove (ʃʌv) *vt,vi* spingere. *n* spinta *f*.

shovel (ˈʃʌvəl) *n* pala *f*. badile *m*. *vt* spalare.

show (ʃou) *vt* **1** mostrare. **2** manifestare. **3** dimostrare. *vi* mostrarsi. **show off** pavoneggiarsi, esibire. ~*n* **1** mostra *f*. spettacolo *m*. **3** sembianza *f*. **4** pompa *f*. **show business** *n* mondo dello spettacolo *m*. **showcase** *n* campionario *m*. vetrina *f*. **showdown** *n* resa dei conti *f*. **show-jumping** *n* concorso ippico *m*. **showmanship** *n* capacità propagandistica *f*. **showroom** *n* sala d'esposizione *f*.

shower (ˈʃauə) *n* **1** doccia *f*. **2** (of rain) acquazzone, rovescio *m*. *vt* inondare. **showerproof** *adj* impermeabile.

shrank (ʃræŋk) *v see* **shrink.**

shred (ʃred) *n* strappo, brandello, frammento *m*. briciola *f*. *vt* fare a brandelli, stracciare.

shrewd (ʃruːd) adj accorto, scaltro. **shrewdness** n accortezza, sagacia f.

shriek (ʃriːk) n grido, strillo m. vi gridare, strillare.

shrill (ʃril) adj acuto, stridulo.

shrimp (ʃrimp) n gamberetto m.

shrine (ʃrain) n 1 tempio, altare m. 2 sacrario m.

shrink* (ʃriŋk) vi restringersi. vt diminuire, raccorciare. **shrink from** rifuggire da, tirarsi indietro.

shrivel (ˈʃrivəl) vi avvizzire, aggrinzarsi.

shroud (ʃraud) n sudario m. vt 1 avvolgere. 2 celare, nascondere.

Shrove Tuesday (ʃrouv) n Martedì Grasso m.

shrub (ʃrʌb) n arbusto m. **shrubbery** n boschetto m. macchia f.

shrug (ʃrʌg) vt scrollare. vi scrollare le spalle. n alzata di spalle f.

shrunk (ʃrʌŋk) v see **shrink.**

shudder (ˈʃʌdə) n brivido, fremito m. vi rabbrividire, fremere.

shuffle (ˈʃʌfəl) vt mischiare, mescolare. vi trascinarsi.

shun (ʃʌn) vt evitare, schivare.

shunt (ʃʌnt) vt deviare, smistare. n scambio m.

shut* (ʃʌt) vt chiudere, serrare. **shut down** chiudere. **shut in** rinchiudere. **shut out** escludere. ~adj chiuso.

shutter (ˈʃʌtə) n imposta f.

shuttlecock (ˈʃʌtəlkɔk) n volano m.

shy (ʃai) adj timido. vi esitare. **shyness** n timidezza f.

Sicily (ˈsisəli) n Sicilia f. **Sicilian** adj,n siciliano.

sick (sik) adj 1 ammalato, indisposto. 2 inf disgustato, stufo. **be sick** vomitare. **sicken** vt nauseare. vi ammalarsi. **sickening** adj disgustoso, nauseante. **sickness** n malattia f. malessere m.

side (said) n 1 lato, fianco m. 2 parte f. 3 bordo m. adj 1 di lato, laterale. 2 indiretto. **sideboard** n credenza f. **side effect** n effetto secondario m. **sidelight** n fanalino m. **sideline** n 1 attività secondaria f. 2 game fuoricampo m. **sideshow** n spettacolo secondario m. **sidestep** vt evitare. **sidetrack** vt distrarre. **sideways** adv lateralmente. **siding** n raccordo m.

sidle (ˈsaidl) vi procedere con timore or furtivamente.

siege (siːdʒ) n assedio m.

siesta (siˈestə) n siesta f.

sieve (siv) n setaccio m. vt setacciare.

sift (sift) vt stacciare, separare, distinguere.

sigh (sai) n sospiro m. vi sospirare.

sight (sait) n 1 vista f. 2 spettacolo m. vt avvistare, intravedere. **sightread** vt leggere a prima vista. **sightseeing** n giro turistico m.

sign (sain) n 1 segno, cenno m. 2 indizio m. traccia f. 3 segnale m. vt 1 firmare, sottoscrivere. **signpost** n indicatore stradale m.

signal (ˈsignl) n segnale m. vi segnalare, fare segnalazioni.

signature (ˈsignətʃə) n firma f.

signify (ˈsignifai) vt significare. **significance** n significato m. **significant** adj significativo, importante.

silence (ˈsailəns) n silenzio m. quiete f. vt ridurre al silenzio. **silencer** n silenziatore m. **silent** adj silenzioso, taciturno.

silhouette (siluˈet) n profilo m. sagoma f. vt profilare.

silk (silk) n seta f. adj di seta. **silkworm** n baco da seta m.

sill (sil) n 1 soglia f. 2 (of a window) davanzale m.

silly (ˈsili) adj sciocco, stupido.

silt (silt) n limo m. sedimenti m pl.

silver (ˈsilvə) n argento m. adj argenteo, d'argento.

similar (ˈsimilə) adj 1 simile. 2 pari. **similarity** n somiglianza f.

simile (ˈsimili) n similitudine f.

simmer (ˈsimə) vt bollire lentamente. vi ribollire. **simmer down** calmarsi.

simple (ˈsimpəl) adj semplice. **simple-minded** adj ingenuo. **simplicity** n semplicità f. **simplify** vt semplificare. **simply** adv semplicemente, assolutamente.

simultaneous (siməlˈteiniəs) adj simultaneo.

sin (sin) n peccato m. colpa f. vi peccare.

since (sins) adv da allora, dopo. prep da quando. conj 1 dacchè, poichè. 2 da quando.

sincere (sinˈsiə) adj sincero, genuino.

sinew (ˈsinjuː) n 1 anat tendine m. 2 struttura, fibra f. tendine m.

sing* (siŋ) vt,vi cantare. **singer** n cantante m,f.

singe (sindʒ) vt scottare, strinare.

single (ˈsiŋgəl) adj 1 singolo, solo. 2 celibe, nubile. v **single out** scegliere, isolare. **single-handed** adj da solo, senza aiuto. **single-minded** adj schietto, semplice. **singly** adv individualmente, ad uno ad uno.

singular ('siŋgjulə) adj,n singolare m. **singularly** adv insolitamente, particolarmente.

sinister ('sinistə) adj sinistro.

sink* (siŋk) vi 1 affondare. 2 abbassarsi. vt affondare. n lavandino, acquaio m.

sinner ('sinə) n peccatore m.

sinus ('sainəs) n cavità f. seno m.

sip (sip) vt sorseggiare. n sorso m.

siphon ('saifən) n sifone m. vt sifonare.

sir (səː) n 1 signore m. 2 cap Sir m.

siren ('sairən) n sirena f.

sirloin ('səːlɔin) n lombo m.

sister ('sistə) n 1 sorella f. 2 rel suora f. 3 med infermiera f. **sisterhood** n sorellanza f. **sister-in-law** n cognata f.

sit* (sit) vi 1 sedere, sedersi. 2 posare. vt far sedere. **sit down** accomodarsi. **sit-in** n sit-in m. **sitting** n 1 seduta, adunanza f. 2 phot seduta di posa f. **sitting room** n salotto m.

site (sait) n sito, luogo m. vt situare.

situation (sitju'eiʃən) n 1 situazione f. 2 posto, lavoro m.

six (siks) adj,n sei m or f. **sixth** adj sesto.

sixteen (siks'tiːn) adj,n sedici m or f. **sixteenth** adj sedicesimo.

sixty ('siksti) adj,n sessanta m. **sixtieth** adj sessantesimo.

size (saiz) n 1 misura f. 2 grandezza f. v **size up** misurare la capacità da.

sizzle ('sizəl) vi sfrigolare. n sfrigolio m.

skate[1] (skeit) n pattino m. vi pattinare. **skating** n pattinaggio m.

skate[2] (skeit) n zool razza f.

skeleton ('skelətn) n 1 scheletro m. 2 telaio m. 3 schema m.

sketch (sketʃ) n 1 bozzetto m. 2 Th scenetta f. vt abbozzare.

skewer ('skjuə) n spiedo m.

ski (skiː) n sci m invar. vi sciare. **skiing** n sci m. **ski-lift** n sciovia f.

skid (skid) n slittamento m. vi slittare.

skill (skil) n abilità f. **skilful** adj pratico, abile.

skim (skim) vt 1 schiumare, scremare. 2 sfiorare. **skim through** scorrere rapidamente.

skimp (skimp) vi fare economie. **skimpy** adj scarso.

skin (skin) n 1 pelle f. 2 (rind) buccia f. vt scorticare. **skin-diving** n immersione senza scafandro f. **skin-tight** adj aderente. **skinny** adj magro, ossuto.

skip (skip) n balzo, saltello m. vi saltellare. v omettere.

skipper ('skipə) n capitano m.

skirmish ('skəːmiʃ) n schermaglia f.

skirt (skəːt) n sottana, gonna f. vt rasentare.

skittle ('skitl) n birillo m.

skull (skʌl) n cranio, teschio m.

skunk (skʌŋk) n moffetta f.

sky (skai) n cielo m. **sky-high** adv alle stelle. **skylark** n allodola f. **skyline** n orizzonte m. **skyscraper** n grattacielo m.

slab (slæb) n lastra, piastra f.

slack (slæk) adj 1 fiacco, inerte. 2 lento. 3 negligente. n imbando m. **slacken** vt rallentare, ridurre. vi rallentarsi.

slacks (slæks) n pl pantaloni m pl.

slalom ('slɑːləm) n slalom m.

slam (slæm) vt,vi sbattere. n sbattuta f.

slander ('slɑːndə) n calunnia, diffamazione f. vt diffamare.

slang (slæŋ) n gergo m.

slant (slɑːnt) vi inclinarsi. vt inclinare. n inclinazione f.

slap (slæp) n schiaffo m. vt schiaffeggiare, dare pacche a. **slapdash** adj noncurante. adv senza riguardi. **slapstick** n commedia grossolana f.

slash (slæʃ) vt 1 tagliare, sfregiare. 2 ridurre. n taglio, spacco m.

slat (slæt) n assicella, stecca f.

slate (sleit) n 1 ardesia f. 2 lavagna f. 3 tegola f.

slaughter ('slɔːtə) n macello, massacro m. vt macellare. **slaughterhouse** n mattatoio m.

slave (sleiv) n schiavo m.

sledge (sledʒ) n slitta f.

sledgehammer ('sledʒhæmə) n mazza f. maglio m.

sleek (sliːk) adj liscio, lustro.

sleep* (sliːp) vi dormire. n sonno, riposo m. **sleeper** n (railway) traversina f. **sleeping-bag** n sacco a pelo m. **sleeping-car** n vagone letto m. **sleeping-pill** n sonnifero m. **sleep-walking** n sonnambulismo m. **sleepy** adj assonnato. **feel sleepy** avere sonno.

sleet (sliːt) n nevischio m. v imp nevischiare.

sleeve (sliːv) n 1 manica f. 2 (of a record) copertina f.

sleigh (slei) n slitta f.

slender ('slendə) adj esile, snello.

slept (slept) v see **sleep.**

slice (slais) n fetta, porzione f. vt affettare.

slick (slik) adj liscio, disinvolto.

slide* (slaid) vi scivolare, scorrere. vt far scorrere. n 1 scivolata f. 2 scivolo m. 3 phot diapositiva f. **slide rule** n regolo calcolatore m.

slight (slait) adj esile. vt disdegnare. n affronto m. **s*ightly** adv leggermente, un po'.

slim (slim) adj smilzo, snello. vi dimagrire.

slime (slaim) n fanghiglia f.

sling* (sliŋ) vt scagliare. n 1 fionda f. 2 med fascia f.

slink* (sliŋk) vi strisciare, camminare furtivamente.

slip [1] (slip) vt, vi scivolare. n 1 scivolata f. 2 passo falso m. 3 federa f. 4 sottoveste m. **slippery** adj scivoloso, viscido.

slip [2] (slip) n (cutting) ritaglio m.

slipper ('slipə) n pantofola f.

slit* (slit) n taglio m. fessura f. vt tagliare, fendere.

slobber ('slobə) n bava f. vi sbavare.

slog (slog) vi sgobbare.

slogan ('slougən) n motto m.

slop (slop) vt schizzare. **slops** n cibi liquidi m pl.

slope (sloup) n pendio m. china f. vi pendere, inclinarsi.

sloppy ('slopi) adj 1 trascurato. 2 sl sdolcinato.

slot (slot) n fessura, scanalatura f.

slouch (slautʃ) vi ciondolare.

slovenly ('slʌvənli) adj sciatto.

slow (slou) adj 1 lento. 2 tardo. 3 (of a clock) indietro. adv piano, adagio. v **slow down** rallentare.

slug (slʌg) n zool lumaca f. **sluggish** adj indolente, tardo.

sluice (slu:s) n chiusa f.

slum (slʌm) n 1 catapecchia f. 2 pl quartieri poveri m pl.

slumber ('slʌmbə) vi dormire pacificamente. n dormita f.

slump (slʌmp) n comm caduta dei prezzi f. ribasso m. vi 1 subire un tracollo. 2 lasciarsi andare.

slung (slʌŋ) v see **sling.**

slur (slə:) vt biascicare. n 1 macchia f. 2 mus legatura f.

slush (slʌʃ) n fanghiglia f.

sly (slai) adj astuto, malizioso, sornime.

smack [1] (smæk) n gusto, sapore m. v **smack of** sapere di.

smack [2] (smæk) vt schiaffeggiare, schioccare. n schiaffo, schiocco m. adv inf in pieno.

small (smɔ:l) adj piccolo, basso. **smallholding** n piccola fattoria f. **small-minded** adj meschino. **smallpox** n vaiolo m.

smart (smɑ:t) adj 1 furbo. 2 elegante. 3 svelto. vi dolere. **smarten** vt abbellire, ravvivare. **smarten up** ravvivarsi.

smash (smæʃ) vt fracassare, rovinare. n 1 fracasso m. 2 disastro m. 3 scontro m.

smear (smiə) vt 1 macchiare. 2 spalmare. n macchia f.

smell* (smel) n 1 odore m. 2 (sense of) odorato m. vt sentire l'odore di, fiutare. vi sentire.

smile (smail) vi sorridere. n sorriso m.

smirk (smə:k) vi sorridere con affettazione. n sorriso affettato m.

smock (smɔk) n grembiule m.

smog (smog) n smog m.

smoke (smouk) n fumo m. vt, vi fumare.

smooth (smu:ð) adj 1 liscio. 2 facile. vt lisciare, appianare.

smother ('smʌðə) vt, vi soffocare.

smoulder ('smouldə) vi bruciare lentamente.

smudge (smʌdʒ) n macchia f. scarabocchio m. vt macchiare.

smug (smʌg) adj soddisfatto.

smuggle ('smʌgəl) vt contrabbandare. **smuggler** n contrabbandiere m. **smuggling** n contrabbando m.

snack (snæk) n spuntino m. **snack-bar** n tavola calda f.

snag (snæg) n ostacolo, intoppo m.

snail (sneil) n chiocciola f.

snake (sneik) n serpe f. serpente m.

snap (snæp) vt, vi schioccare. n schiocco m. adj improvvisa. **snapshot** n istantanea f.

snarl (sna:l) vt aggrovigliare. n intrico, imbroglio m.

snatch (snætʃ) n 1 rapimento m. 2 tentativo di prendere m. 3 brandello, pezzo m. vt afferrare, carpire.

sneak (sni:k) n spione m.

sneer (sniə) vi ghignare. n ghigno m.

sneeze (sni:z) vi sternutire. n sternuto m.

sniff (snif) vt, vi fiutare, annusare. n annusata f.

snip (snip) n forbiciata f. ritaglio m. vi fare tagli.

snipe (snaip) n beccaccino m.

snivel ('snivəl) vi frignare.

snob (snob) n snob m invar.

snooker ('snu:kə) n gioco di biliardo m.

snoop (snu:p) vi curiosare.

snooty ('snu:ti) adj altezzoso.

snooze (snu:z) vi sonnecchiare. n pisolino m.

snore (snɔ:) vi russare. n russare m.

snort (snɔːt) n sbuffata f. vi sbuffare.

snout (snaut) n muso, grugno m.

snow (snou) n neve f. v imp nevicare. **snow-ball** n palla di neve f. **snowdrift** n cumulo di neve m. **snowdrop** n bucaneve m invar. **snowflake** n fiocco di neve m. **snowman** n fantoccio di neve m. **snowplough** n spazzaneve m. **snowstorm** n tormenta di neve f.

snub (snʌb) vt fare un affronto a. n affronto m. adj camuso.

snuff (snʌf) n tabacco da fiuto m.

snug (snʌg) adj comodo, intimo.

snuggle ('snʌgəl) vi rannicchiarsi, accoccolarsi.

so (sou) adv 1 così, talmente. 2 anche. **and so on** e così via. **so many** tanti. **so what?** e allora? ~quindi, perciò. **so-and-so** pron un tale. **so-called** adj cosiddetto. **so-so** adv così così.

soak (souk) vt bagnare, inzuppare. n bagno m.

soap (soup) n sapone m. **soap powder** n detersivo m.

soar (sɔː) vi librarsi, veleggiare.

sob (sɔb) n singhiozzo, singulto m. vi singhiozzare.

sober ('soubə) adj sobrio, lucido. v **sober up** smaltire una sbornia.

social ('souʃəl) adj sociale, socievole. **sociable** adj socievole, affabile. **socialism** n socialismo m. **socialist** n socialista m. **society** n 1 società f. 2 comunità, compagnia f. **sociology** n sociologia f.

sock[1] (sɔk) n calza f. calzino m.

sock[2] (sɔk) sl vt percuotere, colpire. n pugno m. percossa f.

socket ('sɔkit) n 1 incavo m. 2 (electric) presa f. 3 anat orbita f.

soda ('soudə) n soda f. **soda-water** n acqua di selz. selz m invar.

sofa ('soufə) n sofà, divano m.

soft (sɔft) adj soffice, tenero, tenue. **soften** vt ammorbidire. vi placarsi, intenerirsi. **soft-hearted** adj compassionevole. **softly** adv dolcemente.

soggy ('sɔgi) adj fradicio, inzuppato.

soil[1] (sɔil) n terreno m. terra f.

soil[2] (sɔil) vt insudiciare, sporcare.

solar ('soulə) adj solare. **solar plexus** n plesso solare m.

sold (sould) v see **sell.**

solder ('sɔldə) n lega per saldatura f. vt saldare.

soldier ('souldʒə) n soldato, militare m.

sole[1] (soul) adj solo, unico.

sole[2] (soul) n 1 anat pianta del piede f. 2 suola f. vt risuolare.

sole[3] (soul) n zool sogliola f.

solemn ('sɔləm) adj solenne, grave.

solicitor (sə'lisitə) n avvocato, procuratore legale m.

solid ('sɔlid) adj 1 solido, massiccio. 2 posato. **solidarity** n solidarietà f. **solidify** vt solidificare. vi solidificarsi.

solitary ('sɔlitri) adj 1 solitario, isolato. 2 unico, solo.

solitude ('sɔlitjuːd) n solitudine f. isolamento m.

solo ('soulou) n assolo m. **soloist** n solista m.

solstice ('sɔlstis) n solstizio m.

soluble ('sɔljubəl) adj 1 solubile. 2 risolvibile.

solution (sə'luːʃən) n 1 risoluzione f. 2 sci soluzione f.

solve (sɔlv) vt risolvere, chiarire, sciogliere, spiegare. **solvent** adj,n solvente m.

sombre ('sɔmbə) adj tetro, triste, fosco.

some (sʌm) adj 1 qualche, alcuni, dei. 2 un po' di, del. pron 1 alcuni. 2 ne, un po'. adv circa. **somebody** pron qualcuno. **somehow** adv in qualche modo, in un modo o nell'altro. **someone** pron qualcuno. **something** pron qualche cosa. **sometime** adv un tempo, un giorno o l'altro, presto o tardi. **sometimes** adv qualche volta, talvolta, a volte, di quando in quando. **somewhat** adv piuttosto, un po'. **somewhere** adv qualche posto or luogo.

somersault ('sʌməsɔːlt) n capriola f. salto mortale m. vi fare salti mortali.

son (sʌn) n figlio, figliolo m. **son-in-law** n genero m.

sonata (sə'nɑːtə) n sonata f.

song (sɔŋ) n canzone f. canto m.

sonic ('sɔnik) adj sonico.

sonnet ('sɔnit) n sonetto m.

soon (suːn) adv presto, tosto, tra poco. **as soon as** non appena. **the sooner the better** prima è meglio è.

soot (sut) n fuliggine f.

soothe (suːð) vt calmare, placare, lenire. **soothing** adj calmante, riposante.

sophisticated (sə'fistikeitid) adj sofisticato, raffinato.

soprano (sə'prɑːnou) n soprano m,f.

sorbet ('sɔːbit) n sorbetto m.

sordid ('sɔːdid) adj sordido, gretto.

sore (sɔː) adj 1 addolorato. 2 irritato, offeso. n piaga, ulcera f. **soreness** n dolore m.

sorrow ('sɔrou) n 1 dispiacere, dolore m. 2 rincrescimento m. **sorrowful** adj addolorato.

sorry ('sɔri) adj 1 spiacente, dolente. 2 meschino. **be sorry** dispiacersi. ~interj scusate!

sort (sɔ:t) n 1 sorta f. genere m. 2 modo m. maniera f. **out of sorts** giù di giri. ~vt classificare, scegliere.

soufflé ('su:flei) n soufflé, sformato m.

sought (sɔ:t) v see **seek**.

soul (soul) n 1 anima f. 2 creatura f. **not a soul** nessuno. **soul-destroying** adj struggente. **soulful** adj sentimentale, pieno di sentimento.

sound¹ (saund) n rumore, suono m. vt,vi suonare. **soundproof** adj 1 isolato acusticamente. 2 fonoassorbente.

sound² (saund) adj 1 giusto, logico. 2 solido, in buona condizione.

sound³ (saund) vt sondare, scandagliare.

soup (su:p) n zuppa, minestra f. brodo m.

sour (sauə) adj 1 acido, acerbo, stizzoso. 2 aspro.

source (sɔ:s) n fonte, sorgente, origine f.

south (sauθ) n sud, mezzogiorno m. adj del sud, meridionale. **southerly** adj del sud, meridionale. **southern** adj del sud, del meridione. **south-east** n sud-est m. **south-west** n sud-ovest m.

South Africa n Africa del Sud f. **South African** adj,n sud-africano.

South America n America del Sud f. **South American** adj,n sud-americano.

South Pole n polo sud m.

souvenir (su:və'niə) n ricordo m.

sovereign ('sɔvrin) n 1 sovrano m. re m invar. 2 comm sterlina, moneta d'oro f. adj sovrano. **sovereignty** n sovranità f.

Soviet Union ('souviət) n Unione Sovietica f.

sow¹ (sou) vt seminare, spargere, piantare.

sow² (sau) n scrofa f.

soya bean ('sɔiə) n soia f.

spa (spa:) n sorgente minerale, stazione termale f.

space (speis) n spazio m. vt spaziare, disporre ad intervalli. **spaceman** n astronauta m. **spaceship** n astronave f. **spacious** adj spazioso, ampio. **spaciousness** n spazio m.

spade¹ (speid) n vanga f. badile m.

spade² (speid) n game picche f pl.

Spain (spein) n Spagna f. **Spaniard** nm spagnolo m. **Spanish** adj spagnolo. **Spanish** (language) n spagnolo m.

274

span¹ (spæn) n 1 spanna f. palmo m. 2 periodo di tempo m. vt stendersi attraverso.

span² (spæn) v see **spin**.

spaniel ('spæniəl) n spaniel m.

spank (spæŋk) vt sculacciare.

spanner ('spænə) n chiave inglese f.

spare (spɛə) adj 1 d'avanzo, in più, extra. 2 parco, frugale. 3 disponibile. vt 1 risparmiare. 2 fare a meno di.

spark (spa:k) n scintilla, favilla f. lampo m. vi scintillare, emettere scintille. **spark off** lanciare. **spark plug** n candela f.

sparkle ('spa:kəl) n bagliore m. scintilla f. vi emettere scintille, risplendere.

sparrow ('spærou) n passero m.

sparse (spa:s) adj rado, sparso.

spasm ('spæzəm) n spasmo, spasimo m. contrazione f. **spastic** adj spastico.

spat (spæt) v see **spit**.

spatial ('speiʃəl) adj spaziale.

spatula ('spætjulə) n spatula f.

spawn (spɔ:n) n uova f pl. vt,vi deporre.

speak* (spi:k) vi parlare. vt esprimere, pronunciare. **speak out** parlare francamente. **speak up** alzare la voce.

spear (spiə) n lancia, asta, fiocina f. vt fiocinare, trafiggere.

special ('speʃəl) adj 1 speciale, particolare. 2 straordinario. **specialist** n specialista m. **speciality** n specialità f. **specialize** vi specializzarsi.

species ('spi:ʃi:z) n specie f invar. genere, tipo m.

specify ('spesifai) vt specificare, precisare. **specific** adj specifico, particolare.

specimen ('spesimən) n campione, modello, esemplare m.

speck (spek) n granello, punto m. macchiolina f. vt macchiare, chiazzare.

spectacle ('spektəkəl) n 1 spettacolo m. vista f. 2 pl occhiali m pl. **spectacular** adj spettacolare, spettacoloso.

spectator (spek'teitə) n spettatore m.

spectrum ('spektrəm) n spettro m.

speculate ('spekjuleit) vi 1 meditare, considerare. 2 comm speculare. **speculation** n speculazione f. **speculator** n speculatore m.

speech (spi:tʃ) n 1 discorso m. orazione f. 2 favella f.

speed* (spi:d) n velocità, rapidità, sveltezza f. vi affrettarsi. **speedboat** n motoscafo veloce m.

spell* ¹ (spel) vt,vi sillabare, compitare.

spell[2] (spel) *n* fascino, incantesimo *m*. magia *f*. **spellbound** *adj* incantato, affascinato.

spell[3] (spel) *n* periodo, intervallo *m*.

spend (spend) *vt* **1** spendere, sborsare. **2** passare, trascorrere. **3** impiegare. *vi* spendere. **spendthrift** *adj,n* prodigo *m*.

sperm (spə:m) *n* sperma *m*.

sphere (sfiə) *n* **1** sfera *f*. globo *m*. **2** ambiente *m*. **spherical** *adj* sferico.

spice (spais) *n* **1** aroma *f*. **2** *pl* spezie *f pl*. *vt* **1** aromatizzare. **2** rendere piccante. **spicy** *adj* **1** piccante. **2** arguto, mordace.

spider ('spaidə) *n* ragno *m*.

spike (spaik) *n* **1** punta *f*. aculeo *m*. **2** chiodo *m*. *vt* inchiodare.

spill[1] (spil) *vt* versare, spargere. *n* caduta *f*.

spin[*] (spin) *vt* **1** filare. **2** far girare. *vi* girare. *n* **1** giro *m*. rotazione *f*. **2** gita *f*. **spin drier** *n* macchina asciugatrice *f*. **spin-dry** *vt* asciugare colla centrifuga. **spinning wheel** *n* filatoio *m*.

spinach ('spinidʒ) *n* spinaci *m pl*.

spine (spain) *n* **1** spina dorsale *f*. **2** spina, lisca *f*. **3** (of a book) dorso *m*. **spineless** *adj* debole.

spinster ('spinstə) *n* zitella, nubile *f*.

spire[1] (spaiə) *n arch* guglia, cuspide *f*.

spire[2] (spaiə) *n* spira, spirale *f*. **spiral** *adj,n* spirale *f*. **spiral staircase** *n* scala a chiocciola *f*.

spirit ('spirit) *n* **1** spirito *m*. anima *f*. **2** fantasma *m*. **3** coraggio *m*. **4** *pl* liquori *m pl*. **spiritual** *adj* spirituale.

spit[1] (spit) *vt* sputare. *vi* (of rain) piovigginare. *n* sputo *m*. saliva *f*.

spit[2] (spit) *n cul* spiedo *m*.

spite (spait) *n* dispetto, rancore, ripicco *m*. **in spite of** malgrado. **out of spite** per dispetto. ~*vt* contrariare, far dispetto a. **spiteful** *adj* malevolo, dispettoso.

splash (splæ∫) *vt* schizzare, spruzzare. *vi* cadere con un tonfo. *n* spruzzo, schizzo *m*.

splendid ('splendid) *adj* splendido, magnifico. **splendour** *n* splendore, lustro *m*.

splint (splint) *n* **1** scheggia *f*. **2** *med* stecca *f*. **splinter** *n* scheggia *f*. frantume *m*. *vt,vi* frantumare.

split[*] (split) *vt* fendere, spaccare. *vi* fendersi. *n* spaccatura, fessura *f*.

splutter ('splʌtə) *vt,vi* barbugliare.

spoil[*] (spoil) *vt* **1** guastare, rovinare, sciupare. **2** viziare. **spoil-sport** *n* guastafeste *m invar*.

spoke[1] (spouk) *n* (of a wheel) raggio *m*.

spoke[2] (spouk) *v see* **speak.**

spoken ('spoukən) *v see* **speak.**

spokesman ('spouksmən) *n* portavoce *m*.

sponge (spʌndʒ) *n* spugna *f*. *vt* **1** lavare con la spunga. **2** scroccare.

sponsor ('sponsə) *n* **1** garante *m*. **2** padrino *m*. madrina *f*. *vt* essere garante di. **sponsorship** *n* garanzia *f*.

spontaneous (spon'teiniəs) *adj* spontaneo, naturale.

spool (spu:l) *n* rocchetto *m*. bobina *f*.

spoon (spu:n) *n* cucchiaio *m*. **spoonful** *n* cucchiaiata *f*.

sport (spo:t) *n* **1** gioco, divertimento *m*. **2** sport *m invar*. **sportsman** *n* sportivo *m*.

spot (spot) *n* **1** luogo, posto *m*. località *f*. **2** macchia *f*. *vt* **1** macchiare. **2** scoprire, individuare. **spotlight** *n* riflettore *m*. luce della ribalta *f*.

spouse (spaus) *n* coniuge *m,f*.

spout (spaut) *n* tubo di scarico, becco, getto *m*. *vi* **1** scaturire, zampillare. **2** declamare.

sprain (sprein) *n* strappo muscolare, storta *f*. *vt* slogare, storcere.

sprang (spræŋ) *v see* **spring.**

sprawl (spro:l) *vi* sdraiarsi in modo scomposto.

spray[1] (sprei) *n* spruzzo, getto *m*. *vt* spruzzare, polverizzare.

spray[2] (sprei) *n* (of flowers, etc.) ramoscello, rametto *m*.

spread[*] (spred) *vt* **1** distendere. **2** diffondere, propagare. **3** spiegare. **4** spalmare. *vi* **1** stendersi. **2** diffondersi. *n* **1** distesa, estensione *f*. **2** diffusione *f*.

spree (spri:) *n* **1** baldoria *f*. **2** divertimento *m*.

sprig (sprig) *n* ramoscello, rametto *m*.

sprightly ('spraitli) *adj* vivace, spiritoso.

spring[*] (spriŋ) *vi* **1** nascere, sorgere, provenire. **2** balzare, scaturire. *n* **1** fonte, sorgente *f*. **2** primavera *f*. **3** molla *f*. **4** salto *m*. **springboard** *n* trampolino *m*. **spring-clean** *vt* pulire accuratamente. **spring onion** *n* cipollina *f*. **springtime** *n* primavera *f*.

sprinkle ('spriŋkəl) *vt* spruzzare, spargere. *n* spruzzatina *f*. **sprinkling** *n* infarinatura *f*.

sprint (sprint) *vi* correre velocemente. *n* corsa breve *f*. scatto *m*.

sprout (spraut) *vi* germogliare. *n* germoglio *m*.

sprung (sprʌŋ) *v see* **spring.**

spun (spʌn) *v see* **spin.**

spur (spə:) n sperone, sprone m. vt incitare, stimolare, spronare.

spurt (spə:t) n 1 getto m. 2 breve sforzo m. vt, vi spruzzare.

spy (spai) n spia f. vi spiare, fare la spia.

squabble ('skwɔbəl) n bisticcio m. lite f. vi bisticciarsi, accapigliarsi.

squad (skwɔd) n squadra f. plotone m.

squadron ('skwɔdrən) n 1 mil squadrone m. 2 naut, aviat squadriglia f.

squalid ('skwɔlid) adj misero, squallido.

squander ('skwɔndə) vt sprecare, scialacquare, sperperare.

square (skwɛə) adj 1 quadrato. 2 giusto, preciso. 3 inf all'antica. n 1 quadrato m. 2 piazza f. vt quadrare. adv chiaro e tondo. **square root** n radice quadrata f.

squash (skwɔʃ) n 1 spremuta f. 2 sport squash m. vt 1 schiacciare, spremere. 2 umiliare.

squat (skwɔt) adj tarchiato, tozzo. vi 1 rannicchiarsi, accovacciarsi. 2 occupare abusivamente.

squawk (skwɔ:k) vi emettere un grido rauco. n grido rauco m.

squeak (skwi:k) n grido acuto m. vi strillare acutamente, guaire.

squeal (skwi:l) n strillo m. vi strillare.

squeamish ('skwi:miʃ) adj schizzinoso.

squeeze (skwi:z) vt spremere, stringere, comprimere, strizzare. n stretta, spremitura, compressione f.

squid (skwid) n seppia f. calamaro m.

squiggle ('skwigəl) n scarabocchio m.

squint (skwint) vi 1 essere strabico. 2 guardare obliquamente. n strabismo m. adj strabico.

squire ('skwaiə) n gentiluomo, proprietario di terre m.

squirm (skwə:m) vi 1 imbarazzarsi. 2 contorcersi.

squirrel ('skwirl) n scoiattolo m.

squirt (skwə:t) vt spruzzare, schizzare. n schizzetto m.

stab (stæb) n pugnalata, coltellata f. vt pugnalare, accoltellare.

stabilize ('steibəlaiz) vt stabilizzare. vi stabilizzarsi.

stable[1] ('steibəl) n stalla, scuderia f.

stable[2] ('steibəl) adj stabile, permanente.

stack (stæk) n catasta f. mucchio, cumulo m. vt ammucchiare, accatastare.

stadium ('steidiəm) n stadio m.

staff (stɑ:f) n 1 bastone m. 2 personale m. 3 mil stato maggiore m.

stag (stæg) n cervo m.

stage (steidʒ) n 1 palcoscenico, teatro m. 2 stadio m. 3 momento m. vt mettere in scena. **stage manager** n direttore di scena m.

stagger ('stægə) vi vacillare, esitare, barcollare.

stagnate (stæg'neit) vi ristagnare. **stagnant** adj stagnante, fermo, inattivo.

stain (stein) n macchia f. vt macchiare, colorire. **stained glass** n vetro istoriato m. vetrata f. colori f.

stair (stɛə) n 1 scalino, gradino m. 2 pl scale f pl. **staircase** n scala, tromba delle scale f.

stake[1] (steik) n palo m. incudine f. vt cintare, chiudere.

stake[2] (steik) n game 1 scommessa f. 2 pl premio m. vt scommettere, mettere in gioco.

stale (steil) adj stantio, vecchio, raffermo.

stalemate ('steilmeit) n stallo, punto morto m.

stalk[1] (stɔ:k) n stelo, gambo m.

stalk[2] (stɔ:k) vi camminare maestosamente. vt inseguire.

stall[1] (stɔ:l) n 1 chiosco m. edicola, bancherella f. 2 pl Th poltrona f.

stall[2] (stɔ:l) vi 1 agire evasimente. 2 mot fermarsi.

stallion ('stæljən) n stallone m.

stamina ('stæminə) n capacità di resistenza f. vigore m.

stammer ('stæmə) n balbuzie f. balbettamento m. vt, vi balbettare.

stamp (stæmp) n 1 impronta f. 2 (on a letter, etc.) francobollo, bollo m. vt 1 incidere, imprimere. 2 timbrare.

stampede (stæm'pi:d) n fuga precipitosa f.

stand[*] (stænd) vi 1 stare in piedi. 2 stare. 3 essere valido. vt sopportare. **stand out** spiccare. ~n 1 posizione f. 2 pausa f. 3 bancarella f. chiosco m. 4 sport tribuna f. **stand-by** n scorta, riserva f. **standing** n posizione, reputazione f. adj 1 eretto. 2 fermo. **standstill** n 1 arresto m. 2 fermata f. **at a standstill** fermo.

standard ('stændəd) n 1 modello, campione m. 2 bandiera f. stendardo m. 3 livello m. qualità f. 4 base f. supporto m. adj standard invar. normale. **standard lamp** n lampada a stelo f.

stank (stæŋk) v see **stink**.

staple[1] (steipəl) n chiodo ad U m. graffetta f.

staple[2] ('steipəl) adj principale. n prodotto principale m.

star (stɑ:) n 1 stella f. astro m. 2 Th diva f. vi Th

avere il ruolo di protagonista. **starfish** n stella di mare f.

starboard ('stɑːbəd) adj di dritta. n dritta f. triboro m.

starch (stɑːtʃ) n amido m. vt inamidare.

stare (stɛə) n sguardo fisso m. vi spalancare gli occhi. **stare at** fissare, sguardare.

stark (stɑːk) adj 1 rigido. 2 completo. 3 desolato. adv interamente, completamente.

starling ('stɑːliŋ) n storno m.

start (stɑːt) vi 1 cominciare. 2 partire. 3 trasalire. vt 1 dare inizio a. 2 mot mettere in moto. n 1 inizio m. 2 partenza f. 3 soprassalto m. **make an early start** partire di buon'ora.

startle ('stɑːtl) vt spaventare, allarmare.

starve (stɑːv) vt far soffrire la fame. vi morire di fame.

state (steit) n 1 stato m. condizione, situazione f. 2 pol stato m. 3 rango m. adj di stato. vt 1 dichiarare. 2 stabilire. 3 esporre. **stately** adj signorile, maestoso. **statement** n 1 dichiarazione f. 2 rapporto, esposto m. 3 comm bilancio m. **statesman** n uomo di stato, statista m. **statesmanship** n abilità politica f.

static ('stætik) adj statico.

station ('steiʃən) n 1 stazione f. 2 posto, luogo m. 3 base f. vt assegnare un posto a, collocare. **stationmaster** n capostazione m.

stationary ('steiʃənri) adj stazionario, fermo, fisso.

stationer ('steiʃənə) n cartolaio m. **stationer's shop** n cartoleria f. **stationery** n articoli di cancelleria m pl.

statistics (stə'tistiks) n 1 statistica f. 2 pl statistiche f pl. **vital statistics** misure vitali f pl.

statue ('stætjuː) n statua f.

stature ('stætʃə) n statura f.

status ('steitəs) n stato m. condizione sociale f. **status symbol** n oggetto il cui possesso denota un alto stato sociale m.

statute ('stætjuːt) n statuto, regolamento m. **statutory** adj statutario.

stay[1] (stei) vi fermarsi, restare, soggiornare.

stay[2] (stei) n sostegno, supporto m.

steadfast ('stedfɑːst) adj costante, fermo, risoluto.

steady ('stedi) adj 1 fermo, saldo. 2 regolare. 3 serio, equilibrato. vt rafforzare, stabilizzare. vi stabilizzarsi.

steak (steik) n bistecca, fetta di carne f.

steal* (stiːl) vt,vi rubare, sottrarre.

steam (stiːm) n vapore m. vt cucinare a vapore. vi emettere vapore, fumare. **steam-engine** n macchina a vapore f. **steam-roller** n compressore rullo m. **steamship** n piroscafo, vapore m.

steel (stiːl) n acciaio m. vt indurire. **steel oneself** corazzarsi. **stainless steel** n acciaio inossidabile m.

steep[1] (stiːp) adj 1 ripido, erto. 2 inf esorbitante, irragionevole.

steep[2] (stiːp) vt immergere, inzuppare.

steeple ('stiːpəl) n guglia f. campanile m. **steeplechase** n corsa ad ostacoli f.

steer (stiə) vt 1 mot sterzare, manovrare. 2 dirigere. vi sterzare. **steering wheel** n volante m.

stem[1] (stem) n stelo, gambo m.

stem[2] (stem) vt arrestare, arginare.

stencil ('stensəl) n stampino m. vt stampinare.

step (step) n 1 passo m. 2 orma, impronta f. 3 gradino m. 4 grado, avanzamento m. vi camminare, andare, recarsi. **stepladder** n scala a libretto f. **stepping stone** n 1 pietra per guadare f. 2 trampolino m.

stepbrother ('stepbrʌðə) n fratellastro m.

stepdaughter ('stepdɔːtə) n figliastra f.

stepfather ('stepfɑːðə) n patrigno m.

stepmother ('stepmʌðə) n matrigna f.

stepsister ('stepsistə) n sorellastra f.

stepson ('stepsʌn) n figliastro m.

stereo ('steriou) n stereo m. adj stereoscopico.

stereophonic (steriə'fɔnik) adj stereofonico.

stereotype ('steriətaip) n stereotipo m.

sterile ('sterail) adj sterile. **sterilize** vt sterilizzare.

sterling ('stɑːliŋ) adj genuino, puro. n sterlina f.

stern[1] (stɑːn) adj severo, rigido, rigoroso.

stern[2] (stɑːn) n 1 naut poppa f. 2 parte posteriore, coda f.

stethoscope ('steθəskoup) n stetoscopio m.

stew (stjuː) n stufato, umido m.

steward ('stjuːəd) n 1 naut cameriere di bordo m. 2 dispensiere m. 3 intendente, amministratore m.

stick[1] (stik) n bastone m. bacchetta, stecca f.

stick*[2] (stik) vt 1 ficcare. 2 incollare. vi 1 ficcarsi. 2 attaccarsi. **stick out** tirare fuori. **stick up for** prendere le difese di. **sticky** adj appiccicoso, viscoso.

stiff (stif) adj rigido, duro. **stiffen** vt irrigidire, indurire, rassodare. vi irrigidirsi.

stifle ('staifəl) vt reprimere, trattenere.

stigma ('stigmə) *n,pl* **stigmata** marchio, segno, stigma *m*.

stile (stail) *n* barriera *f*.

still[1] (stil) *adj* 1 immobile, fermo. 2 silenzioso. *adv* ancora. **stillborn** *adj* nato morto. **still life** *n* natura morta *f*.

still[2] (stil) *n* alambicco *m*.

stilt (stilt) *n* trampolo *m*.

stilted ('stiltid) *adj* artificioso.

stimulate ('stimjuleit) *vt* stimolare, incitare. **stimulus** *n, pl* **stimuli** stimolo, incentivo *m*.

sting* (stiŋ) *vt,vi* pungere, colpire. *n* pungiglione *m*. puntura d'insetto *f*.

stink* (stiŋk) *vi* puzzare. *n* puzzo, fetore *m*. **stinking** *adj* puzzolente.

stint (stint) *vt* limitare, lesinare. *n* limite *m*. restrizione *f*.

stipulate ('stipjuleit) *vt* stipulare. **stipulation** *n* stipulazione *f*.

stir (stə:) *vt* mescolare, agitare. **stir up** agitare. ~*n* 1 rimescolio *m*. 2 animazione *f*.

stirrup ('stirəp) *n* staffa *f*.

stitch (stitʃ) *n* 1 punto *m*. 2 maglia *f*. 3 *med* fitta, trafitta *f*. *vt* 1 cucire. 2 *med* suturare.

stoat (stout) *n* ermellino *m*.

stock (stɔk) *n* 1 provvista *f*. rifornimento *m*. 2 razza, stirpe *f*. 3 *pl comm* titoli *m pl*. azioni *f pl*. *vt* approvvigionare, fornire. **stockbreeding** *n* allevamento di bestiame *m*. **stockbroker** *n* agente di cambio *m*. **stock exchange** *n* borsa valori *f*. **stockpile** *n* riserva, scorta *f*. *vt* accumulare. **stocktaking** *n* inventario *m*.

stocking ('stɔkiŋ) *n* calza *f*.

stocky ('stɔki) *adj* tozzo, tarchiato.

stodge (stɔdʒ) *n* cibo pesante *m*. **stodgy** *adj* pesante, indigesto.

stoical ('stouikl) *adj* stoico.

stoke (stouk) *vt* 1 accudire alle caldaie. 2 alimentare, caricare. **stoker** *n* fochista *m*.

stole[1] (stoul) *v see* **steal.**

stole[2] (stoul) *n* stola *f*.

stolen ('stoulən) *v see* **steal.**

stomach ('stʌmək) *n* stomaco, ventre *m*. *vt* sopportare, digerire, tollerare. **stomach-ache** *n* mal di stomaco *m*.

stone (stoun) *n* 1 pietra, roccia *f*. sasso *m*. 2 *bot* nocciolo di frutta *m*. *vt* 1 lapidare, colpire a sassate. 2 togliere il nocciolo a.

stood (stud) *v see* **stand.**

stool (stu:l) *n* sgabello, seggiolino *m*.

stoop (stu:p) *vi* abbassarsi, chinarsi, curvarsi. *n* curvatura *f*.

stop (stɔp) *vt* 1 fermare, arrestare, cessare, sospendere, smettere. 2 otturare, tamponare. *vi* fermarsi. *n* 1 sosta *f*. arresto *m*. 2 (bus) fermata *f*. **stopgap** *n* palliativo *m*. **stoppage** *n* 1 blocco *m*. ostruzione *f*. 2 pausa, interruzione *f*. **stopper** *n* turacciolo, tappo *m*. **stopwatch** *n* cronometro *m*.

store (stɔ:) *n* 1 negozio, magazzino *m*. 2 provvista, scorta *f*. *vt* 1 fornire. 2 immagazzinare, conservare. **storage** *n* 1 deposito, immagazzinamento *m*. 2 magazzino *m*.

storey ('stɔ:ri) *n* piano di edificio *m*.

stork (stɔ:k) *n* cicogna *f*.

storm (stɔ:m) *n* 1 temporale *m*. tempesta *f*. 2 tumulto *m*. *vt* assalire, attaccare.

story ('stɔ:ri) *n* storia, favola *f*. racconto, aneddoto *m*.

stout (staut) *adj* grosso, robusto, corpulento. *n* birra scura *f*.

stove (stouv) *n* cucina, stufa *f*. fornello *m*.

stow (stou) *vt* riporre, stipare. **stow away** conservare. **stowaway** *n* passeggero clandestino *m*.

straddle (strædl) *vt* stare a cavalcioni.

straggle ('strægəl) *vi* sparpagliarsi, disperdersi.

straight (streit) *adj* 1 diritto. 2 onesto. 3 (of drinks, etc.) liscio. *adv* 1 in linea retta. 2 direttamente. **straight away** subito. **straighten** *vt* 1 raddrizzare. 2 rassettare. 3 regolare. **straightforward** *adj* franco, leale, schietto.

strain[1] (strein) *vt* 1 tendere. 2 sforzare, mettere a dura prova. 3 filtrare. *vi* sforzarsi. *n* 1 tensione *f*. 2 sforzo *m*. 3 *med* strappo *m*.

strain[2] (strein) *n* razza, tendenza *f*.

strand[1] (strænd) *vt* arenare.

strand[2] (strænd) *n* filo *m*.

strange (streindʒ) *adj* 1 strano, curioso. 2 estraneo, sconosciuto. **stranger** *n* sconosciuto, forestiero *m*.

strangle ('stræŋgəl) *vt* strangolare, strozzare, soffocare.

strap (stræp) *n* cinghia, correggia *f*. *vt* legare con cinghia.

strategy ('strætidʒi) *n* strategia *f*. **strategic** *adj* strategico.

straw (strɔ:) *n* 1 paglia *f*. 2 (for drinking) cannuccia *f*. **the last straw** il colmo. ~*adj* di paglia.

strawberry ('strɔ:bri) *n* fragola *f*. **strawberry plant** *n* fragola *f*.

stray (strei) *adj* 1 randagio, smarrito. 2 isolato,

occasionale. *n* trovatello *m.* *vi* **1** vagare. **2** deviare.

streak (stri:k) *n* striscia, stria *f.* *vt* strisciare.

stream (stri:m) *n* corrente *f.* corso d'acqua *m.* *vi* scorrere, sgorgare. **streamline** *vt* snellire, organizzare.

street (stri:t) *n* strada, via *f.*

strength (streŋθ) *n* **1** forza *f.* vigore *m.* **2** solidità, tenacia *f.* **strengthen** *vt* rafforzare, irrobustire, sviluppare.

strenuous (ˈstrenjuəs) *adj* strenuo, stancante.

stress (stres) *n* **1** tensione *f.* sforzo *m.* **2** accento *m.* enfasi *f* *invar.* *vt* accentuare, sottolineare.

stretch (stretʃ) *vt* stendere, tirare, allungare. **stretch one's legs** sgranchirsi le gambe. ~*n* **1** stiramento *m.* tensione *f.* **2** estensione, distesa *f.* **stretcher** *n* barella, lettiga *f.*

strict (strikt) *adj* **1** severo, rigoroso, rigido. **2** preciso.

stride* (straid) *vi* **1** camminare a passi lunghi. **2** stare a cavalcioni. *n* passo lungo *m.* andatura *f.* **take in one's stride** superare facilmente.

strike* (straik) *vt* **1** battere, colpire. **2** impressionare. **3** accendere. *vi* **1** scioperare. **2** suonare le ore. *n* sciopero *m.*

string* (striŋ) *n* spago *m.* corda *f.* *vt* **1** legare. **2** (pearls) infilare.

stringent (ˈstrindʒənt) *adj* severo, rigoroso.

strip[1] (strip) *vt* spogliare, denudare. *vi* svestirsi. **striptease** *n* spogliarello *m.*

strip[2] (strip) *n* striscia *f.* nastro *m.*

stripe (straip) *n* **1** riga, striscia *f.* **2** *mil* gallone *m.* *vt* striare, rigare.

strive* (straiv) *vi* sforzarsi.

strode (stroud) *v* see **stride.**

stroke[1] (strouk) *n* **1** colpo *m.* percossa *f.* **2** *sport* bracciata, remata *f.* **3** *med* colpo apoplettico *m.*

stroke[2] (strouk) *vt* accarezzare, lisciare. *n* carezza *f.*

stroll (stroul) *n* passeggiatina *f.* **go for a stroll** andar a fare quattro passi. ~*vi* passeggiare, andare a spasso.

strong (strɔŋ) *adj* forte, robusto, efficace. **stronghold** *n* fortezza *f.* **strong-minded** *adj* volitivo.

strove (strouv) *v* see **strive.**

struck (strʌk) *v* see **strike.**

structure (ˈstrʌktʃə) *n* **1** struttura *f.* **2** costruzione *f.*

struggle (ˈstrʌgəl) *n* lotta *f.* sforzo *m.* *vi* lottare, dibattersi, sforzarsi.

strum (strʌm) *vt,vi* strimpellare.

strung (strʌŋ) *v* see **string.**

strut[1] (strʌt) *vi* camminare impettito.

strut[2] (strʌt) *n* puntone, contropalo *m.*

stub (stʌb) *n* **1** mozzicone *m.* rimanenza *f.* **2** *comm* matrice *f.* **3** ceppo *m.* *vt* inciampare. **stub out** spegnere.

stubborn (ˈstʌbən) *adj* ostinato, testardo, cocciuto.

stud[1] (stʌd) *n* **1** chiodo a capocchia larga *m.* **2** bottoncino *m.* *vt* guarnire, ornare.

stud[2] (stʌd) *n* (of horses) scuderia *f.* allevamento *m.*

student (ˈstjuːdnt) *n* studente *m.* studentessa *f.*

studio (ˈstjuːdiou) *n* **1** studio *m.* **2** teatro di posa *m.*

study (ˈstʌdi) *n* **1** studio *m.* **2** esame attento *m.* investigazione *f.* *vt* studiare, esaminare attentamente. **studious** *adj* **1** studioso. **2** attento.

stuff (stʌf) *n* **1** *inf* sostanza, cosa, roba *f.* **2** stoffa *f.* tessuto *m.* *vt* **1** imbottire. **2** *cul* farcire. **3** rimpinzare. **stuffing** *n* **1** imbottitura *f.* **2** *cul* ripieno *m.* **stuffy** *adj* afoso, mal ventilato.

stumble (ˈstʌmbəl) *vi* inciampare. *n* inciampata *f.*

stump (stʌmp) *n* **1** tronco, ceppo *m.* **2** moncone di membro *m.* **3** mozzicone *m.*

stun (stʌn) *vt* stordire, tramortire.

stung (stʌŋ) *v* see **sting.**

stunk (stʌŋk) *v* see **stink.**

stunt[1] (stʌnt) *vt* impedire la crescita a.

stunt[2] (stʌnt) *n* **1** trovata pubblicitaria *f.* **2** bravata *f.*

stupid (ˈstjuːpid) *adj* stupido, sciocco.

sturdy (ˈstəːdi) *adj* forte, robusto, vigoroso.

sturgeon (ˈstəːdʒən) *n* storione *m.*

stutter (ˈstʌtə) *n* balbuzie *f* *invar.* *vi* balbettare, tartagliare.

sty (stai) *n* porcile *m.*

style (stail) *n* **1** stile, modello *m.* **2** moda *f.* *vt* chiamare, designare.

stylus (ˈstailəs) *n* **1** stilo *m.* **2** puntina per grammofono *f.*

subconscious (sʌbˈkɔnʃəs) *adj,n* subcosciente *m.*

subcontract (*n* sʌbˈkɔntrækt; *v* sʌbkənˈtrækt) *n* subappalto *m.* *vt* subappaltare.

subdue (səbˈdjuː) *vt* **1** domare, soggiogare. **2** attenuare.

subject (*n,adj* ˈsʌbdʒikt; *v* səbˈdʒekt) *n* **1** soggetto, argomento *m.* **2** suddito *m.* **3** *educ* materia *f.* *adj* soggetto, assoggettato. *vt* assoggettare, sottomettere, soggiogare. **subjective** adj soggettivo, individuale.

subjunctive (sǝb'dʒʌŋktiv) adj,n congiuntivo m.

sublime (sǝ'blaim) adj sublime.

submachine-gun (sʌbmǝ'ʃiːŋgʌn) n mitra f. fucile, mitragliatore m.

submarine (sʌbmǝ'riːn) n sommergibile m.

submerge (sǝb'mǝːdʒ) vt sommergere, immergere.

submit (sǝb'mit) vi sottomettersi, rassegnarsi. vt presentare. **submission** n sottomissione f.

subnormal (sʌb'nɔːmǝl) adj subnormale, al di sotto della normalità.

subordinate (adj,n sǝ'bɔːdinǝt; v sǝ'bɔːdineit) adj subordinato, secondario. n subalterno, inferiore m. vt subordinare.

subscribe (sǝb'skraib) vt 1 sottoscrivere. 2 abbonarsi a. vi 1 approvare. 2 sottoscrivere. 3 abbonarsi. **subscriber** n abbonato m. **subscription** n 1 abbonamento m. 2 sottoscrizione f.

subsequent ('sʌbsikwint) adj successivo, ulteriore.

subservient (sǝb'sǝːviǝnt) adj servile, subordinato.

subside (sǝb'said) vi 1 decrescere, sprofondare, calare. 2 quietarsi.

subsidiary (sǝb'sidiǝri) adj supplementare, secondario, sussidiario.

subsidize ('sʌbsidaiz) vt sussidiare, sovvenzionare. **subsidy** n sussidio m.

subsist (sǝb'sist) vi sussistere.

substance ('sʌbstǝns) n 1 sostanza, essenza f. 2 solidità f. **substantial** adj 1 sostanzioso, resistente. 2 notevole. **substantive** adj,n sostantivo m.

substitute ('sʌbstitjuːt) n sostituto, delegato, supplente m. vt sostituire.

subtitle ('sʌbtaitl) n sottotitolo m.

subtle ('sʌtl) adj 1 sottile, indefinibile. 2 astuto, scaltro.

subtract (sǝb'trækt) vt sottrarre, detrarre. **subtraction** n sottrazione f.

suburb ('sʌbǝːb) n sobborgo m. periferia f. **suburban** adj suburbano, periferico. **suburbia** n quartieri fuori città m pl.

subvert (sʌb'vǝːt) vt sovvertire.

subway ('sʌbwei) n 1 sottopassaggio m. 2 metropolitana f.

succeed (sǝk'siːd) vi 1 riuscire. 2 raggiungere la fama. **success** n successo m. **succession** n

successione f. serie f invar. **successive** adj successivo, consecutivo.

succulent ('sʌkjulǝnt) adj succulento.

succumb (sǝ'kʌm) vi soccombere.

such (sʌtʃ) adj tale, simile. **in such cases** in casi del genere. **such as it is** così com'è. ~pron tale, questo. **suchlike** adj simile.

suck (sʌk) vt succhiare, poppare. n succhiata, poppata f.

sucker ('sʌkǝ) n 1 sl credulone m. 2 tech pistone m. 3 ventosa f.

suction ('sʌkʃǝn) n risucchio, assorbimento m.

sudden ('sʌdn) adj subitaneo, improvviso, repentino.

suds (sʌdz) n pl schiuma, saponata f.

sue (suː) vt far causa a. vi citare, far causa.

suede (sweid) n camoscio m. pelle scamosciata f. adj di camoscio.

suet ('suːit) n lardo m.

suffer ('sʌfǝ) vt,vi soffrire, patire. vt tollerare, subire.

sufficient (sǝ'fiʃǝnt) adj sufficiente, bastevole.

suffix ('sʌfiks) n suffisso m.

suffocate ('sʌfǝkeit) vt,vi soffocare.

sugar ('ʃugǝ) n zucchero m. vt inzuccherare, addolcire. **sugar beet** n barbabietola da zucchero f. **sugar cane** n canna da zucchero f.

suggest (sǝ'dʒest) vt 1 suggerire, proporre. 2 alludere a. **suggestion** n 1 suggerimento m. proposta f. 2 allusione f. 3 lieve traccia f.

suicide ('suːisaid) n 1 suicidio m. 2 (person) suicida m. **commit suicide** suicidarsi. **suicidal** adj che tende al suicidio.

suit (sjuːt) n 1 abito da uomo m. 2 law causa f. 3 game seme m. vt 1 soddisfare. 2 star bene a. 3 adattare. **suit yourself** fa come vuoi. **suitable** adj adatto, adeguato. **suitability** n convenienza f.

suitcase ('sjuːtkeis) n valigia f.

suite (swiːt) n 1 seguito, corteo m. 2 (of rooms) appartamento m. 3 (of furniture) completo m.

sulk (sʌlk) vi tenere il broncio. n broncio m. **sulky** adj imbronciato.

sullen ('sʌlǝn) adj accigliato.

sulphur ('sʌlfǝ) n zolfo m.

sultan ('sʌltǝn) n sultano m.

sultana (sʌl'tɑːnǝ) n uva sultanina f.

sultry ('sʌltri) adj 1 afoso, soffocante. 2 provocante.

sum (sʌm) n 1 somma f. 2 addizione f. v **sum up** ricapitolare.

summarize ('sʌməraiz) vt riassumere. **summary** n sommario, sunto m.

summer ('sʌmə) n estate f. adj d'estate, estivo. **summerhouse** n chiosco m. **summertime** n **1** stagione estiva f. **2** ora legale estiva f.

summit ('sʌmit) n **1** cima f. **2** culmine, apice m.

summon ('sʌmən) vt convocare, fare appello a. **summon up courage** prendere coraggio. **summons** n **1** chiamata f. **2** law citazione f. vt citare in giudizio.

sun (sʌn) n sole m.

sunbathe ('sʌnbeið) vi fare bagni di sole.

sunburn ('sʌnbə:n) n scottatura f.

Sunday ('sʌndi) n domenica f.

sundial ('sʌndaiəl) n meridiana f.

sundry ('sʌndri) adj parecchi, vari.

sunflower ('sʌnflauə) n girasole m.

sung (sʌŋ) v see **sing.**

sunglasses ('sʌngla:siz) n pl occhiali da sole m pl.

sunk (sʌŋk) v see **sink.**

sunken ('sʌŋkən) adj sprofondato, incavato.

sunlight ('sʌnlait) n luce del sole f.

sunny ('sʌni) adj luminoso, soleggiato.

sunrise ('sʌnraiz) n alba f. sorgere del sole m.

sunset ('sʌnset) n tramonto m.

sunshine ('sʌnʃain) n **1** luce del sole f. **2** bel tempo m.

sunstroke ('sʌnstrouk) n colpo di sole m.

suntan ('sʌntæn) n abbronzatura f.

super ('su:pə) adj eccellente, sopraffino.

superannuation (su:pərænju'eiʃən) n pensione di vecchiaia f.

superb (su:'pə:b) adj eccellente, superbo.

superficial (su:pə'fiʃəl) adj superficiale, poco profondo.

superfluous (su:'pə:fluəs) adj superfluo.

superhuman (su:pə'hju:mən) adj sovrumano.

superimpose (su:pərim'pouz) vt sovrapporre.

superintendent (su:pərin'tendənt) n sovrintendente m.

superior (su'piəriə) adj,n superiore m.

superlative (su'pə:lətiv) adj,n superlativo m.

supermarket (su:pə'ma:kit) n supermercato m.

supernatural (su:pə'nætʃrəl) adj soprannaturale.

supersede (su:pə'si:d) vt rimpiazzare, sostituire.

supersonic (su:pə'sɔnik) adj ultrasonico, supersonico.

superstition (su:pə'stiʃən) n superstizione f. **superstitious** adj superstizioso.

supervise ('su:pəvaiz) vt sorvegliare, sovrintendere. **supervision** n sorveglianza f. **supervisor** n sorvegliante, sovrintendente m.

supper ('sʌpə) n cena f. **have supper** cenare.

supple ('sʌpəl) adj pieghevole, flessibile.

supplement (n 'sʌplimənt; v 'sʌpliment) n supplemento m. vt completare, integrare. **supplementary** adj supplementare.

supply (sə'plai) vt fornire, provvedere. n provvista f. rifornimento m.

support (sə'pɔ:t) n sostegno, appoggio m. vt **1** sostenere, reggere. **2** mantenere.

suppose (sə'pouz) vt supporre, presumere, credere. **supposing** conj se nel caso.

suppress (sə'pres) vt **1** sopprimere, reprimere. **2** tener nascosto.

supreme (sə'pri:m) adj supremo, massimo.

surcharge ('sə:tʃa:dʒ) n soprattassa f.

sure (ʃuə) adj sicuro, certo. adv,interj certamente, davvero. **surely** adv certamente. **surety** n **1** certezza f. **2** garanzia f. pegno m.

surf (sə:f) n risacca f.

surface ('sə:fis) n superficie f. vi affiorare.

surfeit ('sə:fit) n eccesso m.

surge (sə:dʒ) n impeto m. vi gonfiarsi.

surgeon ('sə:dʒən) n chirurgo m. **surgery** n **1** chirurgia f. **2** (place) ambulatorio, studio medico m.

surly ('sə:li) adj scontroso, sgarbato.

surmount (sə'maunt) vt sormontare, superare.

surname ('sə:neim) n cognome m.

surpass (sə'pa:s) vt superare.

surplus ('sə:plis) n sovrappiù m invar. avanzo m.

surprise (sə'praiz) n sorpresa f. stupore m. adj inaspettato. vt sorprendere, stupire.

surrealism (sə'riəlizəm) n surrealismo m.

surrender (sə'rendə) vt cedere. vi arrendersi. n **1** resa f. **2** abbandono m.

surreptitious (sʌrəp'tiʃəs) adj furtivo, clandestino.

surround (sə'raund) vt circondare, cingere. n bordura f. **surrounding** adj circostante. **surroundings** n pl ambiente m. dintorni m pl.

survey (n 'sə:vei; v sə'vei) n **1** perizia f. **2** esame m. indagine f. vt esaminare, ispezionare.

surveyor (sə'veiə) n topografo, ispettore m.

survive (sə'vaiv) vi sopravvivere. vt sopravvivere a. **survival** n sopravvivenza f.

susceptible (sə'septəbəl) adj **1** suscettibile, impressionabile, permaloso. **2** disposto.

suspect (v sə'spekt; n,adj 'sʌspekt) vt **1** sospettare. **2** credere. *n* persona sospetta *f*. *adj* sospetto.

suspend (sə'spend) *vt* **1** sospendere. **2** appendere, tenere sospeso. **suspense** *n* ansia, incertezza *f*. **suspension** *n* sospensione *f*.

suspicion (sə'spiʃən) *n* sospetto, dubbio *m*. **suspicious** *adj* **1** sospettoso, diffidente. **2** losco.

sustain (sə'stein) *vt* **1** sostenere, sopportare. **2** subire. **3** reggere.

swab (swɔb) *n* tampone *m*.

swagger ('swægə) *vi* pavoneggiarsi, muoversi con boria. *n* andatura spavalda *f*.

swallow[1] ('swolou) *vt* inghiottire, ingoiare. *n* sorso *m*.

swallow[2] ('swolou) *n zool* rondine *f*.

swam (swæm) *v see* **swim**.

swamp (swomp) *n* palude *f*. *vt* inondare, sommergere.

swan (swon) *n* cigno *m*.

swank (swæŋk) *vi* darsi arie. *n inf* vanagloria *f*.

swap (swop) *n* scambio *m*. *vt* barattare, scambiare.

swarm (swɔːm) *n* sciame *m*. folla *f*. *vi* **1** sciamare. **2** pullulare, brulicare.

swastika ('swostikə) *n* svastica, croce uncinata *f*.

swat (swot) *vt inf* colpire. *n* acchiappamosche *m*.

sway (swei) *vi* oscillare, ondeggiare. *vt* influenzare, dominare. *n* **1** preponderanza *f*. **2** oscillazione *f*.

swear[*] (swɛə) *vt* giurare. *vi* bestemmiare. **swearword** *n* bestemmia, imprecazione *f*.

sweat (swet) *vi* sudare, traspirare. *n* sudore *m*. traspirazione *f*. **sweater** *n* maglione *m*.

swede (swiːd) *n* rapa svedese *f*.

Sweden ('swiːdn) *n* Svezia *f*. **Swede** *n* svedese *m,f*. **Swedish** *adj* svedese. **Swedish** (language) *n* svedese *m*.

sweep[*] (swiːp) *vt* **1** spazzare, scopare. **2** sfiorare. *vi* **1** muoversi velocemente. **2** scopare. *n* **1** scopata, spazzata *f*. **2** curva *f*. **3** movimento rapido *m*. **sweeping** *adj* **1** generale. **2** vasto. **3** rapido.

sweet (swiːt) *adj* **1** dolce. **2** amabile. *n* dolce *m*. caramella *f*. **sweetbread** *n* animella *f*. **sweet corn** *n* granoturco *m*. **sweetheart** *n* innamorato *m*. **sweet pea** *n* pisello odoroso *m*. **sweeten** *vt* **1** zuccherare. **2** addolcire.

swell[*] (swel) *vt* **1** aumentare. **2** gonfiare. *vi*

gonfiarsi. *n naut* mare lungo *m*. risacca *f*. **swelling** *n* infiammazione *f*.

swept (swept) *v see* **sweep**.

swerve (swəːv) *vi* deviare. *n* deviazione *f*.

swift (swift) *adj* **1** svelto. **2** rapido, agile. *n zool* rondone *m*.

swig (swig) *n inf* bevuta, sorsata *f*. *vt,vi* tracannare.

swill (swil) *n* risciacquatura *f*. *vt* **1** risciacquare. **2** tracannare.

swim[*] (swim) *vi* nuotare. *n* nuotata *f*. **swimmer** *n* nuotatore *m*. **swimming** *n* nuoto *m*. **swimming costume** *n* costume da bagno *m*. **swimming pool** *n* piscina *f*.

swindle ('swindl) *vt* frodare, truffare. *n* frode *f*.

swine (swain) *n* maiale, porco *m*.

swing[*] (swiŋ) *vi* **1** dondolare, oscillare. **2** girare. *vt* agitare. *n* **1** oscillazione *f*. dondolio *m*. **2** altalena *f*. **3** ritmo *m*.

swipe (swaip) *inf n* colpo violento *m*. *vt* colpire con forza.

swirl (swəːl) *n* vortice, turbine *m*. *vi* turbinare.

swish (swiʃ) *n* sibilo *m*. sferzata *f*. *vi* sibilare, fischiare.

switch (switʃ) *n* **1** (electric) interruttore *m*. **2** frustino *m*. *vt* mutare, spostare. **switch on/off** accendere/spegnere. **switchboard** *n* centralino *m*.

Switzerland ('switsələnd) *n* Svizzera *f*. **Swiss** *adj,n* svizzero.

swivel ('swivəl) *n* perno, snodo *m*. *vi* girare. **swivel chair** sedia girevole.

swollen ('swoulən) *v see* **swell**.

swoop (swuːp) *n* attacco, assalto *m*. *vi* assalire, abbattersi.

swop (swop) *n* scambio *m*. *vt* barattare, scambiare.

sword (sɔːd) *n* spada *f*. **swordfish** *n* pesce spada *m*. **swordsman** *n* spadaccino *m*. **swordsmanship** *n* maestria nel maneggiare la spada *f*.

swore (swɔː) *v see* **swear**.

sworn (swɔːn) *v see* **swear**.

swot (swot) *sl vi* sgobbare. *n* sgobbone *m*.

swum (swʌm) *v see* **swim**.

swung (swʌŋ) *v see* **swing**.

sycamore ('sikəmɔː) *n* sicomoro *m*.

syllable ('siləbəl) *n* sillaba *f*.

syllabus ('siləbəs) *n* programma, prospetto *m*.

symbol ('simbəl) *n* simbolo *m*. **symbolic** *adj* simbolico. **symbolism** *n* simbolismo *m*. **symbolize** *vt* simboleggiare.

symmetry ('simitri) n simmetria f. **symmetrical** adj simmetrico.

sympathy ('simpəθi) n 1 simpatia, comprensione f. 2 compassione, solidarietà f. **sympathetic** adj 1 simpatizzante, cordiale. 2 simpatico. **sympathize** vi capire, condividere i sentimenti.

symphony ('simfəni) n sinfonia f.

symposium (sim'pouziəm) n simposio m.

symptom ('simptəm) n sintomo, indizio m.

synagogue ('sinagɔg) n sinagoga f.

synchronize ('siŋkrənaiz) vt sincronizzare.

syndicate ('sindikət) n sindacato m.

syndrome ('sindroum) n sindrome f.

synonym ('sinənim) n sinonimo m.

synopsis (si'nɔpsis) n, pl **synopses** sinossi f invar.

syntax ('sintæks) n sintassi f.

synthesis ('sinθəsis) n, pl **syntheses** sintesi f. **synthetic** adj sintetico.

syphilis ('sifəlis) n sifilide f.

Syria ('siriə) n Siria f. **Syrian** adj,n siriano.

syringe (si'rindʒ) n siringa f.

syrup ('sirəp) n sciroppo m.

system ('sistəm) n sistema, metodo m. **systematic** adj sistematico.

T

tab (tæb) n 1 linguetta f. 2 etichetta f.

tabby ('tæbi) adj tigrato. n gatto soriano m.

table ('teibəl) n 1 tavola f. 2 tabella, classifica f. **lay/clear the table** apparecchiare/sparecchiare la tavola. **tablecloth** n tovaglia f. **tablemat** n tovaglietta f. sottopiatto m. **tablespoon** n cucchiaio m. **table tennis** n Ping-pong Tdmk m.

tablet ('tæblət) n 1 med pastiglia, compressa f. 2 lapide, tavoletta f.

taboo (tə'bu:) adj,n tabù m invar.

tack (tæk) n 1 puntina f. 2 (sewing) imbastitura f. vt 1 attaccare. 2 imbastire. vi naut virare.

tackle ('tækəl) vt 1 affrontare. 2 sport caricare, placcare. n attrezzi m pl.

tact (tækt) n tatto m. **tactful** adj pieno di tatto.

tactics ('tæktiks) n pl tattica f.

tadpole ('tædpoul) n girino m.

taffeta ('tæfitə) n taffettà m.

tag (tæg) n 1 cartellino m. etichetta f. 2 linguetta f.

Tahiti (tə'hi:ti) n Tahiti m. **Tahitian** adj,n tahitiano.

tail (teil) n 1 coda f. 2 pl (of a coin) rovescio m. 3 pl marsina f. franc m.

tailor ('teilə) n sarto m.

taint (teint) vt contaminare, corrompere, inquinare. n 1 infezione f. 2 marchio m.

take* (teik) vt 1 prendere. 2 portare. 3 accompagnare. 4 occorrere. **take after** assomigliare a. **take down** 1 abbassare. 2 smontare. 3 inf umiliare. **take in** 1 comprendere. 2 (clothes) stringere. 3 ingannare. **take off** 1 togliere. 2 aviat decollare. **take-off** n decollo m. **take over** rilevare. **take-over** n rilevamento or assorbimento di una ditta m. **takings** n pl.

talcum powder ('tælkəm) n borotalco, talco m.

tale (teil) n 1 storia f. racconto m. 2 chiacchiera, diceria f.

talent ('tælənt) n talento, ingegno m.

talk (tɔ:k) vi parlare, conversare, chiacchierare. **talk over** discutere su. ~n discorso m. conversazione, chiacchierata f. **talkative** adj loquace, chiacchierone.

tall (tɔ:l) adj 1 alto. 2 incredibile.

tally ('tæli) n talloncino m. etichetta f. vt calcolare, registrare. vi corrispondere.

talon ('tælən) n artiglio m.

tambourine (tæmbə'ri:n) n tamburello m.

tame (teim) adj 1 domestico, docile, mansueto. 2 banale. vt addomesticare, domare.

tamper ('tæmpə) vi alterare, corrompere.

tampon ('tæmpɔn) n tampone m.

tan (tæn) vt 1 abbronzare. 2 (leather) conciare. vi abbronzarsi. n abbronzatura f. adj marrone rossiccio.

tangent ('tændʒənt) n tangente m.

tangerine (tændʒə'ri:n) n mandarino m.

tangible ('tændʒəbəl) adj 1 tangibile. 2 chiaro, manifesto.

tangle ('tæŋgəl) n groviglio, imbroglio m. vt aggrovigliare, ingarbugliare. vi aggrovigliarsi.

tango ('tæŋgou) n tango m.

tank (tæŋk) n 1 vasca, cisterna f. 2 mil carro armato m. **tanker** n nave cisterna f. **oil tanker** n petroliera f.

tankard ('tæŋkəd) n boccale m.

tantalize ('tæntəlaiz) vt tentare, tormentare.

tantrum ('tæntrəm) n 1 accesso d'ira m. 2 pl capricci m pl.

tap[1] (tæp) vt (hit) colpire lievemente. n colpetto.

tap² (tæp) n rubinetto m. vt attingere, utilizzare.

tape (teip) n 1 nastro m. 2 (ribbon) fettuccia f. vt 1 legare con un nastro. 2 incidere su un nastro magnetico. **tape-measure** n metro m. **tape-recorder** n registratore m.

taper ('teipə) n candela sottile f. vt assottigliare.

tapestry ('tæpistri) n arazzo m. tappezzeria f.

tapioca (tæpi'oukə) n tapioca f.

tar (tɑ:) n catrame m. vt incatramare, impeciare.

tarantula (tə'ræntjulə) n tarantola f.

target ('tɑ:git) n bersaglio, obiettivo, traguardo m.

tariff ('tærif) n tariffa f.

Tarmac ('tɑ:mæk) n Tdmk macadam al catrame m.

tarnish ('tɑ:niʃ) vt 1 annerire, ossidare. 2 macchiare. n annerimento m. ossidazione f.

tarragon ('tærəgən) n dragoncello m.

tart¹ (tɑ:t) adj 1 agro, aspro. 2 sarcastico.

tart² (tɑ:t) n 1 cul crostata f. 2 sl meretrice f.

tartan ('tɑ:tn) n tessuto scozzese m.

tartar sauce ('tɑ:tə) n salsa tartara f.

task (tɑ:sk) n compito, dovere m.

tassel ('tæsəl) n nappa f. fiocco m.

taste (teist) vt gustare, assaggiare. **taste of** sapere di. ~n 1 gusto, sapore m. 2 assaggio m. 3 inclinazione f. 4 buon gusto m.

tattoo¹ (tə'tu:) n ritirata militare m.

tattoo² (tə'tu:) n tatuaggio m. vt tatuare.

taught (tɔ:t) v see **teach.**

taunt (tɔ:nt) n sarcasmo, insulto m. vt schernire.

Taurus ('tɔ:rəs) n Toro m.

taut (tɔ:t) adj teso, tirato.

tautology (tɔ:'tɔlədʒi) n tautologia f.

tavern ('tævən) n taverna f.

tax (tæks) n tassa, imposta f. vt 1 tassare. 2 mettere alla prova.

taxi ('tæksi) n tassì m.

tea (ti:) n tè m. **high tea** n pasto serale con tè m. **tea bag** n bustina di tè f. **tea-break** n intervallo per merenda m. **tea cloth** n strofinaccio da cucina. **teacup** n tazza de tè f. **tea-leaf** n foglia del tè f. **teapot** n teiera f. **teaspoon** n cucchiaino m. **tea-tray** n vassoio da tè m.

teach⁺ (ti:tʃ) vt insegnare. **teacher** n insegnante, professore m. professoressa f.

teak (ti:k) n tek m.

team (ti:m) n 1 squadra f. 2 (of horses) tiro m.

tear¹ (tiə) n lacrima f. **teardrop** n lacrima f. **tear gas** n gas-lacrimogeno m.

tear⁺² (tɛə) vt 1 strappare. 2 dividere, lacerare.

vi strapparsi. **tear along** correre. **tear up** fare a pezzi. ~n strappo m. lacerazione f.

tease (ti:z) vt stuzzicare, prendere in giro.

teat (ti:t) n 1 tettarella f. 2 zool capezzolo m.

technical ('teknikəl) adj tecnico. **technician** n tecnico m. **technique** n tecnica f. **technology** n tecnologia f.

teddy bear ('tedi) n orsacchiotto m.

tedious ('ti:diəs) adj tedioso.

tee (ti:) n sport tee m. **to a tee** a puntino. ~vt mettere sul tee.

teenage ('ti:neidʒ) adj adolescente. **teenager** n adolescente m,f.

teetotal (ti:'toutl) adj astemio. **teetotaller** n astemio m.

telegram ('teligræm) n telegramma m.

telegraph ('teligrɑ:f) n telegrafo m. vt,vi telegrafare. **telegraph pole** n palo telegrafico m.

telepathy (ti'lepəθi) n telepatia f.

telephone ('telifoun) n telefono m. vt telefonare a. vi telefonare.

telescope ('teliskoup) n telescopio, cannocchiale m. vi incastrarsi l'uno nell'altro.

televise ('telivaiz) vt teletrasmettere. **television** n televisione f. **television set** n televisore m.

telex ('teleks) n telex m. vt trasmettere per telex.

tell⁺ (tel) vt 1 dire, raccontare. 2 distinguere. **telltale** n chiacchierone, pettegolo m. adj rivelatore.

temper ('tempə) n 1 collera f. 2 umore m. 3 indole f. vt moderare, temperare. **temperament** n temperamento m. indole f. **temperamental** adj capriccioso. **temperate** adj temperato, moderato. **temperature** n temperatura f. **have a temperature** avere la febbre.

tempestuous (tem'pestjuəs) adj 1 tempestoso, burrascoso. 2 agitato.

temple¹ ('tempəl) n rel tempio m.

temple² ('tempəl) n anat tempia f.

tempo ('tempou) n tempo, ritmo m.

temporal ('tempərəl) adj temporale. **temporary** adj temporaneo.

tempt (tempt) vt tentare, indurre al male.

ten (ten) adj,n dieci m or f. **tenth** adj decimo.

tenacious (tə'neiʃəs) adj tenace, ostinato.

tenant ('tenənt) n inquilino m. **tenancy** n affitto m. locazione f.

tend¹ (tend) vi tendere. **tendency** n tendenza, inclinazione f.

tend² (tend) vt curare.

tender[1] ('tendə) adj 1 affettuoso, tenero. 2 delicato, sensibile.

tender[2] ('tendə) vt offrire, presentare. vi fare offerte per un appalto. n offerta f.

tendon ('tendən) n tendine m.

tendril ('tendril) n viticcio m.

tenement ('tenəmənt) n abitazione f.

tennis ('tenis) n tennis m. **tennis court** n campo da tennis m.

tenor ('tenə) n 1 tenore m. 2 mus tenore m.

tense[1] (tens) adj teso. vt tendere. vi innervosirsi. **tension** n tensione f.

tense[2] (tens) n gram tempo m.

tent (tent) n tenda f.

tentacle ('tentəkəl) n tentacolo m.

tentative ('tentətiv) adj sperimentale, di prova.

tenuous ('tenjuəs) adj 1 tenue, sottile. 2 rarefatto.

tepid ('tepid) adj tiepido.

term (tə:m) n 1 termine m. 2 educ trimestre m. 3 termine m. parola f. 4 pl rapporti m pl. vt chiamare, definire.

terminal ('tə:minl) n 1 stazione terminale, capolinea f. 2 tech morsetto m. adj estremo, finale.

terminate ('tə:mineit) vt,vi terminare. **termination** n terminazione f.

terminology (tə:mi'nɔlədʒi) n terminologia f.

terminus ('tə:minəs) n, pl **termini** 1 capolinea f. 2 termine m.

terrace ('terəs) n 1 terrazza f. 2 fila di case f.

terrestrial (tə'restriəl) adj terrestre.

terrible ('teribəl) adj terribile.

terrier ('teriə) n terrier m.

terrify ('terifai) vt atterrire. **terrific** adj 1 terrificante. 2 straordinario, magnifico.

territory ('teritri) n 1 territorio m. 2 zona f.

terror ('terə) n terrore m. **terrorist** n terrorista m. **terrorize** vt terrorizzare.

Terylene ('terili:n) n Tdmk terital m.

test (test) n 1 prova f. esame m. 2 collaudo m. 3 med analisi f invar. vt 1 esaminare, mettere alla prova. 2 collaudare. 3 med analizzare. **test-tube** n provetta f.

testament ('testəmənt) n testamento m.

testicle ('testikl) n testicolo m.

testify ('testifai) vt 1 attestare, dimostrare. 2 testimoniare.

testimony ('testiməni) n attestato m. deposizione, testimonianza f. **testimonial** n testimonianza f. benservito m.

tether ('teðə) vt impastoiare. n pastoia f.

text (tekst) n testo m. **textbook** n libro di testo m. **textual** adj testuale.

textile ('tekstail) adj,n tessile m.

texture ('tekstʃə) n 1 tech grana f. 2 tessuto m.

Thames (temz) n Tamigi m.

than (ðən; stressed ðæn) conj che, di, di quanto, di quello che, che non.

thank (θæŋk) vt ringraziare. **thanks** n pl grazie f pl. **thank you!** grazie! **thankful** adj riconoscente.

that (ðæt) adj quel, quello ms. quella fs. quei, quegli m pl. quelle f pl. pron 1 quello ms. quella fs. quei, quegli m pl 2 ciò. 3 che, il quale ms, la quale fs, i quali m pl, le quali f pl. 4 in cui. conj che.

thatch (θætʃ) n paglia f. vt coprire di paglia.

thaw (θɔ:) vt sgelare. vi sgelarsi. n disgelo m.

the (ðə; stressed ði:) def art il, lo l' ms. la, l' fs. i, gli m pl. le f pl.

theatre ('θiətə) n 1 teatro m. scena f. 2 med sala operatoria f. **theatrical** adj teatrale, drammatico.

theft (θeft) n furto m.

their (ðεə) poss adj 3rd pers pl (il) loro, (la) loro, (i) loro, (le) loro. **theirs** pron 3rd pers pl il loro, la loro, i loro, le loro, di loro.

them (ðəm; stressed ðem) pron 3rd pers pl 1 li m pl. le f pl. loro m,f pl. 2 essi m pl. esse f pl. loro m,f pl. **themselves** pron 3rd pers pl 1 se or si stessi. 2 si, sè.

theme (θi:m) n tema, soggetto m. **thematic** adj tematico.

then (ðen; stressed ðen) adv 1 allora, a quel tempo. 2 poi, dopo. conj in questo caso, quindi, dunque. **by then** ormai. **up to then** fino allora, fino a quel momento.

theology (θi'ɔlədʒi) n teologia f. **theologian** n teologo m. **theological** adj teologico.

theorem ('θiərəm) n teorema m.

theory ('θiəri) n 1 teoria f. 2 opinione f. **theoretical** adj teorico, astratto. **theoretically** adv in teoria. **theorize** vi formulare teorie, teorizzare.

therapy ('θerəpi) n terapia, cura f. **therapeutic** adj terapeutico, curativo.

there (ðεə) adv 1 lì, là. 2 ci, vi. 3 in ciò. interj ecco! **thereabouts** adv 1 là vicino, nei pressi. 2 circa, pressappoco. **thereafter** adv da allora in poi, in seguito. **thereby** adv così, in tal modo. **therefore** adv quindi, dunque, perciò. **thereupon** adv al che, quindi. **therewith** adv con ciò.

thermal ('θɜ:məl) *adj also* **thermic 1** termale. **2** termico.

thermodynamics (θɜ:moudai'næmiks) *n* termodinamica *f*. **thermodynamic** *adj* termodinamico.

thermometer (θə'mɔmitə) *n* termometro *m*.

thermonuclear (θɜ:mou'nju:kliə) *adj* termonucleare.

Thermos ('θɜ:məs) *n Tdmk* termos *m invar*.

thermostat ('θɜ:məstæt) *n* termostato *m*.

these (ði:z) *adj,pron* questi.

thesis ('θi:sis) *n, pl* **theses** tesi *f invar*. teoria *f*.

they (ðei) *pron 3rd pers pl* essi *m pl*. esse *f pl*. loro *m,f pl*.

thick (θik) *adj* **1** grosso, spesso. **2** denso. **3** fitto. **4** stupido. **thick as thieves** amici per la pelle. **thick-skinned** *adj* insensibile. **thicken** *vt* addensare, rendere più denso. *vi* **1** infittirsi. **2** complicarsi. **3** offuscarsi. **thickness** *n* spessore *m*.

thief (θi:f) *n, pl* **thieves** ladro *m*.

thigh (θai) *n* coscia *f*.

thimble ('θimbəl) *n* ditale *m*.

thin (θin) *adj* **1** sottile, fine. **2** magro, snello. **3** rado, scarso. **thin-skinned** *adj* sensibile. **thinness** *n* magrezza *f*.

thing (θiŋ) *n* **1** cosa, roba *f*. oggetto *m*. **2** *pl* effetti *m pl*. **for one thing...for another** in primo luogo...d'altra parte.

think* (θiŋk) *vt,vi* **1** pensare, riflettere. **2** credere, immaginare. **think about/of** pensare di/a. **think over** ripensare, ripensarci.

third (θɜ:d) *adj* terzo. *n* terzo *m*. terza parte *f*. **third party** *n comm* terzi *m pl*. **third person** *n* terza persona *f*. **third-rate** *adj* scadente.

thirst (θɜ:st) *n* sete *f*. *v* **thirst for** bramare, desiderare. **thirsty** *adj* assetato. **be thirsty** avere sete.

thirteen (θɜ:'ti:n) *adj,n* tredici *m* or *f*. **thirteen** *adj* tredicesimo.

thirty ('θɜ:ti) *adj,n* trenta *m*. **thirtieth** *adj* trentesimo.

this (ðis) *adj,pron* questo.

thistle ('θisəl) *n* cardo *m*.

thorn (θɔ:n) *n* spino *m*. spina *f*.

thorough ('θʌrə) *adj* esauriente, accurato. **thoroughbred** *adj* di razza. **thoroughfare** *n* strada, via di transito *f*. **thoroughly** *adv* a fondo, in dettaglio.

those (ðouz) *adj,pron* quei, quegli, quelli *m pl*. quelle *f pl*. **those who** chi.

though (ðou) *conj* **1** sebbene, benchè. **2** anche se. **as though** come se. ~*adv* tuttavia.

thought[1] (θɔ:t) *n* pensiero *m*. idea, opinione *f*. **on second thoughts** ripensandoci. **thoughtful** *adj* **1** pensieroso. **2** premuroso. **thoughtless** *adj* **1** avventato, sbadato. **2** irriguardoso.

thought[2] (θɔ:t) *v see* **think**.

thousand ('θauzənd) *adj* mille. *n* mille *m*. migliaio *m*, *pl* migliaia *f*. **thousandth** *adj* millesimo.

thrash (θræʃ) *vt* battere, colpire, frustare. **thrashing** *n* **1** percosse *f pl*. **2** sconfitta *f*.

thread (θred) *n* filo *m*. *vt* infilare. **threadbare** *adj* logoro.

threat (θret) *n* minaccia *f*. **threaten** *vt* minacciare. **threatening** *adj* minaccioso.

three (θri:) *adj,n* tre *m* or *f*. **three-cornered** *adj* triangolare. **three-dimensional** *adj* tridimensionale. **threequarters** *adv* a tre quarti. **threesome** *n* trio *m*.

thresh (θreʃ) *vt* trebbiare.

threshold ('θreʃhould) *n* soglia *f*.

threw (θru:) *v see* **throw**.

thrift (θrift) *n* economia, parsimonia *f*. **thrifty** *adj* frugale, parco.

thrill (θril) *n* brivido *m*. *vt* eccitare. *vi* fremere. **thriller** *n* romanzo poliziesco, giallo *m*. **thrilling** *adj* eccitante.

thrive* (θraiv) *vi* prosperare. **thriving** *adj* prospero, florido.

throat (θrout) *n* gola *f*. **have a sore throat** avere mal di gola.

throb (θrɔb) *n* battito, palpito *m*. *vi* battere, palpitare, pulsare.

throne (θroun) *n* trono *m*.

throng (θrɔŋ) *n* folla, ressa *f*. *vt* affollare. *vi* affollarsi.

throttle ('θrɔtl) *n* valvola *f*. *vt* strozzare.

through (θru:) *prep* **1** per, attraverso. **2** durante. **3** mediante. *adj* diretto. *adv* completamente. **throughout** *adv* completamente. *prep* in tutto.

throw* (θrou) *n* lancio, tiro *m*. *vt* gettare, lanciare, tirare. **throw away** gettar via. **throw out** cacciar fuori, espellere.

thrush (θrʌʃ) *n* tordo *m*.

thrust* (θrʌst) *n* spinta *f*. colpo *m*. *vt* conficcare.

thud (θʌd) *n* tonfo *m*. *vi* cadere con un tonfo.

thumb (θʌm) *n* pollice *m*. *vt* voltare le pagine di.

thump (θʌmp) n **1** botta f. colpo m. **2** tonfo m. vt battere, colpire.

thunder ('θʌndə) n tuono m. vi tuonare. **thunderstorm** n temporale m.

Thursday ('θə:zdi) n giovedì m.

thus (ðʌs) adv così, quindi.

thwart (θwɔ:t) vt frustrare, contrastare.

thyme (taim) n timo m.

thyroid ('θairɔid) n tiroide f.

tiara (ti'ɑ:rə) n tiara f.

tick¹ (tik) n **1** tic tac, ticchettio, scatto m. **2** segno m. **3** inf attimo m. vi ticchettare. vt segnare. **tick off** spuntare.

tick² (tik) n zool zecca f. acaro m.

ticket ('tikit) n biglietto, scontrino m. **ticket collector** n bigliettaio m. **ticket office** n biglietteria f.

tickle ('tikəl) vt fare il solletico a, stuzzicare. vi prudere. **ticklish** adj **1** sensibile al solletico. **2** difficile.

tide (taid) n marea f. flusso m.

tidy ('taidi) adj ordinato. vt mettere in ordine. **tidiness** n ordine m. accuratezza f.

tie (tai) n **1** legame, vincolo m. **2** (clothing) cravatta f. vt legare, annodare.

tier (tiə) n fila f. ordine m.

tiger ('taigə) n tigre f.

tight (tait) adj **1** stretto, aderente, fermo. **2** inf brillo. adv saldamente. **tight-fisted** adj tirchio. **tightrope** n corda dell'acrobata f. **tightrope walker** n funambolo m. **tighten** vt serrare. vi tendersi. **tights** n pl calzamaglia f. collant m.

tile (tail) n tegola, mattonella, piastrella f. vt lastricare.

till¹ (til) prep fino a. conj finché.

till² (til) vt coltivare.

till³ (til) n cassa f. cassetto m.

tiller ('tilə) n naut barra f.

tilt (tilt) n inclinazione, pendenza f. vt inclinare. vi pendere.

timber ('timbə) n legname m.

time (taim) n **1** tempo m. **2** ora f. **3** volta f. vt,vi cronometrare, scegliere il momento. **from time to time** a volte, di quando in quando. **time bomb** n bomba a orologeria f. **timekeeper** n cronometrista, segnatempo m. **timetable** n orario m. **timely** adj opportuno.

timid ('timid) adj timido.

timpani ('timpəni) n pl timpani m pl.

tin (tin) n **1** min stagno m. **2** barattolo m. lattina

f. vt **1** stagnare. **2** inscatolare. **tin-opener** n apriscatole m invar.

tinge (tindʒ) n **1** tinta f. **2** sfumatura f. vt **1** tingere. **2** sfumare.

tingle ('tiŋgəl) n formicolio m. vi formicolare.

tinker ('tiŋkə) n calderaio m. v **tinker with** armeggiare con.

tinkle ('tiŋkəl) n tintinnio, trillo m. vt far tintinnare. vi trillare.

tinsel ('tinsəl) n lustrino m.

tint (tint) n **1** tinta f. **2** sfumatura f. vt **1** tingere. **2** sfumare.

tiny ('taini) adj piccolo, minuscolo.

tip¹ (tip) n (point) punta f. **tiptoe** n punta di piedi f. vi camminare in punta di piedi.

tip² (tip) n **1** inclinazione, pendenza f. **2** deposito m. vt **1** inclinare. **2** buttare. **tip over** rovesciare.

tip³ (tip) n **1** (gratuity) mancia f. **2** informazione riservata f. vt dare la mancia a. **tip off** avvertire. **tip-off** n avvertimento m.

tipsy ('tipsi) adj brillo, alticcio.

tire ('taiə) vt stancare. vi stancarsi. **tired** adj **1** stanco. **2** stufo.

tissue ('tiʃu:) n **1** tessuto m. **2** fazzoletto di carta m.

tit (tit) n **1** capezzolo m. **2** zool cincia f. **tit for tat** botta e risposta.

title ('taitl) n titolo m.

to (tə; stressed tu:) prep **1** a, da. **2** con, verso, per. **3** fina a. **4** in confronto a. **to and fro** su e giù.

toad (toud) n rospo m. **toadstool** n fungo velenoso m.

toast¹ (toust) n cul pane tostato, toast m. vt tostare, abbrustolire. **toaster** n tostapane m.

toast² (toust) n brindisi m invar. vi brindare.

tobacco (tə'bækou) n tabacco m. **tobacconist** n tabaccaio m.

toboggan (tə'bɔgən) n toboga m invar. slitta f.

today (tə'dei) adv,n oggi m.

toddler ('tɔdlə) n infante m.

toe (tou) n **1** anat dito del piede m. **2** punta f. **toenail** n unghia del piede f.

toffee ('tɔfi) n caramella f.

toga ('tougə) n toga f.

together (tə'geðə) adv **1** insieme. **2** contemporaneamente.

toil (tɔil) n lavoro m. fatica f. vi faticare.

toilet ('tɔilət) n gabinetto m. toletta f. **toilet paper** n carta igienica f. **toilet roll** n rotolo di carta igienica *m.* **toilet water** *n* acqua da toletta *f.*

token ('toukən) *n* segno, pegno *m.*

told (tould) *v* see **tell.**

tolerate ('tɔləreit) *vt* tollerare, sopportare. **tolerance** *n* tolleranza, indulgenza *f.* **tolerant** *adj* tollerante.

toll[1] (toul) *vt* suonare. *n* rintocco *m.*

toll[2] (toul) *n* pedaggio *m.* imposta *f.* **tollgate** *n* barriera di pedaggio *f.*

tomato (tə'mɑːtou) *n, pl* **-toes** pomodoro *m.*

tomb (tuːm) *n* tomba *f.* **tombstone** *n* lapide *f.*

tomorrow (tə'mɔrou) *adv,n* domani *m.*

ton (tʌn) *n* tonnellata *f.*

tone (toun) *n* 1 tono *m.* 2 tonalità *f.* *v* **tone down** attenuare, smorzare. **tone with** armonizzarsi con. **tonality** *n* tonalità *f.*

tongs (tɔŋz) *n pl* pinze, molle *f pl.*

tongue (tʌŋ) *n* lingua *f.* **tongue-tied** *adj* ammutolito, reticente. **tongue-twister** *n* scioglilingua *m.*

tonic ('tɔnik) *adj,n* tonico *m.* **tonic water** *n* acqua tonica *f.*

tonight (tə'nait) *adv* questa sera, stasera, questa notte, stanotte.

tonsil ('tɔnsəl) *n* tonsilla *f.* **tonsillitis** *n* tonsillite *f.*

too (tuː) *adv* 1 anche, inoltre, pure. 2 troppo. **too many** troppi. **too much** troppo.

took (tuk) *v* see **take.**

tool (tuːl) *n* attrezzo, strumento *m.*

tooth (tuːθ) *n, pl* **teeth** dente *m.* **toothache** *n* mal di denti *m.* **toothbrush** *n* spazzolino da denti *m.* **toothpaste** *n* dentifricio *m.* **toothpick** *n* stuzzicadenti *m invar.*

top[1] (tɔp) *n* 1 cima *f.* vertice *m.* 2 coperchio, tappo *m.* adj superiore, principale. *vt* 1 superare. 2 coprire. **top hat** *n* tuba *f.* **top-heavy** *adj* sbilanciato.

top[2] (tɔp) *n* (toy) trottola *f.*

topaz ('toupæz) *n* topazio *m.*

topic ('tɔpik) *n* argomento, soggetto *m.* **topical** *adj* d'attualità.

topography (tə'pɔgrəfi) *n* topografia *f.*

topple ('tɔpəl) *vt* rovesciare. *vi* vacillare, cadere. **topple over** rovesciarsi.

topsoil ('tɔpsɔil) *n* terriccio *m.*

topsy-turvy ('tɔpsi'təːvi) *adj,adv* sottosopra.

torch (tɔːtʃ) *n* torcia, fiaccola *f.*

tore (tɔː) *v* see **tear.**

torment ('tɔːmənt) *n* tormento *m.* pena *f.* *vt* tormentare, molestare.

torn (tɔːn) *v* see **tear.**

tornado (tɔː'neidou) *n, pl* **-does** or **-dos** tornado, uragano, ciclone *m.*

torpedo (tɔː'piːdou) *n, pl* **-does** torpedine *f.* siluro *m.* *vt* silurare.

torrent ('tɔrənt) *n* torrente *m.* **torrential** *adj* torrenziale.

torso ('tɔːsou) *n* tronco, torso *m.*

tortoise ('tɔːtəs) *n* testuggine, tartaruga *f.*

tortuous ('tɔːtʃuəs) *adj* tortuoso.

torture ('tɔːtʃə) *n* tortura *f.* supplizio *m.* *vt* torturare, tormentare.

Tory ('tɔːri) *n* 1 lancio *m.* scrollata *f.* *vt* 1 lanciare. 2 scrollare. *vi* agitarsi.

toss (tɔs) *n* 1 lancio *m.* scrollata *f.* *vt* 1 lanciare. 2 scrollare. *vi* agitarsi.

tot[1] (tɔt) *n* 1 (child) bambino *m.* 2 sorso *m.*

tot[2] (tɔt) *vt* **tot up** sommare.

total ('toutl) *n* totale *m.* adj totale, completo. *vt* sommare. *vi* ammontare. **totalitarian** *adj* totalitario.

totem ('toutəm) *n* totem *m invar.* **totem pole** *n* palo del totem *m.*

totter ('tɔtə) *vi* barcollare, vacillare.

touch (tʌtʃ) *n* 1 tocco, colpetto *m.* 2 tatto *m.* 3 contatto *m.* 4 po', poco di *m.* **get in touch with** mettersi in contatto con. —*vt* 1 toccare. 2 sfiorare. *vi* toccarsi. **touching** *adj* commovente. **touchy** *adj* permaloso, suscettibile.

tough (tʌf) *adj* 1 duro, tenace, violento. 2 forte. 3 difficile. **toughen** *vt* indurire, rafforzare.

toupee ('tuːpei) *n* toupet, parrucchino *m.*

tour (tuə) *n* viaggio, giro *m.* *vt* visitare. *vi* viaggiare. **tourism** *n* turismo *m.* **tourist** *n* turista *m.* adj turistico.

tournament ('tuənəmənt) *n* torneo *m.*

tow (tou) *vt* rimorchiare, trainare. *n* rimorchio *m.* **towrope** *n* cavo da rimorchio *m.*

towards (twɔːdz) *prep also* **toward** verso.

towel ('tauəl) *n* asciugamano *m.* salvietta *f.*

tower ('tauə) *n* torre *f.* *vi* torreggiare. **towering** *adj* dominante, imponente.

town (taun) *n* città *f.* **town clerk** *n* segretario comunale *m.* **town hall** *n* municipio *m.* **town-planning** *n* urbanistica *f.*

toxic ('tɔksik) *adj* tossico, velenoso.

toy (tɔi) *n* giocattolo *m.*

trace (treis) *n* 1 traccia *f.* segno *m.* *vt* 1 tracciare, rintracciare. 2 ricalcare.

track (træk) *n* 1 traccia, impronta *f.* 2 percorso *m.* 3 (railway) binario *m.* *vt* seguire le tracce di, inseguire. **track down** scovare. **tracksuit** *n* tuta ginnica *f.*

tract (trækt) n 1 periodo m. 2 zona f.

tractor ('træktə) n trattore m.

trade (treid) n 1 mestiere m. 2 commercio m. vt scambiare. vi commerciare. **trademark** n marchio di fabbrica. **tradesman** n negoziante, commerciante m. **trade union** n sindacato m.

tradition (trə'diʃən) n tradizione f. **traditional** adj tradizionale.

traffic' ('træfik) n traffico m. vi trafficare, commerciare. **traffic jam** n ingorgo m. **traffic lights** n pl semaforo m. **traffic warden** n addetto al traffico m.

tragedy ('trædʒədi) n tragedia f. **tragic** adj tragico.

trail (treil) n 1 traccia f. 2 scia f. vt 1 trascinare. 2 seguire le tracce di. vi strisciare. **trailer** n rimorchio m.

train (trein) n 1 treno m. 2 seguito m. 3 serie f invar. 4 strascico m. vt addestrare. vi allenarsi. **trainee** n apprendista m. **trainer** n allenatore m. **training** n allenamento m.

traitor ('treitə) n traditore m.

tram (træm) n tram m invar.

tramp (træmp) n vagabondo m. vi camminare con passo pesante.

trample ('træmpəl) n scalpitio m. vt calpestare. vi camminare pesantemente.

trampoline ('træmpəli:n) n trampolino m.

trance (tra:ns) n trance f. sonno ipnotico m.

tranquil ('træŋkwil) adj calmo, tranquillo. **tranquillity** n calma, tranquillità f. **tranquillizer** n tranquillante m.

transact (træn'zækt) vt trattare. **transaction** n trattativa f.

transatlantic (trænzət'læntik) adj transatlantico.

transcend (træn'send) vt trascendere.

transcribe (træn'skraib) vt trascrivere. **transcription** n trascrizione f.

transfer (v træns'fə:; n 'trænsfə:) vt trasferire. n trasferimento, trasporto m.

transform (træns'fɔ:m) vt trasformare. **transformation** n trasformazione f.

transfuse (træns'fju:z) vt travasare. **transfusion** n trasfusione f.

transistor (træn'zistə) n transistor m invar.

transit ('trænsit) n transito, passaggio m.

transition (træn'ziʃən) n transizione f. cambiamento m.

transitive ('trænsitiv) adj transitivo.

translate (trænz'leit) vt tradurre. **translation** n traduzione f. **translator** n traduttore m.

translucent (trænz'lu:sənt) adj traslucido.

transmit (trænz'mit) vt trasmettere. **transmitter** n trasmettitore m.

transparent (træns'pærənt) adj trasparente.

transplant (v træns'plɑ:nt; n 'trænspla:nt) vt 1 trapiantare. 2 med innestare. n trapianto m.

transport (v træns'pɔ:t; n 'trænspɔ:t) vt 1 trasportare. 2 deportare. n 1 trasporto m. 2 slancio m.

transpose (træns'pouz) vt trasporre, trasportare.

trap (træp) n 1 trappola f. 2 calesse m. vt intrappolare, prendere in trappola.

trapdoor (træp'dɔ:) n botola f.

trapeze (trə'pi:z) n trapezio m.

trash (træʃ) n 1 rifiuti m pl. 2 sciocchezze f pl.

trauma ('trɔ:mə) n trauma m. **traumatic** adj traumatico.

travel ('trævəl) vi viaggiare. n viaggi m pl. **travel agency** n agenzia di viaggio f. **traveller** n viaggiatore m. viaggiatrice f. **traveller's cheque** n assegno turistico m.

trawl (trɔ:l) n strascico m. vt pescare con rete. **trawler** n barca da pesca a motore f.

tray (trei) n vassoio m.

treachery ('tretʃəri) n tradimento m. slealtà f.

treacle ('tri:kəl) n melassa f.

tread (tred) vt calpestare, schiacciare. vi camminare. n 1 passo m. 2 battistrada m.

treason ('tri:zən) n tradimento m.

treasure ('treʒə) n tesoro m. vt custodire gelosamente, aver caro. **treasurer** n tesoriere m. **treasury** n tesoreria f. fisco m.

treat (tri:t) vt 1 trattare. 2 med curare. 3 offrire a, pagare a. n 1 festa f. 2 premio m. **treatment** n 1 trattamento m. 2 med cura f.

treatise ('tri:tiz) n trattato m.

treaty ('tri:ti) n trattato m. convenzione f.

treble ('trebəl) adj 1 triplo. 2 mus di soprano. n 1 triplo m. 2 mus soprano m. vt triplicare. 2 triplicarsi.

tree (tri:) n albero m.

trek (trek) n 1 migrazione f. 2 viaggio scomodo m. vi viaggiare senza comodità.

trellis ('trelis) n grata f.

tremble ('trembəl) vi tremare. n tremito, fremito m.

tremendous (tri'mendəs) adj 1 tremendo, terribile. 2 inf straordinario.

tremor ('tremə) n tremore m.

trench (trentʃ) n 1 mil trincea f. 2 fosso m.

trend (trend) n direzione, tendenza f.

trespass ('trespəs) n 1 (of property) trasgressione, violazione f. **2** rel peccato m. offesa f. vi violare, oltrepassare i confini. **trespasser** n trasgressore m.

trestle ('tresəl) n **1** cavalletto m. **2** intelaiatura f.

trial ('traiəl) n **1** law processo m. **2** prova f. esperimento m.

triangle 'traiæŋgəl) n triangolo m. **triangular** adj triangolare.

tribe (traib) n tribù f. **tribesman** n membro di tribù m.

tribunal (trai'bju:nl) n tribunale m.

tributary ('tribjutəri) adj tributario. n tributario, affluente m.

tribute ('tribju:t) n **1** tributo m. **2** omaggio m.

trick (trik) n **1** trucco, espediente m. **2** inganno m. **3** gioco di prestigio m. vt ingannare. **tricky** adj **1** complicato. **2** scaltro.

trickle ('trikəl) n gocciolio m. vi gocciolare.

tricycle ('traisikəl) n triciclo m.

trifle ('traifəl) n **1** sciocchezza f. **2** cul zuppa inglese f. vi baloccarsi, scherzare.

trigger ('triga) n grilletto m.

trill (tril) n trillo m. vi trillare.

trim (trim) adj ordinato, accurato. n ordine m. vt **1** assettare. **2** guarnire, ornare. **3** tagliare.

trio ('triou) n trio m.

trip (trip) n **1** gita f. viaggio m. **2** passo falso, sgambetto m. vi **1** inciampare. **2** camminare con passo svelto.

tripe (traip) n **1** cul trippa f. **2** sl robaccia f.

triple ('tripəl) adj triplo. vt triplicare. vi triplicarsi. **triplet** n bimbo nato da parto trigemino m.

tripod ('traipɔd) n treppiede, tripode m.

trite (trait) adj comune, banale.

triumph ('traiʌmf) n trionfo m. vi trionfare. **triumphant** adj trionfante.

trivial ('triviəl) adj insignificante, banale, frivolo.

trod (trɔd) v see **tread.**

trodden ('trɔdn) v see **tread.**

trolley ('trɔli) n carrello m.

trombone (trɔm'boun) n trombone m.

troop (tru:p) n **1** gruppo m. **2** pl mil truppe f pl.

trophy ('troufi) n trofeo m.

tropic ('trɔpik) n tropico m. **tropical** adj tropicale.

trot (trɔt) n trotto m. trottata f. vi trottare. **trotter** n **1** trottatore m. **2** cul piedino m.

trouble ('trʌbəl) n **1** guaio m. preoccupazione f. **2** fastidio, disturbo m. vt **1** turbare, preoccupare. **2** disturbare. **troublemaker** n sobillatore, attaccabrighe m.

trough (trɔf) n tinozza f.

troupe (tru:p) n troupe, compagnia f.

trousers ('trauzəz) n pl pantaloni, calzoni m pl.

trout (traut) n invar trota f.

trowel ('trauəl) n paletta, cazzuola f.

truant ('truənt) n pigrone m. **play truant** marinare la scuola.

truce (tru:s) n tregua f.

truck (trʌk) n carro, autocarro m.

trudge (trʌdʒ) vi camminare faticosamente.

true (tru:) adj **1** vero, reale. **2** fedele, leale. **truly** adv sinceramente, veramente.

truffle ('trʌfəl) n tartufo m.

trump (trʌmp) n briscola f. vt, vi giocare.

trumpet ('trʌmpit) n tromba f. vi suonare la tromba.

truncheon ('trʌntʃən) n **1** manganello m. **2** mazza f.

trunk (trʌŋk) n **1** (luggage) baule m. cassa f. **2** tronco m. **3** proboscide f. **4** pl calzoni corti m pl. **trunk call** n telefonata interurbana f.

trust (trʌst) n **1** fiducia, fede f. **2** law patrimonio amministrato m. **3** sindacato m. società finanziaria f. vt **1** aver fiducia in, fidarsi di. **2** sperare. vi fidarsi. **trustee** n fiduciario, amministratore m. **trustworthy** adj fidato, degno di fiducia.

truth (tru:θ) n verità f. vero m. **truthful** adj veritiero, sincero.

try (trai) n prova f. tentativo m. vt **1** provare, tentare. **2** mettere alla prova. **3** assaggiare. **4** law processare. **try on** vt provare. **trying** adj **1** difficile. **2** fastidioso.

tsar (tsɑ:) n zar m invar.

T-shirt n maglietta f.

tub (tʌb) n vasca, tinozza f.

tuba ('tju:bə) n tuba f.

tube (tju:b) n **1** tubo m. **2** ferrovia sotterranea f.

tuber ('tju:bə) n tubero m.

tuberculosis (tju:bə:kju'lousis) n tubercolosi f.

tuck (tʌk) n piega f. vt riporre, stipare. **tuck up** rimboccare.

Tuesday ('tju:zdi) n martedì m.

tuft (tʌft) n ciuffo m.

tug (tʌg) n **1** naut rimorchiatore m. **2** strappo m vi dare strattoni.

tuition (tju:'iʃən) n insegnamento m. istruzione f.

tulip ('tu:lip) n tulipano m.

tumble ('tʌmbəl) n caduta f. capitombolo m. vi cadere, ruzzolare. **tumbler** n bicchiere senza stelo m.

tummy ('tʌmi) n *inf* stomaco m. pancia f.

tumour ('tju:mə) n tumore m.

tumult ('tumʌlt) n tumulto m.

tuna ('tju:nə) n tonno m.

tune (tju:n) n 1 motivo m. aria f. 2 tono m. **in/out of tune** intonato/stonato. ~vt accordare. **tuneful** adj armonioso, melodioso.

tunic ('tju:nik) n tunica f.

tunnel ('tʌnl) n galleria f. traforo, tunnel m.

tunny ('tʌni) n tonno m.

turban ('tə:bən) n turbante m.

turbine ('tə:bain) n turbina f.

turbot ('tə:bət) n rombo m.

turbulent ('tə:bjulənt) adj turbolento.

turf (tə:f) n 1 tappeto erboso m. 2 torba f. 3 campo da corse m pl. **turf accountant** n allibratore m.

turkey ('tə:ki) n tacchino m.

Turkey ('tə:ki) n Turchia f. **Turk** n turco m. **Turkish** adj turco. **Turkish (language)** n turco m.

turmeric ('tə:mərik) n curcuma f.

turmoil ('tə:mɔil) n tumulto, scompiglio m.

turn (tə:n) vt 1 girare, voltare. 2 cambiare. 3 rendere, alterare. **turn on/off** accendere/spegnere. **turn out** 1 mandar via. 2 spegnere. 3 risultare. **turn over** rovesciare. **turnover** n 1 *comm* giro d'affari m. 2 *cul* pasticcio m. n 1 giro m. svolta f. 2 volta f. turno m. **a good turn** un favore m. **turning** n svolta, curva f. **turntable** n 1 piattaforma girevole f. 2 piatto del grammofono m.

turnip ('tə:nip) n rapa f.

turpentine ('tə:pəntain) n trementina f.

turquoise ('tə:kwɔiz) adj,n turchese m.

turret ('tʌrət) n torretta f.

turtle ('tə:tl) n tartaruga f.

Tuscany ('tʌskəni) n Toscana f. **Tuscan** adj,n toscano. **Tuscan (dialect)** n toscano m.

tusk (tʌsk) n zanna f.

tussle ('tʌsəl) n zuffa, rissa f. vi azzuffarsi.

tutor ('tju:tə) n 1 tutore m. 2 insegnante privato m. 3 professore universitario m. vt istruire. vi fare il tutore.

tweed (twi:d) n tessuto tweed m.

tweezers ('twi:zəz) n pl pinzetta f.

twelve (twelv) adj,n dodici m or f. **twelfth** adj dodicesimo.

twenty ('twenti) adj,n venti m or f. **twentieth** adj ventesimo.

twice (twais) adv due volte.

twiddle ('twidl) vt,vi girare, giocherellare.

twig (twig) n ramoscello m.

twilight ('twailait) n crepuscolo m.

twin (twin) n gemello m.

twine (twain) n spago m. corda f. vt attorcigliare, intrecciare.

twinge (twindʒ) n fitta f.

twinkle ('twiŋkl) vi scintillare, luccicare. n scintillio, luccichio m.

twirl (twə:l) n giro m. piroetta f. vt girare, roteare. vi girare.

twist (twist) vt 1 torcere. 2 intrecciare, attorcigliare. 3 alterare. n 1 curva f. 2 filo ritorto m.

twitch (twitʃ) n 1 tic nervoso m. 2 strattone m. vt dare uno strattone a. vi contrarsi, contorcersi.

twitter ('twitə) vi cinguettare, pigolare.

two (tu:) adj,n due m. **two-faced** adj falso. **twosome** n coppia f. **two-way** adj reciproco. **two-way traffic** n traffico a senso doppio m.

tycoon (tai'ku:n) n capitalista, magnate m.

type (taip) n 1 tipo, genere m. 2 carattere m. vt,vi dattilografare. **typewriter** n macchina da scrivere f. **typist** n dattilografo m.

typhoid ('taifɔid) n tifoide m.

typhoon (tai'fu:n) n tifone m.

typical ('tipikəl) adj tipico, caratteristico.

tyrant ('taiərənt) n tiranno m. **tyranny** n tirannia f. **tyrannical** adj tirannico.

tyre (taiə) n gomma f. pneumatico m.

Tyrol (ti'roul) n Tirolo m. **Tirolese** adj,n tirolese.

U

ubiquitous (ju:'bikwitəs) adj onnipresente.

udder ('ʌdə) n mammella f.

ugly ('ʌgli) adj brutto, sgradevole. **ugliness** n bruttezza f.

ukulele (ju:kə'le:li) n chitarra hawaiana f.

ulcer ('ʌlsə) n ulcera, piaga f.

ulterior (ʌl'tiəriə) adj 1 ulteriore. 2 segreto.

ultimate ('ʌltimət) adj ultimo, finale. **ultimatum** n ultimatum m.

ultraviolet (ʌltrə'vaiələt) adj ultravioletto.

umbrella (ʌm'brelə) n ombrello m.

umpire ('ʌmpaiə) n arbitro m. vt,vi arbitrare.

umpteen (ʌmp'ti:n) adj innumerevole.

unable (ʌn'eibəl) adj incapace, inabile.

unacceptable (ʌnək'septəbəl) adj inaccettabile.

unaccompanied (ʌnə'kʌmpnid) adj 1 solo. 2 *mus* senza accompagnamento.

291

unanimous (juːˈnænɪməs) adj unanime.

unarmed (ʌnˈɑːmd) adj disarmato.

unattractive (ʌnəˈtræktɪv) adj poco attraente.

unavoidable (ʌnəˈvɔɪdəbəl) adj inevitabile.

unaware (ʌnəˈwɛə) adj ignaro, inconsapevole. **unawares** adv inconsapevolmente, inavvertitamente.

unbalanced (ʌnˈbælənst) adj instabile, squilibrato.

unbearable (ʌnˈbɛərəbəl) adj insopportabile, intollerabile.

unbelievable (ʌnbɪˈliːvəbəl) adj incredibile.

unbend* (ʌnˈbend) vt 1 raddrizzare. 2 slegare, allentare. vi rilassarsi, distendersi.

unbreakable (ʌnˈbreɪkəbəl) adj infrangibile.

unbutton (ʌnˈbʌtn) vt sbottonare.

uncalled-for (ʌnˈkɔːldfɔː) adj superfluo, non meritato.

uncanny (ʌnˈkænɪ) adj misterioso, prodigioso.

uncertain (ʌnˈsɜːtn) adj incerto, dubbio.

uncle (ˈʌŋkəl) n zio m.

unclear (ʌnˈklɪə) adj poco chiaro.

uncomfortable (ʌnˈkʌmftəbəl) adj scomodo, a disagio.

unconscious (ʌnˈkɒnʃəs) adj 1 inconscio, involontario, inconsapevole. 2 privo di sensi.

unconventional (ʌnkənˈvenʃnəl) adj anticonformista, non convenzionale.

uncooked (ʌnˈkʊkt) adj crudo.

uncouth (ʌnˈkuːθ) adj rozzo.

uncover (ʌnˈkʌvə) vt 1 scoprire. 2 rivelare, esporre.

uncut (ʌnˈkʌt) adj non tagliato.

undecided (ʌndɪˈsaɪdɪd) adj incerto, indeciso.

undeniable (ʌndɪˈnaɪəbəl) adj innegabile.

under (ˈʌndə) prep sotto. adv al di sotto.

undercharge (ʌndəˈtʃɑːdʒ) vt far pagare troppo poco.

underclothes (ˈʌndəkləʊðz) n pl biancheria personale f.

undercoat (ˈʌndəkəʊt) n prima mano f.

undercover (ˈʌndəkʌvə) adj segreto.

undercut* (ʌndəˈkʌt) vt 1 colpire da sotto. 2 vendere a minor prezzo di.

underdeveloped (ʌndədɪˈveləpd) adj sottosviluppato.

underdone (ʌndəˈdʌn) adj poco cotto, al dente.

underestimate (ʌndərˈestɪmeɪt) vt sottovalutare.

underfoot (ʌndəˈfʊt) adv sotto i piedi.

undergo* (ʌndəˈgəʊ) vt subire, sopportare, essere sottoposto a.

undergraduate (ʌndəˈgrædjʊət) n studente universitario m.

underground (adv ʌndəˈgraund; adj,n ˈʌndəgraund) adv 1 sotto terra. 2 clandestinamente. adj 1 sotterraneo. 2 segreto, clandestino. n metropolitana f.

undergrowth (ˈʌndəgrəʊθ) n sottobosco m.

underhand (ʌndəˈhænd) adj clandestino, segreto.

underline (ʌndəˈlaɪn) vt sottolineare.

undermine (ʌndəˈmaɪn) vt 1 minare. 2 indebolire, insidiare.

underneath (ʌndəˈniːθ) adv al di sotto. prep sotto, al di sotto di.

underpants (ˈʌndəpænts) n pl mutande f pl.

underpass (ˈʌndəpɑːs) n sottopassaggio m.

underrate (ʌndəˈreɪt) vt sottovalutare.

understand* (ʌndəˈstænd) vt 1 comprendere, capire. 2 sentir dire. 3 dedurre. **understanding** n 1 comprensione, conoscenza f. 2 accordo m.

understate (ʌndəˈsteɪt) vt minimizzare.

understudy (ˈʌndəstʌdɪ) n sostituto m. vt sostituire.

undertake* (ʌndəˈteɪk) vt 1 intraprendere, impegnarsi a. 2 assumere. **undertaker** n imprenditore di pompe funebri m.

undertone (ˈʌndətəʊn) n tono sommesso m.

underwater (ʌndəˈwɔːtə) adj subacqueo.

underwear (ˈʌndəwɛə) n biancheria personale f.

underworld (ˈʌndəwɜːld) n 1 malavita f. 2 bassifondi m pl.

underwrite* (ˈʌndəraɪt) vt 1 sottoscrivere. 2 comm assicurare.

undesirable (ʌndɪˈzaɪərəbəl) adj indesiderabile.

undo* (ʌnˈduː) vt 1 disfare, slacciare. 2 annullare.

undoubted (ʌnˈdaʊtɪd) adj indubitato, incontestato.

undress (ʌnˈdres) vt svestire, spogliare. vi svestirsi.

undue (ʌnˈdjuː) adj 1 non dovuto, ingiusto. 2 indebito.

undulate (ˈʌndʒəleɪt) vi ondeggiare.

unearth (ʌnˈɜːθ) vt scoprire, dissotterrare.

unearthly adv 1 soprannaturale. 2 lugubre, sinistro. 3 assurdo.

uneasy (ʌnˈiːzɪ) adj 1 a disagio, impacciato. 2 ansioso.

unemployed (ʌnɪmˈplɔɪd) adj disoccupato. **unemployment** n disoccupazione f.

unequal (ʌn'i:kwəl) *adj* **1** disuguale. **2** inadeguato, incapace.

uneven (ʌn'i:vən) *adj* **1** ineguale, irregolare. **2** *math* dispari *invar*.

unfair (ʌn'fɛə) *adj* ingiusto.

unfaithful (ʌn'feiθfəl) *adj* infedele, sleale.

unfamiliar (ʌnfə'miliə) *adj* poco conosciuto.

unfit (ʌn'fit) *adj* **1** inadatto, incapace. **2** inabile.

unfold (ʌn'fould) *vt* **1** spiegare, schiudere. **2** rivelare.

unfortunate (ʌn'fɔ:tʃunət) *adj* sfortunato.

unfurnished (ʌn'fə:niʃt) *adj* non ammobiliato.

ungrateful (ʌn'greitfəl) *adj* ingrato.

unhappy (ʌn'hæpi) *adj* **1** infelice. **2** poco opportuno.

unhealthy (ʌn'helθi) *adj* **1** malsano, insalubre. **2** malaticcio.

unicorn ('ju:nikɔ:n) *n* unicorno *m*.

uniform ('ju:nifɔ:m) *n* uniforme, divisa *f*. *adj* uniforme, costante.

unify ('ju:nifai) *vt* unificare.

uninterested (ʌn'intrəstid) *adj* non interessato.

union ('ju:niən) *n* **1** unione *f*. **2** (trade) sindicato *m*.

Union Jack *n* bandiera britannica *f*.

unique (ju:'ni:k) *adj* unico.

unison ('ju:nizən) *n* unisono *m*.

unit (ju:nit) *n* **1** unità *f*. **2** gruppo, insieme *m*. **3** *mil* reparto *m*.

unite (ju:'nait) *vt* unire, congiungere. *vi* unirsi. **unity** *n* **1** unità *f*. **2** armonia *f*. accordo *m*.

United Kingdom *n* Regno Unito *m*.

United States of America *n pl* Stati Uniti *m pl*.

universe ('ju:nivə:s) *n* universo *m*. **universal** *adj* universale.

university (ju:ni'və:siti) *n* università *f*.

unjust (ʌn'dʒʌst) *adj* ingiusto.

unkempt (ʌn'kempt) *adj* trascurato, sciatto.

unkind (ʌn'kaind) *adj* scortese, sgarbato.

unknown (ʌn'noun) *adj* sconosciuto, ignoto.

unlawful (ʌn'lɔ:fəl) *adj* illegale, illecito.

unless (ən'les) *conj* a meno che (non), se non.

unlike (ʌn'laik) *adj* dissimile diverso. *prep* all'inverso di. **unlikely** *adj* improbabile, inverosimile.

unload (ʌn'loud) *vt* scaricare.

unlucky (ʌn'lʌki) *adj* **1** sfortunato. **2** di cattivo augurio.

unnatural (ʌn'nætʃərəl) *adj* innaturale.

unnecessary (ʌn'nesəsri) *adj* superfluo.

unofficial (ʌnə'fiʃəl) *adj* ufficioso.

unorthodox (ʌn'ɔ:θədɔks) *adj* non ortodosso.

unpack (ʌn'pæk) *vt* disfare. *vi* disfare le valigie.

unpleasant (ʌn'plezənt) *adj* spiacevole, sgradevole.

unpopular (ʌn'pɔpjulə) *adj* impopolare.

unravel (ʌnrævəl) *vt* **1** districare, sbrogliare. **2** chiarire.

unreasonable (ʌn'ri:zənəbəl) *adj* irragionevole.

unreliable (ʌnri'laiəbəl) *adj* infido.

unrest (ʌn'rest) *n* agitazione *f*. fermento *m*.

unruly (ʌn'ru:li) *adj* indisciplinato.

unscrew (ʌn'skru:) *vt* svitare.

unsettle (ʌn'setl) *vt* sconvolgere.

unsightly (ʌn'saitli) *adj* brutto, spiacevole a vedersi.

unsound (ʌn'saund) *adj* **1** in cattivo stato. **2** non solido. **3** difettoso.

unsteady (ʌn'stedi) *adj* **1** instabile, vacillante. **2** variabile.

unsuccessful (ʌnsək'sesfəl) *adj* sfortunato, fallito.

untangle (ʌn'tæŋgəl) *vt* districare.

untidy (ʌn'taidi) *adj* disordinato, trasandato.

untie (ʌn'tai) *vt* sciogliere, slegare.

until (ʌn'til) *prep* fino a. *conj* finchè (non), fintanto che.

untrue (ʌn'tru:) *adj* **1** falso, erroneo. **2** infedele.

unusual (ʌn'ju:ʒuəl) *adj* insolito, fuori del comune.

unwanted (ʌn'wɔntid) *adj* indesiderato.

unwell (ʌn'wel) *adj* indisposto, ammalato.

unwind (ʌn'waind) *vt* svolgere, srotolare, dipanare.

unwrap (ʌn'ræp) *vt* disfare, svolgere.

up (ʌp) *adv* **1** su, in su. **2** in piedi. *prep* su, su per. *adj* ascendente. **it's up to you** sta a te.

upbringing ('ʌpbriŋiŋ) *n* educazione *f*.

upheaval (ʌp'hi:vəl) *n* sconvolgimento *m*. sommossa *f*.

uphill (ʌp'hil) *adv* in salita. *adj* **1** in salita. **2** difficile.

uphold* (ʌp'hould) *vt* **1** sostenere. **2** approvare.

upholstery (ʌp'houlstəri) *n* tappezzeria *f*.

upkeep ('ʌpki:p) *n* manutenzione *f*.

uplift (ʌp'lift) *vt* sollevare, alzare. *n* sollevamento *m*.

upon (ə'pɔn) *prep* su, sopra.

upper ('ʌpə) *adj* superiore. **upper-class** *adj* signorile. **upper hand** *n* sopravvento *m*. **uppermost** *adj* il più alto, dominante. *adv* più in alto di tutto.

upright ('ʌprait) *adj* 1 eretto, verticale, diritto. 2 onesto. *adv* in piedi.

uprising ('ʌpraiziŋ) *n* rivolta, insurrezione *f*.

uproar ('ʌprɔː) *n* tumulto, clamore *m*.

uproot (ʌp'ruːt) *vt* sradicare.

upset *v* (ʌp'set; *n* 'ʌpset) *vt* 1 rovesciare, capovolgere. 2 scombussolare. *adj* sconvolto, turbato. *n* 1 scompiglio *m*. 2 rovesciamento *m*.

upshot ('ʌpʃɔt) *n* risultato *m*. conclusione *f*.

upside down ('ʌpsaid 'daun) *adv* sottosopra. **turn upside down** capovolgere.

upstairs (ʌp'stɛəz) *adv* al piano di sopra. *n* piano superiore *m*.

upstream (ʌp'striːm) *adv* controcorrente.

upward ('ʌpwəd) *adv also* **upwards** in su, in alto. *adj* in rialzo, in aumento.

uranium (juː'reiniəm) *n* uranio *m*.

Uranus ('juərənəs) *n* Urano *m*.

urban ('əːbən) *adj* urbano.

urge (əːdʒ) *vt* 1 spronare, esortare. 2 insistere su. *n* impulso, sprone *m*.

urgent ('əːdʒənt) *adj* 1 urgente. 2 insistente. **urgency** *n* urgenza *f*.

urine ('juərin) *n* orina, urina *f*. **urinate** *vi* orinare.

urn (əːn) *n* 1 urna *f*. 2 samovar *m*.

us (ʌs) *pron* 1st *pers pl* 1 noi *m,f*. 2 ci *m,f*. 3 ce *m,f*.

use (*v* juːz; *n* juːs) *vt* usare, adoperare. **use up** esaurire. ~*n* 1 uso *m*. 2 utilità *f*. **usage** *n* uso *m*. usanza *f*. **used** *adj* usato. **used to** abituato a. **useful** *adj* utile, vantaggioso. **useless** *adj* inutile, vano.

usher ('ʌʃə) *n* usciere, cerimoniere *m*. *vt* 1 introdurre. 2 annunciare.

usual ('juːʒuəl) *adj* usuale, consueto. **as usual** come al solito. **usually** *adv* usualmente, di solito.

usurp (juː'zɔːp) *vt* usurpare.

utensil (juː'tensəl) *n* utensile, arnese *m*.

uterus ('juːtərəs) *n,pl* **uteri** utero *m*.

utility (juː'tiliti) *n* utilità *f*. profitto *m*. *adj* utilitario, funzionale.

utmost ('ʌtmoust) *adj also* **uttermost** estremo, ultimo, massimo. **do one's utmost** fare del proprio meglio.

utter[1] ('ʌtə) *vt* 1 emettere. 2 esprimere.

utter[2] ('ʌtə) *adj* totale, assoluto, completo.

V

vacant ('veikənt) *adj* 1 vuoto, non occupato. 2 distratto. **vacancy** *n* posto vacante *m*.

vacate (və'keit) *vt* lasciare libero.

vacation (və'keiʃən) *n* rinuncia *f*. 2 vacanza *f*.

vaccine ('væksiːn) *n* vaccino *m*. **vaccinate** *vt* vaccinare. **vaccination** *n* vaccinazione *f*.

vacillate ('væsəleit) *vi* 1 vacillare. 2 estitare.

vacuum ('vækjuəm) *n* 1 vuoto, vuoto pneumatico *m*. 2 lacuna *f*. **vacuum cleaner** *n* aspirapolvere *m*. **vacuum flask** *n* termos *m*.

vagina (və'dʒainə) *n* vagina *f*.

vagrant ('veigrənt) *adj,n* vagabondo, nomade *m*.

vague (veig) *adj* 1 vago, indeterminato. 2 distratto.

vain (vein) *adj* 1 vano, inutile. 2 vanitoso.

valiant ('væliənt) *adj* valoroso, prode.

valid ('vælid) *adj* valido.

valley ('væli) *n* valle, vallata *f*.

value ('væljuː) *n* 1 valore *m*. 2 utilità *f*. *vt* 1 valutare, stimare, apprezzare. 2 *comm* valutare. **valuable** *adj* 1 prezioso, di gran valore. 2 utile. **valuables** *n pl* oggetti di valore *m pl*.

valve ('vælv) *n* valvola *f*.

vampire ('væmpaiə) *n* vampiro *m*.

van (væn) *n* camioncino, furgone *m*.

vandal ('vændl) *n* vandalo *m*. **vandalism** *n* vandalismo *m*.

vanilla (və'nilə) *n* vaniglia *f*.

vanish ('væniʃ) *vi* svanire, sparire.

vanity ('væniti) *n* vanità *f*.

vapour ('veipə) *n* vapore *m*. esalazione *f*.

variety (və'raiəti) *n* varietà *f*. assortimento *m*. **variety show** *n* spettacolo di varietà *m*.

various ('vɛəriəs) *adj* 1 vario, diverso. 2 parecchi.

varnish ('vɑːniʃ) *n* vernice, lacca *f*. *vt* verniciare, laccare.

vary ('vɛəri) *vi* differire. *vt* variare, cambiare. **variable** *adj* variabile, mutevole. **variant** *adj,n* variante *m*. **variation** *n* variazione *f*.

vase (vɑːz) *n* vaso *m*.

vasectomy (væ'sektəmi) *n* vasectomia *f*.

vast (vɑːst) *adj* vasto, ampio.

vat (væt) *n* tino *m*. tinozza *f*.

Vatican ('vætikən) *n* Vaticano *m*.

vault[1] (vɔ:lt) n **1** volta f. **2** cantina f. **3** sepolcro m.

vault[2] (vɔ:lt) vi volteggiare, saltare. vt saltare. n salto m.

veal (vi:l) n vitello m.

veer (viə) vi cambiare direzione, virare.

vegetable ('vedʒtəbəl) n **1** vegetale, ortaggio m. **2** pl verdura f. adj vegetale. **vegetarian** adj,n vegetariano. **vegetation** n vegetazione f.

vehement ('viːmənt) adj veemente, impetuoso.

vehicle ('viːikəl) n veicolo m.

veil (veil) n velo m. vt velare, nascondere.

vein (vein) n **1** vena f. **2** umore m. vena f.

velocity (və'lɔsiti) n velocità f.

velvet ('velvit) n velluto m. adj di velluto, vellutato.

vendetta (ven'detə) n vendetta f.

veneer (vi'niə) n **1** impiallacciatura f. **2** vernice, maschera f.

venerate ('venəreit) vt venerare, riverire.

venereal disease (vi'niəriəl) n malattia venerea f.

vengeance ('vendʒəns) n vendetta f.

Venice ('venis) n Venezia f. **Venetian** adj,n veneziano.

venison ('venisən) n carne di daino f.

venom ('venəm) n **1** veleno m. **2** cattiveria, malignità f.

vent[1] (vent) n **1** apertura f. foro m. **2** (in a jacket) spacco m.

vent[2] (vent) n sfogo m. **give vent to** sfogare. ~vt sfogare.

ventilate ('ventileit) vt ventilare. **ventilation** n ventilazione f. **ventilator** n ventilatore m.

venture ('ventʃə) n **1** avventura f. **2** comm speculazione f. vt avventurare. vi avventurarsi.

Venus ('viːnəs) n Venere f.

veranda (və'rændə) n veranda f.

verb (vəːb) n verbo m.

verdict ('vəːdikt) n **1** law verdetto m. **2** parere, giudizio m.

verge (vəːdʒ) n orlo, limite m. **on the verge of** sul punto di. ~v **verge on** rasentare, essere vicino a.

verify ('verifai) vt verificare, confermare.

vermicelli (vəːmi'tʃeli) n vermicelli m pl.

vermin ('vəːmin) n insetti parassiti m pl.

vermouth ('vəːməθ) n vermut m.

vernacular (və'nækjulə) adj,n vernacolo m.

versatile ('vəːsətail) adj versatile.

verse (vəːs) n **1** verso m. **2** versi m pl. **3** poesia f.

version ('vəːʃən) n versione f.

vertebrate ('vəːtibreit) adj,n vertebrato m.

vertical ('vəːtikəl) adj,n verticale m.

verve (vəːv) n verve, brio m.

very ('veri) adv molto, assai. adj **1** vero e proprio. **2** esatto. **3** stesso. **4** proprio.

vessel ('vesəl) n **1** naut vascello m. nave f. **2** recipiente, vaso m.

vest (vest) n maglia f.

vestment ('vestmənt) n veste sacerdotale f.

vestry ('vestri) n sagrestia f.

vet (vet) n inf veterinario m. vt esaminare.

veteran ('vetərən) adj,n veterano m.

veterinary surgeon ('vetrinəri) n veterinario m.

veto ('viːtou) n,pl **-toes** veto m. vt vietare.

vex (veks) vt **1** affliggere. **2** irritare.

via ('vaiə) prep via, attraverso.

viable ('vaiəbəl) adj **1** vitale. **2** praticabile.

viaduct ('vaiədʌkt) n viadotto m.

vibrate (vai'breit) vi vibrare, oscillare. vt far vibrare. **vibration** n vibrazione f.

vicar ('vikə) n parroco, curato m.

vicarious (vi'kɛəriəs) adj **1** delegato. **2** insostituzione.

vice[1] (vais) n **1** vizio m. depravazione f. **2** difetto m. imperfezione f.

vice[2] (vais) n tech morsa f.

vice-chancellor n vice-cancelliere m.

vice-president n vice-presidente m.

vice versa ('vəːsə) adv viceversa.

vicinity (vi'siniti) n vicinanza, prossimità f.

vicious ('viʃəs) adj **1** crudele, dispettoso. **2** vizioso.

victim ('viktim) n vittima f. **victimize** vt tormentare.

Victorian (vik'tɔːriən) adj vittoriano.

victory ('viktri) n vittoria f. **victorious** adj vittorioso.

video-tape ('vidiouteip) n nastro televisivo m.

Vietnam (viet'næm) n Vietnam m. **Vietnamese** adj,n vietnamese.

view (vjuː) n **1** vista f. veduta f. panorama m. **3** veduta f. **2** intento, scopo m. **in view of** visto che. ~vt **1** vedere, osservare. **2** ispezionare. **viewfinder** n mirino m.

vigil ('vidʒil) n veglia f. **vigilant** adj vigile, vigilante.

vigour ('vigə) n vigore m. energia f. **vigorous** adj vigoroso.

vile (vail) adj **1** abietto, sordido, vile. **2** pessimo.

villa ('vilə) *n* villa *f.*

village ('vilidʒ) *n* villaggio, paese *m.*

villain ('vilən) *n* furfante, farabutto *m.*

vindictive (vin'diktiv) *adj* vendicativo.

vine (vain) *n* vite *f.* **vineyard** *n* vigneto *m.* vigna *f.*

vinegar ('viniɡə) *n* aceto *m.*

vintage ('vintidʒ) *n* vendemmia, annata *f.*

vinyl ('vainil) *n* vinile *m.*

viola (vi'oulə) *n* viola *f.*

violate ('vaiəleit) *vt* violare, violentare. **violation** *n* violazione *f.*

violence ('vaiələns) *n* violenza *f.* **violent** *adj* violento.

violet ('vaiələt) *n* 1 *bot* viola *m.* 2 (colour) viola *m invar. adj* violetto.

violin (vaiə'lin) *n* violino *m.*

viper ('vaipə) *n* vipera *f.*

virgin ('və:dʒin) *adj,n* vergine *f.*

Virgo ('və:gou) *n* Vergine *f.*

virile ('virail) *adj* virile, maschio.

virtue ('və:tju:) *n* virtù *f.* **virtual** *adj* virtuale, effettivo.

virus ('vairəs) *n* virus *m. adj* virale.

visa ('vi:zə) *n* visto consolare *m.*

viscount ('vaikaunt) *n* visconte *m.*

vision ('viʒən) *n* 1 visione *f.* 2 capacità visiva *f.* 3 intuito *m.* **visible** *adj* visibile, evidente.

visit ('vizit) *vt* 1 visitare, fare una visita a. 2 ispezionare. *n* visita *f.*

visual ('vizjuəl) *adj* 1 visuale, visivo. 2 visibile. **visualize** *vt,vi* immaginarsi, raffigurarsi.

vital ('vait|) *adj* vitale, essenziale. **vitality** *n* vitalità, forza *f.*

vitamin ('vitəmin) *n* vitamina *f.*

vivacious (vi'veiʃəs) *adj* vivace, vispo.

vivid ('vivid) *adj* vivido, vivo.

vixen ('viksən) *n* volpe femmina *f.*

vocabulary (və'kæbjuləri) *n* vocabolario *m.*

vocal ('voukəl) *adj* vocale. **vocal chords** *n pl* corde vocali *f pl.*

vocation (vou'keiʃən) *n* 1 *rel* vocazione *f.* 2 inclinazione, attitudine *f.*

vodka ('vodkə) *n* vodka *f.*

voice (vois) *n* 1 voce *f.* 2 opinione *f. vt* esprimere, dire.

void (void) *adj* 1 vuoto. 2 non valido, nullo. *n* vuoto *m.*

volatile ('volətail) *adj* 1 volatile. 2 volubile.

volcano (vol'keinou) *n,pl* **-noes** or **-nos** vulcano *m.*

vole (voul) *n* topo d'acqua *m.*

volley ('voli) *n* scarica, raffica *f.* **volleyball** *n* palla a volo *f.*

volt (voult) *n* volt *m.*

volume ('volju:m) *n* 1 volume *m.* 2 massa *f.*

volunteer (volən'tiə) *n* volontario *m. vi* 1 offrirsi volontariamente. 2 arruolarsi volontario. **voluntary** *adj* 1 volontario, spontaneo. 2 voluto.

voluptuous (və'lʌptjuəs) *adj* voluttuoso, sensuale.

vomit ('vomit) *vt,vi* vomitare. *n* vomito *m.*

voodoo ('vu:du:) *n* vuduismo *m.*

vote (vout) *n* voto *m.* votazione *f. vt,vi* votare.

vouch (vautʃ) *vi* **vouch for** rispondere di.

voucher ('vautʃə) *n* 1 documento giustificativo *m.* 2 tagliando *m.* 3 garante *m.*

vow (vau) *n* voto *m. vt* 1 fare voto di. 2 promettere.

vowel ('vauəl) *n* vocale *f.*

voyage ('voiidʒ) *n* viaggio *m.*

vulgar ('vʌlɡə) *adj* volgare.

vulnerable ('vʌlnrəbļ) *adj* vulnerabile.

vulture ('vʌltʃə) *n* avvoltoio *m.*

W

wad (wod) *n* 1 pacchetto, rotolo *m.* 2 tampone *m.* **wadding** *n* 1 imbottitura *f.* 2 ovatta *f.*

waddle ('wod|) *vi* camminare ondeggiando. *n* andatura ondeggiante *f.*

wade (weid) *vi* avanzare faticosamente. *vt* guadare.

wafer ('weifə) *n* cialda *f.*

waft (woft) *vt* sospingere. *vi* 1 fluttuare. 2 (of a breeze) soffiare blandamente. *n* soffio *m.*

wag (wæg) *vt* scuotere, agitare. *n* scodinzolio *m.*

wage (weidʒ) *n* salario *m.* paga *f. vt* (war) intraprendere.

waggle ('wægəl) *vt* scuotere, dondolare.

wagon ('wægən) *n* 1 carro *m.* 2 vagone merci *m.*

waif (weif) *n* trovatello *m.*

wail (weil) *vi* gemere, lamentarsi. *n* gemito, lamento *m.*

waist (weist) *n* vita, cintola *f.* **waistband** *n* cintura, fascia *f.* **waistcoat** *n* panciotto, gilè *m.* **waistline** *n* vita *f.* giro di vita *m.*

wait (weit) *vi,vt* aspettare, attendere. **wait on** servire. ~*n* attesa *f.* **waiter** *n* cameriere *m.* **waiting list** *n* lista d'attesa *f.* **waiting**

room n sala d'aspetto f. **waitress** n cameriera f.

waive (weiv) vt rinunciare a, desistere da.

wake *¹ (weik) vt svegliare. vi svegliarsi. **waken** vt svegliare, risvegliare. vi svegliarsi.

wake ² (weik) n naut scia f.

Wales (weilz) n Galles m.

walk (wɔːk) vi camminare, andare a piedi. n 1 passeggiata, camminata f. percorso m. 2 andatura f. **walking stick** n bastone m. **walkout** n sciopero non autorizzato m. **walkover** n inf vittoria facile f.

wall (wɔːl) n muro m. parete f. **wallflower** n 1 violacciocca f. 2 inf ragazza che fa da tappezzeria f. **wallpaper** n carta da parati f.

wallet ('wɔlit) n portafoglio m.

wallop ('wɔləp) inf vt percuotere. n percossa f. colpo m.

wallow ('wɔlou) vi rotolarsi, sguazzare.

walnut ('wɔːlnʌt) n noce f. **walnut tree** n noce f.

walrus ('wɔːlrəs) n tricheco m.

waltz (wɔːls) n valzer m. vi ballare il valzer.

wand (wɔnd) n bacchetta f.

wander ('wɔndə) vi 1 vagare, vagabondare. 2 deviare, smarrirsi. 3 vaneggiare, delirare.

wane (wein) vi 1 (of the moon) calare. 2 diminuire. n declino m. **on the wane** in declino.

wangle ('wæŋgəl) vt brigare, ottenere con intrighi.

want (wɔnt) vt 1 volere, desiderare. 2 aver bisogno di. vi mancare. n 1 mancanza f. 2 necessità f. bisogno m. vt 1 volere, desiderare. 2 aver bisogno di. vi mancare.

wanton ('wɔntn) adj 1 licenzioso, impudico. 2 arbitrario. 3 capriccioso.

war (wɔː) n guerra f. vi guerreggiare. **warfare** n guerra f. stato di guerra m.

warble ('wɔːbəl) vt,vi trillare, gorgheggiare. n trillo, gorgheggio m.

ward (wɔːd) n 1 (of a hospital) reparto m. corsia f. 2 circoscrizione comunale f. 3 law pupillo m. v **ward off** parare. **warden** n guardiano, custode m. **warder** n carceriere m. **wardrobe** n guardaroba f. armadio m.

warehouse ('wɛəhaus) n magazzino, deposito m.

warm (wɔːm) adj 1 caldo. 2 ardente. vt riscaldare. **warm-blooded** adj 1 appassionato. 2 a sangue caldo. **warm-hearted** adj gentile, compassionevole. **warmth** n 1 calore m. 2 zelo m. **warm-up** n esercizio fisico m.

warn (wɔːn) vt mettere in guardia, avvertire. **warning** n allarme, avvertimento m.

warp (wɔːp) vt 1 storcere. 2 pervertire. vi deformarsi. n ordito m.

warrant ('wɔrənt) n autorizzazione f. ordine m. vt assicurare, garantire.

warren ('wɔrən) n garenna f.

warrior ('wɔriə) n guerriero, soldato m.

wart (wɔːt) n verruca f. porro m.

wary ('wɛəri) adj diffidente, prudente.

was (wəz; stressed wɔz) v see **be**.

wash (wɔʃ) vt lavare. vi lavarsi. **wash up** lavare i piatti. ~n lavata f. **washbasin** n lavandino m. **washer** n tech anello m. **washing** n bucato m. **washing machine** n lavatrice f. **washing powder** n detersivo m. **wash-out** n inf disastro m. **washroom** n bagno m.

wasp (wɔsp) n vespa f.

waste (weist) vt rovinare, sprecare. n spreco, sciupio m. **wasteful** adj prodigo. **wastepaper basket** n cestino per carta straccia m.

watch (wɔtʃ) n 1 (wrist) orologio m. 2 sorveglianza f. vt guardare. vi fare la guardia. **watchdog** n cane da guardia m. **watchful** adj attento.

water ('wɔːtə) n acqua f. vt 1 innaffiare. 2 diluire. 3 abbeverare. vi (of eyes) piangere.

water-closet n gabinetto m.

watercolour ('wɔːtəkʌlə) n acquerello m.

watercress ('wɔːtəkres) n crescione m.

waterfall ('wɔːtəfɔːl) n cascata f.

watering-can n annaffiatoio m.

waterlily ('wɔːtəlili) n ninfea f.

waterlogged ('wɔːtəlɔgd) adj inzuppato.

watermark ('wɔːtəmaːk) n 1 livello di marea m. 2 filigrana f.

watermelon ('wɔːtəmelən) n cocomero m.

watermill ('wɔːtəmil) n mulino m.

waterproof ('wɔːtəpruːf) adj impermeabile.

water-ski vi fare lo sci nautico. **water-skiing** n sci nautico m.

watertight ('wɔːtətait) adj ermetico.

waterway ('wɔːtəwei) n canale m.

waterworks ('wɔːtəwəːks) n pl impianto idrico m.

watery ('wɔːtəri) adj acquoso.

watt (wɔt) n watt m invar.

wave (weiv) n 1 onda f. 2 (of the hand) cenno m. vi 1 ondeggiare. 2 far segno di saluto. vt agitare. **waveband** n gamma di lunghezza d'onda f. **wavelength** n lunghezza d'onda f. **wavy** adj ondulato.

waver ('weivə) vi vacillare, fluttuare.

wax[1] (wæks) n cera f.

wax[2] (wæks) vi (of the moon) crescere, aumentare.

way (wei) n 1 via, direzione f. 2 modo m. 3 mezzo m. **by the way** a proposito. **in the way** ingombrante. **wayside** n bordo della strada m. adj sul bordo della strada.

waylay (wei'lei) vt tendere un agguato a.

wayward ('weiwəd) adj capriccioso, ostinato.

we (wi:) pron 1st pers pl 1 noi m,f. 2 si m,f.

weak (wi:k) adj debole. **weaken** vt indebolire. vi indebolirsi. **weak-kneed** adj smidollato. **weakling** n creatura gracile f. **weakness** n debolezza f. **weak-willed** adj indeciso.

wealth (welθ) n ricchezza f. **wealthy** adj ricco.

weapon ('wepən) n arma f, pl armi.

wear* (wɛə) vt portare, indossare. vi logorarsi. **wear out** 1 esaurire. 2 consumare. ~n uso m. **wear and tear** logoramento m.

weary ('wiəri) adj affaticato. vt 1 annoiare. 2 stancare.

weasel ('wi:zəl) n donnola f.

weather ('weðə) n tempo m. vt resistere a.

weave* (wi:v) vt,vi tessere. n tessuto m.

web (web) n 1 (of a spider) ragnatela f. 2 tela f. tessuto m.

wedding ('wediŋ) n matrimonio m. **wedding ring** n fede f.

wedge (wedʒ) n cuneo m. vt incuneare.

Wednesday ('wenzdi) n mercoledì m.

weed (wi:d) n erbaccia f. vt sarchiare.

week (wi:k) n settimana f. **weekday** n giorno feriale m. **weekend** n fine settimana m. **weekly** adj settimanale. **weekly magazine** n settimanale m.

weep* (wi:p) vi piangere.

weigh (wei) vt pesare. **weighbridge** n ponte a basculla m. **weight** n 1 peso m. 2 importanza f. **weight-lifting** n sollevamento di pesi m.

weird ('wiəd) adj strano.

welcome ('welkəm) adj benvenuto, gradito. n benvenuto m. vt dare il benvenuto m.

weld (weld) vt saldare.

welfare ('welfɛə) n benessere m.

well[1] (wel) adv bene. adj in buona salute. **be well** star bene.

well[2] (wel) n pozzo m.

well-bred adj beneducato.

well-built adj robusto.

well-known adj ben noto.

well-off adj benestante, danaroso.

well-paid adj ben retribuito.

well-spoken adj forbito nel parlare.

well-worn adj usato.

Welsh (welʃ) adj gallese. **Welsh** (language) n gallese m. **Welshman** n gallese m.

went (went) v see **go.**

wept (wept) v see **weep.**

were (wə:) v see **be.**

west (west) n ovest, ponente m. adj occidentale, dell'ovest. **westerly** adj dell'ovest. **western** adj occidentale.

West Indies ('indiz) n Indie Occidentali f pl. **West Indian** adj delle Indie Occidentali.

wet (wet) adj 1 bagnato, umido. 2 fradicio. 3 fresco. n umidità f. vt bagnare, inzuppare. **wet blanket** n guastafeste m.

whack (wæk) inf vi bastonare. n percossa f.

whale (weil) n balena f.

wharf (wɔ:f) n banchina f.

what (wɔt) pron 1 che? che cosa? 2 ciò, che. **what for?** perchè? **what's the matter?** che cosa hai? ~adj 1 quale? che? 2 che. **what a** che. **whatever** pron qualsiasi cosa. adj qualunque.

wheat (wi:t) n frumento, grano m.

wheedle ('wi:dl) vt adulare, persuadere con lusinghe.

wheel (wi:l) n 1 ruota f. 2 volante m. vt far ruotare. **wheelbarrow** n carriola f. **wheelchair** n sedia a rotelle f.

wheeze (wi:z) vi ansimare. n respiro affannoso m.

whelk (welk) n buccina f.

when (wen) adv,conj quando. **whenever** adv ogni volta che.

where (wɛə) pron,adv,conj dove. **whereabouts** adv da che parte. **where to?** dove. n luogo m. posizione f. **whereas** conj mentre. **whereby** adv con cui, come. **whereupon** adv dopo di che. **wherever** adv dovunque, in qualunque luogo.

whether ('weðə) conj se.

which (witʃ) pron 1 chi? quale? 2 che, la qual cosa, il quale. adj 1 quale? 2 il quale. **whichever** pron qualsiasi. adj qualunque.

whiff (wif) n soffio, sbuffo m.

while (wail) conj also **whilst** mentre. n momento m.

whim (wim) n capriccio m.

whimper ('wimpə) vi piagnucolare. n piagnuco- lio m.

whimsical ('wimzikəl) adj capriccioso, bizzarro.

whine (wain) vi uggiolare. n 1 (of a dog) uggiolio m. 2 piagnucolio m.

whip (wip) n frusta f. vt frustare.

whir (wə:) vi ronzare, rombare. n ronzio, rombo m.

whirl (wə:l) n vortice, giro rapido m. vi roteare. vt far girare. **whirlwind** n turbine, vortice m. tromba d'aria f.

whisk [1] (wisk) vi muoversi rapidamente. vt spazzare. n movimento rapido m.

whisk [2] (wisk) vt cul frullare. n frullino m.

whisker ('wiskə) n baffo m.

whisky ('wiski) n whisky m invar.

whisper ('wispə) vt,vi sussurrare. n bisbiglio, mormorio m.

whist (wist) n whist m.

whistle ('wisəl) vt,vi fischiare. n fischio, sibilo m.

white (wait) adj 1 bianco, candido. 2 pallido. n 1 bianco m. 2 (of an egg) chiaro m. 3 cap Bianco m. **whiten** vt imbiancare. **whitewash** n calce f. intonaco m. vt imbiancare. **whiting** n merlano m.

Whitsun ('witsən) n Pentecoste f.

whiz (wiz) vi fischiare. n fischio m.

who (hu:) pron 1 chi? 2 che, il quale. **whoever** pron chiunque.

whole (houl) adj 1 intero, tutto. n tutto m. **wholemeal** adj integrale. **wholehearted** adj generoso, sincero. **wholesale** n vendita all'ingrosso f. adv all'ingrosso. **wholesome** adj sano, salubre. **wholly** adv completa- mente, totalmente.

whom (hu:m) pron 1 chi? 2 che, il quale.

whooping cough ('hu:piŋ) n pertosse f.

whore (hɔ:) n puttana f.

whose (hu:z) pron 1 di chi? 2 di cui, del quale, il cui.

why (wai) adv 1 perchè? 2 per cui. conj perchè.

wick (wik) n lucignolo m.

wicked ('wikid) adj cattivo, malvagio.

wicket ('wikit) n 1 sportello, cancelletto m. 2 sport porta f.

wide (waid) adj largo, ampio, esteso. adv 1 lontano, lungi. 2 bene. **widely** adv larga- mente, molto, diffusamente. **widen** vt esten- dere, allargare. vi allargarsi. **widespread** adj esteso, generale. **width** n larghezza, ampiezza f.

widow ('widou) n vedova f.

wield (wi:ld) vt 1 tenere, maneggiare. 2 (power) esercitare.

wife (waif) n, pl **wives** moglie, sposa f.

wig (wig) n parrucca f.

wiggle ('wigəl) vt dimenare. vi contorcersi.

wigwam ('wigwæm) n tenda dei pellirosse f.

wild (waild) adj 1 selvaggio, feroce. 2 incolto. **wilderness** ('wildənəs) n 1 deserto m. 2 solitu- dine m.

wilful ('wilfəl) adj intenzionale, fatto apposta.

will [1] (wil) v mod aux 1 volere. 2 expressed by the future tense.

will [2] (wil) n 1 volontà f. volere m. 2 law testamento m. **willing** adj pronto, disposto. **willpower** n volontà f.

willow ('wilou) n salice m.

wilt (wilt) vi appassire.

win [*] (win) vt,vi vincere, guadagnare. n vincita, vittoria f.

wince (wins) vi trasalire. n smorfia f.

winch (wintʃ) n argano m. manovella f.

wind [1] (wind) n 1 vento m. 2 med flatulenza f. **windfall** n fortuna inaspettata f. **windmill** n mulino a vento m. **windpipe** n trachea f. **windscreen** n parabrezza m. **windscreen wiper** n tergicristallo m. **windswept** adj battuto dai venti. **windy** adj ventoso.

wind [2] (waind) vt avvolgere, girare. vi ser- peggiare. **wind up** caricare.

windlass ('windləs) n verricello m.

window ('windou) n finestra, vetrata f. **win- dow box** n cassetta per fiori f. **window- dressing** n allestimento di vetrine m. **win- dow-shop** vi guardare le vetrine.

wine (wain) n vino m. **wineglass** n bicchiere da vino m.

wing (wiŋ) n 1 ala f. 2 volo m. 3 pl Th quinta f. **wingspan** n apertura d'ali f.

wink (wiŋk) vi ammiccare, strizzare l'occhio. n batter d'occhio, cenno m.

winkle ('wiŋkəl) n chiocciola marina f.

winter ('wintə) n inverno m.

wipe (waip) vt pulire, strofinare. n strofinata f.

wire (' waiə) n 1 filo m. 2 inf telegramma m. vt telegrafare. **wireless** n radio f invar.

wisdom ('wizdəm) n saggezza f.

wise (waiz) adj saggio.

wish (wiʃ) vt,vi 1 desiderare. 2 augurare. n desiderio m. voglia f.

wisp (wisp) n ciuffo m. ciocca f.

wisteria (wis'tiəriə) n glicine m.

wistful ('wistfəl) *adj* pensoso.

wit (wit) *n* arguzia *f.* spirito *m.*

witch (witʃ) *n* strega *f.* **witchcraft** *n* stregoneria *f.*

with (wið) *prep* con, in compagnia di, presso.

withdraw* (wið'drɔ:) *vt* ritirare. *vi* ritirarsi. **withdrawal** *n* ritiro *m.*

wither ('wiðə) *vi* appassire, deperire, avvizzire.

withhold* (wið'hould) *vt* **1** trattenere. **2** nascondere.

within (wið'in) *prep* entro, in meno di. *adv* dentro.

without (wið'aut) *prep* senza (di).

withstand* (wið'stænd) *vt* resistere a.

witness ('witnəs) *n* **1** testimone *m.* **2** testimonianza *f.* *vt* testimoniare, essere testimone di.

witty ('witi) *adj* arguto, spiritoso.

wizard ('wizəd) *n* mago, stregone *m.*

wobble ('wɔbəl) *vi* vacillare.

woke (wouk) *v see* **wake**[1].

woken ('woukən) *v see* **wake**[1].

wolf (wulf) *n, pl* **wolves** lupo *m.*

woman ('wumən) *n; pl* **women** donna *f.* **womanhood** *n* femminilità *f.* le donne *f pl.*

womb (wu:m) *n* utero *m.*

won (wʌn) *v see* **win**.

wonder ('wʌndə) *n* meraviglia *f.* *vi* **1** meravigliarsi. **2** domandarsi. **wonderful** *adj* meraviglioso.

wonky ('wɔŋki) *adj sl* **1** traballante. **2** incostante.

wood (wud) *n* **1** (material) legno *m.* **2** bosco *m.* **woodcock** *n* beccaccia *f.* **wooden** *adj* di legno. **woodland** *n* terreno boscoso *m.* **woodpecker** *n* picchio *m.* **woodpigeon** *n* colombo selvatico *m.* **woodwind** *n* strumenti a fiato *m pl.* **woodwork** *n* lavoro in legno *m.* **woodworm** *n* tarlo *m.*

wool (wul) *n* lana *f.* **woollen** *adj* di lana *f.* **woolly** *adj* **1** lanoso. **2** confuso.

word (wə:d) *n* **1** parola *f.* vocabolo *m.* **2** promessa *f.*

wore (wɔ:) *v see* **wear**.

work (wə:k) *n* **1** lavoro *m.* **2** daffare *m.* *vi* lavorare. *vt* far funzionare. **working** *adj* **1** che lavora. **2** che funziona. **working class** *n* classe operaia *f.* **workman** *n* operaio *m.* **workmanship** *n* abilità, esecuzione *f.* **workshop** *n* officina *f.*

world (wə:ld) *n* mondo *m.* **worldly** *adj* mondano. **worldwide** *adj* in tutto il mondo.

worm (wə:m) *n* verme *m.*

wormwood ('wə:mwud) *n* assenzio *m.*

worn (wɔ:n) *v see* **wear**.

worry ('wʌri) *n* preoccupazione *f.* tormento *m.* *vt* **1** preoccupare. **2** tormentare. *vi* preoccuparsi.

worse ('wə:s) *adj* peggiore, peggio. *adv n* peggio *m.* **worse and worse** sempre peggio. **worsen** *vt* peggiorare, aggravare. *vi* peggiorare, aggravarsi.

worship ('wə:ʃip) *n* adorazione *f.* **His** or **Your Worship** Signor Giudice, Signor Sindaco. ~*vt* adorare.

worst (wə:st) *adj* peggiore. *adv* peggio.

worth (wə:θ) *n* valore, merito *m.* *adj* **1** degno di. **2** del valore di. **3** che merita. **be worth** valere. **worthwhile** *adj* che vale la pena. **worthy** *adj* degno.

would (wəd; *stressed* wud) *v see* **will**[1].

wound[1] (wu:nd) *n* ferita *f.* *vt* ferire, offendere.

wound[2] (waund) *v see* **wind**[2].

wove (wouv) *v see* **weave**.

woven ('wouvn) *v see* **weave**.

wrangle ('ræŋgəl) *vi* discutere. *n* rissa *f.* alterco *m.*

wrap (ræp) *vt* **1** avvolgere. **2** incartare.

wreath (ri:θ) *n* ghirlanda, corona di fiori *f.*

wreathe (ri:ð) *vt* inghirlandare.

wreck (rek) *n* **1** naufragio *m.* **2** rovina *f.* **3** nave che ha fatto naufragio *f.* *vt* distruggere. **wreckage** *n* relitti rottami *m pl.*

wren (ren) *n* scricciolo *m.*

wrench (rentʃ) *vt* storcere. *n* storta *f.* strappo *m.* *vt* storcere.

wrestle ('resəl) *vi* lottare. **wrestling** *n* lotta *f.*

wretch (retʃ) *n* disgraziato *m.* **wretched** *adj* sfortunato, miserabile.

wriggle ('rigəl) *vi* contorcersi, dimenarsi.

wring* (riŋ) *vt* torcere, stringere, strizzare.

wrinkle ('riŋkəl) *n* ruga, crespa *f.* *vt* aggrinzire, corrugare. *vi* corrugarsi.

wrist (rist) *n* polso *m.*

writ (rit) *n* decreto, ordine *m.*

write* (rait) *vt, vi* scrivere. **writer** *n* scrivente *m, f.* **writing paper** *n* carta da lettere *f.*

writhe (raið) *vi* contorcersi.

wrong (rɔŋ) *adj* **1** sbagliato. **2** ingiusto. **be wrong** avere torto. ~*n* **1** torto *m.* **2** ingiustizia *f.* *adv* **1** erroneamente. **2** male.

wrote (rout) *v see* **write**.

wrought iron (rɔ:t) *n* ferro battuto *m.*

wrung (rʌŋ) *v see* **wring**.

wry (rai) *adj* ironico.

X

xenophobia (zenə'foubiə) n xenofobia f.
X-ray n radiografia f. vt radiografare.
xylophone ('zailəfoun) n silofono m.

Y

yacht (jɔt) n panfilo, yacht m. **yachtsman** n 1 proprietario di panfilo m. 2 chi pratica la navigazione su yacht, velista m.
yank (jæŋk) vt tirare con violenza. n strattone, strappo m.
yap (jæp) vi guaire, abbaiare.
yard[1] (jɑːd) n (measurement) iarda f. **yardstick** n pietra di paragone f.
yard[2] (jɑːd) n cortile, recinto m.
yarn (jɑːn) n 1 filato m. 2 inf filastrocca, storia f.
yawn (jɔːn) vi sbadigliare. n sbadiglio m.
year (jiə) n anno m. annata f. **yearly** adj annuale. adv annualmente.
yearn (jəːn) vi desiderare intensamente.
yeast (jiːst) n lievito m.
yell (jel) n urlo, strillo m. vi urlare.
yellow ('jelou) adj,n giallo m.
yelp (jelp) vi guaire. n guaito m.
yes (jes) adv sì.
yesterday ('jestədi) adv ieri.
yet (jet) adv 1 ancora. 2 ma. conj ma, tuttavia.
yew (juː) n tasso m.
Yiddish ('jidiʃ) adj,n yiddish m.
yield (jiːld) vt produrre. vi cedere. n raccolto m.
yodel ('joudl) vi cantare alla tirolese.
yoga ('jougə) n yoga m.
yoghurt ('jɔgət) n yogurt m.
yoke (jouk) n giogo m.
yolk (jouk) n torlo d'uovo m.
yonder ('jɔndə) adj quello. adv laggiù.
you (juː) pron 2nd pers s 1 fam tu, ti, te m,f. 2 fml Lei m. Ella f. 3 pl fam voi, vi, ve m,f. 4 fml pl Loro m,f.
young (jʌŋ) adj giovane. **youngster** n ragazzo m.
your (jɔː; juə) poss adj 2nd pers s 1 fam (il) tuo, (la) tua, (i) tuoi, (le) tue. 2 fml (il) suo, (la) sua, (i) suoi, (le) sue. 3 pl fam (il) vostro, (la) vostra, (i) vostri, (le) vostre. 4 pl fml (il) il, la, i, or le) loro invar. **yourself** pron 2nd pers s 1 fam tu stesso. 2 fam ti, te. 3 fml Lei stesso. 4

pl fam voi stessi. 5 pl fam vi. 6 pl fml Loro stessi.
yours (jɔːz; juəz) poss pron 2nd pers s 1 fam il tuo, la tua, i tuoi, le tue. 2 fml il suo, la sua, i suoi, le sue. 3 pl fam il vostro, la vostra, i vostri, le vostre. 4 pl fml il, la, i, or le loro.
youth (juːθ) n 1 giovinezza, gioventù f. 2 giovane m. **youth hostel** n albergo della gioventù m.
Yugoslavia (juːgou'slɑːviə) n Iugoslavia f. **Yugoslav** adj,n Iugoslavo.

Z

zeal (ziːl) n zelo m. **zealous** adj premuroso.
zebra ('zebrə) n zebra f. **zebra crossing** n passaggio pedonale m.
zero ('ziərou) n,pl **-ros** or **-roes** zero m.
zest (zest) n 1 gusto m. 2 sapore m.
zigzag ('zigzæg) n zigzag m invar. vi andare a zig-zag.
zinc (ziŋk) n zinco m.
Zionism ('zaiənizəm) n sionismo m. **Zionist** adj,n sionista.
zip (zip) n chiusura lampo f.
zither ('ziðə) n cetra f.
zodiac ('zoudiæk) n zodiaco m.
zone (zoun) n zona f.
zoo (zuː) n zoo m.
zoology (zou'ɔlədʒi) n zoologia f. **zoological** adj zoologico. **zoologist** n zoologo m.
zoom (zuːm) vi 1 ronzare, rombare. 2 zumare.